Criminal Procedure
From First Contact to Appeal

Second Edition

JOHN L. WORRALL

University of Texas at Dallas

PEARSON

Boston ■ New York ■ San Francisco
Mexico City ■ Montreal ■ Toronto ■ London ■ Madrid ■ Munich ■ Paris
Hong Kong ■ Singapore ■ Tokyo ■ Cape Town ■ Sydney

Series Editor: David Repetto
Editorial Assistant: Liz DiMenno
Senior Marketing Manager: Kelly May
Production Editor: Won McIntosh
Editorial-Production Service: Progressive Publishing Alternatives
Compositor: Progressive Information Technologies
Composition and Prepress Buyer: Linda Cox
Manufacturing Buyer: Megan Cochran
Interior Designer: Denise Hoffman
Cover Designer: Kristina Mose-Libon

For related titles and support materials, visit our online catalog at www.ablongman.com.

Between the time Website information is gathered and then published, it is not unusual for some sites to have closed. Also, the transcription of URLs can result in typographical errors. The publisher would appreciate notification where these errors occur so that they may be corrected in subsequent editions.

Library of Congress Cataloging-in-Publication Data

Worrall, John L.
    Criminal procedure : from first contact to appeal / John L. Worrall.—2nd ed.
      p. cm.
    Includes index.
    ISBN 0-205-49310-6
    1. Criminal procedure—United States.   2. Appellate procedure—United States.
    I. Title.

    KF9619.W67 2007
    345.73′05—dc22

                                                2006043409

Printed in the United States of America

10 9 8 7 6 5 4 3 2 1   CIN   10 09 08 07 06

Photo Credits: p. xviii: Larry Downing/Landov; p. 28: Spencer Platt/Liaison/Getty Images; p. 34: Jose Azel/Woodfin Camp & Associates; p. 50: Phillip Kamrass/Liaison/Getty Images; p. 66: Bob Daemmrich/Stock Boston; p. 86: AP Wide World Photos; p. 96: Mikael Karlsson/ 911 Pictures; p. 125: Stone Allstock/Getty Images; p. 136: Ron Chapple/Taxi/Getty Images; p. 149: AP Wide World Photos; p. 168: Spencer Grant/PhotoEdit; p. 189: Michael Newman/ PhotoEdit; p. 198: Nancy Richmond/The Image Works; p. 216: A. Ramey/PhotoEdit; p. 226: The Image Works; p. 244: Michael Newman/PhotoEdit; p. 256: Spencer Grant/PhotoEdit; p. 268: The Image Works; p. 280: AP Wide World Photos; p. 286: Marc Asnin/SABA/ Corbis; p. 308: Image Bank/Getty Images; p. 325: David Young-Wolff/Stone Allstock/Getty Images; p. 342: AP Wide World Photos; p. 363: Michael Newman/PhotoEdit; p. 370: Bruce Ayres/Stone Allstock/Getty Images; p. 390: Stone Allstock/Getty Images; p. 402: AP Wide World Photos; p. 408: AP Wide World Photos; p. 434: Hulton Archive Photos/Getty Images; p. 443: Carl J. Single/The Image Works.

To Dylan
for giving me a title far more
meaningful than Ph.D.

CONTENTS

I decided to write this book, *Criminal Procedure: From First Contact to Appeal,* after I had taught criminal procedure for several years. During each course, my students typically asked a litany of "what if?" questions and became curious about the rules of criminal procedure after the police arrest and book a suspect. Students also expressed frustration with the fact that many of the leading books on criminal procedure presupposed a certain degree of familiarity with the criminal process, including an understanding of basic terminology. Students came to loathe these books' excessive use of legalese and obtuse descriptions of criminal procedure topics that had no real-life applications.

In addition, students frequently pointed out, as did I, that there are often significant differences between what the courts require and what happens in the real world of criminal justice. For instance, consider the definition of a *seizure* for the purposes of the Fourth Amendment. Namely, a seizure occurs when a reasonable person would believe he or she is not free to leave. Yet many times, students find this definition wanting and ask, "If a person is not seized according to this definition, is he or she really free to leave?" This question highlights the differences between what this book calls *theory* and *reality.* It and countless other similar questions prompted me to write a criminal procedure book of my own, one that takes a comprehensive yet basic approach to criminal procedure and that connects the material to the real world with examples and exercises.

By way of preview, then, this book presents an introduction to criminal procedure, from the point at which an individual first comes into contact with the police all the way through the appeals process. Approximately half of the book is devoted to traditional criminal procedure topics—notably, search and seizure as well as interrogation and identification procedures. The remainder of the book moves beyond these topics and discusses the pretrial process; the roles of defense attorneys, prosecutors, and grand juries; plea bargaining and guilty pleas; rights of criminal defendants at trial; and appeals and *habeas corpus.*

Presentation

The material in *Criminal Procedure* is covered, in large part, by focusing on the constitutional rights of criminal defendants, as interpreted by the U.S. Supreme Court. To this end, many leading Supreme Court decisions are discussed; however, lengthy excerpts from the actual decisions have been reduced to relevant remarks in order to avoid distracting from the many important concepts introduced. (Note that key cases appear on a supplementary CD.) In order to maintain a real-world focus, the book also incorporates many actual legal documents and excerpts from official policy manuals of police departments and other criminal justice agencies around the United States.

Criminal procedure should not be confused with *evidence procedure* or *trial procedure.* Evidence procedure concerns the rules for presenting evidence to prove guilt (or the lack thereof); thus, evidence courses cover such topics as types of evidence, rules for presenting witness testimony, hearsay, and the like. This book touches on evidence only tangentially—namely, by discussing witness questioning and the police actions used to secure evidence through search and seizure. But the focus on evidence does not move beyond these two issues. Likewise, this book is not about trial procedure. That is, it does not address the nuances of criminal trials, including the order of events at trial, what objections can be raised, instructions to the jury, and so on. Trial procedure is a topic typically covered in law school.

Instead, this book presents a comprehensive introduction to criminal procedure, thoroughly presenting basic legal concepts and issues in a conversational written style and tone. Given this content coverage and the frequent use of examples from actual legal documents and policy guides, readers who are pursuing careers in criminal justice will find this book especially useful. Individuals who are already employed in criminal justice will find the book useful as well. Moreover, because the book constitutes more than a general overview of criminal procedure, it should prove beneficial to aspiring law students. But, it should not be over the heads of students with little or no background in criminal justice.

Features

Criminal Procedure has a number of pedagogical features that will benefit readers. Each chapter begins with an outline of the topics covered, giving readers an at-a-glance preview of the content. Lists of key terms and key cases are also included in the chapter opener, and each term and case is then highlighted where it is discussed in the chapter text. Each chapter ends with a set of Review Questions, which cover the basic content and also ask readers to correlate what they have learned.

The list of key cases is supplemented with a CD that contains the full texts of the Supreme Court decisions associated with each case. Selected *Federal Rules of Criminal Procedure* are also reprinted in the book from time to time in an effort to show how the issue or topic in question is addressed in the federal courts. And, the complete U.S. Constitution is reprinted in an appendix at the end of the book.

Several topics are featured throughout the book as well. Sections entitled "Criminal Procedure in Post–September 11 America" and "Enter the Patriot Act" examine how the legislation that followed the terrorist attacks on New York City and Washington, DC has affected criminal procedure in the United States. Finally, nearly every chapter contains a discussion of some controversial issue in criminal procedure, including racial profiling, police/probation partnerships, "knock and talk," civil liability, plea bargaining, and the like.

To enhance the real-world focus of the text, a series of Decision-Making Exercises are scattered throughout each chapter. Each exercise places the reader in the position of judge, asking him or her to decide a case based on the facts presented. The answers to the exercises, which are provided in a section following the appendix, explain what was decided in the actual case on which a given exercise was based or what likely would be decided given precedent in the area.

As noted earlier, the real-world focus of the book is also achieved through the use of actual legal forms and documents and excerpts from police department policy manuals and other law enforcement publications. Presented as figures, these materials show how professionals working in the field of criminal justice deal with the concepts and issues covered throughout the book.

In short, this book is intended to move beyond the basic introductory approach to criminal procedure that many of the competing books have taken but not to a level that presupposes any knowledge about the criminal process. Many competing texts focus overwhelmingly on search and seizure and on interrogation and confession procedures. This book covers these topics as well, and in great detail. But it also covers many more topics because criminal procedure consists of much more than interactions between the police and criminal suspects.

Content

Criminal Procedure is divided into five parts: (1) "Introduction"; (2) "Search and Seizure"; (3) "Interrogations, Confessions, and Identification Procedures"; (4) "The Beginnings of Formal Proceedings"; and (5) "Trial, Conviction, and Beyond." The latter two topics are rarely covered in conventional criminal procedure books, particularly at the level of detail found in this text. In contrast, the traditional approach to criminal procedure rarely moves beyond the material covered in the first three parts of this text.

Part I contains two chapters. Chapter 1 is introductory and provides readers with the information necessary to begin studying criminal procedure. In particular, it defines criminal procedure; highlights the due process/crime control dilemma, which is at the heart of all controversies in criminal procedure; discusses the relationship among the courts, including a brief section on how to do legal research; and introduces several issues and trends in criminal procedure. Chapter 1 ends with a detailed overview of the text. Chapter 2, the "remedies" chapter, begins by discussing civil and criminal remedies, then considers nonjudicial remedies, and finally examines the exclusionary rule. Remedies are presented early in the text so readers will become aware of how people's rights can be enforced in the U.S. courts.

Part II covers standard search and seizure topics. Chapter 3 provides a framework for studying the Fourth Amendment; specifically, it defines Fourth Amendment terminology and specifies when searches and seizures occur. This chapter also covers the doctrine of justification, focusing on the definitions of probable cause, reasonable suspicion, and what this book calls *administrative justification*. Chapters 4 and 5 go on to cover searches and seizures *with* warrants and *without* warrants, respectively. Chapter 6 covers actions based on reasonable suspicion, including stops-and-frisks and investigative detentions, and Chapter 7 covers actions based on administrative justification and consent, including inventories, inspections, checkpoints, school and office searches, drug and alcohol testing, and the like.

Part III covers interrogations, confessions, and identification procedures. To this end, Chapter 8 focuses heavily on the Fifth Amendment's self-incrimination clause and then summarizes the proper procedures for conducting interrogations and obtaining valid confessions. Chapter 8 also examines how the Sixth and Fourteenth Amendments govern interrogations and confessions. Chapter 9 discusses identification procedures, including the guidelines for proper pretrial identifications, and also introduces identification procedures used during trial, including the proper questioning of witnesses to assist in valid in-court identifications.

The information in Part IV is pretrial in nature. Chapter 10 begins by discussing booking, the initial appearance, the probable cause hearing, pretrial release, the preliminary hearing, and the arraignment. This chapter also introduces the rules surrounding discovery. While discovery can occur well into a trial, most discovery is pretrial in nature; thus, it is appropriate to discuss discovery in this context. Chapter 11 covers prosecutors, grand juries, and defense attorneys, including the constitutional guidelines by which each must abide. Of course, the actions of prosecutors, defense attorneys, and even grand juries matter outside the pretrial context, but readers should be familiar with these important actors before moving into the adjudication section. Finally, Chapter 12 covers plea bargaining and guilty pleas. Again, both can occur well into a trial, but most plea bargains and guilty pleas are undertaken in an effort to avoid trial.

Part V is entitled "Trial, Conviction, and Beyond." Chapter 13, the first of two chapters about the defendant's rights at trial, examines the right to a speedy trial and the right to an impartial judge and jury. Chapter 14 continues the focus on rights at trial, discussing openness, confrontation, compulsory process, double jeopardy, and entrapment. Lastly, Chapter 15 covers important topics in sentencing as well as appeals and *habeas corpus*.

As noted earlier, most texts on criminal procedure give only limited coverage to the topics in Parts IV and V, so readers should benefit by the material presented. Once again, the purpose of this book is to present a comprehensive look at criminal procedure, demonstrating that the Constitution affects much more than the actions of law enforcement personnel.

■ Supplements

Several supplements are available for this book. A CD contains the full texts of the Supreme Court cases cited at the beginning of every chapter. Also, I have written an instructor's manual, which contains test banks as well as detailed lecture outlines. Each is available in electronic format to assist instructors in structuring classroom presentations to their satisfaction.

■ Acknowledgments

Many people contributed to this book, and I will attempt to remember them all.

I would like to thank those individuals who reviewed this text for Allyn and Bacon and offered useful suggestions and remarks: Robert Boyer, Luzerne County Community College; Jack E. Call, Radford University; Kevin Daugherty, Albuquerque TVI Community College; Charles Dreveskracht, Northeastern State University; Russell A. Hunt, Dodge City Community College; David Kramer, Bergen Community College; Donna Nicholson, Manchester Community College; Caryl Anne Poteete, Southern Illinois University at Carbondale; Larry Salinger, Arkansas State University; Philip E. Secret, University of Nebraska at Omaha; and Carol Lynn Tebben, University of Wisconsin–Parkside.

Special thanks go to the following law enforcement personnel: Chief Garrett Zimmon and Sergeant Vince Kilbride of the San Bernardino, California, Police Department; Chief Paul Walters, Captain Mike Lewellen, Corporal Anthony Bertagna, and Sergeant Brian Sheldon of the Santa Ana, California, Police Department; and Chief Walter Tangel of the Gallatin, Tennessee, Police Department.

Thanks also go to my former colleagues in the Department of Criminal Justice at California State University, San Bernardino, especially Larry Gaines, chair, for being supportive of and enthusiastic about this project. I would also like to thank Craig Hemmens at Boise State University for fielding many questions from me. My students throughout the years deserve special thanks as well. Their "What if?" questions and frustration with the traditional, heavy-on-case-law approach to teaching criminal procedure contributed in no small part to this, the final product.

Finally, special thanks go to my family, especially my wife, Sabrina, for her tolerance and understanding. (I had no idea how much work a single-authored text of this magnitude would be!)

ABOUT THE AUTHOR

John L. Worrall is an associate professor in the Crime and Justice Studies program at the University of Texas at Dallas. He received his Ph.D. in political science from Washington State University in 1999. His research interests are crime control policy, prosecution, and legal issues in policing. He is the author of six books, the most recent of which is *Crime Control in America: An Assessment of the Evidence* (Allyn and Bacon, 2006). His work has also appeared in *Evaluation Review, Justice Quarterly*, and *Social Science Research,* among other journals.

CHAPTER 1

Introduction to Criminal Procedure

OUTLINE

KEY TERMS

criminal procedure
court decisions
statutes
state constitutions
Federal Rules of Criminal Procedure
Fourth Amendment
Fifth Amendment
Sixth Amendment
Eighth Amendment
Fourteenth Amendment
substantive due process
procedural due process

incorporation
precedent
stare decisis
distinguish
theory world
real world
due process
crime control
courts of limited jurisdiction
courts of general jurisdiction
superior courts
intermediate appellate courts
state supreme courts

district courts
U.S. courts of appeals
U.S. Supreme Court
defendant
prosecutor
appellant
appellee
petitioner
reverse
remand
vacate
affirm
opinion

INTRODUCTION
What Is Criminal Procedure?

American **criminal procedure** consists of a vast set of rules and guidelines that describe how suspected and accused criminals are to be handled and processed by the justice system. Of great significance is the relationship between the police and the people suspected of criminal activity. Criminal procedure arms the police with the knowledge necessary to preserve the rights of individuals who are seized, searched, arrested, and otherwise inconvenienced by law enforcement officials. It also arms other actors—such as judges, prosecutors, and defense attorneys—with the necessary information to preserve the rights of individuals accused of criminal activity. In short, criminal procedure begins when the police first contact a person and ends well after his or her conviction.

At least three important themes run throughout criminal procedure. First, there is a concern with the constitutional rights of accused persons, as interpreted by the courts. People enjoy a number of important rights in the United States, but the bulk of criminal procedure consists of *constitutional procedure*, or what the U.S. Constitution says— usually through the interpretation of the U.S. Supreme Court (i.e., the Court)—with regard to the treatment of criminal suspects.

Second, criminal procedure contains an important historical dimension, one that defers regularly to how sensitive legal issues have been approached in the past. The role of *precedent*, or past decisions by the courts, cannot be overemphasized. At the same time, though, the world continues to evolve, and it is sometimes necessary to part ways with the past and decide novel legal issues.

Third, criminal procedure creates something of a collision between two different worlds: the world of the courts versus that of law enforcement. What the courts require and what law enforcement actually deals with do not always harmonize. That is, in the

concurring opinion
dissent
writ of certiorari
rule of four
bright-line decisions
case-by-case adjudication
totality of circumstances
subjective reasonableness
objective reasonableness
Warren Court
judicial restraint
judicial activism
trespass doctrine
right to privacy
Patriot Act

KEY CASES

- *Geddes v. Northwest Missouri State College*, 49 F.3d 426 (8th Cir. 1995)
- *Wilson v. Layne*, 526 U.S. 603 (1999)
- *Manson v. Braithwaite*, 432 U.S. 98 (1977)
- *Graham v. Connor*, 490 U.S. 386 (1989)
- *Katz v. United States*, 389 U.S. 347 (1967)
- *United States v. Dionisio*, 410 U.S. 1 (1973)

real world, the influence of the courts may not always be as significant or relevant as might be expected. The following subsections will elaborate more fully on the importance of these three themes.

■ EMPHASIS ON CONSTITUTIONAL RIGHTS

The Preamble to the U.S. Constitution states:

> We the People of the United States, in Order to form a more perfect Union, establish Justice, insure domestic Tranquility, provide for the common defence, promote the general Welfare, and secure the Blessings of Liberty to ourselves and our Posterity, do ordain and establish this Constitution for the United States of America.

Of particular relevance to criminal procedure are the terms *order, justice,* and *liberty*. The Constitution helps ensure these through both setting forth the various roles of government and protecting the rights of people within the nation's borders. Throughout the years, the courts have devoted a great amount of energy to interpreting the Constitution and to specifying what rights are important and when they apply.

However, the Constitution is not the only source of rights; there are others worthy of consideration. In addition, some rights are more important than others, at least as far as criminal procedure is concerned. Finally, the two-tiered system of government in the United States creates a unique relationship between the federal and state levels. Criminal procedure cannot be understood without attention to the interplay between federal and states' rights.

■ Sources of Rights

In addition to the Constitution, important sources of rights include **court decisions**, **statutes**, and **state constitutions**. Most of the court decisions discussed in this section and throughout the text are U.S. Supreme Court decisions.

Whenever the Supreme Court interprets the Constitution, it effectively makes an announcement concerning people's rights. For example, the Fourth Amendment states that unreasonable searches and seizures are impermissible. The term *unreasonable* is not self-explanatory, however, so the Court has taken steps to define it. One definition of *unreasonable* appears in the recent decision of *Wilson v. Layne* (526 U.S. 603 [1999]), in which the Court held that it is unreasonable for the police to bring reporters along when serving a warrant, unless the reporters are there to serve a legitimate law enforcement objective.

Although the Constitution and the court decisions stemming from it reign supreme in criminal procedure, statutes play an important role, as well. Obviously, the Constitution and the courts cannot be expected to protect all of the interests that people represent. Statutes attempt to compensate for that shortcoming by establishing that certain rights exist. An example is Title VII of the 1964 Civil Rights Act. Among other things, it prohibits discrimination in employment. Another statute of relevance in criminal procedure (one that will be considered in some depth in the next chapter) is 42 U.S.C. Section 1983. It allows private citizens to sue local law enforcement officials for violations of federally protected rights.

In addition, each state has its own constitution, which can be considered an important source of rights. The supremacy clause of Article VI to the U.S. Constitution makes *it* the supreme law of the land and binds all states and the federal government to it. However, nothing in the U.S. Constitution precludes individual states from adopting stricter interpretations of the federal provisions. In general, if a state constitution gives *less* protection than the federal Constitution, such a limitation is unconstitutional. But a stricter interpretation of the federal Constitution is perfectly reasonable. For example, the Supreme Court has interpreted the Fifth Amendment in such a way that it requires police to advise a suspect of his or her so-called *Miranda* rights when the suspect is subjected to custodial interrogation—an action that does not necessarily rise to the level of an arrest. A *state*, however, could require that *Miranda* rights be read whenever a person is arrested, regardless of whether he or she is interrogated.

Finally, although it is not a source of rights per se, the **Federal Rules of Criminal Procedure** are worth considering.[1] Excerpts from the *Federal Rules* are reprinted throughout this book because they sometimes clarify important rulings handed down by the U.S. Supreme Court. Additionally, the *Federal Rules* set forth the criminal procedure guidelines by which federal criminal justice practitioners are required to abide.

Rights of Relevance in Criminal Procedure

Of the many rights specified in the U.S. Constitution (which, incidentally, is reprinted in the Appendix), the rights stemming from five amendments are of special importance in criminal procedure. Four of these—the Fourth, Fifth, Sixth, and Eighth Amendments—can be found in the Bill of Rights. Beyond the Bill of Rights, the Fourteenth Amendment is of special relevance in criminal procedure.

The **Fourth Amendment** is perhaps the most well known source of rights in criminal procedure. In fact, it is viewed to be so important that several books on criminal procedure devote the overwhelming majority of their chapters to it. The Fourth Amendment states:

> The right of the people to be secure in their persons, houses, papers, and effects, against unreasonable searches and seizures, shall not be violated, and no Warrants shall issue, but upon probable cause, supported by Oath or affirmation and particularly describing the place to be searched, and the persons or things to be seized.

Several rights can be distinguished by reading the text of the Fourth Amendment. It refers to the right of people to be free from unreasonable searches and seizures, and it provides that specific requirements are to guide the warrant process. That is, a warrant must be issued by a magistrate or judge, supported by probable cause, and sufficiently specific as to what is to be searched and/or seized. Because of the complexity of the Fourth Amendment, this book devotes an entire section to its interpretation (see Part II).

The second constitutional amendment of special relevance to criminal procedure is the Fifth. The **Fifth Amendment** provides:

> No person shall be held to answer for a capital, or otherwise infamous crime, unless on a presentment or indictment of a Grand Jury, except in cases arising in the land or naval forces, or in the Militia, when in actual service in time of War or public danger; nor shall any person be subject for the same offense to be twice put in jeopardy of life or limb; nor shall be compelled in any criminal case to be a witness against himself, nor be deprived of life, liberty, or property, without due process of law; nor shall private property be taken for public use, without just compensation.

This book also examines the Fifth Amendment in detail, focusing in particular on the role of the grand jury, the statement that no person shall be "twice put in jeopardy of life or limb" (known as the *double-jeopardy* clause), the statement that no one can be compelled "to be a witness against himself" (also known as the *self-incrimination* clause), and perhaps most important of all, the requirement that an individual cannot be deprived of life, liberty, or property without due process of law.

[1] *Federal Rules of Criminal Procedure*, issued by the 107th Congress, First Session, December 1, 2001. Available online: <www.house.gov/judiciary/crim2001.pdf>.

The First Amendment and Criminal Procedure

The First Amendment to the U.S. Constitution provides that "Congress shall make no law respecting an establishment of religion, or prohibiting the free exercise thereof; or abridging the freedom of speech, or of the press; or the right of the people peaceably to assemble, and to petition the Government for a redress of grievances." Given what you have read so far, is the First Amendment relevant to criminal procedure?

The **Sixth Amendment** is also of great importance in criminal procedure. It specifies:

In all criminal prosecutions, the accused shall enjoy the right to a speedy and public trial, by an impartial jury of the State and district wherein the crime shall have been committed, which district shall have been previously ascertained by law, and to be informed of the nature and cause of the accusation; to be confronted with the witnesses against him; to have compulsory process for obtaining witnesses in his favor, and to have the Assistance of Counsel for his defence.

Of relevance to criminal procedure is the Sixth Amendment's language concerning speedy and public trials, impartial juries, confrontation, and compulsory process. The Sixth Amendment also suggests that in addition to being public, trials should be open, not closed, proceedings. The Supreme Court has interpreted the Sixth Amendment as providing the right of the accused to be present at his or her trial and to be able to put on a defense.

The **Eighth Amendment** is relevant in criminal procedure but to a limited extent. It states:

Excessive bail shall not be required, nor excessive fines imposed, nor cruel and unusual punishments inflicted.

The Eighth Amendment's language on bail and the nature of cruel and unusual punishment are addressed in Chapters 10 and 15, respectively.

Finally, the **Fourteenth Amendment** has an important home in criminal procedure. It is a fairly long amendment, however, and only a small portion is relevant to the handling and treatment of criminal suspects. That portion states:

All persons born or naturalized in the United States, and subject to the jurisdiction thereof, are citizens of the United States and of the State wherein they reside. No State shall make or enforce any law which shall abridge the privileges or immunities of citizens of the United States, nor shall any State deprive any person of life, liberty, or property, without due process of law; nor deny to any person within its jurisdiction the equal protection of the laws.

The due process language of the Fourteenth Amendment mirrors that of the Fifth. Nonetheless, because the Fifth Amendment is part of the Bill of Rights, it is only binding on the federal government. The Fourteenth Amendment, by contrast, has been used by the Supreme Court to *incorporate*, or make applicable to the states, several of the rights provided for in the Bill of Rights. (The following subsection introduces the so-called incorporation controversy.)

The Fourteenth Amendment's due process clause has been interpreted to consist of two types of due process: (1) **substantive due process** and (2) **procedural due process**. The essence of substantive due process is protection from arbitrary and unreasonable

FIGURE 1.1   Constitutional Amendments Important to Criminal Procedure and
Their Relevant Provisions

- **Fourth Amendment:** Protects from unreasonable searches and seizures.
- **Fifth Amendment:** Provides protection from double jeopardy and self-incrimination and for grand jury indictment in serious crimes.
- **Sixth Amendment:** Provides for a speedy and public trial, impartial jury, confrontation, compulsory process, and assistance of counsel.
- **Eighth Amendment:** Protects from cruel and unusual punishment.
- **Fourteenth Amendment:** Includes the so-called due process clause, which has been used to incorporate various other rights described in the Bill of Rights.

action on the part of state officials. By contrast, a procedural due process violation is one in which a violation of a significant life, liberty, or property interest occurs (e.g., *Geddes v. Northwest Missouri State College*, 49 F.3d 426 [8th Cir. 1995]).

Geddes v. Northwest Missouri State College, 49 F.3d 426 (8th Cir. 1995)

Figure 1.1 lists the constitutional amendments that are of particular importance in criminal procedure. As the following section will describe, certain rights that are provided for in each amendment may not be binding on the states. Also, even though a particular amendment may provide a particular right, the Supreme Court may have interpreted that amendment to apply in only certain circumstances. Such circumstances will be discussed throughout the text.

The Incorporation Controversy

The Bill of Rights, consisting of the first 10 amendments to the U.S. Constitution, places limitations on the powers of the federal government. It does *not* limit the power of the states, however. In other words, the first 10 amendments place no limitations on state and local governments and their agencies. Government power at the state and local levels is clearly limited by state constitutions.

Even though the Bill of Rights does not limit state and local governments, the Supreme Court has found a way to do so through the Fourteenth Amendment. In particular, the Court has used the Fourteenth Amendment's due process clause, which holds that no state shall "deprive any person of life, liberty, or property, without due process of law," to make certain protections specified in the Bill of Rights applicable to the states. This is known as **incorporation**.

The extent to which the Fourteenth Amendment should regulate state and local government power has been the subject of some disagreement—hence, the incorporation controversy. The basic question posed over the years has been, To what degree should the Fourteenth Amendment's due process clause incorporate the various provisions of the Bill of Rights so as to restrict state and local law enforcement in the same way federal law enforcement is restricted by the Bill of Rights?

Significance of the Debate

The incorporation debate is significant because of three concerns. First, since most contact between citizens and the police occurs at the state and local levels, it is critical to determine the role of the federal Constitution at the state level. Comparatively few people have contact with federal law enforcement, so the Bill of Rights actually regulates a limited number of police/citizen contacts. Second, incorporation, according to some, threatens *federalism*. Under the doctrine of federalism, states have the authority to develop their own rules and laws of criminal procedure, but if the Fourteenth Amendment incorporates the Bill of Rights, this authority can be compromised. Third, the incorporation debate raises important concerns about the separation of powers. Namely, the Supreme Court has decided which rights should be incorporated—a decision that may better be reserved for Congress.

Views on Incorporation

There are four leading views on the incorporation debate.[2] One has won out over the others, but all of the views are important to consider, regardless.

First, the *total incorporation* perspective holds that the Fourteenth Amendment's due process clause incorporates the entire Bill of Rights. In other words, all protections specified in the Bill of Rights should be binding on the states. The primary proponent of this view was Supreme Court Justice Hugo Black (e.g., *Adamson v. California*, 332 U.S. 46 [1947]; *Rochin v. California*, 342 U.S. 165 [1952]).

The second leading view on incorporation is that of *selective incorporation*, or the *fundamental rights* perspective. It favors incorporation of certain protections enumerated in the Bill of Rights, not all of them. Further, this perspective deems certain rights as being more critical, or fundamental, than others. The Supreme Court's decision in *Snyder v. Massachusetts* (291 U.S. 97 [1934]) advocates this perspective, arguing that the due process clause prohibits state encroachment on those "principle[s] of justice so rooted in the traditions and consciences of our people as to be ranked as fundamental."

The third view on incorporation can be termed *total incorporation plus*. This view holds that the Fourteenth Amendment's due process clause incorporates the whole Bill of Rights as well as additional rights *not* specified in the Constitution, such as the "right to privacy." This view can be found in such Supreme Court cases as *Adamson v. California* (332 U.S. 46 [1947]) and *Poe v. Ullman* (367 U.S. 497 [1961]).

Finally, some people believe that the topic of incorporation deserves case-by-case consideration. That is, no rights should be incorporated across the board. Rather, the facts and circumstances of each individual case should be weighed in order to determine if any protections listed in the Bill of Rights should apply at the state or local level.

Outcome of the Debate

So, which perspective has won out? Arguably, the selective incorporation, or fundamental rights, perspective is the winner. The Supreme Court has consistently held that some protections listed in the Bill of Rights are more applicable to the states than others. The Fourth Amendment, in its view, lists several *fundamental rights*. By contrast, the Fifth Amendment's grand jury clause has not been deemed fundamental and is not binding on the states (*Hurtado v. California*, 110 U.S. 516 [1884]).

To an extent, part of the total-incorporation-plus perspective has won out, as well. While not all of the Bill of Rights is binding on the states, the Supreme Court has repeatedly emphasized Americans have a fundamental right to privacy. This is despite the fact that the Constitution makes no mention of privacy. It is commonly said (as will be noted in the section on the Fourth Amendment) that people do not enjoy an *expectation of privacy* in public places. It would seem, then, that certain rights not listed in the Constitution have been identified as well as incorporated.

Figure 1.2 lists the rights that have been deemed fundamental by the Supreme Court and, as a result, incorporated to the states.[3] The Supreme Court cases responsible for these incorporation decisions are listed, as well.

[2]J. Dressler, *Law Outlines: Criminal Procedure* (Santa Monica, CA: Casenotes Publishing, 1997), pp. 2-3–2-4.

[3]Some scholars believe that the Ninth Amendment to the U.S. Constitution (also referred to as the *penumbra clause*) implies that all of the rights not specifically spelled out in the Constitution are automatically protected nonetheless. But to demonstrate this, a court would have to recognize a particular right as fundamental in case law. Privacy could be considered one such right.

FIGURE 1.2	Rights Incorporated to the States

Right	Deciding Case
First Amendment freedom of religion, speech, and assembly and the right to petition for redress of grievances	*Fiske v. Kansas,* 274 U.S. 380 (1927)
Fourth Amendment prohibition of unreasonable searches and seizures	*Wolf v. Colorado,* 338 U.S. 25 (1949)
Fifth Amendment protection against compelled self-incrimination	*Malloy v. Hogan,* 378 U.S. 1 (1964)
Fifth Amendment protection from double jeopardy	*Benton v. Maryland,* 395 U.S. 784 (1969)
Sixth Amendment right to counsel	*Gideon v. Wainwright,* 372 U.S. 335 (1963)
Sixth Amendment right to a speedy trial	*Klopfer v. North Carolina,* 386 U.S. 213 (1967)
Sixth Amendment right to a public trial	*In re Oliver,* 333 U.S. 257 (1948)
Sixth Amendment right to confrontation	*Pointer v. Texas,* 380 U.S. 400 (1965)
Sixth Amendment right to an impartial jury	*Duncan v. Louisiana,* 391 U.S. 145 (1968)
Sixth Amendment right to compulsory process	*Washington v. Texas,* 388 U.S. 14 (1967)
Eighth Amendment prohibition of cruel and unusual punishment	*Robinson v. California,* 370 U.S. 660 (1962)

THE IMPORTANCE OF PRECEDENT

To many students of criminal procedure, legal research is a less than desirable pursuit. Even so, it is essential in everyday practice because of the importance of precedent. A **precedent** is a rule of case law (i.e., a decision by a court) that is binding on all lower courts and the court that issued it. A past decision may not be available in each case, but when one is, the courts will defer to it. This is the doctrine of *stare decisis*.

Stare Decisis

Stare decisis is a Latin term that means to abide by or to adhere to decided cases. Most courts adhere to the principle of *stare decisis*. That is, when a court has handed down a decision on a specific set of facts or legal questions, later court decisions that involve similar facts or questions will defer to the previous decision. In short, *stare decisis* is simply the practice of adhering to a previous decision, or precedent.

Why does *stare decisis* occupy such an important position in the U.S. court system? The answer is that it promotes consistency. It is well known that accused criminals enjoy the right to counsel (*Gideon v. Wainwright*, 372 U.S. 335 [1963]), but what if from one year to the next, the Supreme Court vacillated on whether this right were constitutionally guaranteed? The criminal process, not to mention the rights of the accused, would be unpredictable and vary from one point to the next.

It is important to note that the practice of deferring to precedent is not always possible or desirable. First, *stare decisis* is usually only practiced by courts in a single jurisdiction. Suppose, for example, that a federal circuit appeals court handed down a decision. All the district courts within that circuit would then abide by the appeals court decision. Courts outside that circuit would *not* be bound to adhere to the decision (although some courts often do as a matter of professional courtesy). Perhaps more important, if a case coming before a court is unique and does not resemble one decided in the past, the court may *distinguish* it.

■ Distinguishing Cases

When a previous decision does not apply to the current facts, a court will **distinguish** the case, saying, in effect, that this case is different and cannot be decided by looking to past rulings. Another way of understanding what it means to distinguish a case is to think of the present set of facts as unique and never before considered by an appellate court.

Since only a handful of cases make it to the appellate level, and even fewer still arrive at the Supreme Court, there is an untold number of cases waiting to be distinguished. This is a critical point. The case law in place currently addresses only a minute quantity of possible constitutional questions. Countless contacts occur between the police and citizens, and several of them may give rise to important constitutional questions. Yet they may never see the inside of a courtroom. So, while this book may appear heavy on case law, a thorough understanding of criminal procedure would require a review of the nearly infinite possible factual circumstances that could arise in the criminal process.

An example of a case that was distinguished is *Terry v. Ohio* (392 U.S. 1 [1968]). In that case, the Supreme Court held that police officers can stop and frisk suspects with reasonable suspicion, not probable cause (the latter standard appearing in the text of the Fourth Amendment). The Court felt that a stop-and-frisk is different from a search or a seizure and, as such, should be governed by a different set of standards. Had the Supreme Court *not* decided *Terry*, or any case like it, stop-and-frisk encounters would probably still be considered seizures and therefore subject to the Fourth Amendment's requirement for probable cause. *Terry* will be considered in more detail later, as will many other distinguished cases.

DECISION MAKING EXERCISE 1.2

Traditional Legal Doctrine Meets High-Tech Crime

In *United States v. Maxwell* (45 M.J. 406 [C.A.A.F. 1996]), the U.S. Court of Appeals for the Armed Forces dealt with the ability of existing Fourth Amendment case law to cope with searches and seizures in cyberspace. The case was very complex and raised many legal issues, but the facts can be summarized briefly: An agent of the Federal Bureau of Investigation (FBI) learned that child pornography was being exchanged on the Internet by individuals with specific America Online (AOL) screen names. (Note that a *screen name* is not the same as a *user name,* the former being the name the person goes by online. A user name is the actual name used for billing, correspondence, and so on. One household may have several screen names but only one user name.) The FBI agent approached AOL and requested the records associated with each screen name. The AOL employee said the agent would need to obtain a search warrant first. In anticipation of the warrant, AOL employees began compiling the records that the agent sought. The agent then obtained the search warrant, which permitted seizure of the records of each user associated with the screen names identified by the agent. Simply put, the agent was interested in the records for each *screen name* suspected of exchanging child pornography on the Internet but mistakenly sought the records associated with each *user.* The agent argued that this was a so-called "good faith" mistake and that the records associated with each user—as opposed to each screen name—should be admissible. Since the agent obtained records for each user, more incriminating evidence was found than would have been if he had only acquired the records for each screen name of interest. The "good faith" argument has roots in existing case law and has succeeded countless times in the past. Do you think it should succeed here?

In nearly every class on criminal procedure, students ask, "What if . . . ?" The "what if" question reflects a concern over possible factual circumstances not already addressed in published court decisions. In order for a "what if" question to be answered, a court decision must result. Otherwise, the best approach to answering such a question is to look to the past and find a decision that closely resembles the hypothetical scenario posed by the question. In this vein, every case discussed throughout this text should be thought of as a distinguished case. Every decision was based on a different set of factual circumstances and was deemed by the reviewing court as worthy of being distinguished. Were it not for distinguished cases, criminal procedure case law could be adequately covered in a matter of minutes, even seconds.

THEORY VERSUS REALITY

Criminal procedure consists mostly of rules and guidelines that have been handed down by the courts so as to dictate how the criminal process should play out. As already mentioned, many of these rules and guidelines have come from the U.S. Supreme Court, which has decided on thousands of occasions how the Constitution should be interpreted. However, in some circumstances, court decisions may not really have a great deal of influence. That is, some court decisions are made in the **theory world**, which is somewhat disconnected from the day-to-day operations of law enforcement. In contrast, the police occupy a position that is very definitely in the **real world**. Understandably, there can be differences, even tensions, between the worlds of theory and reality.

The fact that theory and reality may differ is a subject that receives little direct attention in criminal procedure textbooks. Indeed, that certain Supreme Court decisions may not really matter, or might even be flatly ignored, is a controversial notion, to say the least. Americans are taught that the courts—and the Supreme Court, in particular—are charged with interpreting the Constitution and the laws of the United States. They are further taught that law enforcement should accept such interpretations uncritically and without much reflection. While this is mostly true, theory and reality can still differ for at least four reasons.

First, the Supreme Court sometimes makes decisions on excruciatingly detailed matters that have almost no applicability to most law enforcement officers most of the time. A good example is the Supreme Court's recent decision in *Atwater v. City of Lago Vista* (533 U.S. 924 [2001]), a case that will be considered more fully later. (See Chapter 5 on warrantless searches and seizures.) The Court decided that the Fourth Amendment does not prohibit the police from arresting people for seatbelt violations. On one level, this decision seems significant, but how many police officers are now going to arrest people for seatbelt violations? Probably very few police will take up this cause because they usually have more important matters to address.

Second, the Supreme Court frequently hands down restrictive decisions that would seem to have dramatic effects on the nature of law enforcement but that actually involve issues already being addressed by many police agencies. For example, the Supreme Court's decision in *Tennessee v. Garner* (471 U.S. 1 [1985]) made it a violation of the Fourth Amendment for the police to use deadly force to apprehend an unarmed and nondangerous fleeing felon. However, prior to *Garner*, many police agencies had already adopted restrictive deadly force policies—policies that, in many instances, were more restrictive than what was handed down in *Garner*. Police agency policy, therefore, can differ from, and even be more restrictive than, decisions reached by the Supreme Court. To illustrate this, several excerpts from police agency manuals and guidelines are reprinted throughout subsequent chapters.

The third reason for the theory/reality dichotomy is that the courts sometimes hand down decisions that can be effectively circumvented or ignored by the police. Clearly, it is not in the best interest of law enforcement to ignore the courts, and it is probably quite rare that the police do so, but it can be done. For example, in *Kyllo v. United States* (533 U.S. 27 [2001]), the Supreme Court held that it is a violation of the Fourth Amendment for the police to scan a private residence with an infrared thermal imager without first obtaining a warrant. The consequence of conducting such a scan without a warrant is that any evidence subsequently obtained will not be admissible in court. However, in reality, what is to prevent the police from scanning someone's house if there is no intent to secure evidence?

DECISION MAKING EXERCISE 1.3

Theory and Reality Collide

In *Miranda v. Arizona* (384 U.S. 436 [1966]), the U.S. Supreme Court decided that the police must advise suspects who are custodially interrogated of their Fifth Amendment privilege against self-incrimination. This case will be revisited in great detail in Chapter 8, but for now, it illustrates that (1) *custody* occurs when a reasonable person would believe the suspect is not free to leave (an arrest being a prime example of such action) and (2) *interrogation* refers to actions by the police that are reasonably likely to elicit a response from the suspect. Assume that the police arrest a man but do not interrogate him. Assume further that the man confesses to a crime. Did the police violate the *Miranda* decision?

Finally, what the courts say and the police do can differ simply as a consequence of the U.S. legal system. It is well known, for example, that a police officer cannot stop a motorist without some level of justification. On how many occasions, though, are motorists stopped without justification? That is, how many people are pulled over every day simply because a police officer is suspicious of them? This cannot be established for certain, but it does happen. It *can* happen because the legal system cannot do much to prevent it. Someone who is wrongfully stopped can file a complaint, but research shows that many such complaints are resolved in favor of the police.[4] A lawsuit can be filed, but as will be noted in Chapter 2, such suits rarely are successful. And if nothing worthy of arresting the motorist is discovered, then it is doubtful that the illegal stop will draw attention in court.

In fairness to the law enforcement community, it is not the case that the police (or other criminal justice officials) regularly trample people's constitutional rights. Most law enforcement officials are responsible, professional, and upstanding enforcers of the law, as are most judges and prosecutors. But the fact cannot be ignored that the reality of everyday law enforcement and the somewhat distant nature of certain court decisions do not always meet. It is for this reason that distinctions between theory and reality are pointed out throughout later chapters.

COMPETING CONCERNS IN CRIMINAL PROCEDURE

Criminal procedure is an exciting topic because of the inherent tension it creates between two competing sets of priorities. On the one hand, there is a serious interest in the United States in controlling crime, with some Americans advocating doing whatever it takes to keep criminals off the streets. On the other hand, because of their country's democratic system of government, Americans value people's rights and become angry when those rights are compromised or threatened. These two competing sets of values have been described by Herbert Packer as the *crime control* and *due process* perspectives.[5]

The values each opposing perspective subscribes to are probably familiar to many readers because the due process/crime control debate invariably pops up all throughout

---

[4]For an informative review, see J. L. Worrall, "If You Build It, They Will Come: Consequences of Improved Citizen Complaint Review Procedures," *Crime and Delinquency* 48 (2002): 355.

[5]H. L. Packer, *The Limits of the Criminal Sanction* (Palo Alto, CA: Stanford University Press, 1968).

criminal justice. Almost without exception, whenever there is disagreement as to how best to approach the crime problem—be it through court decisions or legislative measures—the due process/crime control distinction rears its head. A delicate balance has to be achieved between the two perspectives.

The due process perspective closely resembles a liberal political orientation. Liberals often favor protection of people's rights and liberties to a higher degree than their conservative counterparts. By contrast, the crime control perspective is the one most frequently subscribed to by conservative law-and-order types.

Of course, in reality, there can be a great deal of overlap between the two orientations. Liberals occasionally favor conservative crime control policies, and conservatives can be concerned with protecting the rights of American citizens. That is to say, although the two groups frequently stand in stark contrast to each other, they do sometimes meet in the middle. Regardless, the values espoused by each group—be it an interest in crime control, an interest in civil rights, or an interest in both—are here to stay. Given that, it is useful to consider each perspective in more detail, focusing special attention on the implications for criminal procedure.

■ Due Process

Packer's **due process** model is, first and foremost, concerned with people's rights and liberties. It also gives significant weight to human freedom. Due process advocates believe that the government's primary job is not to control crime but rather to maximize human freedom, which includes protecting citizens from undue government influence. Proponents of due process favor minimizing the potential for mistakes, as explained by Packer:

> People are notoriously poor observers of disturbing events. . . . [C]onfessions and admissions by persons in police custody may be induced by physical or psychological coercion so that the police end up hearing what the suspect thinks they want to hear rather than the truth; witnesses may be animated by a bias or interest that no one would trouble to discover except one specially charged with protecting the interests of the accused (as the police are not).[6]

Due process advocates also believe that each suspect is innocent until proven guilty, just as Americans are taught. In addition, they place greater emphasis on *legal guilt* (whether a person is guilty according to the law) rather than *factual guilt* (whether a person actually committed the crime with which he or she is charged).

Underlying the due process perspective are four ideals: (1) The criminal process looks, or should look, something like an obstacle course; (2) Quality is better than quantity; (3) Formality is preferred over informality; and (4) A great deal of faith is put in the courts.

The Obstacle Course

The "obstacle course" idea is rooted in a metaphor, of course. A criminal process that resembles an obstacle course is one that is complex and needs to be navigated by skilled legal professionals. Further, it is one that is somewhat difficult to operate in a predictable fashion. It is not a process that prides itself on speed and efficiency—values of great importance in the crime control perspective. In fact, the opposite could be said. The obstacle course metaphor also stresses that each case must pass through several complicated twists and turns before a verdict can be rendered.

Quality over Quantity

Another way to distinguish between due process and crime control is in terms of quantity and quality. The due process view favors quality—that is, reaching a fair and accurate

---

[6]Packer, p. 163.

decision at every stage of the criminal process. It stresses that each case should be handled on an individual basis and that special attention should be paid to the facts and circumstances surrounding the event. In addition, the concern with quality is one that minimizes the potential for error. For example, due process advocates are in favor of allowing several death penalty appeals because the possibility of executing the wrong person should be avoided at all costs.

Insistence on Formality

Due process advocates do not favor informal processes. Because of the potential for human error and bias, they favor a full-blown adversarial criminal process. They also believe that early intervention by judges and other presumptively objective parties (besides, say, the police) is in the best interest of people accused of breaking the law.

DECISION MAKING EXERCISE **1.4**

Due Process or Crime Control?

How should the *Miranda* decision from Exercise 1.3 be characterized: as due process oriented or crime control oriented? In other words, does *Miranda* prioritize the suspect's due process rights or the interest of the police in controlling crime? What about the Supreme Court's decision in *Kyllo v. United States*, mentioned in the Theory versus Reality section?

Faith in the Courts

Another value inherent in the due process perspective is intense faith in the courts as opposed to law enforcement. Due process advocates correctly point out that the job of a judge is to interpret the U.S. Constitution. This, they argue, helps provide protection to people charged with crimes. Faith in the courts also corresponds with the above-mentioned insistence on formality. When guilt or innocence is determined in court, an air of fairness and objectivity must be maintained.

Crime Control

In contrast to the due process perspective, the **crime control** model emphasizes the importance of controlling crime, perhaps to the detriment of civil liberties. From a cost/benefit perspective, crime control advocates believe that the benefit of controlling crime to society at large outweighs the cost of infringing on some individuals' due process protections. Another way to distinguish between the due process and crime control perspectives is to consider the distinction between *means* and *ends*: Crime control is more concerned with the *ends*, with wiping out crime, or at a minimum, with mitigating its harmful effects. By contrast, due process is concerned with the *means*, with the methods by which people are treated by criminal justice officials. The result—either crime or the absence of it—is not of great concern to due process advocates.

Additional differences between the due process and crime control perspectives are illustrated in Figure 1.3.

The Assembly Line

The metaphor of an "assembly line" suggests that the criminal process should be automatic, predictable, and uniform. In other words, every criminal should be treated the same, with minimal variations in terms of charges and sentences. The assembly line metaphor further suggests that the criminal process should be quick and efficient. The goal of the crime control perspective is to move criminals through the justice process as

---

FIGURE 1.3   *The Values of Due Process versus Crime Control*

Crime Control Values	Due Process Values
■ Follows "assembly line" metaphor	■ Follows "obstacle course" metaphor
■ Emphasizes quantity over quality	■ Emphasizes quality over quantity
■ Favors informality	■ Prefers formality
■ Has faith in the police	■ Has faith in the courts
■ Makes presumption of guilt	■ Makes presumption of innocence
■ Seeks to benefit society	■ Seeks to benefit suspects
■ Is concerned with ends, not means	■ Is concerned with means, not ends
■ Seeks to maximize police authority	■ Seeks to maximize human freedom
■ Seeks to control crime at all costs	■ Seeks to protect people's rights at all costs
■ Puts emphasis on factual guilt	■ Puts emphasis on legal guilt

---

swiftly as possible. A full-blown adversarial criminal process, replete with hearings and other pauses in the interest of the accused, is anathema to the crime control view.

Quantity over Quality

As just mentioned, the due process model stresses quality over quantity. The crime control model, by contrast, favors quantity over quality, a view that is consistent with the assembly line metaphor. The goal is to move as many offenders as possible through the criminal justice system with as little delay as possible. If mistakes are made along the way and someone is wrongfully charged or convicted, so be it. That is, the *overall* goal of ensuring that as many criminals are dealt with as possible is superior to protecting any individual's constitutional rights.

Insistence on Informality

Whereas the due process perspective favors the formality of the criminal process, with particular emphasis on the courts, the crime control perspective favors informality. The courts are to be avoided; instead, justice should be meted out beyond the walls of a courtroom. Plea bargaining, for instance, is favored because of its swift, behind-the-scenes nature (not to mention that it eliminates the need to go to trial). An insistence on informality suggests further that the law enforcement establishment should be more involved in making determinations of guilt, not the courts.

DECISION MAKING EXERCISE **1.5**

Due Process or Crime Control?

In two decisions, *United States v. Leon* and *Massachusetts v. Sheppard,* the Supreme Court created what is known as the "good faith" exception to the exclusionary rule. This exception, as well as the exclusionary rule, is discussed toward the end of Chapter 2. But for now, realize that both cases are important in that they held that violations of people's constitutional rights are permissible, under limited circumstances, when the police make honest mistakes. For example, if a police officer relies on a search warrant that was obtained on the basis of a reasonable mistake, he or she could serve the warrant, search for evidence, and seize it, even if these actions violated the rights of the person searched. The key is that the mistake must be a *reasonable* one. How, then, would you characterize both the *Leon* and *Sheppard* decisions; as prioritizing crime control or due process?

Faith in the Police

Finally, whereas the due process perspective places a great deal of faith in the courts, the crime control perspective puts a high degree of trust in the police. All Americans are taught that each suspect is innocent until proven guilty in a court of law. Clearly, the courts are charged with making this determination. However, crime control advocates favor so-called street justice, giving the police vast discretion in deciding how to deal with people suspected of being involved in criminal activity. A fitting quote describing the crime control perspective is, therefore, "All criminals are guilty until proven innocent." In other words, all suspects should be considered guilty; if the courts determine otherwise, then so be it.

■ DOING LEGAL RESEARCH AND UNDERSTANDING THE RELATIONSHIP AMONG COURTS

Criminal procedure can be complex, not only because of the many factual questions that arise in day-to-day police/citizen encounters (as well as throughout the rest of the justice process) but also because of the two-tiered structure of the U.S. court system. This two-tiered structure reflects the idea of *dual sovereignty*: that the federal and state governments are considered separate, or *sovereign*, in their own right. Each state, as well as the federal government, has its own court structure.

There is no way to succinctly describe all the variations in state court structures, but, generally, they resemble one another. Typically, the lowest-level courts in a given state are **courts of limited jurisdiction**, which are charged with trying specific types of relatively minor offenses and infractions. A traffic court fits in this category. Next are the trial courts, also called **courts of general jurisdiction**, which try several types of cases. Courts of general jurisdiction are often county-level courts and are frequently called **superior courts**. At the next highest level are the **intermediate appellate courts**; verdicts from courts of general jurisdiction are appealed to these courts. Finally, each state has its own **state supreme court**, the highest court in the state. Figure 1.4 shows a typical state court structure—this one, from the state of California.

The *federal* court structure can be described succinctly because, for the purposes of criminal procedure, it consists of three specific types of courts. The lowest courts at the federal level are the so-called **district courts**. There are 94 federal district courts in the United States (as of this writing), including 89 district courts in the 50 states and 1 each in Puerto Rico, the Virgin Islands, the District of Columbia, Guam, and the Northern Mariana Islands. At the next level are the **U.S. courts of appeals**. There are 13 of these so-called circuit courts of appeals: 12 regional courts and one for the federal circuit. Each is charged with hearing appeals from several of the district courts that fall within its circuit. Finally, the **U.S. Supreme Court** is the highest court in the federal system. As will be discussed, however, the Supreme Court does not only hear federal appeals.[7] Figure 1.5 shows the structure of the federal court system; the courts of relevance in criminal procedure are highlighted. Figure 1.6 presents a map of the federal judicial circuits.

The federal government and each of the 50 states is considered a sovereign entity. That is why each has a court system of its own. There is another set of sovereigns, however: the Native American tribal courts. These tribal courts will receive no further attention in this book because, in general, they do not have to follow the same constitutional requirements as state and federal courts. Rather, they come under the Indian Civil Rights

---

[7]Note that references to the federal-level Supreme Court are always capitalized (e.g., *the U.S. Supreme Court*, *the Supreme Court*, and even *the Court*), whereas those to state-level supreme courts are not (i.e., except in citing a particular state court, such as the *Florida Supreme Court*).

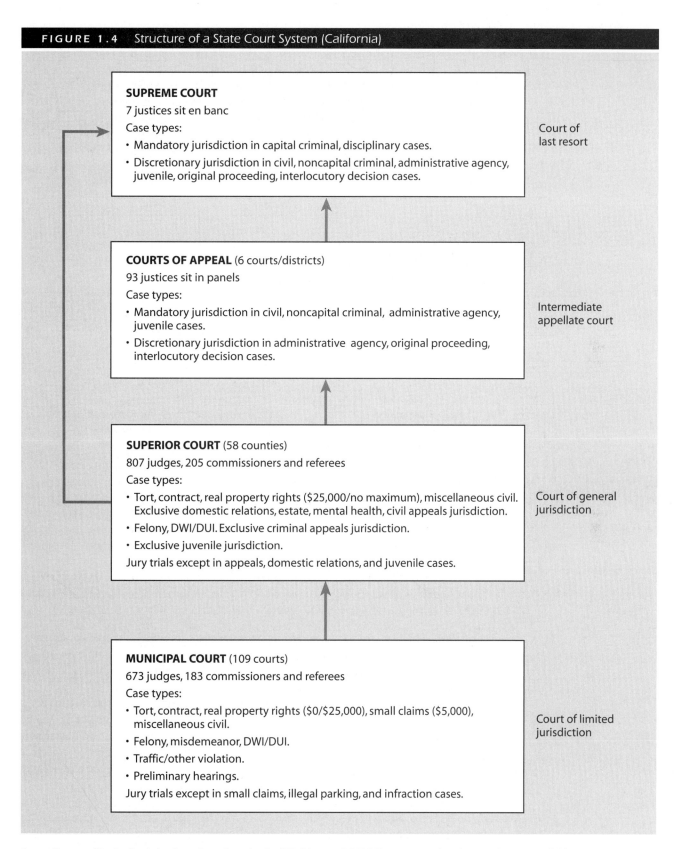

FIGURE 1.4 Structure of a State Court System (California)

SUPREME COURT

7 justices sit en banc

Case types:

• Mandatory jurisdiction in capital criminal, disciplinary cases.

• Discretionary jurisdiction in civil, noncapital criminal, administrative agency, juvenile, original proceeding, interlocutory decision cases.

Court of last resort

COURTS OF APPEAL (6 courts/districts)

93 justices sit in panels

Case types:

• Mandatory jurisdiction in civil, noncapital criminal, administrative agency, juvenile cases.

• Discretionary jurisdiction in administrative agency, original proceeding, interlocutory decision cases.

Intermediate appellate court

SUPERIOR COURT (58 counties)

807 judges, 205 commissioners and referees

Case types:

• Tort, contract, real property rights ($25,000/no maximum), miscellaneous civil. Exclusive domestic relations, estate, mental health, civil appeals jurisdiction.

• Felony, DWI/DUI. Exclusive criminal appeals jurisdiction.

• Exclusive juvenile jurisdiction.

Jury trials except in appeals, domestic relations, and juvenile cases.

Court of general jurisdiction

MUNICIPAL COURT (109 courts)

673 judges, 183 commissioners and referees

Case types:

• Tort, contract, real property rights ($0/$25,000), small claims ($5,000), miscellaneous civil.

• Felony, misdemeanor, DWI/DUI.

• Traffic/other violation.

• Preliminary hearings.

Jury trials except in small claims, illegal parking, and infraction cases.

Court of limited jurisdiction

Source: Bureau of Justice Statistics, *State Court Organization* (Washington, DC: U.S. Department of Justice, 1998), p. 322. Available online:<www.ojp.usdoj.gov/bjs/pub/pdf/sco9808.pdf>.

FIGURE 1.5 Structure of the Federal Court System

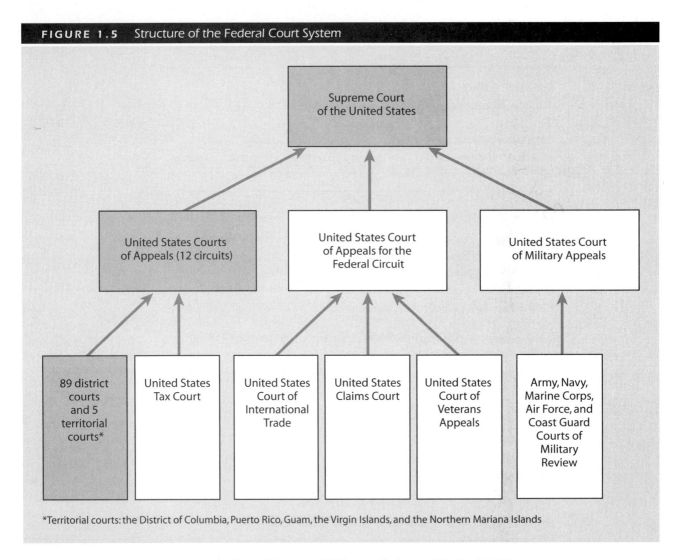

*Territorial courts: the District of Columbia, Puerto Rico, Guam, the Virgin Islands, and the Northern Mariana Islands

Source: Available online:<www.uscourts.gov/understanding_courts/gifs/figure1.gif>. Accessed October 21, 2002.

Act of 1968. The U.S. military also has its own structure, in which the rules of criminal procedure differ markedly from those covered here. Because of the complexity of the Uniform Code of Military Justice, military courts and criminal procedure will not be covered in this book, either.

That said, what decides where a case will be decided? Generally, if the case involves federal law, it will be tried in federal court. If, by contrast, it involves state law, it will be heard in state court. Certain crimes—such as kidnapping, transportation of illegal narcotics across state lines, and robbing a federally insured bank—can be tried in both federal and state courts, if the prosecutors agree. As will be discussed later, such a dual prosecution does not violate the Fifth Amendment's double-jeopardy clause.

As indicated near the outset of this chapter, criminal procedure textbooks—this one included—focus almost exclusively on U.S. Supreme Court decisions. Why focus on *federal* Supreme Court decisions rather than *state* supreme court decisions? The answer is that many important cases move from the state supreme courts to the U.S. Supreme Court, which is the court of last resort. Decisions of the U.S. Supreme Court are, therefore, important because they represent the last word on what conduct is constitutional and what conduct is not.

FIGURE 1.6 Federal Circuit Courts

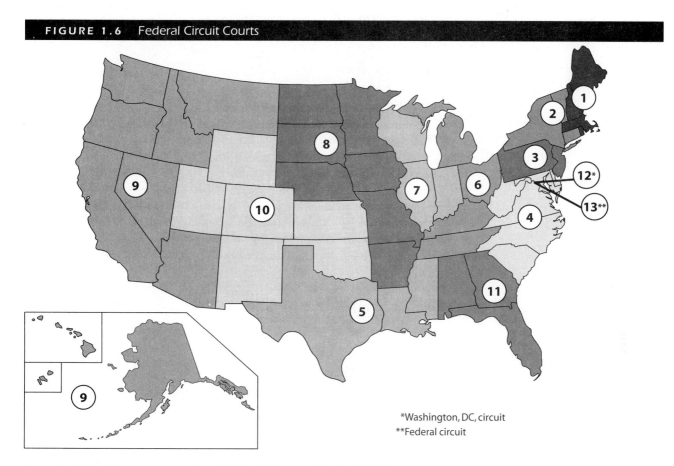

*Washington, DC, circuit
**Federal circuit

Source: Available online: <www.uscourts.gov/links.html>. Accessed October 21, 2002.

To understand the relationship between the federal and state courts, it is necessary to understand first where to find criminal cases and then how to trace the progress of criminal cases as they move from the trial to the appellate level. Following discussion of these topics, attention will turn to what types of cases are decided by the U.S. Supreme Court and how state-level court decisions arrive at the nation's highest court.

Finding Cases

Being able to find court cases requires that readers be familiar with legal citations as well as the publications in which cases can be found. Legal citations are somewhat cryptic but can be deciphered with relative ease. The citation format used throughout this text looks something like this:

Miranda v. Arizona (384 U.S. 436 [1966])

Miranda and *Arizona* refer to the parties to the case. The legal citation format that follows the parties is interpreted as follows: The first part, *384*, is the volume; the second part, *U.S.*, is the publication in which the case can be found; the third part, *436*, is the page on which the case starts; and the fourth, *1966*, is the year the decision was published. See Figure 1.7 for a listing of publications in which court cases can be found.

After becoming familiar with case citations, it is necessary to learn where the cases can actually be found. First, most university libraries have one or several of the so-called reporters listed in Figure 1.7. They can be found in bound form on the library shelves. Online research is also an option. Cases can be found at such Web sites as <www.findlaw.com>.

FIGURE 1.7 Publications Containing Court Cases

Abbreviation	Description
U.S.	*United States Reports:* This is the official publication for U.S. Supreme Court decisions.
S.Ct.	*Supreme Court Reporter:* This West Law publication reports U.S. Supreme Court decisions.
CrL	*Criminal Law Reporter:* This Bureau of National Affairs publication reports U.S. Supreme Court decisions.
L.W.	*United States Law Week:* This Bureau of National Affairs publication reports U.S. Supreme Court decisions.
F.2d	*Federal Reports,* Second Series: This West Law publication reports decisions of the Federal Courts of Appeals.
P.2d	*Pacific Reporter,* Second Series: This West Law publication reports decisions from the Pacific states.
A.2d	*Atlantic Reporter,* Second Series: This West Law publication reports decisions from the Atlantic states.
N.E.2d	*North Eastern Reporter,* Second Series: This West Law publication reports decisions from the northeastern states.
N.W.2d.	*North Western Reporter,* Second Series: This West Law publication reports decisions from the northwestern states.
S.E.2d	*South Eastern Reporter,* Second Series: This West Law publication reports decisions from the southeastern states.
S.W.2d	*South Western Reporter,* Second Series: This West Law publication reports decisions from the southwestern states.
S.2d	*Southern Reporter,* Second Series: This West Law publication reports decisions from the southern states.

U.S. Supreme Court cases can be found at <www.supremecourtus.gov>. Another Web site, maintained by Cornell University, is helpful for finding Supreme Court cases: <supct.law.cornell.edu:8080/supct/>.

Many university libraries also have access to subscription databases, such as West Law and Lexis Nexis, which contain cases from nearly all courts across the country. Both Lexis and West have a feature known as *Shepard's Citations*. This allows researchers to enter a case citation and retrieve every other case that has cited it. Doing a Shepard's search is useful for tracing the history and current status of an important decision.

For those who do not enjoy reading actual court decisions, other sources of legal information may be useful. For example, legal dictionaries and encyclopedias offer clarification of important legal concepts. Legal digests identify and consolidate legal issues, provide commentary on and interpret cases, and otherwise "digest" complex material. Finally, law reviews are useful places to find discussions of various aspects of the law as well as opinions on and interpretations of court cases. Databases such as Lexis Nexis contain full-text articles from nearly all law reviews.

■ Tracing the Progress of a Criminal Case

One of the more frustrating aspects of criminal procedure, especially for those who have little familiarity with the law or legal jargon, is the sometimes laborious task of tracing the progress of a criminal case. If final decisions were reached in a single court, then criminal procedure would be vastly simplified. In reality, though, a single case can bounce back and forth between trial and appellate courts, sometimes for years. Indeed, many U.S. Supreme Court decisions concern matters that occurred a decade or more ago. Thus, it is of particular importance for students of criminal procedure to learn how to trace a criminal case.

There are several essential steps to tracing the progress of a criminal case. First, it is necessary to have a basic understanding of the nation's court structure. This requires knowing where the criminal trial in question took place. If it took place in a federal circuit court, then tracing the progress of the case will be fairly easy. There are only three possible courts—district court, circuit appellate court, and the Supreme Court—that may have handed down decisions on the matter. If the case originated in state court, however, it can be decidedly more difficult to trace the case over time. Familiarity with the state court structure will be needed, as well as an understanding of how cases can jump back and forth between the state and federal courts, which will be discussed later in this section.

Second, to adequately follow the progress of a criminal case, it is also necessary to understand the legal jargon, beginning with the parties to the case. The *parties* to the case are the people involved. At the trial level, the parties of interest are the **defendant**, or the person charged with the crime in question, and the **prosecutor**, or the person representing the government. At the appellate level, these parties are no longer called *defendant* and *prosecutor* but rather **appellant** and **appellee**. The *appellant* is the person who appeals; both the prosecutor and defendant can appeal (see Chapter 15). The *appellee* (sometimes called the *respondent*) is the person appealed against. The term **petitioner** is also used at times. That is how the defendant is referred to when he or she files a *habeas corpus* petition (see Chapter 15). A petitioner is one who petitions an appellate court to hear his or her case.

Next, to follow a criminal case, it is essential to have an understanding of how cases are decided and what possible decisions can be reached. At the trial level, two decisions can result: guilty and not guilty. At the appellate level, however, the picture becomes more complex. Assume, for example, that a defendant is found guilty in a federal district court and appeals to one of the circuit courts of appeals. Assuming that the court agrees to hear the case, it can hand down one of several decisions. It could **reverse** the lower court's decision, which is akin to nullifying or setting aside the trial verdict. A reversal does *not* always have the effect of setting the defendant free, however. The appellate court could also **remand** the case back to the lower court. When a case is remanded, it is sent back to the trial court for further action consistent with the appellate court's decision. Cases can also be reversed and remanded together. Sometimes, an appellate court will even **vacate** a lower court's judgment, which is also akin to setting it aside. The appellate court can also **affirm** the lower court's decision, in which case it agrees with the lower court.

If there was only one appellate court, tracing the progress of a case would be fairly simple. Unfortunately, multiple appellate courts exist, which means the decisions from court to court can change. This is a very important point. Assume, for example, that a defendant is found guilty in a state trial court. He or she could appeal to the state's intermediate appellate court, which could reverse the defendant's conviction. The case could then go to the state's supreme court, which could reverse the appellate court's decision and basically uphold the defendant's conviction. Finally, the case could go to the U.S. Supreme Court, which could again reverse the defendant's conviction. Believe it or not, this is a fairly simple progression. Nothing prevents a single case from going from the trial court to the appellate court, back to the trial court, up to the appellate court again, then up to the state supreme court, back to the intermediate appellate court, and so on.

It is essential to understand what has happened with a criminal case before making any claims as to its importance or influence. In other words, doing incomplete legal research can be a recipe for disaster. If, for instance, a researcher finds a state supreme court decision that supports a point he or she wants to make but that decision was later reversed, say, by the U.S. Supreme Court, whatever argument he or she makes in reliance on that state supreme court case will be inaccurate. Thus, in tracing the progress of a criminal case, it is necessary to understand whether the issue in question has been resolved or may currently be on the docket of an appellate court, which could render an altogether different decision.

In tracing a criminal case, especially when interpreting one decided at the appellate level, it is important to understand the components of a published decision. An appellate court often consists of a panel of judges who may not always agree with one another, even though the court reaches a single decision. For example, a 5 to 4 decision by the U.S. Supreme Court is one in which the Court reached a single decision because of a majority, but four of the justices disagreed. The **opinion** is the voice of the five justices, although one or more of the five may opt to write a **concurring opinion**, which supports the majority's decision but with different legal logic. The four remaining justices will probably write a **dissent**, in which they argue why they disagree with the majority's decision. If they wanted to, each of the four minority justices could write his or her own individual dissent. Either way, it is important to distinguish between a given court's opinion and possible concurring and dissenting opinions.

DECISION MAKING EXERCISE 1.6

Interpreting a Supreme Court Holding

Assume that John Smith was subjected to a search that was not supported by probable cause. Assume further that he was convicted in a federal district court based on evidence obtained from the search. He appealed his conviction to the U.S. court of appeals, which remanded his case back to the district court to determine if the search to which Smith was subjected required probable cause. (Some searches, as will be discussed later, do not require probable cause.) The district court concluded that the search did not require probable cause. The case was then appealed again to the U.S. court of appeals, which reversed the district court's decision, holding that the search *did* need to be supported by probable cause. The U.S. Supreme Court then granted *certiorari* and reversed the U.S. court of appeals decision, holding that the search did not need to be supported by probable cause. In plain English, what happened here? In other words, what is the practical effect of this convoluted case progression?

There is much more to tracing the progress of a criminal case than understanding the terminology encountered along the way. How is it that certain cases are appealed and others are not? Under what circumstances may the defendant appeal but not the prosecution, and vice versa? Why do some defendants file several appeals and others do not? Answers to these questions are presented in the last chapter of this text, where special attention is given to the appellate process and other methods for challenging the verdicts of trial courts throughout the United States.

■ How Cases Arrive at the Supreme Court

Most criminal cases originate at the state level. This should be obvious because there are 50 state court structures and only 1 federal court system. Also, the number of state laws criminalizing certain types of conduct vastly exceeds the number of federal laws with the same objective. But just because most cases are heard in state courts does not mean they cannot be heard at the federal level. State-level cases can arrive at the U.S. Supreme Court.

Stated simply, a state-level case can arrive at the Supreme Court if it raises a federal question, which is usually a question concerning the U.S. Constitution. First, however, such a case must proceed through several steps. It must move all the way to the state supreme court. That is, a case cannot jump from a state-level intermediate appellate court to the U.S. Supreme Court.

Next, like many appellate courts, the U.S. Supreme Court must decide whether it wants to hear the case. The party seeking a decision must file documents with the Court, asking to be heard. If the Supreme Court agrees the case is worth deciding, it issues what is known as a *writ of certiorari*. This is an order by the court, requiring the lower court to send the case and a record of its proceedings to the U.S. Supreme Court for review. Four of the nine U.S. Supreme Court justices must agree to hear a case before a *writ of certiorari* will be issued. This is known as the **rule of four**.

If four justices do not agree to hear the case, that is the end of the road in terms of legal options. When tracing the progress of a case, encountering a statement such as "cert. denied" will indicate this result. The case was denied a hearing by the Supreme Court. Figure 1.8 summarizes how cases arrive at the Supreme Court.

It cannot be overemphasized that only a handful of cases ever reach the U.S. Supreme Court. It is not uncommon for the Supreme Court to review thousands of petitions for review yet grant less than 100 *writs of certiorari*. Most cases that are appealed stop short of reaching the Supreme Court, so it is necessary to find out at what level the final decision was reached. Not tracing a case to its final decision can be fatal to a legal argument. In other words, if a researcher wants to argue a specific point with reference to

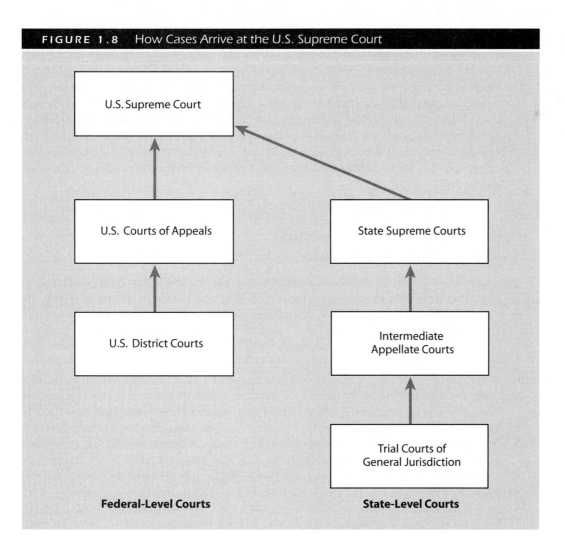

FIGURE 1.8 How Cases Arrive at the U.S. Supreme Court

U.S. Supreme Court

U.S. Courts of Appeals

State Supreme Courts

U.S. District Courts

Intermediate Appellate Courts

Trial Courts of General Jurisdiction

Federal-Level Courts

State-Level Courts

a previously decided case, he or she must be sure that the decision is, if only for the time being, a final one.

Would the Supreme Court Hear This Case?

Assume that a state supreme court heard an appeal from one of the state's intermediate appellate courts. In the appeal, the defendant argued that her conviction should be overturned, as the judge failed to declare that certain testimony provided by the government's lead witness should have been deemed inadmissible according to the state's rules of evidence. In making its decision, the appellate court sided with the government, upholding the defendant's conviction. Would the U.S. Supreme Court likely hear this case? What if, instead, the defendant argued that the original judge mistakenly permitted the prosecutor to comment to the jury concerning the defendant's refusal to take the stand and testify? Would that issue likely get a hearing from the Court?

▪ IMPORTANT TERMS, ISSUES, TRENDS, AND CHANGES IN CRIMINAL PROCEDURE

Criminal procedure, as presented in this text, is mostly about interpreting U.S. Supreme Court decisions regarding certain constitutional rights. In interpreting those decisions, it is worth understanding some important terms, issues, and trends in the Supreme Court's decision-making practices over the years. Also, it is important to realize that criminal procedure has recently changed due to some important legislation. This section focuses on six topics: (1) bright-line decisions versus case-by-case adjudication; (2) the distinction between *subjectivity* and *objectivity*; (3) an increased faith in the police; (4) the notion of judicial restraint; (5) the issue of personal privacy; and (6) the Patriot Act, which was signed into law following the attacks on the Pentagon and the World Trade Center on September 11, 2001.

▪ Bright-Line Decisions versus Case-by-Case Adjudication

There are two types of Supreme Court decisions: (1) **bright-line decisions** and (2) decisions requiring **case-by-case adjudication**. A bright-line decision is one in which the Court hands down a *specific rule*, one subject to very little interpretation. It is like the metaphorical "line drawn in the sand"; in other words, the Court emphatically communicates to the criminal justice community what it can and cannot do. An example of a bright-line decision is *Wilson v. Layne* (526 U.S. 603 [1999]), a case mentioned near the beginning of this chapter. In that case, the Supreme Court said that the police cannot bring the media along on the service of warrants unless its presence serves a legitimate law enforcement objective. It is easy to see that this is a clear, bright-line rule. Exactly what constitutes a "law enforcement objective" may be somewhat vague, but otherwise, this rule is quite clear. The advantage of a bright-line rule is that it promotes clarity and consistency. Also, it is easily understood by criminal justice officials.

  A decision requiring case-by-case adjudication is quite different. In many cases, the Supreme Court refers to the concept of **totality of circumstances**. For example, in the case of *Manson v. Braithwaite* (432 U.S. 98 [1977]), the Supreme Court held that the totality of circumstances determines whether an identification procedure is unreliable. This

▪ *Wilson v. Layne*, 526 U.S. 603 (1999)

▪ *Manson v. Braithwaite*, 432 U.S. 98 (1977)

means that all the facts and circumstances surrounding the case must be examined in order to determine whether a constitutional rights violation has taken place. Deciding whether the totality of circumstances supports the action in question requires looking at each case *individually*. There is no existing recipe specifying what authorities should or should not do. A case-by-case decision is preferable in some instances because it is rarely possible to know in advance all the possible twists and turns in a criminal case. That is, case-by-case decisions promote flexibility, leaving it up to the lower courts (usually, the trial court) to decide if the action in question conforms to constitutional guidelines. However, this approach can also create uncertainty for law enforcement officials.

DECISION MAKING EXERCISE 1.8

A Bright-Line Decision or Case-by-Case Adjudication?

In *Tennessee v. Garner* (471 U.S. 1 [1985]), a Memphis police officer shot and killed an unarmed 15-year-old boy who was fleeing the scene of a residential burglary. The officer called to the boy, Garner, to stop, but he did not. When Garner was about to climb a fence, the officer shot him in the back of the head, fatally wounding him. Garner's surviving family members filed a section 1983 lawsuit, claiming the level of force used was excessive. The Supreme Court agreed, ruling that deadly force may be used only when two criteria are present: (1) It is necessary to prevent the suspect's escape, and (2) the officer has probable cause to believe the suspect poses a serious threat of death or serious physical injury to other people or police officers. Can the Court's decision in *Garner* be characterized as bright line in nature?

Subjectivity versus Objectivity

The terms *subjective* and *objective* are sometimes found in Supreme Court decisions. And although what these terms mean in everyday use is well understood, what they mean in the language of criminal procedure is not necessarily so well defined. Part of the confusion stems from the fact that *subjective* and *objective* are sometimes used directly before the term *reasonable*. It is not uncommon to read a Supreme Court opinion referring to *objective reasonableness* or *subjective reasonableness*. Usually, phrases such as these are considered in the context of the Fourth Amendment because of its language on reasonableness.

Police conduct that is considered subjectively reasonable, or characterized by **subjective reasonableness**, is conduct that would be considered reasonable by the police officer engaged in the conduct. For example, if a police officer arrests a person without probable cause but feels that probable cause was present, his or her actions can be considered subjectively reasonable. **Objective reasonableness**, by contrast, refers to what a reasonable person (usually, a reasonable police officer) would do or feel under the circumstances. A reasonable person would believe that making an arrest without probable cause is unconstitutional.

Objective and subjective language can be found in the Supreme Court's references to people's privacy interests. For example, in deciding whether a person enjoys a reasonable expectation of privacy when engaging in some sort of activity, both terms frequently appear. The Court has been forced to answer a simple question: Should individual people be trusted to identify their privacy interests, or should what a reasonable person would believe determine the expectation of privacy?

In the past few decades, the Supreme Court has moved from subjective analyses to objective analyses in many of its decisions. The reason for this should be fairly clear: A subjective analysis puts a high degree of faith in the individual police officer, citizen, or other person. Assume that a man has a marijuana field on his property, and it is observed by the police in a helicopter fly-over. He will probably argue that he should be able to enjoy privacy in his backyard and that the police should not be able to spy on him. Such an argument is quite predictable in a case like this because it behooves the suspect to assert a privacy interest. However, what the suspect believes and what a reasonable person may believe could be two entirely different things. Indeed, the Supreme Court has moved to an objective analysis in many scenarios such as this for the simple reason that individuals are not entirely without bias in making such determinations. The Court now prefers to defer to what a reasonable person would believe.

In some ways, the term *objective*, as used in court decisions, mirrors its meaning in everyday use. It suggests a more or less unbiased view of a particular matter. By comparison, the term *subjective* suggests more of an individually based determination. Unfortunately, it is not always easy to identify what a reasonable person would believe. The notion of a reasonable person is, in fact, a hypothetical construct. For this reason, the Court usually decides what can be considered an objectively reasonable belief.

The distinction between objective and subjective reasonableness can be clarified with an important Supreme Court decision. In the landmark case of *Graham v. Connor* (490 U.S. 386 [1989]), the leading nondeadly force case decided to date, the Supreme Court declared emphatically that all claims involving allegations of excessive (nondeadly) force against police officers must be analyzed under the Fourth Amendment's reasonableness requirement. Namely, "[A]ll claims that law enforcement officers have used excessive force—deadly or not—in the course of an arrest, investigatory stop, or other 'seizure' of a free citizen should be analyzed under the Fourth Amendment and its 'reasonableness' standard" (p. 386).

■ *Graham v. Connor*, 490 U.S. 386 (1989)

More importantly, in *Garner*, the Court adopted a test of objective reasonableness to decide whether excessive force has been used. This requires focusing on what a *reasonable* police officer would do "without regard to [the officer's] underlying intent or motivation." In trying to decide what a reasonable police officer would do, the Court looked to three factors: (1) the severity of the crime; (2) whether the suspect posed a threat; and (3) whether the suspect was resisting and/or attempting to flee the scene. Courts must, in focusing on these three factors, allow "for the fact that police officers are often forced to make split-second judgments—about the amount of force that is necessary in a particular situation" (p. 386). Note that the Court was not concerned with what the individual officer felt with regard to these three factors. Rather, the preferred focus was on what a reasonable officer would believe.

DECISION MAKING EXERCISE 1.9

Subjective or Objective?

Chapter 2 will discuss civil liability against the police, but for now, realize that a police officer who is sued for violating someone's constitutional rights can assert a defense to such liability. That defense is known as *qualified immunity*. A police officer who is sued enjoys qualified immunity if he or she did not violate clearly established rights that a reasonable person would have known about (*Harlow v. Fitzgerald*, 457 U.S. 800 [1982]). Which type of *reasonableness* is considered in this context: objective or subjective?

■ Increased Faith in the Police

Earl Warren was appointed to the position of Chief Justice of the U.S. Supreme Court in 1953; thus, references to the **Warren Court** reflect the time from 1953 to 1969, during which Warren was Chief Justice. The Warren Court handed down a number of decisions, particularly throughout the 1960s, that provided extensive constitutional protections for criminal defendants. To use Packer's language, the Court was highly concerned with due process during this period. Others describe the Court as being extremely liberal during the Warren era. All in all, the Court did not place a great deal of trust in the police, much less other criminal justice officials. Rather, it was concerned primarily with individual rights.

Warren E. Burger held the position of Chief Justice from 1969 to 1986. During his tenure, the Court moved closer to the center of judicial and political thought and away from the liberal stance of the Warren Court. This movement toward conservatism gained significant momentum with the appointment of William H. Rehnquist as Chief Justice in 1987. The decisions handed down by the Court in the area of criminal procedure began to take on a different orientation, one that placed a great deal of faith in the police. In practice, many of the Court's decisions of late have increased the power of law enforcement as well as granted the police extensive latitude with regard to controlling crime. For example, the Court created the well-known "good faith" exception to the exclusionary rule. (This development is further discussed in the next chapter.) Also, many decisions have carved out exceptions to the Fourth Amendment's warrant requirement, suggesting that judicially authorized search and arrest warrants are not of particular use or importance much of the time.

The reader is encouraged to take note of the dates of the many Supreme Court decisions discussed throughout this text. With only a handful of exceptions, the decisions of the Warren Court in the 1960s were concerned with the rights of criminal suspects and placed significant restrictions on the authority of criminal justice officials. Many of the decisions handed down since approximately the 1980s reflect something of a change in priorities, one that favors increased law enforcement authority and a concern with effective crime control, as opposed to due process.

Judicial Restraint

The term **judicial restraint** identifies the philosophy of limiting decisions to the facts of each case, deciding only the issue or issues that need to be resolved in a particular situation. The practice of judicial restraint also entails avoiding unnecessary decisions on constitutional questions that have yet to be posed. In the area of criminal procedure, a judicially restrained judge will look to the Constitution for guidance and, should the Constitution not be entirely clear, he or she will attempt to understand the framers' intent. Another way to think of judicial restraint is that it is *interpretive*, seeking only to interpret the Constitution. Yet another way to understand judicial restraint is with regard to *precedent*; the judicially restrained judge will defer to precedent as much as possible and avoid setting new guidelines and rules.

The philosophy of judicial restraint can be placed at one end of the large spectrum of judicial philosophies. At the other end is **judicial activism**. A judicially active judge is one who sees his or her role as more than interpreting the Constitution. A judicially active judge avoids precedent, preferring to hand down decisions with sweeping implications for the future. Thus, a judicially active judge looks more to the future than the past. Further, a judicially active judge favors "judge-made" law.

In *Silverman v. United States* (365 U.S. 505 [1961]), the Supreme Court elaborated on the notion of judicial restraint when it was deciding a Fourth Amendment case: "[T]he facts of the present case... do not require us to consider the large questions which have been argued. We need not here contemplate the Fourth Amendment implications of these and other frightening paraphernalia which the vaunted marvels of an electronic age may visit upon human society" (p. 509). The Court basically stated that large questions should not be answered, only the specific question before the court.

Silverman stands in contrast with the Court's recent decision in *Kyllo v. United States* (533 U.S. 27 [2001]), in which it was to decide on the constitutionality of warrantless thermal imaging (infrared) searches. The Court stated, "Where, as here, the Government uses a device that is not in *general public use*, to explore *details of the home* that would previously have been unknowable without physical intrusion, the surveillance is a 'search' and is presumptively unreasonable without a warrant" (p. 2046). Clearly, this language is sweeping and general; the Court did not focus on thermal imagers but instead handed down a decision addressing a wider range of technology. This, according to some critics, violates the philosophy of judicial restraint.

▪ Personal Privacy

▪ *Katz v. United States*, 389 U.S. 347 (1967)

The Supreme Court's landmark 1967 decision in *Katz v. United States* (389 U.S. 347 [1967]), a case that will be revisited later, reflects a high degree of respect for people's privacy. This and other Supreme Court decisions show that people should enjoy protection beyond physical intrusions into their property. In *Katz*, the Court stated that "the Fourth Amendment protects people, not places," emphasizing that the scope of the "Amendment cannot turn upon the presence or absence of physical intrusion." This has come to be known as the *privacy doctrine*.

In the past, the Court required a physical intrusion by authorities into a person's private property. This was known as the **trespass doctrine**. People did not enjoy privacy unless the police or other government officials physically trespassed on their property. Today, fortunately, privacy has been extended to encompass more than personal property. What people say in private telephone conversations (as in *Katz*), for instance, is subject to intense constitutional protection:

> We conclude . . . that the "trespass" doctrine . . . can no longer be regarded as controlling. The Government's activities in electronically listening to and recording the petitioner's words violated the privacy upon which he justifiably relied while using the telephone booth and thus constituted a "search and seizure" within the meaning of the Fourth Amendment. The fact that the electronic device employed to achieve that end did not happen to penetrate the wall of the booth can have no constitutional significance. (p. 353)

The importance of personal privacy has been reaffirmed over the years in many court decisions and even by prominent academics. Sam Ervin's observation on the matter is illustrative:

> The oldest and deepest hunger in the human heart is for a place where one may dwell in peace and security and keep inviolate from public scrutiny one's innermost aspirations and thoughts, one's most intimate associations and communications, and one's most private activities. This truth was documented by Micah, the prophet, 2,700 years ago when he described the Mountain of the Lord as a place where "they shall sit every man under his own vine and fig tree and none shall make them afraid."[8]

DECISION
MAKING
EXERCISE **1.10**

The Issue of Personal Privacy

As will be discussed in detail later, the police may search a person and his or her immediate "grabbing area" pursuant to a lawful arrest. In *New York v. Belton* (453 U.S. 454 [1981]), the Supreme Court said that the police may search the passenger compartment of a person's vehicle pursuant to a lawful arrest, even if the arrested person is handcuffed and seated in the back of a patrol car. Does this decision increase or erode personal privacy?

---

[8]S. J. Ervin, "The Exclusionary Rule: An Essential Ingredient of the Fourth Amendment," *Supreme Court Review* (1983): 283.

The trend toward increased personal privacy is an interesting one because the Fourth Amendment (and the whole Bill of Rights, for that matter) contains no mention of privacy. In other words, there is no constitutional right to privacy. The Supreme Court has seen fit to identify a **right to privacy**, nonetheless. As such, privacy is something of a judicially created right. Another judicial creation is the *exclusionary rule* (discussed in Chapter 2). Because the exclusionary rule is a judicial creation, it has been eroded over the years. It is therefore conceivable that the right to privacy could be eroded in this way, as well. In fact, decisions such as *United States v. Dionisio* (410 U.S. 1 [1973]), in which the Court held that people cannot expect privacy in what they knowingly expose to the public, support such a possibility. Privacy in the home, however, continues to enjoy the highest level of protection.

■ *United States v. Dionisio*, 410 U.S. 1 (1973)

■ The Patriot Act and Criminal Procedure in Post–September 11 America

Criminal procedure is sometimes altered by important changes in federal and state legislation. One example of such legislation is the Antiterrorism and Effective Death Penalty Act of 1996, passed following the 1995 bombing of the Oklahoma City federal building. It has altered federal *habeas corpus* practice (see Chapter 15). An arguably more important piece of legislation, one that has affected several aspects of criminal procedure, was signed into law recently.

On September 14, 2001, in response to the September 11 attacks on the Pentagon and the World Trade Center, President George W. Bush declared a state of emergency, which permitted him to invoke certain presidential powers. Those powers included the ability to summon reserve troops, to marshal military units, and to issue executive orders for the implementation of such things as military tribunals. Congress also took action following September 11. In order to empower the Department of Justice, Congress passed the **Patriot Act** on October 26, 2001.[9] It is very long and complex, consisting of 10 parts and over 300 single-spaced pages. President Bush signed the act into law on October 27. (Note that the word *Patriot* in the Patriot Act is an acronym that stands for "Uniting and Strengthening America by Providing Appropriate Tools Required to Intercept and Obstruct Terrorism.")

The Patriot Act makes several important changes to past law and practice. First, it centralizes federal law enforcement authority in the U.S. Department of Justice. For example, Section 808 of the act reassigns the authority for investigating several federal crimes of violence from law enforcement agencies, such as the Secret Service and the Bureau of Alcohol, Tobacco, and Firearms, to the attorney general. The act also provides for Central Intelligence Agency (CIA) oversight of all domestic intelligence gathering. Prior to the Patriot Act, the CIA's role was primarily concerned with foreign intelligence gathering. The act also expands the definition of the terms *terrorism* and *domestic terrorism* to include activities that

(A) involve acts dangerous to human life that are a violation of the criminal laws of the United States or of any state; (B) appear to be intended (i) to intimidate or coerce a civilian population; (ii) to influence the policy of a government by mass destruction, assassination, or kidnapping; or (iii) to effect the conduct of a government by mass destruction, assassination, or kidnapping; and (C) occur primarily within the territorial jurisdiction of the United States. (USA Patriot Act 802, 115 Stat. at 376)

Of particular relevance in the context of this book are the changes in criminal procedure attributable to the Patriot Act. Before describing these changes, providing some background

---

[9]On March 9, 2006, President Bush signed a law that made the Patriot Act permanent. Certain provisions were changed and some civil liberties protections were added, but most of the original Act remains intact.

A fiery blast rocked the World Trade Center in New York City after both towers were hit by hijacked passenger planes on September 11, 2001. This attack, along with a similar attack on the Pentagon in Washington, DC, prompted passage of the Patriot Act.

will be informative. First, the Supreme Court has traditionally held that the Fifth and Sixth Amendments' rights of due process and access to jury trials apply to *all persons*, not just citizens of the United States (*United States v. Verdugo-Urquidez*, 494 U.S. 259, 264–266 [1990]). In addition, the Supreme Court has held that all undocumented aliens living inside U.S. borders are entitled to the protections enunciated in the Bill of Rights (*Mathews v. Diaz*, 426 U.S. 67 [1976]). Specifically, the Court has stated that "the Fifth Amendment, as well as the Fourteenth Amendment, protects every one of these persons from deprivation of life, liberty, or property without due process of law. Even one whose presence in this country is unlawful, involuntary, or transitory is entitled to constitutional protection" (p. 77). These rights have also applied to the removal of aliens from within U.S. borders. That is, proceedings for the deportation of aliens have had to conform to constitutional requirements, especially due process (*Shaughnessy v. United States ex rel. Mezei*, 345 U.S. 206 [1953]).

In short, legal, illegal, resident, and temporary aliens have *all* historically enjoyed the same constitutional protections as ordinary U.S. citizens. But with the passage of the Patriot Act, that is no longer the case. In several ways, the Patriot Act alters and even abolishes constitutional protections historically available to legal and illegal aliens.

Given that the Patriot Act has far-reaching implications for criminal procedure, it is worth considering throughout this text, as the need arises. To this end, several subsections beginning with "Enter the Patriot Act" will appear in later chapters, briefly describing how the Patriot Act affects certain aspects of criminal procedure, such as the Fourth Amendment's warrant requirement and the Sixth Amendment's jury trial requirement. Sections titled "Criminal Procedure in Post–September 11 America" will also discuss changes in criminal procedure following the terrorist attacks, such as administrative and procedural changes, that do not directly appear in the Patriot Act but are closely tied to it and important for criminal procedure.

THE CRIMINAL PROCESS: AN OVERVIEW

There is no easy or concise way to describe the criminal process. In an attempt to do so, the 1967 President's Crime Commission described the criminal process with the flowchart reprinted in Figure 1.9, but this conceptualization is not perfect. There are

FIGURE 1.9 Sequence of Events in the Criminal Justice System

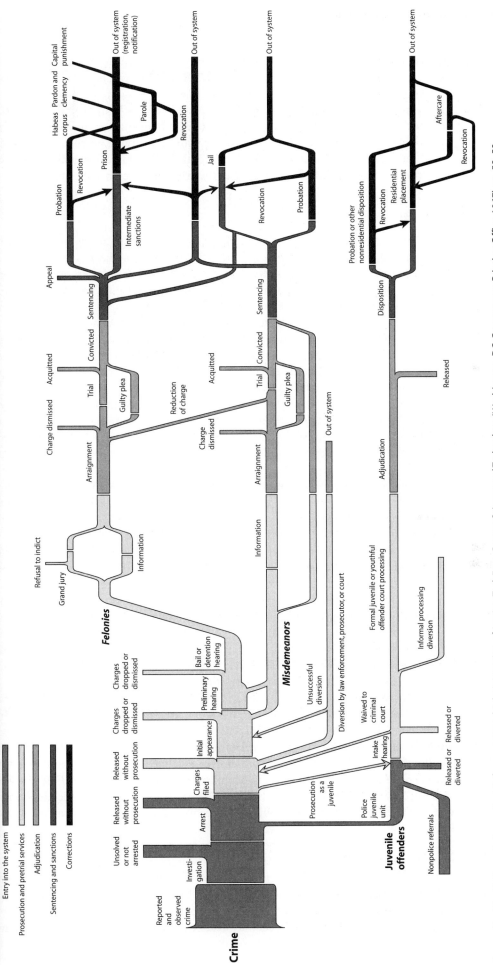

Entry into the system
Prosecution and pretrial services
Adjudication
Sentencing and sanctions
Corrections

Crime

Reported and observed crime

Investigation

Unsolved or not arrested

Arrest

Felonies

Released without prosecution

Charges filed

Initial appearance

Released without prosecution

Charges dropped or dismissed

Preliminary hearing

Charges dropped or dismissed

Bail or detention hearing

Grand jury

Refusal to indict

Information

Arraignment

Charge dismissed

Acquitted

Trial

Guilty plea

Convicted

Sentencing

Appeal

Probation

Revocation

Prison

Habeas corpus

Pardon and clemency

Capital punishment

Parole

Revocation

Out of system (registration, notification)

Intermediate sanctions

Out of system

Misdemeanors

Unsuccessful diversion

Information

Arraignment

Reduction of charge

Charge dismissed

Acquitted

Trial

Guilty plea

Convicted

Sentencing

Jail

Revocation

Probation

Out of system

Diversion by law enforcement, prosecutor, or court

Out of system

Juvenile offenders

Nonpolice referrals

Police juvenile unit

Prosecution as a juvenile

Released or diverted

Intake hearing

Released or diverted

Informal processing diversion

Waived to criminal court

Formal juvenile or youthful offender court processing

Adjudication

Released

Disposition

Probation or other nonresidential disposition

Revocation

Residential placement

Revocation

Aftercare

Out of system

Source: President's Commission on Law Enforcement and Administration of Justice, *Task Force Report: Science and Technology* (Washington, DC: Government Printing Office, 1967), pp. 58–59.

countless variations, at both the federal and state levels, in how criminal cases are handled. Further, depending on the seriousness of a case, the criminal process may assume different forms.

Almost all criminal procedure texts present an overview of the criminal process, like the one that follows. But because of the variation from one jurisdiction to the next, readers should take steps to familiarize themselves with the criminal processes in the areas in which they reside. That said, think of the rest of this section as an overview of the criminal process. The rest of this book will detail the criminal process in this order.

Pretrial

A typical criminal case begins with a *complaint*. It may come in the form of a 911 call from a citizen, a report to the police that someone has been victimized, or a report from a law enforcement officer who observes a crime in progress. If a citizen reports the crime, the police will usually follow up on the complaint by performing an investigation. If an officer observes the crime, not as much investigation is necessary. In the former instance, the police must take steps to confirm the observations of the citizen. A police officer's observations, by contrast, do not require as much investigative scrutiny. In fact, when an officer observes a crime in progress, he or she will probably arrest the suspect on the spot. This arrest will then be subjected to judicial scrutiny in a court hearing, in which a judge will decide if there was probable cause to arrest the suspect.

In a crime reported by a citizen, once the police have identified a suspect, they will approach a judge and seek either an arrest or a search warrant. In either case, the police must be able to show probable cause that the evidence they seek will be found in the place to be searched and/or that the suspect was the one who committed the crime. If this burden is met, an arrest, a search warrant, or both will be issued and the police will go to arrest the suspect or search the premises named in the search warrant. The burden of probable cause that is required for search and arrest warrants is not to be taken lightly and has spawned a great deal of debate in the courts. Probable cause, as well as other such standards of justification, is the focus of Part II, Chapters 3 through 7.

The role of the police during the pretrial process cannot be overemphasized. In the period from the first contact between an officer and suspect up to the point when the suspect is arrested and detained, the police's role is complex and multifaceted. The Constitution, particularly the Fourth Amendment, places significant restrictions on what the police can and cannot do when they investigate crimes and handle suspects. This is why many criminal procedure books (this one included) devote extensive attention to the role of the police in the criminal process. *Criminal* procedure is, in many ways, *police* procedure. However, because the criminal process continues well beyond an arrest and imposing criminal charges, this book takes the additional step of considering the whole of the criminal process.

If, as indicated, a police officer arrests a suspect for a crime committed in his or her presence, no warrant is necessary. But even when arresting a suspect or searching his or her residence based on a citizen complaint, a warrant is not always required. Many situations arise in which the police are permitted to arrest or to search without a warrant. Suspects who evade authorities, seek to destroy evidence, or are likely to inflict harm on others create circumstances in which the police must act quickly. Indeed, in many other areas of law enforcement, the police may be forced to make split-second decisions, whether to arrest or search, without the protection of a warrant. These areas of law enforcement will be considered, as well.

Once a suspect is arrested—be it pursuant to an arrest warrant, a warrant to search his or her residence, or another method—he or she will be searched. This is done to protect the police and also to discover contraband that may be in the suspect's possession. Then, the suspect will be transported to the police station and booked. *Booking* is the process in which the suspect is fingerprinted, processed, photographed, and probably placed in a holding cell. The suspect may also be required to submit to testing (such as a breathalyzer) and possibly be required to participate in a lineup for identification by a witness to the crime.

After this, the police will present their case to the prosecutor, and, assuming the prosecutor believes the evidence is persuasive enough, he or she will bring charges against the suspect, subject to certain restrictions identified by the U.S. Supreme Court. The suspect will now be considered the *defendant*. If the charges are minor, the police may release the suspect, in which case he or she will be required to appear in court at some later date.

Suspects who are booked, placed in detention, and charged with a crime face a number of different court hearings, depending on the seriousness of the crime. Misdemeanors, because of their not-so-serious nature, tend to be fast-tracked through the courts. A misdemeanor defendant may appear at only one court hearing, in which the judge will decide guilt or innocence. Felony defendants, by contrast, face a longer legal road. If, as described already, the suspect is arrested without a warrant, he or she will be granted a probable cause hearing, in which the judge will decide whether the arresting officer had appropriate justification to make the arrest. (This hearing may, in fact, be merged with other hearings, but this book will treat it as a separate event.)

The next step in the criminal process is the *arraignment*. At the arraignment, the suspect comes before a judge and is, at a minimum, informed of the charges against him or her. The defendant will also be notified of the right to counsel, the right to remain silent, and other important rights. He or she will also be allowed to enter a *plea*. Common pleas are guilty, not guilty, and *nolo contendere* (which is akin to a plea of "no contest"). A public defender may be assigned at this stage, particularly if the defendant is unable to afford his or her own representation. Probable cause may also be determined at this stage, if a separate hearing is not required. Finally, for a misdemeanor charge, a trial may take place at the arraignment. A bail determination could be made, as well.

If the bail determination is not fused with the arraignment, a separate hearing may be warranted. (The approach taken in this book is that the bail determination is made in a separate hearing.) In deciding whether bail should be granted, the judge will take such factors into account as the seriousness of the crime as well as the defendant's prior record, likelihood of flight, and level of dangerousness. The defendant's financial status may also be considered.

It is important to note that the prosecutor's method of filing charges varies from one state to the next. Some states require that the prosecutor proceed by *information*, a document that describes the charges the prosecutor is filing. Other states require that the prosecutor proceed by a *grand jury indictment*. That is, a grand jury decides whether charges should be filed, usually with the advice and assistance of the prosecutor. Some states require or allow both methods of filing charges, depending on the nature of the case. What is important in this discussion, however, is that in jurisdictions in which the prosecutor proceeds by information, he or she is usually required to show that the charging decision is appropriate. This is accomplished in a so-called *preliminary hearing*, during which the prosecutor makes out what is known as a *prima facia case* of the defendant's guilt. A preliminary hearing can also be required in a grand jury jurisdiction, requiring the prosecutor to present his or her case before seeking a grand jury indictment.

◼ Adjudication

Once the pretrial process has concluded and the charges have stood, a trial may or may not take place. If, at arraignment, the defendant pleads guilty, then a trial is not necessary. In such an instance, special steps must be taken to ensure that the defendant's guilty plea is valid. The defendant may also agree to a *plea bargain* agreement, in which in exchange for leniency from the prosecutor and/or the court, he or she pleads guilty to the crime with which he or she is charged. Plea bargaining of this nature can occur at any stage of the criminal process, however. That is, a suspect can reach a plea agreement with the prosecutor as early as the pretrial stage, during the trial, and, in fact, well into jury deliberations. In any case, the plea bargain, if there is one, must be accepted by the court. The judge makes this determination.

If the defendant pleads not guilty, the case is set for trial. The trial is usually scheduled for some date well after the arraignment. This allows both sides—the prosecution and the defense—to prepare their respective cases. A balance needs to be achieved between providing enough time for both sides to present effective arguments and protecting the defendant's Sixth Amendment right to a speedy trial. During this preparation process, *discovery* takes place. Discovery is the process by which each side to a criminal case learns what evidence the other side will present. Work product and legal strategy are off limits, but the identities of witnesses who will testify, the physical evidence in possession of both parties, and other items must all be made available in the discovery process.

At trial, the prosecutor bears the burden of proving that the defendant is guilty beyond a reasonable doubt. After the prosecution has presented its case, the defense steps in and presents its case. In doing so, it seeks to cast doubt on the prosecution's evidence. A criminal trial may move back and forth in this fashion until both sides rest. At this point, a verdict must be reached. Depending on the seriousness of the offense, the verdict is decided by either a judge or a jury. A judge decides the defendant's fate in a so-called bench trial but only for an offense that is likely to result in less than six months' imprisonment. A jury decides the verdict when the offense at issue is more serious. Special steps must be taken in either instance to ensure the impartiality of the judge or the jury.

Beyond Conviction

The criminal process does not necessarily end once the verdict has been read. *Sentencing* usually takes place at a separate hearing. The guilty party may be sentenced to death (for a capital crime), committed to prison, fined, placed on probation, or subjected to a host of other possible sanctions. Probation is the most common sanction; imprisonment (and, of course, death) are clearly much more serious. When a person is committed to prison or sentenced to death, it may seem that the criminal process has just begun, as the appeals process can drag on years beyond the criminal trial.

Appeals come in two varieties: automatic and discretionary. Most convicted criminals are entitled to at least one *automatic appeal* (also known as an *appeal of right*). An automatic appeal must be heard by an appellate court. With a discretionary appeal, however, it is up to the appellate court to decide whether the appeal will be heard. The right of a convicted criminal to file excessive discretionary appeals is deplored by supporters of the death penalty and other serious sanctions.

Making an appeal is not the only method of challenging a guilty verdict. The right of *habeas corpus*—a method of what is commonly called *collateral attack*—is guaranteed in the Constitution, providing every convicted criminal the right to petition a court to decide on the constitutionality of his or her confinement. All that is granted, however, is the right to *file* a petition, or to *request* to be heard. The decision whether to grant a prisoner's *habeas* petition is up to the reviewing court. If a prisoner exhausts all available appellate mechanisms and is denied *habeas* review, he or she will remain in prison for the full term of his or her sentence.

CONCLUSION

This first chapter has provided a foundation for the study of criminal procedure. Throughout the remainder of this book, the reader should be attuned to several important concerns. First, criminal procedure is mostly about constitutional rights. What's more, it is about constitutional rights as primarily interpreted by the U.S. Supreme Court. State laws, agency policies, time-honored practices, and the like also set forth rules and guidelines, but the focus here is almost exclusively on rights spelled out in the U.S. Constitution—notably, those found in the Fourth, Fifth, Sixth, Eighth, and Fourteenth Amendments.

Criminal procedure and history cannot be divorced from one another because of the importance of precedent. Before making decisions, courts almost always look to the past for the purpose of determining whether a case with similar facts has already been decided. If one has not, the court will distinguish the present case and hand down a decision that may be relied on by some other court, at some other date.

Even though criminal procedure, as presented in this text, is mostly about court decisions, it would be a crucial mistake to become hopelessly mired in the world of judicial decision making. In the real world, the police and other criminal justice officials must act, and what they do does not always agree with decisions handed down by the courts. That is, the theoretical world of the courts can differ in important ways from the real world of law enforcement. Understanding that these two different worlds exist and that they can be at odds with one another allows looking at court decisions with a critical eye but also a dose of reality.

Throughout criminal procedure—indeed, throughout all of criminal justice—two competing concerns can almost always be heard. The crime control perspective favors controlling crime at whatever cost, and the due process perspective is concerned with protecting people's rights. Every court decision, every crime control policy, and even every reaction by the criminal justice system to the threat of crime must balance both of these concerns. Some decisions and policies lean too far in the direction of crime control and, for that reason, become quite controversial. The same holds true for decisions and policies that cater to due process. For the justice process to flow smoothly, a balance needs to be achieved.

The United States has a two-tiered court structure consisting of federal and state courts. At the federal level, three types of courts are relevant: district courts, circuit courts of appeals, and the U.S. Supreme Court. The district courts try cases involving violations of federal laws. The decisions of district courts are appealed to circuit courts of appeals and then to the U.S. Supreme Court. State court structures vary from one state to the next but generally consist of courts of limited jurisdiction, trial courts of general jurisdiction, intermediate appellate courts, and supreme courts. Most criminal cases originate in trial courts of general jurisdiction; the decisions of these courts are appealed to intermediate appellate courts and then to the state supreme court. A state supreme court decision can be appealed to the U.S. Supreme Court but will only be heard if it raises a constitutional question. This is usually true for federal cases, as well.

Several important topics, issues, and trends need to be understood before reading too much into court decisions. First, some decisions consist of specific bright-line rules, whereas others favor case-by-case adjudication. Next, the courts—in particular, the U.S. Supreme Court—have moved from a subjective to an objective focus, meaning that they are now more concerned with how a reasonable person would act under the circumstances. Third, Supreme Court decisions of late have reflected an increased faith in the police. Fourth, to understand why court decisions often focus on excruciating legal details, one must understand the notion of judicial restraint: the practice of deciding only the specific legal question before the court. Finally, throughout criminal procedure there is a concern with people's privacy, even though the Constitution contains no mention of the term.

There is no one best way to describe the criminal process; there are simply too many variations from state to state. Even so, a more or less accurate description can be offered. The description set forth in this chapter and followed throughout the remainder of the book begins with the police/citizen encounter and then moves into arrest, booking, pretrial hearings, trial, and appeals. Along the way, special attention is given to constitutional rights stemming from several amendments to the Constitution and to the four important actors—the police, prosecutors, defense attorneys, and judges—whose decisions affect the whole of the criminal process. The reader is strongly encouraged to become familiar with the details of the criminal process in his or her area of residence.

REVIEW QUESTIONS

1. Identify several sources of rights.
2. What is the incorporation controversy? What are the leading perspectives describing it?
3. What rights have been incorporated? What rights have not?
4. In what ways can *theory* differ from *reality*?
5. Compare and contrast the due process and crime control perspectives.
6. Explain the federal court structure.
7. How does a case arrive at the U.S. Supreme Court?
8. Distinguish between a bright-line decision and case-by-case adjudication.
9. How are the terms *subjective* and *objective* used in criminal procedure?
10. In what ways have recent Supreme Court decisions shown increased faith in the police?
11. What is judicial restraint? How does it compare to judicial activism?
12. Is privacy a right? If not, why is it so important in many Supreme Court opinions?
13. What happens, briefly, during the pretrial phase?
14. What happens, briefly, during the adjudication phase?
15. What happens, briefly, beyond conviction?

 Answers to the Decision-Making Exercises for this chapter can be found on pages 487–488.

CHAPTER 2

Remedies for Constitutional Violations

OUTLINE

KEY TERMS

remedy
extralegal remedies
legal remedies
civil litigation
damages
injunctive relief
42 U.S.C. Section 1983
color of law
constitutional rights violation
culpability
theory of liability
supervisory liability
municipal/county liability
individual liability

substantive due process
procedural due process
Bivens claims
absolute immunity
sovereign immunity
qualified immunity
state tort claim
intentional tort
neglience tort
public duty doctrine
18 U.S.C. Section 242
public duty defense
internal review
civilian review

civilian input
civilian monitor
mediation
ombudsman
exclusionary rule
"silver platter" doctrine
"good faith" exception
impeachment exception
"fruit of the poisonous tree" doctrine
"purged taint" exception
independent source
inevitable discovery

INTRODUCTION
Remedies for Constitutional Rights Violations

A fitting point with which to begin a review of criminal procedure is a discussion concerning remedies. A **remedy** provides a method of rectifying wrongdoing. That is, when a person believes he or she has been harmed in some way, he or she may seek to ease the pain, make the person who caused the harm "pay," or both. For example, if Sandy is unjustifiably assaulted by Jim, an on-duty police officer, she may opt to remedy the wrong inflicted on her. A remedy is the mechanism for enforcing violations of people's rights.

Remedies fall into two categories: (1) legal and (2) extralegal. **Extralegal remedies** are those conducted outside the legal process. A good example of an extralegal remedy is vigilantism. For example, if one man is assaulted by another, the assaulted individual may seek revenge and opt to solve the perceived injustice with his fists. This type of remedy is not the kind discussed in this chapter or anywhere else throughout the text. Instead, this chapter focuses on **legal remedies**—that is, remedies made available by the law, by a court decision, or by a police agency policy or procedure.

The most frequently discussed remedy in criminal procedure is the *exclusionary rule*. As such, a large section of this chapter is devoted to it. It is an example of a remedy made available because of court decisions; that is, it has no statutory basis. However, in order to place the exclusionary rule in context, this chapter first focuses on other types of remedies, such as those provided in law and agency practice. These and other remedies are important because the exclusionary rule applies only in limited contexts.

The bulk of criminal procedure concerns *constitutional* procedure. That is, it focuses on the various forms of government action permitted and not permitted by the U.S.

KEY CASES

Civil Remedies

- *Monroe v. Pape*, 365 U.S. 167 (1961)
- *Rizzo v. Goode*, 423 U.S. 362 (1976)
- *Monell v. Department of Social Services*, 436 U.S. 658 (1978)
- *City of Canton v. Harris*, 489 U.S. 378 (1989)
- *Tennessee v. Garner*, 471 U.S. 1 (1985)
- *Estelle v. Gamble*, 429 U.S. 97 (1976)
- *Hudson v. McMillian*, 503 U.S. 1 (1992)
- *Rochin v. California*, 342 U.S. 165 (1952)
- *Bivens v. Six Unknown Agents*, 403 U.S. 388 (1971)
- *Malley v. Briggs*, 475 U.S. 335 (1988)

Criminal Remedies

- *Screws v. United States*, 325 U.S. 91 (1945)

Exclusionary Rule

- *Weeks v. United States*, 232 U.S. 383 (1914)
- *Mapp v. Ohio*, 367 U.S. 643 (1961)
- *United States v. Leon*, 468 U.S. 897 (1984)
- *Walder v. United States*, 347 U.S. 62 (1954)
- *Silverthorne Lumber Co. v. United States*, 251 U.S. 385 (1920)
- *Wong Sun v. United States*, 371 U.S. 471 (1963)
- *Segura v. United States*, 468 U.S. 796 (1984)
- *Nix v. Williams*, 467 U.S. 431 (1984)

Constitution. Accordingly, the bulk of the discussion in this chapter is on remedies for constitutional rights violations. These include *42 U.S.C. Section 1983*, a statute that provides for civil litigation against governmental officials, as well as the exclusionary rule. However, there are several occasions when neither the exclusionary rule nor 42 U.S.C. Section 1983 applies. Therefore, this chapter also focuses on additional remedies that are available to people whose *constitutional* rights are not violated but whose *rights* are violated, nonetheless. These include state tort litigation, disciplinary procedures, civilian review, mediation, and the criminal law.

This chapter contains four primary sections. The first section includes *civil remedies*. This is where 42 U.S.C. Section 1983 fits in; state tort law also provides for civil remedies. Civil remedies are sought by filing lawsuits. Next, this chapter focuses on *criminal remedies*, both federal and state. Criminal remedies are limited in their applicability, but if a law enforcement officer violates the law and commits a crime, a criminal prosecution may be in order. Third, *nonjudicial remedies* are discussed, including internal review, civilian review, and mediation. This chapter concludes with an in-depth look at the *exclusionary rule*, including the many exceptions that have been identified since its creation.

◼ CIVIL REMEDIES

When a person's constitutional or other federal civil rights are violated, he or she can sue. Even if a person merely *believes* his or her rights have been violated, litigation is still an option. The worst (or best) that can happen is that the lawsuit will be dismissed. Litigation is also an option for *tort violations*, which are civil wrongs that do not rise to the level of a constitutional rights violation or a violation of federally secured rights. This section begins with constitutional and federal civil rights litigation; then it turns attention to state tort litigation.

What is the purpose of **civil litigation**? Aside from sometimes being the only remedy available, civil lawsuits are attractive because money can be awarded. Lawsuits in which people seek monetary compensation are called **damages** suits. The *plaintiff*, or the person filing the lawsuit, seeks payment for injuries or perceived injuries suffered. In addition to damages, the plaintiff can also seek **injunctive relief**, which basically means he or she wants the court to bring the injurious or offensive action to a halt. Figure 2.1 (pages 38–39) provides an overview of the stages of a typical civil lawsuit.

◼ 42 U.S.C. Section 1983: Liability of State Officials

42 U.S.C. Section 1983 (hereafter referred to as Section 1983) provides a remedy in federal court for the "deprivation of any rights . . . secured by the Constitution and laws" of the United States. Specifically, Section 1983 states:

> Every person who, under color of any statute, ordinance, regulation, custom, or usage, of any State or Territory, subjects, or causes to be subjected, any citizen of the United States or other persons within the jurisdiction thereof to the deprivation of any rights, privileges, or immunities secured by the Constitution and laws, shall be liable to the party injured in an action at law, suit in equity, or other proper proceeding for redress.

Section 1983 was originally enacted as part of the Ku Klux Klan Act of April 20, 1871 (also known as Section 1 of the Civil Rights Act of 1871). The act was designed to address atrocities being committed by Klan members in the wake of the Civil War, but it did not target Klan members as such. Instead, Section 1983 imposed liability on state representatives who failed to enforce state laws against illegal Klan activities. The statute was rarely used, however, and remained effectively dormant for some 90 years after it was signed into law.

Section 1983 enjoyed a resurgence in *Monroe v. Pape* (365 U.S. 167 [1961]). In that case, a group of police officers allegedly entered the home of James Monroe without warning and then forced the occupants to stand naked in the living room while the house was searched and ransacked. Monroe brought a Section 1983 action against the police officers and the city of Chicago. The case eventually reached the U.S. Supreme Court, where eight justices held that the alleged misuse of authority could support a Section 1983 action against the police officers. That is, the Supreme Court held that Section 1983 could be used as a vehicle to sue the police.

■ *Monroe v. Pape,*
365 U.S. 167 (1961)

Since *Monroe*, Section 1983 litigation has become quite popular. The reasons for this increase are many, but the Supreme Court's decision in *Monroe* almost certainly had a strong influence. For example, as cited in Lieberman, Chief Justice Rehnquist has referred to *Monroe* as "the fountainhead of the torrent of civil rights litigation of the last 17 years."[1] In a similar reference to Section 1983 as the "cornerstone of police federal liability litigation," Kappeler and his colleagues have observed that "[t]he increased use of the 1871 Civil Rights Act may be attributable to expanded interpretation of the legislation by the Supreme Court."[2] And Vaughn and Coomes have noted that "Section 1983 is extremely controversial because of its widespread impact on criminal justice personnel, particularly police officers."[3]

The next four subsections focus carefully on Section 1983. The first discusses the concept of *color of law*, a requirement for any successful Section 1983 claim. Second, the types of actions that amount to constitutional rights violations are considered. Third, theories of liability under Section 1983 are reviewed. Finally, qualified immunity, the main defense available to defendants in Section 1983 actions, is introduced.

Color of Law

One of the requirements for a successful Section 1983 lawsuit is that the *defendant*, the person being sued, acted under color of law. The Supreme Court has stated that someone acts under **color of law** when he or she acts in an official capacity (*Lugar v. Edmondson Oil Co.*, 457 U.S. 922 [1982]). For example, a police officer who is on duty acts under color of law. By contrast, someone acting in a private capacity, such as an ordinary citizen, cannot be said to have acted under color of law.

Offering further clarification, Vaughn and Coomes have shown that police officers act under color of law when one or more of the following conditions are satisfied:

1. They have identified themselves as officers.
2. They are performing a criminal investigation.
3. They have filed official police documents.
4. They are making an arrest.
5. They are invoking police powers in or outside their jurisdiction.
6. They are settling a personal vendetta with police power.
7. They are displaying weapons or police equipment.[4]

Interestingly, plaintiffs *can* sue private parties under Section 1983 when private parties conspire with state officers. With regard to this point, the Supreme Court has held that "a state normally can be held responsible for a private decision only when it has exercised coercive power or has provided such significant encouragement, either overt or

[1]J. K. Lieberman, *The Litigious Society* (New York: Basic Books, 1983), p. 152.
[2]V. E. Kappeler, S. F. Kappeler, and R. V. del Carmen, "A Content Analysis of Police Civil Liability Cases: Decisions of the Federal District Courts, 1978–1990," *Journal of Criminal Justice* 21 (1993): 327.
[3]M. S. Vaughn and L. F. Coomes, "Police Civil Liability under Section 1983: When Do Police Officers Act under Color of Law?" *Journal of Criminal Justice* 23 (1995): 396.
[4]Vaughn and Coomes, p. 409.

FIGURE 2.1 Stages of a Civil Lawsuit

1. *Citizen complaint*: The first step in filing a lawsuit normally involves a citizen complaint. In a citizen complaint, the aggrieved party can do one of two things: call attention to inappropriate police conduct *or* demand some form of remedial action (e.g., injunctive relief or monetary damages). This latter form of citizen complaint is considered a *demand*.

2. *Demand*: If the complaint filed with the police by a citizen (the *complainant*) requests some action on the part of the police, then the complainant will make a more or less informal demand of the police, who will then send a *response*. This may lead to informal discussions between the two sides. The complainant may retain the services of an attorney, but the procedure remains largely informal at this early juncture.

3. *Citizen complaint board*: In some jurisdictions (e.g., Spokane, WA), the complainant can further file a complaint with a local citizen complaint board if the police agency in question fails to take satisfactory action. Citizen complaint boards vary considerably in use, authority, and terminology, so they are only mentioned here in passing as one mechanism for dispute resolution. Other avenues of dispute resolution may well be in place.

4. *Lawyer's letter*: If the complainant and the police cannot work things out informally, the complainant usually brings in an attorney. The attorney will send a so-called lawyer's letter to the police agency, the officer(s) in question, and/or the city or county. While this letter may not

have any legal significance, it usually gets a serious response.

5. *Prelitigation settlement discussion*: An informal prelitigation settlement discussion is often held, in which the police and/or their representatives and the complainant and/or his or her representatives work together to try to reach a settlement. If no settlement is reached, the complaint/demand will likely evolve into a full-blown lawsuit.

6. *Claim with city/county clerk*: Before being able to proceed with a lawsuit, the citizens in some states and counties are first required to file a claim with the city or county against which the complaint is made or to give the police agency a chance to respond to a formal complaint or a request for damages. This *claim* should be distinguished from a *citizen complaint*, discussed above. This claim is an explicit prerequisite that must be completed before a lawsuit can move forward; it is mandated by law. The purpose of such a claim is primarily to inform officials of what is about to transpire. Often, a lawsuit cannot be filed until the parties in question are given the opportunity to respond to a claim.

7. *Lawsuit*: A citizen complaint/demand evolves into a full-blown lawsuit when none of the informal proceedings discussed satisfy the complainant. To reach the stage of a lawsuit, two actions must occur: First, a *complaint* must be filed with the clerk of the court in which the lawsuit will be heard. (This complaint is a legal requirement and

---

covert, that the choice must in law be deemed to be that of the state" (*Blum v. Yaretsky*, 457 U.S. 991 [1982], p. 1004).

DECISION
MAKING
EXERCISE **2.1**

Section 1983 Civil Liability

Officer Webster regularly patronized a bar. One night, while off duty, he got into a fight, drew his gun, and shot and killed James Ramos. Ramos's heirs filed a Section 1983 lawsuit against the city for which Webster worked, alleging that it failed to adequately train him as to whether and how to react during off-duty altercations. Furthermore, Ramos's heirs alleged that this failure caused Webster, acting under color of law, to deprive Ramos of his constitutional rights. Will this lawsuit succeed?

Constitutional Violation

The second requirement for a successful Section 1983 lawsuit is that a constitutional rights violation has taken place. In determining whether a **constitutional rights violation** has taken place, the plaintiff must establish that the defendant's conduct violated a specific constitutional provision, such as the Fourth Amendment. As noted in *Daniels v. Williams* (474 U.S. 327 [1986], "[I]n any given Section 1983 suit, the plaintiff must still prove a violation of the underlying constitutional right" (p. 330).

differs from the citizen complaint already filed.) Second, the court or an attorney must issue a *summons* to be *served* on the agencies or people named in the complaint. Sometimes, the summons is personally delivered; other times, it is sent by registered or certified mail. The parties named in the complaint (e.g., the police, their agencies, municipalities, etc.) are now known as the *defendants*, and the aggrieved party or parties filing the lawsuit are now known as the *plaintiffs*.

8. *Answer*: Once the defendants have been served with the summons, they must provide their formal answer within a prescribed timeframe. For obvious reasons, defendants in police civil liability cases rarely fail to acknowledge the summons.

9. *Discovery*: A lawsuit may involve pretrial discovery, in which one or both parties attempt to get evidence as to what happened in the alleged incident, perhaps by taking the testimony of witnesses or examining documents or physical evidence.

10. *Motions*: In a lawsuit, either side may make motions to try to narrow the issues, to compel the other side to do something, or even to have the court decide the matter without actually conducting a trial. In police civil liability cases, two motions are commonly raised by the defendants: The first is the motion to *dismiss*, in which the defendants attempt to have the case thrown out on the grounds that it does not raise a question of law or other legitimate legal issue. Motions to dismiss are rarely granted. The second common type of motion calls for a *summary judgment*, in which the defendants ask the court to find in favor of the police without going to trial. The majority of these motions succeed, leaving only a few lawsuits that actually progress to the trial stage.

11. *Pretrial conference*: Before the start of the trial, the court will typically order a pretrial conference to narrow the issues still further and perhaps to get the parties to agree to a settlement. Again, the aim is to avoid a lengthy trial proceeding.

12. *Trial, judgment, and posttrial motions and appeals*: If a lawsuit progresses all the way to trial, it will either be decided by a judge alone or by a jury that decides the facts and a judge that decides the law. After the trial, the court will enter a judgment, in which the plaintiff, for example, might be entitled to a fixed amount of money. Posttrial motions might also be raised, in which the losing party tries to convince the judge that some other judgment would be more appropriate (e.g., perhaps more money, added relief, or none at all). Finally, the losing party might appeal to a higher court.

13. *Collecting the judgment*: The party who wins the lawsuit may have received a judgment stating what he or she is entitled to recover. It is then his or her job to collect the judgment. This can be a difficult and time-consuming process, so it is typically put on hold until all relevant appeals have been exhausted.

Recently, the courts have begun to require that constitutional rights violations alleged under Section 1983 be committed with a certain level of **culpability**. That is, the plaintiff generally has to prove that the defendant officer intended for the violation to occur. There is a very clear reason for this: Not all constitutional rights violations are (or should be) actionable under Section 1983. In other words, Section 1983 is generally reserved for the most egregious of civil rights violations. The level of culpability required for a constitutional rights violation varies, depending on the type of unconstitutional conduct alleged by the plaintiff.[5] Some of the specifics of this issue will be addressed in the following section on individual liability.

Theories of Liability

The term **theory of liability** refers mostly to whom the defendant is. Typically, in Section 1983 cases, the plaintiff's lawsuit will target an individual officer, that officer's supervisor, the city or municipality for which the officer works, or any combination of each. While the individual officer responsible for inflicting harm should arguably be held liable, it is often attractive to plaintiffs to go after the "bigger fish" because that is likely where the greatest rewards will be. Governmental entities, in particular, are attractive targets for civil litigation. Following is a discussion of the three most common theories of liability under Section 1983.

[5]See J. L. Worrall, "Culpability Standards in Section 1983 Litigation against Criminal Justice Officials: When and Why Mental State Matters," *Crime and Delinquency* 47 (2001): 28–59.

■ *Rizzo v. Goode*,
423 U.S. 362 (1976)

Supervisory Liability. The only Supreme Court case concerning **supervisory liability** in the Section 1983 context was *Rizzo v. Goode* (423 U.S. 362 [1976]). In *Rizzo*, the plaintiffs sued the mayor of Philadelphia, the city's managing director, the police commissioner, and two other police department supervisors, alleging a "pervasive pattern of illegal and unconstitutional mistreatment by police officers . . . directed against minority citizens in particular and against all Philadelphia residents in general" (pp. 366–367). The plaintiffs further charged supervisors with "conduct ranging from express authorization or encouragement of this mistreatment to failure to act in a manner so as to assure that it would not recur in the future" (p. 367). The lower federal courts found in favor of the plaintiffs, but the Supreme Court stated, disapprovingly, that "there was no *affirmative link* between the occurrence of the various incidents of police misconduct and the adoption of any plan or policy by [the supervisors]—express or otherwise—showing their authorization or approval of such misconduct" (p. 371, emphasis added). In other words, for a Section 1983 lawsuit to succeed against a supervisor, there must be a clear link between the supervisor and the constitutional violation committed by a subordinate. Figure 2.2 provides a summary of the supervisory liability process under Section 1983.

■ *Monell v. Department of Social Services*, 436 U.S. 658 (1978)

Municipal/County Liability. Cities and counties can be held liable under Section 1983 if they adopt and implement policies or adopt customs that become responsible for constitutional rights violations (see *Monell v. Department of Social Services*, 436 U.S. 658 [1978]). In general, a plaintiff will not succeed with a Section 1983 **municipal/county liability** claim if a common practice is engaged in by lower-ranking officials who have no authority to make policy in the traditional sense of the term. For example, if a group of police officers regularly use excessive force but do so on their own, with no authorization from the city or county, then the city or county cannot be held liable for these officers' actions.

■ *City of Canton v. Harris*, 489 U.S. 378 (1989)

In another city/county liability case, *City of Canton v. Harris* (489 U.S. 378 [1989]), the Supreme Court held that counties (and, by extension, cities) can be held liable for inadequately training their law enforcement officers. The facts of the case in *Canton* were that Harris was arrested and brought to the police station in a patrol wagon. On arrival, the officers found Harris lying on the floor of the wagon. She was asked if she needed medical attention, but she responded incoherently. After she was brought into the station, she slumped to the floor on two occasions. Eventually, she was left lying on the floor; no medical attention was summoned for her. Harris later sued, seeking to hold the city liable for a violation of her Fourteenth Amendment right, under the due process clause, to receive medical attention while in police custody. However, the Court held that "only where a municipality's failure to train its employees in a relevant respect evidences a 'deliberate indifference' to the rights of its inhabitants can such a shortcoming be properly thought of as a city 'policy or custom' that is actionable under [Section] 1983" (p. 389).

DECISION MAKING EXERCISE 2.2

Municipal Liability

Danny Koller, 17 years old, stole a van from a car lot by driving it through the showroom window. Almost immediately, members of the local police department began to pursue him. After a dangerous, lengthy, high-speed chase, the van was forced to stop. Danny emerged from the van unarmed. When the pursuing officers approached him, they hit him and pulled his hair. In the scuffle, one of the officer's pistol discharged. The bullet struck Danny in the head and hand, and he died as a result of these wounds. Danny's parents brought suit under 42 U.S.C. Section 1983, seeking damages from the city. They argued that the city maintained a formal policy of using excessive police force that caused Danny's death. Assuming this tragedy is an isolated event, will the plaintiffs succeed with their lawsuit?

FIGURE 2.2   Supervisory Liability under Section 1983

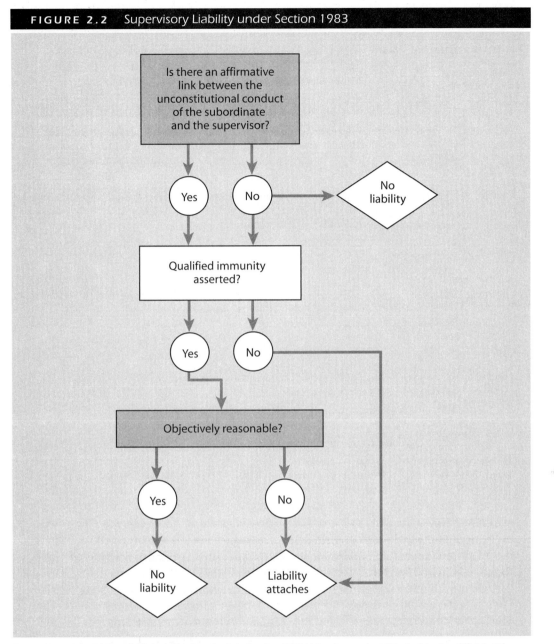

Source: From John L. Worrall, "Culpability Standards in Section 1983 Litigation against Criminal Justice Officials: When and Why Mental State Matters," *Crime and Delinquency* 47 (2001):28–59 (p. 47). Copyright © 2001 by Sage Publications, Inc. Reprinted by permission of Sage Publications, Inc.

In *Board of Commissioners of Bryan County v. Brown* (520 U.S. 397 [1997]), the Supreme Court revisited the city/county liability issue. In particular, the question before the Court was whether a single hiring decision by a municipality's policymaker could give rise to an inadequate hiring claim under Section 1983. In that case, Brown's claim was fueled by the injuries she suffered at the hands of Bryan County Reserve Deputy Stacy Burns during a high-speed pursuit and by the fact that Burns had two previous misdemeanor convictions for assault and battery (both of which were overlooked during the pre-employment screening process). Brown seemed to have a good case, but the Court felt otherwise, finding for Bryan County and setting a high standard for claims against a municipality for inadequate hiring. Specifically, the Court held that "[e]ven

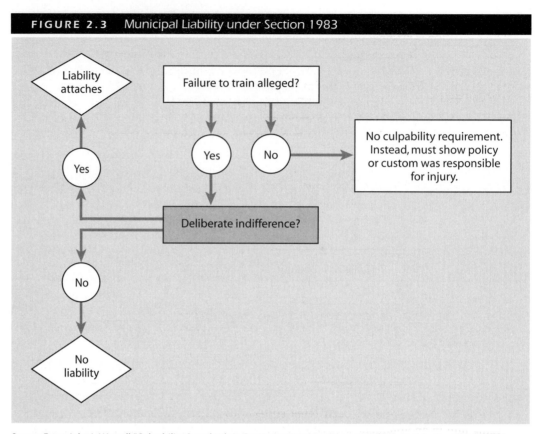

FIGURE 2.3 Municipal Liability under Section 1983

Source: From John L. Worrall, "Culpability Standards in Section 1983 Litigation against Criminal Justice Officials: When and Why Mental State Matters," *Crime and Delinquency* 47 (2001): 28–59 (p. 48). Copyright © 2001 by Sage Publications, Inc. Reprinted by permission of Sage Publications, Inc.

assuming without deciding that proof of a single instance of inadequate screening could ever trigger municipal liability, [the county commissioners'] failure to scrutinize Burns's record cannot constitute' deliberate indifference' to [the] respondent's federally protected right to be free from the use of excessive force" (p. 412).

Figure 2.3 offers a summary of the municipal liability process under Section 1983. Note that there is no reference in Figure 2.3 to *qualified immunity* (discussed later). This omission is deliberate; cities and counties cannot assert qualified immunity.

Individual Liability. For a finding of **individual liability**, Section 1983 requires a plaintiff to demonstrate that his or her constitutional rights were violated by someone acting under color of state law. Accordingly, numerous constitutional amendments have been implicated in Section 1983 cases, including the First Amendment (e.g., *Pickering v. Board of Education*, 391 U.S. 563 [1968]), the Fourth Amendment (e.g., *Tennessee v. Garner*, 471 U.S. 1 [1985]), the Fifth Amendment (e.g., *Veilleux v. Perschau*, 94 F.3d 732 [1st Cir. 1996]), the Sixth Amendment (e.g., *Weatherford v. Bursey*, 429 U.S. 545 [1977]), the Eighth Amendment (e.g., *Estelle v. Gamble*, 429 U.S. 97 [1976]), the Fourteenth Amendment (e.g., *County of Sacramento v. Lewis*, 118 S. Ct. 1708 [1998]), and others. The amendments most commonly invoked, however, have been the Fourth, Eighth, and Fourteenth. What is the pertinent case law surrounding each?

The language of the Fourth Amendment clearly suggests that unreasonable searches and seizures are prohibited. Of course, what conduct should be deemed *unreasonable* is not immediately clear, but the Supreme Court has attempted to clarify the text of the Fourth Amendment by reference to a standard of *objective reasonableness*

■ *Tennessee v. Garner*, 471 U.S. 1 (1985)

■ *Estelle v. Gamble*, 429 U.S. 97 (1976)

(*Tennessee v. Garner*). As the Court remarked in *Graham v. Connor* (490 U.S. 386 [1989]), "[T]he question is whether the officers' actions are' objectively reasonable' in light of the facts and circumstances confronting them, without regard to their underlying intent or motivation" (p. 397). Thus, allegations of Fourth Amendment violations must be evaluated objectively from the standpoint of the reasonable officer.

The Eighth Amendment states, "Excessive bail shall not be required, nor excessive fines imposed, nor cruel and unusual punishments inflicted." Cruel and unusual punishment can be understood as arising in two separate and distinct contexts: conditions of confinement and excessive force. In general, Section 1983 lawsuits alleging Eighth Amendment violations can be filed only by prison and jail inmates. Excessive force claims arising outside the prison/jail context are better approached under the Fourth Amendment (see, e.g., *Graham v. Connnor*).

First, the courts have applied a standard of *deliberate indifference* in evaluating Eighth Amendment conditions of confinement claims. However, the criterion set by this standard has been said to lie somewhere between *inadvertence* and *intent*. In *Whitley v. Albers* (475 U.S. 312 [1986]), for example, the Court held that "inadvertence or error" will not trigger the Eighth Amendment, but that "[a]n express intent to inflict unnecessary pain is not required" (p. 319). Similarly, in *Estelle v. Gamble*, the Court held that the "inadvertent failure to provide adequate medical care" or "negligence in diagnosing or treating a medical condition does not state a valid claim . . . under the Eighth Amendment" (pp. 105–106).

Second, something more than deliberate indifference is necessary for an Eighth Amendment claim alleging excessive force. The *malicious and sadistic* standard was therefore created in *Hudson v. McMillian* (503 U.S. 1 [1992]), a case in which an inmate in a Louisiana state penitentiary sued three corrections officers for allegedly beating and kicking him in an argument with one of the officials. Importantly, this case involved a lawsuit filed by a prison inmate. Had the plaintiff not been in prison and had the excessive force allegedly been used by police officers, he would have invoked the Fourth Amendment.

■ *Hudson v. McMillian,* 503 U.S. 1 (1992)

Finally, the Fourteenth Amendment contains two primary components, both of which are actionable under Section 1983. These are the so-called *substantive* and *procedural* components (*Daniels v. Williams*). The essence of **substantive due process** is protection from arbitrary and unreasonable action on the part of state officials. A so-called *"shocks the conscience"* standard has been used in cases involving allegations of Fourteenth Amendment substantive due process. In *Rochin v. California* (342 U.S. 165 [1952]), the Supreme Court held that the pumping of a suspect's stomach by police officers to obtain evidence violated substantive due process because it shocked the conscience and constituted such force as to "offend even hardened sensibilities" (p. 172).

■ *Rochin v. California,* 342 U.S. 165 (1952)

DECISION MAKING EXERCISE 2.3

Culpability under Section 1983

A police officer was in pursuit of a motorcycle carrying a passenger. During the pursuit, the motorcycle crashed in the road, directly in front of the officer. Despite his attempt to stop his cruiser in time, it slid into the back of the motorcycle, killing the passenger. The passenger's family members brought a Section 1983 lawsuit against the officer and the county for whom he worked, alleging that the passenger's substantive due process rights were violated. The case worked its way up to a federal circuit court, where it was decided that the appropriate standard for Section 1983 civil liability for a substantive due process violation is deliberate indifference and that the officer acted in a deliberately indifferent fashion. Finally, the case reached the U.S. Supreme Court. As a Justice of that Court, would you affirm or reverse?

A deliberate indifference standard has been applied in **procedural due process** cases. At the risk of simplification, this violation is one involving a significant life, liberty, or property interest (*Geddes v. Northwest Missouri State College*, 49 F.3d 426 [8th Cir. 1995]). To clarify, in *Howard v. Grinage* (82 F.3d 1343 [6th Cir. 1996]), the court distinguished between *procedural* and *substantive* due process as follows: "[S]ubstantive due process prohibits the government's abuse of power or its use for the purpose of oppression, and procedural due process prohibits arbitrary and unfair deprivations of protected life, liberty, or property interests without procedural safeguards" (p. 1350).

In a recent case (*Castle Rock v. Gonzales*, 125 S.Ct. 2796 [2005]), a woman sued police for their failure to respond to her repeated requests over several hours for assistance in enforcing a restraining order against her husband. He took their children and murdered them. The woman argued that her procedural due process rights were violated because she had a protected property interest in enforcement of the restraining order. Basically, she argued that she was *owed* enforcement of the order. The Supreme Court disagreed. It stated, in relevant part, that the order did not entitle the woman to its enforcement because officials had discretion to grant or not to grant the order in the first place. What happened in this case is clearly tragic, but the Court felt it would be risky to open the "can of worms" the woman was effectively calling for.

Bivens Claims against Federal Officials

■ *Bivens v. Six Unknown
Agents*, 403 U.S. 388
(1971)

Prior to 1971, it was not clear whether federal officials could be sued under Section 1983. In *Bivens v. Six Unknown Named Agents* (403 U.S. 388 [1971]), however, the Supreme Court held that federal law enforcement officers can be sued for Fourth Amendment violations. *Bivens* claims must meet two essential requirements, which are effectively the same requirements as for a Section 1983 lawsuit: namely, (1) the official acted under color of state law and (2) the official deprived someone of his or her constitutional rights. *Bivens* claims are not limited to the Fourth Amendment, however. Since the *Bivens* decision, many other constitutional rights violations have been recognized. For example, *Davis v. Passman* (442 U.S. 228 [1979]) and *Sonntag v. Dooley* (650 F.2d 904 [7th Cir. 1981]) both dealt with the Fifth Amendment, and *Carlson v. Green* (446 U.S. 14 [1980]) was an Eighth Amendment case.

Bivens **claims** are primarily limited to law enforcement officers, as other federal officials enjoy absolute immunity. **Absolute immunity** means the official cannot be sued under any circumstances. Federal officials who enjoy absolute immunity include federal judges (*Bradley v. Fisher*, 80 U.S. 335 [1871]) and federal prosecutors (*Yaselli v. Goff*, 275 U.S. 503 [1927]). By contrast, heads of federal agencies (*Butz v. Economou*, 438 U.S. 478 [1978]), presidential aides (*Harlow v. Fitzgerald*, 457 U.S. 800 [1982]), and federal law enforcement officers *can* be sued. However, these and other federal officials enjoy *qualified immunity*, the same defense that applies to state officials in the Section 1983 context. Also, *Bivens* claims cannot be brought against federal agencies (*FDIC v. Meyer*, 510 U.S. 471 [1994]) or private corporations performing federal functions (*Correctional Svcs. Corp. v. Malesko*, 534 U.S. 61 [2001]).

Defenses to Section 1983 Civil Liability

Two defenses to Section 1983 civil liability can be identified: sovereign immunity and qualified immunity. The former stems from the Eleventh Amendment to the U.S. Constitution, and the latter stems from U.S. Supreme Court decisions.

Sovereign Immunity

The Eleventh Amendment states, "The judicial power of the United States shall not be construed to extend to any suit in law or equity, commenced or prosecuted against one of the United States by citizens of another State, by citizens or subjects of any foreign state." In simple terms, the defense of **sovereign immunity** means that states and state officials acting in their official capacities cannot be sued in federal court. However, lawsuits against other government employees, as well as lower-level units of government such as cities and counties, are still permissible. Also, the Eleventh Amendment only limits the jurisdiction of the *federal courts*, which means that lawsuits against state officials can be heard in *state courts*, just not Section 1983 lawsuits (see *Will v. Michigan Department of State Police*, 491 U.S. 58 [1989]). Finally, the Eleventh Amendment does not prevent federal courts from issuing injunctions restraining state officers who are acting in an unconstitutional fashion (see *Ex parte Young*, 209 U.S. 123 [1908]).

Qualified Immunity

Qualified immunity is a judicially created defense; it does not appear in the language of Section 1983. Qualified immunity can also serve as more than an affirmative defense. In some cases, it affords immunity from suit.

Qualified immunity was developed to accommodate two conflicting policy concerns: effective crime control vis-à-vis the protection of people's civil liberties. While the Supreme Court has clearly intimated that Section 1983 should serve as a deterrent to official misconduct, the Court has also recognized that it is not fair to hold officials liable for lapses in judgment and honest mistakes. These issues were addressed in the seminal cases of *Harlow v. Fitzgerald* (457 U.S. 800 [1982]) and *Wood v. Strickland* (420 U.S. 308 [1975]).

Similar to the Fourth Amendment's test for reasonableness, an objective reasonableness standard has been applied in order to determine if qualified immunity should be extended to criminal justice officials who are defendants. For the purposes of qualified immunity, a defendant is said to have acted in an objectively reasonable fashion if he or she does not violate clearly established rights about which a reasonable person would have known (*Harlow v. Fitzgerald*). In some Section 1983 cases, defendants have benefited from qualified immunity even for violating clearly established constitutional rights, provided that the defendants' mistaken belief was objectively reasonable (see *Anderson v. Creighton*, 483 U.S. 635 [1987]; *Malley v. Briggs*, 475 U.S. 335 [1988]).

In *Baker v. Putnal* (75 F.3d 190 [5th Cir.1996]), the Fifth Circuit developed a two-pronged test for determining whether qualified immunity should be granted: "First, the court must determine whether the plaintiff has alleged a violation of a clearly established constitutional right. If the plaintiff fails at this step, the defendant is entitled to qualified immunity. If she is successful, the issue becomes the objective legal reasonableness of the defendant's conduct under the circumstances" (p. 198). This two-pronged test was recently reaffirmed in *Saucier v. Katz* (533 U.S. 194 [2001]). Qualified immunity thus affords protection to defendant criminal justice officials for reasonably mistaken beliefs. In essence, it offers a defense for ignorance, provided that the ignorance in question is reasonable.

DECISION MAKING EXERCISE **2.4**

The Fourth Amendment and Qualified Immunity

In a recent Supreme Court case, *Wilson v. Layne* (526 U.S. 603 [1999]), the Supreme Court considered (1) whether law enforcement officers violated the Fourth Amendment by allowing members of the media to accompany them on the service of warrants and (2) whether the officers were nonetheless entitled to qualified immunity if such activity violates the Fourth Amendment. The Court decided that "a media 'ride-along' in a home violates the Fourth Amendment, but because the state of the law was not clearly established at the time the entry in this case took place, respondent officers are entitled to qualified immunity" (p. 603). Do you see any problems with this decision?

■ *Malley v. Briggs,*
475 U.S. 335 (1988)

One of the best examples of a reasonably mistaken belief was in the case of *Malley v. Briggs* (475 U.S. 335 [1988]). In *Malley*, the plaintiffs filed a Section 1983 suit alleging that a police officer applied for and obtained a warrant that failed to establish probable cause. Rather than focus on the probable cause issue, the Supreme Court stated that the "question in this case is whether a reasonably well-trained officer in petitioner's position would have known that his affidavit failed to establish probable cause and that he should not have applied for the warrant" (p. 345). The Court went on to note that "[o]nly where the warrant application is so lacking in indicia of probable cause as to render official belief in its existence unreasonable will the shield of immunity be lost" (pp. 344–345).

In summary, qualified immunity poses the last (or one of the first) questions in the Section 1983 process. If a criminal justice official acts on a reasonably mistaken belief, as gauged from the standpoint of a reasonable officer, then qualified immunity can be granted. Figure 2.4 provides an overview of the Section 1983 process for lawsuits against individual police officers. Note that individual officers can enjoy qualified immunity if they act in an objectively reasonable fashion.

■ State Tort Liability

A **state tort claim** is reserved for the plaintiff who does not wish to seek recovery under the provisions of Section 1983. This is an important avenue of redress because a negligent act by the police and/or misconduct that results in minor injury is usually not serious enough to make Section 1983 litigation a viable option for the plaintiff. In other words, state tort actions are reserved for matters not reaching the level of constitutional significance.

Two types of state tort claims are relevant here. First, an **intentional tort** occurs when a police officer's behavior is highly likely to cause injury or damage and the officer knowingly engages in the behavior. To be liable for an intentional tort, an officer need not have *intended* to do harm; it need only be shown that the officer intended to engage in the behavior that *led* to the harm. Common forms of intentional torts applicable to policing include wrongful death, assault and battery, false arrest, and false imprisonment.

A second, and clearly further reaching, variety of tort claim is one based on negligence. In a **negligence tort**, the mental state of the defendant officer is not at issue. The plaintiff needs only to demonstrate the presence of four elements to succeed with a negligence claim: (1) a legal duty between the officer and the plaintiff; (2) a breach of that duty; (3) proximate (i.e., direct) causation between the officer's actions and the alleged harm; and (4) actual damage or injury.

Defenses against State Tort Liability

Police officers who are sued under state tort law benefit from the so-called **public duty doctrine**, which states that police protection (as well as other governmental functions) is owed to the general public, not to individuals. This means that if a police officer is not present to thwart a criminal act, then he or she cannot be held liable for failure to protect. The reason for this barrier to liability is clear: It would be unreasonable to hold law enforcement officials liable every time they do *not* intervene in criminal activity. The law enforcement presence is simply spread too thin to accommodate such a notion.

There are situations, however, in which police officers owe a legal duty to an individual and, as such, can be held liable for failure to perform that legal duty. For example, if a police officer stops a motorist and confirms that he or she is drunk, a special relationship has been created between these two individuals. The officer should arrest the drunk driver or, at a minimum, ensure that he or she will not drive anymore in this condition. If the motorist is released, the officer could be held liable under state tort law for negligent failure to protect.

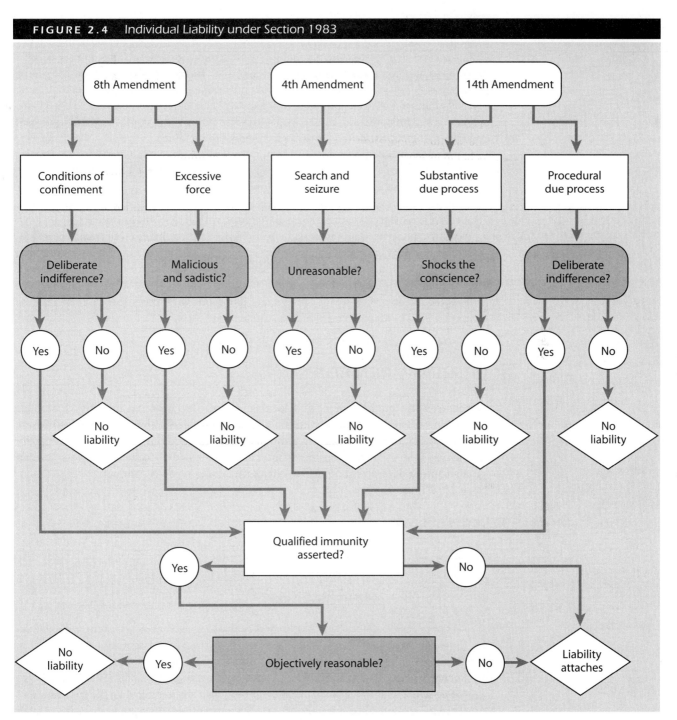

FIGURE 2.4 Individual Liability under Section 1983

Source: From John L. Worrall, "Culpability Standards in Section 1983 Litigation against Criminal Justice Officials: When and Why Mental State Matters, "*Crime and Delinquency* 47 (2001): 28–59 (p. 49). Copyright © 2001 by Sage Publications, Inc. Reprinted by permission of Sage Publications, Inc.

However, even in situations in which a special relationship exists between a police officer and a private citizen, the officer may be able to assert one of several defenses to liability. The first such defense is known as *contributory negligence*. This defense holds that if an officer can show that the plaintiff was also negligent in, say, causing an accident, the officer will not be held liable. Contributory negligence can arise not only from a criminal defendant but from a third party, as well. If, for example, during the course of a high-speed pursuit, a third motorist runs a red light, is struck by the officer, and later sues, the officer may not be found liable because the motorist contributed to the crash by running a red light.

A second defense to state tort liability is *comparative negligence*. This defense is not a total bar to liability, unlike contributory negligence. Instead, it looks at who is to blame and assigns liability accordingly. If it is found that the police officer is 20 percent liable and the plaintiff is 80 percent liable, damages will be awarded in accordance with these percentages. The comparative negligence defense permits the courts to determine fault and the extent to which each party contributed to an incident.

Yet another defense to state tort liability is *assumption of risk*. This defense provides that if the plaintiff voluntarily engaged in a dangerous activity that led to his or her injury, then the police officer sued will not be held liable. For instance, if the suspect is injured during the course of a high-speed pursuit and sues the officer, the court may decide that the suspect assumed the risk of injury by fleeing from the police.

Finally, police defendants in state tort claims enjoy a defense referred to as *sudden peril*. This is basically an emergency defense for situations in which officers are required to make split-second decisions. This defense only applies in situations in which injury or death is *clearly* attributed to the heat of the moment. If the officer asserting such a defense contributed in any way to the emergency situation, the courts (and juries) may be inclined to find in favor of the plaintiff.

CRIMINAL REMEDIES

Various statutes at the federal and local levels provide criminal remedies for police misconduct. Some states make it criminal for police officers to trespass and/or to falsely arrest people. In fact, most criminal sanctions that apply to ordinary citizens also apply to police officers. Likewise, various statutes at the federal level make it not only improper but also criminal for police officers to engage in certain types of conduct.

Federal Law

At the federal level, the most common statute for holding police officers criminally liable is **18 U.S.C. Section 242**. Section 242 is to criminal liability what Section 1983 (discussed earlier) is to civil liability. It can be used to prosecute either a state or a federal law enforcement officer. Section 242 states:

> Whoever, under color of any law, statute, ordinance, regulation, or custom, willfully subjects any inhabitant of any State, Territory, or District to the deprivation of any rights, privileges, or immunities secured or protected by the Constitution or laws of the United States, or to different punishments, pains, or penalties, on account of such inhabitant being an alien, or by reason of his color, or race, than are prescribed for the punishment of citizens, shall be fined not more than $1,000 or imprisoned not more than one year, or both; and if death results shall be subject to imprisonment for any term of years or for life.

Screws v. United States,
325 U.S. 91 (1945)

To be held liable under Section 242, a law enforcement officer must act with specific intent to deprive a person of important constitutional (or other federal) rights (*Screws v. United States*, 325 U.S. 91 [1945]). Also, for criminal liability under Section 242, a constitutional right must be clearly established (*United States v. Lanier*, 520 U.S. 259 [1997]). Together, these restrictions have resulted in the filing of relatively few Section 242 cases. In fact, criminal liability under Section 242 is reserved for the most egregious forms of police misconduct.

Despite its relatively infrequent application, there is a handful of noteworthy cases invoking Section 242. For example, in *Miller v. United States* (404 F.2d 611 [5th Cir. 1968]), a police officer was held criminally liable for allowing his canine unit to bite a suspect. In *Williams v. United States* (341 U.S. 97 [1951]), a defendant had been beaten, threatened, and physically punished for several hours, so a police officer was held criminally liable. And in *Lynch v. United States* (189 F.2d 476 [5th Cir. 1951]), Section 242 was applied in the wake of the assault and battery of several criminal defendants.

Additional federal statutes make it a criminal act to unlawfully search and seize individuals (18 U.S.C. Section 2236), although applications of this statute are rare, as well. Section 2235 of 18 U.S.C. makes it criminal to maliciously procure a warrant, and Section 2234 makes it criminal to exceed the authority of a warrant. Regardless of which criminal statute applies, an important distinction needs to be made between the various criminal statutes and 42 U.S.C. Section 1983. An officer who is held *criminally* liable will receive a criminal conviction and can even go to prison. Section 1983, by contrast, is *civil*, meaning that it is used independently of the criminal process. A successful Section 1983 lawsuit will never result in imprisonment of the defendant.

State Law

The same laws that apply to ordinary citizens also apply to police officers. For example, if a police officer knowingly and intentionally kills someone and is not legally justified in doing so (e.g., to prevent injury to a third party), that officer can be held criminally liable for murder. Similarly, if a police officer trespasses on private property without appropriate justification, he or she can be held criminally liable. Criminal liability can extend to a police officer for virtually any conceivable offense.

Some crimes are committed by police officers more often than other crimes. Birzer places such offenses into three categories: (1) violent and sex crimes; (2) drug crimes; and (3) other crimes.[6] With respect to violent crimes, the so-called Miami River Cops were charged with murdering drug smugglers. As for sex crimes, a police officer in Fort Myers, Florida, was charged with sexual assault against a 19-year-old female. Indeed, U.S. Border Patrol agents along the Arizona/Mexico border have become the targets of almost *daily* criminal complaints for a variety of violent acts.

Given the staggering amount of money associated with the illegal drug trade, it is no wonder that some police officers attempt to profit from such activities. This appears to be the case with the now-infamous Rampart scandal in the Los Angeles Police Department. Officers in other cities have faced similar charges. For example, seven officers in the Chicago Police Department's tactical unit were charged with stealing and extorting drug money; seven more officers in Atlanta, Georgia, were arrested in 1995 on drug charges; a deputy in Tucson, Arizona, was arrested during 1999 for conspiracy to distribute drugs; and the list goes on.[7]

Police officers have also been held liable for offenses ranging from burglary to shoplifting and fabrication of evidence to perjury. Lyman has actually reported that in the city of Detroit, federal agents arrested three city police officers who were planning a home invasion in Michigan to steal $1 million in cash.[8] This is not to suggest that police officers frequently engage in criminal activity but only that it happens. No one is above the law, even police officers.

Clearly, police officers also engage in many actions that would be crimes if performed by ordinary citizens. Police officers, however, enjoy immunity from criminal liability for these actions, if the actions are committed (justifiably) as part of their official duties. The so-called law enforcement or **public duty defense** to criminal liability is what shields police officers from criminal liability on most occasions. It is useful to think of this defense in terms of deadly force and nondeadly force.

[6]M. L. Birzer, "Crimes Committed by Police Officers," in *Police Misconduct*, ed. M. J. Palmiotto (Upper Saddle River, NJ: Prentice Hall, 2001), pp. 171–178.
[7]See Birzer.
[8]M. W. Lyman, *The Police: An Introduction* (Upper Saddle River, NJ: Prentice Hall, 1999).

New York City Police Officer Sean Carroll becomes emotional during testimony about his suspected involvement in the Amadou Diallo shooting, one of the most infamous cases of criminal behavior by police.

As a general rule, *deadly force* cannot be used to effect an arrest for or to prevent a misdemeanor. Indeed, rarely can deadly force be applied in the felony context. A police officer can only use deadly force to prevent a felony if he or she reasonably believes that the other person is about to commit an "atrocious" or "forcible" felony (see *People v. Ceballos*, 526 P.2d 241 [Cal. 1974]). And with regard to arrest, deadly force can only be used to effect an arrest if (1) the force is necessary to prevent the suspect's flight; (2) the officer can attempt to warn the suspect of his or her intention to use deadly force (e.g., "Stop or I'll shoot!"); and (3) the officer has probable cause to believe that the suspect, if not immediately apprehended, poses a significant threat of death or serious bodily injury to the officer or others (*Tennessee v. Garner*, 471 U.S. 1 [1985]).

DECISION MAKING EXERCISE 2.5

Use of Deadly Force

Officer Howe had been chasing Rupert DeHeil and his companion through a swamp after a high-speed car chase. When Howe caught up with DeHeil, he held a gun to his head and yelled to DeHeil's companion to come back or he would shoot DeHeil. DeHeil told his companion to keep running and that Howe couldn't shoot him because he was unarmed. Officer Howe began screaming and pushing the gun into the side of DeHeil's head, threatening to shoot him. Eventually, DeHeil's companion came back. At that point, Howe had DeHeil put his face in the mud and asked DeHeil why he had run; DeHeil answered that he had an outstanding arrest warrant. Officer Howe then shot DeHeil at close range in the back. DeHeil asked Howe why he did that, and Howe said, "The swamp's a hell of a place to die, ain't it?" Did Howe use appropriate force in this situation?

As for *nondeadly force*, the standard is objective reasonableness. A police officer enjoys immunity from criminal liability if when applying nondeadly force, he or she does so in an objectively reasonable fashion (*Graham v. Connor*). This requires asking whether a reasonable officer would, under the circumstances, have acted in the same way. If the answer is no, criminal liability may attach.

Beyond the realms of deadly and nondeadly force, police officers do not have much in the way of defense against criminal liability. If a police officer who committed burglary for his or her own personal gain attempted to assert a public duty defense, he or she would almost certainly fail. Similarly, if a police officer shoots and kills a person not for the purpose of preventing a crime or effecting an arrest but, say, for vengeance, that officer will almost certainly be convicted of some degree of homicide and probably sentenced to prison.

NONJUDICIAL REMEDIES

Three nonjudicial remedies for police misconduct can be identified. First, an *internal review* refers to a police department investigating complaints against its own officers. Typically, an internal affairs division takes up this task. The second, *civilian review*, refers to mechanisms by which private citizens serve in some capacity to review complaints of police misconduct. Not to be confused with civilian review, *mediation* asks an objective third party, such as an ombudsman, to resolve a grievance between a police officer and a citizen who complains of wrongdoing.

Internal Review

Many police agencies have developed innovative and highly respected **internal review** mechanisms. The internal affairs division of the Oakland, California, Police Department, for instance, is respected throughout the United States.[9] According to Perez and Muir, the "Internal Affairs Section of the Oakland Police Department works closely with the chief of police, who sets the tone for its rigorous investigations."[10] Officers who have worked at internal affairs (IA) "help to pass on its knowledge about citizens' complaints and educate the everyday cop about how I.A. works. Ideally these dynamics combine to make I.A. respected, understood, and feared by the cops it polices" (p. 208).

In its model police misconduct policy, the Police Executive Research Forum listed three ways that the police themselves can implement effective complaint procedures:

> (1) [T]hrough the provision of meaningful and effective complaint procedures, citizen confidence in the integrity of police increases and this engenders community support and confidence in the police department; (2) through disciplinary procedures that permit police officials to monitor officers' compliance with departmental procedures; and (3) by clarifying rights and ensuring due process protection to citizens and officers alike.[11]

Figure 2.5 (page 52) shows the Boston Police Department's internal complaint review process, depicting one agency's approach to internal discipline.

Geller is a defender of internal review. In particular, he has argued that civilian review procedures (described more fully below) suffer from a number of drawbacks:

1. They ignore existing legal resources at citizens' disposal.
2. It is difficult for people disconnected from the police department to have an adequate understanding of the internal operations of a civilian review board.
3. Citizen review damages morale.
4. Civilian review invites abdication of authority by line supervisors.
5. Such boards weaken the ability of top management to achieve conformity through discipline.
6. They are tantamount to admitting that the police are incapable of policing themselves.[12]

In sum, Geller believes that internal review of complaints of police misconduct is preferable.

[9]J. Douglas and J. Johnson, *Official Deviance* (New York: Lippincott 1977), p. 265; D. Guyot, *Policing as Though People Matter* (Philadelphia: Temple University Press, 1991), p. 181.
[10]D. W. Perez and W. K. Muir, "Administrative Review of Alleged Police Brutality," in *And Justice for All: Understanding and Controlling Police Abuse of Force*, ed. W.A. Geller and H. Toch (Washington, DC: Police Executive Research Forum, 1995), p. 207.
[11]Police Executive Research Forum, *Police Agency Handling of Officer Misconduct: A Model Policy Statement* (Washington, DC: Author, 1981), p. 1.
[12]W. A. Geller, *Police Leadership in America* (New York: Praeger, 1985), pp. 157–198.

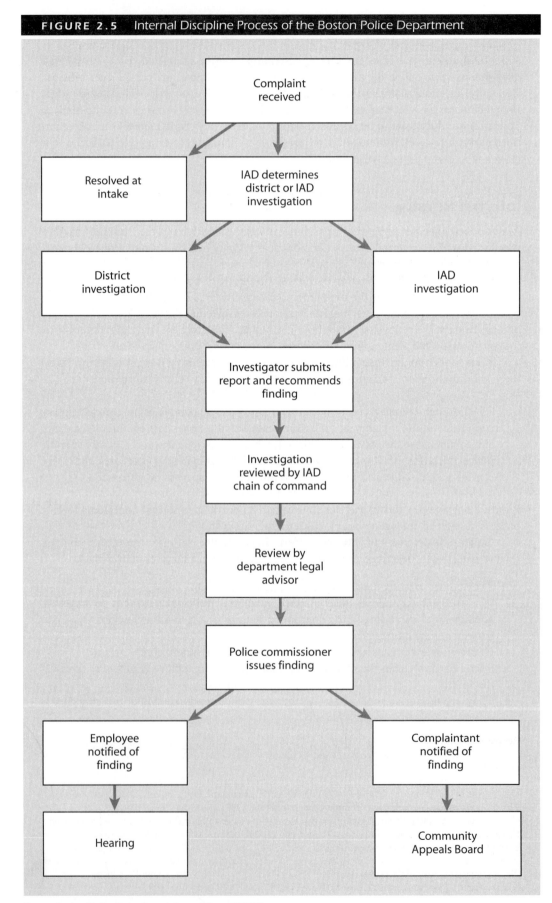

FIGURE 2.5   Internal Discipline Process of the Boston Police Department

Source: Boston Police Department, *Annual Report* (1997).

▪ Civilian Review

Walker and Bumphus found that since 1986, there has been an increase in the number of cities involving citizens at some stage of the complaint review process.[13] This has occurred, as noted, because of the demand for some form of external input in the investigation process. In essence, civilian review boards are comprised of several individuals, some of them (and perhaps all of them) members of the community, who evaluate alleged police misconduct.

An example of a civilian review model is the Berkeley, California, Police Review Commission. Although most citizen review boards report to the chief of police,[14] the Berkeley board reports directly to the city manager with its recommendations. According to Perez and Muir, the Berkeley Police Review Commission is "the most 'independent' and long standing civilian review operation in existence in the country."[15] California law requires police agencies to investigate complaints internally, so the Berkeley Commission only investigates complaints that people wish to make public.

A similar external complaint review mechanism is Portland, Oregon's, Police Internal Investigations Auditing Committee. A city ordinance authorized the committee to (1) monitor the complaint process to ensure fairness and efficiency; (2) report the findings; and (3) provide an avenue of appeal for citizens who were dissatisfied with the police handling of their complaints.[16] Other examples of external review mechanisms include Chicago's Office of Professional Standards,[17] Kansas City's Office of Citizen Complaints,[18] and Detroit's Board of Police Commissioners.[19] Whatever its form, the most often cited advantage to having an external review system is that it helps address the lack of trust between the police and minority citizens.[20]

Varieties of Civilian Review

West has identified three distinct forms of citizen review: (1) civilian review; (2) civilian input; and (3) civilian monitor.[21] Pure **civilian review** is the strongest form; a civilian panel investigates, adjudicates, and recommends punishment to the police chief. The second strongest form is **civilian input**; in this form, a civilian panel receives and investigates a complaint, leaving adjudication and discipline with the department itself. Finally, the **civilian monitor** form, the weakest of the three, leaves investigation, adjudication, and discipline inside the department; a civilian is allowed to review the adequacy and impartiality of the process. The research reported by West focused only on the first two forms: civilian review and civilian input. Both place investigative authority with an independent body and are arguably more satisfactory to disgruntled citizens than the third form, civilian monitor.

---

[13]S. Walker and V. W. Bumphus, *Civilian Review of the Police: A National Survey of the 50 Largest Cities* (Omaha: University of Nebraska at Omaha, 1992).

[14]Walker and Bumphus.

[15]Perez and Muir, p. 209.

[16]A. I. Jolin and D. C. Gibbons, "Policing the Police: The Portland Experience," *Journal of Police Science and Administration* 12 (1984): 315–322.

[17]S. T. Lethan, "Chicago's Answer to Police Brutality: The Office of Professional Standards," *The Police Chief* 1 (1980): 16–17.

[18]Kansas City Police Department, "General Order 80–4" (Kansas City, MO: Author, 1980).

[19]R. J. Terrill, "Complaint Procedures: Variations on the Theme of Civilian Participation," *Journal of Police Science and Administration* 10 (1982): 398–407.

[20]T. Hensley, "Civilian Review Boards: A Means to Police Accountability," *The Police Chief* 9 (1988): 45–47.

[21]P. West, *Investigations of Complaints against the Police: Summary Findings* (Washington, DC: Police Executive Research Forum, 1987).

Mediation

Some have argued that **mediation** is a desirable approach to address the problem of police misconduct. In it, the decision of a neutral third party, or **ombudsman**, is sought.[22] As Whitebread and Slobogin observe:

> [Another] remedial system which, like the civilian review board, operates outside the judicial and internal police spheres, is the Scandanavian ombudsman system. The ombudsman is, most simply, an external critic of administration. His goal is improvement of administration rather than punishment of administrators or redress of individual grievances. Thus, instead of conducting formal hearings associated with adjudicating individual complaints, he relies primarily on his own investigations to gather information. On the basis of his findings, he may recommend corrective measure to the department, although he cannot compel an official to do anything.[23]

A key characteristic of the ombudsman system is that it is independent of the complainant and the person being complained against. The ombudsman should be a person to whom people may come with grievances connected with the government. The ombudsman stands between the citizen and the government, acting as something of an intermediary.

As another alternative, Chief Justice Burger suggested in *Bivens* that a quasi-judicial body be appointed for the purpose of recovering damages against the government. Under his plan, if damages are awarded, the record of what transpired will become part of the offending officer's permanent file. Neither of these systems has gained widespread acceptance, much less adoption.

THE EXCLUSIONARY RULE

By far the most significant remedy in criminal procedure is the **exclusionary rule**. It is, simply, a rule of exclusion, such that evidence obtained in violation of the Constitution cannot be used in a criminal trial to prove guilt. It is a rule, as opposed to a constitutional provision, because nowhere in the Constitution does it say that illegally obtained evidence must be excluded at trial.

The Rule and Its History

Somewhat surprisingly, the U.S. Constitution contains no provisions for enforcing the protections enunciated in the Bill of Rights. For example, even though people enjoy the right to be free from unreasonable searches and seizures, the Constitution does not specify how this right is to be enforced.

For a time, then, the Bill of Rights was more or less a sham, especially when it came to criminal procedure. Without a means for remedying an unlawful search, improperly obtained confession, or similar violation, evidence obtained in flagrant violation of the Constitution could be admissible at trial.

Fortunately, as early as 1886, the U.S. Supreme Court suggested that improperly obtained evidence be excluded. In *Boyd v. United States* (116 U.S. 616 [1886]), the Court held that business records should have been excluded because "a compulsory production of the private books and papers of the owner of goods . . . is compelling him to be a witness against himself, within the meaning of the Fifth Amendment to the Constitution, and is the equivalent of a search and seizure—and an unreasonable search and

---

[22]The term *ombudsman* is traditional and used to identify either a man or a woman serving in this role.
[23]C. H. Whitebread and C. Slobogin, *Criminal Procedure*, 4th ed. (New York: Foundation Press, 2000), p. 65.

seizure—within the meaning of the Fourth Amendment" (p. 634). This statement is interesting because the Supreme Court argued that evidence should be excluded not only on Fourth Amendment grounds but on Fifth Amendment grounds, as well.

Then, in *Weeks v. United States* (232 U.S. 383 [1914]), the Court relied solely on the Fourth Amendment as a basis for exclusion. In that case, the Court held that papers seized following a search that was in violation of the Fourth Amendment should have been returned, rather than used in a criminal trial against the petitioner. Later, in *Silverthorne Lumber Co. v. United States* (251 U.S. 385 [1920]), Justice Holmes stated that without an enforcement mechanism, "the Fourth Amendment [is reduced] to a form of words" and little else (p. 392).

■ *Weeks v. United States*, 232 U.S. 383 (1914)

It is important to note that *Boyd, Weeks*, and *Silverthorne Lumber* were all *federal* cases. Following these decisions, the Supreme Court continued for several years to apply the exclusionary rule only in federal cases (e.g., *Agnello v. United States*, 269 U.S. 20 [1925]). Then, in 1949, the Court began to turn its attention to constitutional rights violations occurring at the *state* level. For example, in *Wolf v. Colorado* (338 U.S. 25 [1949]), the Court decided that evidence resulting from a Fourth Amendment violation can be excluded under the due process clause of the Fourteenth Amendment. However, the Court was hesitant to require that from that point forward, states must adopt the exclusionary rule:

> Granting that in practice the exclusion of evidence may be an effective way to deterring unreasonable searches, it is not for this Court to condemn as falling below the minimal standards assured by the Due Process Clause a State's reliance upon other methods which, if consistently enforced, would be equally effective. . . . We cannot brush aside the experience of the States which deem the incidence of such conduct by the police too slight to call for a deterrent remedy not by way of disciplinary measure but by overriding the relevant rules of evidence. (p. 31)

Even though the Court was hesitant to mandate exclusion in state courts of improperly obtained evidence, at the time of the *Wolf* decision, many states had already adopted their own versions of the exclusionary rule. By 1960, 26 states had adopted exclusionary rules (see *Elkins v. United States*, 364 U.S. 206 [1960]).

Various other Supreme Court decisions focused on the issue of exclusion, but it was not until 1961 that the exclusionary rule was formally applied to the states. For example, as noted earlier in *Rochin v. California*, the Court noted that a search in violation of the Fourth Amendment could be so serious as to shock the conscience and should be excluded as a matter of due process. As in *Wolf*, the Court was focusing on due process, not on the Fourth Amendment per se.

Elkins v. United States (364 U.S. 206 [1960]) took another step toward applying the exclusionary rule to the states. In that case, the Court denounced the so-called "**silver platter**" **doctrine**, which permitted the use of evidence in *federal* court that had been obtained illegally by *state* officials. For example, federal officials could not expect illegally obtained evidence to be admissible if they seized it (the decision in *Weeks*), but under the silver platter doctrine, they could ask state law enforcement officials to seize the evidence, even in violation of the Constitution, and it would be admissible in federal court. The silver platter doctrine, then, was a convenient means of circumventing the *Weeks* decision. The Court caught on to this practice and scrapped the doctrine.

The year 1961 marked a watershed in criminal procedure, as it was the year the Supreme Court decided the landmark case of *Mapp v. Ohio* (367 U.S. 643 [1961]). Arguably this was, and continues to be, the most significant criminal procedure case the Supreme Court has decided. In that case, the Court decided 5 to 4 that the exclusionary rule applies to the states. The Court concluded that other remedies, such as reliance on the due process clause to enforce Fourth Amendment violations, had proven "worthless and futile." Justice Clark, in a related case, stated that the exclusionary rule is the

■ *Mapp v. Ohio*, 367 U.S. 643 (1961)

"imperative of judicial integrity," noting, "The criminal goes free, if he must, but it is the law that sets him free. Nothing can destroy a government more quickly than its failure to observe its own law, or worse, its disregard of the charter of its own existence" (*Elkins v. United States*, p. 222).

Insofar as *Mapp* applied the exclusionary rule to the states, it did not do so fully. In the later case of *Ker v. California* (374 U.S. 23 [1963]), the Supreme Court noted that it had no "supervisory authority over state courts, . . . and, consequently, [*Mapp*] implied no *total* obliteration of state laws relating to arrests and searches in favor of federal law" (p. 31). In essence, the Court was deferring to the states to decide what made up a reasonable search or seizure, but only to the extent such decisions were "consistent with federal constitutional guarantees." Thus, whenever determining the reasonableness of a questionable Fourth Amendment action, federal standards must be applied. However, if a state adopts procedures that are *more restrictive* than federal standards, doing so follows the *Mapp* decision.

One final restriction concerning *Mapp* is that it only mandates exclusion of evidence obtained in violation of the federal Constitution. If, instead, evidence is obtained in violation of a rule or state law that is not of constitutional dimension, exclusion is not required under *Mapp* (*Cady v. Dombrowski*, 413 U.S. 433 [1973]). Such evidence may be excluded, however, under another decision.

Applicability of the Rule beyond the Fourth Amendment

There is a measure of debate concerning the applicability of the exclusionary rule to violations of constitutional rights besides those stemming from the Fourth Amendment. People have asked, Should the exclusionary rule be applied to the Fifth Amendment? What about the Sixth Amendment? The short answer to both questions is that it does. As a general rule, evidence obtained in violation of either the Fifth or Sixth Amendment will be excluded at a criminal trial. The long answer, unfortunately, leaves the issue somewhat unresolved.

On the one hand, some people believe that because the Fourth Amendment contains no specific reference to what should happen when an improper search or seizure takes place, the purpose of the exclusionary rule is to enforce the Fourth Amendment. They argue, furthermore, that because the exclusionary rule operates differently outside the Fourth Amendment context, it was not meant to apply to Fifth and Sixth Amendment violations. For example, just because a confession is improperly obtained does not mean that any subsequently obtained physical evidence will be excluded.

On the other hand, some observers argue that evidence can still be excluded because of Fifth, Sixth, and even Fourteenth Amendment violations. Improperly obtained confessions are not admissible; that is, they will be excluded from a criminal trial. Coercive confessions will be excluded under the Fourteenth Amendment's due process clause, identifications stemming from Sixth Amendment violations will not be admissible, and so on. These observers' point is that evidence can technically be excluded when any constitutional provision giving rise to such evidence is violated.

The perspective adopted in this book is that the exclusionary rule applies across the board. Any constitutional provision that governs law enforcement's efforts to secure evidence that could be used in a criminal prosecution falls under the purview of the exclusionary rule. That is, whenever law enforcement violates one or more of the Fourth, Fifth, Sixth, and Fourteenth Amendments—the most common amendments in criminal procedure—the evidence resulting from such a violation will not be admissible in a court of law. It is important to note, however, that the exclusionary rule and its close cousin—the "fruit of the poisonous tree" doctrine (discussed later in this chapter)—do not always operate in the same manner outside the Fourth Amendment context.

Arguments for and against the Rule

The debate over the exclusionary rule centers on three important issues: (1) whether the rule deters police misconduct; (2) whether the rule imposes unnecessary costs on society; and (3) whether alternative remedies would be effective and should be pursued.

With regard to deterrence, critics argue that the exclusionary rule does not deter police misconduct. They claim that most constitutional rights violations are unintentional and that such mistakes are undeterrable. And regarding police officers who act in bad faith, critics argue that such officers will commit perjury to mask a constitutional rights violation. Supporters of the deterrence argument, by contrast, state that the rule is not intended to deter individual officers (i.e., *specific deterrence*) but that it is intended to have a broader, systemic deterrent effect (i.e., *general deterrence*). This perspective is well supported because many police departments have amended their policies in the wake of the *Mapp* decision and encouraged their officers to adhere to constitutional safeguards.

As for social costs, critics make a number of claims. First, they believe that the exclusionary rule requires throwing out some of the most reliable forms of evidence (e.g., confessions), letting suspected criminals go free. Second, critics believe that innocent people have nothing to gain from the exclusionary rule because they have nothing to be seized by law enforcement officers who would infringe on constitutional protections. Critics also believe that the exclusionary rule creates public cynicism because it allows some individuals to escape prosecution. Finally, critics believe that the exclusionary rule is too extreme, in that a relatively trivial violation by a police officer may result in the exclusion of significant evidence.

Supporters of the exclusionary rule, by contrast, believe the benefits outweigh the costs. For example, they argue, quite persuasively, that the exclusionary rule is rarely applied. Indeed, this is true; motions to exclude evidence because of alleged constitutional rights violations are relatively rare, and they succeed even more rarely. Second, supporters believe the rule is beneficial because it *does* help innocent people. That is, since *Mapp* and other significant decisions, innocent people have been subjected to fewer unconstitutional searches, not necessarily because the police fear the exclusion of evidence but because of the potential for civil liability, citizen complaints, and the like. Supporters of the exclusionary rule also argue that public cynicism, to the extent it exists, should be directed at wayward government officials, not the exclusionary rule. Finally, supporters argue that the exclusionary rule is not disproportionate in terms of its consequences but rather is intended to serve as a general deterrent.

Opinions about the exclusionary rule are also divided along the notion of alternative remedies. Critics of the rule claim that effective alternatives do exist and should be pursued, including civil litigation, criminal prosecution, and internal discipline. Their view is that overzealous law enforcement officers can be deterred from violating the Constitution by these enforcement mechanisms. Others do not believe that the alternatives will likely prove effective. They claim, for example, that juries are more likely to favor police officers in civil trials, that immunity is often extended to police officers in civil litigation cases, and that internal police discipline is something of a sham (i.e., disciplinary decisions tend to favor the officer, not the citizen filing the complaint).

Needless to say, there are many divergent opinions concerning the exclusionary rule. Both sides to the debate make interesting points, and their arguments are persuasive. However, given the relatively small number of celebrated cases in which serious criminals have gone free, the exclusionary rule is probably more beneficial than it is harmful. In addition, just because evidence may be excluded because of police misconduct, this does not mean the defendant will "walk." In many cases, the prosecutor possesses other evidence. For example, suppose a defendant's confession is excluded but several witnesses are still willing to testify that the defendant committed the crime. He or she will, in all likelihood, be convicted.

In order to inject something of an empirical (as opposed to anecdotal) perspective into this discussion, Figure 2.6 (page 58) summarizes the scholarly research on the effect of the exclusionary rule on policing.

FIGURE 2.6 Summary of Empirical Research on the Exclusionary Rule

The question of whether the exclusionary rule is beneficial or harmful has been subjected to a fair amount of empirical research. Of particular interest to researchers have been the effects of the rule on police policy and procedure as well as on the outcomes of criminal cases. Thus, most of the research can be organized around two topics: (1) the impact of the rule on the police and prosecutors and (2) the incidence of cases in which the rule resulted in the suppression of evidence and/or the extent to which search and seizure concerns dictated the decision to prosecute. The information that follows comprises the main findings of leading studies. Citations are also provided so readers can examine the findings and research designs in more detail, as desired.

Effects of the Rule on Police and Prosecutors

1. Following *Mapp*, arrests declined among detectives in the narcotics bureau but increased for other detectives (Comment, "Effect of *Mapp v. Ohio* on Police Search and Seizure Practices in Narcotics Cases," *Columbia Journal of Legal and Social Problems* 4 [1968]: 87).

2. The exclusionary rule has virtually no effect on the arrest behavior of police (Oaks, "Studying the Exclusionary Rule in Search and Seizure," *University of Chicago Law Review* 37 [1970]: 665).

3. The exclusionary rule has no deterrent effect on illegal search practices and exacts a high cost on society because of its potential to free guilty criminals (Spiotto, "Search and Seizure: An Empirical Study of the Exclusionary Rule and Its Alternatives," *Journal of Legal Studies* 2 [1973]: 243).

4. Law enforcement search and seizure practices changed significantly following *Mapp*; namely, police officers were more likely to comply with search warrant procedures (Canon, "Is the Exclusionary Rule in Failing Health? Some New Data and a Plea against a Precipitous Conclusion," *Kentucky Law Journal* 62 [1974]: 681).

5. Interviews with narcotics detectives in Chicago led a researcher to conclude that the exclusionary rule had "significant deterrent effects . . . . [It] changed police, prosecutorial, and judicial procedures . . . . [It] educated police officers in the requirements of the Fourth Amendment and punished them when they violated requirements" (Orfield, "The Exclusionary Rule and Deterrence: An Empirical Study of Chicago Narcotics Officers," *University of Chicago Law Review* 54 [1987]: 1016).

Research on the Incidence of Lost Cases and Related Issues

1. Of 2,804 cases analyzed between July 1 and August 31, 1978, successful motions for the exclusion of evidence were made in only 1.3 percent of prosecuted cases: that is, 1.3 percent of the 16 percent whose cases were accepted for prosecution (General Accounting Office, *Report of the Comptroller General of the United States, Impact of the Exclusionary Rule on Federal Criminal Prosecutions* [Washington, DC: Government Printing Office, 1979]).

2. An estimated 4.8 percent of cases rejected for prosecution were rejected because of search and seizure problems. Approximately half of those individuals released because of the exclusionary rule were rearrested within two years of their release (National Institute of Justice, *The Effects of the Exclusionary Rule: A Study in California* [1982]).

3. In a reanalysis of the previous study, one researcher found that prosecutors rejected only 0.8 percent of felony arrests because of Fourth Amendment concerns. He concluded further that "only about 2.35% of felony arrests are lost because of illegal searches" (Davies, "A Hard Look at What We Know (and Still Need to Learn) about the 'Costs' of the Exclusionary Rule: The NIJ Study and Other Studies of 'Lost' Arrests," *American Business Foundation Research Journal* 3 [1983]: 611).

4. A nine-county study of 7,500 felony court cases revealed that motions to suppress were filed in less than 5 percent of all cases, and the success rate of such motions was reported to be 0.69 percent. The study concluded that less than 0.6 percent of all cases were lost due to the exclusion of evidence (Nardulli, "The Societal Cost of the Exclusionary Rule: An Empirical Assessment," *American Business Foundation Research Journal* 3 [1983]: 585).

5. "[M]otions to suppress were successful in only 0.9% of the primary warrants (15 of 1,748). Judges sustained motions for 2% of all defendants (27 of 1,355) in our warrant-based sample. Few cases were 'lost' as a result of the exclusionary rule in seven jurisdictions when police used search warrants. Twenty-one of 1,355 defendants (1.5%) were 'allowed to go free' as a result of a successful motion to suppress physical evidence" (Uchida and Bynum, "Search Warrants, Motions to Suppress, and 'Lost Cases': The Effects of the Exclusionary Rule in Seven Jurisdictions," *Journal of Criminal Law and Criminology* 81 [1991]: 1034).

When the Exclusionary Rule Does Not Apply

As indicated already, the exclusionary rule applies in criminal trials. But what of other proceedings, both criminal and noncriminal? The answer is that it depends. More specifically, it depends on whether the rule's remedial objective in a given context is deterrence. In other words, if in a particular circumstance the exclusion of evidence would not in theory deter misconduct, the rule does not apply.

First, the exclusionary rule does not apply in the context of grand jury investigations. In *United States v. Calandra* (414 U.S. 338 [1974]), a witness called before a grand jury refused to answer questions that were based on evidence obtained from him during an unlawful search. Worried that enforcement of the exclusionary rule would impede grand jury investigations, the Court held that it did not apply in those proceedings. The Court noted that "[a]ny incremental deterrent effect which might be achieved by extending the rule to grand jury proceedings is uncertain at best" (p. 351). The reason for this is that grand juries serve investigative functions, and the evidence would still be excluded at trial.

The rule also does not apply in *habeas corpus* proceedings. The topic of *habeas corpus* will be discussed later in this book (see Chapter 15), but it is worth defining the term here. Basically, every state or federal prisoner in the United States enjoys the constitutional right to challenge his or her conviction in federal court on the grounds that his or her constitutional rights were violated. *Habeas corpus* is not an appeal; it is known as a *collateral attack*.

As far as the exclusionary rule goes, since a *habeas corpus* petition always *follows* a criminal trial, the Court removed Fourth Amendment issues from the list of violations that can be raised in such a petition, assuming the petitioner had a "full and fair" opportunity to challenge such violations at trial. In other words, the Court reasoned that since the exclusionary rule applies at trial, any deterrent effect is most likely served there. (Deterrence *after* the trial would essentially be pointless.) In the Court's words, "The view that the deterrence of Fourth Amendment violations would be furthered rests on the dubious assumption that law enforcement authorities would fear that federal habeas review might reveal flaws in a search or seizure that went undetected at trial and on appeal" (*Stone v. Powell*, 428 U.S. 465 [1976], p. 493).

The third type of criminal proceeding in which the exclusionary rule does not apply is a parole revocation hearing. This was the decision reached in *Pennsylvania v. Scott* (524 U.S. 357 [1998]), in which the majority argued that application of the exclusionary rule in a parole revocation hearing "would both hinder the function of state parole systems and alter the traditionally flexible administrative nature of parole revocation proceedings" (p. 364). The Court further noted that the relationship between a *parole officer* and a *parolee* (as opposed to the relationship between a *police officer* and a *suspect*) is supervisory rather than adversarial, so it would be "unfair to assume that the parole officer bears hostility against the parolee that destroys his neutrality" (p. 368). Although this view is clearly debatable, it is one of the main reasons the Court offered for its decision not to apply the exclusionary rule in parole revocation proceedings. Finally, in line with the Court's decision in *Scott*, several lower courts have decided that the exclusionary rule is inapplicable in sentencing hearings (e.g., *United States v. Schipani*, 315 F. Supp. 253 [E.D.N.Y 1970]; *United States v. McCrory*, 930 F.2d 63 [D.C.Cir. 1991]).

DECISION MAKING EXERCISE **2.6**

When Does the Exclusionary Rule Not Apply?

Two officers from the state liquor control board, acting without a warrant, stopped and searched an automobile. They found that the car contained many cases of liquor not bearing state tax seals. The driver was arrested, and his car was seized. The government sought to forfeit the automobile, but the trial judge, concluding that the officers had acted without probable cause, did not permit it on the grounds that doing so depended on the admission of evidence illegally obtained in violation of the Fourth Amendment. Should the exclusionary rule apply in a civil forfeiture case, such as that described here?

Moving into the realm of civil proceedings, the exclusionary rule does not apply in civil actions brought by the Internal Revenue Service (IRS) to collect taxes. This was the decision reached in *United States v. Janis* (428 U.S. 433 [1976]). Janis had successfully excluded evidence in his prior criminal trial, citing officer misconduct, and then moved to have the same evidence excluded in a civil action brought against him by the IRS. The

Court held that the IRS case fell "outside the offending officer's zone of primary interest." Thus, excluding the evidence a second time would not deter the officer's misconduct; that was remedied at the criminal trial in which the evidence was first excluded.

In another case, the Court held that the exclusionary rule does not apply in deportation hearings brought by the Immigration and Naturalization Service (INS), which are noncriminal. In *INS v. Lopez-Mendoza* (468 U.S. 1032 [1984]), the Court moved away from the "zone of interest" language expressed in *Janis* and adopted a balancing test similar to that espoused in *Calandra*. Specifically, the Court looked at the social benefits of applying the exclusionary rule versus the costs to society of excluding evidence. In support of its decision, the Court noted that since most illegal aliens do not defend themselves in deportation hearings and agree to leave voluntarily, it is doubtful that the exclusionary rule would deter border agents from committing Fourth Amendment violations. On the other hand, the Court noted that releasing illegal aliens into the United States because of constitutional rights violations would frustrate the purpose of the INS.

There are *some* civil proceedings in which the exclusionary rule *does* apply. In particular, if the civil proceeding is the primary focus of the investigating law enforcement officer (e.g., a civil forfeiture investigation in lieu of a criminal investigation), then the exclusionary rule may apply. The Supreme Court has not directly confronted this issue, but some lower courts have. For example, lower courts have applied the exclusionary rule in juvenile delinquency proceedings (e.g., *State in Interest of T.L.O.,* 94 N.J. 331 [1983]; *New Jersey v. T.L.O.,* 469 U.S. 325 [1985]) and in some administrative proceedings (e.g., *Donovan v. Sarasota Concrete Co.,* 693 F.2d 1061 [11th Cir. 1982]). The key in each situation was that the investigating law enforcement officer worked directly with the adjudicating body. Contrast this with, for example, *Janis*, in which the IRS's civil case was secondary to a criminal prosecution and the investigating officer was involved only with the criminal prosecution.

Exceptions to the Rule

Critics of the exclusionary rule routinely argue that it constitutes a loophole in the criminal justice process and is responsible for otherwise guilty criminals going free. On the whole, this argument is somewhat deceptive, in part because of the exceptions allowed to the exclusionary rule. The Supreme Court has seen fit over the years to *allow* evidence in light of honest mistakes as well as for other purposes. There are two exceptions to the exclusionary rule: (1) the "good faith" exception and (2) the impeachment exception.

DECISION
MAKING
EXERCISE **2.7**

An Act of "Good Faith"?

After learning from an informant that some businesses had been broken into during the previous night and without making any effort to corroborate the information supplied by the informant, County Deputy Smith signed a complaint naming Mark Laurel and Carl Rogers as those who had broken into the buildings. After receiving this complaint, a judge issued a warrant for the arrests of Laurel and Rogers. Deputy Smith then sent out a police radio bulletin, describing both suspects, the car they were likely to be driving, and items that had been taken from the buildings. Police Officer Wesson, who was employed by the city, stopped a car that met the description in the radio bulletin. Wesson observed that the car had two men in it and that one of the men met Laurel's description in the radio bulletin. Officer Wesson arrested both occupants and searched the car. He found items that had been taken from one of the buildings and described in the radio bulletin in the interior of the car and burglars' tools in the trunk. Assuming the warrant is invalid (which it is because it lacks any corroboration), should Officer Wesson's arrest come under the "good faith" exception to the exclusionary rule?

As a general rule, when an honest mistake is made during the course of a search or seizure, any subsequently obtained evidence will be considered admissible. Two cases decided together were responsible for this "**good faith**" **exception**: *United States v. Leon* (468 U.S. 897 [1984]) and *Massachusetts v. Sheppard* (468 U.S. 981 [1984]). In both *Leon* and *Sheppard*, the Supreme Court concluded that evidence obtained in reasonable (good faith) reliance on a defective warrant was admissible:

> [W]e cannot conclude that admitting evidence obtained pursuant to a warrant while at the same time declaring that the warrant was somehow defective will in any way reduce judicial officers' professional incentives to comply with the Fourth Amendment, encourage them to repeat their mistakes, or lead to the granting of all colorable warrant requests. (*United States v. Leon*, p. 917)

■ *United States v. Leon*, 468 U.S. 897 (1984)

The good faith exception enunciated in *Leon* and *Sheppard* is not unqualified, however. If, for example, a warrant is "so lacking in indicia of probable cause as to render official belief in its existence entirely unreasonable, then evidence obtained following its service will not be admissible" (*United States v. Hove*, 848 F.2d 137 [9th Cir. 1988], p. 139). Similarly, if a warrant is "so facially deficient—i.e., in failing to particularize the place to be searched or things to be seized—that the executing officers cannot reasonably presume it to be valid, then the exception does not apply" (*United States v. Leary*, 846 F.2d 592 [10th Cir. 1988], p. 607). Furthermore, if the judge issuing the warrant is deliberately misled by information in the affidavit, as when a police officer acts in *bad* faith, then the good faith exception will not apply (*Lo-Ji v. State of New York*, 442 U.S. 319 [1979]). Also, if the judge issues a search warrant without sufficient consideration, then good faith cannot later be asserted.

The good faith exception is not held in the highest regard by some. Critics believe that it gives police officers an incentive to "forum shop," or to find judges who will be quick to sign off on a warrant. Justice Brennan argued in opposition to the exception as follows:

> Creation of this new exception for good faith reliance upon a warrant implicitly tells magistrates that they need not take much care in reviewing warrant applications, since their mistakes will from now on have virtually no consequence: If their decision to issue a warrant is correct, the evidence will be admitted; if their decision was incorrect but [not "entirely unreasonable" and] the police rely in good faith on the warrant, the evidence will also be admitted. Inevitably, the care and attention devoted to such an inconsequential chore will dwindle. (*United States v. Leon*, p. 956)

The good faith exception has been extended to other situations besides searches and seizures based on defective warrants. For instance, if a police officer acts in reasonable reliance on a statute that is later found to be unconstitutional, then the good faith exception will not apply (see *Michigan v. DeFillippo*, 443 U.S. 31 [1979]). In addition, if evidence is obtained following a search or seizure that is conducted in reasonable reliance on computer records that turn out to be inaccurate, then, again, the exception will not apply. In *Arizona v. Evans* (514 U.S. 1 [1995]), for example, a defendant was arrested during a traffic stop because the officer's computer showed an outstanding warrant that, unknown to the officer, had been quashed 17 days earlier. Evidence obtained from a search of the vehicle was admissible because, according to the Court, "there is no basis for believing that application of the exclusionary rule in these circumstances will have a significant effect on court employees responsible for informing the police that a warrant has been quashed" (p. 15).

The next leading exception to the exclusionary rule is the so-called **impeachment exception**. If one of the good faith exceptions does not apply, then the prosecution cannot use, as part of its case, evidence resulting from an illegal search or seizure. However, if the prosecution seeks to use such evidence for the purpose of impeaching (i.e., attacking the credibility of) a witness, then it will be considered admissible for that purpose. In *Walder v. United States* (347 U.S. 62 [1954]), a narcotics case, the Supreme Court permitted the introduction of heroin that had been illegally seized from the defendant two years earlier

■ *Walder v. United States*, 347 U.S. 62 (1954)

in order to attack his statement that he had never purchased, used, or sold drugs. An important restriction concerning the impeachment exception is that it applies only to criminal defendants, not other witnesses (*James v. Illinois*, 493 U.S. 307 [1990]).

DECISION MAKING EXERCISE 2.8

The Impeachment Exception

Dewey and Rodriguez, both attorneys, boarded a flight from Lima, Peru, and flew to Miami, Florida. In Miami, a customs officer searched Rodriguez and found cocaine sewn into makeshift pockets in the T-shirt he was wearing under his clothing. Rodriguez was arrested and he implicated Dewey, who had previously cleared customs. Dewey was located and arrested. His luggage was then seized and searched without a warrant. The officers found no drugs but seized a T-shirt from which pieces had been cut that matched the pieces sewn to Rodriguez's T-shirt. Because Dewey's luggage had been searched without a warrant, the T-shirt and other evidence were suppressed prior to trial. Dewey took the stand at his trial on narcotics offenses and denied having any connection to the incriminating T-shirt. Could the shirt be readmitted as evidence for any reason?

Good faith and impeachment are, again, the only two recognized exceptions to the exclusionary rule. Three additional exclusionary rule–type exceptions (i.e., inevitable discovery, independent source, and purged taint) are sometimes blended together with these two, but they should be kept separate. They are actually exceptions to the "fruit of poisonous tree" doctrine, to which the discussion turns now.

The "Fruit of the Poisonous Tree" Doctrine

■ *Silverthorne Lumber Co. v. United States*, 251 U.S. 385 (1920)

In *Silverthorne Lumber Co. v. United States* (251 U.S. 385 [1920]), the Supreme Court created the **"fruit of the poisonous tree" doctrine**.[24] In that case, Silverthorne Lumber Company was convicted on contempt charges for failing to produce documents that were learned of during the course of an illegal search. The Court reversed the conviction, stating that forcing the company to produce documents that were learned of strictly because of an illegal search violated the Fourth Amendment. The *Silverthorne* holding was reaffirmed in the case of *Nardone v. United States* (308 U.S. 338 [1939]). In it, the Court noted that it should be left to the discretion of "experienced trial judges" to determine whether "a substantial portion of the case against [the accused] was a fruit of the poisonous tree" (p. 341).

The metaphor of the "fruit of the poisonous tree" can be traced to the biblical story of the Garden of Eden. As the story goes, Adam and Eve ate the apple, the forbidden fruit, from the tree, bringing original sin into the world. The poisonous tree, then, is the initial unconstitutional search or seizure. Anything obtained from the tree is considered forbidden fruit.

In short, the exclusionary rule applies not only to evidence obtained as a direct result of a constitutional rights violation but also to evidence *indirectly* derived from a constitutional rights violation. In many ways, the fruit of the poisonous tree doctrine resembles a "but for" test, in which the courts have to ask, But for the unconstitutional police conduct, would the evidence have been obtained regardless? If the answer is no, then the evidence will be excluded. If the answer is yes, then the issue becomes more complicated. The Supreme Court has carved out three important exceptions to the fruit of the poisonous tree doctrine.

---

[24]Courts often speak in terms of *derivative evidence* in the same breath as "fruit of the poisonous tree." The term refers simply to evidence *derived* from a previous unconstitutional search or seizure.

Exceptions to the Doctrine

The first exception to the fruit of the poisonous tree doctrine is known as the *attenuation*, or **"purged taint" exception**. In *Nardone*, Justice Frankfurter observed that in some cases, "sophisticated argument may prove a causal link obtained through [illegality] and the Government's proof. As a matter of good sense, however, such a connection may have become so attenuated as to dissipate the taint" (p. 341). This observation was somewhat prophetic in the sense that the Court did not actually admit evidence because of attenuation. Several years later, in the case of *Wong Sun v. United States* (371 U.S. 471 [1963]), however, the Court did admit evidence because of attenuation.

■ *Wong Sun v. United States*, 371 U.S. 471 (1963)

In making an attenuation analysis, the court must decide whether the derivative evidence was obtained by exploitation of the initial unconstitutional act or instead by other means that are purged of the primary taint. In *Wong Sun*, the Court determined that statements provided by a defendant who was illegally arrested and released but later returned to the police stationhouse on his own initiative were admissible because the statements did not result from the illegal arrest. Instead, the defendant decided to come back *later*, following his release. The Court noted that his statement had become attenuated to the extent that it dissipated the taint of the initial unconstitutional act.

In *Brown v. Illinois* (422 U.S. 590 [1975]), the Supreme Court pointed to several factors that should be considered in determining whether the purged taint exception applies: (1) whether the *Miranda* warnings were given prior to a voluntary confession; (2) the "temporal proximity" of the illegal police conduct and verbal statements made by a suspect; (3) the presence of intervening events or circumstances; and (4) the "purpose and flagrancy of the official misconduct." Several later cases focused on these four factors, to varying degrees.

DECISION MAKING EXERCISE 2.9

The "Purged Taint" Exception

Officer Lewis was taking a break in a flower shop and conversing with an employee of the shop when she noticed an envelope with money protruding from it lying on the cash register. Lewis examined the envelope and found that it contained not only money but betting slips. She placed the envelope back on the register, and without telling the employee what she had found, she asked who it belonged to. The employee told Lewis that the envelope belonged to Steve Stevens, the store's owner. The officer reported this information to local detectives, who interviewed Stevens some four months later without referring to the incident at the flower shop. About six months after that incident, Stevens was summoned before a grand jury, where he testified that he had never taken bets at his flower shop. However, the store employee testified to the contrary. Stevens was then indicted for perjury. Should the employee's statement be ruled inadmissible at trial?

For example, in *Dunaway v. New York* (442 U.S. 200 [1979]), the Court chose to decide whether a confession obtained following a questionable stationhouse detention was admissible. The *Miranda* warnings had been given, but the Court still held that stationhouse detention intruded "so severely on interests protected by the Fourth Amendment as necessarily to trigger the traditional safeguards against illegal arrest" (p. 216). The Court then held that despite the *Miranda* warnings, Dunaway's statements should not be admissible. To hold differently would allow "law enforcement officers to violate the Fourth Amendment with impunity, safe in the knowledge that they could wash their hands in the 'procedural safeguards' of the Fifth" (p. 219).

In another case, *Taylor v. Alabama* (457 U.S. 687 [1982]), the Court held that the purged taint exception should not apply even under these circumstances: (1) the defendant had been advised of his *Miranda* rights; (2) six hours had elapsed between the defendant's illegal arrest and confession; and (3) the defendant had been permitted to visit with friends before making his confession.

Contrast *Taylor* with *Rawlings v. Kentucky* (448 U.S. 98 [1980]), in which the Court held that statements made 45 minutes after an illegal arrest *were* admissible because the defendant (1) had been advised of his *Miranda* rights just before making an incriminating statement; (2) had been in a house instead of a police station; and (3) had made spontaneous statements that did not result from direct questioning. Furthermore, the Court noted that the illegal arrest was not flagrant and that the defendant never argued that his admission was an involuntary product of police questioning.

The second exception to the fruit of the poisonous tree doctrine is the so-called **independent source** exception. The first case to affirmatively establish this type of exception was *Segura v. United States* (468 U.S. 796 [1984]). There, the Court held that evidence found in an apartment pursuant to a valid search warrant was admissible, even though the police had entered the apartment illegally *prior* to serving the search warrant because the warrant was based on information totally disconnected with the initial illegal search. In other words, even though the police first entered the apartment illegally, the warrant they later served was based on information independent from that search.

■ *Segura v. United States*, 468 U.S. 796 (1984)

DECISION MAKING EXERCISE 2.10

The Independent Source

Suspecting that people were storing marijuana in a warehouse, several police officers entered the building without obtaining a warrant to do so. (Later, they argued that they had suspected that evidence would be destroyed or that the people would escape if they had waited to obtain a warrant.) In fact, the search revealed bales of marijuana but no people. The police then applied for a warrant to search the building, deliberately failing to mention their previous search. The warrant was granted, the search was conducted, and the police "discovered" the marijuana. Should the marijuana be considered admissible at trial?

The third exception to the fruit of the poisonous tree doctrine is known as the **inevitable discovery** exception. Stated simply, if evidence would be found regardless of unconstitutional police conduct, then it is admissible. This exception was first recognized by the Supreme Court in *Nix v. Williams* (467 U.S. 431 [1984]). In that case, the evidence was the body of a young girl, which was discovered after the police had illegally questioned the defendant concerning the body's whereabouts. Under ordinary circumstances, the body would not have been considered admissible, but the prosecution was able to prove that at the time of the illegal questioning, a search party looking for the girl's body had narrowed in on its target and would have "inevitably discovered" the body. The Iowa Supreme Court affirmed the lower court's decision to admit the body into evidence because "(1) the police did not act in bad faith for the purpose of hastening discovery of the evidence in question, and (2) . . . the evidence in question would have been discovered by lawful means" (*Iowa v. Williams*, 285 N.W.2d 248 [Iowa 1979], p. 260).

■ *Nix v. Williams*, 467 U.S. 431 (1984)

The inevitable discovery exception bears striking resemblance to the independent source exception. For all practical purposes, evidence that would be inevitably discovered comes from an independent source. The search that was underway in *Nix v. Williams*, for example, was totally disconnected from the questioning of the defendant. In light of the similarities between these two exceptions to the fruit of the poisonous tree doctrine, some courts have simply opted to call the inevitable discovery exception the *hypothetical independent source* exception (see *Nix*, p. 438).

CONCLUSION

A number of legal remedies are available for addressing violations of people's rights, including those provided by the law, court decisions, and police policy and procedures. The most common remedies in criminal procedure are (1) civil litigation; (2) criminal liability; (3) nonjudicial mechanisms; and (4) the exclusionary rule.

Civil lawsuits against government officials—the police, mainly—come in three common varieties. The first, Section 1983 litigation, requires the plaintiff to show that a constitutional rights violation was committed by an official acting under color of state law. Section 1983 lawsuits can be filed against individual police officers, supervisors, and municipalities/counties. The courts are increasingly requiring the plaintiff to show that the constitutional rights violation was committed with a certain level of culpability on the part of the defendant. *Bivens* claims are virtually identical to Section 1983 claims but are intended to target federal, instead of state, officials. Finally, state tort law provides another avenue for litigation. Regardless of what avenue a plaintiff chooses, defendants have at their disposal a number of defenses to liability.

Police can be held *criminally* liable, as well. For instance, both state and federal law enforcement officers can be held criminally liable for violating certain federal laws. Officers are also bound by the criminal law at the state level. They can, of course, engage in certain authorized public duties (e.g., to use deadly force in appropriate circumstances) that would be crimes if committed by regular citizens.

Nonjudicial remedies include internal review, civilian review, and mediation. In the most common of these remedies, internal review, a police agency investigates its own for allegations of misconduct. Internal affairs divisions engage in this sort of activity. Civilian review occurs when citizens get involved in the investigation process; numerous varieties of citizen review are in place around the United States. Finally, a less common method of rectifying constitutional rights violations is mediation, in which a neutral third party decides on issues in dispute.

The exclusionary rule is the main remedy that will be focused on throughout the remainder of this book. It requires that evidence obtained in violation of certain constitutional amendments (notably the Fourth, Fifth, Sixth, and Fourteenth) be excluded from criminal trial. Exceptions to the exclusionary rule have been recognized in cases in which (1) the police acted in good faith but nonetheless violated the Constitution and (2) the prosecutor sought to impeach a witness at trial by pointing to contradictions in his or her out-of-court statements, even if such statements were obtained in an unconstitutional manner.

The exclusionary rule has been extended to require that derivative evidence obtained from a constitutional rights violation also be excluded. This is known as the "fruit of the poisonous tree" doctrine. Exceptions to this doctrine include inevitable discovery, independent source, and purged taint. That is, if evidence would have been discovered inevitably, if it was arrived at by means of an independent source, or if the taint of an initial unconstitutional act has been purged, then derivative evidence will be considered admissible at trial.

REVIEW QUESTIONS

1. Define the term *remedy*, and distinguish between two types of remedies.
2. Explain three methods of civil litigation.
3. What are the requirements of a successful Section 1983 lawsuit against an individual police officer? A supervisor? A city or county?
4. What is a *Bivens* claim?
5. What defense is available to a law enforcement officer charged in a Section 1983 lawsuit?
6. Distinguish among three types of state torts.
7. What defenses are available to a police officer in a state tort lawsuit?
8. How does the criminal law operate as a remedy?
9. Distinguish among three types of nonjudicial remedies.
10. What are the varieties of civilian review? How do they differ from one another?
11. What is the exclusionary rule? Is it applicable beyond the Fourth Amendment?
12. Explain the arguments for and against the exclusionary rule.
13. When does the exclusionary rule *not* apply?
14. What are the two exceptions to the exclusionary rule?
15. Define the "fruit of the poisonous tree" doctrine, and explain the three exceptions to it.

 Answers to the Decision-Making Exercises for this chapter can be found on pages 489–491.

CHAPTER 3

Introduction to the Fourth Amendment

OUTLINE

KEY TERMS

Fourth Amendment
reasonableness clause
warrant clause
person
house
papers and effects
search

seizure
government action
reasonable expectation of privacy
reasonableness
curtilage
open field

seizure of property
seizure of a person
justification
probable cause
reasonable suspicion
administrative justification
standing

INTRODUCTION

The Core Purpose and Elements of the Fourth Amendment

The **Fourth Amendment** to the U.S. Constitution reflects one of the primary grievances early American colonists had toward the Crown. The British Parliament, intent on rooting out smuggling activities taking place in the American colonies, issued writs of assistance, which permitted unlimited searches. Officials needed no justification to obtain writs of assistance, and there was no judicial supervision designed to limit the scope of the searches authorized by the writs. By adopting the Fourth Amendment, the framers of the Constitution placed significant restrictions on searches conducted by government officials.

Despite the Fourth Amendment's seemingly simple language, the 54 words that make up its text have been subjected to incredible amounts of scrutiny and interpretation. There are literally millions of pages of text—in the forms of case opinions, law review articles, and legal treatises—devoted to interpreting the language of the Fourth Amendment. The Supreme Court alone has added several layers of interpretation to the Fourth Amendment through hundreds of significant decisions. As a result, a complete understanding of Fourth Amendment rules and procedures comes with considerable difficulty. In fact, it is probably impossible to fully understand the scope, reach, and language of the Fourth Amendment because of its continued evolution. Almost without exception, the Supreme Court will decide a Fourth Amendment case during every term.

Nevertheless, the Fourth Amendment contains two basic clauses: The **reasonableness clause**, which proscribes unreasonable searches and seizures, is followed by the **warrant clause**, which says that "no Warrants shall issue, but upon

KEY CASES

Searches

- *Burdeau v. McDowell*, 256 U.S. 465 (1921)
- *Camara v. Municipal Court*, 387 U.S. 523 (1967)
- *Coolidge v. New Hampshire*, 403 U.S. 443 (1971)
- *United States v. Jacobsen*, 466 U.S. 109 (1984)
- *Katz v. United States*, 389 U.S. 347 (1967)
- *California v. Greenwood*, 486 U.S. 35 (1988)
- *Hoffa v. United States*, 385 U.S. 293 (1966)
- *United States v. On Lee*, 343 U.S. 747 (1952)
- *United States v. Dionisio*, 410 U.S. 1 (1973)
- *Oliver v. United States*, 466 U.S. 170 (1984)
- *United States v. Knotts*, 460 U.S. 276 (1983)
- *United States v. Place*, 462 U.S. 696 (1983)

Seizures

- *United States v. Jacobsen*, 466 U.S. 109 (1984)
- *Terry v. Ohio*, 392 U.S. 1 (1968)

Justification Doctrine

- *Beck v. Ohio*, 379 U.S. 89 (1964)
- *Brinegar v. United States*, 338 U.S. 160 (1949)
- *Aguilar v. Texas*, 378 U.S. 108 (1964)
- *Spinelli v. United States*, 393 U.S. 410 (1969)
- *Illinois v. Gates*, 462 U.S. 213 (1983)
- *Terry v. Ohio*, 392 U.S. 1 (1968)
- *Alabama v. White*, 496 U.S. 325 (1990)
- *Camara v. Municipal Court*, 387 U.S. 523 (1967)
- *Skinner v. Railway Labor Executives' Association*, 489 U.S. 602 (1989)

probable cause, supported by Oath or affirmation, and particularly describing the place to be searched, and the persons or things to be seized."

A fundamental question has been raised about these two clauses. They are joined in the text of the Fourth Amendment by the conjunction *and*, which has led to a great deal of debate over whether the two clauses are related or separate. Some people have argued that the warrant clause gives meaning to the reasonableness clause, in that it automatically renders unreasonable a search that is not conducted with a warrant. Justice Frankfurter took this position in *United States v. Rabinowitz* (339 U.S. 56 [1950]): "What is the test of reason which makes a search reasonable?... There must be a warrant to permit search, barring only inherent limitations upon that requirement when there is a good excuse for not getting a search warrant" (p. 83). This is the *warrant requirement* interpretation, requiring that a neutral magistrate come between the officer conducting the search and the citizen being the target of the search.

Others have argued that the search-and-seizure clause and the warrant clause should be read separately. Their position is that the reasonableness of a search should not depend on whether a warrant was obtained or on whether there was a good excuse for not obtaining a warrant. Instead, they argue that the courts should focus on the factual circumstances justifying the search. They argue, specifically, that the courts should consider the manner in which the search was executed, not whether a warrant was secured. The main protection offered by the Fourth Amendment should lie, then, not with a judge *prior* to the search but with the courts *after* the search. In this view, the courts should reflect on what occurred and seek to determine whether the search was reasonable at the time it was actually conducted.

A third view, known as the *warrant preference view*, has come to the forefront in recent years. As a result, much of the confusion surrounding the nexus of the search-and-seizure clause and the warrant clause has been cleared up. As the Supreme Court stated in *Mincey v. Arizona* (437 U.S. 385 [1978]), "The Fourth Amendment proscribes all unreasonable searches and seizures, and it is a cardinal principle that searches conducted outside the judicial process, without prior approval by judge or magistrate, are per se unreasonable under the Fourth Amendment, subject to a few specifically established and well delineated exceptions" (p. 390) (see also *Vale v. Louisiana*, 399 U.S. 30 [1970]). Basically, the rule of thumb is that a search warrant (or an arrest warrant, in the case of a seizure of a person) should be procured whenever practical. If, however, there is an emergency or other such exception, such as a significant risk to public safety, a warrant may not be necessary. This third view is most common today.

■ BASIC TERMINOLOGY

The Fourth Amendment protects *persons, houses, papers, and effects* from unreasonable searches and seizures. Few court cases have turned on the meanings of these terms, but it is still important to define them.

The term **person** encompasses the individual as a whole, both internally and externally. An arrest, for example, is a seizure of a person. If a police officer pulls up the sleeves of a suspected drug user to look for needle tracks, this is a search of a *person* within the meaning of the Fourth Amendment.

In the early twentieth century, the Supreme Court ruled that the Fourth Amendment applied only to searches and seizures of tangible items (*Olmstead v. United States*, 277 U.S. 438 [1928]). Oral communications fell outside the scope of the Fourth Amendment, so surveillance of conversations, regardless of how it was pursued, did not trigger constitutional protections. Today, however, in the wake of *Katz v. United States* (389 U.S. 347 [1967]), the Supreme Court has stated emphatically that oral communications trigger the protections of the Fourth Amendment. Thus, the definition of *person* for purposes of the Fourth Amendment not only includes the person's internal and external physical body but also (most) oral communications made by people.

House is a term that is broadly construed to mean any structure that a person uses as a residence (and frequently a business) on either a temporary or long-term basis. A hotel room is a prime example of a short-term house. Also, a garage or other structure not connected to a house can also fall within the meaning of the Fourth Amendment. Whether a garage is actually a house, though, depends on the notion of *curtilage*. An open field, by contrast, does not trigger the protection of the Fourth Amendment because it is not a house. (Open fields and curtilage are defined later on in this chapter.)

Next, **papers and effects** include nearly all personal items. Business records, letters, diaries, memos, and countless other forms of tangible evidence can be defined as *papers*. *Effects* is the catch-all category. Anything that is not a person, house, or paper is probably an effect. Effects can include cars, luggage, clothing, weapons, contraband, and the fruits of criminal activity. Given these broad definitions, then, it is easy to understand why few court cases have turned on the meanings of *persons*, *houses*, *papers*, and *effects*.

If the police activity in question does not involve a person, house, paper, or effect, no Fourth Amendment protections exist. In reality, though, almost any conceivable tangible item or form of communication falls within the protection of the Fourth Amendment. What becomes important, then, is determining precisely when the Fourth Amendment applies and when a search or seizure can be considered reasonable.

A FRAMEWORK FOR ANALYZING THE FOURTH AMENDMENT

For the sake of clarifying a fairly complex body of law, this book approaches the Fourth Amendment in a specific format. This chapter introduces basic Fourth Amendment terminology, focusing in particular on (1) which police activities trigger the protections of the Fourth Amendment and (2) what justification is required for the police to engage in certain types of activities. Later chapters focus on the types of law enforcement activity authorized (and not authorized) by the Fourth Amendment as well as on relevant procedures.

In determining when the Fourth Amendment is triggered, it is important to draw a distinction between a **search** and a **seizure**. Each action triggers the protections of the Fourth Amendment, but each is distinctly different. In addition, the law that governs searches is not the same as the law that governs seizures.

A search is, as the term suggests, an activity geared toward finding evidence to be used in a criminal prosecution. To define when a search takes place, two important factors need to be considered: (1) whether the presumed search is a product of **government action** and (2) whether the intrusion violates a person's **reasonable expectation of privacy**.

The term *seizure*, on the other hand, has a dual meaning in criminal procedure. First, *property* can be seized. Often, the result of a search is a seizure of evidence. For example, if the police successfully serve a search warrant to look for illegal weapons at 345 Oak Street, the weapons they find will be seized. Second, *people* can also be seized. Seizures of people can occur almost anywhere and at any time. An arrest, for example, is considered a seizure within the meaning of the Fourth Amendment.

The second stage in the Fourth Amendment analysis requires focusing on the **reasonableness** of the search or seizure. In other words, once the protections of the Fourth

Amendment are triggered, did the police act in line with Fourth Amendment requirements? For example, if a person is arrested, did the police have adequate reason to believe the person arrested in fact committed the crime? When the courts focus on the reasonableness of a search or seizure, they speak in terms of *justification*. If the police (or other government actors) engage in a search or seizure without justification, they violate the Fourth Amendment.

The only justification mentioned in the Fourth Amendment is *probable cause*. The untrained observer may be inclined to think that any search or seizure based on a lesser degree of certainty than probable cause would violate the Fourth Amendment. For a time, this was the case. In recent decades, however, the Supreme Court has carved out exceptions to the Fourth Amendment's probable cause requirement. Basically, the Court has ruled that there are certain situations in which the police can seize people and/or look for evidence with a lesser degree of certainty than probable cause.

Think of this chapter as being almost pre–Fourth Amendment in its orientation. It is designed to supply the reader with the tools for approaching any situation resembling a search or a seizure. Without an understanding of (1) when the Fourth Amendment applies and (2) what justification is required for the police to act, it will be impossible to judge the constitutionality of the police conduct under examination.

WHEN A SEARCH OCCURS

Again, generally speaking, a *search* can be defined as the act of looking for evidence. However, not every act of looking for evidence can be considered a search *within the meaning of the Fourth Amendment*. For example, a private citizen may look for evidence, but because private citizens are not government actors, their actions are not bound by the Fourth Amendment. The Fourth Amendment protects citizens from *government* action. Thus, one requirement in determining when a search occurs is to ascertain *who* is looking for evidence.

Even though the Fourth Amendment restricts government action, it is not the case that government actors always engage in searches when looking for evidence. The police can do many things to look for evidence, such as looking in open fields, without being bound by the strictures of the Fourth Amendment. To draw a distinction between a search and a nonsearch, then, the courts will focus on *where* the police look for evidence. This requires that attention be given to the notion of *reasonable expectation of privacy*.

Government Action, Not Private Action

The Fourth Amendment's protection against unreasonable searches and seizures has been limited by the courts to conduct that is governmental in nature. Thus, when a private individual seizes evidence or otherwise conducts a search, the protections of the Fourth Amendment are not triggered. For example, if Angela knows that her neighbor Larry has a large supply of stolen stereo equipment in the garage behind his house, she could conceivably enter his garage, seize the evidence, and turn it over to the police. They, in turn, could use the evidence, and other information provided by Angela, to arrest Larry. Of course, Angela could be found guilty of criminal trespass, but as far as the Fourth Amendment is concerned, she committed no constitutional violations. Assuming that Angela acted independent of the police, she acted in a private capacity.

■ *Burdeau v. McDowell,*
256 U.S. 465 (1921)

The inapplicability of the Fourth Amendment to searches or seizures carried out by private individuals was first recognized by the Supreme Court in *Burdeau v. McDowell* (256 U.S. 465 [1921]). In that case, some individuals illegally entered McDowell's business office and seized records. The records were later turned over to the Attorney General of the United States, who planned to use them against McDowell in court. McDowell sought return of the records, and the district court granted his petition. But

The Scope of a Private Search

Glen Olson stands accused of poisoning dogs in his neighborhood by means of feeding them dog biscuits lined with a harmful chemical. Olson's girlfriend, in a desperate attempt to bring her boyfriend's cruelty to a halt, turned a bag of dog biscuits over to the police that presumably contained the chemical used to poison the helpless animals. Since the police were not sure what the substance in the biscuits was, they took the biscuits to a laboratory and subjected them to a chemical analysis. Laboratory technicians found that the substance was a chemical known to bring about violent illness. May Olson move to suppress the evidence on the grounds that the laboratory analysis triggered the protections of the Fourth Amendment?

In *United States v. Jacobsen* (466 U.S. 109 [1984]), however, the Supreme Court modified its earlier opinion in *Walter* and instead noted that the subsequent governmental search must be *substantially more intrusive* in order for the Fourth Amendment to be triggered. In *Jacobsen*, Federal Express employees opened a damaged package and found several packages containing a suspicious white powder. They closed the package and then summoned federal agents, who reopened the packages and conducted a field test on the substances. The Court held, "The agent's viewing of what a private party had freely made available for his inspection did not violate the Fourth Amendment" (p. 119), and the field test had nothing more than a "de minimus [minimal] impact on any protected property interest."

■ *United States v. Jacobsen,* 466 U.S. 109 (1984)

■ Infringement on Reasonable Expectation of Privacy

Governmental action alone is not enough to implicate the Fourth Amendment. Coupled with governmental action, the Fourth Amendment is triggered only when the law enforcement activity in question infringes on a person's reasonable expectation of privacy. In other words, there are times when police officers and other governmental officials look for evidence (as in an open field, for instance) but do not act intrusively enough so as to trigger the Fourth Amendment.

Prior to 1967, the definition of a *search* was closely tied to property interests. Police action would only be deemed a search if it physically infringed on an individual's property. The activity basically had to amount to common-law trespassing for it to be considered a search. Any police activity that was not trespassory in nature was not considered a search. This definition became outdated in the landmark decision of *Katz v. United States* (389 U.S. 347 [1967]).

■ *Katz v. United States,* 389 U.S. 347 (1967)

In *Katz*, federal agents placed a listening device outside a phone booth in which Katz was having a conversation. Katz made incriminating statements during the course of his conversation, and the FBI sought to use the statements against him at trial. The lower court ruled that the FBI's activities did not amount to a search because there was no physical entry into the phone booth. The Supreme Court reversed that decision, holding that the Fourth Amendment "protects people, not places," and so its reach "cannot turn upon the presence or absence of a physical intrusion into any given enclosure" (p. 353). Instead, the Fourth Amendment definition of a *search* turns on the concept of privacy. In the Court's words, "The Government's activities in electronically listening to and recording words violated the privacy upon which [Katz] justifiably relied while using the telephone booth and thus constituted a 'search and seizure' within the meaning of the Fourth Amendment" (p. 353).

Despite the seemingly profound change in the search-and-seizure definition following *Katz,* several subsequent decisions have interpreted the *Katz* ruling rather narrowly. For

■ *California v. Greenwood,*
486 U.S. 35 (1988)

instance, in *California v. Greenwood* (486 U.S. 35 [1988]), the Supreme Court ruled that a Fourth Amendment search or seizure occurs only when (1) the citizen has a manifested subjective expectation of privacy and (2) the expectation of privacy is one that society (through the eyes of a court) is willing to accept as objectively reasonable.

Recall from the discussion in Chapter 1 that a *subjective* interest focuses on what one individual thinks (in this case, the person presumably being subjected to a search) and that an *objective* interest focuses either on what society thinks or what a reasonable person would think. With regard to *Greenwood*, then, this means that just because someone *feels* he or she should enjoy privacy in a particular activity is not enough to trigger the Fourth Amendment. His or her activity needs to be one that society perceives as reasonable, also. In other words, it is not enough for someone to believe his or her rights have been infringed upon; his or her belief must also be an objectively reasonable one.

Today, the courts scarcely look toward the *subjective* issue and focus almost exclusively on the *objective* expectation of privacy. The reason for this is that it is pointless to dwell on an individual's expectation of privacy because if the seizure is questionable at all, the defendant will almost certainly proclaim he or she expected privacy. Focusing on an objective (instead of a subjective) expectation of privacy seems eminently more sensible.

One important observation in *Katz* deserves further mention: The Court stated that "[w]hat a person knowingly exposes to the public, even in his own home or office, is not subject to Fourth Amendment protection" (p. 351). Protection is only afforded for "what he seeks to preserve as private" (p. 351).

Defining the vague notions of *reasonableness* and *knowing exposure* has been the focus of a number of Supreme Court cases. These cases can be placed into four categories: (1) the undercover agents cases; (2) the physical characteristics cases; (3) the open fields and curtilage cases; and (4) the enhancement device cases.

Undercover Agents, Institutional Agents, and Informants

■ *Hoffa v. United States,*
385 U.S. 293 (1966)

What happens when a person privately conveys information to a third party who is, in fact, an undercover agent, or as some people describe them, a "false friend"? In *Hoffa v. United States* (385 U.S. 293 [1966]), the Supreme Court sought to answer this question. In that case, the defendant, Hoffa, had a conversation with a union official who was in Hoffa's private suite by invitation but who was, in fact, a government informant. The informant reported what Hoffa said to government officials, and Hoffa sought to have the evidence excluded on the grounds that it was an illegal search. The Supreme Court disagreed with this decision, noting that the informant "was not a surreptitious eavesdropper" (p. 302) but a person who "was in the suite by invitation and every conversation which he heard was either directed to him or knowingly carried on in his presence" (p. 302).

DECISION MAKING EXERCISE 3.4

A "False Friend" Scenario

John Quinn was put in jail after being arrested as a homicide suspect. The prosecutor did not think she had enough evidence to proceed to trial, so she asked a police officer to dress in street clothes, pose as a jail inmate, and strike up a conversation with Quinn. The officer was placed in the same cell with Quinn and began to make small talk with him. Eventually, Quinn mentioned that he was involved in the murder of Valerie Hutton but that he was not the "trigger man." The police officer reported this conversation to the prosecutor, who then sought to use Quinn's incriminating statements against him at trial. Quinn's attorney moved to have the statements suppressed on the grounds that a Fourth Amendment violation took place.

In particular, the defense attorney argued that Quinn had a reasonable expectation of privacy that his conversation would not be shared with or repeated to other individuals. Does Quinn have a reasonable expectation of privacy in this regard?

A more difficult question arose in *United States v. On Lee* (343 U.S. 747 [1952]). *On Lee* addressed the issue of whether an undercover agent could wear a recording device during a conversation with a suspected criminal. The majority ruled that this activity did not constitute a search, again, because the informant was invited into the area where the conversation took place. Justice Burton dissented, however, noting that the recorder "amount[s] to [the agent] surreptitiously bringing [the police] with him" (p. 766). The majority countered by arguing that the listening device was simply designed to improve the accuracy of the evidence obtained by the informant. Other cases have been decided in a similar fashion (e.g., *United States v. White*, 401 U.S. 745 [1971]; *Lopez v. United States*, 373 U.S. 427 [1963]).

■ *United States v. On Lee* 343 U.S. 747 (1952)

Still other questions have been posed in the cases involving so-called *institutional agents*: individuals who are not undercover agents or informants per se but nonetheless third parties who turn evidence over to authorities. For example, in *United States v. Miller* (425 U.S. 435 [1976]), the Supreme Court held that a subpoena of records of financial information voluntarily surrendered to a bank is not a search within the meaning of the Fourth Amendment. Similarly, in *Smith v. Maryland* (442 U.S. 735 [1979]), the Court ruled that a person does not have a reasonable expectation of privacy in the phone numbers he or she dials, as he or she should know that a record of the calls, as well as the numbers, is kept with the phone company. In *California v. Greenwood* (486 U.S. 35 [1988]), the Court ruled:

> [G]arbage bags left on or at the side of a public street are readily accessible to animals, children, scavengers, snoops, and other members of the public. Moreover, respondents placed their refuse at the curb for the express purpose of conveying it to a third party, the trash collector, who might himself have sorted through respondents' trash or permitted others, such as the police, to do so. Accordingly, having deposited their garbage in an area particularly suited for public inspection and, in a manner of speaking, public consumption, for the express purpose of having strangers take it, respondents could have no reasonable expectation of privacy in the inculpatory items they discarded. (p. 40)

Generally speaking, then, when people voluntarily convey information or provide material to third parties, they cannot have a reasonable expectation of privacy (even if those third parties are best friends) because the third parties could easily turn the information over to authorities. Similarly, when people abandon their property (as in *Greenwood*), a Fourth Amendment search does not take place.

Privacy in One's Physical Characteristics

The courts have also held that people's external physical characteristics are knowingly exposed to the public and are thus outside the scope of the Fourth Amendment. As noted in *United States v. Dionisio* (410 U.S. 1 [1973]), for example, "No person can have a reasonable expectation that others will not know the sound of his voice, any more than he can reasonably expect that his face will be a mystery to the world" (p. 13). To this end, the government can require handwriting samples (as in *Dionisio*) and other forms of physical evidence, such as locks of hair, voice exemplars, and fingerprints (e.g., *Davis v. Mississippi*, 394 U.S. 721 [1969]).

■ *United States v. Dionisio*, 410 U.S. 1 (1973)

Physical attributes not on public display, however, generally fall within the protection of the Fourth Amendment. For example, in *Skinner v. Railway Labor Executives' Association* (489 U.S. 602 [1989]), the Court ruled that blood, urine, and breath analysis all amount to searches because "they intrude upon expectations of privacy as to medical information" (p. 616) (see also *Schmerber v. California*, 384 U.S. 757 [1966]; *Winston v. Lee*, 470 U.S. 753 [1985]; and *Cupp v. Murphy*, 412 U.S. 291 [1973]).

Just because external physical characteristics are knowingly exposed does not mean, however, that the police are not restricted in other ways by the Fourth

Amendment. If a suspect is at home in his or her private residence, for instance, and the police wish to obtain his or her fingerprints, in almost all circumstances, they will need appropriate justification to do so. This could be accomplished by demonstrating probable cause and obtaining a warrant. Think of it this way: A person may not enjoy a reasonable expectation of privacy with regard to his or her physical characteristics that are on public display, but he or she will *always* enjoy a reasonable expectation of privacy in his or her residence, provided the police attempt to find him or her at that location.

Open Fields and Curtilage

The physical setting in which police activity takes place is also important in determining whether the Fourth Amendment applies. Clearly, the inside of a residence is protected by the Fourth Amendment, but what about the outside? And if the outside is protected, how far beyond the residence can the strictures of the Fourth Amendment be expected to apply?

In providing answers to these questions, the courts refer to the term *curtilage.* According to the Supreme Court (*Oliver v. United States*, 466 U.S. 170 [1984]), **curtilage** is the "area to which extends the intimate activity associated with the sanctity of a man's home and the privacies of life" (p. 225). This definition should be contrasted with the definition of an **open field**, which is any unoccupied or undeveloped real property falling outside the curtilage of a home (p. 170). Figure 3.1 distinguishes among a house, curtilage, and open field.

■ *Oliver v. United States,* 466 U.S. 170 (1984)

Open fields do not enjoy Fourth Amendment protection, but homes and curtilage do. Note, however, that open fields need not be *open* or *fields* to fall beyond the reach of the Fourth Amendment. If a barn that is located 50 yards from a house is not used for "intimate activities," it *can* be considered an open field, even though it is located on private property (see *United States v. Dunn*, 480 U.S. 294 [1987]). This is because "[o]pen fields do not provide the setting for those intimate activities that the [Fourth] Amendment is intended to shelter from government interference or surveillance" (*Oliver v. United States*, p. 179).

In *Oliver*, the Court went on to observe that

> there is no societal interest in protecting the privacy of those activities, such as the cultivation of crops, that occur in open fields. Moreover, as a practical matter, these lands usually are accessible to the public and the police in ways that a home, office or commercial structure would not be. It is not generally true that fences or [No Trespassing] signs effectively bar the public from viewing open fields in rural areas. (p. 179)

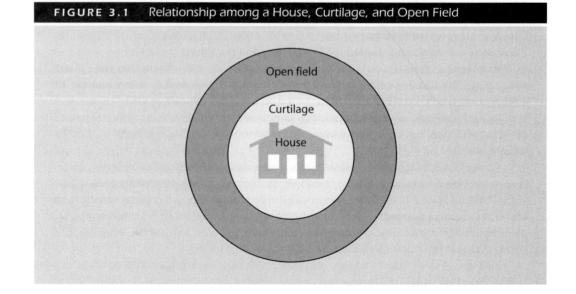

FIGURE 3.1 Relationship among a House, Curtilage, and Open Field

FIGURE 3.2   Factors Used to Distinguish between a Curtilage and Open Field

1. Is the area close to a house or residence?
2. Is the area contained by a fence or similar enclosure?
3. To what use is the area being put?
4. What steps have been taken to protect the area from observation?

The courts consider four factors when distinguishing between an open field and cur-tilage: (1) the proximity of the area to the house; (2) whether the area is included within a fence or another enclosure surrounding the house; (3) the nature of the use to which the land/property is being put; and (4) the steps taken by the resident to protect the area from observation (*United States v. Dunn*). These four issues were considered by the Court in *United States v. Dunn.* In that case, police entered the defendant's property without a war-rant, climbed over several fences, and peered inside his barn. They eventually obtained a warrant to search the barn, but the Court ruled that their earlier activity was a search within the meaning of the Fourth Amendment. See Figure 3.2 for a summary of these factors.

DECISION MAKING EXERCISE **3.5**

Is a Public Street an Open Field?

Officer Perez suspects that a local man is growing marijuana in his backyard but cannot tell for certain because of the large fence surrounding the house. To find out, Perez places a stepladder on a nearby public sidewalk, climbs up to the top, peers over the fence, and observes several dozen marijuana plants growing in the man's garden. Has a search occurred in this situation?

A twist in the aforementioned scenarios occurs when the police perform so-called flyovers, or aerial surveillance from a fixed-wing aircraft and/or helicopter. In *California v. Ciraolo* (476 U.S. 207 [1986]), the Supreme Court ruled that naked-eye observation of a fenced-in backyard from a height of 1,000 feet did not constitute a search. The logic offered by the Court was that in "an age where private and commercial flight in the public airways is routine, it is unreasonable for respondent to expect that his marijuana plants were constitutionally protected" from such observation (p. 215).

Similarly, in *Florida v. Riley* (488 U.S. 445 [1989]), the Court held that the Fourth Amendment was not implicated when the police flew a helicopter at an altitude of 400 feet over the defendant's partially covered greenhouse, which was found to contain marijuana. "Riley no doubt intended and expected that his greenhouse would not be open to public inspection, and the precautions he took [including placing a wire fence around the greenhouse and a Do Not Enter sign] protected against ground-level observation" (p. 450). The fact that any person could position himself or herself over the greenhouse in a helicopter was not enough to amount to a Fourth Amendment violation. The Court supported its position in this matter by noting that the helicopter's altitude was within legal parameters and Federal Aviation Administration (FAA) guidelines.

A similar decision was reached in *Dow Chemical Co. v. United States* (476 U.S. 227 [1986]), a case in which the Environmental Protection Agency (EPA) hired an aerial photographer to take pictures of the defendant's plant. Despite the photographer's use of a camera to take pictures (as opposed to simple, naked-eye observation), the Supreme

Court ruled that aerial photography of the type used in *Dow Chemical* did not amount to a search, thereby triggering Fourth Amendment protections (see also *Air Pollution Variance Bd. v. Western Alfalfa Corp.*, 416 U.S. 861 [1974]).

Enhancement Devices

The rules become significantly more complicated when law enforcement officials use socalled *enhancement devices* to look for evidence. Enhancement devices can include flashlights, drug dogs, satellite photography, thermal imagery, and so on. Whatever their form, the devices are designed to enhance or replace the ability of the police to identify and discern criminal evidence or crime itself.

In determining what level of sensory enhancement is appropriate, the courts generally give consideration to six specific factors: (1) the nature of the place surveilled; (2) the nature of the activity surveilled; (3) the care taken to ensure privacy; (4) the lawfulness of the vantage point; (5) the availability of sophisticated technology; and (6) the extent to which the technology used enhances or replaces the natural senses.[1]

■ *United States v. Knotts*, 460 U.S. 276 (1983)

Illustrating the first consideration, the Court in *United States v. Knotts* (460 U.S. 276 [1983]) decided on the constitutionality of federal agents' actions of placing a "beeper" (a tracking device) in a container and tracking the container to the defendant's cabin. The Court concluded that "[a] person travelling in an automobile on public thoroughfares has no reasonable expectation of privacy in his movements from one place to another" (p. 281) (see also *United States v. Karo*, 468 U.S. 705 [1984]). The determinative factor in *Knotts* (and *Karo*) was that the nonsearch was conducted outside a residence. Had the beeper entered the residence, the outcome would have almost certainly been different.

With regard to the lawfulness of the police's vantage point, one thing is clear: If the police are not in a lawful vantage point but continue to look for evidence, a search occurs. Examples of lawful vantage points include sidewalks, streets, and, of course, public airways. As the Court ruled in *United States v. Dunn* (480 U.S. 294 [1987]), the police can take up positions anywhere outside the home or the curtilage of the home and still be in a lawful vantage point. In fact, even if the police find themselves in curtilage that is open to the public, they may still find themselves in a lawful vantage point (see *Minnesota v. Carter*, 525 U.S. 83 [1998]).

The availability of sophisticated technology is also determinative in deciding which sensory enhancement devices the police can use. The previous discussion of *Dow Chemical* showed that the use of a camera from a publicly navigable airspace does not necessarily amount to a search. The Court deemed this activity beyond the scope of the Fourth Amendment because the camera equipment was available on the open market. However, the Court also pointed out that "using highly sophisticated surveillance equipment *not* generally available to the public, such as satellite technology, might be constitutionally proscribed absent a warrant" (p. 238, emphasis added). Moreover, the use of "an electronic device to penetrate walls or windows so as to hear and record confidential discussions of chemical formulae or other trade secrets would raise very different and far more serious questions" (p. 238).

The recent Supreme Court case of *Kyllo v. United States* (S33 U.S. 27 [2001]) fits clearly into a discussion of law enforcement's use of technology. In that case, law enforcement officials were suspicious that marijuana was being grown in Kyllo's home. Agents scanned his home using a thermal imaging device (also known as FLIR, for Forward Looking Infrared). The scan revealed that Kyllo's garage roof and side wall were relatively hot compared to the rest of his home. Based in part on the results from the thermal imager, a federal magistrate issued a warrant to search Kyllo's home. However, the Supreme Court declared that "[w]here . . . the Government uses a device that is not in general public use, to explore details of a private home that would previously have

---

[1]C. H. Whitebread and C. Slobogin, *Criminal Procedure*, 4th ed. (New York: Foundation Press, 2000), pp. 120–125.

been unknowable without physical intrusion, the surveillance is a Fourth Amendment 'search,' and is presumptively unreasonable without a warrant" (p. 40).

The courts will also consider the extent to which a sensory enhancement device actually enhances the natural senses. In doing this, several courts have distinguished between devices that *enhance* the senses versus those that *replace* the senses. Generally, an enhancement device that is used to assist the senses (as binoculars do, for instance) is less likely to implicate the Fourth Amendment than a device that replaces the senses (as some satellites do). The permissibility of the use of binoculars can be attributed to the argument that police officers sometimes wish to avoid detection during the course of observation. Flashlights are clearly devices that enhance the natural senses, and courts have ruled that, when used, they do not trigger the Fourth Amendment (*Texas v. Brown*, 460 U.S. 730 [1983]; *United States v. Dunn*, 480 U.S. 294 [1987]).

DECISION MAKING EXERCISE 3.6

Drug Dogs as Sensory Enhancement Devices

A woman traveler paid for a plane ticket to Miami. When she checked in at the airport, the ticket agent took her luggage and placed it on a conveyor belt so it could be loaded onto the plane. As the luggage was traveling along the conveyor, it passed a narcotics agent, whose dog sniffs every bag in an attempt to find drugs. The dog was alerted to the woman's bag, so the narcotics officer grabbed it and opened it. Several kilogram packages of cocaine were inside. Before the woman could board her flight, she was arrested. Was the arrest valid?

A slightly more controversial device is a drug dog. Some courts have ruled that their use does not trigger the Fourth Amendment under certain circumstances (e.g., *United States v. Place*, 462 U.S. 696 [1983]), but the issue is unresolved because one could argue that a drug dog's senses are used to *replace* an officer's senses. In fact, in *Commonwealth v. Johnston* (515 Pa. 454 [1987]), the court ruled that law enforcement officers' use of drug dogs violated the state constitution because "a free society will not remain free if police may use this, or any other crime detection device, at random and without reason" (p. 465). The courts also need to consider *where* drug-sniffing dogs are used. For example, the Second Circuit held that the use of a drug dog adjacent to the defendant's apartment to determine the presence of narcotics *within* was a search, triggering the amendment's protection (see *United States v. Thomas*, 757 F.2d 1359 [2nd Cir. 1985]).

■ *United States v. Place,* 462 U.S. 696 (1983)

■ WHEN A SEIZURE OCCURS

The Fourth Amendment is clearly implicated when a search occurs. The same applies to a seizure. That is, whenever a person or piece of property is seized, then the Fourth Amendment applies.

The definition of *seizure* has a very specific meaning in criminal procedure. It is not the case that something must be physically grasped for a seizure to take place. Indeed, the police can stop short of actually touching a person, but their actions can still constitute a seizure. At the other extreme, though, there are certain things the police can do to inconvenience people without triggering the Fourth Amendment. It is important to distinguish between two types of seizures: (1) seizures of property and (2) seizures of persons.

Seizures of Property

United States v. Jacobsen,
466 U.S. 109 (1984)

As the Supreme Court declared in *United States v. Jacobsen* (466 U.S. 109 [1984]), a **seizure of property** occurs "when there is some meaningful interference with an individual's possessory interest in that property."

In determining if a piece of property is seized, courts often refer to people's *actual* and *constructive* possessions. A piece of property is in a person's actual possession if he or she is physically holding or grasping the property. Constructive possession, by comparison, refers to possession of property without physical contact (e.g., a bag that is next to a person on the ground but not in his or her hands). A piece of property is seized, therefore, if the police remove it from a person's actual or constructive possession, such as when they take a person's luggage at an airport and move it into another room to be searched (see *United States v. Place*, 462 U.S. 696 [1983]).

Relatively few cases are encountered concerning seizures of property. Usually, property is seized *after* a search occurs. When a search is declared unlawful, the seizure of the property that follows is generally unconstitutional under the "fruit of the poisonous tree" doctrine (see Chapter 2). However, there are certain cases in which seizure occurs apart from a search (*Soldal v. Cook County*, 506 U.S. 56 [1992]). Otherwise, most of the remaining chapters in the search-and-seizure section of this text refer to searches of people and property and seizures of persons.

Seizures of Persons

Subject to significant clarification in later chapters, a **seizure of a person** occurs when a police officer—by means of physical force or show of authority—intentionally restrains an individual's liberty in such a manner that a reasonable person would believe that he or she is not free to leave (*Terry v. Ohio*, 392 U.S. 1 [1968]; *United States v. Mendenhall*, 446

Terry v. Ohio,
392 U.S. 1 (1968)

U.S. 544 [1980]). Another way of understanding what a Fourth Amendment seizure involves is to ask this question: Would a reasonable person believe that he or she is free to decline the officer's requests or otherwise terminate the encounter? (*Florida v. Bostick*, 501 U.S. 429 [1991]). A yes answer means a seizure has occurred.

The seizure of a person can take place in a number of ways. For example, a person is seized when he or she is arrested and taken to the police station for questioning (*Dunaway v. New York*, 442 U.S. 200 [1979]). A person is also seized if he or she is physically restrained on the street so that he or she may be frisked (e.g., *Terry v. Ohio*, 392 U.S. 1 [1968]) or if he or she is pulled over by the police in his or her car.

The seizure of a person does not have to be *physical* for the Fourth Amendment to be implicated. For example, a seizure can occur when a police officer simply questions a person. The Supreme Court stated in *Terry v. Ohio* that "not all personal intercourse between policemen and citizens involves 'seizures' of persons" (p. 20, n. 16). Even so, a seizure *does* occur when the officer's conduct in conjunction with the questioning would convince a reasonable person that he or she is not free to leave.

Another way a seizure can occur is by *pursuit*, even if the person sought by the police is never caught. However, it is not always clear whether a pursuit constitutes a seizure. This is important because if the pursuit of a suspect is *not* a seizure, then the police may lawfully chase people without justification. Moreover, if the person discards anything during the chase, the police may lawfully seize the item because the Fourth Amendment does not apply. In fact, as the Supreme Court noted in *California v. Hodari D.* (499 U.S. 621 [1991]), when an officer chases a suspect but does not lay hands on him or her, a seizure does not occur until which point the suspect submits to police authority.

In *Hodari D.*, a police officer chased a suspect on foot. The officer did not have justification to stop or arrest the suspect. The suspect discarded an item during the chase, which the officer stopped to pick up. The Supreme Court upheld the officer's action because the suspect was still in flight at the time the officer picked up the object. The Supreme Court did state in *Hodari D.*, however, that a seizure *does* occur the instant a police officer lays hands on a suspect during a chase, even if the suspect is able to break away from the officer's grasp.

The definitions of seizure offered in this section are general. The cases on which they are based will be encountered in the next three chapters as the topics of stop-and-frisk and arrest are considered. For now, remember that there are different types of seizures. An arrest, for example, is a type of seizure, but a seizure does not have to rise to the level of an arrest for the Fourth Amendment to be implicated. The following chapters will take care to ensure that the reader will be able to distinguish among different types of seizures.

THE DOCTRINE OF JUSTIFICATION

To this point, only the threshold question of whether the Fourth Amendment applies has been addressed—that is, Has a search or seizure occurred? If the answer is no, then the issue will go no further, and justification will not matter because a search or seizure did not occur. However, if the government's action constitutes a search or seizure, the next issue involves deciding whether the police acted within the limits of the Fourth Amendment. If they did not, then any evidence they obtained during the course of such an illegal search or seizure cannot be used in a criminal proceeding to determine guilt.

Once it has been determined *whether* the Fourth Amendment applies, it is then necessary to consider *what* the Fourth Amendment requires. The warrant requirement will be considered later, but the first and most fundamental inquiry in terms of Fourth Amendment requirements concerns the doctrine of justification. Put simply, the police need to have **justification**, or cause, before they can conduct a search or a seizure. Justification needs to be in place *a priori*—that is, before a person or evidence is sought in an area protected by the Fourth Amendment. The police cannot conduct an illegal search to obtain evidence and then argue *after the fact* that what they did was appropriate.

Although the language of the Fourth Amendment suggests that probable cause is the only important standard of justification, the Supreme Court has also focused on the amendment's reasonableness clause to carve out exceptions to the probable cause requirement. So-called *Terry* stops, for instance, do not require probable cause, but they are still required to be reasonable. (*Terry* stops are discussed in the next chapter.) At the other extreme, a quick reading of the Fourth Amendment would lead one to believe that the probable cause requirement is only necessary when a warrant is used. In actuality, however, the Supreme Court has held that the probable cause requirement applies in *warrantless* search and seizure situations, as well (see *Wong Sun v. United States*, 371 U.S. 471 [1963]).

Justification can be viewed as something of a sliding scale that hinges on the type of intrusion the police make. Generally, the more intrusive the police action, the higher the level of justification required. Conversely, the lower the level of intrusion, the lower the justification needed. Three primary levels of justification recognized by the courts will be considered throughout the remainder of this chapter: (1) probable cause, the standard for searches and seizures; (2) reasonable suspicion, the standard for stop-and-frisk; and (3) administrative justification, the standard for administrative searches.

Probable Cause

In principle, the definition of **probable cause** does not vary, regardless of the conduct in which the police engage. It was defined by the Supreme Court in *Beck v. Ohio* (379 U.S. 89 [1964]) as more than bare suspicion; it exists when "the facts and circumstances within [the officers'] knowledge and of which they [have] reasonably trustworthy information [are] sufficient to warrant a prudent man in believing that the [suspect] had committed or was committing an offense" (p. 91). In *Brinegar v. United States* (338 U.S. 160 [1949]), the Court added, "The substance of all the definitions of probable cause is a reasonable ground for belief of guilt" (p. 175).

Beck v. Ohio, 379 U.S. 89 (1964)

Brinegar v. United States, 338 U.S. 160 (1949)

FIGURE 3.3 Ingredients in the "Recipe" for Probable Cause

1. **Prior Record**
   - A man suspected of operating a methamphetamine lab had a prior conviction for the same activity (*People v. Wilson*, 182 Cal.App.3d 742 [1986], p. 754)
   - A man suspected of murdering two boys "had a record for physical abuse of a nine-year-old" (*People v. Memro*, 11 Cal.4th 786 [1995], p. 843)
   - A man suspected of robbery was "known as a burglar" (*People v. Franklin*, 171 Cal.App.3d 627 [1985], p. 631)
   - A man suspected of possessing stolen property "had been active as a receiver of stolen property" (*People v. Martin*, 9 Cal.3d 687 [1973], p. 693)

2. **Flight from the Scene**
   - Flight from an apartment known for drug dealing, coupled with an anonymous tip (*U.S. v. Lane*, 909 F.2d 895 [6th Cir. 1990])
   - Upon seeing police, the suspects rose and ran away (*People v. Britton*, 91 Cal. App. 3d 1112 [2001], pp. 1118–1119)
   - Two men fled the scene of a jewelry store robbery (*People v. Dolliver*, 181 Cal.App.3d 49 [1986])
   - A man approached a stolen car as if to open the door but then spotted officers and ran away (*People v. Superior Court*, 83 Cal.App.3d 609 [1978], p. 615)

3. **Suspicious Conduct**
   - A suspect failed to make eye contact with officers (*U.S. v. Montero-Camargo*, 208 F.3d 1122 [9th Cir. 2000], p. 1136)
   - A suspect showed extreme inattention to officers (*United States v. Arvizu*, 534 U.S. 266 [2002])
   - A suspect showed extreme attention to officers (*Flores v. Superior Court*, 17 Cal. App. 3d 219 [1971], p. 224)
   - A suspect appeared startled by police and quickly looked away (*People v. Fields*, 159 Cal. App. 3d 555 [1984], p. 564)

   - A suspect showed nervousness (*People v. Guajardo*, 23 Cal. App. 4th 1738 [1994], p. 1743)
   - A suspect was apparently "casing" a setting (*Terry v. Ohio*, 392 U.S. 1 [1968], p. 23)

4. **Admissions**
   - A suspect told an informant that he "could do a small thing of boy (sell a small amount of heroin)" (*People v. Veasey*, 98 Cal. App. 3d 779 [1979], pp. 784–785)
   - An officer overheard two men talking about "point spreads" for professional football while investigating an illegal bookmaking operation (*People v. Rooney*, 175 Cal. App. 3d 634 [1985], p. 648)
   - An officer arrived at a suspect's home to discuss graffiti vandalism and the suspect said, "Take me to jail" (*In re Trinidad V.*, 212 Cal App. 3d 1077 [1989], p. 1080)
   - As an officer approached two burglary suspects, one told the other, "I told you not to do it" (*People v. Stokes*, 224 Cal. App. 3d 715 [1990], p. 721)

5. **Incriminating Evidence**
   - A suspect was found in possession of the fruits or instrumentalities of a crime (*People v. Hagen*, 6 Cal. App. 3d 35 [1970], p. 43)
   - Two burglary suspects were found with pillowcases full of loot (*People v. Valdez*, 138 Cal. App. 3d 995 [1983], p. 1001)
   - A man suspected of possessing drugs was carrying a "big stack or wad of bills" (*People v. Brueckner*, 223 Cal. App. 3d 1500 [1990], p. 1505)
   - Inside a robbery suspect's car, police found live shotgun shells and a ski mask (*People v. Jardine*, 116 Cal. App. 3d 907 [1981], p. 913)

6. **Unusual Hour**
   - 2:35 a.m.: An officer sees a man "exiting from darkened private property where valuable merchandise was located" (*People v. Allen*, 50 Cal. App. 3d 896 [1975], p. 901)
   - 3:00 a.m.: An officer saw a man riding a bicycle to which was attached a large axe (*People v. Foranyic*, 64 Cal. App. 4th 186 [1998], p. 190)

Source: Alameda County District Attorney's Office, *Probable Cause* (Oakland, CA: District Attorney's Office, 2002). Available online: <www.co.alameda.ca.us/da/pov/POV_index.shtml>.

Unfortunately, these legal definitions are of little use to those on the frontlines of law enforcement. A more practical definition of probable cause is *more than 50 percent certainty*. As such, it lies somewhere below absolute certainty and proof beyond a reasonable doubt (the latter of which is necessary to obtain a criminal conviction) and somewhere above a hunch or reasonable suspicion (the latter of which is required to conduct a stop-and-frisk).

The notion of a *prudent man* is akin to the idea of objective reasonableness already discussed. Basically, it means that courts consider what the average person on the street

- 3:30 A.M.: Two men walking in a business area started to run when they saw the police (*Crofoot v. Superior Court*, 121 Cal. App. 3d 717 [1981], p. 724)
- 4:00 A.M.: A suspect was standing alone next to a business in which a silent burglar alarm was triggered (*People v. Lloyd*, 4 Cal. App. 4th 724 [1992], pp. 733–734)

7. The Suspect Resembles the Perpetrator

- A suspect wore clothes similar to those of the perpetrator (*People v. Anthony*, 7 Cal. App. 3d 751 [1970])
- A suspect was the occupant of a car similar in appearance to the car used by the perpetrator (*People v. Hill*, 89 Cal. App. 4th 48 [2001])
- A suspect was with one or more other people who matched the general descriptions of the perpetrators (*In re Brian A.*, 173 Cal. App. 3d 1168 [1985])
- The number of suspects in the vehicle was the same as the number of suspects involved in the crime (*People v. Soun*, 34 Cal. App. 4th 1499 [1995])

8. Evasive and Untruthful Responses to Questions

- A suspect was caught in a lie about where he was coming from (*People v. Suennen*, 114 Cal. App. 3d 192 [1980], p. 199)
- A suspect gave a false name or date of birth (*People v. Superior Court*, 137 Cal. App. 3d 90 [1982], p. 97)
- A suspect was using an alias (*United States v. Sokolow*, 490 U.A. 1 [1989], p. 9)
- A suspect denied owning car that was registered to him (*People v. Carrillo*, 37 Cal. App. 4th 1662 [1995], pp. 1668–1671)
- A suspect gave vague and confusing answers to questions (*People v. Adams*, 175 Cal. App. 3d 855 [1985], p. 861)
- A suspect told unbelievable stories (*People v. Fields*, 159 Cal. App. 3d 555 [1984], p. 564)

9. An Obvious Attempt to Hide Something

- Officers heard the sound of a toilet flushing when they arrived to serve a search warrant (*People v. Clark*, 262 Cal. App. 2d 471 [1968], p. 475)

- Officers observed a suspect pushing something under the seat of the car (*People v. Superior Court*, 272 Cal. App. 2d 383 [1969], p. 387)
- Officers observed a group of men looking at a TV set in the trunk of a car; the men then slammed the trunk lid when they saw the officers (*People v. Gravatt*, 22 Cal. App. 3d 133 [1971], p. 137)

10. Presence in a High-Crime Area and/or Near a Crime Scene

- An officer witnessed a car leaving the scene of a burglary; no other vehicles or people were around (*People v. Conway*, 25 Cal. App. 4th 385 [1994], p. 390)
- A suspect was the only pedestrian near the scene of the burglary (*People v. Juarez*, 35 Cal. App. 3d 631 [1973], p. 635)
- A suspect was the only person found riding a motorcycle near the scene of a reckless motorcycling incident (*In re Frank V.*, 233 Cal. App. 3d 1232 [1991], p. 1238, fn.2)
- Officers observed an apparent drug transaction in an area known for narcotics activity (*People v. Souza*, 9 Cal. 4th 224 [1994], p. 240)

11. Furtive Gestures

- Officers spotted the suspect's car and saw one person duck from view (*In re Jonathan M.*, 117 Cal. App. 3d 530 [1981], p. 535)
- A suspect made a quick hand-to-mouth movement, as though secreting drugs (*People v. Johnson*, 231 Cal. App. 3d 1 [1991], p. 12)
- A suspect turned away from officers when they announced their presence (*People v. Valdez*, 196 Cal. App. 3d 799 [1987], p. 806)
- A driver reached under the seat (*People v. Clayton*, 13 Cal. App. 3d 335 [1970])

12. Knowing Too Much

- A suspect volunteered information that only the perpetrator would know (*People v. Spears*, 228 Cal. App. 3d 1 [1991])

would believe, not what a person who has received special training in the identification and apprehension of lawbreakers (e.g., police officer, judge, etc.) would believe. This is not to say, however, that the experience of a police officer is not relevant to a probable cause determination. On the contrary, in *United States v. Ortiz* (422 U.S. 891 [1975]), the Court ruled that "officers are entitled to draw reasonable inferences from these facts in light of their knowledge of the area and their prior experience with aliens and smugglers" (p. 897) and, by extension, other people suspected of criminal activity.

Figure 3.3 lists a number of the ingredients in the "recipe" for probable cause as well as examples of each ingredient in practice with relevant case citations. Each in isolation is rarely, if ever, enough. Rather, a combination of the factors listed in Figure 3.3 is necessary for probable cause to be established.

Probable cause is always required in the following scenarios: (1) arrests with warrants; (2) arrests without warrants; (3) searches and seizures of property with warrants; and (4) searches and seizures of property without warrants. When a warrant is required, the probable cause determination is made by the magistrate charged with issuing the warrant; when a warrant is not used, the police officer makes the probable cause determination. In general:

> Probable cause can be obtained from police radio bulletins, tips from "good citizen" informers who have happened by chance to see criminal activity, reports from victims, anonymous tips, and tips from "habitual" informers who mingle with people in the underworld and who themselves may [even] be criminals. Probable cause can be based on various combinations of these sources.[2]

When the police make an *arrest*, the probable cause determination concerns whether an offense has been committed and whether the suspect did, in fact, commit the offense. In the case of a search, however, the probable cause issue concerns whether the items to be seized are connected with criminal activity and whether they can be found in the place to be searched. This means, then, that the courts sometimes treat the probable cause requirement differently, depending on the conduct in which the police engage.

One point needs to be underscored: Probable cause to search does not necessarily create probable cause to arrest, and, alternatively, probable cause to arrest does not necessarily create probable cause to search. With regard to the latter point, consider this hypothetical: Police officers pursue a drug suspect into her residence and, based on a hot-pursuit exigency, arrest her in her living room. Assuming probable cause was in place to pursue the suspect, the police do not possess unfettered latitude once in the house to search the place up and down. The courts have placed restrictions on what can be done in a situation such as this—that is, on how far the police can go with a search following (i.e., incident) to arrest. Searches incident to arrest will be covered in a later chapter, but this example illustrates that the ingredients in the probable cause recipe are not always the same for arrests as they are for searches.

In several arrest cases, the courts have had the opportunity to decide what sources of information meet the probable cause burden. Three sources of information can be identified: (1) informants; (2) firsthand knowledge; and (3) information that turns out, after the fact, to be mistaken but is reasonably relied on.[3]

Other information may help establish probable cause to arrest, but the courts have been most vocal about these three sources.

Informants and Other Third Parties

The police routinely rely on information supplied to them by a sophisticated network of *informants*. Informants are not necessarily shady characters connected to the criminal lifestyle; they can also be victims of crime, witnesses of crime, and other police officers.

■ *Aguilar v. Texas,* 378 U.S. 108 (1964)

As to the first type of informant, the courts have attempted to create tests to ensure that information supplied by informants is credible. In *Aguilar v. Texas* (378 U.S. 108 [1964]), the Supreme Court ruled that an affidavit based on a tip from an informant must show (1) sufficient information to demonstrate how the informant reached his or her conclusion and (2) sufficient information to establish the reliability of the informant. Stated differently, the first prong asks, Why should the police believe this person? and the second prong asks, How does the informant know what he or she claims to know?

[2]J. G. Miles Jr., D. B. Richardson, and A. E. Scudellari, *The Law Officer's Pocket Manual* (Washington, DC: Bureau of National Affairs, 1988–1989), p. 6:4.
[3]Whitebread and Slobogin, pp. 120–125.

Informants and Probable Cause

A police officer applied for a warrant to search the apartment of Marcus Bell, who is suspected of running an illegal gambling operation from this location. The officer's application for a warrant asserted that an informant had attested that Bell was, in fact, running an illegal gambling operation out of his apartment. (The officer neglected to mention that the informant had provided reliable information in the past.) The informant had described how the illegal operation worked (i.e., the procedure for placing bets over the phone) and had given the police an unlisted phone number that could be used to place illegal bets. The police had then contacted the phone company, and an investigation had revealed that phone number was one used by Bell. The police had also found that Bell's most recent phone bill had been for an amount in excess of $1,400. Should the judge issue a warrant?

For both prongs of the *Aguilar* test to be satisfied, the police need to supply specific information in their affidavit. A statement to the effect that "this informant has provided reliable information in the past" is not enough. More appropriate is a statement such as "This informant has supplied information in the past that led to the conviction of John Doe" (see also *United States v. Freitas*, 716 F.2d 1216 [9th Cir. 1983]).

In *Spinelli v. United States* (393 U.S. 410 [1969]), the Supreme Court clarified the meaning of the first prong. It concluded that insufficient knowledge about the details of the reported criminal activity can be overcome if "the tip describe[s] the accused's criminal activity in sufficient detail that the magistrate knows that he is relying on something more substantial than a casual rumor . . . or an accusation based merely on a individual's general reputation" (p. 416). Similarly, in *Draper v. United States* (358 U.S. 307 [1959]), the Court ruled that the first prong—the credibility prong—may also be satisfied when the informant implicates himself or herself in criminal activity, provided that such a statement is against self-interest. An example of a self-interested admission of criminal activity would be one in which the informant seeks to curry favor with the police and/or prosecutors in exchange for supplying information (see *United States v. Harris*, 403 U.S. 573 [1971]; *United States v. Jackson*, 818 F.2d 345 [5th Cir. 1987]).

The *Aguilar* and *Spinelli* tests were heavily modified in *Illinois v. Gates* (462 U.S. 213 [1983]), when the Supreme Court basically abandoned the two-pronged probable cause analysis and replaced it with a *totality of circumstances* test. Thus, if "a particular informant is known for the unusual reliability of his predictions of certain types of criminal activities in a locality, his failure, in a particular case, to thoroughly set forth the basis of his knowledge surely should not serve as an absolute bar to a finding of probable cause based on his tip" (p. 233). In other words, a deficiency in one prong can be compensated for with an abundant supply of information in the other.

Interestingly, *Aguilar*, *Spinelli*, and *Gates* were all search cases, which would seem to limit their applicability in the arrest context. Actually, the *Illinois v. Gates* totality of circumstances test is now used for determining probable cause based on information from informants in both the arrest and search/seizure contexts. However, relying on *Draper v. United States* (358 U.S. 307 [1959]), the courts will still give consideration to five factors in determining whether the totality of circumstances creates probable cause: (1) when the informant describes how he or she found out about the criminal activity; (2) when the informant gives a detailed description of that activity; (3) when evidence for the informant's reliability exists; (4) when the informant predicts criminal activity that is later corroborated by the police; and (5) when the informant implicates himself or herself in criminal activity.

What happens when the informant is a victim or an eyewitness? In both situations, the Supreme Court has relaxed the *Aguilar/Spinelli/Gates* tests. In *Jaben v. United States* (381 U.S. 214 [1965]), for instance, the Court held that "whereas some supporting information

Spinelli v. United States,
393 U.S. 410 (1969)

Illinois v. Gates,
462 U.S. 213 (1983)

Police officers use informants on a regular basis to gather information.

concerning the credibility of informants in narcotics cases or other common garden varieties of crime may be required, such information is not so necessary in the context of the case before us" (p. 224). Also, in *Chambers v. Maroney* (399 U.S. 42 [1970]), the Court upheld an arrest for robbery of a suspect who was arrested by police based on information supplied by two teenagers who happened to witness the event. Similar rulings have been applied when the informants have been other police officers. For example, in *United States v. Ventresca* (380 U.S. 102 [1965]), the Supreme Court ruled that "[o]bservations of fellow officers of the Government engaged in a common investigation are plainly a reliable basis for a warrant applied for by one of their number" (p. 111). Of course, probable cause is still required. When probable cause is found lacking, the arrest will most likely be deemed unconstitutional (see *Whiteley v. Warden*, 401 U.S. 560 [1971]).

Firsthand Knowledge

The second major category of probable cause to arrest cases hinges on information that results from *firsthand knowledge*. That is, when is probable cause established by someone other than a third party—namely, the arresting officer? The courts usually do not worry about the truthfulness or accuracy of the arresting officer's observations but, instead, whether probable cause to arrest was in place. In particular, the courts have required that probable cause *to* arrest must be determined independently from the arrest itself, meaning that probable cause to arrest must be required *before* the arrest. In *Sibron v. New York* (392 U.S. 40 [1968]), the Supreme Court stated, "It is axiomatic that an incident search may not precede an arrest and serve as part of its justification" (p. 63). In simple terms, this means that police cannot search people and illegally seize evidence simply for the purpose of establishing probable cause to arrest. Stated differently, probable cause cannot be established in hindsight. It should be pointed out, though, that evidence encountered during law enforcement activity that does not constitute an arrest or a search (a patdown, for instance) can create or be used to establish probable cause to arrest or conduct a further search, depending on the circumstances. (Patdown searches are discussed in a following section.)

Having Probable Cause to Arrest

An observant police officer was on foot patrol and noticed a suspicious person standing at the counter in a convenience store. The person, who had one hand in his coat pocket, appeared to be carrying on a conversation with the clerk, who was reaching into the cash register and appeared to be very nervous. On a hunch that she was witnessing a robbery in progress, the officer quickly entered the store, surprised the person talking to the clerk, arrested him, and upon searching him incident to the arrest, found a handgun in his coat pocket. His attorney moved to suppress the handgun on the grounds that the police officer did not have probable cause to arrest. What should the courts decide?

In another case, *United States v. Di Re* (332 U.S. 581 [1948]), the Supreme Court held that a suspect's proximity to criminal activity is not enough to establish probable cause to arrest. In that case, officers arrested Di Re from the front seat of a car on the grounds that there were two other men in the car passing counterfeit ration coupons between one another. The Court noted that had Di Re even seen the activity, "it would not follow that he knew they were ration coupons, and if he saw that they were ration coupons, it would not follow that he would know them to be counterfeit" (p. 593). Simply put, then, proximity to criminal activity does not create probable cause to arrest (see also *Johnson v. United States*, 333 U.S. 10 [1948]).

In another case, one in which the police had a valid warrant authorizing them to search a tavern, the Court held that the search warrant did not give them permission to search the patrons of the bar, including the petitioner, because they were not named in the warrant (*Ybarra v. Illinois*, 444 U.S. 85 [1979]). If, however, the arresting officer were armed with additional information (from an third-party informant, for example), then probable cause would be easier to establish (see *Ker v. California*, 374 U.S. 23 [1963]). What is more, courts regularly defer to officers' judgments as to whether probable cause was in place (see *Maryland v. Pringle*, 540 U.S. 366 [2003]).

Reasonable Reliance on Mistaken Information

Interestingly, if information supplied by an informant or by an officer's firsthand observations later proves to be false, the courts will uphold the earlier action (see *Henry v. United States*, 361 U.S. 98 [1959]; *United States v. Garofalo*, 496 F.2d 510 [8th Cir. 1974]), so long as the mistake was a reasonable one (*Franks v. Delaware*, 438 U.S. 154 [1978]). When such a mistake is deemed *unreasonable*, however, the courts will almost always reach a different conclusion. An unreasonable mistake can be found in *Albright v. Oliver* (510 U.S. 266 [1994]), in which the Supreme Court implied that it was unreasonable (and a violation of the Fourth Amendment) for a police officer to rely on an informant who had provided false information on 50 previous occasions.

Challenging a Probable Cause Determination

It is appropriate at this juncture to mention the procedures for challenging a probable cause determination. Occasionally, a defendant will argue in a suppression hearing that the officers who made the arrest or conducted the search did not have probable cause to do so. A source of frequent contention is the officer's (i.e., the *affiant's*) statements made in the affidavit used to obtain the warrant.

In *Franks v. Delaware* (483 U.S. 154 [1978]), the Court set forth explicit criteria for challenging statements included in an affidavit submitted in attempt to obtain a warrant. First, the allegation of false information must (1) allege that false statements were made deliberately or with reckless disregard for the truth; (2) point specifically to the portion of the warrant that is purportedly false; (3) be accompanied by supporting reasoning; and (4) furnish additional affidavits of sworn or otherwise reliable statements of witnesses concerning the statements.

In *Franks v. Delaware*, the Court also ruled that defendants can only challenge information supplied by police officers. This decision was designed to ensure that informants' identities are kept confidential where necessary. In *McCray v. Illinois* (386 U.S. 300 [1967]), for example, the Court held that despite an accused's right to confront witnesses, an informant's identity may be kept confidential when the trial judge believes the informant's testimony will not contradict any information already before the court. The Court also imposed a third restriction on defendants who seek to challenge the probable cause finding—namely, that the defendant must show that the true material in the warrant application would not be enough to establish probable cause.

Reasonable Suspicion

To recap, the justification required to conduct a search or a seizure within the meaning of the Fourth Amendment is probable cause. But much police activity does not reach the level of intrusion that occurs when a search or seizure is carried out. For example, the

---

FIGURE 3.4 Example of Law Enforcement Definition of Reasonable Suspicion

In order for an investigative stop or detention to be valid, you must have a "reasonable suspicion" that: (1) criminal activity may be afoot; and (2) the person you are about to detain is connected with that possible criminal activity. (*Wardlow* (2000) 120 S.Ct. 673, 675; *Sokolow* (1989) 490 U.S. 1, 7–8; *Justin B.* (1999) 69 Cal. App. 4th 879, 886; *Bennett* (1998) 17 Cal. 4th 373, 386; *Daugherty* (1996) 50 Cal. App. 4th 275, 285; *Ross* (1990) 217 Cal. App. 3d 879, 884; *Ornelas* (1996) 517 U.S. 690, 695–696; *Johnson* (1991) 231 Cal. App. 3d 1, 10; *Limon* (1993) 17 Cal. App. 4th 524, 532.)

"The determination of reasonable suspicion must be based on commonsense judgments and inferences about human behavior." (*Wardlow* (2000) 120 S.Ct. 673, 676.) "The quantum of proof needed for reasonable suspicion is less than a preponderance of evidence, and less than probable cause. It is merely a particularized and objective basis for suspecting the person stopped of criminal activity." (*Tiong* (9th Cir. 2000) 224 F.3d 1136, 1140; *internal footnotes and quotation marks deleted.*)

Remember, however, that even though the court will consider the "totality of the circumstances," you must have specific facts which you can articulate to a court. The court will then decide if these facts—together with your training and experience—were enough to make your suspicion objectively reasonable. (*Wright* (1988) 206 Cal. App. 3d 1107; *Lloyd* (1992) 4 Cal. App. 4th 724, 733.)

You cannot make a valid detention based solely on a hunch, rumor, intuition, instinct, or curiosity. (*Wardlow* (2000) 120 S.Ct. 673, 676; *Tony C.* (1978) 21 Cal.3d 888; *Raybourn* (1990) 218 Cal.App.3d 308.) However, for "reasonable suspicion," both the

quality and quantity of the information you need is considerably less than the "probable cause" you need to arrest or search. (*White* (1990) 496 U.S. 325, 330; *Bennett* (1998) 17 Cal.4th 373, 387; *Johnson* (1991) 231 Cal.App.3d 1, 11.) "'[R]easonable suspicion' is a less demanding standard than probable cause and requires a showing considerably less than preponderance of the evidence . . . ." (*Wardlow* (2000) 120 S.Ct.673, 675–676.)

In addition, in the vast majority of situations, your subjective thinking, i.e., the purpose behind your search or seizure (detention or arrest), should have no bearing on a court's determination of the legality of your action. As the Supreme Court has put it repeatedly, "Subjective intentions play no role in ordinary, probable-cause Fourth Amendment analysis." (*Sullivan* (2001) 121 S.Ct. 1876, 1878; *Whren* (1996) 517 U.S.806, 813; see also *Robinette* (1996) 519 U.S. 33, 38; *Scott* (1978) 436 U.S. 128, 138; *Hull* (1995) 34 Cal. App.4th 1448, 1454; *Lloyd* (1992) 4 Cal. App.4th 724, 733.)

Note: In at least two non–probable cause situations, however, your subjective intent is still relevant, namely, administrative inspections and vehicle inventories. (See, for example, *Valenzuela* (1999) 74 Cal. App.4th 72.)

Example: Officers saw two males loading a TV set into the trunk of their car at 7.30 p.m., when most nearby businesses were closed. There were no television shops nearby, and the neighborhood had been plagued by burglaries. When they saw the officers, the men looked "shocked," slammed down the trunk lid, and walked swiftly toward a bar. They ignored the officers' requests to talk and had to be forcibly detained. The court ruled there were enough specific facts to make the detention valid. (*Garcia* (1981) 121 Cal. App.3d 239.)

Source: From *California Peace Officers Legal Sourcebook,* electronic edition, revision 113 (Sacramento, CA: California Department of Justice, Office of the Attorney General), pp. 2.8–2.12c.

police routinely have to confront people on the street in order to question them and to pull over automobiles to enforce traffic laws. If probable cause were required under such circumstances, the police could do little in terms of investigating suspicious activity.

Recognizing how essential these *lesser intrusions* are to the police mission, the Supreme Court established in *Terry v. Ohio* (392 U.S. 1 [1968]) a different level of justification for such activities. The Court created the standard of **reasonable suspicion**—something below probable cause but above a hunch. *Terry* dealt with so-called stop-and-frisk activities (the topic of Chapter 6), but reasonable suspicion as a standard of justification permeates other arenas of criminal procedure (e.g., traffic stops).

■ *Terry v. Ohio*, 392 U.S. 1 (1968)

In *Terry*, an officer's attention was drawn to two men on a street corner who appeared to the officer to be "casing" a store for a robbery. The officer approached the men and asked them to identify themselves. The officer then proceeded to pat down the men and found a gun on each one. The men were placed under arrest. They tried to suppress the guns, but the Supreme Court eventually held the officer's actions valid in the interest of "effective crime prevention and detection" (p. 22). Balancing an intrusion that was arguably less serious than a search with the interests of society in apprehending lawbreakers, the Court held that a lower standard than probable cause was required because "street encounters between citizens and police officers are incredibly rich in diversity" (p. 13).

1. Specific Factors

In deciding whether your suspicion was reasonable, the court will look at all the factors—the "totality of the circumstances." (*Sokolow* (1989) 490 U.S. 1, 7–8; *Souza* (1994) 9 Cal.4th 224, 231.)

a. Nighttime/High Crime Area

Certain factors, such as "nighttime" and "high crime" or "high narcotics" area, will not suffice, alone, to justify a detention. However, they are important and relevant, and in combination with one or more other suspicious factors, may justify a reasonable suspicion. (*Wardlow* (2000) 120 S.Ct. 673; *Souza* (1994) 9 Cal.4th 224, 240–241; *Mims* (1992) 9 Cal. App.4th 1244, 1248.)

b. Race (see chapter 5)

c. Flight

If you approach someone or a group and one or more of them walks or runs away, and you give chase, your act of chasing after the person does not constitute a detention. As the United States Supreme Court has made clear, there is no "seizure" until you have actually physically stopped the person, or he stops on his own and submits to your authority. (*Hodari D.* (1991) 499 U.S. 621, 626.)

Example: When officers drove around the corner in their unmarked vehicle, a group of males who had been standing around a red car took off, and so did the car. One officer got out, ran around the block the other way, and approached within a few feet of the suspect, who was looking over his shoulder while running towards the officer, before the suspect looked up and saw him, whereupon he discarded a rock of cocaine before being tackled. The Supreme Court held that the suspect was not "seized" until he was tackled, because up to that moment, he had not submitted to the officer's assertion of authority. (*Hodari D.* (1991) 499 U.S. 621, 626; see also *Chesternut* (1988) 486 U.S. 567—driving along beside fleeing suspect did not constitute a detention; and *Arangure* (1991) 230 Cal.App.3d 1302, 1306.)

d. Your Experience

Don't overlook your experience. "The specialized knowledge of a police officer experienced in police narcotics work may render suspicious what would appear innocent to a layman.'" (*Mims* (1992) 9 Cal. App.4th 1244, 1248; *Brown* (1985) 169 Cal. App.3d 159, 165; *Limon* (1993) 17 Cal.App.4th 524, 532.)

Example: The suspect was in a park where marijuana sales often took place, doing nothing. An apparent stranger drove up, approached the suspect, gave him money for two small, thin, white, filterless cigarettes, and then drove away. Because of the officer's experience and the specifics of what he'd seen exchange hands, the court found probable cause to justify an arrest. (*Stanfill* (1985) 170 Cal.App.3d 420.)

e. Officer Safety

Officer safety, as a justification for certain police action, exists in many areas of the law. It is perhaps best known as the basis for permitting a limited search for weapons, also known as a patdown or frisk. (*Terry* (1968) 392 U.S. 1.)

However, there are also some cases, and helpful language in still more cases, which permit you to detain someone in the first place (but not necessarily to take the additional basis of patting them down), on the basis of officer safety.

f. Drug Courier Profile (see chapter 6)

There is no clear definition of *reasonable suspicion*, just as there is no clear definition of *probable cause*. As stated in *United States v. Cortez* (449 U.S. 411 [1981]):

> Courts have used a variety of terms to capture the elusive concept of what cause is sufficient to authorize police to stop a person. Terms like "articulable reasons" and "founded suspicion" are not self-defining; they fall short of providing clear guidance dispositive of the myriad factual situations that arise. But the essence of all that has been written is that the totality of circumstances—the whole picture—must be taken into account. Based upon that whole picture the detaining officers must have a particularized and objective basis for suspecting the particular person stopped of criminal activity. (p. 417)

As a level of justification lying below probable cause, then, reasonable suspicion is "considerably less than proof of wrongdoing by a preponderance of evidence" (*United States v. Sokolow,* 490 U.S. 1 [1989], p. 7) but more than an unparticularized hunch. Figure 3.4 contains portions of the *California Peace Officers Legal Sourcebook* that address the definition of *reasonable suspicion*.

Like probable cause, reasonable suspicion can be based on a number of different sources, including informants. But because the reasonable suspicion standard falls below that for probable cause, less information is required. In *Adams v. Williams* (407 U.S. 143 [1972]), for example, the Supreme Court held that reasonable suspicion may be based on an anonymous telephone tip, so long as the police can corroborate certain details from the informant. In a similar case, *Alabama v. White* (496 U.S. 325 [1990]), the Supreme Court observed, "Reasonable suspicion is a less demanding standard than probable cause not only in the sense that reasonable suspicion can be established with information that is different but also in the sense that reasonable suspicion can arise from information that is less reliable than that required to show probable cause" (p. 330).

■ *Alabama v. White,*
496 U.S. 325 (1990)

DECISION MAKING EXERCISE 3.9

Is There Reasonable Suspicion?

Officer Hopper was on patrol in a high-crime area at 3:00 a.m. and was waved over to the curb by a woman on the sidewalk. She told Hopper that there was a person sitting in a car nearby who had illegal narcotics and a gun on his/lap. Officer Hopper approached the car and asked the driver to open the door. Instead, the driver started to roll down the window. Hopper quickly reached into the window and grabbed the gun from the driver's lap. Was the officer's conduct justified?

In *United States v. Hensley* (469 U.S. 221 [1985]), the Supreme Court unanimously held that the reasonable suspicion standard is satisfied when the police rely on "wanted" flyers, even those from other jurisdictions. A restriction on this ruling was that the flyer, regardless of its place of origin, must be based on articulable facts that connect the suspect to criminal activity. The Court in *Hensley* also had to decide if a stop based on reasonable suspicion of *prior* criminal activity was permissible under the Fourth Amendment's reasonableness standard. All decisions up to that point had dealt with suspected criminal activity immediately before the officer's arrival or criminal activity likely to have occurred but for the officer's arrival. In *Hensley,* the police stopped a man 12 days after the commission of a robbery for which he was suspected. The Court upheld the police's action and stated that it "would not only hinder the investigation, but might also enable the suspect to flee in the interim and to remain at large" (p. 229).

To further illustrate the meaning of reasonable suspicion, consider the case of *Sibron v. New York* (392 U.S. 40 [1968]). In that case, the Court held that talking to known addicts and reaching into their pockets does not produce reasonable suspicion that criminal activity is afoot. In yet another case, *Brown v. Texas* (443 U.S. 47 [1979]), two police officers observed Brown and another man walking away from one another. One of the officers later testified that he thought the officers' arrival broke up some suspicious activity. Officer Venegas approached Brown and asked him to identify himself. Brown refused and was later convicted under a statute that made it illegal to refuse to give an officer one's name and address. According to the Court:

> There is no indication in the record that it was unusual for people to be in the alley. The fact that the appellant was in a neighborhood frequented by drug users, standing alone, is not a basis for concluding that the appellant himself was engaged in criminal conduct. In short, the appellant's activity was no different from the activity of other pedestrians in that neighborhood. (p. 52)

Contrast *Brown v. Texas* with the Supreme Court's decision in *Illinois v. Wardlow* (528 U.S. 119 [2000]). In that case, Chicago police officers were patrolling an area known for narcotics traffic. Upon seeing the officers, Wardlow ran and was chased down by the police. When he was patted down, the officers found a Colt .38 pistol and arrested him. Wardlow appealed his conviction, arguing that the stop-and-frisk was illegal because the officers did not have reasonable suspicion. The Court disagreed, noting that "a location's characteristics are relevant in determining whether the circumstances are sufficiently suspicious to warrant further investigation" (p. 119). In addition, the Court noted that "it was Wardlow's unprovoked flight that aroused the officers' suspicion" and that "nervous, evasive behavior is another pertinent factor in determining reasonable suspicion, and headlong flight is the consummate act of evasion" (p. 124). Thus, in the Court's view, the officers *did* have reasonable suspicion to stop and frisk Wardlow.

Recently, in *United States v. Arvizu* (534 U.S. 266 [2002]), the Supreme Court highlighted the importance of the totality of circumstances as well as officers' experience in making a determination of reasonable suspicion. In that case, a border patrol agent in a remote part of Arizona became suspicious of a van that slowed upon seeing him. Also, the driver failed to acknowledge the agent. The agent stopped the van, and the Supreme Court upheld this decision. The Court stated the agent was "entitled to make an assessment of the situation in light of his specialized training and familiarity with the customs of the area's inhabitants" (p. 276).

Because reasonable suspicion is of fundamental importance in criminal procedure, this text will devote an entire chapter to the role it plays in law enforcement activities. In particular, Chapter 4 will cover *Terry* stops in detail, focusing carefully on the definitions of *stop* and the scope of the *frisk*. Before continuing with that, though, it is necessary to turn attention to yet another level of justification of importance in Fourth Amendment jurisprudence. Actually, it could more appropriately be labeled a form of *nonjustification*. Either way, *administrative justification* is something of a fallback—a lower standard that permits fairly significant intrusions with little or no justification.

■ Administrative Justification

A third level of justification has arisen by virtue of the fact that government entities occasionally conduct searches in circumstances other than criminal investigations. As noted earlier, a search-and-seizure aimed at obtaining evidence for use in a criminal proceeding cannot occur without appropriate justification. Noncriminal searches also occur, however, so the Supreme Court has created a different level of justification. Instead of being based on reasonableness, the **administrative justification** adopts a balancing approach, weighing the privacy interests of individuals with the interests of society in preserving a measure of public safety.

The first case creating an administrative form of justification was *Camara v. Municipal Court* (387 U.S. 523 [1967]), which involved a health code inspection of residential dwelling units. The Supreme Court held that such inspections were subject to Fourth

■ *Camara v. Municipal Court*, 387 U.S. 523 (1967)

Amendment restrictions but rejected the argument that the appropriate level of justification was probable cause (or reasonable suspicion, for that matter). Invoking the Fourth Amendment's reasonableness clause, the Court balanced the public interest in enforcing safety codes with the "relatively limited invasion of the urban citizen's privacy," given that "the inspections are neither personal in nature nor aimed at the discovery of evidence of crime" (p. 537). The Court further noted that such searches are permissible, so long as "reasonable legislative or administrative standards for conducting an area inspection are satisfied with respect to a particular dwelling" (p. 538). In other words, administrative searches should not be conducted arbitrarily or with selective enforcement.

DECISION MAKING EXERCISE 3.10

Metal Detectors and Administrative Justification

Jack Marceau was in a hurry to make his flight. On the way to the gate, he had to go through security, including a metal detector, just like all other passengers did. He had forgotten that there was a .45 pistol in his pocket, and of course, it set off the metal detector and alerted the authorities. Marceau was arrested and charged with illegal possession of a firearm. He moved to have the gun suppressed on the grounds that the use of the metal detector was a search conducted without justification. Will he succeed?

More recently, in *Colorado v. Bertine* (479 U.S. 367 [1987]), the Court stated that the "standard of probable cause is peculiarly related to criminal investigations, not routine, noncriminal procedures.... The probable-cause approach is unhelpful when analysis centers upon the reasonableness of routine administrative caretaking functions, particularly when no claim is made that the protective procedures are a subterfuge for criminal investigations" (p. 317). Accordingly, the courts have required that administrative searches be conducted according to objective, standardized procedures. Also important, authorities cannot use an administrative search as a pretext for a full-blown search.

An informative example of the balancing approach taken in justifying administrative searches can be found in *Vernonia School District v. Acton* (115 S. Ct. 2386 [1995]). In that case, the Court decided the fate of a school policy that required athletes to submit to random urinalysis for drugs. The Court allowed the search because it was not geared toward any particular individual. Further, the Court reasoned that athletes in public schools enjoy a lesser expectation of privacy because they must participate in other examinations, they dress together in the locker room, and they participate in the sports *voluntarily*. The government interest cited by the Court was preventing "drug use by our Nation's school children" (p. 2395). This was a controversial decision, indeed, as it seemed to reduce the need for justification set forth explicitly in the Fourth Amendment.

The administrative search rationale has been applied in a number of related situations. For example, the courts have been rather liberal in terms of upholding questionable searches of highly regulated business establishments. In *New York v. Burger* (482 U.S. 691 [1987]), for instance, the Supreme Court authorized a warrantless search of an automobile junk yard. In *Donovan v. Dewey* (452 U.S. 594 [1981]), the Court upheld the warrantless inspection of mines. The same logic carried over to a case involving the inspection of a gun dealership (*United States v. Biswell*, 406 U.S. 311 [1972]). In support of its decisions, the Court argued that people who choose to conduct business in highly regulated environments enjoy a reduced expectation of privacy.

Other decisions have involved such varied enterprises as arson investigations (*Michigan v. Clifford*, 464 U.S. 286 [1984]; *Michigan v. Tyler*, 436 U.S. 499 [1978]); border checkpoints to stop vehicles in an effort to detect illegal aliens (e.g., *United States v. Martinez-Fuerte*, 428 U.S. 543 [1976]); searches of impounded vehicles (*Colorado v. Bertine*, 479 U.S. 367 [1987]) and other personal items in need of inventorying (*Illinois v. Lafayette*, 462 U.S. 640 [1983]); and mandatory drug testing of public and private employees (e.g., *National*

Treasury Employees Union v. Von Raah, 489 U.S. 656 [1989]; *Skinner v. Railway Labor Executives' Assn.*, 489 U.S. 602 [1989]). In *Skinner*, the Court observed:

■ *Skinner v. Railway Labor Executives' Association*, 489 U.S. 602 (1989)

> In light of the limited discretion exercised by the railroad employers under the [drug testing] regulations, the surpassing safety interest served by toxicological tests in this context, and the diminished expectation of privacy that attaches to information pertaining to the fitness of covered employees, we believe it is reasonable to conduct such tests in the absence of a warrant or reasonable suspicion that any particular employee may be impaired. (p. 602)

It should be noted that the courts have placed significant restrictions on the scope of so-called administrative searches. For example, in *Marshall v. Barlow's, Inc.* (436 U.S. 307 [1978]), the Court ruled as unconstitutional searches based on the Occupational Safety and Health Act of businesses that had not been heavily regulated in the past. At the same time, however, administrative searches can give great latitude in terms of seizing contraband and evidence of a crime to whomever conducts the search. As stated in *New York v. Burger* (482 U.S. 691 [1987]), "The discovery of evidence of crimes in the course of an otherwise proper administrative inspection does not render that search illegal or the administrative scheme suspect" (p. 716).

Further, if the purpose of an administrative search is to detect evidence of criminal activity, probable cause is required. This was the decision reached in the recent Supreme Court case *City of Indianapolis v. Edmond* (531 U.S. 32 [2000]). In it, the Court decided whether a city's suspicionless checkpoints for detecting illegal drugs were constitutional. The court held that stops such as those conducted during checkpoint operations require individualized suspicion. In addition, "because the checkpoint program's primary purpose [was] indistinguishable from the general interest in crime control" (p. 32), it was deemed violative of the Fourth Amendment.

Moving on, the administrative search justification that has been applied to regulatory inspections has also been applied to situations involving "special needs beyond the normal need for law enforcement" (*Skinner v. Railway Labor Executives' Association*, p. 619). In *New Jersey v. TLO* (469 U.S. 325 [1985]), a student's purse was searched by an assistant principal, who suspected that the student was violating the school's policy against smoking. The search turned up marijuana, but according to the Supreme Court, "the schoolchild's legitimate expectation of privacy and the school's equally legitimate need to maintain an environment in which learning can take place" (p. 340) did not need a warrant or even probable cause. Similarly, in *O'Connor v. Ortega* (480 U.S. 709 [1987]), a case involving the warrantless search of a government employee's office, and in *Griffin v. Wisconsin* (483 U.S. 868 [1987]), a case in which a probation officer searched the home of a probationer under the officer's supervision, the Court invoked the logic of special needs beyond normal law enforcement to dispense with the warrant requirement.

■ STANDING

Standing is a topic closely tied to the Fourth Amendment. Basically, it means that a person cannot object to a wrongful search or seizure unless he or she can show standing to bring the issue to the court's attention. A person who does not have standing will not even be able to have his or her argument heard by a judge.

A person has *standing* if he or she is the victim of a Fourth Amendment violation. Basically, this means that person A cannot complain about an infringement on person B's rights. According to the Supreme Court in *Jones v. United States*, the victim of a Fourth Amendment violation should be distinguished from one "who claims prejudice only through the use of evidence gathered as a consequence of a search or seizure directed at someone else" (p. 261). Or as stated in *Rakas v. Illinois*, "A person who is aggrieved by an illegal search and seizure only through the introduction of damaging evidence secured by a search of a third person's premises or property has not had any of his Fourth Amendment rights infringed" (p. 134).

Originally, standing was tied to property interests. Only if one had a *possessory interest* in the thing to be seized or the place to be searched was he or she considered to have standing. However, in *Jones v. United States*, the Supreme Court declared that "it is unnecessary and ill-advised to import into the law surrounding the constitutional right to be free from unreasonable searches and seizures subtle distinctions, developed and refined by the common law in evolving the body of private property law" (p. 266). The Court conferred standing, instead, on anyone legitimately on the premises. Also in *Jones*, the Court declared that when defendants are charged with possessory offenses (e.g., possession of an illegal firearm), they automatically enjoy standing. The reason for this was that certain defendants had to admit the contraband was theirs and incriminate themselves in order to show standing.

The automatic-standing doctrine was overturned in *United States v. Salvucci* (1980), and the legitimately on-the-premises-standard has been replaced with a new standard based on a person's expectation of privacy (*Katz v. United States*). The courts now focus on the *totality of circumstances* to determine whether a person has a reasonable expectation of privacy.

The courts have referred to at least three specific situations in which a person can be said to have standing. First, if a person has the right to exclude others from the premises, he or she has standing (e.g., *Rawlings v. Kentucky*). Second, if a person has continuing access plus possessory interest, he or she can be said to have standing. For example, in *United States v. Jeffers*, the Court declared that a man who did not have a key to his aunt's apartment, as well as possession of some items within the apartment, had standing, even though he could not technically exclude others from the premises. Third, in *Minnesota v. Olson*, the Supreme Court ruled that a person who is legitimately on the premises and has a possessory interest in the item seized can also have standing. An example of such a person is a woman who visits a friend in her friend's house. Although as the guest she cannot exclude anyone from the house and does not have continuing access, she can still have standing if an item in her possession is seized unlawfully.

■ The Link between Standing and the Definition of a Search

In *Rakas v. Illinois*, the Supreme Court recognized the similarity between the *standing* analysis and the definition of a *search*. Both focus on a person's reasonable expectation of privacy. In essence, the standing and search analyses collapse into one when there is a questionable search on the part of the police.

Why discuss standing separately from the definition of a search? There are three reasons. First, it is important to realize that while a search may occur, the person targeted by that search does not always have a reasonable expectation of privacy. In other words, a search may occur, but if evidence is not seized and used against that person at trial, the person cannot claim any Fourth Amendment protection. Second, there may be situations in which a search is legal but a seizure is illegal, thus requiring that the search and the seizure be analyzed separately. Finally, as Justice Blackmun observed in *Rawlings v. Kentucky*, it is possible for a defendant to demonstrate standing to challenge a search but fail to prove that the search was unlawful (p. 112). Alternatively, a defendant may show that a Fourth Amendment violation took place but not have the standing to contest it.

For all practical purposes, the standing analysis is regularly merged into the Fourth Amendment search analysis and rarely requires discussion in and of itself. Indeed, rare are the situations in which standing and the Fourth Amendment receive individual attention. As such, standing will not be revisited elsewhere in this book. Readers should understand that it is an important threshold issue, however.

FIGURE 3.5	Fourth Amendment Checklist

1. Did a search or seizure take place?
   a. For a search, did a government actor violate a reasonable expectation of privacy?
   b. For a seizure, would a reasonable person have believed that he or she was not free to leave?

   If either of these questions can be answered no, then the Fourth Amendment does not apply. If either can be answered yes, continue with item 2.

2. Was the search or seizure justified?
   a. Identify the level of the intrusion: seizure, stop, nonstop, and so on.
   b. Identify the level of justification appropriate to the intrusion.

   If the justification was not appropriate, the search or seizure was not reasonable.

3. Was the search or seizure conducted in accordance with constitutional guidelines?
   See Chapters 4–7 to answer this question.

CONCLUSION

This chapter introduced the Fourth Amendment, including basic terminology associated with this important constitutional provision. Importantly, a search occurs when government actors infringe on a legitimate expectation of privacy while looking for evidence. Seizures of property occur when a meaningful possessory interest is interfered with. Seizures of persons occur when a reasonable person would believe he or she is not free to leave.

The doctrine of justification asserts that police must have cause before they can conduct a search or a seizure. There are three standards of justification. Probable cause, which falls between 51 and 100 percent certainty, is required for arrests and searches with and without warrants. Reasonable suspicion, which falls below 51 percent certainty but above a hunch, is required for stops and investigative detentions that fall short of arrests. Finally, administrative justification is required in administrative and "special needs beyond law enforcement" searches. The constitutionality of a search based on administrative justification is determined by balancing the interests of society with the privacy interests of the individual. Finally, a person must have standing in order to raise a Fourth Amendment challenge. Figure 3.5 summarizes this chapter's Fourth Amendment introduction in question-and-answer form.

REVIEW QUESTIONS

1. Explain the various perspectives on the relationship between the warrant and reasonableness clauses of the Fourth Amendment.
2. Define *person*, *house*, *paper*, and *effect*, each for Fourth Amendment purposes.
3. When does the Fourth Amendment apply?
4. When does a search take place? Explain both elements of a search, and discuss pertinent cases.
5. When can private parties be considered government actors?
6. What can authorities *not* do following a private-party search?
7. Explain the notion of reasonable expectation of privacy. When does a person *not* enjoy an expectation of privacy? Cite relevant cases.

8. What is a seizure? Distinguish between seizures of persons and seizures of property.
9. What is the doctrine of justification? Why is it important?
10. Explain probable cause as well as acceptable sources of information for the establishment of probable cause.
11. How can a mistake serve as a source of information in the probable cause determination?
12. What is the procedure for challenging a probable cause determination?
13. What is reasonable suspicion? How does it differ from probable cause and other standards of justification?
14. What is administrative justification? How does it differ from reasonable suspicion and probable cause?
15. Explain the balancing of interests associated with administrative justification.

 Answers to the Decision-Making Exercise for this chapter can be found on pages 491–493.

CHAPTER 4

Searches and Arrests with Warrants

KEY TERMS

arrest warrant
search warrant
neutral and detached magistrate
probable cause
particularity
stop
arrest

seizure
nonstop
"knock and announce"
   requirement
deadly force
nondeadly force
Federal Communications Act

Title III of the Omnibus Crime
   Control and Safe Streets Act
Electronic Communications
   Privacy Act
civil asset forfeiture
administrative search warrant
anticipatory search warrant

INTRODUCTION
Provisions of the Fourth Amendment

Five types of activities are governed by the Fourth Amendment: (1) arrests with warrants; (2) arrests without warrants; (3) searches with warrants; (4) searches without warrants; and (5) the seizure of evidence. This chapter's primary focus is on arrests and searches *with warrants*. Warrantless actions are discussed in the next three chapters.

The seizure of evidence is often a consequence of arrests and searches with and without warrants. However, if a search or arrest with or without a warrant violates the Fourth Amendment, any evidence seized will be inadmissible in court. As has been shown already, this is due to the *exclusionary rule*. Because of the exclusionary rule, little attention is given here (or in the next three chapters) to the seizure of evidence independent of an arrest or search. While it is possible for a seizure to take place in the absence of a search or arrest (e.g., *Soldal v. Cook County*, 506 U.S. 56 [1992]), rare is the occasion in which the police (or a private individual acting in a governmental capacity) can seize evidence without a search or an arrest.

The Fourth Amendment seems fairly clear with respect to warrants: "and no Warrants shall issue, but upon probable cause, supported by Oath or affirmation, and particularly describing the place to be searched, and the persons or things to be seized." Despite this seemingly simple language, however, the Fourth Amendment's warrant requirement has been litigated extensively in the courts. As indicated in Chapter 3, the courts have focused on the meaning of *probable cause* as well as acceptable sources of information used to determine the presence of probable cause. Many decisions have also focused on the Fourth Amendment's requirement that warrants be supported by "Oath or affirmation" and on the particularity requirement. This chapter gives special attention to these latter issues.

KEY CASES

Warrant Components
- *Coolidge v. New Hampshire*, 403 U.S. 443 (1971)
- *Lo-Ji Sales, Inc. v. New York*, 442 U.S. 319 (1979)
- *Maryland v. Garrison*, 480 U.S. 79 (1987)
- *Andresen v. Maryland*, 427 U.S. 463 (1976)

Arrests with Warrants
- *Florida v. Royer*, 460 U.S. 491 (1983)
- *Davis v. Mississippi*, 394 U.S. 721 (1969)
- *Carroll v. United States*, 267 U.S. 132 (1925)
- *Payton v. New York*, 445 U.S. 573 (1980)
- *Steagald v. United States*, 451 U.S. 204 (1981)

- *Atwater v. City of Lago Vista*, 532 U.S. 318 (2001)
- *Ker v. California*, 374 U.S. 23 (1963)
- *Sabbath v. United States*, 391 U.S. 585 (1968)
- *Tennessee v. Garner*, 471 U.S. 1 (1985)
- *Graham v. Connor*, 490 U.S. 386 (1989)

Searches with Warrants
- *Gooding v. United States*, 416 U.S. 430 (1974)
- *Harris v. United States*, 331 U.S. 145 (1947)
- *Michigan v. Summers*, 452 U.S. 692 (1981)
- *City of West Covina v. Perkins*, 525 U.S. 234 (1999)
- *Wilson v. Layne*, 526 U.S. 603 (1999)

Even though there are many cases involving searches and arrests with warrants, the law is actually very clear with respect to *when* a warrant is required. Generally, a search warrant is required for *any* type of search, regardless of where it is conducted, provided that (1) there are no exigent (i.e., emergency) circumstances and (2) the search is not one justified on so-called administrative grounds. Even searches pursuant to arrest and searches under the automobile exception are justified in terms of exigencies. Arrest warrants, by contrast, are required for arrests in private places, provided exigent circumstances are absent.

■ COMPONENTS OF WARRANTS

An **arrest warrant** and a **search warrant** each have three essential components. First, it must be issued by a neutral and detached magistrate. Second, a showing of probable cause is required. Finally, it must conform to the Fourth Amendment's particularity requirement. The first requirement—a neutral and detached magistrate—is the same regardless of the type of warrant. However, the probable cause and particularity requirements differ, depending on the type of warrant in question. These requirements are considered in the following subsections.

■ A Neutral and Detached Magistrate

The logic for requiring a **neutral and detached magistrate** in the issuance of an arrest or search warrant was described by the Supreme Court over 50 years ago in *Johnson v. United States* (333 U.S. 10 [1948]):

> The point of the Fourth Amendment . . . is not that it denies law enforcement the support of the usual inferences reasonable men draw from evidence. Its protection consists in requiring that those inferences be drawn by a neutral and detached magistrate instead of being judged by the officer engaged in the often competitive enterprise of ferreting out crime. (pp. 13–14)

Most judges are considered neutral and detached. Even so, the Supreme Court has focused, in a number of cases, on this first critical warrant requirement. For example, in *Coolidge v. New Hampshire* (403 U.S. 443 [1971]), the Court declared that a state attorney general cannot issue a search warrant. State attorneys general are chief prosecutors and thus inclined to side with law enforcement officers. Similarly, in *United States v. United States District Court* (407 U.S. 297 [1972]), the Court decided that the president, acting through the attorney general of the United States, cannot authorize electronic surveillance without judicial approval. Justice Powell observed:

Coolidge v. New Hampshire,
403 U.S. 443 (1971)

> The Fourth Amendment does not contemplate the executive officers of Government as neutral and detached magistrates. Their duty and responsibility is to enforce the laws, to investigate and to prosecute . . . . [T]hose charged with this investigative and prosecutorial duty should not be the sole judges of when to utilize constitutionally sensitive means in pursuing their tasks. The historical judgment, which the Fourth Amendment accepts, is that unreviewed executive discretion may yield too readily to pressures to obtain incriminating evidence and overlook potential invasions of privacy and protected speech. (p. 317)

Lo-Ji Sales, Inc. v. New York,
442 U.S. 319 (1979)

There have also been some cases in which the Court has focused on the extent to which judge can be viewed as neutral and detached. For example, in *Lo-Ji Sales, Inc. v. New York*

(442 U.S. 319 [1979]), a magistrate issued a warrant for two obscene items, but he also authorized the police to seize any other items that he might find obscene upon examination of the location to be searched. The magistrate then accompanied the officers on the search, discovered items that he deemed to be obscene, and added them to the initial warrant. The items were then admitted into evidence against the defendants. The Supreme Court declared that the magistrate was not acting in a neutral and detached capacity: "[H]e was not acting as a judicial officer but as an adjunct law-enforcement officer" (p. 327).

Finally, if a magistrate has a financial interest in the issuance of warrants, he or she cannot be considered neutral and detached. This issue was presented to the Supreme Court in *Connally v. Georgia* (429 U.S. 245 [1977]). A Georgia statute authorized unsalaried magistrates to receive five dollars for each warrant issued but no money for warrant applications that were denied. The Court unanimously held that the statute violated the Constitution, citing that "judicial action by an officer of a court who has 'a direct, personal, substantial, pecuniary interest' in his conclusion to issue or to deny the warrant" (p. 250) cannot possibly be considered neutral and detached.

A Showing of Probable Cause

Probable cause was defined in Chapter 3; as such, there is no need to revisit the definition here. However, it is important to point out that probable cause is required as a component of a valid warrant. Also, the meaning of probable cause—as opposed to the sources of information that give rise to it—differs, depending on whether an arrest or search warrant is issued.

Showing of Probable Cause in an Arrest Warrant

The showing of probable cause in an arrest warrant is not particularly complex. The officer applying for the warrant must simply show probable cause that the person to be arrested committed the crime. Acceptable sources of information for a probable cause showing were described in Chapter 3. When applying for an *arrest* warrant, the officer is not required to show probable cause that the suspect will be found at a particular location. In *Payton v. New York* (445 U.S. 573 [1980]), the majority stated, "If there is sufficient evidence of a citizen's participation in a felony to persuade a judicial officer that his arrest is justified, it is constitutionally reasonable to require him to open his doors to the officers of the law" (pp. 602–603).

Showing of Probable Cause in a Search Warrant

The showing of probable cause in a search warrant is twofold. First, the officer applying for the search warrant must show probable cause that the items to be seized are connected with criminal activity. Second, the officer must show probable cause that the items to be seized are in the location to be searched. Note that this second requirement does not apply to an arrest warrant.

Particularity

The Fourth Amendment expressly provides that warrants particularly describe the "place to be searched, and the persons or things to be seized." Not surprisingly, the **particularity** requirement differs, depending on the type of warrant issued. For an arrest warrant, the particularity requirement is easily satisfied. The particularity requirement for a search warrant, however, is far more complex.

Particularity in an Arrest Warrant

There are two ways to satisfy the Fourth Amendment's particularity requirement with regard to an arrest warrant. First, if the suspect's name is known, then simply supplying his or her name is enough to meet the particularity requirement. In some situations, however, the suspect's name is *not* known. Then, a specific description of the suspect is sufficient and a "John Doe" warrant will be issued. As long as other officers may locate the suspect with reasonable effort, the suspect's name is not required.

Who Was That Bald Man?

The police have in their possession the video from a security camera at a bank that was recently robbed. The suspect is a white male, six feet tall, and has a mustache, a bald head, a scar on his left cheek, and a tattoo of a skull and crossbones on his neck. May the police apply for an arrest warrant based on this information, even if they never learned of the suspect's name prior to applying for the warrant?

Even so, an arrest warrant is rarely issued without the suspect's name. This is not to suggest, however, that the police almost always know the suspect's name. Remember, there are many occasions involving warrantless arrests (e.g., after a suspect is caught fleeing the bank he or she just robbed) in which an arrest can be made without knowledge of the suspect's name. As long as probable cause is in place, the name of the suspect is not essential (regardless of whether a warrant is issued).

Particularity in a Search Warrant

The particularity requirement for a search warrant is twofold. First, the warrant must specify the *place* to be searched. Next, the warrant must specify the *items* to be seized. The reason for this particularity requirement stems from the framers' concerns with so-called general warrants. *General warrants*, which were issued by the English Crown, permitted basically limitless searches for evidence of treason.

Contrary to popular belief, a search warrant does not need to state with absolute precision the place to be searched. It "is enough if the description is such that the officer with a search warrant can, with reasonable effort, ascertain and identify the place intended" (*Steele v. United States*, 267 U.S. 498 [1925], p. 503). However, the items mentioned in the warrant should be described with sufficient specificity that a reasonable officer would know where to look for them.

In situations in which the warrant incorrectly specifies the place to be searched, the courts will focus on the reasonableness of the officers' mistake. For example, in *Maryland v. Garrison* (480 U.S. 79 [1987]), police officers obtained a warrant to search the person of Lawrence McWebb and the premises known as "2036 Park Avenue, third-floor apartment." They believed that McWebb's apartment occupied the entire third floor when, in fact, there were two apartments on that floor—one of which belonged to Garrison. The Court held that the warrant was valid for several reasons: It was based on information by a trusted informant, and the police had inquired with the local utility company and were given the impression that there was only one apartment on the third floor.

As for the items to be seized, the warrant must clearly specify what the police wish to seize. The case of *Lo-Ji Sales, Inc. v. New York* (442 U.S. 319 [1979]) is again illustrative. Recall from the discussion about the neutral and detached magistrate requirement that the magistrate in *Lo-Ji Sales* issued a warrant that named two specific items but also permitted the police to seize anything the magistrate considered obscene. The Court unanimously held that the warrant failed to "particularly describe . . . the things to be seized" (p. 319).

■ *Maryland v. Garrison,* 480 U.S. 79 (1987)

DECISION MAKING EXERCISE **4.2**

The Fourth Amendment's Particularity Requirement

A police officer obtained a search warrant from a judge that authorized the seizure of "numerous marijuana plants and growing equipment" at 123 Main Street. Does this warrant comport with the Fourth Amendment's particularity requirement? What if the warrant also authorized the seizure of "stolen stereo equipment"?

Contrast *Lo-Ji Sales* with *Andresen v. Maryland* (427 U.S. 463 [1976]), in which the Court upheld a warrant that authorized the seizure of several items "together with other fruits, instrumentalities and evidence of crime at this [time] known" (p. 479). The Court noted that the crime in question was particularly complex and "could be proved only by piecing together many bits of evidence" (p. 482). This is a controversial decision, indeed, because it suggests that, under certain circumstances, the police can circumvent the Fourth Amendment's particularity requirement (see also *United States v. DeLuna*, 763 F.2d 897 [8th Cir. 1985]; *United States v. Alexander*, 761 F.2d 1294 [9th Cir. 1985]; *Groh v. Ramirez*, 540 U.S. 551 [2004]).

■ *Andresen v. Maryland*, 427 U.S. 463 (1976)

If the police have a hunch that an item is in a place to be searched but do not include the item in the application for a warrant, the item can be seized under the doctrine of plain view as long as the police are legally authorized (by obtaining a warrant) to be on the premises. *Plain view* is discussed in the next chapter. Also, if a warrant does not particularly describe the items to be seized (or the place to be searched), then it is not automatically deemed in violation of the Fourth Amendment. If there is an objectively reasonable basis for the officers' mistaken belief, then the warrant will most likely be upheld (see *Massachusetts v. Sheppard*, 468 U.S. 981 [1981]). Also, just because an item is not listed in a warrant does not mean that it cannot be seized. As will be considered in the next chapter, items in plain view can be seized, provided certain conditions are met. Figure 4.1 (pages 102–103) provides a copy of an actual search warrant that satisfies the Fourth Amendment's particularity requirement.

ARRESTS WITH WARRANTS

Justice Powell once stated that "a search may cause only an annoyance and temporary inconvenience to the law-abiding citizen, assuming more serious dimensions only when it turns up evidence of criminality [but an] arrest . . . is a serious personal intrusion regardless of whether the person seized is guilty or innocent" (*United States v. Watson*, 423 U.S. 411 [1976], p. 428). Even so, an unconstitutional arrest has little significance by itself in criminal procedure. The reason for this is that the remedy for an illegal arrest is simply a release from custody. It is possible that a person unlawfully arrested may sue, but little recourse is generally available to a person who is unlawfully arrested. Why, then, focus attention on the constitutionality of arrests? The answer is that the constitutionality of an arrest is frequently critical in determining whether seized evidence is admissible in court.

Consider this example: Assume that a police officer arrests a defendant without probable cause. Such an arrest is automatically unconstitutional. Assume also that the officer finds an illegal firearm on the defendant and turns it over to the prosecutor, who decides to use it against the defendant at his trial on firearm charges. The defendant will almost certainly seek to have the firearm excluded as evidence on the grounds that it resulted from an unlawful arrest. In other words, the defendant will argue that the firearm is "fruit of the poisonous tree," as discussed in Chapter 2.

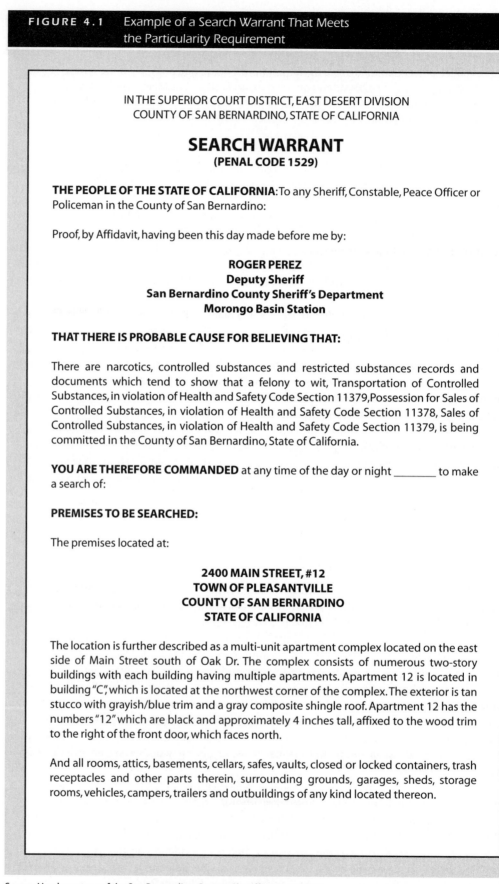

FIGURE 4.1   *Example of a Search Warrant That Meets the Particularity Requirement*

IN THE SUPERIOR COURT DISTRICT, EAST DESERT DIVISION
COUNTY OF SAN BERNARDINO, STATE OF CALIFORNIA

SEARCH WARRANT
(PENAL CODE 1529)

THE PEOPLE OF THE STATE OF CALIFORNIA: To any Sheriff, Constable, Peace Officer or Policeman in the County of San Bernardino:

Proof, by Affidavit, having been this day made before me by:

ROGER PEREZ
Deputy Sheriff
San Bernardino County Sheriff's Department
Morongo Basin Station

THAT THERE IS PROBABLE CAUSE FOR BELIEVING THAT:

There are narcotics, controlled substances and restricted substances records and documents which tend to show that a felony to wit, Transportation of Controlled Substances, in violation of Health and Safety Code Section 11379, Possession for Sales of Controlled Substances, in violation of Health and Safety Code Section 11378, Sales of Controlled Substances, in violation of Health and Safety Code Section 11379, is being committed in the County of San Bernardino, State of California.

YOU ARE THEREFORE COMMANDED at any time of the day or night _____ to make a search of:

PREMISES TO BE SEARCHED:

The premises located at:

2400 MAIN STREET, #12
TOWN OF PLEASANTVILLE
COUNTY OF SAN BERNARDINO
STATE OF CALIFORNIA

The location is further described as a multi-unit apartment complex located on the east side of Main Street south of Oak Dr. The complex consists of numerous two-story buildings with each building having multiple apartments. Apartment 12 is located in building "C", which is located at the northwest corner of the complex. The exterior is tan stucco with grayish/blue trim and a gray composite shingle roof. Apartment 12 has the numbers "12" which are black and approximately 4 inches tall, affixed to the wood trim to the right of the front door, which faces north.

And all rooms, attics, basements, cellars, safes, vaults, closed or locked containers, trash receptacles and other parts therein, surrounding grounds, garages, sheds, storage rooms, vehicles, campers, trailers and outbuildings of any kind located thereon.

Source: Used courtesy of the San Bernardino County Sheriff's Department.

And all persons located on or at the premises. And all vehicles belonging to or in the control of said persons.

And you are hereby authorized to answer all incoming telephone calls received at the premises and the vehicles to be searched and to further seize and record all the incoming telephonic pager numbers and messages received at the premises and the vehicles to be searched and to seize all telephonic "fax" messages received at the premises and the vehicles to be searched. And to determine if the aforementioned telephone calls, telephonic messages, or "faxed" messages are related to illegal activities.

FOR THE FOLLOWING PROPERTY:

Methamphetamine and paraphernalia commonly associated with the possession, packaging, and sale of methamphetamine such as scales, weighing devices and measuring devices; packaging materials including paper bindles, glass vials, plastic baggies, foil; processing materials including sifters, filters, screens and cutting agents; recordation of the purchase and/or sales of methamphetamine including ledgers, notebooks, pay/owe sheets, customer lists, video tapes and phone answering machine tape recordings, personal phone books; personal photographs which document the possession, sales and/or possession for sales of methamphetamine; and proceeds from the sales of methamphetamine consisting of currency.

Financial records including expenses incurred in obtaining chemicals and apparatus and income derived from sales of narcotics and other controlled substances as well as records showing legitimate income or the lack thereof and general living expenses.

Serial numbers, model numbers, identifying marks and descriptions of all personal property including, but not limited to, televisions, radios, stereo equipment, and other electrical devices, appliances, hand and power tools, firearms, bicycles, items of jewelry, silver, gold and coins which can be identified as stolen and/or evidence of the crime of Burglary and/or Possession of Stolen Property or property which is readily traded for narcotics in lieu of cash.

All articles of personal property which will identify persons in control of the premises, storage areas or containers where controlled substances may be found, including keys to those areas that may be locked, rental agreements and receipts, deeds of trust, documents or papers bearing names, canceled mail, paycheck stubs and other employment records, tax documents and personal identification.

AND IF YOU FIND THE SAME OR ANY PART THEREOF, to bring it forthwith before me at my courtroom

GIVEN UNDER MY HAND, and dated this _17th_ day of September 2002.

James D. Franklin

Judge of the Superior Court
East Desert Division
County of San Bernardino
State of California

This hypothetical situation is the main reason it is important to study the law of arrest. It is not that the legality of an arrest matters by itself. What is important is that an illegal arrest can lead to the exclusion of evidence. Virtually all arrest cases that make it to the Supreme Court have something in common: A convicted defendant is seeking to have his or her *arrest* declared unconstitutional so the evidence that led to his or her conviction will be suppressed and/or the conviction reversed.

■ The Definition of *Arrest*

Invariably, students of criminal procedure become confused when instructors toss around terms like *seizure, stop,* and *arrest* with little attention to the fact that each term has a very distinct meaning. Think of **stops** and **arrests** as being different types of seizures. Additionally, think of each type of **seizure** as falling along a scale of seriousness: An arrest is the most intrusive type of seizure, and a stop is the next most intrusive.

Another source of confusion is that the term *seizure* can refer to two totally different types of actions. As shown in Chapter 3, the seizure of a person occurs when a police officer, by means of physical force or show of authority, intentionally restrains an individual's liberty in such a manner that a reasonable person would believe that he or she is not free to leave (*Terry v. Ohio*, 392 U.S. 1 [1968]; *United States v. Mendenhall*, 446 U.S. 544 [1980]). However, law enforcement officers can also seize property.

As indicated near the beginning of this chapter, the seizure of evidence per se is not the focus here. Instead, the focus is on the seizures of persons—namely, stops and arrests. Why distinguish between stops and arrests? Arrests require probable cause; stops (the focus of Chapter 6) only require reasonable suspicion. If the circumstances surrounding a stop are such that it evolves into an arrest, then the arrest will be declared unconstitutional and the evidence will be thrown out, assuming the officer did not have probable cause.

Prior to the civil rights era, the Supreme Court suggested that anything the police do to restrict a person's movement constitutes an arrest. For example, in *Henry v. United States* (361 U.S. 98 [1959]), the Court found that an arrest occurred when the police stopped a car whose occupants were suspected of transporting illegal alcohol. According to the Court, "When the officers interrupted the two men and restricted their liberty of movement, the arrest, for purposes of this case, was complete" (p. 103). Since the police in *Henry* did not have probable cause to stop the men, the so-called arrest was deemed unconstitutional.

Recently, though, the Supreme Court has held that the police must do more than restrict a person's movement for an arrest to occur. In *Terry v. Ohio* (392 U.S. 1 [1968]), the case that essentially altered the definition of arrest for all time, the Court ruled that a suspect's movements can be restricted without such activity being considered an arrest. The Court distinguished between arrests that "eventuate in a trip to the station house and prosecution for crime" and lesser intrusions that can occur "whenever a police officer accosts an individual and restrains his freedom to walk away" (p. 16).

In one sense, distinguishing between an arrest and a lesser type of intrusion is easy. For example, when a suspect is handcuffed, placed in the back of a patrol car, and driven to the police station for booking, an arrest has clearly occurred. Alternatively, if a person is accosted by a single police officer and asked general questions about his or her suspected involvement in a crime, an arrest has not occurred. However, there are many police/citizen encounters that fall between these two extremes. A stop can evolve into an arrest if the circumstances are just so. A seizure that falls short of a formal arrest may be so intrusive as to constitute a *de facto* arrest, in which case probable cause, rather than reasonable suspicion, would be required to make the encounter constitutional.

Distinguishing between a Stop and an Arrest

Generally, the courts will weigh (1) the duration of a stop and (2) the degree of the intrusion in assessing whether a stop evolved into an arrest. Sometimes, the courts also refer to the officers' intentions and the manner in which the stop took place. The importance of these issues—particularly, degree and duration—is evidenced by the Supreme Court's opinion in *Florida v. Royer* (460 U.S. 491 [1983]):

■ *Florida v. Royer,* 460 U.S. 491 (1983)

> The predicate permitting seizures on suspicion short of probable cause is that law enforcement interests warrant a limited intrusion on the personal security of the suspect. The scope of the intrusion permitted will vary to some extent with the particular facts and circumstances of each case. *This much, however, is clear: an investigative detention must be temporary and last no longer than is necessary to effectuate the purpose of the stop. Similarly, the investigative methods employed should be the least intrusive means reasonably available to verify or dispel the officer's suspicion in a short period of time.* (p. 500, emphasis added)

Several Supreme Court cases are illustrative. Four categories of such cases can be identified: (1) cases involving detention in a stationhouse or similar structure, such as the investigation room in an airport; (2) cases involving an encounter between police and citizens on the street; (3) cases involving a border detention; and (4) cases involving detention in the home. Each category is briefly considered in the paragraphs that follow.

What Type of Seizure?

The police concluded that a man who was suspected of rape was also responsible for a recent burglary/rape. Without a warrant and without probable cause, the police went to the suspect's home to obtain fingerprints. Arriving at the home, the police spoke to the suspect on his front porch, and when he expressed reluctance to accompany them to the stationhouse, one officer said that they would arrest him. The suspect then replied that he would rather go to the station than be arrested. He was then taken to the station and fingerprinted. Does the police action constitute an arrest?

With regard to stationhouse detentions, in *Davis v. Mississippi* (394 U.S. 721 [1969]), several youths, including Davis, were taken into custody and fingerprinted as part of a rape investigation. The officers did not have probable cause, and Davis was held for two days and interrogated throughout his detention. On the basis of his fingerprints and confession, Davis was charged, convicted, and sentenced to death. The Supreme Court reversed Davis's conviction on the grounds that detention was too long, too intrusive, and unsupported by probable cause. The Court did not explicitly address the distinction between a stop and an arrest, but it intimated that because probable cause was required to detain Davis, the police officers had effectively arrested him.

■ *Davis v. Mississippi,* 394 U.S. 721 (1969)

In a similar case, *Dunaway v. New York* (442 U.S. 200 [1979]), the Supreme Court ruled that stationhouse detentions require probable cause. In that case, police officers took a man into custody during the course of a robbery/murder investigation. They read the man the *Miranda* warnings and subjected him to questioning—without probable cause. The Supreme Court reversed the man's subsequent conviction. Again, the Court did not decide on the arrest issue, but it did declare that custodial interrogation, such as that in *Dunaway*, must be supported by probable cause. The Court further declared that *Terry* was inapplicable because it permits only a "limited violation of individual privacy" while ensuring "interests in both crime prevention and detection and in the police officer's safety" (p. 209).

In *Florida v. Royer* (460 U.S. 491 [1983]), mentioned earlier, the Court ruled again that certain forms of detention can require probable cause, rather than reasonable suspicion. In that case, officers in an airport asked a man to accompany them into a room because he was suspected of carrying narcotics. The officers found drugs in the man's luggage, and he was arrested. The Court declared that the detention, which lasted 15 minutes, constituted an arrest, which required probable cause. As Justice White stated, "What had begun as a consensual inquiry in a public place had escalated into an investigatory procedure in a police interrogation room, where the police, unsatisfied with previous explanations, sought to confirm their suspicions" (p. 503). What is important in this case, as well as the preceding two, was that the detention was not consensual. If a person consents to the detention, he or she is not considered under arrest.

It is important to note, also, that not all *nonconsensual* encounters between police and citizens amount to arrests. As will be addressed later, detentions at the national borders and in other locations are permissible under certain circumstances. In addition, there are situations in which the courts have declared that holding a person for investigative purposes may not arise to the level of an arrest, requiring probable cause. For example, even though the Court reversed a defendant's conviction in *Davis v. Mississippi* (394 U.S. 721 [1969]), it did state that "because of the unique nature of the fingerprinting process, [detentions for the purpose of obtaining fingerprints] might, under narrowly defined circumstances, be found to comply with the Fourth Amendment even though there is no probable cause in the traditional sense" (p. 727).

There are also situations in which encounters on the street (as opposed to questioning in a stationhouse or its equivalent) can evolve into arrests. In *Terry*, the Supreme Court noted that a stop must be *brief*, suggesting that any stop that is not brief may require probable cause. While the Supreme Court has been hesitant to put a precise time limit on the length of a stop, it made this statement in *United States v. Sharpe* (470 U.S. 675 [1985]):

> While it is clear that "the brevity of the invasion of the individual's Fourth Amendment interests is an important factor in determining whether the seizure is so minimally intrusive as to be justifiable on reasonable suspicion," we have emphasized the need to consider the law enforcement purposes to be served by the stop as well as the time reasonably needed to effectuate these purposes . . . . Much as a "bright line" rule would be desirable in evaluating whether an investigative detention is unreasonable, common sense and ordinary human experience must govern over rigid criteria. (p. 685)

As already noted, Fourth Amendment requirements are significantly relaxed at the nation's borders. Recall that in *United States v. Montoya de Hernandez* (473 U.S. 531 [1985]), the Supreme Court upheld law enforcement officials' 16-hour detention of a suspected drug "balloon swallower" while they waited for nature to take its course, so to speak. The majority approved of the delay because the defendant's detention "resulted solely from the method by which she chose to smuggle illicit drugs into the country" (p. 559). Justices Brennan and Marshall strongly dissented, however, pointing out that the detention in this case— "indefinite confinement in a squalid back room cut off from the outside world, the absence of basic amenities that would have been provided to even the vilest of hardened criminals, repeated strip searches" (p. 556)—was effectively an arrest, thus requiring probable cause.

DECISION MAKING EXERCISE 4.4

Detention of a Third Party during an Arrest

As officers arrived at a house to serve a search warrant, they encountered Larry McVee descending the front steps. The officers asked McVee to help them gain entry into the house. McVee replied that he did not have keys to the house but would ring someone over the intercom. When he did so, another occupant answered the door but refused to allow the officers into the house. The officers then forced the door open and detained McVee as well as eight other people who were in the house. All nine people were frisked because the officers feared for their safety. One of the people had a gun on his person. The officers arrested that man, and in his later trial for weapons offenses, he moved to suppress the gun on the grounds that the officers did not have justification to detain him (or the other people in the house) during the execution of a search warrant. Will his motion be granted?

Finally, a handful of cases have involved detentions in the home, focusing, in particular, on the extent to which detention of a person (e.g., owner, renter, or guest) in a home can evolve into a full-blown arrest. Somewhat surprisingly, nonconsensual encounters in the home between residents and the police do not always rise to the level of an arrest. For example, in *Beckwith v. United States* (425 U.S. 341 [1976]), the Supreme Court ruled that questioning by Internal Revenue Service (IRS) agents of a defendant in his living room was not an arrest or even custodial in nature. Contrast this decision with that of *Rawlings v. Kentucky* (448 U.S. 98 [1980]), in which several individuals were detained at a house where officers had served an arrest warrant but had failed to find the person named in the warrant. The Court declared that this type of detention amounted to an arrest because there was no probable cause to detain the individuals not named in the warrant. In addition, the detention lasted 45 minutes, which was unnecessarily long, under the circumstances (though not as long as some detentions that the Supreme Court has upheld).

The Supreme Court seemed to backpedal on the *Rawlings* decision in *Michigan v. Summers* (452 U.S. 692 [1981]), decided a year later. In *Summers*, the Court held that an individual *can* be detained during a search of his or her house, without such activity rising to the level of an arrest, as long as the police have a search warrant and even if there is no probable cause to arrest him or her. In support, the Court noted that (1) such detentions are not as embarrassing or stigmatizing as public detentions and (2) when there is probable cause to search for evidence of criminal activity, it is reasonable to assume that the person who lives on the premises is involved. See Figure 4.2 for a summary of this discussion.

Distinguishing between a Stop and a Nonstop

Remember that it is important to distinguish not just between a stop and an arrest but between a stop and a **nonstop**. If a stop occurs when a reasonable person *would not* believe that he or she is free to leave, then a nonstop occurs when a reasonable person *would* believe that he or she is free to leave. A nonstop requires no justification at all because it is not considered a seizure within the meaning of the Fourth Amendment. As will be discussed in Chapter 6, police officers are free to confront people and ask questions of them, as long as the people are free to leave. If the people are stopped, however, then reasonable suspicion is required. And again, if an arrest is made, the requisite standard of justification is probable cause.

FIGURE 4.2   *Factors Used to Distinguish between a Stop and an Arrest*

All four of these criteria should be considered together. For example, if a police/citizen encounter occurs at the stationhouse, the encounter may not be considered an arrest. However, if the encounter is overly lengthy and the citizen is not free to leave, then an arrest has taken place.

1. Purpose
   a. Intent to arrest = Arrest
   b. No intent to arrest = *Terry* stop or nonstop
2. Manner
   a. Person not free to leave = Arrest or *Terry* stop
   b. Person free to leave = Nonstop
3. Location
   a. At police station or in private = Arrest or *Terry* stop
   b. Public = Arrest, *Terry* stop, or nonstop
4. Duration
   a. Lengthy = Arrest
   b. Short = *Terry* stop or nonstop

Summary. Clearly, distinguishing between arrests and lesser intrusions, such as investigative stops, can be confusing. At one extreme, a seizure that is accompanied by handcuffs, or words to the effect that the person is "under arrest," is always considered an arrest. At the other extreme, when a person is confronted by a police officer and not free to leave, but nevertheless briefly detained and not interrogated, an arrest has not occurred. Where the distinction is confusing is in the gray area between a stop and an arrest. A stop can evolve into a *de facto* arrest in a number of circumstances. The courts will give weight to four factors in making their decision: (1) the purpose of the stop (e.g., to question or interrogate a person); (2) the manner in which the stop takes place (e.g., one officer or several); (3) the location in which the stop takes place (e.g., stationhouse, street, or home); and (4) the duration of the stop. No single factor is necessarily determinative. If, however, a person is detained by several officers in a stationhouse for several days so as to be interrogated, then the court will almost certainly consider such police activity tantamount to an arrest.

In closing, this section has endeavored to provide a definition of *arrest*, but in fact, no clear definition really exists. The courts must weigh each case individually. Fortunately, most people know an arrest when they see it.

■ When an Arrest Warrant Is Required

Under common law, if an arresting officer had probable cause to believe that (1) a person was committing or had committed a felony or (2) a person was committing a certain misdemeanor in the officer's presence, then an arrest warrant was not required. This held true regardless of where the arrest took place, even if it was effected in someone's private home (e.g., *Trupiano v. United States*, 334 U.S. 699 [1948]). The only real situation in which an arrest warrant *was* required was for a misdemeanor committed out of view of the arresting officer. The logic for this was set forth by the Supreme Court in *Carroll v. United States* (267 U.S. 132 [1925]):

■ *Carroll v. United States*, 267 U.S. 132 (1925)

> The reason for arrest for misdemeanors without warrant at common law was to promptly suppress breaches of the peace . . . while the reason for arrest without a warrant on a reliable report of a felony was because the public safety and the due apprehension of criminals charged with heinous offenses required that such arrests should be made at once without warrant. (p. 157)

Since 1925, the Supreme Court has stuck to the rule set forth in *Carroll*, subject to two exceptions. First, an arrest in someone's private home cannot be made without a warrant, unless exigent circumstances are present. Second, an arrest in the home of a third party is impermissible without a warrant, again providing no exigent circumstances are in place. An example of a third-party situation is one in which the police seek to arrest a person who is visiting a friend's house. One additional restriction was recognized in *Gerstein v. Pugh* (420 U.S. 103 [1975]); namely, a judicial determination of probable cause is required when an arrest is made without a warrant (see Chapter 9).

The remainder of this section considers two types of arrest: (1) arrests in the home and (2) arrests in third-party homes. With rare exceptions, a warrant is required for each.

Arrests in the Home

■ *Payton v. New York*, 445 U.S. 573 (1980)

In the landmark decision of *Payton v. New York* (445 U.S. 573 [1980]), the Supreme Court held that the Fourth Amendment prohibits a warrantless, nonconsensual entry into a private home for the purpose of making an arrest. In that case, police officers, after two days of investigation, had assembled enough evidence to establish probable cause to believe that Payton had murdered the manager of a gas station. The officers went to Payton's apartment to arrest him. When no one answered the door, they used a crowbar to open the door and entered the apartment. They did not find Payton, but they did find, in plain view, a .30 caliber shell casing lying on the floor. They seized it and admitted it into evidence at Payton's trial. Payton ultimately surrendered to the police and was indicted for murder. The lower court admitted the shell casing into evidence, but the Supreme Court reversed, stating, "In terms that apply equally to seizures of property and to seizures of persons, the Fourth Amendment has drawn a firm line at the entrance to the house. Absent exigent circumstances, that threshold may not reasonably be crossed without a warrant" (p. 590). Justice Stevens also stated, citing an earlier case (*United States v. United States District Court*, 407 U.S. 297 [1972]), that "physical entry of the home is the chief evil against which the wording of the Fourth Amendment is directed" (p. 585). In *Payton*, then, the Court handed down a bright-line rule: An arrest in the home must be accompanied by a warrant in the absence of exigent circumstances. The decision in *Kirk v. Louisiana* (536 U.S. 635 [2002]) recently reaffirmed this.

DECISION MAKING EXERCISE 4.5

A Public or Private Arrest?

Federal drug agents had probable cause to arrest John Crook. They knew he was staying at the local motel, but they did not know what room he was in. The agents asked hotel personnel to supply the room number, which they did, and then the agents went to that room. Standing in the hall, one of the agents identified himself to a housekeeping employee and asked him to knock on the door of the room and check whether anyone was in it. The employee knocked and called out, "Housekeeping." Crook opened the door. The agents recognized him immediately, at which point one of the agents drew his weapon, pointed it at Crook, and ordered him to raise his hands. Crook immediately raised his hands and said to the agents, "I won't give you guys any trouble. I've got a gun in my right pocket." Both agents, with their weapons drawn, entered the room. Crook's gun was removed, and he was advised that he was under arrest. Was a warrant required in this situation? Or, in other words, could this be considered a public arrest? Note that based on the facts supplied, there are no exigent circumstances in place.

Arrests in Third-Party Homes

Not long after *Payton*, the Supreme Court decided *Steagald v. United States* (451 U.S. 204 [1981]). Justice Marshall expressed concern that although an arrest warrant may protect a person "from an unreasonable seizure, it [does] absolutely nothing to protect [a third party's] privacy interest in being free from an unreasonable invasion and search of his home" (p. 213). Accordingly, the Court decided that in such situations, the police must obtain not only an arrest warrant for the person they seek but also a *separate* warrant to search the third-party residence for the arrestee.

The facts in *Steagald* were as follow: Acting on an arrest warrant issued for a person by the name of Lyons, Drug Enforcement Administration (DEA) agents entered the home of Steagald. This entry was made without a warrant. While searching Steagald's home for Lyons, the agents found cocaine and other incriminating evidence, but they did not find Lyons. Steagald was arrested and convicted on federal drug charges. He appealed, and the Supreme Court eventually reversed Steagald's conviction. The Court offered the following in support of its position:

> Two distinct interests were implicated by the search in this case—Ricky Lyons' interest in being free from an unreasonable seizure and petitioner's [Steagald's] interest in being free from an unreasonable search of his home. Because the arrest warrant for Lyons addressed only the former interest, the search of petitioner's home was no more reasonable from

■ *Steagald v. United States*, 451 U.S. 204 (1981)

petitioner's perspective that it would have been if conducted in the absence of any warrant. (p. 216).

The Court's decision in *Steagald* was not without opposition. Justices Rehnquist and White dissented, arguing that the police and judges "will, in their various capacities, have to weigh the time during which a suspect for whom there is an outstanding arrest warrant has been in the building, whether the dwelling is the suspect's home, how long he has lived there, whether he is likely to leave immediately, and a number of related and equally imponderable questions" (p. 213). The majority countered by pointing out that if the police did not need warrants to enter third-party residences, "[a]rmed solely with an arrest warrant for a single person, [the police] . . . could search all the homes of that individual's friends and acquaintances" (p. 215). Such a possibility would be controversial, indeed.

DECISION MAKING EXERCISE 4.6

Serving a Search Warrant in a Third-Party Residence

Sue Lyons leases an apartment and lives by herself. However, when she found out that her old boyfriend, Fred Taber, had been on the run from authorities for several months, she offered to let him stay at her apartment. She gave him a key so he could come and go at will. After eight weeks, during which time Fred continued to live with Sue, the police were alerted as to his presence by a vigilant neighbor. Officers then entered Sue's apartment without a warrant and arrested Fred. Will the arrest hold up?

Thus, having an arrest warrant does *not* allow authorities to enter a third-party residence. A warrantless entry into a third-party residence violates the third party's rights. There are two exceptions to this rule, however: If *consent* is given and/or *exigent circumstances* are in place, the police may make a warrantless entry into a third-party's residence. Figure 4.3 offers a summary of this discussion.

▪ Arrests for Minor Offenses

The Supreme Court recently declared that "the Fourth Amendment does not forbid a warrantless arrest for a minor criminal offense, such as a misdemeanor seatbelt violation punishable only by a fine" (*Atwater v. City of Lago Vista*, 532 U.S. 318 [2001]). Texas law makes it a misdemeanor for a front-seat passenger in a car equipped with seatbelts not to

▪ *Atwater v. City of Lago Vista*, 532 U.S. 318 (2001)

FIGURE 4.3 Summary of Arrest Warrant Requirements

1. When an arrest warrant is required:
   a. In a home/residence absent exigent circumstances
   b. In a third-party home; a separate search warrant is also required
2. When an arrest warrant is not required:
   a. In public, regardless of whether the offense was committed in the officer's presence
   b. If one or more of the following exigencies is in place:
      (1) hot pursuit
      (2) danger to officers
      (3) danger to third parties
      (4) possible escape
      (5) possible destruction of evidence

wear the seatbelt. The law states that the police may arrest or issue only a citation to the passenger. Atwater was arrested and later filed suit under Section 1983, arguing that the officer violated her Fourth Amendment rights. In the Court's words, "Atwater has cited no particular evidence that those who framed and ratified the Fourth Amendment sought to limit peace officers' warrantless misdemeanor arrest authority to instances of actual breach of the peace, and the Court's review of framing-era documentary history has likewise failed to reveal any such design" (p. 336).

On its face, *Atwater* seems to be a controversial case. On closer examination, though, the decision is likely to have little impact on criminal procedure. The reason for this is, simply, that it is unpractical (and usually undesirable) to arrest people for violations as trivial as failing to wear a seatbelt. Just because the Court has now said that such warrantless arrests do not violate the Fourth Amendment does not mean that the police will alter their behavior consistent with the *Atwater* decision.

Arrests for Offenses Committed Out of an Officer's Presence

The courts have stated that if probable cause exists, the police can arrest anyone for any offense, as long as the arrest is made in a public place. It is useful, though, to distinguish between (1) various types of offenses and (2) whether the offense in question was committed in the presence of the officer. Generally, any offense committed in an officer's presence permits an arrest. Also, there is no requirement that the offense for which a person is arrested be "closely related" to the conduct that led to the confrontation between officer and suspect (*Devenpeck v. Alford*, 543 U.S. 146 [2004]). Additionally, serious offenses (felonies) committed *out* of the officer's view permit a warrantless, public arrest—provided that probable cause exists. Less clear is the issue of a warrantless, public arrest for a misdemeanor committed out of the officer's presence.

In *Welsh v. Wisconsin* (466 U.S. 740 [1984]), a case covered in more detail in Chapter 5, the Supreme Court frowned on the warrantless arrest of a suspect in his home for what the Court perceived to be a relatively minor offense. Also significant (though not mentioned in the Court's opinion in *Welsh*) was that the offense took place out of the officers' presence. What, then, of minor offenses committed in public and out of the view of the police? Generally, the courts do not favor arrest of a person for a minor offense committed out of the view of a police officer.

Executing an Arrest Warrant

Assuming a valid warrant is in place, the police cannot use any means available to effect the arrest. For example, they cannot kick in a door without having any reason to do so. Similarly, they cannot use deadly force unless absolutely necessary and for the most dangerous of criminal offenders. In almost all cases, the procedures for executing an arrest warrant are laid out in police department policy manuals. One such policy from the Gallatin, Tennessee, Police Department is reprinted in Figure 4.4 (page 112).

The following subsections focus on two important issues with regard to the service of arrest warrants: (1) when the police are required to "knock and announce" their presence and (2) when deadly force can be used. A later section discusses the consequences of arresting the wrong person.

The Announcement Requirement

Under common law, the police were entitled to break into a house to make an arrest after announcing their presence and their reason for being there. Today, the method of entry the police can use to serve warrants (arrest and search) is usually set forth in legislation.

9.2.2 Arrest with Warrant(s)

As much as is reasonably possible, an arrest warrant will be served in an order that will most protect life and property in the community. This will usually be in the order of urgency, such as mental detainers, felonies, criminal misdemeanors, traffic, and others.

9.2.3 Arrest Warrant Requirements

When executing a warrant, an officer must be especially diligent in identifying the person to be arrested as the person named in the warrant. This is important in cases where the suspect claims not to be the person wanted. An officer will also determine if the warrant is good on its face. When in doubt, an officer must utilize simple and direct means of verifying identification when such means exist. At a minimum, an officer will contact Communications to establish if the warrant is still outstanding prior to serving. If the warrant cannot be verified, it should be returned to Records with an explanation attached.

In order for a warrant to be valid, it must be signed by the issuing magistrate, along with his/her title, have the date issued, name of the court to which it is to be returned, name and description of the defendant, and name of the complainant.

Source: From *General Directives Manual,* Gallatin, Tennessee, Police Department (December 28, 1999). Used courtesy of the Gallatin Police Department.

With regard to federal law enforcement, for example, 18 U.S.C. Section 3109 states that an officer "may break open any outer or inner door or window of a house . . . to execute a search warrant, if, after notice of his authority and purpose, he is refused admittance."

Almost without exception, the law requires that police officers announce their presence and state their authority (e.g., "Police officers! Search warrant!"). Doing so is important for several reasons: (1) it helps avoid needless destruction of property; (2) it helps prevent violence resulting from unnecessary surprise; and (3) it helps preserve people's dignity and privacy. Of course, in certain situations, these reasons for a "**knock and announce**" **requirement** do not serve their intended purposes. In fact, the second reason can work opposite from what is intended: If the police are required to announce their presence for all manner of suspects, such an announcement could *result* in violence, rather than reduce the possibility for it. What, then, are the criteria for determining when a "knock and announce" is not required? It is useful to turn to Supreme Court precedent to answer this question.

The first cases in which the Court addressed the constitutionality of the commonlaw knock and announce requirement were *Ker v. California* (374 U.S. 23 [1963]) and *Wilson v. Arkansas* (514 U.S. 927 [1995]). The Court was most vocal on the issue in *Wilson.* In that case, Wilson had conducted several narcotics transactions with an informant over a period of several months. Based on the informant's information about those transactions, police officers obtained an arrest warrant for Wilson as well as a search warrant for her home. When the officers arrived at Wilson's residence, they identified themselves and declared that they had a warrant *as they entered the home through an unlocked door.* They did not knock and wait for an answer. In addition to finding evidence, the officers found Wilson in the bathroom, flushing marijuana down the toilet. At her trial, Wilson moved to suppress the evidence collected by the officers on the grounds that the search was invalid because the officers did not follow the common-law "knock and announce" requirement before entering her home to serve the warrants. The Supreme Court ruled that the officers *were* required to follow the "knock and announce" requirement. According to the Court, "An examination of the common law of search and seizure . . . leaves no doubt that the reasonableness of a search of a dwelling may depend in part on whether law enforcement officers announce their presence and authority prior to entering" (p. 931).

■ *Ker v. California,*
374 U.S. 23 (1963)

The Supreme Court later clarified its position in the case of *Richards v. Wisconsin* (520 U.S. 385 [1997]). There, the Court held that police can dispense with the "knock and announce" requirement if they have *reasonable suspicion* that such a requirement "would be dangerous or futile, or that it would inhibit the effective investigation of the crime by, for example, allowing the destruction of evidence" (p. 394). Basically, then, if the police have reasonable suspicion to believe that exigent circumstances are present, they do not necessarily have to knock on the door and announce their presence.

In *Ker v. California* (374 U.S. 23 [1963], the case predating *Wilson*, Justice Brennan offered guidance concerning the link between exigent circumstances and the common-law "knock and announce" requirement:

> [T]he Fourth Amendment is violated by an unannounced police intrusion into a private home, with or without an arrest warrant, except (1) where the persons within already know of the officers' authority and purpose, or (2) where the officers are justified in the belief that persons within are in imminent peril of bodily harm, or (3) where those within, made aware of the presence of someone outside (because, for example, there has been a knock at the door), are then engaged in activity which justifies the officers in the belief that an escape or the destruction of evidence is being attempted. (p. 47)

DECISION MAKING EXERCISE 4.7

A Properly Served Arrest Warrant?

DEA agents and county police officers executed a search warrant at a drug dealer's house. In executing the warrant, the agents and officers gathered on the back porch of the house, knocked on the back door, yelled "Police, arrest warrant!" several times, and then broke down the door. During the search that followed, the officers seized a fully loaded revolver, 150 vials of cocaine, and cash in excess of $27,000. Did this action comport with the federal "knock and announce" requirement enunciated in 18 U.S.C. Section 3109, which states that officers "may break open any outer or inner door or window of a house . . . to execute a search warrant, if, after notice of his authority and purpose, he is refused admittance"?

It is critical that when an announcement is required, police officers announce their authority *and* their intentions. This came to light in *Miller v. United States* (357 U.S. 301 [1958]). In that case, police officers arrived at Miller's apartment at 3:45 a.m. without a warrant but for the purpose of arresting Miller. One of the officers knocked on Miller's door. When Miller asked who it was, the officers did nothing more than answer "Police." Miller then opened the door slightly, as it was secured by a chain, and inquired as to the officers' intentions. At that point, Miller attempted to close the door, but one of the officers reached through the opening and disconnected the chain. The officers then entered the apartment and arrested Miller. The Supreme Court ultimately reversed Miller's conviction on the grounds that the officers never adequately announced their intention to arrest Miller.

In a recent case (*United States v. Banks*, 540 U.S. 31 [2003]), the Supreme Court considered how long the police should wait after announcing their presence and intentions. In that case, police served a warrant by first knocking on the door and then calling out "Police, search warrant." They waited 15 to 20 seconds and, after getting no response, broke down the door with a battering ram. The Supreme Court upheld this action, arguing that the 15- to 20-second wait—coupled with the announcement—was sufficient. The Court did *not*, however, require that police always wait 15 to 20 seconds before entering.

Property Damage

■ *Sabbath v. United States,* 391 U.S. 585 (1968)

In *Sabbath v. United States* (391 U.S. 585 [1968]), the Supreme Court focused on the extent to which police officers can *break and enter* for the purpose of serving a warrant. In particular, the Court focused on the part of 18 U.S.C. Section 3109 that permits officers to "break open an outer door or window." In *Sabbath*, police officers enlisted the help of a man named Jones, whom they had caught trying to smuggle drugs into the country, to apprehend Sabbath, the man who was to receive the shipment of drugs. Jones agreed to deliver the drugs to Sabbath while the police looked on. After Jones entered the apartment, the officers knocked on the door. Not hearing a response, the officers opened the unlocked door, entered the apartment with guns drawn, and arrested Sabbath. The court of appeals affirmed Sabbath's conviction on the grounds that because the officers did not enter by force, the knock and announce requirement of Section 3109 was not triggered.

The Supreme Court disagreed with this reasoning, however, and reversed Sabbath's conviction. According to the Court, "An unannounced intrusion into a dwelling—what Section 3109 basically proscribes—is no less an unannounced intrusion whether officers break down a door, force open a chain lock on a partially open door, open a locked door by use of a passkey, or, as here, open a closed but unlocked door" (p. 590). This case seems to suggest that whether physical damage to the premises is inflicted is immaterial. Instead, what is important is merely that officers knock and announce their presence.

In cases in which physical damage to the premises *is* significant, even excessive, the Fourteenth Amendment enters in. As this chapter indicates, the service of arrests warrants (and, by extension, search warrants) is governed by the Fourth Amendment. However, some *attempts* to seize people are governed by the Fourteenth Amendment's due process clause. This was the unanimous holding in *County of Sacramento v. Lewis* (523 U.S. 833 [1998]). In that case, a police officer ran over the passenger on a motorcycle, killing her, while pursuing the driver. This was another case that arrived at the Supreme Court by way of a civil lawsuit.

The Court held that since a stop had not occurred (see the discussion of *California v. Hodari D.* in the previous chapter), the Fourth Amendment was not implicated. Instead, the Court held that the Fourteenth Amendment's due process clause was relevant because it protects citizens from arbitrary government action. The Court went on to note that had the police conduct in *Lewis* "shocked the conscience," then the police would have been liable. The Court observed that "[w]hile prudence would have repressed the [officer's] reaction, the officer's instinct was to do his job as a law enforcement officer, not to induce [the driver of the motorcycle's] lawlessness, or to terrorize, cause harm, or kill" (p. 855).

Applying *Lewis* to the service of warrants, complaints about excessively destructive police conduct during the service of warrants are also governed by the Fourteenth Amendment. If the police's conduct shocks the conscience, then they may be liable under the due process clause. But there is no easy way to define what conduct shocks the conscience. At least one case has suggested that when police officers show "deliberate or reckless indifference," their conduct can be seen as conscience shocking (see *Estelle v. Gamble*, 429 U.S. 97 [1976]).

Permissible Degree of Force

It is appropriate at this juncture to consider what level of force is permitted against people who are the targets of arrest warrants. Almost every state has a law or regulation concerning police use of force. The American Law Institute adopted just one such regulation, which resembles many others in place around the United States. Section 120.7 states that a police officer "may use such force as is reasonably necessary to effect the arrest, to enter premises to effect the arrest, or to prevent the escape from custody of an arrested person." Further, **deadly force** is authorized when the crime in question is a felony and when such force "creates no substantial risk to innocent persons" and the officer reasonably believes that there is a substantial risk that the fleeing felon will inflict harm on other people or police officers.

In *Tennessee v. Garner* (471 U.S. 1 [1985])—which involved the shooting death of a young, unarmed, fleeing felon—the Supreme Court adopted a rule similar to the American Law Institute's formulation. The result was the leading Supreme Court precedent concerning the use of deadly force to apprehend fleeing felons. The *Garner* decision declared unconstitutional a Tennessee statute that authorized police officers who give notice of the intent to arrest to "use all the necessary means to effect the arrest" if the suspect flees or resists.

> ■ *Tennessee v. Garner,*
> 471 U.S. 1 (1985)

The Court ruled that deadly force may be used when (1) it is necessary to prevent the suspect's escape and (2) the officer has probable cause to believe the suspect poses a serious threat of death or serious physical injury to other people or police officers. One would think that the Supreme Court would be unanimous in a decision such as this, but three justices dissented, noting that the statute struck down by the majority "assist[s] the police in apprehending suspected perpetrators of serious crimes and provide[s] notice that a lawful police order to stop and submit to arrest may not be ignored with impunity" (p. 28).

> **DECISION MAKING EXERCISE 4.8**
>
> **Deadly Force beyond Present Dangerousness**
>
> *Garner* seems to be concerned with *present dangerousness*. That is, police officers contemplating the use of deadly force have to consider, among other factors, how dangerous the suspect is before resorting to deadly force. But what if the suspect committed the crime days or even months earlier? Can the police use deadly force to apprehend, say, an unarmed, fleeing individual who is the suspect in a weeks-old robbery?

Four years after *Garner*, the Supreme Court decided the landmark case of *Graham v. Connor* (490 U.S. 386 [1989]), which set the standard for **nondeadly force**. The Court declared emphatically that *all* claims involving allegations of excessive force against police officers must be analyzed under the Fourth Amendment's reasonableness requirement. Further, the Court adopted a test of objective reasonableness to decide when excessive force is used. This requires focusing on what a *reasonable* police officer would do "without regard to [the officer's] underlying intent or motivation." In determining what a reasonable police officer would do, the Court looked to three factors: (1) the severity of the crime; (2) whether the suspect posed a threat; and (3) whether the suspect was resisting and/or attempting to flee the scene. Courts must, in focusing on these three factors, allow "for the fact that police officers are often forced to make split-second judgments—about the amount of force that is necessary in a particular situation" (p. 386). Generally, then, if the crime in question is a serious one and the suspect is dangerous and resists arrest, then he or she will have difficulty succeeding with an excessive force claim.

> ■ *Graham v. Connor,*
> 490 U.S. 386 (1989)

Incidentally, both the *Garner* and *Graham* decisions resulted from Section 1983 lawsuits (see Chapter 2). Garner's surviving family members and Graham himself both sued on the grounds that their constitutional rights were violated. Whereas many of the cases examined in this book focus on the evidence of crimes (e.g., weapons, drugs, confessions, etc.), *Garner* and *Graham* do not. How evidence was obtained was not at issue because there was none. Thus, the only remedy available to Garner's family and Graham was *civil litigation*.

Garner and *Graham* are both necessarily general. States, cities, and counties around the country have adopted more restrictive guidelines for their officers concerning the use of force. To illustrate, the San Bernardino, California, Police Department's policy on use of force is reprinted in Figure 4.5 (page 116).

Arresting the Wrong Person

On occasion, the police have a warrant to arrest someone but end up arresting the wrong person. The most obvious consequence of arresting the wrong person is that he or she

Purpose

To provide guidelines and parameters for police personnel concerning their use of less than lethal force to accomplish their lawful duties and objectives.

Policy

Police personnel have a duty and responsibility to use the appropriate amount of force to protect themselves and the public from assaultive criminal behavior. However, the amount of force used must be both necessary and reasonable. Personnel shall use only that amount of force which reasonably appears necessary based upon articulable facts and the totality of circumstances known to personnel at the time of the event. Personnel should choose the appropriate force response to overcome active resistance or aggressive behavior. Therefore, personnel should be reasonable in their actions and demonstrate good common sense when employing force.

The primary objective in the application of force is to ensure control of a resistant or combative subject with the minimal amount of force necessary. No specific guidelines or policies can apply to all situations; therefore, personnel should be constantly evaluating all force applications. The use of force will either escalate or de-escalate based upon the totality of circumstances during the course of an arrest or detention.

The scale of force options in order of increasing severity are: verbal persuasion, compliance control techniques, intermediate force (chemical agents, lateral vascular neck restraint, or electronic disabling devices), and impact weapons. It is not necessary for personnel to exercise each option before escalating to the next level of force but flexibility is essential to maintain control during the dynamics of a physical confrontation.

When choosing a particular force option, these factors should be taken into consideration:

1. The severity of the crime/s involved or suspected.
2. The conduct/behavior of the subject/s being confronted.
3. Whether the subject/s poses an immediate threat to the officer/s or others.

4. Does the subject/s have, use, or display a weapon.
5. The proximity of weapons.
6. Officer/suspect factors (age, physical size, relative strength, skill level, injury/exhaustion, number of officer/s versus number of suspect/s).
7. Influence of drugs or alcohol.
8. Potential for injury to bystanders.
9. Availability of other options.
10. Other exigent circumstances.

Procedure

Personnel shall only possess that equipment authorized or issued by the department. Only those defensive tactics or arrest control techniques authorized by or instructed by department personnel or other authorized persons are permitted excluding exigent circumstances. The level of force utilized should be that level which would quickly, safely, and humanely bring a resisting subject under physical control. Personnel should employ escalating scale of force options in order of increasing severity to overcome the subject/s resistance.

1. Scale of Force

   A. Persuasion
      The presence of a confident uniformed police officer displaying professional demeanor coupled with good verbal communication will generally convince a resistant subject to submit to your authority without the necessity of an escalation in force. Good verbalization may be advising, admonishing, warning, or persuading a subject to submit to your authority without the use of profanity or derogatory language. Officers should use their verbal techniques to deescalate confrontations.

   B. Compliance Control Techniques
      Compliance techniques consist of the physical application of force in the form of handcuffing, joint manipulations, blocks, pain compliance, and takedowns. These empty handed techniques should be coupled with a police officer's verbal commands.

Source: Chapter 35, Procedure 1, "Use of Force," from *Standard Operating Procedure*, San Bernardino, California, Police Department (rev. July 16, 2002). Used courtesy of the San Bernardino Police Department.

must be let go (and will possibly file a lawsuit). What the courts have focused on, though, is the admissibility of *evidence* resulting from a wrongful arrest. An example of such a situation would be one in which the police serve an arrest warrant at the wrong house and, during the course of arresting the wrong person, discover evidence of another crime. To what extent would such evidence be admissible? It depends on the reasonableness of the police action.

In *Hill v. California* (401 U.S. 797 [1971]), the Supreme Court focused on an arrest of the wrong person. In that case, the police arrived at Hill's apartment to arrest him, but Miller answered the door. Since Miller fit Hill's description, the police arrested Miller.

C. Intermediate Force
1. Chemical Agents
Police personnel may use chemical agents as an intermediate level of force for controlling or subduing combative persons. Chemical agents are defensive control weapons to be used to control or subdue subjects who are physically resisting arrest. Chemical agents should not be used indiscriminately and shall not be used against noncombative persons. It should not be used against a subject who is under restraint unless that subject is physically assaulting officers or others.
2. Lateral Vascular Neck Restraint
The lateral vascular neck restraint (LVNR) is a means of subduing physically combative persons. This technique is a method which permits personnel to apprehend violent subjects who cannot be controlled or restrained with compliance or control holds.
3. Taser
The electronic disabling device (taser) is a device which may be used to subdue physically combative person/s in violent or potentially violent situations lessening the injury to the subject/s or officers involved. The taser may be used if other apprehension methods or restraints have failed or are deemed impractical and there is a reasonable expectation that it would be hazardous for personnel to approach and physically contact the subject/s.

D. Impact Weapons
Impact weapons are methods of subduing physically combative persons or immediately impeding the threatening actions of a violently resistant subject with physical strikes to the subject's body. These physical strikes shall be directed to those areas which are easily accessible, effective for quickly subduing the subject/s, and unlikely to cause serious injury. Other self defense techniques, kicks or arm strikes, can be used if the officer's baton is unavailable. Other authorized police equipment may be used as an impact weapon in exigent circumstances.

2. Reporting the Use of Force
Any physical use of force by personnel of this department shall be documented in an appropriate report depending upon the nature of the incident. When a use of force greater than a compliance control technique occurs, personnel shall promptly make an oral report to their watch commander or supervisor. Personnel shall note the name of the supervisor notified in their report; however, supervisory notification shall be made immediately following the application of any force which has caused physical injury or complaint of pain.

Medical assistance shall be obtained for subjects who have sustained injury, expressed a complaint of pain, or who have been rendered unconscious.

Any supervisor notified of a use of force incident greater than a compliance control technique *shall* generate a Use of Force report to be forwarded to the appropriate division commander. The Use of Force report will be completed on the department approved form. The supervisor will forward all corresponding documentation with the use of force report.

Each Use of Force report will be distributed to the appropriate area or unit commander (lieutenant) for review. The area or unit commander will review the Use of Force report to make a determination whether the use of force is consistent with department policy and training. The area or unit commander will generate a staff report with his/her findings for the division commander.

When a officer uses physical force greater than a compliance control technique, or a subject complains of pain, or there is a visible injury; the officer shall ensure that photographs are taken of the injured subject.

When a subject/s is hospitalized or receives a serious injury due to a use of force incident, the watch commander will notify the officer's division commander and the Internal Affairs Unit.

Miller even provided identification to prove that he was not Hill, but the Court stated that "aliases and false identifications are not uncommon" (p. 803). A pistol and ammunition clip were in plain view. These were admitted into evidence, and the Supreme Court focused on their admissibility. The Court ruled that the police could have reasonably believed that Miller was Hill. Furthermore, the Court pointed out that "sufficient probability, not certainty, is the touchstone of reasonableness under the Fourth Amendment and on the record before us the officers' mistake was understandable and the arrest a reasonable response to the situation facing them at the time" (p. 803).

■ SEARCHES WITH WARRANTS

Searches with warrants are subjected to many of the same restrictions that arrests with warrants are. However, because the purpose of obtaining a search warrant is to search for something, as opposed to seizing a person, the courts have placed significant restrictions on what the police can do when searching for evidence with warrants. Just because a warrant is obtained does not mean that the police can look anywhere and take unlimited time to search for the item(s) named in the warrant.

FIGURE 4.6   Example of a Search Warrant Policy

9.7.5 Search Warrants

For the purposes of the Gallatin Police Department, *Search Warrant* will be defined as an order in writing, signed by a judicial authority, and directed to a law enforcement officer, commanding him/her to search for described personal property at a specific location and to bring such property before said judicial authority.

The primary objectives of a search warrant, as defined herein, may be to obtain the following:

1. *Fruits of a crime*: Items that have been stolen or embezzled;

2. *Instruments of a crime*: Items such as weapons, tools, and such other items which have been used in the commission of a crime;

3. *Contraband*: Items whose mere possession is a violation of law; and/or

4. *Mere evidence of a crime*: Items that tend to connect the accused with the commission of the crime.

Before any search warrant may be issued, a signed, sworn statement (affidavit) must be filed with a judicial authority, or a statement under oath must be taken by a judicial authority, from the officer or other witness, and reduced to writing and signed by the officer seeking the warrant. The statement must set out the underlying facts which establish "probable cause" for believing that the property sought is in the place to be searched and is of the type or kind which may be seized. If necessary, affidavits of other witnesses may be presented to the judicial authority in order to establish "probable cause."

In the affidavit itself, the officer making the affidavit, the affiant, must set out all the facts, in detail, upon which he/she is relying to establish probable cause. The facts set out in the affidavit must be detailed enough to enable judicial authority to make an independent determination that there are sufficient grounds to support the issuance of the search warrant.

In the event an officer makes his/her affidavit based upon information received from an informant, it will be necessary to state that the information was received from an informant. In such instances, the affidavit must contain some statement as to why the informant's information should be considered credible. In other words, the affidavit must contain some statement by the officer that information given by the informant in the past has been true and correct or that the officer has corroborating evidence.

A search warrant must specifically state the location and a description of the premises to be searched. This should be done so that an officer not familiar with the case will be able to find and identify the location. A search warrant must also specifically describe the property for which the search is being made. This will prevent the officer from indiscriminately seizing items and ensure that the officer knows what to search for.

9.7.6 Search Warrant Executions

It is the policy of this law enforcement agency to:

1. Provide techniques to accomplish a thorough and legal search;

2. Observe the constitutional rights of the person(s) the warrant is being served upon;

3. Minimize the level of intrusion experienced by those who are having their premises searched;

4. Provide for the highest degree of safety for all persons concerned; and

5. Establish a record of the entire execution process.

For the purposes of this section of the Manual, the following definitions will apply.

1. A *Search Site* is the premises or person to be searched, as explicitly stated in the search warrant.

2. *Search Personnel* are law enforcement officers and supporting personnel taking part in the execution of a search warrant.

3. An *Evidence Collector* is a member of the search team responsible for the possession, packaging, sealing, and marking of all items seized.

4. The *Supervisor* is a supervising officer within the Department.

When a search warrant is to be executed, the search team will include the officer to whom the warrant is addressed and at least one uniformed officer. All non-uniformed officers will be clearly identified as law enforcement officers by wearing a distinctive armband, jacket, or some other indicator of office. All members of the search team will wear body armor, a safety holster, and a departmentally-issued firearm for the duration of the search warrant execution.

A search warrant will be executed and returned to the issuing magistrate within five days of its issuance, as stated

Source: From *General Directives Manual*, Gallatin, Tennessee, Police Department (December 28, 1999). Used courtesy of the Gallatin Police Department.

Executing a Search Warrant

Two specific issues arose with regard to the *service* of arrest warrants: (1) whether the police were required to knock and announce their presence and (2) whether the police could use force to effect an arrest.

The "knock and announce" requirement, discussed earlier, carries over to the service of search warrants. As indicated before, the police do not have to announce their presence if they have reasonable suspicion that exigent circumstances are present.

in Tennessee Code Annotated. Circumstances that may necessitate a delay in executing a search warrant include, but are not limited to:

1. The need to have many searches occur at the same time, which requires coordination and mobilization of law enforcement resources.

2. The seizable items have not arrived at the search site.

3. The probability that substantial resistance will be encountered.

4. A particular person(s) is absent from the search site, and the supervisory officer feels that the search would best be conducted if that person were present.

5. The need to protect an informant's identity.

It is to be stressed that absent court approval, necessity, or authorization by law, a search warrant will be executed during daylight hours.

Prior to entering the premises, the supervisory officer will conduct a pre-entry briefing of the execution process with all search team personnel. The briefing will include a review of the actual order of operations and procedures the search personnel will follow, a simulation of the conditions of the search site (using maps, charts, and diagrams, when appropriate), and tactics and equipment to be used in the event of forced entry. The supervisory officer will also attempt to determine if any circumstances have changed which make executing the search warrant at that time undesirable. Finally, the supervisory officer will ensure that the entire search warrant execution process is documented, from beginning to end, and continued until the search team leaves the premises. This documentation will include, but is not limited to, every officer using a tape recorder to record his/her verbal contacts during the search; a written record supported by photographs, and; when practical, a videotaping of the entire search site from start to finish.

On approaching the scene where the search warrant is to be executed, the approach will be conducted without use of sirens or emergency lights. If a pre-execution surveillance team is on the scene, radio contact will be made to ensure that it is an appropriate time to serve the search warrant. Prior to arriving on the scene, the supervisory officer should examine the search warrant to ensure its validity and that the property about to be searched is the property listed on the warrant. The supervisory officer will also ensure that the entry

is tape-recorded. For the purposes of entry into the structure that is to be searched, search personnel will position themselves in the following manner:

1. All exits from the premises will be covered;

2. When feasible, uniformed officers will be the most visible members of the search team and will announce the search warrant; and

3. Non-uniformed officers will be the last officers to enter the search site.

Notification of the warrant to inhabitants of the structure will be conducted by a uniformed officer when practical. The officer will speak in a voice loud enough to be heard inside the premises, state that he/she is a police officer, has a warrant to search the premises, and demands entry to the premises immediately. In the event that the officer is refused entry after giving notice of his/her authority and purpose, and that entry will be made by force if necessary, forced entry will be made. It should be noted that "no-knock entries," where an announcement of the officers' presence *is not made* prior to the entry, are only permitted when previously authorized by a judge. Whenever forced entry is made, it will be done so as to cause as little damage as possible. If damage occurs during an entry to premises that will be left vacant, and the damage may leave the premises vulnerable to security problems, arrangements will be made to guard the premises until it can be secured. If any damage occurs at any time during the search, a report will be prepared by the Shift Commander on the actions that caused the damage and a detailed description of the nature and extent of the damage.

During the execution of the search warrant, the supervisory officer will ensure that a security sweep of the search site is conducted by other officers and/or himself/herself. After the search site has been secured, search personnel will develop a prioritized strategy that details the likely whereabouts of the items to be seized and an order of operation for conducting the search. One person will be designated as responsible for collecting, preserving, and documenting all items seized until possession is transferred to the evidence custodian.

A search warrant must be executed and returned to the issuing authority within five days after it was issued, to the hour. The returned warrant must state any property that was seized. If a search warrant is not executed and returned within five days, it is void, and any search conducted would be illegal.

Use of force is rarely an issue that arises during the service of a search warrant because, strictly speaking, a search warrant authorizes the police to look for evidence. If a person gets in the way during the service of a search warrant, however, he or she may be arrested and force may be applied, if need be (i.e., subject to the restrictions discussed earlier).

Finally, if the police mistakenly search the wrong residence, the search will not automatically be declared invalid. As pointed out earlier, as long as the mistake is a reasonable one, any evidence seized during a search of the wrong residence will be admissible in a criminal trial. The key, however, is that the mistake must be an *objectively reasonable* one, gauged from the standpoint of a reasonable officer.

In addition to the "knock and announce" requirement, several issues are relevant to the service of a search warrant: (1) time restrictions, both for when the warrant can be served and for how long the police can look for evidence; (2) the scope and manner of the search; (3) the procedure after the service of the search warrant; and, most recently, (4) the presence of the media during the service of a search warrant. To illustrate the complexity inherent in search warrant procedure, the Gallatin, Tennessee, Police Department's search warrant policy is reprinted in Figure 4.6 (pages 118–119).

It is important to note that the police can sometimes request a search warrant with special instructions, which can include night service, no knock authorization, and the like. An example of the face sheet for a special instructions warrant from the state of California is reprinted in Figure 4.7.

Time Constraints

There are three means by which the courts impose time constraints on the police when it comes to the service of search warrants. First, the service of a search warrant should take place promptly after its issuance. Clearly, probable cause could dissipate if an excessive amount of time elapses between the time the warrant is issued and the time it is served. To avoid this potential problem, a warrant will sometimes specify that the search be conducted within a certain period of time.

A second time restriction that is occasionally imposed pertains to the time of day. Judges commonly restrict the service of warrants to the daytime hours or at least favor daytime service (see *Gooding v. United States*, 416 U.S. 430 [1974]). The *Federal Rules of Criminal Procedure*, for example, restrict the service of warrants to daytime hours, unless the issuing judge specifically authorizes execution at another time. *Daytime hours*, according to the *Federal Rules*, are between the hours of 6:00 a.m. and 10:00 p.m.

▪ *Gooding v. United States,* 416 U.S. 430 (1974)

DECISION MAKING EXERCISE **4.9**

Defining Daytime

On August 26, at approximately 7:30 p.m., the Sunny County Sheriff's Department executed a search warrant on the premises of 5678 Cherry Lane. The defendants later argued that the search warrant and its execution were defective because the warrant directed that it be executed during the *daytime*. In fact, the warrant was executed at approximately 7:30 p.m., and sunset occurred at 6:43 p.m., according to the National Weather Service. Given this, was the warrant therefore defective?

The third time restriction concerns how long the police can search for evidence. The general rule is that a search cannot last indefinitely. Once the item in the warrant has been discovered, the search must be terminated. If the police have difficulty finding the item or items named in the warrant, they can take as long as necessary to find them. If the police do not succeed in finding the evidence named in the warrant and then leave and come back later, they will be required to obtain another warrant. Steps should always be taken to avoid the appearance of arbitrariness, and people's Fourth Amendment privacy interests should always be respected.

FIGURE 4.7   *Example of a Special Instructions Warrant*

SUPERIOR COURT OF CALIFORNIA
County of _____

SEARCH WARRANT
◆ Special Instructions ◆

THE PEOPLE OF THE STATE OF CALIFORNIA to: Warrant No. _____
Any peace officer in _____ **County**
The affidavit filed herewith by _____, sworn to and subscribed before me, has established probable cause for this warrant which you are ordered to execute as follows:

Place(s) to be searched: Described in Exhibit 1A, *attached* hereto and incorporated by reference.

Property to be seized: Described in Exhibit 1B, attached hereto and incorporated by reference.

Disposition of property: All property seized pursuant to this search warrant shall be retained in the affiant's custody pending further court order pursuant to Penal Code §§ 1528(a), 1536.

◆ SPECIAL INSTRUCTIONS ◆

The Statement of Probable Cause, filed herewith, has demonstrated legal justification for the following special procedures which are authorized if checked:

☐ **Night Service:** This warrant may be served at any hour of the day or night.

☐ **No Knock Authorization:** Compliance with Penal Code § 1531 is excused *unless* a change in circumstances negates the need for non-compliance.

☐ **Special Master:** The search shall be conducted by a Special Master pursuant to Penal Code §§ 1524(c)-(g). The Special Master shall be _____.

☐ **Sealing Order:** The following documents shall be sealed and delivered into the custody of the Clerk of the Superior Court pending further court order: ☐ All documents filed herewith. ☐ Documents listed in Exhibit 2. Grounds for sealing: ☐ Informant protection (Evid. Code § 1041) ☐ Official information (Evid. Code § 1040)

☐ **Nondisclosure Order:** The financial institution served with this warrant, including its employees and agents, shall not disclose any information regarding its content, existence, or execution pending further court order.

☐ **Blood draw:** (Not for HIV testing per Penal Code § 1524.1): A blood sample shall be drawn from the person described in Exhibit 1A by trained medical personnel in accordance with accepted medical practices.

☐ **Anticipatory Warrant:** Having determined that probable cause for this search will exist upon the occurrence of the triggering event(s) described in Exhibit 3, and that there is probable cause said triggering event(s) will occur, this warrant shall be executed promptly after said triggering event(s) occur. Exhibit 3 is *attached* hereto and incorporated by reference.

☐ **Covert Warrant:** The property described in Exhibit 1B shall not be removed from the premises. An inventory shall be prepared showing the location of all such property discovered on the premises. Said property shall be photographed or videotaped to show its location when discovered. Compliance with the receipt requirements of Penal Code § 1535 is excused until _____ unless an extension is granted by this court. [Initial compliance date must not be more than 7 days following execution of the warrant.] Within two days after executing this warrant, the following shall be filed with this court: (1) the inventory, and (2) the original or copy of all photographs and/or videotape recordings made during the execution of this warrant.

☐ **Additional instructions:** Additional instructions pertaining to this search warrant are contained in Exhibit 4, *attached* hereto and incorporated by reference.

_____   _____
Date and time warrant issued   Judge of the Superior Court

Source: Superior Court of California. Available online:<www.co.alameda.ca.us/da/sw_multi.pdf>.

Scope and Manner of the Search

Two additional restrictions with regard to the service of a search warrant concern the scope and manner of the search. *Scope* refers to where the police can look for evidence. *Manner* refers to the physical steps the police can take to find the evidence in question, including breaking down doors, forcibly opening locked cabinets, and so on.

The scope of the search must be reasonable, based on the object of the search. In other words, the police are restricted in looking for evidence insofar as they can only look where the item could reasonably be found. For example, assume the evidence in question is a stolen diamond ring. Such an item is relatively small, so the police will be authorized to look almost anywhere for the ring. However, if the evidence in question is large in size—for example, a stolen big-screen television set—then the police cannot look in small places, where such an item could not possibly be found. The Supreme Court's statement in *Harris v. United States* (331 U.S. 145 [1947]) provides further clarification: "[T]he same meticulous investigation which would be appropriate in a search for two small canceled checks could not be considered reasonable where agents are seeking a stolen automobile or an illegal still" (p. 152).

■ *Harris v. United States*, 331 U.S. 145 (1947)

The police may also detain people as needed while serving a search warrant. According to the Court in *Michigan v. Summers* (452 U.S. 692 [1981]), "[A] warrant to search for contraband founded on probable cause implicitly carries with it the limited authority to detain the occupants of the premises while a proper search is conducted" (p. 704). Although the police may detain people who are on the premises to be searched, they cannot search the people unless probable cause exists (*Ybarra v. Illinois*, 444 U.S. 85 [1979]). A frisk is permissible, though, as long as the police have a reasonable suspicion that there is a risk to officer safety. If a person does not live on the premises, does not house personal belongings there, and is not a threat, he or she will probably be allowed to leave.

■ *Michigan v. Summers*, 452 U.S. 692 (1981)

DECISION MAKING EXERCISE **4.10**

Where Can Police Reasonably Look?

Sheriff's deputies had a search warrant to look for a rare, stolen koala in the house of the local taxidermist. When serving the warrant, they looked through the kitchen cupboards, wherein they found small baggies of a white, powdery substance as well as a scale. They seized the items and arrested the taxidermist for drug possession. The koala was never found. May the seized items be admitted into evidence? What if the officers had been looking for a stolen circus elephant?

As was discussed in the arrest warrant section, federal law authorizes the police to break open doors and containers if they are refused admittance (18 U.S.C. Section 3109). Still, there are restrictions. Basically, the manner of the search must be limited to what is reasonably necessary to find the evidence in question. The Supreme Court has stated that "[e]xcessive or unnecessary destruction of property in the course of a search may violate the Fourth Amendment, even though the entry itself is lawful and the fruits of the search not subject to suppression" (*United States v. Ramirez*, 523 U.S. 65 [1998], p. 71). Additionally, the occupant of the place searched can be detained—even in handcuffs—for the duration of the search (*Muehler v. Mena*, 125 S.Ct. 1465 [2005]).

Procedure after Service of a Search Warrant

After a search warrant has been served, the police are required to inventory the items that were seized. Doing so not only protects against theft but also helps assure the person whose premises were searched that his or her property has been accounted for. A copy of the inventory is given to the person whose property was searched, and if no one was on the premises during the time of the search, the list must be left at the scene in a prominent place. Also, the police typically have to complete some type of a search record form to be kept on file with the department. An example of such a form from Lexington-Fayette Urban County is reprinted in Figure 4.8.

Interestingly, the police are not required to notify the property owner of the steps necessary for the return of the property or to remedy any perceived constitutional violation (see *City of West Covina v. Perkins*, 525 U.S. 234 [1999]). Also, it is not clear whether *failure* to provide persons whose premises are searched with an inventory of items seized is constitutionally required. The Supreme Court has suggested that failure to do so is a matter of state law (*Cady v. Dombrowski*, 413 U.S. 433 [1973]), not necessarily an issue of constitutional concern.

■ *City of West Covina v. Perkins*, 525 U.S. 234 (1999)

Media Presence

In a recent case, *Wilson v. Layne* (526 U.S. 603 [1999]), the Supreme Court decided whether the police can bring members of the media along during the service of a search warrant. The facts of the case are as follow: Early in the morning on April 16, 1992, deputy U.S. marshals and Montgomery County police officers entered the suspected home of Dominic Wilson. They were joined by a *Washington Post* reporter and a photographer as part of a marshals' service ride-along policy. Dominic's parents were asleep in bed when the officers arrived. They heard the officers enter the home and ran into the living room to investigate the disturbance. A verbal altercation ensued, and both the Wilsons were subdued. Dominic Wilson was never found. Even though the reporter observed what occurred and the photographer took pictures of what transpired, the story was never printed and the pictures were never published. The parents, Charles and Geraldine Wilson, nonetheless brought a *Bivens* action (the Section 1983 counterpart for lawsuits against *federal* officials) against the marshals, alleging the officers violated their Fourth Amendment rights by bringing the media into their home.

■ *Wilson v. Layne*, 526 U.S. 603 (1999)

The case worked its way up through the courts and was ultimately heard by the Supreme Court, which decided that media presence during the service of search warrants violates the Fourth Amendment, as long as the presence serves no "legitimate law enforcement objectives." The Court declared that "it is a violation of the Fourth Amendment for police to bring members of the media or other third parties into a home during the execution of a warrant when the presence of the third parties in the home was not in aid of the execution of the warrant" (p. 614).

Chief Justice Rehnquist, writing for the majority, began by stating that the Fourth Amendment embodies the "centuries-old principle of respect for the privacy of the home" (p. 610). He went on to note that although the law enforcement officers were authorized to enter the Wilsons' home, "it does not necessarily follow that they were entitled to bring a newspaper reporter and photographer with them" (p. 611). The Court then considered whether the actions of both parties—the reporters and the police—were related to the objectives of the intrusion into the Wilsons' home. It ruled that they were not. Since the reporters were in the Wilsons' residence for their own purposes, they "were not present for any reason related to the justification for police entry into the home" (p. 611). However, if media presence *does* serve legitimate law enforcement objectives, then the Fourth Amendment will not be violated.

To many observers, the Court's decision in *Wilson v. Layne* seemed to decide the fate of the so-called reality-based police television shows—and to an extent, it did. The police cannot take a camera crew with them when a search warrant is served. Media accompaniment is still permissible outside people's homes, however. Figure 4.9 provides a summary of the restrictions on the servicing of search warrants. The last sections of this chapter focus on special circumstances that arise in the search warrant context.

FIGURE 4.8 Example of a Search Record Form

SEARCH RECORD — **FORM 349** (1/00)

NAME (L, F, M)

ADDRESS

CITY	STATE	ZIP

ID TYPE STATE	ID NUMBER

DATE OF BIRTH	AGE	SEX	RACE

☐ MALE   ☐ WHITE   ☐ BLACK   ☐ HISPANIC   ☐ ASIAN
☐ FEMALE   ☐ AM.INDIAN/ALASKA   ☐ OTHER

VEH MAKE	MODEL	YEAR	REG STATE	COLOR

REGISTRATION NO.	DATE	TIME	SECTOR/BEAT

EXACT LOCATION OF SEARCH:

SEARCH OF: **CONSENT**
☐ **Person;**   ☐ *pedestrian*   ☐ *driver*   ☐ *occupant*   ☐ No
☐ **Vehicle;**   ☐ *occupied*   ☐ *unoccupied*   ☐ Yes, *Oral*
☐ **Building/Residence**   ☐ Yes, *Written*
☐ **Property**   ☐ **Canine Utilized**

Was Evidence/Contraband located?   ☐ No   ☐ Yes (*specify below*)
Arrest Made?   ☐ No   ☐ Yes   Citation Issued?   ☐ No   ☐ Yes

DETAILS: (Indicate the object of, and grounds for search)

☐ Additional on back

CASE NO.	SUPERVISOR SIGNATURE

OFFICER SIGNATURE	EMPLOYEE NO.	Enter as **F.I.** ☐

FIGURE 4.9   *Summary of Search Warrant Restrictions*

1. Time Constraints
   a. Search must be executed promptly after issuance
   b. Search must be conducted during daylight hours if possible
   c. Search must not last indefinitely
2. Scope and Manner
   a. Search must be based on object sought
   b. Search must avoid causing excessive and unnecessary property damage
   c. Cannot search guests or third parties if probable cause to do so is lacking

---

SPECIAL CIRCUMSTANCES

Electronic surveillance law is something of a creature in and of itself and, as such, does not fit neatly into the discussion of searches with warrants just presented. In addition, important restrictions govern bodily intrusions and civil asset forfeiture, as do the Fourth Amendment's probable cause and warrant requirements. Finally, there are two types of search warrants that differ markedly from the types discussed thus far: (1) administrative search warrants and (2) anticipatory search warrants.

Electronic Surveillance

The term *electronic surveillance* includes a variety of methods for spying on the activities of suspected criminals, including conversations as well as criminal actions. The methods used to spy on criminal suspects are quite diverse and include wiretapping, "bugging," hacking into computer transmissions, tracking movements of persons and equipment, video surveillance, and seeing through opaque surfaces using devices such as thermal imagers and "gun detectors."

   Electronic surveillance law is exceedingly complex and rapidly changing, so a thorough introduction is beyond the scope of this text. However, by focusing some attention

The laws about electronic surveillance are very complex and rapidly changing.

on legislative developments over time, sufficient familiarity can be developed with the general contours of the law in this important area of criminal procedure. The following subsections begin by looking at early legislative requirements in the area of electronic surveillance, then move into Title III of the Omnibus Crime Control and Safe Streets Act of 1968 (and its 1986 amendments), and finally consider the Patriot Act, which was passed following the September 11 terrorist attacks.

Most of the law in this area, especially Title III and the Patriot Act, restricts government interception of private communications. Thus, the bulk of the discussion that follows concerns the use of wiretaps and similar strategies to intercept people's communications. Other types of electronic surveillance—namely, the use of tracking devices, video recorders, and detection devices—are discussed in a separate subsection, as these types of activities are governed mostly by Supreme Court decisions.

The Old Law

Prior to the Supreme Court's decision in *Katz v. United States* (389 U.S. 347 [1967]), the constitutionality of searches and seizures was governed by the so-called trespass doctrine (see Chapter 3). The leading case was *Olmstead v. United States* (277 U.S. 438 [1928]), in which the Court held that a warrantless wiretap was constitutional because it did not "trespass" on the defendant's property. Then, in *Goldman v. United States* (316 U.S. 129 [1942]), the Court upheld the use of a "detectaphone" placed against an office wall because it did not amount to a trespass. But in *Katz v. United States*, the Supreme Court abandoned the trespass doctrine, holding that the appropriate inquiry is whether the law enforcement action in question infringed on a person's reasonable expectation of privacy.

Following *Katz*, the Supreme Court decided *Berger v. New York* (388 U.S. 41 [1967]), in which it decided on the constitutionality of a statute that permitted eavesdropping orders to be issued by magistrates if the police showed reasonable grounds that evidence of a crime would be discovered. The Court declared the statute unconstitutional, holding that a warrant supported by probable cause is necessary to secure permission to intercept people's communications. Importantly, though, *Katz* and *Berger* do not apply to the interception of communications that can be considered consensual, such as when the government plants a listening device on an informant (see *On Lee v. United States*, 343 U.S. 747 [1952]; *Lopez v. United States*, 373 U.S. 427 [1963]).

In addition to being governed by the Supreme Court's decisions in *Olmstead*, *Katz*, and *Berger*, electronic surveillance was also subject to the restrictions in Section 605 of the **Federal Communications Act** of 1934. In it, Congress provided that "no person not being authorized by the sender shall intercept any communication and divulge or publish the existence, contents, purport, effect or meaning of such intercepted communications to any person." However, if the person whose conversation was intercepted consented to the conversation, any resulting evidence would be admissible (see *Rathbun v. United States*, 355 U.S. 107 [1957]). In summary, Supreme Court decisions and Section 605 restricted the surveillance of conversations in which the suspect did not consent to the conversation. Importantly, the suspect did not have to consent to the use of a recording device, only the conversation during which it was used.

Title III of the Omnibus Crime Control and Safe Streets Act of 1968

In 1968, Congress passed **Title III of the Omnibus Crime Control and Safe Streets Act** (18 U.S.C. Sections 2510–20). Then, in 1986, Congress amended the act by passing the **Electronic Communications Privacy Act** (Pub. L. No. 99-508 [1986]). Both acts govern law enforcement electronic surveillance activities at both the federal and state levels. Both acts are of particular importance in the present context because they preempt state laws addressing electronic surveillance. That is, for electronic surveillance to conform to constitutional requirements, it must not only abide by state law but also by the 1968 and 1986 acts. Another federal statute, the Foreign Intelligence and Surveillance Act, also permits certain forms of electronic surveillance, but it is not reviewed here because of space limitations.

Protected Activities

Title III restricts the *interception* of "wire, oral or electronic communications," unless such interception is authorized by statute (see the act for definitions of each). The 1986 amendments to the act added *electronic communications* to the list of protected activities. The amendments also covered the electronic storage and processing of information. In short, both acts protect virtually all wire, oral, and electronic communications among private parties. That is to say, for the government to intercept such information, it must obtain a valid search warrant.

In contrast to communications between private parties, communications among government employees and communications between private parties and the general public are not protected. For example, if an individual posts a message to the World Wide Web, it will not be protected in any way. Also, as discussed earlier, communications that are consensual in nature—such as between a suspect and a government informant—do not come under the protection of Title III or its amendments.

Requirements for Obtaining a Title III Warrant

The requirements for obtaining a Title III warrant go beyond those for obtaining a typical warrant, as discussed earlier in this chapter. First, the application for a Title III warrant must identify both the officer filing and the officer approving the application. Second, the warrant application must contain "a full and complete statement of the facts and circumstances relied upon by the applicant to justify his belief that an order should be issued." Third, the application should contain "a particular description of the nature and location of the facilities from which or the place where the communication is to be intercepted." Fourth, the application must contain a "full and complete statement as to whether or not other investigative procedures have been tried and failed or why they reasonably appear to be unlikely to succeed if tried or to be too dangerous."

Fifth, the application must contain "a statement of the period of time for which the interception is required to be maintained," including, if deemed necessary, "a particular description of facts establishing probable cause to believe that additional communications of the same type will occur" after "the described type of communication has been first obtained." Sixth, the warrant application must contain "a full and complete statement of the facts concerning all previous applications . . . involving any of the same persons, facilities, or places specified in the application, and the action taken by the judge on each such application." Finally, the warrant application must contain "a statement setting forth the results thus far obtained from the interception, or a reasonable explanation of the failure to obtain such results."

If the applying law enforcement officer meets these seven requirements, a Title III warrant will be issued. Judges take four factors into account in determining whether such a warrant will be issued:

1. Whether there is probable cause that an offense is being or has been committed
2. Whether there is probable cause to believe that the communications concerning the offense can be obtained through electronic interception
3. Whether normal investigative procedures have been tried and failed, seem reasonably unlikely to succeed if tried, or are too dangerous
4. Whether there is probable cause to believe that the facilities to be subjected to surveillance are connected with the communications in question

If these four factors are present and are to the judge's satisfaction, he or she will issue a Title III warrant. However, like the warrant application requirements, the contents of a Title III warrant are different than those of a typical warrant, as well. Specifically, a Title III warrant must meet these requirements:

1. Identify the person whose communications are to be intercepted.
2. Describe "the nature and location of the communications facilities as to which, or the place where, authority to intercept is granted."
3. Describe "the type of communications sought to be intercepted, and a statement of the particular offense to which it relates."
4. Identify the person authorizing the application and the agency serving the warrant.
5. Show "that the authorization to intercept shall be executed as soon as practicable."
6. Show "the period of time during which such interception is authorized" and "whether or not the interception shall automatically terminate when the described communication has been first obtained."
7. State that the interception "be conducted in such a way as to minimize the interception of communications not otherwise subject to interception."
8. Possibly "require reports to be made to the judge who issued the order showing what progress has been made toward achievement of the authorized objective and the need for continued interception."

Executing the Warrant and Related Issues

The service of a Title III warrant is subject to the restrictions listed in the previous section (e.g., the service should minimize the possibility of intercepting other communications not specified in the warrant application). In addition, the service of a Title III warrant, as well as the evidence thereby obtained, should be well documented. The act states, for instance, that all interceptions "shall, if possible, be recorded on tape or wire or other comparable device . . . in such way as will protect the recording from editing or other alterations."

When preparing to serve a Title III warrant, authorities can covertly enter the place where the interception is to take place (see *Dalia v. United States*, 441 U.S. 238 [1979]). The entry must be reasonable and not result in excessive property damage. Indeed, too much, if any, property damage would alert that suspect that an investigation is taking place. Also, if the circumstances of the interception change during the course of the investigation, the Title III warrant will need to be amended. For example, if when listening to conversations, the police are alerted to additional criminal conduct that they would like to hear about, they must seek an amendment to the original warrant.

If the requirements set forth above are not satisfied, the remedy is suppression. That is, the exclusionary rule will apply. In fact, Title III has its own set of exclusionary rules, but they are more or less the same as the rule described in Chapter 2. For example, if a Title III warrant fails to describe with particularity the communications to be intercepted, and assuming this is called to the attention of the court, any evidence resulting from the interception will be inadmissible in court. However, if authorities make a reasonable mistake, then the "good faith" exception announced in *Leon* (468 U.S. 897 [1984]) will apply. Also, only those persons who have *standing* (i.e., who can show that the interception infringed on a reasonable expectation of privacy) can succeed in having intercepted communications excluded from trial (see *Alderman v. United States*, 394 U.S. 165 [1969]). Finally, in *United States v. Giordano* (416 U.S. 505 [1974]), the Court held that suppression of evidence is only required when the part of the act that has been violated "was intended to play a central role in the statutory scheme." In other words, trivial violations of the act will not likely result in suppression. For example, if fewer than all of the law enforcement officers involved in the investigation are identified in the warrant, then evidence will not be suppressed (see *United States v. Donovan*, 429 U.S. 413 [1977]).

Tracking Devices, Video Recordings, and Detection Devices

Tracking devices are somewhat different from devices used to intercept people's conversations. One of the more common types of tracking devices, known as a *beeper*, emits a signal that can be tracked by law enforcement officials. Beepers have been around for some time and are relatively crude in terms of their technology. Far more sophisticated types of devices are being developed currently. These newer devices have attracted little attention by the courts, but beepers have. For example, in *United States v. Knotts* (460 U.S. 276 [1983]), federal agents placed a beeper in a container of chloroform in a store without a warrant but with the consent of the store's owner. The container was later picked up, and the police tracked it to a cabin. The officers then obtained a warrant to search the cabin. The Supreme Court upheld their actions, even though they did not obtain a warrant in advance.

A key feature of *Knotts* was that the beeper led the police *to* the cabin, not inside it. When the police use beepers to track persons and items indoors, the story is different. In *United States v. Karo* (468 U.S. 705 [1984]), the police, using a beeper, tracked a suspect's movements *inside* a residence. The beeper was placed inside a can of ether. The Court ruled that this action was a violation of the Fourth Amendment.

Video recordings are another method of conducting electronic surveillance. Whether using such devices requires a warrant depends on whether the recording is of a private or a public place. With regard to private places, video recordings are usually governed, according to certain courts anyway, by Title III of the Omnibus Crime Control and Safe Streets Act of 1968, even though the act does not explicitly refer to video recorders. A key case in this area is *United States v. Torres* (751 F.2d 875 [7th Cir. 1984]). In it, the Federal Bureau of Investigation (FBI) obtained authorization from a judge to place cameras in so-called safehouses used by a Puerto Rican separatist group. The agents followed the guidelines set forth in Title III, and the Seventh Circuit Court of Appeals upheld their actions. Other courts, however, have held that Title III's restrictive guidelines need not apply to video recordings. Rather, they have argued that the traditional Fourth Amendment approach should be used (see, e.g., *United States v. Cuevas-Sanchez*, 821 F.2d 248 [5th Cir. 1987]).

The foregoing does not apply to video cameras in public places. The city of Palm Springs, California, for example, has several video cameras strategically mounted on a busy stretch of road that is a popular place for tourists and locals to congregate. While this may smack of Orwellian society, to date, the use of such cameras has been entirely constitutional. In a similar vein, several cities throughout the United States are using so-called red-light cameras to capture motorists who run red lights. Similar cameras are used to catch speeders, as well. While civil libertarians groan at the increased use of such cameras, they remain an effective law enforcement tool and are not considered unconstitutional.

Finally, detection devices are another method of engaging in what amounts to electronic surveillance. One of these devices, the thermal imager (infrared heat sensor), was discussed in Chapter 3. The Supreme Court decided in *Kyllo v. United States* (533 U.S. 27 [2001]) that a thermal imager cannot be used to scan a private residence without a warrant. Other types of detection devices, such as gun detectors—which can actually help police determine when persons are armed—are being developed, and some are even being used. It will be interesting to see if and when these come to the attention of the Supreme Court, as they almost certainly will.

Enter the Patriot Act

The Patriot Act, passed in 2001, has had greater effects on electronic surveillance law than on any other aspect of criminal procedure. For example, it has amended parts of the Foreign Intelligence Surveillance Act (FISA) to permit surveillance in cases in which foreign intelligence is a significant purpose rather than the only purpose (Pub. L. No. 107-56, 218, 115 Stat. 272, 291 [2001]). This and other changes to FISA have given federal authorities enhanced opportunities to engage in intelligence gathering that is only remotely connected to national security. Naturally, civil libertarians are concerned.

The Patriot Act has also amended FISA to permit wiretap warrants against unspecified persons, and it has increased the time period for FISA warrants from 90 to 120 days for a wiretap order and from 45 to 90 days for a physical search. Moreover, the Patriot Act has given law enforcement more authority to use *pen registers*: devices that record telephone and Internet service provider numbers dialed by a telephone for outgoing communications. The act has also granted more authority for the use of *"trap-and-trace" devices*, which record telephone numbers dialing in to a particular location. With regard to both these devices, the Patriot Act states that they can be used "to obtain foreign intelligence information not concerning a United States person or to protect against international terrorism or clandestine intelligence activities" (Pub. L. No. 107-56, 208, 115 Stat. 272 [2001]). The act also expanded the geographic area in which pen registers and "trap-and-trace" devices can be used.

In addition, the Patriot Act has changed Title III of the Omnibus Crime Control and Safe Streets Act of 1968. It was generally more difficult to get a wiretap order (i.e., a Title III warrant) under Title III than it was under FISA, but the Patriot Act has amended Title III to allow any investigative or law enforcement officer or prosecutor to obtain foreign intelligence information that will help the United States protect itself from terrorism (USA Patriot Act 202, 115 Stat. at 280). Specifically, the Patriot Act has amended Title III to permit wiretap orders for *terrorism* investigations, *chemical weapons* investigations, and *computer fraud and abuse* investigations (Pub. L. No. 107-56, 201–202, 115 Stat. 272, 278 [2001]). Some critics of the Patriot Act have expressed concern that these terms are too broadly defined and thus give law enforcement too much authority.

The Patriot Act has also amended Title III to permit wiretaps of voice-mail messaging systems. In the past, wiretaps of this nature were only permissible in accordance with Title III's restrictive guidelines. Also, under Title III, stored voice-mail messages fell into the category of *wire communications*, which meant that it was difficult to obtain a Title III warrant to intercept them. In effect, voice-mail messages were treated in the same way as actual communications between two parties. The Patriot Act has reclassified voice-mail messages into the category of an *electronic communication system*, which makes it easier for authorities to obtain warrants to intercept them. In a similar vein, the Patriot Act also permits authorities to obtain so-called *administrative subpoenas*, which, in turn, allows them to obtain telephone and Internet/e-mail service provider records of customers' accounts (see, e.g., USA Patriot Act 204, 115 Stat. at 283). This means that authorities can now easily access a wealth of information with little more than a person's telephone number.

Yet another change in criminal procedure attributable to the Patriot Act, though certainly not the last, is that it permits federal law enforcement officials to delay giving notice that a search warrant is about to be served until *after* it has been served (USA Patriot Act, Pub. L. No. 107-56, 213, 115 Stat. 272, 286 [2001]). Recall from the discussion earlier in this chapter that authorities are generally required to knock and announce their presence. The standard for delaying notice under the Patriot Act is one of reasonableness. That is, if authorities have reasonable cause to believe that giving notice would have an "adverse effect," it can be delayed until after the warrant has been served (USA Patriot Act 213, 115 Stat. at 285–86). What constitutes an *adverse effect* is not altogether clear according to the act. If delay is necessary, notice only needs to be provided "within a reasonable period" of the warrant's execution and can be extended for "good cause" (USA Patriot Act Act 213, 115 Stat. at 285–86).

This is just a sampling of the changes to search warrant protocol that have resulted from the Patriot Act. It has had effects on other aspects of criminal procedure, as well, including the Fifth Amendment right to indictment by a grand jury and the Sixth Amendment right to counsel provision. These issues are discussed in later chapters.

Search Warrants and Bodily Intrusions

The Supreme Court has been especially restrictive with regard to intrusions into the human body. The most well-known case that serves as an example is *Rochin v. California* (342 U.S. 165 [1952]). In that case, the police had information that a man was selling narcotics. They entered his home and forced their way into his bedroom. When the police asked the man about two capsules that were lying on his bed, he put the capsules in his mouth. The officers could not successfully remove the drugs from the man's mouth, so they took him to the hospital, where his stomach was pumped. Drugs were found and the man was convicted in California state court for possession of morphine. *Rochin* was decided in 1952, prior to when the exclusionary rule was applied to the states. As a result, the Court ruled that the way the police handled the man shocked the conscience, thereby violating his Fourteenth Amendment right to due process.

In another case, *Winston v. Lee* (470 U.S. 753 [1985]), the Supreme Court decided whether the government could require a bullet to be surgically removed from a suspected robber. The Court required that a warrant be obtained before allowing such an intrusion but also that the suspect's safety and privacy interests should be weighed against society's interest in capturing lawbreakers. The Court noted:

> A compelled surgical intrusion into an individual's body for evidence . . . implicates expectations of privacy and security of such magnitude that the intrusion may be "unreasonable" even if likely to produce evidence of a crime . . . . The reasonableness of surgical intrusions beneath the skin depends on a case-by-case approach, in which the individual's interests in privacy and security are weighed against society's interests in conducting the procedure. In a given case, the question whether the community's need for evidence outweighs the substantial privacy interest at stake is a delicate one admitting of few categorical answers. (pp. 759–760)

The Court did not expressly decide what the appropriate procedure would be before surgery would be permitted, but it did cite a lower court decision, *United States v. Crowder* (543 F.2d 312 [1977]), in which the D.C. Circuit Court of Appeals decided that before surgery would be permissible (even if a warrant were obtained), an adversarial hearing with appellate review must occur. Thus, under certain circumstances, it would appear that certain types of bodily intrusions require more than a warrant.

Given the importance of bodily intrusions vis-à-vis civil liberties, police departments should take special care for engaging in them. Accordingly, the San Bernardino, California, Police Department's policy for strip and body cavity searches is reprinted in Figure 4.10 (page 132). The body cavity discussion, in particular, deserves careful attention, as this type of search enjoys a high level of Fourth Amendment protection.

Civil Asset Forfeiture

Civil asset forfeiture involves the seizure (i.e., taking) and eventual forfeiture (i.e., giving up of ownership) of property derived from or used to facilitate the commission of a

FIGURE 4.10   Example of a Strip and Body Cavity Search Policy

Purpose

A. To establish a policy governing strip and body cavity searches, and to protect arrested persons from unwarranted intrusions.

B. To conform to the requirements of Penal Code Section 4030.

Definitions

A. *Strip Search*—Means a search that requires a person to remove or arrange some or all of his/her clothing so as to permit a visual inspection of the underclothing, breasts, buttocks, or genitalia of that person.

B. *Body Cavity*—Means the stomach or rectal cavity of any person and the vagina of a female person.

C. *Visual Body Cavity Search*—The visual inspection of a body cavity.

D. *Physical Body Cavity Search*—Mean physical intrusion into a body cavity for the purpose of discovering any object concealed in that cavity.

Procedures

A. When an arrestee is taken into custody, that person may be subjected to a pat down search, metal detector search, and thorough clothing search in order to discover and retrieve concealed weapons and/or contraband prior to being transported to County Jail.

B. Before requesting authority for a strip search or body cavity search, an officer must determine there is a reasonable suspicion based on specific and articulable facts to believe an arrestee is concealing a weapon or contraband, and that a strip search or body cavity search will result in the discovery of the weapon or contraband.

No strip search or visual body cavity search may be conducted on a misdemeanor or infraction arrestee, without the prior written authorization of the supervisor on duty. A copy of the written authorization shall remain with the case file and shall be made available upon request. The time, date, and place of the search, the name and sex of the person conducting the search, and a statement of the results of the search, including a list of any items removed from the person searched shall be recorded in the case file and made available upon request of the person search or his/her authorized representative. The authorization shall include specific and articulable facts and circumstances upon

which the reasonable determination was made by the supervisor.

C. No arrestee shall be subjected to a physical body cavity search except under the authority of a search warrant issued by a magistrate specifically authorizing the physical body cavity search.

A physical body cavity search shall be conducted under sanitary conditions, and only by a physician, nurse practitioner, registered nurse, licensed vocational nurse, or emergency medical technician licensed to practice in the State of California. Any physician engaged in providing health care to detainees or inmates of a facility may conduct the physical body cavity search. A copy of the warrant shall remain in the case file and shall be made available upon request of the person searched or his/her authorized representative. The time, date, and place of search, the name and sex of the person conducting the search, and a statement of the results of the search including a list of items removed from the person searched shall be recorded in the case file.

D. A person conducting a strip search or a visual body cavity search shall not touch the breasts, buttocks, or genitalia of the person being searched.

E. All persons conducting or present during a strip search or visual or physical body cavity search shall be of the same sex as the person being searched, except for physicians or licensed medical personnel.

F. All strip, visual, and physical body cavity searches shall be conducted in an area of privacy so that the search cannot be observed by persons not participating in the search. A person is considered to be participating in the search if his/her official duties relative to search procedure require him/her to be present at the time the search is conducted.

G. No strip or body cavity search shall be conducted on persons not under arrest, without their consent, or a valid search warrant for that person and the rules herein apply to infraction or misdemeanor arrestees. Officers will also adhere to all procedures when dealing with felony arrestees, except that no prior written authorization of the supervisor is required.

H. Employees are reminded that willful violations of Penal Code Section 4030 relating to strip searches and body cavity searches by persons authorizing or conducting such searches are punishable as misdemeanors and civil actions as well punitive damages are available to a person improperly searched.

Source: Chapter 29, Procedure 1, "Strip and Body Cavity Searches," from *Standard Operating Procedure,* San Bernardino, California, Police Department (rev. April 8, 1991). Used courtesy of the San Bernardino Police Department.

crime. Various state and federal statutes permit law enforcement authorities to forfeit assets. Civil asset forfeiture begins with the seizure of property. Property will be forfeited if the government can prove that it was derived from or used to facilitate a crime. Forfeiture of this sort is permissible even if the person whose property is sought is never charged or convicted criminally.

A warrant is rarely required for the seizure of property pursuant to a forfeiture statute. However, when *real property*, such as a house or a piece of land, is involved, the courts have required that an opportunity be made available for the property owner to be heard *prior* to the act of seizing that property (see *United States v. James Daniel Good Real* Property, 510 U.S. 43 [1993]). In the case of *personal property*, the courts (as well as most forfeiture statutes) provide for a hearing *after* the seizure has taken place to determine its validity.

Note that such hearings are not always held in the criminal context. If the police have probable cause to seize evidence, their judgment is not always challenged at a later court hearing. The only exception is when the courts require a probable cause hearing. Thus, civil asset forfeiture statutes, not to mention the courts, impose certain restrictions that are not always found in criminal proceedings.

Other constitutional restrictions on civil asset forfeiture activities also deserve mention. Assuming the police have probable cause to seize property and that such probable cause is eventually demonstrated in an adversarial proceeding, the Eighth and Fourteenth Amendments may call into question the constitutionality of the seizures. First, the due process clause of the Fourteenth Amendment requires notice and an opportunity to be heard prior to a seizure, unless the police can demonstrate that exigent circumstances exist (e.g., that the property may be destroyed). Second, forfeiture can be in violation of the Eighth Amendment's excessive fines clause (*Austin v. United States*, 509 U.S. 602 [1993]; *United States v. Bajakajian*, 524 U.S. 321 [1998]).

Administrative Search Warrants

Warrants are also required to conduct administrative searches. An **administrative search warrant** is not issued on particularized probable cause (e.g., on probable cause that evidence will be found in a particular location), however. Instead, it is issued once it has been shown that the location to be inspected has been chosen according to a prescribed plan and relying on neutral criteria (e.g., the date of the last search). This requirement is designed to overcome the appearance of bias or bad faith, but probable cause is not required.

Anticipatory Search Warrants

Another special situation concerns an **anticipatory search warrant**. In some situations, a warrant is issued based on the *expectation* that evidence will be present or will arrive at a particular location. Assume, for example, that the police believe a freighter arriving from Colombia has drugs aboard, but they do not want to wait until the drugs arrive to obtain a warrant for fear that the drugs will disappear. In such a circumstance, a judge can issue a search warrant based on the expectation that the drugs will arrive, as long as the police have probable cause.

A circuit court judged explained the reasons for the issuance of anticipatory search warrants in deciding *United States v. Garcia* (882 F.2d 699 [2d. Cir. 1989]):

> Courts—though not yet the Supreme Court, to be sure—have upheld the anticipatory warrant, in large part, because they see it as desirable, whenever possible, for

police to obtain judicial approval before searching private premises. Indeed, the Fourth Amendment mandates that, with few exceptions, a warrant be obtained before any search of a dwelling occurs. Yet one of the major practical difficulties that confronts law enforcement officials is the time required to obtain a warrant. In many instances, the speed with which government agents are required to act, especially when dealing with the furtive and transitory activities of persons who traffic in narcotics, demands that they proceed without a warrant or risk losing both criminal and contraband . . . . [T]he purposes of the Fourth Amendment are best served by permitting government agents to obtain warrants in advance if they can show probable cause to believe that the contraband will be located on the premises at the time that search takes place. (p. 703)

CONCLUSION

A warrant has three required components: (1) a neutral and detached magistrate; (2) a showing of probable cause; and (3) particularity. A prosecutor or law enforcement official cannot be considered neutral and detached. Neither can a judge who is paid for issuing warrants.

Probable cause was defined in Chapter 3, but in this chapter, it was pointed out that the showing of probable cause differs, depending on the type of warrant. An *arrest warrant* requires showing probable cause that the person to be arrested committed the crime. A *search warrant* requires showing probable cause that the evidence to be seized was connected with a crime *and* that it will be found in the place to be searched.

Particularity in an arrest warrant is satisfied when the suspect's name or a detailed description of him or her is given. Particularity in a search warrant is satisfied when the place to be searched and the item or items to be seized are described in detail.

This chapter devoted special attention to arrests with warrants. Unfortunately, the Supreme Court has defined *seizure* with regard to the same reasonable person standard regardless of whether an arrest or a stop occurs. As such, the courts focus on several specific factors to draw a distinction between a stop and an arrest, including the purpose, manner, location, and duration of the seizure.

Arrest warrants are required in two situations: (1) arrests in the home and (2) arrests in third-party homes. Arrests in public do not require warrants. Similarly, arrests in the presence of exigent circumstances do not require warrants, regardless of location. The police are required to announce their presence during the execution of a search warrant unless exigent circumstances are present.

The police will generally not be liable for property damage during the service of a warrant; however, due process can be violated if the property damage is excessive. Deadly force can be used to effect an arrest, but only when the suspect seeks to escape and poses a significant threat to other officers or citizens. Finally, the courts will admit evidence resulting from a wrongful arrest, as long as the mistake was a reasonable one.

Searches with warrants are subject to many of the same restrictions as *arrests* with warrants. However, search warrants are also constrained in terms of time, insofar as the police cannot wait too long to serve the warrant or take too long to look for evidence. Also, the courts frequently require that search warrants be served during daylight hours. The scope of the search must be limited to the object of the search, the seized evidence must be inventoried and a list given to the homeowner, and the police cannot bring members of the media along when serving a search warrant if the media presence serves no legitimate law enforcement objectives.

The traditional Fourth Amendment approach to determining constitutionality does not always work in the case of electronic surveillance. The interception of communications, in particular, is governed by a restrictive body of law (e.g., Title III of the Omnibus Crime Control and Safe Streets Act of 1968). However, the recently enacted Patriot Act has undercut some of these restrictions. Likewise, the Fourth Amendment's warrant requirement may not suffice in the case of bodily intrusions. Similarly, civil asset forfeiture is governed by restrictions beyond the Fourth Amendment's warrant requirement. Administrative search warrants and anticipatory search warrants are special situations and require careful consideration.

REVIEW QUESTIONS

1. Explain the three components of a valid warrant.
2. How does the showing of probable cause differ for an arrest warrant versus a search warrant?
3. How does particularity differ for an arrest warrant versus a search warrant?
4. Distinguish between a stop and an arrest.
5. Distinguish between a stop and a nonstop.
6. When is an arrest warrant required?
7. Summarize the Supreme Court's view on arrests for minor offenses.
8. What reasons have been offered for the so-called announcement requirement with regard to arrest and search warrants?
9. When can the announcement requirement be dispensed with?
10. Briefly summarize the Supreme Court's view on property damage during the service of a warrant.
11. Summarize the Supreme Court's decisions in *Tennessee v. Garner* and *Graham v. Connor.* Why are these decisions important to criminal procedure?
12. What restrictions exist concerning the scope and manner of a search with a warrant?
13. What is the Supreme Court's view on the media's presence during the service of a search warrant? What is the leading case in this area?
14. Explain the two leading cases that address bodily intrusion during the course of a search.
15. What is an anticipatory search warrant?

 Answers to the Decision-Making Exercises for this chapter can be found on pages 493–496.

CHAPTER 5

Searches and Arrests without Warrants

OUTLINE

KEY TERMS

exceptions to the warrant requirement
search incident to arrest
armspan rule
protective sweep

exigent circumstances
hot pursuit
evanescent evidence
automobile exception
racial profiling

disparate impact
"plain view" doctrine
lawful access
immediately apparent

INTRODUCTION
Moving beyond the Warrant Requirement

If it was not for exceptions to the warrant requirement, the Fourth Amendment would take substantially less effort to understand. At the same time, however, the many exceptions to the Fourth Amendment's warrant requirement are what make it interesting. The so-called warrantless searches and seizures discussed in this chapter are based on Supreme Court decisions in which it was believed that to require a warrant would constitute an undue burden on law enforcement officials. Still, though, a warrant is *always* preferable; whenever circumstances permit, one should be obtained.

The exceptions to the Fourth Amendment's warrant requirement considered in this chapter are those requiring probable cause. There are other exceptions to the warrant requirement that do not require probable cause; they are discussed in the next two chapters. Chapter 6 examines the law of stop-and-frisk, and Chapter 7 looks at searches and seizures based on administrative justification as well as consent.

EXCEPTIONS TO THE WARRANT REQUIREMENT

Broadly, there are five types of warrantless searches and seizures that require probable cause. They are called **exceptions to the warrant requirement** because the actions at issue do not need to be supported by a search or arrest warrant. The five types of warrantless searches and seizures are (1) searches incident to (i.e., following) arrest;

KEY CASES

Searches Incident to Arrest
- *Chimel v. California*, 395 U.S. 752 (1969)
- *Knowles v. Iowa*, 525 U.S. 113 (1998)
- *Preston v. United States*, 376 U.S. 364 (1964)

Searches Based on Exigent Circumstances
- *Warden v. Hayden*, 387 U.S. 294 (1967)
- *Welsh v. Wisconsin*, 466 U.S. 740 (1984)
- *Minnesota v. Olson*, 495 U.S. 91 (1990)
- *Breithaupt v. Abram*, 352 U.S. 432 (1957)
- *Cupp v. Murphy*, 412 U.S. 291 (1973)

Automobile Searches
- *Carroll v. United States*, 267 U.S. 132 (1925)
- *California v. Carney*, 471 U.S. 386 (1985)
- *New York v. Belton*, 453 U.S. 454 (1981)

Arrests in Public Places
- *United States v. Watson*, 423 U.S. 411 (1976)
- *United States v. Santana*, 427 U.S. 38 (1976)

Plain View
- *Coolidge v. New Hampshire*, 403 U.S. 443 (1971)
- *Arizona v. Hicks*, 480 U.S. 321 (1987)
- *Horton v. California*, 496 U.S. 128 (1990)

(2) searches and seizures in the presence of exigent circumstances; (3) searches involving automobiles; (4) arrests in public places; and (5) searches based on the "plain view" doctrine.

■ Searches Incident to Arrest

Imagine a situation in which a police officer has lawfully (i.e., with probable cause) arrested a suspect, is leading him away, and observes the suspect reach into his pocket. What would be going through the police officer's mind as she observed this behavior? Scenarios like this illustrate the reasoning behind the **search incident to arrest** exception. Namely, police officers must be permitted to engage in a search of a suspect incident to arrest (i.e., following an arrest). It would be impractical, even dangerous, to wait for a warrant before conducting such a search.

■ *Chimel v. California*, 395 U.S. 752 (1969)

The leading case in the area of incident searches is *Chimel v. California* (395 U.S. 752 [1969]). As the Supreme Court stated, a search incident to arrest is permitted "to remove any weapons that the [arrestee] might seek to use in order to resist arrest or effect his escape" and to "seize any evidence on the arrestee's person in order to prevent its concealment or destruction" (p. 763).

On the Importance of a Lawful Arrest, the Offense, and Custody

The most basic requirement concerning searches incident to arrest—and one that often goes overlooked—is that the arrest must be lawful. When the arrest itself is not lawful (i.e., when it is not based on probable cause), any search that follows is unlawful (see *Draper v. United States*, 358 U.S. 307 [1959]).

Another important threshold issue with regard to searches incident to arrest concerns the nature of the offense. Courts have grappled with the question as to whether a search should be permitted when the offense on which the arrest is based is not serious. Because the rationale of the exception is to provide officer safety, then is officer safety likely to be compromised when a minor offense, as opposed to a serious offense, justifies the arrest?

Two important Supreme Court cases have sought to answer these questions. First, in *United States v. Robinson* (414 U.S. 218 [1973]), the Court reversed a lower court's decision that only a patdown of the suspect's outer clothing was permissible following an arrest for driving with a revoked license. And in a companion case to *Robinson*, *Gustafson v. Florida* (414 U.S. 260 [1973]), the Court upheld the search of a suspect after his arrest for failure to have his driver's license.

The Supreme Court offered two reasons for its opinions in *Robinson* and *Gustafson*. First, according to Chief Justice Rehnquist, "It is scarcely open to doubt that the danger to an officer is far greater in the case of the extended exposure which follows the taking of a suspect into custody and transporting him to the police station than in the case of the relatively fleeting contact resulting from the typical *Terry*-stop" (*United States v. Robinson*, p. 234). Second, the Court believed a bright-line rule was in order given the stakes involved (i.e., officer safety): "A police officer's determination as to how and where to search the person of a suspect whom he has arrested is necessarily a quick *ad hoc* judgment which the Fourth Amendment does not require to be broken down in each instance into an analysis of each step in the search" (p. 235).

Thus, *any* arrest justifies a warrantless search incident to that arrest. A key restriction, however, is that the arrest must result in a person being *taken into custody*. This was

■ *Knowles v. Iowa*, 525 U.S. 113 (1998)

the ruling from *Knowles v. Iowa* (525 U.S. 113 [1998]). In that case, a police officer stopped a person for speeding, and rather than arresting him (which the officer had justification to do), the officer issued him a citation. Then, the officer conducted a search of the car and found a marijuana pipe. The Court noted that traffic stops rarely pose the same threat to officer safety as arrests. This is not to suggest, however, that police officers cannot search people incident to lawful arrest for minor vehicle-related infractions. If the authority to arrest is present, an incident search is permissible. The key restriction is that the person must actually be arrested and taken into custody. Otherwise, the search will not conform with Fourth Amendment requirements.

Timing of the Search

Another key restriction pertaining to searches incident to arrest has to do with the timing of the search. In particular, probable cause to arrest must *precede* the warrantless search (*Sibron v. New York*, 392 U.S. 40 [1968]). The reason for this is to restrict officers from engaging in "fishing expeditions," or searches based on less than probable cause that would presumably result in probable cause to make an arrest. Note, however, that if probable cause to arrest is in place, the officer is not required to formally arrest the suspect before engaging in the search (see *Rawlings v. Kentucky*, 448 U.S. 98 [1980]).

If the search follows an arrest, then it must take place *soon* after the arrest. In legal parlance, the search must be *contemporaneous* to the arrest. In *Preston v. United States* (376 U.S. 364 [1964]), the case that established this rule, Justice Black observed that the "justifications [for the search incident to arrest] are absent where a search is remote in time or place from the arrest" (p. 367). In *Preston* police officers arrested the occupants of a car and took them to jail. After this, the officers searched the car, which had been towed to an impound lot. The Supreme Court noted that the possibilities of destruction of evidence and danger to the officers were no longer in place, as the suspects were no longer even present(see also *Chambers v. Maroney*, 399 U.S. 42 [1970]).

■ *Preston v. United States,*
   376 U.S. 364 (1964)

DECISION
MAKING
EXERCISE **5.1**

Timing of a Search Incident to Arrest

A locked suitcase was transported by police officers to the police station, after having been lawfully seized from the open trunk of a parked automobile during the arrests of those who were in its possession. After being back at the police station for over an hour, the officers opened the suitcase. They acted without a search warrant and without the consent of the arrested persons, but they did have probable cause to believe that the container held contraband. In fact, the suitcase contained large amounts of marijuana. Can this be considered a valid search incident to arrest?

Note that while a noncontemporaneous search is not justified under the search incident to arrest exception, it is authorized under the automobile exception discussed later. Also, the Supreme Court authorizes inventory searches of automobiles that have been lawfully impounded. Inventory searches are discussed later, as well.

There is one significant exception to the contemporaneousness requirement. In *United States v. Edwards* (415 U.S. 800 [1974]), the Supreme Court, in a 5 to 4 decision, upheld the warrantless search and seizure of an arrestee's clothing 10 hours after his arrest, during which time he was in jail. The Court noted that "searches and seizures that could be made on the spot at the time of arrest may legally be conducted later when the accused arrives at the place of detention" (p. 803). The Court did point out, however, that the taking of the individual's clothing at the time of the arrest would have been impractical because it "was late at night[,] no substitute clothing was then available for Edwards to wear, and it would certainly have been unreasonable for the police to have stripped respondent of his clothing and left him exposed in his cell throughout the night" (p. 805). Thus, the *Edwards* decision established the rule that a noncontemporaneous search incident to arrest is permissible when (1) an immediate search is nearly impossible and (2) the exigency still exists at the time of the later search.

Scope of the Search

The case of *United States v. Rabinowitz* (339 U.S. 56 [1950]) was the first to set limits on the scope of a search incident to arrest. In that case, the officers, armed with a valid arrest warrant, arrested a man and then conducted a warrantless search of his one-room business, including the desk, safe, and file cabinets. The Supreme Court upheld the search because the room "was small and under the immediate and complete control of the respondent" (p. 64).

Nearly 20 years after *Rabinowitz*, however, the Supreme Court voted to overturn its earlier decision. In the case of *Chimel v. California* (395 U.S. 752 [1969]), the Court argued that the *Rabinowitz* decision had been construed to mean that "a warrantless search 'incident to a lawful arrest' may generally extend to the area that is considered to be in the 'possession' or under the 'control' of the person arrested" (p. 759). Further, the Court noted that the *Rabinowitz* standard gave police "the opportunity to engage in searches not justified by probable cause, [but] by the simple expedient of arranging to arrest suspects at home rather than elsewhere" (p. 767). To get around this problem, Justice Stewart argued in favor of a new **armspan rule**. In the Court's words, a search incident to arrest would now be limited to the area "within [the] immediate control" of the person arrested—that is, "the area from within which he might have obtained either a weapon or something that could have been used as evidence against him" (p. 768).

An interesting twist on the aforementioned cases can be found in *Washington v. Chrisman* (455 U.S. 1 [1982]). In that case, an officer stopped a student on suspicion of drinking under age, an action that the Court considered an arrest. The officer asked the student for his identification and followed him to his dorm room, where the student's identification was presumably located. While at the student's room, the officer observed in plain view marijuana and drug paraphernalia. The officer seized the evidence. The Supreme Court upheld the seizure of the evidence, stating that "[e]very arrest must be presumed to present a risk of danger to the arresting officer. . . . Moreover, the possibility that an arrested person will attempt to escape if not properly supervised is obvious" (p. 7). Thus, "it is not unreasonable, under the Fourth Amendment for an officer, as a matter of routine, to monitor the movements of an arrested person, as his judgment dictates, following the arrest" (p. 7).

The cases discussed thus far have focused narrowly on the scope of the incident search exception with reference to the arrestee. What if another person *besides* the arrestee poses a threat to the police? This concern has led to several exceptions to the armspan rule.

First, in *Maryland v. Buie* (494 U.S. 325 [1990]), the Supreme Court expanded the scope of the incident search in two ways. It held that the police may, as part of a search incident to arrest, look in areas immediately adjoining the place of arrest for other persons who might attack the officers; no justification is required. The key, however, is that such a search must occur incident to arrest. Next, the Court held that at any point up to the time the arrest is completed, the police may engage in a **protective sweep** (i.e.,"a cursory visual inspection of those places in which a person might be hiding"), but reasonable suspicion must exist for such a sweep to be justified. Thus, no justification is required *after* arrest, but reasonable suspicion is required to engage in a sweep up to the point of the arrest.

Aside from the possible danger to police officers from "confederates," there is the potential for such third parties to engage in the destruction of evidence. Only one Supreme Court case appears to address this issue: *Vale v. Louisiana* (399 U.S. 30 [1970]). In that case, police officers had warrants authorizing the arrest of the defendant. While engaged in surveillance of the house, the officers observed the defendant come out of the house and engage in what appeared to be a drug sale. They arrested the defendant outside the home but then went back inside and searched it, according to the officers, because two of the defendant's relatives had arrived at the house in the meantime and could have destroyed evidence. *Vale* was actually a case concerning exigent circumstances (see later in this chapter), and the Court reversed the Louisiana Supreme Court's decision that upheld the search. But, in fact, the Court's opinion was not particularly instructive. It stated, in relevant part, that "no reason, so far as anything before us appears, to suppose that it was impracticable for [the officers] to obtain a search warrant as well" (p. 35), but it did not expressly state that related searches would always be unconstitutional. Indeed, several lower courts have upheld warrantless searches of homes for evidence after arrest on less than probable cause (e.g., *United States v. Hoyos*, 892 F.2d 1387 [9th Cir.1989]; *United States v. Rubin*, 474 F.2d 262 [3rd Cir. 1973]).

Another type of warrantless search of a house following a lawful arrest has been authorized based on the need to secure the premises, usually pending the procural of a search warrant. Thus, if the police believe another person or persons are in the house and could potentially destroy evidence, the house may be secured but not searched until a warrant has been obtained. This was the decision reached in *Segura v. United States* (468 U.S. 796 [1984]). In that case, the Supreme Court, in another 5 to 4 decision, declared "that where officers, having probable cause, enter premises . . . , arrest the occupants . . . and take them into custody and, for no more than the period here involved [19 hours in this case], secure the premises from within to preserve the status quo while others, in good faith, are in the process of obtaining a warrant, they do not violate the Fourth Amendment's proscription against unreasonable seizures" (p. 798).

DECISION
MAKING
EXERCISE **5.2**

Proper Scope for a Search Incident to Arrest

Two police officers arrived at Bobby Sheen's house with a valid warrant for his arrest. The officers were informed by a nosy neighbor that two of Sheen's accomplices were in the house with him. The officers knocked, announced their presence, and entered the house. They encountered Sheen as he was descending the stairs. He was placed under arrest. Immediately after the arrest, one of the officers went upstairs and found drug paraphernalia on a nightstand. May this evidence be lawfully seized? What if the drug paraphernalia had been found in a drawer instead?

It is appropriate at this juncture to note that the Court has authorized the police to rely on the incident search exception to engage in searches well beyond the arrestee's armspan—and when no threat exists from people sympathetic to the arrestee. In particular, the Supreme Court has held that officers may engage in a warrantless, suspicionless search of a car and and containers within it following the lawful arrest of the car's driver (*New York v. Belton*, 453 U.S. 454 [1981]). This decision came to be known as the *Belton* rule and is discussed at greater length later in this chapter in the section on automobile searches.

Summary. A search incident to arrest may be conducted without a warrant, but it is subject to four restrictions. First, the arrest must be based on probable cause and result in custodial detention. Second, the search must follow the arrest closely in time (i.e., be contemporaneous). Third, the police must limit their search to (1) the person arrested and any containers discovered from that search; (2) the arrestee's immediate grabbing area; (3) a protective sweep of the premises without justification following an arrest but with reasonable suspicion leading up to the arrest; and/or (4) securing the premises, if they have a reasonable belief that evidence may be destroyed by someone sympathetic to the arrestee (see Figure 5.1). Finally, the premises to be searched can be secured prior to procural of a warrant, but reasonable suspicion is required. Figure 5.2 (page 142) presents the Gallatin, Tennessee, Police Department's policy for a search incident to arrest.

FIGURE 5.1 Permissible Scope of a Search Incident to Arrest
(assuming a valid arrest)

Level of Intrusion	Justification Required
Search of arrestee	None
Search of arrestee's grabbing area	None
Protective sweep	Reasonable suspicion that confederates are present
Secure residence	Reasonable suspicion to fear destruction of evidence

■ Searches Based on Exigent Circumstances

As indicated earlier, the exceptions to the search warrant requirement are premised on the impracticality of obtaining a warrant. Perhaps no exception illustrates this better than the **exigent circumstances** exception. Simply put, when the esigencies, or emergencies, of the situation require the police to act immediately at the risk of danger to themselves, danger to others, the destruction of evidence, or the escape of the suspect, it would be unresonable to require the police to take time to obtain a warrant.

Generally, three types of exigencies are recognized by the courts as authorizing the police to act without a warrant: (1) hot pursuit; (2) likelihood of escape or danger to others; and (3) evanescent evidence. Despite the fact that these exceptions allow the police to act without a warrant, probable cause is still required. For example, probable cause that the person being pursued is the suspect is required before the police can enter a home or building without a warrant to arrest him or her.

FIGURE 5.2 Example of a Policy for a Search Incident to Arrest

9.7.2 Incident to Arrest

When an officer places a person under arrest, the officer will conduct a thorough search of the person and the area in his/her immediate reach. All items on the person of the subject will be removed and secured by the officer. The search of the immediate reach of the subject is intended to disclose weapons and any possible evidence. If these kinds of items are found, they may also be secured by the officer and placed into evidence.

A search incident to arrest will be conducted only after the subject has been placed in restraints (i.e., handcuffs). Whenever possible, the search will be conducted by two officers, one conducting the search, the other providing cover. The search should begin in the immediate are around the subject's hands, including an inspection of the subject's waistband. The officer should then search the subject methodically by searching one-half of the subject's body from head to foot and then returning to the top of the head and search the other side of the subject's body in the same manner. Only by searching a subject in such a methodical manner will an officer ensure his/her safety in knowing that the subject is not in possession of any weapons.

This method for searching an individual incident to an arrest is only offered as one way to search a subject. Under no circumstances is this method considered as the only option an officer has in searching a subject; however, it is a method that has been demonstrated to be effective when used consistently. Any method is acceptable as long as the search is thorough, complete, and effective in discovering weapons and evidence that are occasionally concealed on a subject's person.

Source: From *General Directives Manual,* Gallatin, Tennessee, Police Department (December 28, 1999). Used courtesy of the Gallatin Police Department.

Hot Pursuit

The Supreme Court first recognized the **hot pursuit** exception in the case of *Warden v. Hayden* (387 U.S. 294 [1967]), in which the police were called by taxi cab drivers who reported that their taxi company had been robbed. The police followed the suspect to a house, where they were granted entry by the suspect's wife. The suspect was upstairs in the house, pretending to be asleep. While searching the house for the suspect, the police found and seized clothing, a shotgun, and a pistol, all of which were used against the suspect at trial. The Court found the warrantless entry reasonable because the "exigencies of the situation made that course imperative" (p. 298). Several reasons were offered for the decision. First, Justice Brennan stated that "[t]he Fourth Amendment does not require police officers to delay in the course of an investigation if to do so would gravely danger their lives or the lives of others" (pp. 298–299). Also, "[s]peed . . . was essential, and only a thorough search of the house for persons and weapons could have insured that Hayden was the only man present and that the police had control of all weapons which could be used against them or to effect an escape" (p. 299).

■ *Warden v. Hayden,*
387 U.S. 294 (1967)

Despite the sweeping language from the *Hayden* decision, the Supreme Court has imposed a number of restrictions on searches and seizures premised on hot pursuit. First, hot pursuit permits warrantless entry only when, first, the police have probable cause to believe that the person they are chasing has committed a crime and is on the premises entered.

Second, the police are also required to have reason to believe the suspect will escape or that further harm, either to evidence or to other people, will occur if the suspect is not immediately apprehended. With regard to this second restriction, one court has observed that "[a] hot pursuit, by itself, creates no necessity for dispensing with a warrant" (*State v. Wren*, 115 Idaho 618 [1989], p. 625). Similarly, the Ninth Circuit has stated that police officers must reasonably believe (1) "that the suspect either know[s] or will learn at any moment that they are in immediate danger of apprehension;" (2) that "evidence is being currently removed or destroyed and it is impractical to advert the situation without immediately arresting the suspects or seizing the evidence;" or (3) that "a suspect is currently endangering the lives of themselves or others" (*United States v. George*, 883 F.2d 1407 [9th Cir. 1989]).

Third, although it often goes without saying, the police must begin hot pursuit from a lawful starting point. If, for example, officers are unlawfully on someone's private property, they will not succeed in claiming hot pursuit to justify any further warrantless action. However, in *United States v. Santana* (427 U.S. 38 [1976]), the Supreme Court upheld the warrantless arrest of a woman in her house when the police *observed* a crime on private property from a public vantage point. In that case, police officers observed Santana standing in the open doorway of her house with a brown paper bag, which they had probable cause to believe contained narcotics. They pursued her into the house and arrested her. This decision suggests that the police can pursue from a public vantage point a suspect whom they observe on private property.

Fourth, the hot pursuit doctrine only applies to serious offenses, including felonies and some misdemeanors (see, e.g., *Welsh v. Wisconsin*, 466 U.S. 740 [1984]). This restriction on the hot pursuit doctrine—and, indeed, on exigent circumstance searches in general—is perhaps the most important one. As such, it is treated in a section by itself later.

■ *Welsh v. Wisconsin,*
466 U.S. 740 (1984)

DECISION
MAKING
EXERCISE 5.3

Exigent Circumstances and the Severity of the Offense

Brian Corman was suspected of burglarizing an apartment while no one was home and stealing a checkbook and a television. But apparently, someone in the apartment complex witnessed Corman leaving the victim's unit and called the police. Officers responded and confronted Corman at the door to his apartment, which was in the same building. Without a warrant, the officers then entered Corman's apartment, searched it, found the items stolen in the burglary, and arrested him. Are these actions constitutionally valid?

A fifth restriction on hot pursuits concerns the scope of the search. Generally, the scope of a search based on hot pursuit is broad. In *Hayden*, for example, the Supreme Court stated, "The permissible scope of search must, at the least, be as broad as may reasonably be necessary to prevent the dangers that the suspect at large in the house may resist or escape" (*Warden v. Hayden*, 387 U.S. 294 [1967], p. 299). However, the search must be "prior to or immediately contemporaneous with" the arrest of the suspect. Also, officers may only search where the suspect or weapons might reasonably be found. A simple rule of thumb, then, is that the nature of the exigency defines the scope of the search. Another rule of thumb with regard to hot pursuit is that if the police have a reasonable amount of time to obtain a warrant, they should always do so. In *Welsh*, for example, Justice Brennan argued that the government's "claim of hot pursuit . . . [was] . . . unconvincing because there was no immediate or continuous pursuit of the petitioner from the scene of [the] crime" (*Welsh v. Wisconsin*, 466 U.S. 740 [1984], p. 753).

Escape and Endangerment to Others Absent Hot Pursuit

■ *Minnesota v. Olson,*
495 U.S. 91 (1990)

Hot pursuit is justified, as just discussed, when, among other things, the suspect may escape or inflict harm on police officers or others. In some situations, however, a suspect can potentially escape or inflict harm absent hot pursuit. In *Minnesota v. Olson* (495 U.S. 91 [1990]), for example, the prosecution sought to justify a warrantless entry and arrest of a suspect in a duplex that the police had surrounded. There was probable cause to believe that Olson, the man in the duplex, had been the driver of a getaway car involved in a robbery/murder the day before. The Supreme Court ruled that the officers acted unconstitutionally under the circumstances because Olson was only the driver, not the murder suspect, and the weapon had been recovered, which diminished the urgency of the situation. In addition, it was unlikely Olson would escape because the building was surrounded. On its face, then, this case is not useful on this point. However, the Court seemed to suggest that had Olson *not* been the driver (i.e., had been the murderer), had the weapon *not* been recovered, and had the building *not* been fully surrounded, the warrantless action would have been lawful.

DECISION MAKING EXERCISE 5.4

Are Exigent Circumstances Present?

Assume that the day after a robbery, uniformed police officers observe a man who fits the description of the robber. The man sees that he has been spotted and flees into a nearby house. May the police pursue him inside, without a warrant, and arrest him? (Keep in mind that the police action called into question has taken place the day *after* the robbery.) What if, instead, the police surrounded and staked out the house for three hours and then entered in order to effect the arrest? Finally, what if the police did not wait three hours but instead chased the robbery suspect into a building from which they knew with confidence that there was no way to escape, endanger others, or destroy evidence?

Evanescent Evidence

In situations in which the search incident to arrest or hot pursuit exceptions do not apply, the Court has recognized an additional exception to the warrant required, one that permits warrantless searches for **evanescent evidence** (i.e., disappearing evidence). This can include evidence inside a person, as well as a house, a paper, or an effect.

■ *Breithaupt v. Abram,*
352 U.S. 432 (1957)

The best example of vanishing or disappearing evidence inside a person is alcohol in the blood. In *Breithaupt v. Abram* (352 U.S. 432 [1957]), the Court upheld the warrantless intrusion (via a needle) into a man's body for the purpose of drawing blood to see if he had been drinking. The key in this case, however, was that medical personnel had conducted a *routine* blood test. The majority noted "that the indiscriminate taking of blood under different conditions or by those not competent to do so" (p. 438) would not be allowed. (Indeed, this is why *Breithaupt v. Abram* is an isolated case; police officers rarely, if ever, draw blood from suspects. Breathalyzers usually provide sufficient evidence of intoxication.)

The *Breithaupt* decision also established that warrantless searches for evanescent evidence are only permissible when (1) there is not time to obtain a warrant; (2) there is a "clear indication" that the search will result in obtaining the evidence sought; and (3) the search is conducted in a "reasonable manner." In support of the reasonable manner requirement, the Court offered the following from a later decision, *Schmerber v. California* (384 U.S. 757 [1966]):

> The interests in human dignity and privacy which the Fourth Amendment protects forbid any such intrusions on the mere chance that desired evidence might be obtained. In the absence of a clear indication that in fact such evidence will be found, these fundamental human interest require law officers to suffer the risk that such evidence may disappear unless there is an immediate search. (pp. 769–770)

In *Rochin v. California* (342 U.S. 165 [1952]), a case in which the *police* used a stomach pump to obtain evidence from a man's stomach, the Court declared that a due process violation occurred and that the officers' conduct shocked the conscience. The reason was that the police, not medical personnel, extracted the evidence. Another view is that the use of a stomach pump falls somewhat short of a routine medical procedure.

As for the clear indication requirement, the Court has been somewhat flexible. For example, in *United States v. Montoya de Hernandez* (469 U.S. 1204 [1985]), the Court treated the clear indication requirement from *Breithaupt* as being identical to the reasonable suspicion standard set forth in *Terry v. Ohio*. This case involved the detention for several hours of a woman who was suspected of smuggling narcotics in her alimentary canal.

Finally, it is important to remember that, like the hot pursuit exception, the exigency used to justify a warrantless search for evanescent evidence must be immediate. In other words, there must be good reason to believe that an immediate search will result in the seizure of the evidence in question. A good example can be found in *Cupp v. Murphy* (412 U.S. 291 [1973]). In that case, a man who had been informed of his wife's strangulation volunteered to come to the police station for questioning. While he was at the station, officers observed what appeared to be dried blood on the man's fingernails. The officers asked if they could take a scraping from his fingernails, and the man refused. He then started rubbing his hands behind his back and placing them in his pockets. At that point, the officers forcibly removed some of the material from under the man's fingernails. The Court upheld this action on the grounds that the police had probable cause to believe that "highly evanescent evidence" was in the process of being destroyed.

■ *Cupp v. Murphy,* 412 U.S. 291 (1973)

DECISION MAKING EXERCISE 5.5

Immediacy and Evanescent Evidence

A motor home that federal drug agents believed to contain a methamphetamine laboratory was parked in a secluded area near a river. The agents maintained visual surveillance throughout the afternoon. Around 4 p.m., one of the agents smelled chemicals "cooking." Shortly after that, the agents observed a man dash out of the motor home, gasping for air. In light of this incident, the agents decided to search the motor home. They ordered all of the occupants out of the motor home and placed them under arrest. The agents then entered the motor home to see if any other people were inside, to turn off any cooking apparatus, and to inventory the contents. They found a methamphetamine laboratory behind a drawn curtain at the back of the motor home. Was this action justified?

In certain rare situations, the police may have reason to suspect that evidence may be lost or destroyed not because of the actions of a person (the suspect or the suspect's confederates) but because of other causes. In *United States v. Chadwick* (433 U.S. 1 [1977]), for example, the Supreme Court noted that a warrant would not be required to search a footlocker if the officers believed that it contained evidence that would lose its value unless the footlocker were opened at once or if the officers had reason to believe that the footlocker contained explosives or other inherently dangerous items.

The American Law Institute's Code of Pre-Arraignment Procedure summarizes the law concerning exigencies. Section 206.5 of the code provides that warrantless entries based on reasonable cause are permissible when (1) individuals are in imminent danger of death or serious bodily harm; (2) items are present that are imminently likely to burn, explode, or otherwise cause death, serious bodily harm, or destruction of property; and/or (3) items subject to seizure are present that will cause or be used to cause death or serious bodily injury if not immediately seized.

Offense Seriousness and Exigent Circumstances

The Supreme Court has also noted that the *seriousness* of the offense for which the warrantless arrest is to be made may be relevant in determining whether exigent circumstances are present. For example, in *Welsh v. Wisconsin* (466 U.S. 740 [1984]), a witness one night reported that an automobile was being driven erratically. Eventually, the car swerved off the road and stopped in a field. The driver walked away before police could arrive at the scene. When they did arrive, the police checked the registration of the car and found out it belonged to Welsh. They went to Welsh's house, gained entry, and arrested Welsh without a warrant. The Supreme Court held that the warrantless nighttime entry of a suspect's home to make an arrest for a *nonjailable* offense is a violation of the Fourth Amendment:

> Before government agents may invade the sanctity of the home, it must demonstrate exigent circumstances that overcome the presumption of unreasonableness that attaches to all warrantless home entries. An important factor to be considered when determining whether any exigency exists is the gravity of the underlying offense for which the arrest is being made . . . [A]pplication of the exigent circumstances exception in the context of home entry should rarely be sanctioned when there is probable cause that only a minor offense has been committed. (p.750)

The majority also cited another case, *McDonald v. United States* (335 U.S. 451 [1948]), in its decision: "When an officer undertakes to act as his own magistrate, he ought to be in a position to justify it by pointing to some real immediate and serious consequences if he postponed action to get a warrant" (p. 460).

Welsh is controversial for at least two reasons. First, it is not always clear what constitutes a minor offense. The Court declared that warrantless entry to make an arrest for drunk driving is in violation of the Fourth Amendment, even though drunk driving is considered a serious offense in every state of the union. Second, although the Court did not say so, it implied that warrants are *not* required for warrantless home arrests in serious cases. The D.C. Circuit's opinion in *Dorman v. United States* (435 F.2d 385 [D.C. Cir. 1970]) highlighted seven factors that may permit warrantless entry, only one of which is an exigency discussed thus far:

1. The offense is serious.
2. The suspect is believed to be armed.
3. The police have a high degree of probable cause for arrest.
4. There is an especially strong reason to believe the suspect is on the premises.
5. Escape is likely.
6. The entry can be made peaceably.
7. The entry can be made during the day.

Various lower courts have applied these criteria in their decisions (e.g., *United States v. Reed*, 572 F.2d 412 [2nd Cir. 1978]; *State v. Gregory*, 331 N.W.2d 140 [Iowa 1983]), but it is doubtful that the Supreme Court would uphold any one of the criteria besides the fifth and possibly the second.

The Role of Police-Created Exigencies

Some lower courts have held that the government cannot claim exigent circumstances if the exigency is created by the police. For example, in *United States v. Curran* (498 F.2d 30 [9th Cir. 1974]), the Ninth Circuit Court of Appeals ruled unconstitutional a warrantless entry when it occurred after law enforcement officials knocked on the door of a house they knew contained marijuana. In the court's words, "[T]he officers consciously established the condition which the government now points to as [an] exigent circumstance" (p. 34). In other words, the police cannot claim exigency to justify warrantless searches or seizures in bad faith. By contrast, *good faith* means not acting with the intent to improperly circumvent the warrant requirement by purposefully precipitating a situation in which the destruction of evidence or contraband is likely.

DECISION MAKING EXERCISE **5.6**

Police-Created Exigencies

The police knocked on the door of Patrick Warner, whom they suspected was an armed and dangerous narcotics dealer. When Warner came to the door, the police ordered him to place his hands on the glass door and then to slowly reach down and unlock it. Warner said he did not have a key and would need to go to another room to obtain one. Believing he would retrieve a gun from the other room, the officers kicked down the door and entered as the suspect retreated to another room. Once inside, the officers conducted a protective sweep of the apartment. During the course of the sweep, they found bales of marijuana. Were the entrance and the sweep justified?

Summary. The common types of exigent circumstances recognized by the courts include hot pursuit, threats to persons, and threats to evidence. Warrantless action based on a hot pursuit exigency is constitutional only if the police have probable cause to believe any of the following:

1. The person they are pursuing has committed a serious offense.
2. The person will be found on the premises the police seek to enter.
3. The suspect will escape or harm someone or evidence will be lost or destroyed.
4. The pursuit originates from a lawful vantage point.
5. The scope and timing of the search are reasonable.

In situations in which the hot pursuit exception does not apply (and, presumably, the automobile and search incident to arrest exceptions do not apply), a warrantless search for evanescent evidence is permissible when (1) there is probable cause to believe that evidence will be destroyed, lost, or devalued; (2) the procedures employed are reasonable; and (3) the exigency was not police created. A broad interpretation of the latter condition suggests that the same applies in the case of hot pursuit, but the Supreme Court has not ruled on the problem of police-created exigencies.

Also, a warrantless search is permissible absent hot pursuit or the potential for damage or destruction to evidence if probable cause exists to believe a person on the premises is in imminent danger of death or serious bodily harm. Figure 5.3 (page 148) presents relevant portions from the *California Peace Officers Legal Sourcebook* that address warrantless searches intended to prevent imminent danger to life.

A. To Prevent Imminent Danger to Life

1. "Protective Sweep"

If you are already lawfully inside or outside a house and have some factual basis for believing there may be others inside who pose a danger to you or others, you may undertake a "protective sweep," that is, a limited, quick, visual inspection of those places where a person might be hiding. (*Buie* (1990) 494 U.S. 325, 327; *Furrow* (9th Cir. 2000) 229 F.3d 805, 811.)

In *Buie* itself, the U.S. Supreme Court decided that if you legally arrest a dangerous felon inside a residence, you are entitled to ensure your own safety by:

- looking into "closets and other spaces immediately adjoining the place of arrest from which an attack could be immediately launched," without needing any probable cause or reasonable suspicion; and

- conducting a protective sweep throughout the remainder of the residence, i.e., looking anywhere else where another person could be hiding, if you have reasonable suspicion, based on specific facts, "that the area swept harbors an individual posing a danger to the officer or others." (*Buie* (1990) 494 U.S. 325.)

Although *Buie* and most "protective sweep" cases involve your presence to make an arrest, the doctrine has occasionally been successfully applied to other situations. In every "sweep," however, you are entitled to search (enter and/or look into) only areas where a person could possibly be hiding (therefore not into drawers, small cabinets, etc.).

If you see crime-related evidence in plain view during a protective sweep, you may seize it, or call for someone else to confirm your suspicions. (*Duncan* (1986) 42 Cal.3d 91.) It is normally better, however, to get a warrant, because that way you can search more thoroughly for other similar evidence which may be on the premises.

Example: An officer responding to a burglary call talked to a neighbor who said two teenagers had just fled with a TV. Investigating, the officer found an open window with a box on the ground beneath it containing a TV and other items. The officer entered to see if the burglars, or more of them, or victims, might still be inside—only to find a clandestine drug lab. This warrantless entry was upheld by the state Supreme Court. (*Duncan* (1986) 42 Cal.3d 91.)

2. Victim, Injured or Ill Person Inside

Because exigent circumstances exist, you may enter a home without a warrant if (1) you reasonably believe an imminent threat exists to the life or welfare of someone inside; (2) you have probable cause to believe that a person reliably reported as missing is inside, or (3) you reasonably believe that someone inside is in need of aid. (*Coddington* (2000) 23 Cal.4th 529, 580; *Tamborino* (1986) 41 Cal.3d 919; *Wharton* (1991) 53 Cal.3d 522, 577; (The same is true where animals are in danger. (Pen. Code, § 597.1; *Broden* (1999) 70 Cal.App.4th 1212, 1220–1222).)

Remember, however, that once you are lawfully inside, your "scope" is limited. You may only search or do whatever is necessary to resolve the emergency—such as determining the presence of victims—nothing more. (*Ray* (1999) 21 Cal.4th 464, 477; *Tamborino* (1986) 41 Cal.3d 919.)

Example: Officers responded to a house where there had been reports of "screams." They knocked on the door and requested permission to enter and investigate. The man who answered the door appeared very nervous and ran back into the house toward a bedroom. Fearing for their own safety and that of a possible victim, the officers followed the man and found weapons and contraband (narcotics) in the bedroom in plain view. After the defendant had been arrested and taken to the living room, one officer went back to the bedroom and looked around more closely. He found more narcotics in a cigar box. The court found the entry of the house proper. However, the search of the cigar box was invalid since it was not justified by either the emergency or "plain view." (*Frazier* (1977) 71 Cal.App.3d 690.)

3. Suspected Child Abuse

Courts will go fairly far in finding an exigency and permitting a warrantless entry into premises to prevent possible child-abuse offenses.

Example: Late one evening, the brother of the victim personally reported hearsay information to the police that his father was right then having sexual intercourse forcibly with the cerebral-palsied and retarded daughter of the family. The officer had heard other information about prior acts of sexuality in the house from a probation officer who was working with the family. Accompanied by the brother, the officer entered the house and the father's closed bedroom, finding the sex offense in progress. The warrantless entries were upheld. (*Brown* (1970) 12 Cal.App.3d 600.)

4. Suspected Domestic Violence

It may be legal to enter a residence, without consent or a warrant, at the scene of possible domestic violence, on the basis of exigent circumstances, if the circumstances indicate that such entry is necessary to protect the victim by preventing ongoing or additional violence.

Example: At 11:00 p.m., officers responded to report of "a man shoving a woman around." After knocking without success, they saw a man inside and heard a shout. Thirty seconds after knocking again, a woman answered. Although she claimed she was alright, she was extremely frightened, appeared (to the experienced officer) to have been the victim of felony battery, lied about being alone, and gave a suspicious story about having fallen down the stairs. Believing that she might be under the threat of continued violence and that there might be others in peril inside, the officers entered the residence where they encountered Higgins and observed signs of marijuana activity. After obtaining consent to search from Higgins, the officers discovered more contraband. HELD: The warrantless entry was valid. The entry was motivated by the officers' legitimate safety concerns, and their belief was objectively reasonable here. The court warned, however, that officers must exercise discretion rather than "blindly following" a departmental policy to contact all parties at the scene "without considering the facts at hand." (*Higgins* (1994) 26 Cal.App.4th 247, 251–255.)

Source: From *California Peace Officers Legal Sourcebook*, electronic edition, revision 113 (Sacramento, CA: California Department of Justice, Office of the Attorney General), Sections 3.10, 3.11, and 3.12a.

Automobile Searches

In the landmark case of *Carroll v. United States* (267 U.S. 132 [1925]), the Supreme Court carved out an **automobile exception** to the Fourth Amendment's warrant requirement. The Court declared that the warrantless search of an automobile is permissible when (1) there is probable cause to believe the vehicle contains evidence of a crime and (2) securing a warrant is impractical. *Carroll*, which was decided in 1925, resulted from the vehicle stop of a suspect who was known to have previously engaged in the sale of bootleg whiskey (i.e., during Prohibition). A warrantless search of the car revealed 68 bottles of illegal liquor. The Supreme Court upheld the warrantless search on the grounds that the evidence would be lost if the police had been required to take the time to secure a warrant.

■ *Carroll v. United States,* 267 U.S. 132 (1925)

Rationale

Three arguments can be offered in support of the automobile exception. First, because of the inherent mobility of vehicles, it is impractical to obtain warrants. According to the Court in *Carroll*:

> The guaranty (sic) of freedom from unreasonable searches and seizures by the Fourth Amendment has been construed, practically since the beginning of the Government, as recognizing a necessary difference between a search of a store, dwelling house or other structure in respect of which a proper official warrant readily may be obtained, and a search of a ship, motor boat, wagon or automobile, for contraband goods, where it is not practicable to secure a warrant because the vehicle can be quickly moved out of the locality in which the warrant must be sought. (p. 153)

The second reason for the automobile exception focuses on people's reasonable expectation of privacy. In particular, because vehicles are typically operated in public spaces, a lesser expectation of privacy is enjoyed. As the Court observed in *Cardwell v. Lewis* (417 U.S. 583 [1974]), people have a lesser expectation of privacy in an automobile because it

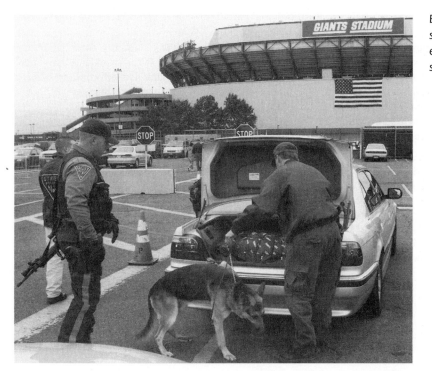

Because vehicles are operated in public spaces, a lesser expectation of privacy is enjoyed, which means warrantless searches may be allowed.

serves a transportation function, not a privacy function; a car "seldom serves as one's residence or the repository of personal effects" (p. 590). Also, people have a lesser expectation of privacy in their automobiles because by their very nature, automobiles travel "public thoroughfares where [their] occupants and [their] contents are in plain view" (p. 590).

The third reason for the automobile exception hinges on the government regulations to which vehicles are subjected. The old adage that "driving is a privilege, not a right" applies in this context. The Court's opinion in *United States v. Chadwick* (433 U.S. 1 [1977]) is illustrative. There, in deciding that the warrantless search of a man's footlocker, based on the automobile exception (because the footlocker was mobile), was unconstitutional, the Court pointed to five issues concerning the regulated nature of automobiles: Automobiles (1) travel on public roads; (2) are subject to state regulations and licensing requirements; (3) are subject to other strict regulations; (4) are subject to periodic inspections; and (5) may be impounded for public safety reasons. Thus, the

---

FIGURE 5.4   Example of a Vehicle Search Policy

9.7.4 Motor Vehicle Searches

It is the policy of this Department to conduct motor vehicle searches that are both legal and thorough. Such searches are to be conducted in strict observance of the constitutional rights of the owner and occupants of the motor vehicle being searched, and with due regard for the safety of all officers, other persons, and property involved.

For the purposes of this policy, a *motor vehicle* is any vehicle operating or capable of being operated on public streets or highways to include automobiles, trucks, trailers, recreational vehicles, mobile homes, motor homes, and any other type of vehicle, whether self-propelled or towed. This policy does not apply to vehicles of any type that have been immobilized in one location for use as a temporary or permanent residence or storage facility, or which are otherwise classified by the law as residences or buildings.

Also, for the purposes of this section of the policy manual, a *search* is an examination of all or a portion of the vehicle with an investigatory motive (i.e., for the purpose of discovering fruits, instrumentalities, or evidence of a crime or contraband, or to enter the vehicle to examine the vehicle identification number or to determine the ownership of the vehicle). Inventories of personal property conducted pursuant to impoundment of the vehicle are not covered by this policy.

Whenever feasible, a warrant will be obtained prior to conducting a search of a vehicle. Warrantless searches are allowed only under exigent circumstances, such as lack of time or when it is impractical for the officer to obtain a warrant. When there is no significant chance the vehicle will be driven away or any evidence contained within will be removed or destroyed, a warrant should be obtained prior to a search. Other circumstances under which a vehicle may be searched include:

1. Probable cause;
2. Consent;
3. Incident to arrest;
4. Frisk for weapons; and/or
5. To examine the VIN or determine ownership.

The scope of vehicle searches is limited as follows:

1. Searches with a warrant: When conducting a search with a warrant, the officer may search all areas of the vehicle unless otherwise stated in the warrant.
2. Probable cause searches: Probable cause searches may extend to all areas of the vehicle, unless the probable cause is limited to a specific area of the vehicle.
3. Consent: The extent of a consented search is limited to terms of consent. The consent will be taped and whenever possible, a signed consent form will be made.
4. Incident to arrest: Searches incident to the arrest of an occupant of a vehicle will include the entire passenger area of the vehicle, as well as the trunk and the engine compartment; however, any locked container found within the vehicle may not be searched without a warrant or absent consent.
5. Frisks for weapons: Frisks for weapons normally must be confined to the passenger area of the vehicle. Areas not immediately accessible to the vehicle's occupants, such as a locked glove compartment, may not be searched.
6. Attempts to examine the VIN or determine ownership: Vehicle searches conducted under these premises will be limited to the reasonable accomplishments of these goals.

Whenever an officer is conducting a limited search discovers an item that creates probable cause to believe that other portions of the vehicle may contain evidence of a crime, any additional portions of the vehicle that could reasonably contain the items being sought may be searched.

Source: From *General Directives Manual,* Gallatin, Tennessee, Police Department (December 28, 1999). Used courtesy of the Gallatin Police Department.

Court declared that the automobile exception should not apply to the warrantless search of personal items, despite their mobility.

Requirements

Three general requirements must be met for a valid warrantless vehicle search: (1) the exception must only apply to automobiles; (2) with one exception, such a search must be premised on probable cause; and (3) it must be impractical to obtain a warrant (i.e., the vehicle stop must be such that it is impractical, burdensome, or risky to take time to obtain a warrant). The third requirement is unresolved, as the courts have relied on lesser expectation of privacy analysis rather than an exigency argument to support warrantless searches of automobiles. Figure 5.4 presents the vehicle search requirements of the Gallatin, Tennessee, Police Department.

In no instance will a container in a motor vehicle be searched unless it could contain the item(s) being sought. In addition:

1. In a probable cause search, any unlocked containers such as paper bags, cardboard boxes, etc., wherever found in the vehicle, may be opened.
2. When the passenger compartment of a vehicle is being searched incident to an arrest, such containers found within the passenger compartment may be opened if unlocked.
3. Containers discovered during a consent search of the vehicle may be opened provided that the terms of the consent expressly permit or reasonably imply that the particular container may be opened.
4. Containers found in or discarded from a vehicle under circumstances that do not justify their search under probable cause rules or in connection with a search incident to arrest should be secured but not searched until a warrant is obtained to search them.
5. Locked containers found during a vehicle search will only be opened with consent or under a warrant. If these conditions are not met, locked containers will be secured by the officer and opened only after a warrant has been obtained.

Whenever possible, the search of a vehicle and any containers therein will be conducted at the location where the vehicle was discovered or detained. Under unusual circumstances, the search may be delayed until after the vehicle or container has been moved to a secure location. Searches will always be conducted as soon as is reasonably practical, taking in to consideration personnel needs and the safety of the officer, other persons, and the property itself.

Vehicle searches will be conducted in a manner which minimizes the intrusiveness of the search and the inconvenience caused to the vehicle owner, occupants and other persons involved. When possible, damage to the vehicle or other property involved will be avoided. When damage is unavoidable, such damage will be limited to that which is reasonably necessary to conduct the search.

Examination of a vehicle that has been abandoned on a public thoroughfare is technically not a search. If an officer can determine in advance that the vehicle has been abandoned, examination of the interior of the vehicle will be conducted only in accordance with the provisions of this policy and the law.

Any evidentiary items discovered in the course of any motor vehicle search will be collected, handled, packaged, marked, transported, and stored in accordance with applicable policies and procedures of this Department. Where appropriate and feasible, itemized receipts for seized property will be given to the owner and/or occupants of the vehicle.

Searches of motor vehicles are to be conducted in strict compliance with all applicable laws, governmental regulations, and departmental policies and procedures pertaining to the protection of departmental personnel from communicable diseases and hazardous substances. Any exposure of search personnel or others to such substances will be reported in accordance with Chapter 9, Section 16, of this Manual.

If a search of a vehicle leaves the vehicle or any property contained therein vulnerable to unauthorized entry, theft, or damage, search personnel will take such steps as are reasonably necessary to secure and/or preserve the vehicle or property from such hazards.

An officer supervising a vehicle search will be responsible for ensuring that it is conducted in accordance with this policy. In the event that the vehicle search is conducted under a warrant, the officer will ensure that the execution of the warrant is properly reported to the issuing court or other authority. The officer will also be responsible for making any other reports regarding the search that may be required by law, policy, or procedure.

So far, the term *automobile* has been tossed around with wild abandon. Note, though, that *automobile* has a very specific meaning. In other words, precise types of vehicles are covered by the automobile exception. Cars, boats (e.g., *United States v. Lee*, 274 U.S. 559 [1927]), and planes are all considered automobiles. However, what about the hybrid situation involving a vehicle serving the dual purpose of transportation and residence, such as a motor home or a tractor trailer with a sleeper cab?

■ *California v. Carney,* 471 U.S. 386 (1985)

The Court was confronted with this question in the case of *California v. Carney* (471 U.S. 386 [1985]). Unfortunately, the Court adopted another objective reasonableness standard and refused to define explicitly the types of automobiles covered by the automobile exception. The Court held that the test of whether a vehicle serves a transportation or residence function requires looking at the *setting* in which the vehicle is located. If the setting "objectively indicates that the vehicle is being used for transportation" (p. 386), then the automobile exception applies.

Four factors are used in determining whether a vehicle serves a transportation function: (1) whether it is mobile or stationary; (2) whether it is licensed; (3) whether it is connected to utilities; and (4) whether it has convenient access to the road. If, for example, a trailer is on blocks, unlicensed, connected to utilities, and in a trailer park, then it will almost certainly be treated in the same way that a residence is for purposes of the Fourth Amendment.

In *Carroll*, the Court noted that "where seizure is impossible except without warrant, the seizing officer acts unlawfully and at his peril unless he can show the court probable cause" (p. 156). Simply put, despite the fact that a vehicle search is permissible without a warrant, the search must still be based on probable cause. Note, however, that probable cause to *search* and probable cause to *arrest* are not one in the same. While probable cause to search may exist, this does not automatically create probable cause to arrest. In *Carroll*, for example, the police had probable cause to search the vehicle but not probable cause to arrest the occupants. Similarly, probable cause to arrest does not authorize a full search of a vehicle, including the trunk, but it does authorize a search of the

■ *New York v. Belton,* 453 U.S. 454 (1981)

passenger compartment (*New York v. Belton*, 453 U.S. 454 [1981]). Belton was recently extended to include searches where the initial contact between the officer and the suspect took place outside the vehicle, in a parking lot (*Thoraton v. United States* 541 U.S. 615 [2004]). In *Preston v. United States* (376 U.S. 364 [1964]), for example, the police arrested the occupants of a car, but the Court declared that this action did not give the police probable cause to search the entire vehicle, including the trunk.

There is one important exception to the rule that probable cause must be in place before a vehicle search can be conducted. In *New York v. Class* (475 U.S. 106 [1986]), the Court held in a 5 to 4 decision that the warrantless, suspicionless search of a car for the purpose of ascertaining the vehicle identification number (VIN) is permissible. All that is required is a valid traffic stop. This exception does not, however, authorize the police to enter cars at will, without any basis for a search. In support of its opinion, the Court pointed to the lesser expectation of privacy argument. Also, it noted that the search was minimally intrusive. The lower court in *Class* was not in agreement with the Supreme Court's decision: "The fact that certain information must be kept, or that it may be of a public nature, does not automatically sanction police intrusion into private space in order to obtain it" (p. 124).

A general rule concerning warrants is that they should be obtained whenever practical. However, given the circumstances surrounding most vehicle stops, it would seem foolish to require that the police obtain a warrant before engaging in the search of an automobile. As the Court observed in *Carroll*, in cases in which the securing of a warrant is reasonably practicable, a warrant must be used. In most situations involving the stop of an automobile, securing a warrant is not practical. In *Husty v. United States* (282 U.S. 694 [1931]), for example, a police officer followed up on a tip from an informant and found contraband in Husty's unattended car. Given that the car was unattended, one could argue that a warrant should have been secured, but the Court argued that the officer "could not know when Husty would come to the car or how soon it would be removed"

(p. 701). Contrast *Husty* with *Coolidge v. New Hampshire* (403 U.S. 443 [1971]). In that case, the Court ruled that the automobile exception did not apply to a warrantless search and seizure of two cars located on the defendant's property because the police had probable cause to act more than two weeks before the search.

Husty and *Coolidge* suggest that the warrantless search of an automobile will only be upheld if it was impractical to obtain a warrant. As mentioned at the outset of this section, however, this third requirement is unresolved. In *Chambers v. Maroney* (399 U.S. 42 [1970]), for example, the Court held that as long as the vehicle is readily mobile, a warrantless search is permissible, even if it is conducted away from the scene at the stationhouse. The actual search of the automobile in *Chambers* was made at the police station many hours after the car had been stopped on the highway, when the car was no longer movable. Furthermore, at that point, exigent circumstances no longer existed and a magistrate could likely have been found to issue a warrant. Yet the court sanctioned the search (see also *Texas v. White*, 423 U.S. 67 [1975]).

One relatively recent case, *United States v. Johns* (469 U.S. 478 [1985]), seems to suggest that the rationale for the automobile exception is, at least in part, an exigency. In that case, the Court held that the warrantless search of an automobile is impermissible if it "adversely affect[s] a privacy [or] possessory interest" (p. 487). This argument seems to suggest that a search under the automobile exception needs to be premised on the urgency of the situation; otherwise, a warrant should be secured. Nevertheless, the Court in *Johns* did state that a three-day delay between the initial stop and the arrest was permissible, partly because the car's owner did not claim that the delay caused hardship.

So, what is the role of exigency in the automobile exception? A safe rule of thumb is that the presence or absence of exigent circumstances is irrelevant. Instead, a showing that the automobile was readily mobile is enough to justify a warrantless search under the automobile exception (as long as probable cause is in place and the target of the search is, in fact, an automobile, as defined earlier).

Scope of the Search

A number of court decisions have considered the scope of the search authorized under the automobile exception. Most of the decisions have focused on whether a container in an automobile can also be searched if probable cause to search the vehicle exists. In *Arkansas v. Sanders* (442 U.S. 753 [1979]), the Court ruled that the warrantless search of a suitcase was not permissible when the police waited for the suitcase to be placed in the vehicle. Similarly, in *Robbins v. California* (453 U.S. 420 [1981]), the Court held that a container discovered during a warrantless vehicle search can be seized but not searched until a warrant can be obtained.

DECISION MAKING EXERCISE 5.7

A Twist on Carroll

Two police detectives have probable cause to believe that several illegal automatic weapons are in the trunk of Carmine Lord's car. However, Lord's car is broken down and has been left with the local auto mechanic. Furthermore, Lord has proven to be a difficult customer and has refused to pay for the full amount of the repair. As such, the mechanic has locked Lord's car in a bay at his service station and refused to release it until he receives payment. Assuming they have the mechanic's blessing, may the detectives search Lord's car for the weapons while it is at the station?

Just one year after *Robbins*, the Court handed down its decision in *United States v. Ross* (456 U.S. 798 [1982]), which overturned *Robbins*. The Court declared that as long as the police have justification to conduct a warrantless vehicle search, they may conduct a search "that is as thorough as a magistrate could authorize in a warrant" (p. 800). The only limitation is "defined by the object of the search and the places in which there is probable cause to believe that it may be found" (p. 824). Accordingly, if the contraband sought is small (e.g., a syringe), the scope of the vehicle search exception is almost limitless. Recently, the Supreme Court held that even passengers' personal belongings can be searched (*Wyoming v. Houghton*, 526 U.S. 295 [1999]).

Fewer cases have focused on precisely how far the police can go during a vehicle search in terms of inflicting damage to the vehicle. On the one hand, based on a reading of the previous chapter, a due process violation may occur if the damage inflicted is excessive. On the other hand, it would appear that a certain degree of physical damage to an automobile is permissible. The *Carroll* decision, for example, was based on a warrantless search in which the police sliced open the vehicle's upholstery to look for contraband.

DECISION MAKING EXERCISE 5.8

Proper Scope for an Automobile Search

Joan Lee was pulled over on Interstate 10 after a highway patrol officer observed her aggressively weaving from one lane to another. The officer had probable cause to search the vehicle for drugs. Accordingly, Lee opened the trunk, at which point the officer's attention was drawn to the spare tire. To the officer, it looked as though the spare was the wrong one for the vehicle. In addition, there appeared to be a white, powdery substance on the rubber. Based on his knowledge that narcotics are smuggled in such a fashion, the officer pulled the spare out of the vehicle, slashed it open with a knife, and found drugs inside. The drugs were seized and Lee was arrested. In terms of scope, was this search justified?

In a recent case, the Supreme Court considered whether allowing a drug dog to sniff a vehicle during a traffic stop violated the Fourth Amendment. In *Illinois v. Caballes* (543 U.S. 405 [2005]), an Illinois state trooper stopped a vehicle while speeding. During the 10-minute stop, while the trooper was going through all the usual motions associated witha a traffic stop, another trooper arrived and allowed a drug dog to sniff the vehicle. The dog was alerted to the trunk. Marijuana was found, and the driver was arrested. The Supreme Court upheld the dog sniff, citing three factors: (1) the legality of the stop; (2) the short duration of the stop; and (3) no one can claim legal ownership to—and thereby assert a privacy interest in—contraband. This was a controversial decision, but one that clearly errs on the side of law enforcement.

When Other Doctrines Govern Searches of Automobiles

Keep in mind that the automobile exception cases are *not* the only cases governing warrantless searches of vehicles. Many warrantless searches of vehicles are better analyzed under other exceptions to the Fourth Amendment's warrant requirement. For example, the Supreme Court has rejected the use of the automobile exception in analyzing searches of automobiles crossing international borders. Such cases are better analyzed under the border checkpoints exception discussed in Chapter 7.

Still other warrantless searches of automobiles are permissible based on other decisions unrelated to the automobile exception initially set forth in *Carroll*. These include searches (1) incident to arrest (see earlier discussion); (2) during the course of a stop-and-frisk (e.g., *Adams v. Williams*, 407 U.S. 143 [1972]; see Chapter 6); (3) under the plain view doctrine (see later discussion); (4) based on the inventory search exception (see Chapter 7); and (5) with consent by the automobile's occupant (see Chapter 7). Therefore, searches of automobiles—like searches of other places as well as people—can

FIGURE 5.5	Levels of Justification for Automobile Searches	
Level of Intrusion	**Justification Required**
Search of entire car, including containers	Probable cause to search
Search of passenger compartment and containers	Probable cause to arrest occupant
Weapons search of passenger compartment	Reasonable suspicion/fear for safety
Order occupants out of car	Reasonable suspicion to stop
Inventory search	Administrative

simultaneously be governed by several different doctrines. Figure 5.5 summarizes the levels of justification required to conduct various types of vehicle searches.

Racial Profiling

The Supreme Court has permitted the police to stop a car based on the belief that a crime has been committed, which includes any traffic violation (*Whren v. United States*, 517 U.S. 806 [1996]). In addition, once a person has been stopped, the officer can order him or her to stand outside the vehicle without any justification (*Maryland v. Wilson*, 519 U.S. 408 [1997]; *Pennsylvania v. Mimms*, 434 U.S. 106 [1997]). The police can also engage in searches with consent (*Ohio v. Robinette*, 519 U.S. 33 [1996]), seize items that are in plain view (*Horton v. California*, 496 U.S. 128 [1990]), frisk the driver and/or search the passenger compartment of the vehicle out of concerns for safety (*Michigan v. Long*, 463 U.S. 1032 [1983]), and search the entire car if probable cause to arrest and/or search is developed (*New York v. Belton*, 453 U.S. 454 [1981]). Finally, police are not required to provide the *Miranda* warnings when asking questions pursuant to a routine vehicle stop (*Miranda v. Arizona*, 384 U.S. 436 [1966]).

All this means that police have numerous opportunities to detect contraband during the course of a vehicle stop. And since almost every driver commits a violation of traffic law at some point or other, there is plenty of justification for stopping motorists to begin with. But whether every motorist is stopped for *legitimate* reasons is questionable. Further, even if the police have legal grounds to stop someone in his or her car, the question of pretext presents itself: Should the police be able to use traffic laws to stop people when they really have other motivations in mind (i.e., to gain consent to search)? The Supreme Court has yet to answer this question, which has led to the concern that the police have *too* much discretion in terms of their authority to stop motorists. Closely tied to this concern are allegations of **racial profiling**, which have emerged in recent years. Racial profiling occurs when the police use race or ethnicity as a factor in determining whether to stop someone. Figure 5.6 (page 156) presents the guidelines for using race or ethnicity as the criterion for conducting a stop from the *California Peace Officers Legal Sourcebook*.

A driver's race or ethnicity obviously does not provide the justification to stop him or her. But many argue that the police use existing traffic laws, which are numerous and easy to violate, to single out certain drivers based on their race or ethnicity. The Supreme Court has yet to decide on the constitutionality of this type of conduct directly, but at least one of its decisions has come close. For example, in *Whren v. United States* (517 U.S. 806 [1996]), Washington, D.C., police made a traffic stop and observed two bags of crack cocaine in the hands of a passenger who was seated in the front of the car. The police testified that they stopped the driver because he had violated traffic laws. In contrast, the defendants claimed that the stop was made based on their race and that the police used alleged traffic violations as a reason to stop them.

> **FIGURE 5.6** *Example of Guidelines for Using Race as a Criterion for Conducting a Stop*
>
> Reasonable suspicion may not be based, in whole or in part, "on broad profiles which cast suspicion on entire categories of people without any individualized suspicion of the particular person to be stopped." (*Montero-Camargo* (9th Cir. 2000) 208 F.3d 1122, 1129–1130, quoting an earlier Ninth Circuit case.) In other words, generally speaking, race is simply not a factor which you may consider in calculating reasonable suspicion.
>
> Indeed, racial profiling, that is, "the practice of detaining a suspect based on a broad set of criteria which casts suspicion upon an entire class of people without individualized suspicion of the particular person being stopped," is specifically outlawed. (Pen. Code, § 13519.4.)
>
> On the other hand, race or ethnicity is still a proper factor to consider if it is part of a description of a specific suspect you are looking for. "Hispanic appearance, or any other racial or ethnic appearance, including Caucasian, may be considered when the suspected perpetrator of a specific offense has been identified as having such an appearance." (*Montero-Camargo* (9th. Cir. 2000) 208 F.3d 1122, 1134, fn. 22.) Even in such a situation, however, there would have to be additional factors, in addition to the suspect's race, which provide reasonable suspicion and thus justify the detention.
>
> *Example:* Suspect in 1 a.m. convenience-store robbery was described as 19-year-old Mexican with a moustache, wearing a dark jacket. Seven minutes later and one-half mile away, an officer stopped a Mexican, approximately 20 years old, who had a moustache. The detention was valid—even though it was based primarily on race—because race was just part of a matching description. (*McCluskey* (1981) 125 Cal.App.3d 220.)
>
> *Example:* It was proper to detain two Hispanics seen sleeping in public at about 8:30 a.m. within one and a half miles of the place a woman had been raped by a group of six young Hispanic males, one of whom had been wearing a red shirt, where both suspects were wearing red shirts, and otherwise fit the general description of race and age. (*Carlos M.* (1990) 220 Cal.App.3d 372.)

Source: From *California Peace Officers Legal Sourcebook*, electronic edition, revision 113 (Sacramento, CA: California Department of Justice, Office of the Attorney General), Section 12.10d.

The Supreme Court concluded that the "constitutional reasonableness of traffic stops" does not depend "on the actual motivations of the individual officers" (p. 813). The Court also concluded that the only relevant inquiry is whether the officer had cause to stop the car (pp. 813–814). It rejected the argument that the Fourth Amendment requires a court to consider whether "the officer's conduct deviated materially from usual police practices, so that a reasonable officer in the same circumstances would not have made the stop for the reasons given" (p. 814). Simply put, the Supreme Court has stated that individual officers' motivations—whether racial or of any other substance— are irrelevant. The only question worth asking and answering, according to the Court, is whether the officer had cause to stop. Needless to say, this decision did not satisfy critics of racial profiling.

Justice Kennedy's dissent in *Maryland v. Wilson* (519 U.S. 408 [1997]) summarizes the voices of racial profiling critics everywhere:

> The practical effect of our holding in *Whren*, of course, is to allow the police to stop vehicles in almost countless circumstances. When *Whren* is coupled with today's holding, the Court puts tens of millions of passengers at risk of arbitrary control by the police. If the command to exit were to become commonplace, the Constitution would be diminished in a most public way. As the standards suggested in dissent are adequate to protect the safety of the police, we ought not to suffer so great a loss. (p. 422)

The Court's opinion in *Whren* effectively closed the door on Fourth Amendment claims of racial discrimination. What is left, perhaps, is the Fourteenth Amendment's equal protection clause as well as Title VI of the Civil Rights Act of 1964, the latter of which provides a remedy for acts of racial discrimination. Each of these remedies is briefly discussed in the following subsections.

Fourteenth Amendment Equal Protection Claims

Motorists can sue, based on 42 U.S.C. 1983, for racial discrimination under the equal protection clause of the Fourteenth Amendment. At least two types of Fourteenth Amendment claims can be identified. The first is a challenge to a law or policy that intentionally classifies people based on race or some other classification. Second, plaintiffs can argue that a racially neutral policy or statute is being enforced in a discriminatory fashion.

For the first type of Fourteenth Amendment claim to succeed, it must be shown that (1) a practice or policy intentionally classifies persons based on race and (2) the practice or policy withstands "strict judicial scrutiny" (*Adarand Constructors, Inc. v. Pena*, 515 U.S. 200 [1995], p. 227). These are known as *Pena's* first and second prongs.

Concerning *Pena's* first prong, one court has said that racial discrimination can be shown by a law that "expressly classifies persons on the basis of race" (*Hayden v. County of Nassau*, 180 F.3d 42 [2nd Cir. 1999]) or by a practice or policy that treats one differently from members of other racial groups. For example, if a police department's policy authorizes stops based on racial or ethnic characteristics, it would be discriminatory. According to another court, racial discrimination exists when law enforcement personnel "adopt a policy, employ a practice, or in a given situation take steps to initiate an investigation . . . based solely upon the citizen's race" (*United States v. Avery* 128 F.3d 974 [6th Cir. 1997], p. 985).

In most situations, however, there are no formal policies or practices that authorize traffic stops based on race. What is necessary in such situations is to use statistical evidence to show that the police acted with intent to discriminate. However, because the saying "you can prove anything with statistics" is at least partly true, the courts have been mixed in terms of their willingness to rely on statistical evidence of racial discrimination. In *Hunter v. Underwood* (471 U.S. 222 [1985]), for instance, the Supreme Court sustained an equal protection claim by African Americans who claimed they were deprived of important rights for convictions under an Alabama law. The Court accepted statistical evidence to the effect that blacks were disenfranchised under the law at a rate 1.7 times more than whites.

However, in *McCleskey v. Kemp* (481 U.S. 279 [1987]), the Court rejected a statistical analysis related to the application of the death penalty in Georgia. The study presented in that case claimed that the race of the victim was the factor most likely to influence jury members in their death penalty decisions. The Court claimed that the study showed only a correlation between the race of the victim and the death penalty decision. The Court took a similar approach in *United States v. Armstrong* (517 U.S. 456 [1996]), in which it rejected the defendants' argument that the federal government engaged in the racially selective prosecution of "crack" cocaine offenders. It held that the defendants "failed to satisfy the threshold showing. . . that the Government declined to prosecute similarly situated suspects of other races" (p. 458). Both decisions suggest that it would be exceedingly difficult to show Fourteenth Amendment discrimination in the context of racial profiling.

As for *Pena's* second prong—that a policy or practice must withstand "strict judicial scrutiny"—the government must show the necessity of the classification scheme. Specifically, a Fourteenth Amendment equal protection claim will not succeed if the government can show that it has a compelling interest justifying the practice or policy. Or stated differently, if the government can show that unequal treatment is necessary to further some clear government purpose, an equal protection claim will not succeed (see, e.g., *Heller v. Doe*, 509 U.S. 312 [1993]; *Romer v. Evans*, 517 U.S. 620 [1996]). However, if the government cannot meet this strict scrutiny test, an equal protection claim will probably succeed, provided that *Pena's* first prong is also satisfied.

As for the second type of Fourteenth Amendment claim, courts sometimes hear lawsuits in which plaintiffs allege that a racially neutral policy or statute has been enforced in a racially discriminatory fashion. Indeed, as early as 1886, the Supreme Court recognized that laws and policies can be enforced in a discriminatory fashion. In *Yick Wo v. Hopkins* (118 U.S. 356 [1886]), the Supreme Court held that a racially neutral statute had been enforced "with a mind so unequal and oppressive as to amount to a practical denial by the state of that equal protection of the laws . . . which is secured . . . by the broad and benign provisions of the Fourteenth Amendment to the Constitution of the United States" (p. 373, n. 46).

Relatedly, some plaintiffs have argued that legal searches and seizures conducted with appropriate justification violate the Fourteenth Amendment if they are used to selectively target certain individuals over others. For example, a plaintiff may argue that even though he or she was detained lawfully, the police violated the Fourteenth Amendment's equal protection clause because they selectively targeted individuals for such actions based solely on race. These types of claims are fairly rare and not often successful, but one New Jersey court has stated that if a police department embarks "upon an officially sanctioned de facto policy of targeting minorities for investigation and arrest," then it may be held liable (*State v. Kennedy*, 588 A.2d 834 [N.J. Super. 1991]).

The recent case of *United States v. Travis* (62 F.3d 170 [6th Cir. 1995]) illustrates this type of Fourteenth Amendment–based allegation. In it, a woman argued that she was selected for questioning based on her race. A detective, who was assigned to the Cincinnati/Northern Kentucky Airport, focused his attention on people arriving on a flight from Los Angeles because numerous passengers from the same flight had been arrested for drug offenses in the past. The woman was stopped by the detective and consented to a search. Drugs were found in her purse. The court held that because the detective did not need reasonable suspicion or probable cause (because of the woman's consent), no constitutional violation took place. However, the court did point out that consensual encounters based solely on race may violate the equal protection clause of the Fourteenth Amendment, even if the Fourth Amendment is not violated (see *Travis*, pp.173–174).

Title VII of the Civil Rights Act of 1964

As the Supreme Court has stated, the Fourth Amendment is not relevant to racial profiling claims. Further, based on *Armstrong* and *McKleskey*, it is exceedingly difficult, if not currently impossible, to succeed with a Fourteenth Amendment equal protection–based claim. The remaining available remedy is Title VII of the Civil Rights Act of 1964, which requires a showing of **disparate impact**. Disparate impact is, in general, a method of acting that treats one group in a markedly different fashion than another. (In the present context, the focus is on police actions.)

Title VII states, in relevant part, that recipients of federal funds "may not . . . utilize criteria or methods of administration which have the effect of subjecting individuals to discrimination based on their race, color, national origin, or have the effect of defeating or substantially impairing accomplishment of the objectives of the program as respects individuals of a particular race, color, or national origin" (28 C.F.R. 42.104[b][2]).

This legislation looks attractive on its face, but it is primarily a method by which the federal government enforces certain rules against entities that receive federal funds—usually state and local units of government. The question of whether private parties (i.e., average citizens) can enforce Title VII is one that has been litigated extensively in the courts. Of particular interest has been the issue of *standing*. Specifically, a plaintiff must show that he or she was a direct participant in or intended beneficiary of a state or local program or activity that receives federal funds. Fortunately, the Civil Rights Act of 1987 defines *program or activity* as all operations of a governmental entity that receives federal funds. Thus, traffic stops would appear to fall within the meaning of the legislation. That is, in theory, people should be able to sue under Title VII for racially discriminatory traffic enforcement policies. The Supreme Court has not ruled on this issue, however.

Recent Developments in Racial Profiling Case Law

Many racial profiling claims have been filed in the nation's courts, and many continue to be filed. This is an area of rapidly developing case law, so a comprehensive overview of the current state of racial profiling litigation is beyond the scope of this book. Most states have implemented or are about to implement record-keeping systems that provide specific numbers concerning the use of race in traffic stops and other encounters. Prior to the implementation of such record-keeping systems, lawsuits alleging racial discrimination against the police did not succeed very often. A few examples of relatively recent racial profiling cases from around the United States will prove useful here.

First, in *Brown v. City of Oneonta* (195 F.3 111 [2nd Cir. 1999]), a 77-year-old woman was attacked near Oneonta, New York. She reported to the police that her assailant was a young, black male and that he had cut his hand with a knife during the attack. A police canine unit tracked the suspect's smell from the scene of the crime to the nearby campus of the State University of New York at Oneonta. Only 2 percent of the students at the college were black, so the police obtained a list of records and attempted to locate and question all black students at the college. This effort failed, so the police then conducted a sweep of the town, during which nonwhite persons were questioned and their hands inspected for evidence of knife wounds. A lawsuit was brought, alleging that the police conduct violated the Fourth and Fourteenth Amendments. The court held that the stops were consensual and, as such, did not violate the Fourth Amendment. And as for the equal protection claims, the court held that the plaintiffs had not been "questioned solely on the basis of their race. They were questioned on the altogether legitimate basis of a physical description given by the victim of the crime" (p. 119).

In another case, *Chavez v. Illinois State Police* (27 F.Supp.2d 1053 [N.D.Ill. 1998]), the American Civil Liberties Union (ACLU) brought a lawsuit against Illinois state troopers, alleging that their practice of stopping, detaining, and searching Hispanic Americans and African Americans based on their race and ethnicity was unconstitutional. The court decided in favor of the defendants—the troopers—by concluding that because no records of such stops were kept, a disparate impact could not be determined and thus the troopers' actions were perfectly legitimate. In effect, the court stated that even if the plaintiffs could have shown that a disproportionate number of minorities were stopped for traffic violations, they could not have proven that claim without showing that other similarly situated nonminority drivers had also been treated differently.

The *Chavez* decision was controversial, to say the least. In response to it, recent federal district court decisions in New York and California have permitted claims of racial profiling to go forward even in the absence of evidence of similarly situated individuals being treated differently. For example, in *Rodriguez v. California Highway Patrol* (89 F.Supp.2d 1131 [N.D.Cal.2000]), a court stated:

> In the present action, the class of similarly situated individuals necessarily would include all motorists present in areas where Defendants were patrolling. It is highly doubtful that Defendants or any other law enforcement agency maintain records identifying law-abiding individuals who are not stopped. The only similarly situated persons as to whom records might be maintained would be the relatively small subset of individuals who were stopped and questioned by the police but not arrested, and even for this group, it is difficult to conceive what data Plaintiffs could obtain absent discovery which have not been alleged in the First Amended Complaint already. (p. 1131)

A comparable decision was reached in *Congress for Puerto Rican Rights v. New York City* (191 F.R.D. 52 [S.D.N.Y. 1999]). In that case, the plaintiffs cited the Second Circuit's decision in *Brown v. Oneonta* (195 F.3d 111 [2d Cir. 1999]), in which it was held that plaintiffs need not identify similarly situated nonminority individuals in order to sustain an equal protection claim. At issue in *Congress for Puerto Rican Rights* were actions by New York City's Street Crime Unit (SCU), an elite squad of police officers whose mission is to interdict violent crime in New York City and remove illegal firearms from the streets. The plaintiffs alleged that SCU officers subjected residents of high-crime areas, particularly African American and Hispanic American men, to stops-and-frisks because of their race and ethnicity.

In closing, the New Jersey Supreme Court recently handed down an interesting decision. The decision followed a study conducted by the Attorney General of New Jersey, in which it was determined that of all the consensual searches of cars on the New Jersey Turnpike, 77.2 percent were searches of minorities and blacks.[1] In *State v. Carty* (170 N.J. 632 [2001]), the court imposed strict limits on consensual automobile searches, interpreting the state's constitution to mean that before asking for a driver's permission to search, a police officer must have "reasonable and articulable suspicion" of criminal activity. In reaching its decision, the court noted, "In the context of motor vehicle stops, where the individual is at the side of the road and confronted by a uniformed officer seeking to search his or her vehicle, it is not a stretch of the imagination to assume that the individual feels compelled to consent" (p. 644).

Interestingly, Hawaii appears to be the only other state with similar restrictions on consensual stops. If and how other states choose to address racial profiling problems remains to be seen.

■ Arrests Based on Exigent Circumstances

Exigent (i.e., emergency) circumstances justify warrantless entry into a private home for the purpose of making an arrest. The five exigencies identified earlier in this chapter justify warrantless entry for this purpose. In other words, a warrantless arrest, with probable cause, is permissible if any of the following is present: (1) hot pursuit; (2) danger to officers; (3) danger to third parties; (4) escape; and (5) destruction of evidence. Figure 5.7 presents the San Bernardino, California, Police Department's policy for making warrantless arrests based on exigent circumstances.

■ Arrests in Public Places

■ *United States v. Watson,*
423 U.S. 411 (1976)

Unlike arrests made in the home (or in a third-party residence), arrests made in public do not require warrants. In *United States v. Watson* (423 U.S. 411 [1976]), the Supreme Court upheld the common-law rule that arrests made in public do not need to be predicated on a warrant. The Court expressed confidence in the ability of police officers to make probable cause determinations: "[W]e decline to transform [a] judicial preference [for arrest warrants] into a constitutional rule when the judgment of the Nation and Congress has for so long been to authorize warrantless public arrests on probable cause" (p. 423).

■ *United States v. Santana,*
427 U.S 38 (1976)

The court extended this decision to the curtilage of a home in *United States v. Santana* (427 U.S 38 [1976]). In that case, the police, who had probable cause to arrest Santana, arrived at her house to find her standing in the opening of her front door. When she saw the officers approaching, she retreated into the house. The officers followed her into the house and made the arrest. The Supreme Court declared that the officers' actions were

[1]Peter Verniero, Attorney General of New Jersey, *Interim Report of the State Police Review Team Regarding Allegations of Racial Profiling* (April 20, 1999), pp. 26–28. Available online: <www.state.nj.us/lps/intm_419.pdf>.

FIGURE 5.7   Example of a Policy for Effecting Warrantless Arrests Based on Exigent Circumstances

The "Ramey Decision" by the California Supreme Court commands that a police officer may not enter the residence of a suspect *for the purpose of effecting an arrest* without a warrant of arrest, unless "exigent (emergency) circumstances" justify such action, or lawful consent for entry is obtained.

The opinion defines exigent circumstances as "an emergency situation requiring swift action to prevent (1) *imminent* danger to life, (2) or *serious* damage to property, (3) or to forestall the *imminent* escape of a suspect, (4) or destruction of evidence."

The burden of proof of the existence of one or more of the exigent circumstances defined by the court will be upon the prosecution, and it appears that the courts will closely scrutinize any such claim of justification.

The prohibition includes arrests for felonies or misdemeanors whether by day or by night, and the prohibition encompasses arrest of adults and minors.

The Ramey rule will be applied to temporary residences such as hotels and motels. With the application of the "vicarious exclusionary rule," which acts to suppress evidence against any defendant when such evidence is obtained in the violation of any third party's rights, it appears that the prohibition will extend to residences of others where the suspect may be a guest regardless of the temporary nature of the suspect's tenancy.

The opinion of the court does not discuss the circumstances of "hot pursuit" or close pursuit from another place into a residence. It is believed that if probable cause for arrest exists during a pursuit but the arrest is not made due purely to the actions of the suspect in evading the officers and going into a residence, then the entry and arrest will be reasonable and justifiable in light of the imminent danger of escape.

Since the issue addressed by the court is the entry into a residence for the purpose of effecting the arrest and the necessity for judicial review of such process before the entry, it can be assumed that entry by means of a valid search warrant would satisfy the requirement for judicial review, and an arrest based on evidence uncovered during the search would be proper and not in violation of the rule in Ramey.

It appears also that if the officer enters the residence lawfully for any purpose other than the arrest of a suspect (in response to a call for service or in the legitimate course of an investigation) an ensuing arrest would be proper, although the courts would certainly scrutinize these circumstances.

In light of this opinion, the policy of the San Bernardino Police Department will be:

A warrant of arrest shall be obtained prior to any arrest of a suspect from a residence at any time for any offense except:

1. When one or more of the defined exigent circumstances are readily evident.

2. As a result of close pursuit wherein the arrest would have been lawful except for the suspect's evading the arrest and going into a residence.

3. When probable cause is developed during the execution of a valid search warrant for the residence and the suspect is present.

4. When entry has been lawfully made for another purpose (such as investigation of an offense or response to a call for service) and was not for the purpose of effecting an arrest.

5. When lawful consent for entry for the purpose of effecting an arrest is obtained. In the case of minors, proper consent may be obtained from the parent/s or responsible adult in charge, or, in the absence of a responsible adult, from the minor himself.

During normal business hours, an arrest warrant may be obtained by contacting the District Attorney's Office. Outside of normal business hours, it will be necessary to contact the "on call" deputy district attorney for review and assistance and then a magistrate for the issuance of a warrant. There is no statutory provision for a telephonic arrest warrant, consequently it will be necessary to contact the magistrate in person.

A list of on-call deputies will be maintained in the watch commander's office along with a list of judges' telephone numbers and home addresses.

As has been the case prior to Ramey, it does not appear that the actual physical possession of a warrant of arrest is necessary as long as there is knowledge of the existence of a properly endorsed warrant.

Source: Chapter 2, Procedure 9, "Arrest in Residence without Warrant," from *Standard Operating Procedure*, San Bernardino, California, Police Department (rev. May 4, 1989). Used courtesy of the San Bernardino Police Department.

---

constitutional because when Santana was standing in the doorway, "[s]he was not in an area where she had any expectation of privacy" (p. 42). The entry into Santana's house was justified on exigent circumstances—namely, hot pursuit.

   Watson and *Santana* therefore combine to permit another type of warrantless action authorized by the Fourth Amendment. As long as probable cause is in place, the police can make a warrantless arrest in a public place. A warrantless arrest in the curtilage of someone's home is also authorized. The key in *Santana*, though, was that the arrest was initiated by the police observing what they perceived to be criminal activity from a public place. This important qualification ensures that the police cannot just wander onto private property, looking for opportunities to make arrests. A crime must be observed from a lawful vantage point; otherwise, a warrant will be required.

■ The Doctrine of Plain View

Untrained observers frequently suggest that "plain view" applies in situations in which evidence can be seen without having to search for it. While this may be a *literal* interpretation of what it means for something to be in plain view, it is not the interpretation the courts use. Plain view has a very specific meaning in criminal procedure, and the doctrine only applies in certain situations.

■ *Coolidge v. New Hampshire,*
403 U.S. 443 (1971)

The "**plain view**" **doctrine** first emerged in the Supreme Court's decision in *Coolidge v. New Hampshire* (403 U.S. 443 [1971]). The issue in *Coolidge* was whether evidence seized during a search of cars belonging to Coolidge was admissible. The police had a warrant to search the cars, but it was later deemed invalid, so the state argued that the evidence should still be admissible because the cars were in plain view from a public street and from the house in which Coolidge was arrested. The Court did not accept this argument, pointing out that just because the police could *see* the cars from where they were was not enough to permit seizure of the evidence in question. However, the Court did point out that had the police been *in* an area, such as a car or a house, evidence that was "immediately apparent as such" and was discovered "inadvertently" would have been admissible. In other words, part of the reason the evidence was not admissible in Coolidge was that the police officers were not lawfully in the cars when the evidence was seized.

To summarize, the Court decided in *Coolidge* that a plain view seizure is authorized when (1) the police are lawfully in the area where the evidence is located; (2) the items are immediately apparent as subject to seizure; and (3) the discovery of the evidence is inadvertent. The first prong of the *Coolidge* ruling—the lawful access prong—has remained relatively stable over time. The second and third prongs, however, have undergone significant interpretation in recent years. The remainder of this section is therefore based on these three requirements.

The Lawful Access Requirement

For the "plain view" doctrine to apply, the police must have **lawful access** to the object to be seized. As the Supreme Court decided in *Coolidge*:

> [P]lain view *alone* is never enough to justify the warrantless seizure of evidence. This is simply a corollary of the familiar principle . . . that no amount of probable cause can justify a warrantless search or seizure absent "exigent circumstances." Incontrovertible testimony of the senses that an incriminating object is on premises belonging to a criminal suspect may establish the fullest possible measure of probable cause. But even where the object is contraband, this Court has repeatedly stated and enforced the basic rule that the police may not enter and make a warrantless seizure. (p. 468)

This excerpt from the Court's opinion in *Coolidge* reinforces the requirement that just because the police may *see* contraband does not necessarily mean they can *seize* it. If, for example, evidence is seen lying in a vacant lot or other public place, it may be seized. In such a situation, a search has not occurred. However, evidence that may be viewed from a public place but is, in fact, on private property cannot be seized unless a warrant is obtained or exigent circumstances are present. So, if a police officer on foot patrol observes a marijuana plant in the window of a private residence, he or she may not enter the premises and seize the plant, even though such observation establishes "the fullest possible measure of probable cause."

What is meant by *lawful vantage point?* There are four specific situations in which police officers can be found in a lawful vantage point for purposes of the "plain view" doctrine. The first is during a warranted search. For example, if an officer comes upon an article during the execution of a valid search warrant, the "plain view" doctrine may apply (subject to further restrictions described later). Second, officers are in a lawful vantage point during a valid arrest. This includes warrantless arrests in public, warrantless arrests based on exigent circumstances, and arrests with warrants. Third, when a warrantless search is conducted, the police officer is in a lawful vantage point—assuming, of course, that the warrantless search is based on probable cause. Finally, as illustrated in the previous paragraph, officers are always in a lawful vantage point during nonsearches.

The "Immediately Apparent" Requirement

In addition to the requirement that the police have lawful access to an object for the "plain view" doctrine to apply, it must also be **immediately apparent** that the object is subject to seizure. *Immediately apparent* means that the officer has probable cause to seize the object.

This was the decision reached in *Arizona v. Hicks* (480 U.S. 321 [1987]). In that case, the police entered the defendant's apartment without a warrant because a bullet had been fired through his floor into the apartment below, injuring a person there. The warrantless entry was based on the exigency of looking for the shooter, for other potential victims, and for the weapon used in the incident. Once inside the apartment, the officer observed new stereo equipment that seemed out of place, given the surroundings. The officer suspected the stereo equipment was stolen but did not have probable cause to believe as such, so he picked up a turntable in order to obtain its serial number. He then called in the information and confirmed that it was stolen. The Court held that this warrantless action did not satisfy the "plain view" doctrine. It was not immediately apparent to the officer that the stereo equipment was stolen.

■ *Arizona v. Hicks*, 480 U.S. 321 (1987)

> **DECISION MAKING EXERCISE 5.9**
>
> ### Considering the "Immediately Apparent" Requirement for Plain View
>
> Police officers have a warrant for the arrest of Randy Whitbeck, who is the suspect in a rape. They lawfully execute the warrant and arrest Whitbeck in his home. While there, one of the officers observes a rifle leaning up against the wall in an adjacent bedroom. Suspecting that it is an illegal assault weapon, she enters the room and seizes the gun. May the gun be introduced into evidence? Assume further that the gun is not connected in any way to the rape. Does it matter that the seizure of the gun is not connected with the rape? Finally, if the officers knew the rifle was contraband *prior* to serving the warrant and if the rifle was not named in the search warrant accompanying the arrest warrant, could they still seize it lawfully?

Keep in mind that *probable cause to seize* and *immediately apparent* are one and the same. An officer does not need to be absolutely certain that the object is subject to seizure for the "plain view" doctrine to apply. That was the decision reached in *Texas v. Brown* (460 U.S. 730 [1983]). In that case, Brown was stopped late at night at a routine driver's license checkpoint. When he opened the glove box in order to look for his license, an opaque balloon, knotted at the opening, fell out onto the floor of the passenger side of the vehicle. The officer making the stop observed what he perceived to be drug paraphernalia in the glove compartment and ultimately seized the balloon and its contents. The balloon was later proven to contain heroin. Brown was convicted of narcotics offenses. The Texas

Court of Criminal Appeals reversed Brown's conviction, pointing out that the plain view doctrine did not apply because the officer did not *know* incriminatory evidence was before him when he seized the balloon. A unanimous Supreme Court reversed the decision, stating, "The fact that [the officer] could not see through the opaque fabric of the balloon is all but irrelevant; the distinctive character of the balloon itself spoke volumes as to its contents—particularly to the trained eye of the officer" (p. 743).

The Role of Inadvertency

The role of *inadvertency* in the plain view determination has received considerable attention. The original position of the Supreme Court in *Coolidge v. New Hampshire* was that an object seized under the "plain view" doctrine must not have been anticipated by the police. For example, assume that a police officer obtains a warrant to search a suspect's home for the proceeds from a robbery. Assume further that the officer *expects* to find guns in the house but does not state in the warrant that guns will be sought. If, during the search, the officer finds guns, under the Supreme Court's old ruling, the guns will not be admissible because the officers expected to find them. This restriction on the "plain view" doctrine came to be known as the *inadvertency requirement*. The rationale for this restriction was that an officer who anticipates discovering evidence of a crime should seek prior judicial authorization (i.e., a warrant). Further, the Fourth Amendment's particularity requirement would be compromised if general searches were permitted.

■ *Horton v. California,*
496 U.S. 128 (1990)

In *Horton v. California* (496 U.S. 128 [1990]), the Court declared that inadvertency, although a "characteristic of most legitimate 'plain view' seizures, . . . is not a necessary condition" of the doctrine (p.130). The Court offered two reasons for abandoning the inadvertency requirement imposed in *Coolidge*. First, according to *Horton*, as long as a warrant particularly describes the places to be searched and the objects to be seized, the officer cannot expand the area of the search once the evidence has been found. In other words, it is unlikely that once officers have found the evidence listed in the warrant, they will go on a "fishing expedition," looking for evidence not listed in the warrant. According to the Court, the particularity requirement itself ensures that people's privacy is protected.

Second, the Court noted that "evenhanded law enforcement is best achieved by the application of objective standards of conduct, rather than standards that depend upon the subjective state of mind of the officer" (p. 138). An inadvertency requirement would force the courts to dwell on police officers' subjective motivations, which would be both time consuming and distracting. The Court went on to note that "[t]he fact that an officer is interested in an item of evidence and fully expects to find it in the course of a search should not invalidate its seizure if the search is confined in area and duration by the terms of the warrant or a valid expection to the warrant requirement" (p. 138).

Plain Touch, Feel, and Smell

The term *plain view* suggests that the "plain view" doctrine is limited to items that the police can see with their eyes. Actually, in recent years, the Court has extended the "plain view" doctrine to incorporate items discovered using additional senses, especially smell (*United States v. Place*, 462 U.S. 696 [1983]) and feel (Cf., *Minnesota v. Dickerson*, 508 U.S. 366 [1993]). In *Dickerson*, for example, a police officer spotted Dickerson acting suspiciously near a notorious "crack house." The officer frisked Dickerson for a weapon, pursuant to *Terry v. Ohio*, but instead of finding a weapon, the officer found a small lump that he could not immediately identify. Instead of terminating the frisk, the officer carefully examined the object in Dickerson's pocket, which turned out to be cocaine. The Court ruled that this action was unlawful, arguing that the officer's actions fell outside the permissible scope of a seizure based on plain touch. Had it been immediately apparent to the officer that the object was contraband, the seizure would have been permissible. Additionally, the "plain view" doctrine can be extended to what police officers hear, as long as probable cause is in place and all the aforementioned requirements have been satisfied (see *United States v. Jackson*, 588 F.2d 1046, 5th Cir., *cert. deined*, 442 U.S. 941 [1979]).

Plain Smell?
Sheriff's deputies have a valid search warrant to look for stolen jewelry in a man's house. While serving the warrant, the deputies smell what they recognize to be marijuana. They then observe an ashtray containing what appears to be a smoldering marijuana cigarette. May the officers seize the cigarette?

In one interesting case (*State v. Jones*, 653 S.2d 1040 [Md. Ct. Spec. App. 1995]), a court predicted what is likely to happen to the "plain view" doctrine in the future:

> [B]ecause of their common doctrinal base, [the plain view and plain feel doctrines] will in all likelihood come to be seen, probably within a decade, as nothing more than instances or variations of an omnibus Plain Sense Doctrine or Plain Perception Doctrine, which will embrace plain view and plain feel and, by a logically compelling growth process, plain hearing, plain smell, and plain taste. (p. 1044)

Some people are vehemently opposed to this predicted progression, however.[2] Nevertheless, in all likelihood, the "plain view" doctrine will continue to undergo significant modifications in years to come.

Plain View as a Fallback Measure

There are countless situations in which the "plain view" doctrine would seem to apply but in which the courts have based their decisions on other doctrines. An example of such a case can be found in *Colorado v. Bannister* (449 U.S. 1 [1980]). In that case, a police officer approached a stopped vehicle and observed on the passenger seat chrome lug nuts of the same type that had reportedly been stolen in the vicinity. The occupants of the car also matched the description of those described by the victim. The officer engaged in a warrantless search of the vehicle and seized the lug nuts. The Supreme Court did not apply the "plain view" doctrine in this case but instead relied on the automobile exception to the warrant requirement set forth in *Carroll v. United States* (see earlier discussion). The Court argued that the warrantless search and seizure of the evidence was permissible, given the inherent mobility of the car, so the "plain view" doctrine did not apply.

Thus, the "plain view" doctrine can be thought of as something of a fallback measure. If a warrantless search and/or seizure is not authorized by any other doctrine (e.g., search incident to arrest, search in the presence of exigent circumstances, etc.), plain view may apply. Consider, for example, the discussion concerning search warrant requirements in Chapter 4. Specifically, the particularity requirement states that the warrant must explicitly describe what is to be seized. However, if during the course of a warranted search, the police stumble across evidence that they believe can be seized but is not set forth in the search warrant, the "plain view" doctrine may apply. In such a situation, the original authorization to engage in the search (i.e., the search warrant) does not clearly permit seizure of the evidence, yet plain view provides another form of authorization to do so.

[2]See "The Case against a Plain Feel Exception to the Warrant Requirement," *Chicago Law Review* 54 (1987): 683.

Similarly, evidence noticed during a hot pursuit (e.g., *Warden v. Hayden*, 387 U.S. 294 [1967]), when accompanying an arrestee to his or her room (*Washington v. Chrisman*, 455 U.S. 1 [1982]), when investigating a fire in a home (e.g., *Michigan v. Tyler*, 436 U.S. 499 [1978]), and many other such situations can be seized but not always on the warrantless action itself. For example, assume police officers during the course of a hot pursuit find a cache of illegal weapons in a house. The hot pursuit exception to the warrant requirement does not authorize seizure of the weapons, but the plain view doctrine does. Again, the plain view doctrine serves as a fallback measure. Another such fallback measure is the inventory search exception, discussed in Chapter 7.

In summary, the "plain view" doctrine will only apply in situations in which the police have lawful access to the object in question. Provided that the appropriate level of justification is in place to engage in the warrantless action in question (e.g., probable cause, reasonable suspicion, administrative justification, or when engaged in a non-search), then the lawful access requirement will automatically be satisfied.

CONCLUSION

The situations in which law enforcement officials *can* search without a warrant almost outnumber the number of situations in which they *cannot* search without a warrant. The Supreme Court has carved out several exceptions to the Fourth Amendment's warrant requirement. While the exceptions vary considerably, a common thread runs through them: The Court has decided that it is not always practical to obtain a warrant.

Searches incident to arrest are constitutionally permissible, but the arrest must, of course, be legal (i.e., based on probable cause). Also, the arrest must result in someone being taken into custody. Next, the search must follow the arrest closely in time. Finally, the search incident to arrest is limited to (1) the person arrested and any containers discovered from that search and (2) the arrestee's immediate grabbing area. Prior to an arrest, the police may engage in a protective sweep of the premises, if they have a reasonable belief that evidence may be destroyed by someone sympathetic to the arrestee. They may also engage in a protective sweep following arrest. No justification is required for such a postarrest sweep. Finally, the Supreme Court appears to agree that the premises can be searched for evidence that is likely to be destroyed, and probable cause is not required.

Hot pursuit, threats to persons, and threats to evidence are exigent circumstances that permit dispensing with the Fourth Amendment's warrant requirement. Warrantless searches and arrests based on hot pursuit are constitutional only if the police have probable cause to believe (1) that the person they are pursuing has committed a serious offense; (2) that the person will be found on the premises the police seek to enter; (3) that the suspect will escape or harm someone or that evidence will be lost or destroyed; (4) that the pursuit originates from a lawful vantage point; and (5) that the scope and timing of the search are reasonable. When hot pursuit does not apply,

a warrantless search for evanescent evidence is permissible when (1) there is probable cause to believe that evidence will be destroyed, lost, or devalued; (2) the procedures employed are reasonable; and (3) the exigency was not police created. Finally, if neither hot pursuit nor the potential for damage or destruction to evidence exists, a warrantless search is permissible if the police have probable cause to believe a person on the premises is in imminent danger of death or serious bodily harm.

Warrantless automobile searches are constitutionally permissible because (1) automobiles are mobile, making it difficult to obtain warrants; (2) people enjoy a lesser expectation of privacy when in their cars; and (3) automobiles are subject to a host of government regulations. Even so, for an automobile search to be constitutional, it must be (1) directed at a vehicle ready to serve a transportation function; (2) premised on probable cause to believe the vehicle contains evidence of a crime; and (3) completed without unnecessary delay.

Racial profiling occurs when the police use race or ethnicity as a factor in determining whether they will stop someone. While a driver's race or ethnicity clearly does not provide justification to stop him or her, critics of profiling claim that the police can use existing traffic laws to single out certain individuals—say, for instance, pulling someone over for speeding regardless of whether that actually occurred. The Supreme Court has yet to decide directly on the constitutionality of this type of conduct, but at least one decision has come close to the issue. In *Whren*, the Court stated that the "constitutional reasonableness of traffic stops" does not depend "on the actual motivations of the individual officers" (p. 813). Despite this controversial decision, Fourteenth Amendment due process claims and claims under Title VI of the Civil Rights Act of 1964 can still be raised.

Two types of warrantless arrests have been authorized by the Supreme Court. First, if exigent circumstances are present, the police may make a warrantless arrest. Probable cause is required, however. Second, an arrest in public can be made without a warrant. Even an arrest that originates in public but then proceeds indoors is constitutional without a warrant, but only if hot pursuit results in the arrest being completed indoors.

Items in plain view can be seized if the police have lawful access to the items and if it is immediately apparent that the items are contraband. The discovery of such items does not have to be inadvertent. The "plain view" doctrine has been extended to include plain smell and plain feel. Finally, the "plain view" doctrine should be viewed as something of a fallback measure because the seizure of evidence can often be justified by other doctrines, such as hot pursuit, search incident to arrest, automobile searches, and so on.

REVIEW QUESTIONS

1. Explain the term *exceptions* as applied to the Fourth Amendment.
2. Summarize the requirements for a valid search incident to arrest.
3. What type of law enforcement activities fall under the banner of exigent circumstances?
4. To what extent do police-created exigencies factor into the exigent circumstances analysis?
5. Explain the Supreme Court's rationale for permitting warrantless searches of automobiles.
6. Summarize the requirements for a valid automobile search.
7. Explain the leading cases in the area of racial profiling.
8. What types of arrest are permissible without a warrant?

9. Why does the term *plain view* mean something different in criminal procedure than in everyday use?
10. Explain the lawful access prong of the plain view doctrine.
11. Explain the immediately apparent prong of the plain view doctrine.
12. To what extent is inadvertency relevant in the plain view context?
13. How has the plain view doctrine been extended by the Supreme Court?
14. What other Fourth Amendment doctrines may permit the seizure of evidence if the plain view doctrine does not apply?
15. Has the Supreme Court become too generous with exceptions to the Fourth Amendment's warrant requirement?

 Answers to the Decision-Making Exercises for this chapter can be found on pages 496–499.

CHAPTER 6

Actions Based on Reasonable Suspicion

OUTLINE

KEY TERMS

reasonable suspicion

stop

frisk

protective sweep

drug courier profiling

investigative detention

INTRODUCTION

Loosening the Fourth Amendment's Restraints

Chapter 3 introduced reasonable suspicion as the appropriate standard of justification required for a police officer to conduct a stop-and-frisk. **Reasonable suspicion** was defined as a lesser degree of certainty than probable cause but a greater degree of certainty than a hunch or unsupported belief.

The term *reasonable suspicion* is found nowhere in the Constitution. Rather, reasonable suspicion is a standard created by the Supreme Court. The reason that the Court declared that certain confrontations between police and citizens can be based on reasonable suspicion is that crime control could not be accomplished without a lower standard than probable cause. If probable cause was always required, police officers would not even be able to question people about suspected involvement in criminal activity without a high degree of justification.

Reasonable suspicion can be understood in terms of the due process/crime control distinction raised in the first chapter. The law governing stop-and-frisk attempts to achieve a balance between due process and crime control. On the one hand, most people find it desirable for the police to control crime. If crime ran rampant, people would curtail their activities by, for example, not going out at night. On the other hand, the Constitution is a highly prized guarantor of personal freedoms. Many people, despite their desire to see crime decline, would object to aggressive search-and-seizure tactics by the police. Reasonable suspicion is something of a compromise, then, between the conflicting goals of crime control and due process. It can be seen as achieving a balance between having unrestricted law enforcement and being able to apprehend lawbreakers.

KEY CASES

Stop

- *Terry v. Ohio*, 392 U.S. 1 (1968)
- *United States v. Mendenhall*, 446 U.S. 544 (1980)
- *California v. Hodari D.*, 449 U.S. 621 (1991)
- *Florida v. Bostick*, 501 U.S. 429 (1991)
- *United States v. Montoya De Hernandez*, 473 U.S. 531 (1985)

Frisk

- *Pennsylvania v. Mimms*, 434 U.S. 106 (1977)
- *Ybarra v. Illinois*, 444 U.S. 85 (1979)
- *Minnesota v. Dickerson*, 508 U.S. 366 (1993)
- *Sibron v. New York*, 392 U.S. 40 (1968)

Expansion of Stop and Frisk

- *Delaware v. Prouse*, 440 U.S. 648 (1979)
- *Maryland v. Buie*, 494 U.S. 325 (1990)
- *Papachristou v. City of Jacksonville*, 405 U.S. 156 (1972)
- *Kolender v. Lawson*, 461 U.S. 352 (1983)

Drug Courier Profiling

- *Reid v. Georgia*, 448 U.S. 438 (1980)
- *United States v. Mendenhall*, 446 U.S. 544 (1980)
- *Florida v. Royer*, 460 U.S. 491 (1983)
- *United States v. Sokolow*, 490 U.S. 1 (1989)

Recall two critical points from Chapter 3. First, when police activity does not constitute a search, the Fourth Amendment does not apply. By extension, then, when the Fourth Amendment does not apply, probable cause is not required. Much the same logic applies to a stop and a frisk. If police conduct falls short of a stop or a frisk, the Fourth Amendment does not apply. Thus, when the Fourth Amendment does not apply, reasonable suspicion is not required. And if the police confront a person but such activity does not constitute a stop or a frisk, no justification is required. At the opposite extreme, though, if police conduct amounts to a more significant intrusion than a stop or a frisk, then a different standard of justification will be required—most likely, probable cause.

STOP AND FRISK: TWO SEPARATE ACTS

A *stop* is separate from a *frisk*. A stop always precedes a frisk, but a stop *does not* give a police officer permission to conduct a frisk. Rather, the officer must have separate justification for each act. Reasonable suspicion is required to stop a person, and it is also required to frisk a person.

■ *Terry v. Ohio,*
392 U.S. 1 (1968)

In *Terry v. Ohio* (392 U.S. 1 [1968]), the Supreme Court ruled that in addition to the suspicion required to justify a stop, the officer must have reasonable suspicion that the person stopped is *armed* and *dangerous* in order to conduct a frisk. In support of this position, the Court used a balancing test: Each intrusion by the government must be justified by a legitimate objective. In other words, no legitimate law enforcement objective is served when a police officer frisks a person whom the officer does not perceive as threatening.

For example, assume a police officer observes two men in an area with much drug traffic activity, whispering to each other and passing items back and forth. Arguably, the officer would have reasonable suspicion that criminal activity is afoot, thus permitting him or her to question the men. However, if the officer does not perceive that either suspect is armed and dangerous, then a frisk would be inappropriate.

Between Reasonable Suspicion and Stop-and-Frisk

In *Terry*, the Supreme Court also held that before a frisk can take place, the officer must identify himself or herself as a police officer. However, if exigent circumstances exist, the identification may not be necessary. In *Adams v. Williams* (407 U.S. 143 [1972]), an officer, acting on a tip that a man in a nearby car had a gun at his waist, approached the car and asked the man to open the door. When the suspect rolled down his car window instead of opening the door, the officer reached into the car and removed a gun from the man's waistband. The officer did not identify himself, but the Supreme Court ruled that the seizure of the weapon was reasonable in light of the circumstances (see also Decision Making Exercise 3.9).

In addition to requiring that an officer identify himself or herself, the Court in *Terry* also required an officer to make a "reasonable inquiry." Few cases have addressed the definition of *reasonable inquiry*, but as will be considered in the later discussion of confession and interrogation law, if the officer's questions become too accusatory, then they may fall outside the type permitted during the course of a *Terry* stop.

THE STOP

In many situations, it is clear when a police officer has stopped someone. For instance, when a patrol officer legally pulls a motorist over, it is safe to say that such activity constitutes a stop. Similarly, if a police officer handcuffs a suspect, that person has clearly been stopped (and arrested). But what about a simple confrontation between a foot patrol officer and a pedestrian? If the officer directs general questions—such as "What is your name?"—at the pedestrian, can this be considered a stop? Given that there are many situations such as this, the definition of a *stop* must be given special attention.

Definition of a Stop

Why does the definition of a **stop** matter? Remember, if the police officer's activities do not amount to a stop, then the Fourth Amendment does not apply. This is because a stop is the same thing as a seizure of a person. As the Court observed in *Terry v. Ohio*, "[W]henever a police officer accosts an individual and restrains his freedom to walk away, he has 'seized' that person" (p. 16).

In *Terry*, the Supreme Court stated that "obviously not all personal intercourse between policemen and citizens involves seizures of persons" (p. 20, n. 16). Instead, the Fourth Amendment applies only "when the officer, by means of physical force or show of authority, has in some way restrained the liberty of [a] citizen" (p. 20, n. 16). Thus, there is an important distinction to be drawn between (1) a forcible seizure or a stop and (2) a less intrusive type of confrontation in which, for example, the officer merely questions a person who is free to ignore the officer and leave. The seizure or stop requires reasonable suspicion (provided it is considered a *Terry* stop and not an arrest), but the simple questioning requires no justification.

There is no easy way to distinguish a *stop* from a *nonstop*, but the Supreme Court has attempted to clarify the differences with an objective test. In *United States v. Mendenhall* (446 U.S. 544 [1980]), the Court observed:

> [A] person has been "seized" within the meaning of the Fourth Amendment only if, in view of all the circumstances surrounding the incident, a *reasonable person would have believed that he was not free to leave*. Examples of circumstances that might indicate a seizure, even where the person did not actually attempt to leave, would be the threatening presence of several officers, the display of a weapon by an officer, some physical touching of the person of the citizen, or the use of language or tone of voice indicating that compliance with the officer's request might be compelled. (p. 554, emphasis added)

■ *United States v. Mendenhall,* 446 U.S. 544 (1980)

The Court's decision in *Mendenhall* stemmed from a confrontation between plainclothes Drug Enforcement Agency (DEA) agents and a 22-year-old African American woman in the Detroit airport. The agents had asked the woman for her ticket and identification, and she complied. When they realized the name on the ticket did not match her name, the agents asked the woman to accompany them into a nearby private room. The Court did not actually decide whether the woman had been stopped, but it did create the objective test described in the previous quote. Figure 6.1 (page 172) lists several criteria used to distinguish between a stop and a consensual encounter.

DECISION
MAKING
EXERCISE 6.1

Looking for Illegal Aliens

The Immigration and Naturalization Service (INS) routinely conducts so-called factory surveys to determine whether illegal aliens are employed at certain worksites. In these surveys, uniformed and armed agents disperse themselves through the building and approach each employee in order to inquire about his or her citizenship. While this is going on, employees are free to continue with their work and move about the building. Does such activity amount to a stop, thereby implicating the Fourth Amendment?

FIGURE 6.1	Factors Used to Distinguish between a Stop and a Consensual Encounter

1. Threatening behavior on the part of officers
2. The presence of several officers
3. Display of a weapon by an officer
4. Physical touching of the person by the officer
5. The issuing of orders as opposed to requests
6. The use of intimidating language or tone of voice
7. A lengthy time period
8. Intrusive actions, such as a full-body search
9. Use of lights or sirens
10. The officer blocking the person's path
11. Coercive police behavior
12. Taking place out of public view

Florida v. Royer (460 U.S. 491 [1983]) was the first case to apply the test set forth in *Mendenhall* in order to determine the conditions under which a seizure or stop may take place. The facts in *Royer* were virtually identical to the facts in *Mendenhall*, except that the officers did not return the detained individual's plane ticket or driver's license. The Supreme Court held, in a 5 to 4 decision, that given the circumstances, when the officers did not indicate that the individual was free to leave, a seizure had taken place. The Court wrote:

> The predicate permitting seizures on suspicion short of probable cause is that law enforcement interests warrant a limited intrusion on the personal security of the suspect. The scope of the intrusion permitted will vary to some extent with the particular facts and circumstances of each case. This much, however, is clear: *an investigative detention must be temporary and last no longer than is necessary to effectuate the purpose of the stop. Similarly, the investigative methods employed should be the least intrusive means reasonably available to verify or dispel the officer's suspicion in a short period of time.* (p. 500, emphasis added)

The detained individual was subjected to the functional equivalent of an arrest, and as a result, the agents needed probable cause to detain him for as long as they did (which, incidentally, was only about 15 minutes). Moving the subject from a public location to a private location was one of the key factors that helped turn the encounter from a stop into an arrest.

Contrast *Royer* with the Supreme Court's decision in *Florida v. Rodriguez* (469 U.S. 1 [1984]). In that case, the Court ruled that a seizure had *not* taken place when a plainclothes officer approached a man in an airport, displayed his badge, asked permission to talk with the man, and requested that he move approximately 15 feet to where the man's companions were standing with other police officers. The Court described this type of confrontation as "clearly the sort of consensual encounter that implicates no Fourth Amendment interest" (p. 5). It seems, therefore, at least in the airport context, that certain confrontations that take place in common areas do not amount to stops within the meaning of the Fourth Amendment.

In another case, *Michigan v. Chestnut* (486 U.S. 567 [1988]), police officers in their car followed a man who fled on foot when he spotted their patrol car. The officers did not activate their siren or lights, display weapons, ask the man to stop, or attempt to block the defendant's path. The Court acknowledged that this type of conduct can be "somewhat intimidating," but it ruled, nevertheless, that the act of police officers following the man did not amount to a stop. The situation would have been different, however, if the police officers had visibly chased the defendant. In the Court's words, "[W]hat constitutes a restraint on liberty prompting a person to conclude that he is not free to leave will vary, not only with the particular police conduct at issue, but also with the setting in which the conduct occurs" (p. 573).

Yet another case has applied the objective test set forth in *Mendenhall*. The case of *California v. Hodari D.* (449 U.S. 621 [1991]) involved the apprehension of an individual who was chased by the police on foot. The Court ruled that the individual had not been seized at the time he threw away a rock of cocaine because the police had not yet caught up with him. The individual argued that he was "stopped" when he was being pursued by the police officers because the chase was sufficient to cause a reasonable person to believe he was not free to leave. In other words, he argued that he was subjected to a "show of authority" stop. Accordingly, the individual argued in court that the cocaine should not be admissible as evidence. Rejecting his argument, the Court ruled that the seizure of a person during a pursuit occurs only when there is an application of force by the police or the suspect submits to police authority (i.e., gives up).

■ *California v. Hodari D.*, 449 U.S. 621 (1991)

DECISION MAKING EXERCISE 6.2

Creating a "Constitutionally Cognizable" Policy

The city mayor, frustrated with a wave of serious and violent crime in the area, instructs the police to stop and demand identification from each citizen they encounter. As the mayor's legal counsel, what would you advise regarding the constitutionality of these instructions to the police?

Another recent case seeks to give meaning to the definition of a *stop*. In *Florida v. Bostick* (501 U.S. 429 [1991]), police officers approached a passenger on a bus and asked to inspect his ticket and identification and also his luggage. Both actions were conducted pursuant to a policy that permitted police officers to conduct suspicionless *Terry* stops for the purpose of detecting drug activity. The Supreme Court refused to adopt the Florida Supreme Court's analysis, which held that such drug sweeps were seizures, implicating the Fourth Amendment. Instead, the Court ruled that "in order to determine whether a particular encounter constitutes a seizure, a court must consider all the circumstances surrounding the encounter to determine whether the police conduct would have communicated to a reasonable person that the person was not free to decline the officer's requests or otherwise terminate the encounter" (p. 439). The Supreme Court remanded the case back to the Florida Supreme Court, instead of reversing it. Nevertheless, a portion of Justice O'Connor's opinion suggests that the majority was not satisfied with the Florida court's decision: The bus passenger's perception of not being free to leave was, according to O'Connor, "the natural result of his decision to take the bus."

■ *Florida v. Bostick*, 501 U.S. 429 (1991)

Recently, in *United States v. Drayton* (536 U.S. 194 [2002]), the U.S. Supreme Court held that *Bostick*-like bus detentions are permissible and that passengers need not be advised of their right to deny consent to search. And another recent decision requires suspects to provide identification if an officer so requests it (*Hiibel v. Sixth Judicial District of Nevada*, 5YZ U.S. 177 [2004]).

■ Alternative Definitions of a Stop

It is instructive to look toward the lower courts for further elaboration of the definition of a *stop*. Of course, the Supreme Court has the last word on that definition, but other courts have created interesting standards and/or looked to different factors than the reasonable person in their *Terry*-based analyses.

Instead of adopting the reasonable person test, some lower courts have, for example, focused on the degree of police coercion in determining what constitutes a stop. In *State v. Tsukiyama* (56 Haw. 8 [1974]), one of the leading state-level cases in this area, the Hawaii Supreme Court found that no search had occurred when police questioned a man after he had asked them for a flashlight so he could repair his car. The man was arrested and charged for weapons and drug offenses because when one of the officers on the scene asked him for his identification, he attempted to reach into the glove box of the car for a weapon. At issue in the case before the Hawaii Supreme Court, though, was whether the initial confrontation between the man and the police was a stop.

The Hawaii Supreme Court pointed to the lack of "command, authority, force, threat, coercion, physical stopping or restraint" (p. 17) at the point when the man asked for a flashlight. It further stated, "Since there was no 'stop' or 'seizure' of the defendant prior to his overtly unlawful act, we do not have to decide whether the circumstances could have given rise to a belief that 'criminal activity may have been afoot' and thus justify a 'stop' or 'seizure'" (pp. 17–18). Had the court declared the initial confrontation a stop, the "fruit of the poisonous tree" doctrine (see Chapter 2) could have potentially applied.

In another case, *Login v. State* (394 So.2d 183 [1981]), the Florida District Court of Appeals had occasion to define when a stop took place. In that case, a man walking in the Miami airport was confronted by a police officer, who displayed his badge and asked the man for identification. The officer asked the man if he could talk for a minute, at which point the officer observed cocaine residue around the man's nostrils. This raised a question similar to that in the *Tsukiyama* case: Did a stop occur when the officer asked the man if they could talk?

The court declared that a stop had not occurred and went on to note that it would be risky to rule that a stop automatically occurs the moment a person is confronted. In the court's words, a rule that a stop occurs the moment a person is confronted by a police officer

> would cover a multitude of police-citizen encounters which in no way approach a police seizure of the person, such as police questioning of a probable witness to a crime or police inquiries directed to a stranded motorist in need of assistance. To label all police encounters with the public as seizures when accompanied by questioning, no matter how cordial, would tremendously impede the police in the effective performance of both their criminal investigation and community assistance functions. (p. 14)

However, the court did note that a *seizure* does occur when the language used by the police "in tone and content bespeak[s] an order to stop, particularly when employed during a fast moving criminal investigation on the street" (p. 13). This observation is similar to the analysis offered by the Hawaii Supreme Court in *Tsukiyama*. Perhaps the most significant factor, then, in determining when a stop occurs is the tone and content of the police officer's questioning.

Other cases, though, would seem to suggest that even the act of asking a person to halt, such as the rider of a bicycle, does not constitute a stop within the meaning of the Fourth Amendment (see *People v. King*, 72 Cal. App.3d 346 [1977]; *State v. Davis*, 543 So.2d 375 [Fla. 3d D.C.A. 1989]).

■ Duration of a Stop

The decision reached in *Florida v. Royer* suggests that a 15-minute detention does not fall within the meaning of a *Terry* stop. However, in certain exceptional circumstances, the courts have permitted detentions lasting as long as 16 hours. For example, in *United States v. Sharpe* (470 U.S. 675 [1985]), officers followed two vehicles suspected of involvement in drug trafficking. One vehicle was stopped and the driver was detained for

40 minutes while the officers sought and stopped the second car and its driver. The Court did not establish a bright-line rule for what time period is considered permissible, but it did state that "in evaluating whether an investigative detention is unreasonable, common sense and ordinary human experience must govern over rigid criteria" (p. 685). Thus, the 40-minute detention of the driver of the first car was permissible.

In another case, *United States v. Montoya De Hernandez* (473 U.S. 531 [1985]), a woman who was traveling from Colombia was detained for 16 hours in an airport because she was suspected of being a "balloon swallower" (i.e., a person who smuggles narcotics by hiding them in his or her alimentary canal). This was actually a very controversial case. The woman was given two options: (1) to return on the next available flight to Colombia or (2) to remain in detention until she was able to produce a monitored bowel movement. She chose the first option, but officials were unable to place her on the next flight, and she refused to use toilet facilities. Officials then obtained a court order to conduct a pregnancy test (she claimed to be pregnant), an X-ray exam, and a rectal exam. The exams revealed 88 cocaine-filled balloons in her alimentary canal. She was convicted of numerous federal drug offenses, but the court of appeals reversed that decision, holding that her detention violated the Fourth Amendment. The Supreme Court, in turn, reversed the court of appeals decision and ruled that the 16-hour detention was permissible. According to the Court, "The detention of a traveler at the border, beyond the scope of a routine customs search and inspection, is justified at its inception if customs agents, considering all the facts surrounding the traveler and her trip, reasonably suspect that the traveler is smuggling contraband in her alimentary canal" (p. 541).

> *United States v. Montoya De Hernandez,* 473 U.S. 531 (1985)

> **DECISION MAKING EXERCISE 6.3**

Stretching the Time Limits of a Stop

Law enforcement officers had a plane under surveillance because they had reasonable suspicion to believe that it was being used to transport narcotics. They approached the aircraft, which was ready for takeoff. Standing near the left wing of the plane, one of the officers raised his badge, identified himself, and, shouting over the noise of the speeding engine, ordered the pilot to shut off the engine and get down. The pilot looked from side to side and appeared hesitant about what to do. At that moment, the officer moved in front of the aircraft, drew his gun, pointed it at the pilot, and again yelled to him to shut off the engine and get out of the plane. The officer identified himself and said he wanted to speak to the pilot because he was suspected of narcotics smuggling. He then patted down the pilot in search of weapons; finding none, he placed his gun back in the holster. The officers then questioned the pilot about the plane's ownership. The pilot was evasive and ended up supplying inaccurate and contradictory information about who owned the plane. The officers then detained him for over an hour while *they* attempted to determine who owned the plane. Was this action justified?

In another case, *Courson v. McMillian* (939 F.2d 1479 [11th Cir. 1991]), the Eleventh Circuit Court ruled that an officer's act of stopping a car and holding the occupants at gunpoint for 30 minutes was not illegal because most of the time was spent waiting for backup to arrive. Citing *Adams v. Williams* (407 U.S. 143 [1972]), the court observed:

> The Fourth Amendment does not require a policeman who lacks the precise level of information necessary for probable cause to arrest to simply shrug his shoulders and allow a crime to occur or criminal to escape. On the contrary, *Terry* recognizes that it may be the essence of good police work to adopt an intermediate response. A brief stop of a suspicious individual, in order to determine his identity or to maintain the status quo momentarily while obtaining more information, may be most reasonable in light of the facts known to the officer at the time. (pp. 145–146)

Contrast the decision reached in *Courson v. McMillian* with that reached in *United States v. Luckett* (484 F.2d 89 [1973]). In *Luckett*, the Second Circuit Court declared a jaywalker's detention invalid because it was based on a hunch that there was a warrant for the jaywalker's arrest. The court ruled that the stop effectively turned into an arrest, not just because of the duration of the stop but because there was no basis for an arrest at the time of the stop.

Are there any clear answers, then, as to what the appropriate duration of a stop is? Unfortunately, no, but the Supreme Court has stated that "the reasonableness of a stop turns on the facts and circumstances of each case. In particular, the Court has emphasized (1) the public interest served by the seizure, (2) the nature and scope of the intrusion, and (3) the objective facts upon which the law enforcement officer relied in light of his knowledge and expertise" (*United States v. Mendenhall*, 46 U.S. 544 [1980], p. 561). Moreover, the Court has ruled that "the use of a particular method to restrain a person's freedom of movement does not necessarily make police action tantamount to an arrest" and that "police may take reasonable action, based upon the circumstances, to protect themselves . . . or to maintain the status quo" (*United States v. Kapperman*, 764 F.2d 786 [11th Cir. 1985], p. 790, n. 4).

The Meaning of Free to Leave

If a person is confronted but not stopped, is he or she *really* free to leave? This question invariably arises in criminal procedure class. Many people tend to feel intimidated by police officers, even when asked nonincriminating, innocuous questions. Would it not appear strange to an officer for someone to simply walk away during a conversation with him or her? Would the officer just let the person walk away and go about his or her business? There are no easy answers to questions such as these, but they highlight the differences between theory and reality, as considered in Chapter 1.

Even though the Supreme Court has stated emphatically that a stop does not take place when a reasonable person would believe he or she is free to leave, actually leaving during the course of a conversation with a police officer could prove to be something of a risky endeavor. Much the same controversy applies to situations in which a motorist is legally permitted to decline to give a police officer permission to search his or her surroundings, even though doing so may create suspicion.

In a similar vein, does a person who is stopped have the right to refuse to answer questions? The answer is yes, for an obvious reason: A person cannot be *forced* to talk. However, refusing to answer questions could create enough fear on the part of the officer to justify a stop and could also factor into a probable cause determination that could justify an arrest. Despite all Supreme Court rulings to the contrary, then, it is risky to simply walk away from an inquisitive police officer and/or to refuse to provide answers to his or her inquiries.

Can Effects Be Seized?

Terry v. Ohio and subsequent similar cases have mostly focused on stops of *persons*, but a handful of cases have addressed the stop (i.e., seizure) of property based on less than probable cause. As indicated in Chapter 3, probable cause is required for the seizure of a person if that seizure amounts to an arrest. The same applies to *effects*, which are usually a person's personal items. If the detention or seizure of a person's effects amounts to an arrest, then probable cause is required.

The question, then, is, when does the seizure of a person's effects rise to the level of an arrest? The Supreme Court attempted to answer this question in *United States v. Place* (462 U.S. 696 [1983]). In that case, the Court ruled that a 90-minute detention of a person's luggage in an airport to arrange for a drug dog "sniff" to detect drugs was unconstitutional because the detention was too long. Also, the Court stated that "the failure of the agents to accurately inform respondent of the place to which they were transporting his luggage, of the length of time he might be dispossessed, and of what arrangements would be made for return of the luggage if the investigation dispelled the suspicion" (p. 710) contributed to the unconstitutional nature of the detention. The Court went on to note that "some brief detentions of personal effects may be so minimally intrusive of Fourth Amendment interests that strong countervailing governmental interests will justify seizure based only on specific articulable facts that the property contains contraband or evidence of a crime" (p. 706).

> ⚖ DECISION MAKING EXERCISE 6.4
>
> ### Was the Mobile Home Seized?
>
> A mobile home park owner sought unsuccessfully to have some tenants evicted for failure to pay the rent. The park owner then notified the sheriff's department that she was going to have the tenants' trailer removed from the park and that she wanted deputies there in order to prevent the owner from interfering with removal of the trailer. Five deputies arrived at the scene and stood by as park employees disconnected the tenants' utilities and removed their trailer from the park, causing significant damage to the trailer. The tenants never resisted, and the deputies never came into contact with the tenants. Does such activity constitute a seizure of an effect within the meaning of the Fourth Amendment?

In another case, *United States v. Leeuwen* (397 U.S. 249 [1970]), the Supreme Court confirmed that there are some situations in which restraints on people's effects do not amount to a Fourth Amendment seizure. In that case, the police, who were contacted by a suspicious postal clerk, asked post office officials to hold two packages for 29 hours while they investigated the situation and obtained a search warrant. A unanimous Court ruled that the circumstances "certainly justified detention, without a warrant, while an investigation was made" (p. 252). Also, the Court ruled that "[n]o interest protected by the Fourth Amendment was invaded by forwarding the packages the following day rather than the day when they were deposited" (p. 253). In short, because the detention of the package did not invade any privacy interest in the package, a Fourth Amendment seizure did not take place.

Summary. A *Terry* stop/seizure is characterized by two specific events: (1) The police question a person or communicate with him or her and (2) a reasonable person would believe that he or she is not free to leave. Reasonable suspicion is required in order to make a *Terry* stop conform to Fourth Amendment requirements. Conversely, if an officer detains a person in such a manner that a reasonable person would believe he or she *is* free to leave, the protections of the Fourth Amendment do not apply and reasonable suspicion is not required. If the officer wishes to conduct a frisk—a separate act from a stop—he or she must have reasonable suspicion that the suspect is armed and dangerous, not just reasonable suspicion, as required for a *Terry* stop.

There are no clear answers as to what is the appropriate duration for a stop. However, as the Supreme Court suggested in *United States v. Mendenhall*, a lengthy stop is constitutionally permissible when (1) the public interest is served by the seizure; (2) the nature and scope of the intrusion are not excessive; and (3) the officer possesses enough in the way of objective facts to justify the stop (p. 561). Thus, if a person is stopped and detained for a long time based on an officer's hunch but poses no threat to public safety, then the stop will probably be declared illegal. In such a situation, the stop would need to be justified by probable cause because it would amount to a *de facto* arrest.

What Constitutes a Proper Stop?

On a Wednesday afternoon at 3:00 p.m., Officer Weber was on patrol in a neighborhood that had experienced several daytime burglaries. Her attention was drawn to a car in the driveway of one residence, which had its trunk open. In the trunk were several plastic trash bags of the type reportedly used by the burglar to carry away the loot. Weber pulled her cruiser into the driveway behind the vehicle, blocking its path. At that point, the driver of the car was closing the trunk and preparing to leave. The driver approached Weber, appearing quite nervous, and asked her to move the cruiser. Instead of doing so, Weber asked the driver for identification, which he produced. The identification indicated an address on the other side of town. Weber then frisked the driver, found a gun in his left coat pocket, and arrested him. No evidence connected the driver to the burglaries, but he was prosecuted for unlawfully carrying a concealed weapon. He moved to exclude the gun on the grounds that the initial stop was illegal and that the gun was the fruit of that illegal stop. What should the court decide?

THE FRISK

As indicated, the additional step of frisking a suspect is a Fourth Amendment intrusion that requires justification apart from that required to stop the person. Specifically, in order to conduct a **frisk**, the officer needs reasonable suspicion that the suspect is armed and dangerous. This is in addition to the reasonable suspicion required to stop the person for questioning.

Permissible Grounds for a Frisk

While *Terry* held that a frisk is permissible only when an officer reasonably fears for his or her safety, there is still considerable dispute over the situations in which a frisk is appropriate. What does it mean, in other words, to *fear for one's safety*? A number of court decisions have wrestled with this question.

■ *Pennsylvania v. Mimms,*
434 U.S. 106 (1977)

For example, in *Pennsylvania v. Mimms* (434 U.S. 106 [1977]), police officers observed a man driving a vehicle with expired plates. The officers stopped the vehicle in order to issue the man a traffic summons. When the officers asked the man to step out of the car, the officers observed a large bulge in the pocket of his jacket. Fearing that the bulge might be a weapon, one of the officers frisked the man. It turned out that the bulge was a .38 caliber revolver. The man claimed at his trial that the gun was seized illegally, but the Supreme Court upheld the frisk. Even though a bulge in one's pocket does not necessarily indicate he or she has a weapon, the Court granted some latitude in its decision to law enforcement personnel.

■ *Ybarra v. Illinois,*
444 U.S. 85 (1979)

However, in *Ybarra v. Illinois* (444 U.S. 85 [1979]), the Court ruled that officers did not have grounds to frisk 12 bar patrons during a search of the bar itself. Justice Stewart stated in *Ybarra* that "[t]he 'narrow scope' of the *Terry* exception does not permit a frisk for weapons on less than reasonable belief or suspicion directed at the person to be frisked, even though that person happens to be on premises where an authorized narcotics search is taking place" (p. 94). Thus, just because someone happens to be in an area in which criminal activity is supposedly taking place does not make him or her eligible for a frisk.

■ *Minnesota v. Dickerson,*
508 U.S. 366 (1993)

Despite the limitations on frisks imposed by the *Ybarra* decision, the Court has since gone back somewhat on its decision in that case. In *Minnesota v. Dickerson*

FIGURE 6.2   When a Frisk Is Permissible

1. When the person has a reputation for dangerousness
2. When the person is suspected of having committed a dangerous felony
3. When visual cues suggest the presence of a weapon or similar dangerous instrument
4. When the suspect makes suggestive or furtive gestures

(508 U.S. 366 [1993]), police officers observed a man leaving a "crack" house. As he approached and saw the officers, he turned and began walking in the opposite direction. The officers stopped and frisked him and found drugs on him. The frisk was conducted without reasonable suspicion or any other level of justification. The Court ruled that the police exceeded the bounds of a valid frisk when they found drugs on the man's person, but the Court did *not* rule that the frisk was unconstitutional. It would seem, then, that under certain circumstances, a frisk is permissible on less than reasonable suspicion. Apparently, the act of leaving a "crack" house and acting evasively was sufficient justification to conduct a frisk, even though the police went too far in doing so.

So, are there any clear rules that establish when an officer can reasonably fear for his or her safety? The answer is no. Ultimately, the determination of a potential threat is a subjective one. Almost without exception, the courts will defer to the judgment of the officer, assuming that he or she is able to articulate some specific facts that contributed to reasonable suspicion that the suspect was armed and dangerous. Figure 6.2 summarizes the circumstances as to when a frisk is permissible.

Scope of a Frisk

A number of cases have focused specifically on the permissible scope of a frisk. Two issues have been raised: (1) the definition of a *frisk*—that is, what the officer can physically do to a person that does not rise to the level of a search; and (2) the items that can be felt for during the course of a frisk.

With regard to the first issue, the Supreme Court in *Terry* described a *frisk* as "a carefully limited search of the outer clothing . . . in an attempt to discover weapons which might be used to assault [a police officer]" (p. 30). In *Sibron v. New York* (392 U.S. 40 [1968]), the Court offered additional clarification by declaring that the act of reaching into a suspect's pockets is impermissible when the officer makes "no attempt at an initial limited exploration for arms" (p. 65). Generally, then, a frisk is little more than an open-handed patdown of someone's outer clothing. Only if the officer feels something that resembles a weapon can he or she then reach into the suspect's pocket (or other area used to conceal it) to determine what the item is. And as the Supreme Court observed in *United States v. Richardson* (949 F.2d 851 [6th Cir. 1991]), "When actions by the police exceed the bounds permitted by reasonable suspicion, the seizure becomes an arrest and must be supported by probable cause" (p. 856).

Sibron v. New York, 392 U.S. 40 (1968)

With regard to the second issue, or the items that can be felt for during the course of a frisk, the Supreme Court in *Ybarra v. Illinois* (444 U.S. 106 [1977]) emphasized that frisks must be directed at discovering weapons, not criminal evidence. In *Ybarra*, one of the police officers had removed what he described as a "cigarette pack with objects in it" from the suspect. The Court basically decided that the officer's actions were too intrusive; the package could not have been considered a threat to the safety of the officers conducting the search. Significantly, the Court did not declare the seizure illegal because the officer was not looking for weapons but because the officer did not have reasonable suspicion to frisk every patron in the bar. Nevertheless, a frisk should not be used as a "fishing expedition" to see if some kind of usable evidence can be found on the person.

The Permissible Scope of a Frisk

Two police officers were approached by a person (previously unknown to them) who stated that Jack Smith was in the Valley Grill on First Street and that he had several bags of cocaine for sale. The person provided detailed information concerning Smith and described the clothing he was wearing. The officers went to the Valley Grill and found no one of that description. After the officers left the bar, however, they observed a person walking on the sidewalk who matched the description they had been given. The officers approached him, blocked his path, and asked for his identification. The man's identification revealed that his name was Jack Smith. At that point, the officers asked Smith to remove his shoes. He did so as the officers continued to ask him questions. Was this action appropriate?

Two points concerning the scope of a frisk need to be underscored at this juncture. First, just because the Supreme Court has declared that a frisk should be conducted based on the motive to preserve officer safety, this does not mean the officer cannot seize contraband found during the course of a lawful frisk. This issue is discussed in the section on plain touch and feel later in this chapter. What is important now, though, is that a frisk is supposed to be *motivated* by the desire to remove weapons and other instruments of potential harm from a criminal suspect.

Second, bear in mind that a valid frisk can always evolve into a Fourth Amendment search, provided that probable cause develops along the way. For example, assume that a Chicago police officer frisks a suspect because she fears he may be carrying a gun. If it turns out that the suspect is carrying a pistol, which is illegal in the city of Chicago, she could arrest the suspect and conduct a full search incident to arrest. In this example, though, the object seized during the frisk (i.e., the gun) must be immediately apparent to the officer for the seizure to be legal. As the Supreme Court stated in *Minnesota v. Dickerson* (508 U.S. 366 [1993]):

> Although the officer was lawfully in a position to feel the lump in respondent's pocket, because *Terry* entitled him to place his hands upon respondent's jacket, the court below determined that the incriminating character of the object was not immediately apparent to him. Rather, the officer determined that the item was contraband only after conducting a further search, one not authorized by *Terry* or by any other exception to the warrant requirement. (p. 379)

In the example, then, had the seizure followed careful manipulation of the object by the officer, then a seizure based on the frisk would not conform to Fourth Amendment requirements. Figure 6.3 provides additional examples of proper frisks from the *California Peace Officers Legal Sourcebook.*

Summary. A frisk is permissible when an officer reasonably fears for his or her safety. However, there is no easy way to discern the facts that would *cause* an officer to reasonably fear for his or her safety. If an officer can offer no facts or testimony to support the frisk, it will probably be declared unconstitutional. On the other hand, if the officer possesses some objective information that served as the basis for a frisk (e.g., observing a bulge in a suspect's pocket), the frisk will probably be legal.

A number of cases have focused on the permissible scope of a frisk, and three important restrictions have been imposed. First, a frisk can be nothing more than a patdown of someone's outer clothing. Groping or squeezing is not permissible. Second, a frisk must be motivated by the desire to promote officer safety, not by the desire to seek out any form of contraband. That is, the sole purpose of a *Terry* patdown is to protect the

FIGURE 6.3 Examples of Proper and Improper Frisks

Proper Frisks

Example: It was illegal for a deputy to frisk a man who was sitting in a stopped car, engine running, in the middle of a onelane rural dirt road, even though the man had no license or other identification, refused to let the deputy search his vehicle, and was nervous and sweating, and even though the deputy had discovered a film canister containing baking soda, since none of these factors would lead an officer to reasonably believe that a weapon might be used against him. (The frisk produced cocaine.) Despite the fact that every encounter between a citizen and a police officer holds some potential that the citizen may be armed, "specific and articulable" facts are necessary which show that the suspect may be armed and dangerous. (*Dickey* (1994) 21 Cal. App. 4th 952, 956.)

Example: Officer made a DUI stop at night for erratic driving. The driver gave false identification, admitted he had recently done time for robbery, and was wearing a bulky jacket which he had trouble keeping his hands out of. HELD: It was legal to order him out, pat him down, and remove what felt like syringes from his jacket pockets. (*Autry* (1991) 232 Cal.App.3d 365; see also *Mimms* (1977) 434 U.S. 106, 112—bulge under sportcoat was enough to justify patdown.)

Example: At 1:15 a.m., officers made a valid stop of a vehicle which had been driving slowly with its lights out in a high crime area. The driver got out of the car to meet the officers, leaving two other males inside. When asked for his license, the driver said it was in his sock. Fearing for his safety, the officer conducted a quick, cursory patdown search of the driver and found a knife inside the sock. Under all the circumstances, the patdown was justified. (*Barnes* (1983) 141 Cal.App.3d 854; *Guillermo M.* (1982) 130 Cal.App.3d 642.)

Example: While on routine patrol one morning, two officers spotted a young man looking into two parked cars in an alley where many complaints of criminal activity—including vehicle tampering—had originated. As the officers drove by slowly, the suspect tried to stay out of view behind a dumpster. When they approached him and began talking to him, he became very nervous, boisterous, angry and antagonistic— "borderline combative." The court said it was proper to pat him down (he was nearly 6' tall, 190 lbs.). "Under such circumstances, they were not required to await an actual assault before assuring themselves that the detainee was not armed with a lethal weapon." (*Michael S.* (1983) 141 Cal.App.3d 814.)

Example: An officer who responded to a report of several suspicious persons in a Taco Bell parking lot was justified in detaining and immediately patting down one male who turned away when the officer arrived, since the officer saw a large heavy object in the suspect's jacket pocket which he reasonably believed might be an illegally concealed weapon. (*Miles* (1987) 196 Cal.App.3d 612.)

Example: Pat down of man and woman in parked car upheld where lone officer was responding to a reported "prowler" late at night in closed business district, occupants could not produce ID and spoke only in Spanish, which he could not understand. (*Castaneda* (1995) 35 Cal. App. 4th 1222, 1230.)

Example: An officer properly detained a male who was walking along a street in a high burglary area, carrying a television set and tan jacket, items which had been reported stolen from a nearby residence earlier that same day. A patdown was justified. "It is reasonable for an officer to believe that a burglar may be armed with weapons, or tools such as knives and screwdrivers which could be used as weapons, and that a patdown is necessary for the officer's safety. (*Myles* (1975) 50 Cal. App. 3d 423.)

Example: An officer, who was validly inside a motel room and who had a legal basis to detain one of the occupants, was justified in patting down clothing for possible weapons before handing the clothing to the detainee. (*Wright* (1988) 206 Cal. App. 3d 1107.)

Example: During the execution of a narcotics search warrant, it was legal for an officer to pat down a man who was sitting on a couch in the living room, even though (1) the man was completely passive and not saying or doing anything threatening, (2) there was nothing beyond the inherent danger of the situation to specifically indicate that the man might be armed and dangerous, and (3) the search warrant did not authorize a search of his person. (*Thurman* (1989) 209 Cal. App. 3d 817.)

Example: An officer who intended to ask a few questions of a man during a consensual street encounter was entitled to grab the man's wrist when he started to reach into a pocket which had a weapon-like bulge, since those circumstances provided a basis to detain him to check for weapons. (*Rosales* (1989) 211 Cal. App. 3d 325, 330.)

Example: It was legal for an officer, responding to a "panhandler" complaint, to pat down the suspect where he saw a large bulge in the front waistband of the suspect's trousers. "Our courts have never held that an officer must wait until a suspect actually reaches for an apparent weapon before he is justified in taking the weapon. Such a holding would eviscerate the reason, officer safety, for a limited pat down during a *Terry* stop." (*Snyder* (1992) 11 Cal. App. 4th 389, 393.)

Example: Officer could lawfully pat down a person who put his hands back inside his bulky jacket after being told to take them out, at least where the person being contacted was in a gang neighborhood at night and had just left a house known for gang activity. (*Frank* V. (1991) 233 Cal. App. 3d 1232, 1240.)

Example: It was proper to detain and pat down a man who had been standing on a corner in a high narcotics area for several minutes, where two other persons nearby, believed to be sellers, had yelled "rollers" to him, after which he had started to leave, then turned towards the approaching officers and reached into his jacket. (*Lee* (1987) 194 Cal. App. 3d 975, 982.)

Source: From *California Peace Officers Legal Sourcebook*, electronic edition, revision 113 (Sacramento, CA: California Department of Justice, Office of the Attorney General), section 2.20.

FIGURE 6.4 Example of a Stop-and-Frisk Policy

9.7.1 Pat-Down Searches

An officer has the right to conduct a pat-down search of the outer garments of a person to look for weapons if the officer legitimately stops the person with reasonable suspicion and has reasonable fear for his/her own or another person's safety. Not every field interview creates the basis for a pat-down search. The following are some criteria that may form the basis for conducting a pat-down search. This list is not all-inclusive and more than one of these criteria may be required to support the needed reasonable suspicion for a search.

1. The type of crime suspected, particularly violent crimes with the use or threat of deadly weapons;

2. More than one suspect being handled by a single officer;

3. The time of day and location of the stop;

4. Prior knowledge of the suspect's use of force and/or propensity to carry weapons;

5. The suspect's appearance and demeanor;

6. Any visual indications that the suspect is carrying a weapon; and/or

7. The age and gender of the suspect.

When an officer decides to perform a pat-down search, the officer will do so with extreme caution, restraint, and sensitivity. These searches are justified only for the safety of the officer, not to look for evidence. Whenever possible, the search will be conducted by two officers, one conducting the search, the other providing cover. Also, whenever possible, the search will be conducted by an officer of the same sex as the suspect. The officer will place the suspect in a standing position, offbalance, with feet spread apart. If an officer sees a weapon, a more secure position will be used, such as the kneeling or prone position. An officer is only allowed to feel the outer clothing of the suspect. An officer may not reach into the suspect's pockets unless they feel an object they reasonably determine to be a weapon or is an item that by its very nature is immediately known to be contraband. If the suspect is carrying an object that may contain a weapon, such as a purse or briefcase, the officer will not search it, but place it out of the reach of the suspect. If the officer finds a weapon or contraband, he/she may retrieve that item only. If the simple possession of the weapon is illegal or if the officer finds contraband, the officer may arrest the suspect and conduct a full-custody search incident to the arrest. If the search does not reveal a weapon or contraband, no further search may be conducted.

Source: From *General Directives Manual,* Gallatin, Tennessee, Police Department (December 28, 1999). Used courtesy of the Gallatin Police Department.

officer from weapons that might be used by the suspect during the encounter. Finally, for an officer to legally seize an item during the course of a frisk, that item must be immediately apparent to the officer as contraband.

For something of a summary of stop-and-frisk law, see Figure 6.4, which contains the Gallatin, Tennessee, Police Department's stop-and-frisk policy. It succinctly summarizes the discussion thus far.

EXPANSION OF STOP-AND-FRISK LAW

In *Terry v. Ohio,* the Supreme Court created an exception to the Fourth Amendment's requirement that probable cause is required for searches by holding that police officers can stop and frisk people based on reasonable suspicion. In the wake of *Terry,* a number of significant and controversial Supreme Court decisions have essentially expanded the scope of the stop-and-frisk exception to the Fourth Amendment's probable cause requirement to include other types of law enforcement action. Four such actions include

(1) vehicle stops and weapons searches of automobiles; (2) protective sweeps of residences; (3) plain touch and feel; and (4) stops for loitering.

Vehicle Stops and Weapons Searches of Automobiles

Automobile searches were covered in Chapter 5, but it is appropriate to mention here, during the discussion of stop-and-frisk, what police officers can do with automobiles in the presence of reasonable suspicion. *Delaware v. Prouse* (440 U.S. 648 [1979]) set forth the rule that police officers, in addition to being able to accost people for the purpose of an investigative stop, can also stop and detain motorists in their vehicles so long as the officers have "at least articulable and reasonable suspicion" that the motorists are violating the law. For example, if a police officer observes a driver run a stop sign, the officer is justified in pulling the person over and detaining him or her because reasonable suspicion is present. The decision in *Pennsylvania v. Mimms* (434 U.S. 106 [1977]) also authorizes a police officer to order a driver out of a car. The logic is that doing so is a minimal intrusion that can be justified by safety concerns. Finally, these decisions (as well as *Terry*) permit a police officer to frisk a motorist who has been pulled over if the officer reasonably fears for his or her safety.

■ *Delaware v. Prouse,* 440 U.S. 648 (1979)

DECISION
MAKING
EXERCISE **6.7**

A Vehicle Search

A police officer pulled a woman motorist over for exceeding the posted speed limit. The officer then ordered the woman out of the car. Without her consent and without probable cause, the officer searched the interior passenger compartment of the vehicle. He found marijuana and a "pot pipe" under the seat and so arrested the woman. Was the search of the passenger compartment justified?

Interestingly, if a police officer orders a driver (or a passenger or both) out of the car, is reasonably suspicious that the driver is armed and dangerous, and frisks the driver, the officer may also search the area of the interior of the car within the suspect's immediate control. Such a search is permissible even when the driver has already been ordered to step out of the vehicle. The case that established this ruling was *Michigan v. Long* (463 U.S. 1032 [1983]). In that case, police officers saw a car swerve into a ditch and after stopping to investigate, they observed that the driver was intoxicated and that there was a large hunting knife on the floor of the vehicle. The Supreme Court ruled that the officers were justified in searching the passenger compartment and frisking the driver.

Michigan v. Long is an important decision because a search almost always requires probable cause. Note, however, that the scope of the search in this case was limited to the vehicle occupant's grabbing area, which included the whole of the interior of the car. Neither containers inside the car nor any in the trunk of the car (if any) can be searched during the course of a vehicle weapons search based on reasonable suspicion.

Protective Sweeps of Residences

Another decision that essentially expands *Terry* is *Maryland v. Buie* (494 U.S. 325 [1990]). If police lawfully make an arrest in a person's residence, a **protective sweep** of the home is permitted based on the *Terry* rationale. A *sweep* is when one or more officers disperse throughout the home with the intent of looking for other people that could pose a threat

■ *Maryland v. Buie,* 494 U.S. 325 (1990)

to the officers making the arrest. In the Court's words, a *protective sweep* is a "quick and limited search of the premises, incident to arrest, and conducted to protect the safety of police officers or others" (p. 325). This protective sweep, which requires reasonable suspicion, should be distinguished from the automatic but more limited sweep that is permitted incident to a lawful arrest (see Chapter 5).

According to the Supreme Court, a sweep is permitted if the officer possesses "a reasonable belief based on specific and articulable facts that an area to be swept harbors an individual posing a danger to those at the arrest scene" (p. 337). In addition, a sweep "may extend only to a cursory inspection of those spaces where a person may be found" and may last only as long as is necessary to eliminate the suspicion of danger. The case of *Maryland v. Buie* thus expands *Terry* in the sense that police officers can do more than just frisk a person who is arrested in a private residence. Note, however, that this case does not permit officers to *search* but only to *sweep* the area. A search would have to be supported by probable cause. However, items in plain view can be seized (see Chapter 5).

The Court's decision in *Maryland v. Buie* is not without its critics, however—the dissenters in the case being perhaps the most vocal. Consider Justice Brennan's observations in the dissent he wrote:

> *Terry* and its early progeny permitted only brief investigative stops and extremely limited searches based on reasonable suspicion . . . but this Court more recently has applied the rationale underlying *Terry* to a wide variety of more intrusive searches and seizures prompting my continued criticism of the emerging tendency on the part of the Court to convert the *Terry* decision from a narrow exception into one that swallows the general rule that [searches] are reasonable only if based on probable cause. (p. 339)

The exception Justice Brennan refers to is Terry's exception to the Fourth Amendment's requirement that reasonable searches be supported by probable cause. In a sense, *Terry* chipped away at the Fourth Amendment. Brennan's concern in this case, then, is that the Fourth Amendment continues to be weakened in cases that continue to uphold police actions that would otherwise be considered searches, but for the Court's decision in *Terry v. Ohio*.

This is an important area of law about which to remain informed. No doubt, the Supreme Court will continue to decide cases that involve the relationship among probable cause, reasonable suspicion, and the police activities that each permits.

Plain Touch and Feel

In *Minnesota v. Dickerson* (508 U.S. 366 [1993]), discussed earlier in this chapter, the ruling was that police officers exceeded the bounds of *Terry* when they frisked the suspect because the officer "squeezed, slid, and otherwise manipulated the packet's content" before learning that it was cocaine. Despite that decision, *Dickerson* is considered by many to be the case that officially recognized the doctrine known as *plain touch* (sometimes called *plain feel*). The Supreme Court has long recognized that the items in plain view fall outside Fourth Amendment protections because they are in plain view to the police. *Dickerson* is something of a cross between a *Terry*-based frisk and the "plain view" doctrine. According to one source, "[I]f the officer, while staying within the narrow limits of a frisk for weapons, feels what he has probable cause to believe is a weapon, contraband or evidence, the officer may expand the search or seize the object."[1]

[1]S. L. Emanuel and S. Knowles, *Emanuel Law Outlines: Criminal Procedure* (Larchmont, NY: Emanuel, 1998), p. 129.

The Bounds of a Proper Frisk

An officer on foot patrol observed a known gang member leaving a notorious "crack" house. When the gang member spotted the officer, he turned and ran in the opposite direction. The officer gave chase, caught up with him, and ordered him to stop. The gang member did stop, at which point the officer administered a patdown frisk. No weapons were revealed, but the officer felt a lump in the gang member's pocket. Upon careful examination with her fingers, the lump was revealed to a be a package of cellophane of the type commonly used to package "crack" cocaine. The officer seized the bag. May it be introduced as evidence at the gang member's trial for narcotics possession?

The reason the Supreme Court frowned on the frisk conducted by the police in *Dickerson* was that it was not immediately apparent to the officers that the suspect had contraband in his pocket. Thus, for the plain feel doctrine to apply, two conditions must be met: (1) Police must have reasonable suspicion to frisk, *and* (2) contraband must be immediately apparent for it to be lawfully seized. Stated more formally, "[T]he police may seize contraband detected solely through the officer's sense of touch, if, as with the plain-view doctrine, the officer had a right to touch the object in question (lawful vantage point and lawful access) and, upon tactile observation, the object's identity as contraband was immediately apparent."[2] Figure 6.5 presents examples of proper seizures based on plain view, touch, and feel during stop-and-frisk situations.

FIGURE 6.5 Examples of Proper Seizures Based on Plain View, Feel, and Touch during the Course of Stops-and-Frisks

Plain View, Smell or Touch

Example: During a patdown, the officer felt an unusual lumpy object by the suspect's knee. In combination with other suspicious factors which the officer had already discovered (a gram scale, the smell of methamphetamine, a small empty baggie, and beepers), this provided probable cause to arrest. Therefore, it was legal to seize the suspected contraband. (*Dibb* (1995) 37 Cal. App. 4th 832, 837.)

Example: While pat-searching a detainee for weapons, an officer felt a clump of small resilient objects. He knew it was not a weapon, but believed, based on his experience, that he had touched heroin-filled balloons. Because he now had probable cause to arrest, it was legal to reach inside the suspect's jacket and retrieve two clear bags, each containing 50 rolled toy balloons. (*Lee* (1987) 194 Cal. App. 3d 975.)

Example: While patting down a man who was present in a house where a search warrant was being executed, an officer felt a large bulge in the man's jacket which he thought could be a gun. Believing that it might be a weapon, he put his hand in the pocket and felt the object, which he then recognized as very large rocks of cocaine. He retrieved the cocaine, and the court upheld all of his actions. (*Thurman* (1989) 209 Cal. App. 3d 817.)

Example: An officer, responding to a "panhandler" complaint, noticed a large bulge in the front waistband of the suspect's trousers. For his own safety, he patted the suspect down, felt the object, concluded it was a bottle, and withdrew it. HELD: The officer's actions were legal. He had the right to feel and retrieve the bottle (a full fifth of brandy) because it constituted a potentially dangerous weapon. (*Snyder* (1992) 11 Cal. App. 4th 389, 392–393.)

Source: From *California Peace Officers Legal Sourcebook*, electronic edition, revision 113 (Sacramento, CA: California Department of Justice, Office of the Attorney General), section 2.21.

[2]J. Dressler, *Law Outlines: Criminal Procedure* (Santa Monica, CA: Casenotes, 1977), pp. 12–5.

Stops for Loitering

A somewhat lesser known but equally controversial expansion of *Terry* has been applied to stops for loitering. Generally, a person cannot be stopped with anything less than reasonable suspicion. However, certain statutes, known collectively as *loitering statutes*, authorize the police to stop or arrest suspicious-looking individuals based on a lesser degree of certainty than even reasonable suspicion. Because these statutes often permit the police to stop people based on less than reasonable suspicion, many of them have been declared unconstitutional on the grounds that they are too vague.

■ *Papachristou v. City of Jacksonville*, 405 U.S. 156 (1972)

An illustrative case is *Papachristou v. City of Jacksonville* (405 U.S. 156 [1972]). In that case, the Supreme Court declared unconstitutional a municipal ordinance that targeted "vagrants" and "rogues and vagabonds, or dissolute persons who go about begging . . . common drunkards, lewd, wanton and lascivious persons, . . . persons wandering or strolling around from place to place without any lawful purpose or object, habitual loafers, [and] disorderly persons" (p. 157, n. 1). The Court concluded that the ordinance provided "no standards governing the exercise of . . . discretion" and thereby "permit[ted] and encourage[d] an arbitrary and discriminatory enforcement of the law" and resulted "in a regime in which the poor and the unpopular are permitted to 'stand on the sidewalk . . . only at the whim of any police officer'" (p. 170).

■ *Kolender v. Lawson*, 461 U.S. 352 (1983)

In a more recent case, *Kolender v. Lawson* (461 U.S. 352 [1983]), the Supreme Court struck down another statute that made a misdemeanant of any person "[w]ho loiters or wanders upon the streets or from place to place without apparent reason or business and who refuses to identify himself and to account for his presence when requested by any peace officer to do so, if the surrounding circumstances are such as to indicate to a reasonable man that the public safety demands such identification" (p. 354, n. 1). The Court ruled that the statute was too vague because it "vests virtually complete discretion in the hands of the police to determine whether the suspect has satisfied the statute and must be permitted to go on his way in the absence of probable cause to arrest" (p. 358).

Even after *Kolender*, a number of jurisdictions have attempted to devise sufficiently specific loitering statutes. For example, the city of Chicago passed a statute providing that "whenever a police officer observes a person whom he reasonably believes to be a criminal street gang member loitering in any public place with one or more other persons, he shall order all such persons to disperse and remove themselves from the area" (Chicago Municipal Code, § 8-4-015, June 17, 1992). *Loitering* was defined as "to remain in any one place with no apparent purpose." Despite the more specific language of this statute, though, the Supreme Court also struck it down. Specifically, in *Chicago v. Morales* (527 U.S. 41 [1999]), the Supreme Court ruled that the statute was unconstitutionally vague. The majority believed that the statute still gave police too much discretion to decide which people could be classified as gang members. The Court suggested it may have upheld the statute if it had applied to gang members or to those with "an apparently harmful purpose or effect," but instead, that statute applied to "everyone in the city who may remain in one place with one suspected gang member as long as their purpose is not apparent to an officer observing them" (p. 41).

Stops, even arrests, for loitering, then, would seem to be constitutionally questionable. Several of the statutes that authorized stops for loitering have been struck down by the Supreme Court. Certainly, loitering statutes can still be found on the books elsewhere in the United States (some of which might not be too vague), but to be safe, the police should limit their stops of people to those that are based on reasonable suspicion that criminal activity is afoot. Any stop based on less than reasonable suspicion opens the police officer's actions to a great deal of constitutional scrutiny.

Other Situations

Chapter 3 introduced *administrative justification*. The courts have recognized a number of situations in which stops and searches can occur in the absence of any suspicion. Such situations include inspections of highly regulated facilities, fire inspections, border in-spections, and checkpoints for illegal immigrants, sobriety, and so on. These types of stops/searches should not be confused with the *Terry*-based stops discussed in this chapter. Administrative stops/searches technically require *no* suspicion, which is why they are not discussed in this chapter.

The discussion of the expansion of *Terry* applies to situations in which *some* degree of suspicion is required for a stop. For example, loitering statutes (despite the fact that these all have been declared unconstitutional) at least require a modicum of suspicion on the part of the police. For this reason, loitering statutes—as well as vehicle weapons searches, plain touch, and protective sweeps—are appropriate to consider in the stop-and-frisk context.

DECISION MAKING EXERCISE 6.9

Putting It All Together

Deputy Smith was on patrol in his police cruiser when he heard a report over the radio that a bank had just been robbed and that four male perpetrators had fled in a blue 1976 Ford pickup without license plates. Several minutes later, Smith observed a vehicle matching the description given over the radio except that it *had* license plates. He followed the truck and, after turning on his flashers, ordered the driver of the truck to pull over to the side of the road, which he did. Smith approached the truck and observed three men and a woman inside, each of whom appeared nervous and upset by the fact that they had been pulled over. After Smith ordered the occupants out of the car, he observed a bulge in the driver's pocket. He frisked the driver and found a weapon. Was Smith justified in stopping the vehicle and frisking the driver?

▦ Enter the Patriot Act

The Patriot Act, passed in 2001 following the September 11 terrorist attacks, has relevance to stop-and-frisk. In particular, Section 412 of the act requires the attorney general to take into custody any alien whom he or she has "reasonable grounds to believe" is "engaged in any other activity that endangers the national security of the United States" (USA Patriot Act, Pub. L. No. 107–56, 412, 115 Stat. 272, 350 [2001]). The alien can then be held for seven days, after which he or she must be released, charged criminally, or deported. Importantly, if an alien is detained for purposes related to immigration, rather than suspected criminal activity, he or she can be detained indefinitely.

This legislation has provided a powerful tool in the war on terrorism, in that authorities can indefinitely detain illegal immigrants. This obviously raises serious due process concerns, however. Too lengthy of a detention may catch the eye of a court. For example, in *Zadvydas v. Davis* (533 U.S. 678 [2001]), it was decided that the detention of an illegal alien beyond six months violated due process.

On the subject of due process, it is also worth pointing out that the Patriot Act permits the seizure of certain assets without due process protections. Specifically, Section 106 of the act increases the president's power over the property and assets of foreign persons and organizations. This portion of the Patriot Act permits the president to "confiscate any property, subject to the jurisdiction of the United States, of any foreign person, foreign organization, or foreign country that he determines has planned, authorized, aided, or engaged in such hostilities or attacks against the United States" (USA Patriot Act 106, 115 Stat. at 277). Relatedly, the act also allows the president to direct other agencies and individuals to use or transfer such property as deemed necessary. Without delving too far into the realm of civil asset forfeiture, it is sufficient to say that the Supreme Court has required due process protections for individuals whose property is targeted for forfeiture (*United States v. Good*, 510 U.S. 43 [1993]). The Patriot Act's forfeiture provisions appear to run counter to the Court's view.

DRUG COURIER PROFILING

An especially controversial variety of *Terry*-like investigative stops includes those based on so-called drug courier profiles. This chapter gives detailed attention to **drug courier profiling** not just because it is a controversial criminal justice topic but also because it is an appropriate topic for a chapter on stop-and-frisk. Almost without exception, drug courier profiling occurs in the stop-and-frisk context—that is, when a person is stopped and questioned because he or she appears suspicious in some way. Drug courier profiling is most common in airports but also occurs on U.S. highways and elsewhere.

Indeed, profiling of offenders occurs for other offenses, as well. Law enforcement officials have developed profiles of a number of other varieties of offenders, including car thieves (*People v. Martinez*, 12 Cal. Rptr. 2d 838 [Cal. Ct. App. 1992]), child abusers (*Flanagan v. State*, 586 So.2d 1085 [Fla. Dist. Ct. App. 1991]), child batterers (*Commonwealth v. Day*, 569 N.E.2d 397 [Mass. 1991]), and sexual abusers (*State v. McMillan*, 590 N.E.2d 23 [Ohio Ct. App. 1990]), among others.

The carrying of controlled substances by airline passengers is a common way that drugs enter the United States from foreign countries. Law enforcement agents *could* conceivably search every person who passes through an airport, but such an effort would be costly, time consuming, unacceptable to passengers, and almost certainly unconstitutional. Warrantless searches that are based on no articulable justification are always unreasonable under the Fourth Amendment, unless one of a few "specifically established and well-delineated exceptions" applies (*Katz v. United States*, 389 U.S. 347 [1967], p. 357). In other words, such searches violate the Fourth Amendment because they are not based on probable cause, as the amendment requires.

Given that suspicionless searches are illegal, then, the police are left with two options when it comes to confronting people suspected of being drug couriers. These two options are "consensual encounters in which contact is initiated by a police officer without any articulable reason whatsoever and the citizen is briefly asked some questions [and] a temporary involuntary detention . . . which must be predicated on 'reasonable suspicion'" (*United States v. Bueno*, 21 F.3d [1978]). Both consensual encounters and investigative detentions are not considered searches, so they fall outside the Fourth Amendment's probable cause requirement.

Consent searches are covered in Chapter 7, but suffice it to say for now that when a person gives consent to the police to conduct a search or ask questions, the Fourth Amendment does not apply. Assuming the citizen remains free to decline the officer's request to conduct a search, the officer can legally ask a person to look in his or her car, bag, house, or other area. The logic behind consent searches was touched on in *Terry v. Ohio*, in which the Supreme Court stated that "there is nothing in the Constitution which prevents a policeman from addressing questions to anyone on the streets" (p. 27). There is one significant restriction, though, for a consent search (or stop) to be truly consensual, and it goes directly to the definition of *stop* covered earlier in this chapter: "[T]he Fourth Amendment permits police officers to approach individuals at random in airport lobbies and other public places to ask them questions and to request consent to search their luggage, so long as a reasonable person would understand that he or she could refuse to cooperate" (*Florida v. Bostick*, p. 431). In other words, the constitutionality of a consent search is premised on the requirement that the person is truly free to decline when asked by a police officer to allow a search.

Perhaps more common in the practice of drug courier profiling is the use of investigative detentions, or *Terry* stops. *Terry*, as addressed throughout the bulk of this

Drug courier profiling occurs most often in airports.

chapter, permits police officers to stop people based on reasonable suspicion that criminal activity is afoot. *Terry* stops occur in airports and elsewhere when a person is involuntarily detained. For this type of stop to occur, however, the officer needs to show that
there is, in fact, reasonable suspicion that the person is a drug courier. The primary question that makes drug courier profiling a controversial topic is, What characteristics must
a person display for reasonable suspicion to be established?

Clearly, not every person walking through an airport can be stopped. Thus, law
enforcement officials must look for specific characteristics of drug couriers. As the
Supreme Court observed in *United States v. Mendenhall* (446 U.S. 544 [1980]),
"Much . . . drug traffic is highly organized and conducted by sophisticated criminal
syndicates . . . . And many drugs . . . may be easily concealed. As a result, the obstacles
to detection . . . may be unmatched in any other area of law enforcement" (pp. 545–546).
Further, one of the most significant impediments in the war on drugs is the "extraordi-
nary and well-documented difficulty of identifying drug couriers" (*Florida v. Royer*, 460
U.S. 491 [1983], p. 519).

The drug courier profile is generally attributed to Paul Markonni, a DEA agent who
identified a number of suspicious characteristics of likely drug couriers when he was
assigned to a drug interdiction unit at the Detroit airport. That profile has since been
described as an "informally compiled abstract of characteristics thought typical of
persons carrying illicit drugs" (*United States v. Mendenhall*, p. 547). There is no single,
nationally recognized drug courier profile or set of characteristics indicative of drug
courier profiling. Instead, specific cases must be considered to ascertain which types of
characteristics fit the drug courier profile.

The first drug courier profile case of note, *United States v. Van Lewis* (409 F. Supp.
535 [E.D. Mich. 1976]), listed several characteristics to be used in identifying drug couriers: (1) the use of small denominations of currency for ticket purchase; (2) travel to and
from major drug import centers; (3) the absence of luggage or use of empty suitcases on
trips that normally require extra clothing; and (4) travel under an alias. In a similar case,

the Fifth Circuit Court, in *Elmore v. United States* (595 F.2d 1036 [5th Cir. 1979]), described these common characteristics of drug couriers:

(1) arrival from or departure to an identified source city; (2) carrying little or no luggage; (3) unusual itinerary, such as rapid turnaround time for a very lengthy airplane trip; (4) use of an alias; (5) carrying unusually large amounts of currency in the many thousands of dollars, usually on their person, or in briefcases or bags; (6) purchasing airline tickets with a large amount of small denomination currency; and (7) unusual nervousness beyond that ordinarily exhibited by passengers. (p. 1039, n. 3)

Some secondary characteristics of drug couriers were also identified in *Elmore v. United States*, including "(1) the almost exclusive use of public transportation, particularly taxicabs, in departing from the airport; (2) immediately making a phone call after deplaning; (3) leaving a false or fictitious call-back telephone number with the airline being utilized; and (4) excessively frequent travel to source or distribution cities" (p. 1039, n. 3).

Still other characteristics of drug couriers include unusual dress, age between 25 and 35, and extreme paleness consistent with being extremely nervous.[3] Another study points to characteristics such as "not checking bags at the airport, not using identification tags on luggage, purchasing tickets on the day of a flight, exiting first or last from the plane, visually scanning the terminal for law enforcement, making no eye contact with airport personnel, walking quickly through the terminal while continuously checking over one's shoulder, and quickly leaving the airport on arrival."[4] See Figure 6.6 for a fairly comprehensive list of the typical characteristics of drug couriers.

FIGURE 6.6 Typical Characteristics of Drug Couriers

1. Use small denominations of currency for ticket purchases
2. Travel to and from major drug import centers
3. Have no luggage or use empty suitcases on trips that normally require extra clothing
4. Travel under an alias
5. Have an unusual itinerary, such as a rapid turnaround time for a very lengthy airplane trip
6. Carry unusually large amounts of currency (i.e., many thousands of dollars)
7. Display unusual nervousness beyond that ordinarily exhibited by passengers
8. Use public transportation almost exclusively upon departing the airport
9. Immediately make a phone call after deplaning
10. Leave a false or fictitious call-back telephone number with the airline
11. Dress in an unusual manner
12. Are between 25 and 35 years old
13. Are extremely pale (consistent with being extremely nervous)
14. Do not use identification tags on luggage
15. Purchase tickets on the day of the flight
16. Exit first or last from the plane
17. Walk quickly through the terminal while continuously checking over his or her shoulder
18. Quickly leave the airport on arrival

[3]B. Wilson, "The War on Drugs: Evening the Odds through the Use of the Airport Drug Courier Profile," *Boston University Public Interest Journal* 6 (1994): 202–232.
[4]C. R. Williams and B. A. Arrigo, "Discerning the Margins of Constitutional Encroachment: The Drug Courier Profile in the Airport Milieu," *American Journal of Criminal Justice* 24, no. 1 (1999): 31–46.

Landmark Cases

A number of Supreme Court cases, some of which have already been mentioned in passing throughout this chapter, have addressed the constitutionality of profiling and stopping people on less than reasonable suspicion. Significantly, the Supreme Court has yet to rule definitively on the constitutionality of drug courier profiling and is not likely to do so soon. Even so, the Court's differing decisions and opinions lend a great deal of insight into this highly controversial drug war enforcement tactic.

Reid v. Georgia

Reid v. Georgia (448 U.S. 438 [1980]) was one of the first Supreme Court cases to address drug courier profiling. The petitioner, Reid, arrived at the Atlanta airport on an early morning flight. A narcotics agent on duty at the time observed that Reid repeatedly looked over his shoulder at another man and that both were carrying shoulder bags. As the two men left the airport, the narcotics officer approached them and asked them for identification and to consent to a search. Reid tried to run away and, in doing so, left his bag behind, which turned out to contain cocaine. He was later apprehended and brought to trial on drug possession charges. He attempted to have the cocaine thrown out under the exclusionary rule, claiming that he had been unconstitutionally detained as he was leaving the airport with the other man.

> *Reid v. Georgia,*
> 448 U.S. 438 (1980)

The trial court granted Reid's motion to suppress the cocaine; however, the Georgia Court of Appeals reversed the lower court's decision and ruled that the narcotics agent had performed a permissible stop based on the so-called drug courier profile. In its decision, the Georgia Court of Appeals noted that Reid (1) had arrived from Fort Lauderdale, Florida, a place of origin for drugs; (2) was traveling at an unusual hour; (3) was attempting to conceal that fact that he was traveling with another person; and (4) was not traveling with any luggage, other than the shoulder bag (p. 441).

The U.S. Supreme Court granted *certiorari*, holding that "the judgment of the appellate court cannot be sustained insofar as it rests on the determination that the DEA agent lawfully seized the petitioner when he approached him" (p. 441). The Court went on to note that the agent "could not . . . have reasonably suspected the petitioner of criminal activity on the basis . . . that the petitioner preceded another person and occasionally looked backward at him" (p. 441). The other reasons for stopping Reid were also criticized by the Court because the unusual hour, lack of luggage, and place of origin "describe a very large category of presumably innocent travelers, who would be subject to virtually random seizures were the Court to conclude that as little foundation as there was in this case could justify the seizure" (p. 441). The Court declared that the DEA agent did not have reasonable suspicion to detain Reid.

United States v. Mendenhall

By now, *United States v. Mendenhall* (446 U.S. 544 [1980]) should be something of a familiar case; it was covered at length in defining the *stop* in stop-and-frisk. However, *Mendenhall* has also had important implications for drug courier profiling in the United States. In that case, DEA agents who were "present for the [purpose] of detecting unlawful traffic in narcotics" (p. 545), observed Mendenhall in the Detroit airport. They approached her in the airport and identified themselves. They then asked Mendenhall for her identification and airline ticket. When she complied, they noticed that the plane ticket was in another name. At that point, the agents asked Mendenhall if she would accompany them to a private room and consent to a search of her bags. She was told that she had the right to decline, but she handed over her purse and agreed to the search. A female police officer then arrived to search Mendenhall's person. When she removed her clothing, a package that appeared to contain heroin was revealed.

> *United States v.*
> *Mendenhall,*
> 446 U.S. 544 (1980)

The agents would later testify that Mendenhall's conduct was consistent with the "characteristics of persons unlawfully carrying narcotics" (p. 567). In particular, the agents testified that Mendenhall fit the profile because she was arriving on a flight from a source city (Los Angeles), was last to leave the plane, appeared to be nervous, was scanning the area around her, and did not claim any luggage. The trial court concluded that the agents' actions were justified because they were "based on specific and articulable facts that justified a suspicion of criminal activity" (*United States v. McCaleb*, 552 F.2d 717 [1977], p. 720).

On appeal, the agents' actions were declared illegal. The court ruled that the officers could not have been reasonably suspicious of criminal activity because Mendenhall's "activities were consistent with innocent behavior" (p. 570). Also, the appeals court pointed out that the act of bringing Mendenhall to a private room was intrusive to the extent that it should have been considered an arrest, requiring probable cause.

The Supreme Court then reversed this decision and remanded the Mendenhall case. The Court ruled that Mendenhall *was* seized because "a reasonable person would have believed that he was not free to leave" (p. 573). In addition, Justice Powell noted that "the [DEA] agents had reasonable suspicion that the respondent [Mendenhall] was engaging in criminal activity, and . . . did not violate the Fourth Amendment by stopping [her] for questioning" (*Brown v. Texas*, p. 52). The Court declared that a certain degree of deference should be given to law enforcement agents to interpret the circumstances in each case, based on their experience and expertise. The Court reasoned that an experienced law enforcement officer may be "able to perceive and articulate meaning in given conduct which would be wholly innocent to the untrained observer" (*United States v. Mendenhall*, p. 557).

The Court was sharply divided in its decision, however. Four justices disagreed with the majority opinion, believing that the agents' actions were violative of the Fourth Amendment. For example, Justice White argued that the Court's decision was "inconsistent with its recognition that consent cannot be presumed from a showing of acquiescence to authority" (*Terry v. Ohio*, p. 17). The dissenters also argued that the agents did not have reasonable suspicion to stop Mendenhall. In their words, "To establish that there was a reasonable suspicion for the stop, it was necessary for the police to be able to point to specific and articulable facts which, taken together with rational inferences from those facts, reasonably warrant that intrusion" (*United States v. Mendenhall*, p. 565). Instead, the dissenters believed that the agents' decision to stop Mendenhall was based on "inchoate and unparticularized suspicion or 'hunch,' rather than specific reasonable inferences which entitled [them] to draw from the facts in light of [their] experience" (*Florida v. Royer*, p. 491; see also following section).

Florida v. Royer

■ *Florida v. Royer,*
460 U.S. 491 (1983)

Another significant drug courier profiling case decided by the Supreme Court is *Florida v. Royer* (460 U.S. 491 [1983]). In that case, two detectives at the Miami International Airport observed Royer, who had purchased a one-way ticket to New York under an assumed name. Believing that Royer displayed characteristics associated with the drug courier profile, the officers approached him. Royer produced his ticket and identification after being requested to do so. The officers did not return his ticket and identification and instead asked Royer to accompany them to a nearby room. One of the detectives retrieved the luggage that Royer had checked and brought it to the room. Royer produced a key for the suitcases, and upon opening one of them, marijuana was found. Royer was convicted for felony possession; however, the Florida Court of Appeals reversed the trial court's decision, holding that the officers detained Royer without probable cause, which was required because of the intrusive nature of the stop.

The detectives argued that Royer fit the drug courier profile for a number of reasons. First, he was carrying luggage that appeared to be heavy. Second, he was young, dressed casually, and appeared nervous. Finally, he paid for his plane ticket in cash and did not complete the airline identification tag, opting instead to write only his name and destination on the tag. The court argued on appeal, however, that "any of these factors relied upon by Miami police may have been as consistent with innocence as with guilt" (p. 492) and that the drug courier profile alone was insufficient to establish reasonable suspicion, much less probable cause, to detain Royer.

The case worked its way up to the U.S. Supreme Court, and the Court upheld the appeals court decision. According to the Supreme Court, Royer was detained illegally, in part because the detectives did not indicate at any point that he was free to leave. Further, the Court argued that "the detention . . . was a more serious intrusion on his personal liberty than is allowable on mere suspicion of criminal activity. What had begun as a consensual encounter . . . escalated into an investigatory procedure in an interrogation room, and [Royer] . . . was under arrest" (p. 503).

Royer was also a sharply divided decision. Four out of the nine justices believed that the police conduct was appropriate as well as "minimally intrusive." Justice Blackmun, writing for the dissenters, argued that given the importance of "overcoming extraordinary obstacles to the detection of drug traffickers, such [police] conduct should not be subjected to the requirement of probable cause" (p. 504). Interestingly, though, the dissent did not comment on the reasonable suspicion issue.

United States v. Sokolow

In *United States v. Sokolow* (490 U.S. 1 [1989]), DEA agents stopped Sokolow upon his arrival at Honolulu International Airport and found a large quantity of cocaine in his carry-on luggage. In support of the stop, the agents noted that Sokolow (1) had paid $2,100 for his airline ticket with a roll of $20 bills; (2) traveled under an assumed name; (3) had flown in from a major "source city," Miami; (4) had stayed in Miami for only 48 hours; (5) appeared nervous; and (6) did not check any luggage.

■ *United States v. Sokolow, 490 U.S. 1 (1989)*

The district court denied Sokolow's motion to suppress the drugs, finding that the agents had reasonable suspicion to stop him in the airport. However, the court of appeals declared that the stop was illegal, a violation of the Fourth Amendment. The court relied on a two-pronged test to assess the legality of the stop. It required a showing that (1) there was "ongoing criminal activity" and that there were (2) "personal characteristics" of drug courier profiles. While the second prong would seem to have been met in this case, the appeals court decided that the first prong had not been met because the government did not offer "empirical documentation that the combination of facts at issue did not describe the behavior of significant numbers of innocent persons" (p. 2). In other words, the court of appeals found no evidence of ongoing criminal activity and thus ruled that the stop was in violation of the Fourth Amendment.

The U.S. Supreme Court reversed the appeals court decision. It held that the agents *did* have reasonable suspicion that Sokolow was engaged in the transportation of narcotics. In criticizing the two-pronged test used by the appeals court, the Supreme Court noted that the test "created unnecessary difficulty in dealing with one of the relatively simple concepts embodied in the Fourth Amendment" (p. 3). In reference to the suspicious conduct observed by the agents, the Court went on to note that "although each of these factors [e.g., paying $2,100 for a plane ticket with small denomination bills] is not by itself proof of illegal conduct and is quite consistent with innocent travel, taken together they amount to reasonable suspicion that criminal activity was afoot" (p. 4).

The Supreme Court was careful not to rule on the constitutionality of drug courier profiling. Instead, the Court explained, "[T]he fact that the agents believed that respondent's behavior was consistent with one of the DEA's 'drug courier profiles' does not alter this analysis, because the factors in question have evidentiary significance regardless of whether they are set forth in a 'profile'" (p. 4). The dissenters, however, believed that the profile was of great significance to the case. For example, Justice Marshall argued:

In my view, a law enforcement officer's mechanistic application of a formula of personal and behavioral traits in deciding whom to detain can only dull the officer's ability and determination to make specific and fact-specific inferences "in light of his experience" . . . particularly in ambiguous or borderline cases. Reflexive reliance on a profile of drug courier characteristics runs a far greater risk than does ordinary, case-by-case police work of subjecting innocent individuals to unwarranted police harassment and detention. (p. 24)

Somewhat telling of cases to come, Marshall then went on to write that "[i]n asserting that it is not 'somehow' relevant that the agents who stopped Sokolow did so in reliance on a prefabricated profile of criminal characteristics . . . the majority thus ducks serious issues relating to a questionable law enforcement practice, to address the validity of which we granted *certiorari* in this case" (pp. 26–27).

As the most recent of the drug courier profiling cases reviewed here, *Sokolow* seems to suggest that profiling is acceptable, as long as law enforcement officers give special attention to the characteristics of couriers without relying on a predefined profile. In other words, the Court seems to have held that the commonly identified characteristics of drug couriers can contribute to reasonable suspicion, but several such characteristics must be displayed at the same time for the stop to be valid.

Race and Drug Courier Profiling

Critics of drug courier profiling have argued that the practice is racially discriminatory. One commentator has argued, for example, that "[a]lthough the DEA has refused to commit the entire profile to writing, the profile clearly contains a racial component."[5] In fact, in *United States v. Taylor* (956 F.2d 572 [6th Cir. 1992]), a case before the Sixth Circuit Court, an officer admitted that 75 percent of the persons detained through use of drug courier profiling were African American (p. 581, n. 1). In a strong dissent to that case, Judge Damon Keith wrote, "The disproportionate number of African-Americans who are stopped indicates that a racial imbalance against African-Americans does exist and is implicitly sanctioned by the law enforcement agency . . . . We cannot allow law enforcement officers to cloak what may fairly be characterized as a racist practice in a generic drug profile that openly targets African-Americans" (pp. 581–582).

Those who argue that race is not a factor in profiling claim, perhaps accurately, that the profile targets minorities because they are, in fact, more likely to be drug couriers than nonminorities. Nevertheless, if a disproportionate number of minorities are stopped during profiling, a serious problem is posed—that of a self-fulfilling prophecy. One author's observations regarding this matter are quite telling:

If the profile assumes that racial minorities are more likely than Whites to be couriers, then the percentage of minorities in the group of people stopped will be higher than the percentage of minorities in the overall population. Even if minorities are in reality no more predisposed than Whites to serve as drug couriers, they will nevertheless appear to be more predisposed, because they will make up a larger proportion of the pool of those persons stopped.[6]

The race issue in drug courier profiling has yet to be addressed by the Supreme Court, just as the use of profiling itself has yet to be decided. It is likely, however, that the Court, in the not too distant future, will have an opportunity to settle this controversial

[5]S. L. Johnson, "Race and the Decision to Detain a Suspect," *Yale Law Journal* 93 (1983): 234.
[6]T. Yin, "The Probative Values and Pitfalls of Drug Courier Profiles as Probabilistic Evidence," *Texas Forum on Civil Liberties and Civil Rights* 5 (2000): 151.

issue once and for all. For now, though, it cannot be said with complete certainty that race is a factor in drug courier profiling.

DECISION MAKING EXERCISE 6.10

An Application of Drug Courier Profiling

DEA agents at the Dallas/Fort Worth airport observed a woman exiting a plane that had just arrived from Miami. She was carrying a small bag on her shoulder and looking around as if she was expecting to meet another person. Still alone, she walked quickly into a restroom. When she came out, she went directly to a pay phone, where she made a phone call lasting 30 minutes. Finding her conduct suspicious, the DEA agents approached the woman, identified themselves, and asked if they could speak with her. The woman appeared very nervous, and her voice cracked when she conversed with them. The agents asked for the woman's identification and plane ticket. She furnished her plane ticket but stated that she had lost her identification. The agents asked how long she was going to stay in the Dallas/Fort Worth area. She replied that she would remain for one week, but one of the agents noticed that her ticket indicated that she would be leaving later that same day. Do the agents have justification to further detain the woman?

INVESTIGATIVE DETENTIONS

The Supreme Court has held that certain police station detentions are justifiable on less than probable cause. One type of **investigative detention**, a stationhouse detention, is less intrusive than an arrest but more intrusive than a *Terry* stop. Stationhouse detentions are used in many locations for such purposes as obtaining fingerprints and photographs, ordering lineups, administering polygraph examinations, and securing other types of evidence.

In *Davis v. Mississippi* (394 U.S. 721 [1969]), the Court excluded fingerprint evidence obtained from 25 rape suspects, but it did note that detention for fingerprinting could have been permissible if "narrowly circumscribed procedures" were in place. In other words, the Court suggested that to justify the detention, there had to be some objective basis for detaining a person, a clear investigation underway, and a court order stating that adequate evidence exists. In another case, *Hayes v. Florida* (470 U.S. 811 [1985]), the Court stated:

> Our view continues to be that the line is crossed when the police, without probable cause or a warrant, forcibly remove a person from his home or other place in which he is entitled to be and transport him to the police station, where he is detained, although briefly, for investigative purposes. We adhere to the view that such seizures, at least where not under judicial supervision, are sufficiently like arrests to invoke the traditional rule that arrests may constitutionally be made only on probable cause. (p. 816)

The key in *Hayes*, however, is that the detention was not consensual. In cases in which consent is obtained, probable cause is not necessary. In short, a stationhouse detention for the purpose of fingerprinting is permissible when (1) there is reasonable suspicion to believe the suspect has committed a crime; (2) there is a reasonable belief that the fingerprints will inculpate or exculpate the suspect; and (3) the procedure is carried out promptly. (Note that the Supreme Court has not addressed stationhouse detentions *not* involving fingerprinting.)

CONCLUSION

A number of specific conclusions can be drawn from the stop-and-frisk discussion in this chapter and from the introduction to reasonable suspicion presented in Chapter 3. First, a police/citizen encounter is not governed by the Fourth Amendment unless it is considered a *stop*, which is one type of *seizure*. When the police activity in question rises to the level of a stop, then the Fourth Amendment applies, and the officer is required to have the appropriate level of justification for the stop to be legal.

Factors to consider in determining whether a stop has taken place include (1) whether the police action was threatening; (2) how long the detention lasted; (3) whether the person was physically detained or physically touched by the police; (4) whether the detention took place in public view or removed from public view, such as in a private room; and perhaps most importantly, (5) whether a reasonable person would, under the circumstances, have believed that he or she was free to leave. With regard to the last factor, it is not necessary that police communicate to the detainee that he or she is free to leave. A situation involving only brief questioning, then, is unlikely to be considered a stop, implicating the Fourth Amendment.

The Fourth Amendment generally requires that probable cause be in place before a Fourth Amendment seizure can occur. However, the Supreme Court in *Terry* ruled that a person can be seized on less than probable cause to arrest. The second conclusion, then, focuses on when this can occur. Generally, a seizure based on less than probable cause (i.e., reasonable suspicion) can occur under three circumstances: (1) when the officer observes a person engaging in unusual activity and can point to specific, articulable facts that contribute to reasonable suspicion that criminal activity is afoot; (2) when the officer receives information from an informant who is reliable; and (3) when the officer receives a communication from another police department that the person to be stopped is suspected of involvement in criminal activity.

When reasonable suspicion is in place and a police officer is entitled to make a stop, he or she must make reasonable inquiries. These inquiries should be limited to testing the officer's suspicion. If the questioning becomes unreasonable, excessive, or too intrusive, probable cause may be required. Then, if the officer reasonably believes, during the course of questioning, that the person is armed and dangerous, he or she can frisk the person. Factors used in determining whether a frisk is reasonable include (1) whether the person has a reputation for dangerousness; (2) the type of criminal activity in which the person is presumably involved; (3) visual cues that suggest the presence of a weapon; and/or (4) suggestive or furtive gestures on the part of the suspect.

Frisks are limited. If one is authorized because the officer reasonably fears for his or her safety, the frisk is limited to a patdown of the person's outer clothing. Recent decisions, however, permit a limited search of the area immediately surrounding the person, such as in automobiles and other situations in which several people may be found. Weapon-like objects and contraband can be removed during the course of the frisk, but both must be immediately apparent to the frisking officer. If a weapon or other item is not immediately apparent, then the officer risks exceeding the limits of a frisk, especially if he or she feels, gropes, or otherwise manipulates the object in an attempt to determine what it is. Such activity may arise to the level of a search, requiring probable cause.

Drug courier profiling remains a controversial practice. While the courts do commonly recognize characteristics of drug courier profiles, a number of cases concerning drug courier profiling have reached the Supreme Court. Even so, the Court has yet to rule on the constitutionality of drug courier profiling. Finally, racial discrimination is also at issue in drug courier profiling. There is no shortage of criticism concerning the role of race in profiling, but since the Supreme Court has not decided on the legality of profiling, it is unlikely that racially motivated investigative stops, to the extent they exist, will cease.

REVIEW QUESTIONS

1. Why is it important to view a stop and a frisk as two separate acts?
2. Assuming a police officer has reasonable suspicion to stop a person, what must the officer do before stopping him or her?
3. Define a *stop*.
4. Why is the duration of a stop important?
5. Can *effects* be seized? Explain.
6. Summarize the permissible grounds for a frisk.
7. Summarize the Supreme Court's view on the proper scope of a frisk.

8. In what ways has stop-and-frisk law been expanded? Summarize pertinent cases.

9. Why is it important to distinguish between theory and reality when discussing stop-and-frisk?

10. What is drug courier profiling?

11. Identify several characteristics of drug couriers.

12. Summarize the Supreme Court's view on drug courier profiling, citing relevant cases.

13. In what ways is race relevant to the drug courier profile?

14. What are investigative detentions? How do they differ from stops?

15. Reasonable suspicion is not mentioned in the Fourth Amendment. Has the Supreme Court overstepped its authority by essentially creating this level of justification? Why or why not?

 Answers to the Decision-Making Exercises for this chapter can be found on pages 499–501.

CHAPTER 7

Actions Based on Administrative Justification and Consent

OUTLINE

KEY TERMS

vehicle inventory
person inventory
inspection
closely regulated business
checkpoints

airport checkpoints
school disciplinary searches
drug and alcohol testing
   programs
police/probation partnerships

consent search
common authority
apparent authority
"knock and talk"

INTRODUCTION

Casting Off the Fourth Amendment's Restraints

As mentioned in Chapter 3, administrative searches are those in which the primary purpose is noncriminal. Because such searches nonetheless intrude on people's privacy—and can lead to the discovery of evidence—the Fourth Amendment is implicated. However, instead of focusing on probable cause or reasonable suspicion, the courts use a balancing test, weighing citizens' privacy interests against the interest to ensure public safety. When the latter outweighs the former, an administrative search is allowed, subject to certain limitations (e.g., department policy). This chapter briefly introduces several types of searches that the Supreme Court has authorized based on administrative justification.

This chapter also introduces the topic of consent searches. When a person gives valid consent to search, neither a warrant nor probable cause is required. Closely tied to consent searches is the controversial police practice known as "knock and talk." The consent search section also delves into third-party consent, or the extent to which one person can grant consent to have another person's property searched.

SEARCHES BASED ON ADMINISTRATIVE JUSTIFICATION

The Supreme Court has authorized numerous varieties of searches under the administrative justification exception to the Fourth Amendment's probable cause and warrant requirements. Sometimes they are described as *special needs beyond law enforcement searches*; other times, they are called *regulatory searches*. To avoid confusion, this book

KEY CASES

Inventories
- *South Dakota v. Opperman*, 428 U.S. 364 (1976)
- *Colorado v. Bertine*, 479 U.S. 367 (1987)
- *Illinois v. Lafayette*, 462 U.S. 640 (1983)

Inspections
- *Camara v. Municipal Court*, 387 U.S. 523 (1967)
- *Wyman v. James*, 400 U.S. 309 (1971)
- *Colonnade Catering Corp. v. United States*, 397 U.S. 72 (1970)
- *United States v. Biswell*, 406 U.S. 311 (1972)
- *Michigan v. Tyler*, 436 U.S. 499 (1978)
- *United States v. Ramsey*, 431 U.S. 606 (1977)

Checkpoints
- *Carroll v. United States*, 267 U.S. 132 (1925)
- *United States v. Martinez-Fuerte*, 428 U.S. 543 (1976)
- *Michigan Dept. of State Police v. Sitz*, 496 U.S. 444 (1990)
- *Delaware v. Prouse*, 440 U.S. 648 (1979)

- *Illinois v. Lidster*, 540 U.S. 419 (2004)
- *City of Indianapolis v. Edmond*, 531 U.S. 32 (2000)

Other Administrative Searches
- *New Jersey v. T.L.O.*, 469 U.S. 325 (1985)
- *O'Connor v. Ortega*, 480 U.S. 709 (1987)
- *Skinner v. Railway Labor Executives' Association*, 489 U.S. 602 (1989)
- *Ferguson v. Charleston*, 532 U.S. 67 (2001)
- *Vernonia School District 47J v. Acton*, 515 U.S. 646 (1995)
- *Board of Education v. Earls*, 536 U.S. 822 (2002)
- *Griffin v. Wisconsin*, 483 U.S. 868 (1987)

Consent
- *Schneckloth v. Bustamonte*, 412 U.S. 218 (1973)
- *Florida v. Jimeno*, 500 U.S. 248 (1991)
- *United States v. Matlock*, 415 U.S. 164 (1974)
- *Illinois v. Rodriguez*, 497 U.S. 177 (1990)

lumps all such searches under the category of *administrative justification*. The types of searches that are considered include (1) inventory searches; (2) inspections; (3) checkpoints; (4) school disciplinary searches; (5) searches of government employees' offices; (6) drug and alcohol testing; and (7) probation supervision searches.

Inventory Searches

Like seizures based on plain view, inventory searches can be viewed as another fallback measure. An inventory search can be of a vehicle and/or of a person's personal items. Usually, a search occurs under the automobile exception (in the case of an automobile) or a search incident to arrest (when a person is involved), and an inventory is taken after the fact for the purpose of developing a record of what items have been taken into custody. Both types of inventory searches are fallbacks in the sense that they often occur *after* an earlier search.

Vehicle Inventories

South Dakota v. Opperman, 428 U.S. 364 (1976)

A **vehicle inventory** occurs in a number of situations, usually after a car has been impounded for traffic or parking violations. In *South Dakota v. Opperman* (428 U.S. 364 [1976]), the Supreme Court held that a warrantless inventory is permissible on administrative/regulatory grounds. However, it must (1) follow a *lawful* impoundment; (2) be of a routine nature, following standard operating procedures; and (3) not be a "pretext concealing an investigatory police motive." Thus, even though an inventory search can be perceived as a fallback measure, which permits a search when probable cause is lacking, it cannot be used in lieu of a regular search requiring probable cause.

Why did the Court opt for another standard besides probable cause for the inventory search, despite the fact that it is still a search in the conventional sense of the term? The Court noted that the probable cause requirement of the Fourth Amendment is "unhelpful" in the context of administrative care-taking functions (e.g., inventory searches) because the concept of probable cause is linked to criminal investigations. Probable cause is irrelevant with this type of administrative search, "particularly when no claim is made that the protective procedures are a subterfuge for criminal investigations" (p. 371).

The Court offered three reasons in support of vehicle inventories. First, an inventory search protects the owner's property while it is in police custody. Second, an inventory search protects the police against claims of lost or stolen property. Finally, an inventory search protects the police and public from dangerous items (e.g., weapons) that might be concealed in a car.

Colorado v. Bertine, 479 U.S. 367 (1987)

Note that an exception to the inventory search includes containers discovered during the search. That is, the police may search *any* container discovered during the course of a vehicle inventory search, but searches of containers should be mandated by departmental procedures governing inventory searches. This was the decision reached in *Colorado v. Bertine* (479 U.S. 367 [1987]). That decision also helped the police insofar as the Court refused to alter the vehicle inventory search exception to the Fourth Amendment when secure impound facilities are accessible. As the Court stated, "[T]he security of the storage facility does not completely eliminate the need for inventorying; the police may still wish to protect themselves or the owners of the lot against false claims of theft or dangerous instrumentalities" (p. 373).

In *Bertine*, the Court also rejected an argument that car owners should be able to make their own arrangements if their vehicles are impounded (e.g., have it towed by a private company, have a friend drive it home, etc.). The Court stated, "The reasonableness of any particular governmental activity does not necessarily or invariably turn on the existence of alternative 'less intrusive' means" (p. 374).

Reading *Opperman* and *Bertine* would suggest that inventory searches are relatively standard and intended mainly to take note of a car's contents. However, in

Michigan v. Thomas (458 U.S. 259 [1982]), the Supreme Court concluded that the police could go even further. In that case, officers found a loaded .38 revolver in one of the impounded vehicle's air vents. The Court upheld the officers' actions because marijuana had been found in the vehicle shortly before the gun was.

DECISION MAKING EXERCISE **7.1**

Inventoried and Inventoried Again

At the time of the defendant's arrest, police officers inventoried his automobile and seized several items. Approximately eight hours after the car was impounded, an officer, without obtaining a warrant, searched the car a second time, seizing additional evidence. Note that both searches were inventory searches. Do these searches appear, as many courts have stated it, to "pass Fourth Amendment muster"? What if only the second search was deemed unconstitutional?

In conclusion, two important issues must be understood with regard to vehicle inventory searches. First, if during the course of a valid inventory search, the police discover evidence that gives rise to probable cause to search, then a more extensive search is permissible. However, according to *Carroll v. United States* (267 U.S. 132 [1925]), discussed in Chapter 5, one of the requirements for such action to be constitutional is the impracticality of securing a warrant.

Second, despite the Supreme Court's apparent willingness to give police wide latitude with vehicle inventory searches, what makes them constitutional is clear guidelines as to how the search should be conducted. In other words, the Court has authorized inventory searches without probable cause or a warrant only if, in addition to the other requirements discussed above, the search is conducted in accordance with clear departmental policies and procedures. Requiring the police to follow appropriate policies minimizes discretion and the concern that inventory searches may be used for criminal investigation purposes. The inventory search policy from the *California Peace Officers Legal Sourcebook* is reprinted in Figure 7.1 (pp. 202–203).

Person Inventories

The inventory search exception to the Fourth Amendment's warrant requirement applies in the case of a **person inventory**, as well. Such a search is often called an *arrest inventory*. The general rule is that the police may search an arrestee and his or her personal items, including containers found in his or her possession, as part of a routine inventory incident to the booking and jailing procedure. As decided in *Illinois v. Lafayette* (462 U.S. 640 [1983]), neither a search warrant nor probable cause is required. According to the Court:

■ *Illinois v. Lafayette,* 462 U.S. 640 (1983)

> Consistent with the Fourth Amendment, it is reasonable for police to search the personal effects of a person under lawful arrest as part of the routine administrative procedure at a police station incident to booking and jailing the suspect. The justification for such searches does not rest on probable cause, and hence the absence of a warrant is immaterial to the reasonableness of the search. Here, every consideration of orderly police administration—protection of a suspect's property, deterrence of false claims of theft against the police, security, and identification of the suspect—benefiting both the police and the public points toward the appropriateness of the examination of respondent's shoulder bag. (pp. 643–648)

It is important to understand that an inventory search of person must follow a lawful arrest, so the probable cause to search requirement is essentially satisfied at the arrest stage.

FIGURE 7.1 Example of an Inventory Search Policy

IX. VEHICLE INVENTORIES

A. In General

Vehicle inventories are supported by three rationales:

- protection of an owner's property while it is in police custody;

- protection of police against claims of lost, stolen, or vandalized property; and

- officer safety. (*Bertine* (1987) 479 U.S. 367, 372; *Opperman* (1976) 428 U.S. 364, 369; *Needham* (2000) 79 Cal.App.4th 260, 266.)

Although vehicle inventories must be "reasonable" under the Fourth Amendment, agencies may go as far as they wish in their inventory policies. For example, it would be valid for a policy to include not only looking into every part of the vehicle, but also opening closed personal containers, such as a suitcase. (*Bertine* (1987) 479 U.S. 367, 372; *Wells* (1990) 495 U.S. 1.)

Example: An officer conducted an inventory following a DUI arrest and prior to towing. Behind the front seat, he found a backpack; inside the backpack he observed a nylon bag containing metal canisters; and inside the canisters he discovered cocaine, drug paraphernalia and cash. In an outside zippered pouch of the backpack, the officer found more cash in a sealed envelope. After completing the inventory of the van, the officer had it towed to an impound lot and took the backpack, money and contraband to the police station. All his actions were legal. (*Bertine* (1987) 479 U.S. 367.)

There are essentially only two conditions or requirements for conducting a lawful inventory. First, you must undertake it in good faith for the legitimate inventory purposes set out above. That is, you may not undertake an inventory simply as a "pretext" or "ruse" for conducting an investigatory search for contraband or evidence of a crime.

Second, to be lawful, you must carry out any inventory in accordance with the "standardized procedure" or "established routine" of your department or agency, i.e., some standard other than suspected criminal activity. (*Bertine* (1987) 479 U.S. 367, 376; *Wells* (1990) 495 U.S. 1, 4; *Needham* (2000) 79 Cal. App. 4th 260, 266.)

However, having a "standardized procedure" authorizing inventories does not mean that it must be reduced to writing. (*Needham* (2000) 79 Cal.App.4th 260, 266; *Steeley* (1989) 210 Cal.3d 887.)

"Standardizing" your procedure likewise does not mean that it must be an "all or nothing" policy, under which you must either open every single container, or no containers at all.

Rather, your policy will be sufficiently "standardized" as long as your department actually has one, that is, as long as your department in fact has an established routine that all the officers know about and are supposed to follow when it comes to vehicle inventories.

Furthermore, it is permissible for your standardized procedure to leave some discretion in the hands of a field officer, for instance, about whether to open a given container, as

Source: From *California Peace Officers Legal Sourcebook*, electronic edition, revision 113 (Sacramento, CA: California Department of Justice, Office of the Attorney General), page 4.18.

The Supreme Court's decision in *Opperman*, discussed in the vehicle inventory search section, has essentially been extended to person inventories. That is, as part of inventorying a person's possessions pursuant to a valid arrest, the police may search containers. The Court felt that it would be unduly burdensome on the police to require them to distinguish between which containers may or may not contain evidence of criminal activity.

■ Inspections

A variety of **inspections** are permissible without a warrant or probable cause. For all practical purposes, they are *searches*. Even so, the courts have continually stressed that the justification for such searches is the "invasion versus need" balancing act—that is, the benefits of some inspections outweigh the costs of inconveniencing certain segments of the population. Most of these exceptions to the warrant requirement are based on the Court's decision in *Camara v. Municipal Court* (387 U.S. 523 [1967]), where it was concluded that "there can be no ready test for determining reasonableness other than by balancing the need to search against the invasion which the search entails" (pp. 536–537).

■ *Camara v. Municipal Court,* 387 U.S. 523 (1967)

long as he doesn't have too much latitude. As stated by the United States Supreme Court:

"A police officer may be allowed sufficient latitude to determine whether a particular container should or should not be opened in light of the nature of the search and characteristics of the container itself."(*Wells* (1990) 495 U.S.1,4.)

Example: Inventory of motorcycle upheld, including bags, pouches and any other container temporarily or permanently attached to it or built into it, where officer was within the discretion of his department's unwritten policy, and where there was no evidence he undertook the inventory as a ruse or pretext to search for evidence of a crime. (*Needham* (2000) 79 Cal.App.4th 260,266–268.)

All the foregoing principles apply not just to the inventory itself, but also to your initial decision to impound. In other words, if you decide to impound a car so that you will be able to conduct an inventory and maybe find some contraband, the evidence will be suppressed. (*Aquilar* (1991) 228 Cal.App.3d 1049.)

Example: A Florida Highway Patrol trooper stopped Wells for speeding, then arrested him for DUI and took him into custody. During a subsequent inventory of the impounded car, a locked suitcase in the vehicle's trunk was forced open, revealing a garbage bag full of marijuana. The court found the discovery to be illegal since the Patrol had no policy whatsoever concerning whether or what types of containers should be opened. The absence of any policy left the officer with so much discretion that he could turn the supposed inventory into "a purposeful and general means of discovering evidence of crime," i.e., "a general rummaging in order to discover incriminating evidence."(*Wells* (1990) 495 U.S.1,4.)

Note: However, in *Green* (1996) 46 Cal.App.4th 367,a 2–1 opinion,the Second District upheld an impound and inventory even where the department had no policy beyond the Vehicle Code itself, where there was no evidence that the inventory was a "ruse" to search for evidence of a crime! Nevertheless, some sort of a standardized policy is still highly advisable.

Example: Following a lawful traffic stop for an equipment violation, the officer discovered that the driver had a suspended license and therefore decided to issue a citation. To prevent the driver from simply driving away afterwards, it was the officer's policy to have the vehicle towed and impounded. During the inventory, he discovered narcotics, so he arrested the driver and took him into custody, leaving the car, locked, on the side of the road. Although the citation was never issued and the vehicle was never towed, the inventory was legal. (*Burch* (1986) 188 Cal.App. 3d 172.)

Example: Officer's discretionary decision to impound and tow was valid, despite the absence of a written manual or guidelines, where the decision complied with verbal training and statutory guidelines and was done to ensure the security of the van. (Additionally, once the officer opened the rear door of the van and observed weapons, he also had probable cause to search the rest of the vehicle.) (*Benites* (1992) 9 Cal.App.4th 309,327–328.)

Home Inspections

Two types of home inspection have been authorized by the Court. The first concerns health and safety inspections of residential buildings, such as public housing units. In *Frank v. Maryland* (359 U.S. 360 [1959]), for example, the Court upheld the constitutionality of a statute designed to punish property holders for failing to cooperate with warrantless health and safety inspections. The Court noted that such inspections "touch at most upon the periphery of the important interests safeguarded by the Fourteenth Amendment's protection against official intrusion" (p. 367). In 1967, however, the Court overruled the *Frank* decision.

In *Camara v. Municipal Court*, the Court noted that nonconsensual administrative searches of private residences amount to a significant intrusion upon the interests protected by the Fourth Amendment. Today, a warrant is required for authorities to engage in a home inspection. However, the meaning of *probable cause* in such a warrant differs from that discussed earlier. The Court has stated that if an area "as a whole" needs inspection, based on factors such as the time, age, and condition of the building, then the probable cause requirement will be satisfied. The key is that probable cause in the inspection context is not *individualized* as in the typical warrant. That is to say, inspections of this sort are geared toward buildings, not persons.

Welfare-Related Home Inspections

These are the paraphrased facts from a real case, *Calabretta v. Floyd* (189 F.3d 808 [9th Cir. 1999]): An anonymous party called the Department of Social Services and said that she was awakened by a child screaming "No, Daddy, no" at 1:30 a.m. at the Calabretta home. Four days after the call, a social worker went to the Calabretta home to investigate. Mrs. Calabretta, the mother, refused to let the social worker in. Then, 10 days after the first visit, the social worker returned to the Calabretta house with a police officer. The officer met the social worker at the Calabretta house, knowing nothing about the case except that he had been assigned to assist her. She told him that they had received a report of the children crying, and he understood her to mean that they might have been beaten. When the police officer knocked on the door of the home, Mrs. Calabretta responded but did not open the door. The police officer said they were checking on the children's welfare because someone had reported children crying. Mrs. Calabretta still did not open the door and said she was uncomfortable letting them in without her husband at home. The police officer had the opinion that any check on the welfare of children involved an exigent circumstance and thus that no search warrant was needed. Once the two gained entry, the social worker took the children into one room while the officer remained in another room with the mother. The social worker asked the 12-year-old to pull down the 3-year-old's pants to check for bruises on her buttocks. The 12-year-old refused and the 3-year-old began crying. At that point, the mother rushed in. The social worker then demanded that the mother pull down the 3-year-old's pants, which she did. There were no bruises. The Calabrettas sued the social worker, the police officer, and other defendants for, among other things, a violation of their Fourth Amendment rights. Was the entrance into the Calabretta home constitutional?

■ *Wyman v. James,*
400 U.S. 309 (1971)

A second type of home inspection is a welfare inspection. In *Wyman v. James* (400 U.S. 309 [1971]), the Supreme Court upheld the constitutionality of a statute that allowed welfare case workers to make warrantless visits to the homes of welfare recipients. The purpose of such inspections is to ensure that welfare recipients are conforming with applicable guidelines and rules. The Court declared that welfare inspections are not searches within the meaning of the Fourth Amendment, which means they can be conducted without a warrant *or* probable cause. Of course, such inspections should be based on neutral criteria and should not mask intentions to look for evidence of criminal activity.

Business Inspections

Far more case law exists in the arena of business inspections. *See v. Seattle* (387 U.S. 541 [1967]), which was a companion case to *Camara*, was one of the first to focus on the constitutionality of business inspections. *See* involved a citywide inspection of businesses for fire code violations. The Court noted that "[t]he businessman, like the occupant of a residence, has a constitutional right to go about his business free from unreasonable official entries upon his private commercial property" (p. 543) and therefore that warrants were required to engage in business inspections.

However, soon after *See*, the Court created what came to be known as the **closely regulated business** exception to the warrant requirement set forth in *Camara* and *See*. Specifically, in *Colonnade Catering Corp. v. United States* (397 U.S. 72 [1970]), the Court upheld a statute criminalizing refusal to allow warrantless entries of liquor stores by government inspectors. According to the Court:

■ *Colonnade Catering Corp. v.*
United States, 397 U.S. 72
(1970)

We agree that Congress has broad power to design such powers of inspection under the liquor laws as it deems necessary to meet the evils at hand. The general rule laid down in *See v. City of Seattle* . . . — "that administrative entry, without consent, upon the portions of commercial premises which are not open to the public may only be compelled through prosecution or physical force within the framework of a warrant procedure"—is therefore not applicable here. In *See*, we reserved decision on the problems of "licensing programs" requiring inspections, saying they can be resolved "on a case-by-case basis under the general Fourth Amendment standard of reasonableness.". . . What we said in *See* reflects this Nation's traditions that are strongly opposed to using force without definite authority to break down doors. We deal here with the liquor industry long subject to close supervision and inspection. As respects that industry, and its various branches including retailers, Congress has broad authority to fashion standards of reasonableness for searches and seizures. (pp. 76–77)

Similarly, in *United States v. Biswell* (406 U.S. 311 [1972]), the Court upheld the warrantless inspection of a firearms dealership. In *Biswell*, the Court observed that "[w]hen a dealer chooses to engage in this pervasively regulated business and to accept a federal license, he does so with the knowledge that his business records, firearms and ammunition will be subject to effective inspection" (p.311). A key restriction on this ruling, however, is that authorities cannot use unauthorized force for the purpose of gaining entrance.

 United States v. Biswell,
406 U.S. 311 (1972)

In a later case, *Donovan v. Dewey* (452 U.S. 494 [1981]), the Court modified the closely regulated business exception. The Court decided that it is not enough that an industry is "pervasively regulated" for the business inspection exception to apply. Three additional criteria must be met: (1) the government must have a "substantial" interest in the activity at stake; (2) warrantless searches must be necessary to the effective enforcement of the law; and (3) the inspection protocol must provide "a constitutionally adequate substitute for a warrant."

Business Inspections

Komfortable Kitty Drug Company manufactures and packages veterinary drugs. Several times during a one-year period, Federal Drug Administration (FDA) agents inspected the company's premises to ensure compliance with the Food, Drug, and Cosmetic Act (actual legislation). The agents cited Komfortable Kitty for several violations. Drugs that were allegedly in violation of the act were seized pursuant to an *in rem* arrest warrant (i.e., a warrant authorizing the arrest of property). Altogether, over $100,000 worth of drugs and equipment was seized. Komfortable Kitty has contested the constitutionality of the seizure. Do the company have a valid case?

The Court clarified the *Dewey* criteria in *New York v. Burger* (482 U.S. 691 [1987]). In that case, the Court upheld the warrantless inspection of a vehicle junkyard for the purpose of identifying "vehicle dismantlers." Justice Blackman noted that *Dewey's* first criterion was satisfied because vehicle theft was a serious problem in New York. The second criterion was satisfied because surprise inspections were necessary if stolen vehicles and parts were to be identified, and the third criterion—adequate substitute—was satisfied because junkyard operators were notified that inspections would be unannounced and conducted during normal business hours. In the Court's words:

The New York regulatory scheme satisfies the three criteria necessary to make reasonable warrantless inspections pursuant to [the statute in question]. First, the State has a substantial interest in regulating the vehicle-dismantling and automobile-junkyard industry because motor vehicle theft has increased in the State and because the problem of theft is associated with this industry. . . . Second, regulation of the vehicle-dismantling industry reasonably serves the State's substantial interest in eradicating automobile theft . . . [and third, the statute] provides a "constitutionally adequate substitute for a warrant." . . . . The statute informs the operator of a vehicle dismantling business that inspections will be made on a regular basis. . . . Thus, the vehicle dismantler knows that the inspections to which he is subject do not constitute discretionary acts by a government official but are conducted pursuant to the statute. (pp. 708–709)

It is important to point out, though, that when business searches become nonregulatory (e.g., for the purpose of criminal investigation/prosecution), then a warrant is required (see *G.M. Leasing Corp. v. United States*, 429 U.S. 338 [1977]).

Fire Inspections

■ *Michigan v. Tyler,*
  436 U.S. 499 (1978)

In *Michigan v. Tyler* (436 U.S. 499 [1978]), the Supreme Court authorized the warrantless inspection of a burned building/residence (i.e., fire inspection) immediately after the fire has been put out. The key is that the search must be contemporaneous, not several days or weeks after the fire. The justification offered by the Court was that it is necessary to determine the cause of a fire as soon as possible after it has been extinguished. A warrant in such an instance, felt the Court, would be unduly burdensome.

In a related case, *Michigan v. Clifford* (464 U.S. 287 [1984]), the Court decided on the constitutionality of a warrantless arson-related search that was conducted five hours after the fire was extinguished. The search began as an inspection, but when evidence of arson was found, a more extensive search was conducted. The Court required a warrant because the officials engaging in the search admitted it was part of a criminal investigation. According to the Court:

> The warrantless intrusion into the upstairs regions of the Clifford house presents a telling illustration of the importance of prior judicial review of proposed administrative searches. If an administrative warrant had been obtained in this case, it presumably would have limited the scope of the proposed investigation and would have prevented the warrantless intrusion into the upper rooms of the Clifford home. An administrative search into the cause of a recent fire does not give fire officials license to roam freely through the fire victim's private residence. (p. 298)

Interestingly, in *Clifford*, the Court stated that "the home owner is entitled to reasonable advance notice that officers are going to enter his premises for the purposes of ascertaining the cause of the fire" (p. 303), which suggests that notice, but not a warrant, is required for the typical fire inspection. More extensive searches, however, still require warrants supported by probable cause.

International Mail Inspections

■ *United States v. Ramsey,*
  431 U.S. 606 (1977)

The Supreme Court has permitted government officials to open incoming international mail. For example, in *United States v. Ramsey* (431 U.S. 606 [1977]), customs agents opened mail that was coming into the United States from Thailand, a known source of drugs. Further, the agents felt that a specific envelope was heavier than what would have been considered usual. Considering these factors, the Supreme Court upheld the warrantless search:

> The border-search exception is grounded in the recognized right of the sovereign to control, subject to substantive limitations imposed by the Constitution, who and what may

enter the country. It is clear that there is nothing in the rationale behind the bordersearch exception which suggests that the mode of entry will be critical. It was conceded at oral argument that customs officials could search, without probable cause and without a warrant, envelopes carried by an entering traveler, whether in his luggage or on his person. . . . Surely no different constitutional standard should apply simply because the envelopes were mailed, not carried. The critical fact is that the envelopes cross the border and enter this country, not that they are brought in by one mode of transportation rather than another. It is their entry into this country from without it that makes a resulting search "reasonable." (p. 620)

Checkpoints

Several types of **checkpoints** are constitutionally permissible without warrants. A checkpoint is a means of investigating a large number of people and should be distinguished from an inspection. Whereas an *inspection* targets particular homes and/or businesses, a *checkpoint* possesses an element of randomness. Either *everyone* is stopped or every *n*th person (e.g., every tenth person) is stopped. A checkpoint is similar to an investigation insofar as its purpose is not criminal in the sense that a typical search is. And to the extent that some checkpoints border on looking for evidence of crime (e.g., illegal immigrants), they are often justified because they are not based on individualized suspicion.

Border Checkpoints

In *Carroll v. United States* (267 U.S. 132 [1925]), the Supreme Court stated that brief border detentions are constitutionally permissible. Further, it is in the interest of "national self protection" to permit government officials to require "one entering the country to identify himself as entitled to come in, and his belongings as effects which may be lawfully brought in" (p. 154). More recently, in *United States v. Montoya de Hernandez* (473 U.S. 531 [1985]), the Court reaffirmed the need for warrantless border inspections: "Routine searches of the persons and effects of entrants [at the border] are not subject to any requirement of reasonable suspicion, probable cause, or a warrant . . . [O]ne's expectation of privacy [is] less at the border" (p. 538). The Court wrote:

> [This case reflects] longstanding concern for the protection of the integrity of the border. This concern is, if anything, heightened by the veritable national crisis in law enforcement caused by smuggling of illicit narcotics . . . and in particular by the increasing utilization of alimentary canal smuggling. This desperate practice appears to be a relatively recent addition to the smugglers' repertoire of deceptive practices, and it also appears to be exceedingly difficult to detect. (pp. 538–539)

Border checkpoints have also been upheld on U.S. waterways (*United States v. Villamonte-Marquez*, 462 U.S. 579 [1983]), at highway checkpoints well inside the international borders (*Almeida-Sanchez v. United States*, 413 U.S. 266 [1973]), and at international airports (*Illinois v. Andreas*, 463 U.S. 765 [1983]). According to a recent Supreme Court decision (*United States v. Flores-Montano*, 541 U.S. 149 [2004]), it also appears that more than just a detention is permissible at the border. In that case, the Supreme Court sanctioned the removal, disassembly, and reassembly of a vehicle's fuel tank.

Illegal Immigrant Checkpoints

In *United States v. Martinez-Fuerte* (428 U.S. 543 [1976]), the Court upheld the decision of the Immigration and Naturalization Service (INS) to establish roadblocks near the Mexican border for the purpose of discovering illegal aliens. The Court offered a number

Carroll v. United States,
267 U.S. 132 (1925)

United States v.
Martinez-Fuerte,
428 U.S. 543 (1976)

of reasons for its decision. First, "[t]he degree of intrusion upon privacy that may be occasioned by a search of a house hardly can be compared with the minor interference with privacy resulting from the mere stop for questioning as to residence" (p. 565). Second, motorists could avoid the checkpoint if they so desired. Third, the Court noted that the traffic flow near the border was heavy, so individualized suspicion was not possible. Fourth, the location of the roadblock was not decided by the officers in the field "but by officials responsible for making overall decisions" (p. 559). Finally, a requirement that such stops be based on probable cause "would largely eliminate any deterrent to the conduct of well-disguised smuggling operations, even though smugglers are known to use these highways regularly" (p. 557). Importantly, law enforcement officers must have justification to search the bags and personal effects of individuals who are stopped at immigration checkpoints (or during any immigration check) (*Bond v. United States*, 529 U.S. 334 [2000]).

DECISION MAKING EXERCISE 7.4

Detecting Illegal Aliens

The U.S. Border Patrol relies on checkpoints north of the Mexican border to look for illegal aliens. (In California, these can be found as far as 90 miles north of the border.) These checkpoints are often stationed in the middle of major freeways, where every car must slow down and, at a minimum, be waved through by one of several agents standing between the lanes. In addition, there is little, if any, opportunity to exit the freeway in order to avoid the checkpoints. Can these checkpoints be considered administrative? What if, instead of having the cars slow down, the border patrol required all vehicles to *stop*, at which point they would briefly search the trunk, cargo compartment (i.e., for a pickup truck, van, or tractor trailer), and so on in an effort to detect illegal aliens? Could they legally do this?

Sobriety Checkpoints

■ *Michigan Dept. of State Police v. Sitz*, 496 U.S. 444 (1990)

In *Michigan Dept. of State Police v. Sitz* (496 U.S. 444 [1990]), the Court upheld a warrantless, suspicionless checkpoint designed to detect evidence of drunk driving. In that case, police checkpoints were set up, at which all drivers were stopped and briefly (approximately 25 seconds) observed for signs of intoxication. If such signs were found, the driver was detained for sobriety testing, and if the indication was that the driver was intoxicated, an arrest was made. The Court weighed the magnitude of the governmental interest in eradicating the drunk-driving problem against the slight intrusion to motorists stopped briefly at such checkpoints. Key to the constitutionality of Michigan's checkpoint were two additional factors: (1) evenhandedness was ensured because the locations of the checkpoints were chosen pursuant to written guidelines and every driver was stopped; and (2) the officers themselves were not given discretion to decide whom to stop. Significantly, the checkpoint was deemed constitutional even though motorists were *not* notified of the upcoming checkpoint *or* given an opportunity to turn around and go the other way. According to the Court:

> No one can seriously dispute the magnitude of the drunken driving problem or the State's interest in eradicating it. Media reports of alcohol-related death and mutilation on the Nation's roads are legion. The anecdotal is confirmed by the statistical. . . . For decades, this Court has "repeatedly lamented the tragedy." . . . Conversely, the weight bearing on the other scale—the measure of the intrusion on motorists stopped briefly at sobriety checkpoints—is slight. . . . In sum, the balance of the State's interest in

preventing drunken driving, the extent to which this system can reasonably be said to advance that interest, and the degree of intrusion upon individual motorists who are briefly stopped, weighs in favor of the state program. We therefore hold that it is consistent with the Fourth Amendment. (pp. 451–455)

License and Safety Checkpoints

In *Delaware v. Prouse* (440 U.S. 648 [1979]), the Supreme Court held that law enforcement officials cannot randomly stop drivers for the purpose of checking their drivers' licenses. The Court's reasoning is interesting:

■ *Delaware v. Prouse,* 440 U.S. 648 (1979)

> An individual operating or traveling in an automobile does not lose all reasonable expectation of privacy simply because the automobile and its use are subject to government regulation. Automobile travel is a basic, pervasive, and often necessary mode of transportation to and from one's home, workplace, and leisure activities. Many people spend more hours each day traveling in cars than walking on the streets. Undoubtedly, many find a greater sense of security and privacy in traveling in an automobile than they do in exposing themselves by pedestrian or other modes of travel. Were the individual subject to unfettered governmental intrusion every time he entered an automobile, the security guaranteed by the Fourth Amendment would be seriously circumscribed. . . . Accordingly, we hold that except in those situations in which there is at least articulable and reasonable suspicion that a motorist is unlicensed or that an automobile is not registered, or that either the vehicle or an occupant is otherwise subject to seizure for violation of the law, stopping an automobile and detaining the driver in order to check his driver's license and the registration of the automobile are unreasonable under the Fourth Amendment. (pp. 662–663)

The Court did note, however, that "this holding does not preclude the State of Delaware or other States from developing methods for spot checks that involve less intrusion or that do not involve the unconstrained exercise of discretion" (p. 663). In particular, "Questioning of all oncoming traffic at roadblock-type stops is one possible alternative" (p. 663). If officers stopped every fifth, tenth, or twentieth vehicle, then this action would probably conform to the Court's requirement that roadblocks and checkpoints restrict individual officers' discretion to the fullest extent possible.

Crime Investigation Checkpoints

In *Illinois v. Lidster* (540 U.S. 419 [2004]), the Supreme Court decided that checkpoints are also authorized for officers to ask questions related to crimes that had occurred earlier at the same area. In *Lidster*, police briefly detained motorists to ask them if they had any information about a hit-and-run accident between a vehicle and a bicycle that had taken place a week prior at the same location. A driver entered the checkpoint, swerved, and nearly hit an officer. He was stopped and subjected to a field sobriety test. He was convicted of drunk driving and later challenged the constitutionality of the checkpoint. The Supreme Court disagreed, thus permitting yet another type of checkpoint.

■ *Illinois v. Lidster,* 540 U.S. 419 (2004)

Other Types of Checkpoints

Still other types of checkpoints have come to the Supreme Court's attention. In *United States v. Villamonte-Marquez* (462 U.S. 579 [1983]), for example, the Court distinguished stops of boats on water from stops of vehicles on land. In that case, customs officers stopped and boarded a person's boat to inspect documents in accordance with 19 U.S.C. Section 1581(a), which permits officers to board any vessel, at any time, without justification, to examine the vessel's manifest or other documents. While onboard the defendant's boat, one of the customs officers smelled what he thought was marijuana. Looking through an open hatch, the officer spotted bales that turned out to contain marijuana. The Court noted that fixed checkpoints are not possible, given the expansiveness of open water, so it relied on different reasoning. The Court noted that boardings such as that in *Villamonte-Marquez* are essential to ensure enforcement of the law in waters, "where the need to deter or apprehend drug smugglers is great" (p. 593). Key restrictions the Court *did* impose, though, were that such detentions be brief and limited to the inspection of documents. The reason the seizure of the marijuana was upheld in *Villamonte-Marquez* was that the contraband was in plain view.

Airport checkpoints are also authorized, and there is no need for probable cause or reasonable suspicion in such situations. According to the Ninth Circuit, "The need to prevent airline hijacking is unquestionably grave and urgent. . . . A pre-boarding screening of all passengers and carry-on articles sufficient in scope to detect the presence of weapons or explosives is reasonably necessary to meet the need" (*United States v. Davis*, 482 F.2d 893 [9th Cir. 1973]). Another court reached a similar conclusion (*United States v. Lopez*, 328 F. Supp. 1077 [E.D.N.Y. 1971]). And the Fifth Circuit's opinion in *United States v. Skipwith* (482 F.2d 1272 [5th Cir. 1971]) is particularly helpful:

> [T]he intrusion which the airport search imposes on the public is not insubstantial. It is inconvenient and annoying, in some cases it may be embarrassing, and at times it can be incriminating. There are several factors, however, which make this search less offensive to the searched person than similar searches in other contexts. One such factor is the almost complete absence of any stigma attached to being subjected to search at a known, designated airport search point. . . . In addition, the offensiveness of the screening process is somewhat mitigated by the fact that the person to be searched must voluntarily come to and enter the search area. He has every opportunity to avoid the procedure by not entering the boarding area. Finally, the circumstances under which the airport search is conducted make it much less likely that abuses will occur. Unlike searches conducted on dark and lonely streets at night where often the officer and the subject are the only witnesses, these searches are made under supervision and not far from the scrutiny of the traveling public. Moreover, the airlines, which have their representatives present, have a definite and substantial interest in assuring that their passengers are not unnecessarily harassed. The officers conducting the search under these circumstances are much more likely to be solicitous of the Fourth Amendment rights of the traveling public than in more isolated, unsupervised surroundings. (pp. 1275–1276)

Note that airport screenings are now conducted by *public* as opposed to *private* actors. Prior to the September 11, 2001, terrorist attacks on the World Trade Center and the Pentagon, airport searches were conducted by private security companies. Now, they are conducted by Transportation Safety Administration (TSA) officials, who are employed by the federal government. This change is of no consequence to the constitutionality of airport screenings, however, even though such searches are today sometimes more intrusive than prior to September 11 (e.g., "shoe searches" and searches at the boarding gate in addition to at the main security checkpoint).

Unconstitutional Checkpoints

The administrative search rationale is *not* acceptable, by comparison, to detect evidence of criminal activity. This was the decision reached in a recent Supreme Court case, *City of Indianapolis v. Edmond* (531 U.S. 32 [2000]). There, the Court decided whether a city's suspicionless checkpoints for detecting illegal drugs were constitutional. Here is how the Supreme Court described the checkpoints:

■ *City of Indianapolis v. Edmond*, 531 U.S. 32 (2000)

> The city of Indianapolis operated a checkpoint program under which the police, acting without individualized suspicion, stopped a predetermined number of vehicles at roadblocks in various locations on city roads for the primary purpose of the discovery and interdiction of illegal narcotics. Under the program, at least one officer would

(1) approach each vehicle, (2) advise the driver that he or she was being stopped briefly at a drug checkpoint, (3) ask the driver to produce a driver's license and the vehicle's registration, (4) look for signs of impairment, and (5) conduct an open-view examination of the vehicle from the outside. In addition, a narcotics-detection dog would walk around the outside of each stopped vehicle. (p. 32)

The Court held that stops such as those conducted during Indianapolis's checkpoint operations require individualized suspicion. In addition, "because the checkpoint program's primary purpose [was] indistinguishable from the general interest in crime control" (p. 44), it was deemed violative of the Fourth Amendment.

DECISION MAKING EXERCISE 7.5

A Constitutionally Valid Checkpoint?

The facts from an actual case follow. Was this action constitutional?

During the spring and summer of 1992, street crime, including four drive-by shootings, escalated in the Soundview neighborhood of the Bronx. In response, the 43rd precinct instituted the so-called Watson Avenue Special Operation. This involved a temporary vehicular checkpoint in an eight square-block narcotics-ridden area where most of the drive-by shootings had taken place. The checkpoint was to be active three days a week on a random basis and for approximately six hours a day, primarily in the evening hours. When the checkpoint was in operation, officers manning the barricade were to stop every vehicle seeking to enter the area in order to ascertain the driver's connection to the neighborhood. Drivers who approached the checkpoint were to be allowed to avoid questioning by driving around the area or by parking their cars and entering the area on foot. Area residents and commercial vehicles were to be allowed into the neighborhood. Officers manning the barricades were verbally instructed that they could also allow cars dropping off small children or visiting the local church to enter the area. Other than that, vehicles were not permitted beyond the barricades. The operation was in effect for six weeks, between August 26 and October 10, 1992. (*Maxwell v. City of New York*, 102 F.3d 664 [2d Cir. 1996], p. 665)

School Disciplinary Searches

Public school administrators and teachers may search a student without a warrant if they possess reasonable suspicion that the search will yield evidence that the student has violated the law or is violating the law or rules of the school. However, such **school disciplinary searches** must not be "excessively intrusive in light of the age and sex of the students and the nature of the infraction" (p. 381). This was the decision reached in *New Jersey v. T.L.O.* (469 U.S. 325 [1985]). In *T.L.O.*, a high school student was caught smoking in a school bathroom (in violation of school policy) and was sent to the vice principal. When the vice principal searched the student's purse for cigarettes, he also found evidence implicating the student in the sale of marijuana. The Court held that the evidence was admissible because the administrator had sufficient justification to search the purse for evidence concerning the school's antismoking policy.

In support of its decision in *T.L.O.*, the Court noted that a warrant requirement "would unduly interfere with the maintenance of the swift and informal disciplinary procedures needed in the schools . . . [and] . . . the substantial need of teachers and administrators for freedom to maintain order in the schools" (p. 376). The majority further stated that the reasonableness test for school disciplinary searches involves a twofold inquiry: "First, one must consider 'whether the . . . action was justified at its inception . . .'

New Jersey v. T.L.O., 469 U.S. 325 (1985)

second, one must determine whether the search as actually conducted 'was reasonably related in scope to the circumstances which justified the interference in the first place'" (p. 341).

Note that *T.L.O.* concerns students in kindergarten through grade 12. A different story emerges in the context of public and private universities. The courts have generally held that the Fourth Amendment is applicable at the university level. That is, for university personnel to conduct searches of students' dorm rooms, lockers, and so on, some level of justification is required.

Locker Searches and Drug Dog "Sniffs"

A handful of lower court decisions concern searches of public school students' lockers as well as drug dog "sniffs" for the purpose of detecting illicit drugs. With regard to locker searches, random, suspicionless locker searches are generally permissible, assuming the students have been given some notification in advance that their lockers are subject to search at any time (see *Commonwealth v. Cass*, 709 A.2d 350 [Pa. 1998]). However, searches of *specific* lockers would still be subject to the reasonableness test set forth in *T.L.O.*

With regard to the use of drug dogs, the Fifth Circuit held that so-called sniffs of lockers and cars in public schools are constitutional (*Horton v. Goose Creek Independent School District*, 690 F.2d 470 [5th Cir. 1982]). The court reasoned that lockers and cars were inanimate objects located in a public place. Compare this decision with the Seventh Circuit's controversial holding in *Doe v. Renfrow* (631 F.2d 91 [7th Cir. 1980]) that the exploratory sniffing of *students* (as opposed to their property) was not a search because "the presence of the canine team for several minutes was a minimal intrusion at best and not so serious as to invoke the protections of the Fourth Amendment" (p. 1020). Note that in both cases, the dogs were handled by law enforcement, not school officials.

■ Searches of Government Employees' Offices

■ *O'Connor v. Ortega,* 480 U.S. 709 (1987)

In a case very similar to *T.L.O.*, although not involving a public school student, the Court held that neither a warrant nor probable cause was required to search a government employee's office, but the search must be "a noninvestigatory work-related intrusion or an investigatory search for evidence of suspected work-related employee misfeasance" (*O'Connor v. Ortega*, 480 U.S. 709 [1987]). Justice O'Connor summarized the Court's reasoning: "[T]he delay in correcting the employee misconduct caused by the need for probable cause rather than reasonable suspicion will be translated into tangible and often irreparable damage to the agency's work, and ultimately to the public interest" (p. 724). It is important to note, however, that the Court was limiting its decision strictly to work-related matters: "[W]e do not address the appropriate standard when an employee is being investigated for criminal misconduct or breaches of other nonwork-related statutory or regulatory standards" (p. 729). The Court further noted in *Ortega* that the appropriate standard by which to judge such searches is *reasonableness*:

> We hold, therefore, that public employer intrusions on the constitutionally protected privacy interests of government employees for noninvestigatory, work-related purposes, as well as for investigations of work-related misconduct, should be judged by the standard of reasonableness under all the circumstances. Under this reasonableness standard, both the inception and the scope of the intrusion must be reasonable. (pp. 725–726)

Searches of Government Employees

Federal law enforcement agents suspected that several employees in a government agency were engaged in criminal wrongdoing. Several of the agency's records were subpoenaed. To ensure that the records were being prepared in accordance with the subpoena, the agents visited the government agency. During the course of their visit, the director of the agency was asked to open an employee's office. Upon looking in the employee's office, the agents found incriminating documents and seized them. They also searched the employee's file cabinet and found more incriminating documents, which were also seized. Is this a valid search of a government employee's office, as authorized by *O'Connor v. Ortega* (480 U.S. 709 [1987])?

At the risk of confusing matters, it should be pointed out that *reasonableness* in the context of public school student and government employee searches is not the same as *reasonable suspicion*. The latter refers to a certain level of suspicion while the former focuses on the procedural aspects of the search (e.g., did authorities go too far in conducting the search?). The distinction between *reasonableness* and *reasonable suspicion* is a subtle but important one—hence, the reason for discussing disciplinary and work-related searches in the section on administrative justification. The searches in this section are based not on suspicion but on administrative need.

Perhaps more important, none of the foregoing applies to individuals employed in *private* companies. The reason for this should be fairly clear: Private employees work for private employers, the latter not being bound by the strictures of the Fourth Amendment. Stated simply, private employers can search private employees' lockers, desks, and the like without infringing on any constitutional rights.

Drug and Alcohol Testing

The Supreme Court has, especially recently, decided on the constitutionality of **drug and alcohol testing programs**. Three lines of cases can be discerned: (1) employee testing; (2) hospital patient testing; and (3) school student testing. Cases involving drug and alcohol testing of each of these three groups are reviewed in the following subsections.

Drug and Alcohol Testing of Employees

The Supreme Court has permitted warrantless, suspicionless drug and alcohol testing of employees. In *Skinner v. Railway Labor Executives' Association* (489 U.S. 602 [1989]) and *National Treasury Employees Union v. Von Raab* (489 U.S. 656 [1989]), the Court upheld the constitutionality of certain regulations that permit drug and alcohol testing, citing two reasons for its decision. The first was deterrence; without suspicionless drug testing, there would be no deterrent to employees to stay off drugs. The second reason was that drug testing promotes businesses' interest in obtaining accurate information about accidents and who is responsible. In *Skinner*, Justice Stevens made this observation:

> Most people—and I would think most railroad employees as well—do not go to work with the expectation that they may be involved in a major accident, particularly one causing such catastrophic results as loss of life or the release of hazardous material requiring an evacuation. Moreover, even if they are conscious of the possibilities that such an accident might be a contributing factor, if the risk of serious personal injury does

■ *Skinner v. Railway Labor Executives' Association,* 489 U.S. 602 (1989) not deter their use of these substances, it seems highly unlikely that the additional threat of loss of employment would have any effect on their behavior. (p. 634)

Two interesting limitations should be noted about both these cases. The first is that the Court did not decide whether warrantless, suspicionless drug testing could be used for *law enforcement* purposes. Rather, such testing was held to be constitutional for *regulatory* reasons. Second, both cases focused on federal regulations: Federal Railroad Administration guidelines in *Skinner* and U.S. Customs Service Policy in *National Treasury Employees Union*. Left open was the question of private business policy. Nevertheless, the courts have since upheld drug and alcohol testing of teachers, police officers, and several other groups.[1]

This line of cases would seem to suggest that employee drug testing is becoming increasingly common across the United States. While it is certainly true that more employees are subject to drug testing now than in the past, the Supreme Court has clearly stated that certain drug testing policies are unconstitutional. For example, in *Chandler v. Miller* (520 U.S. 305 [1997]), the Court struck down a Georgia statute that required every person seeking nomination or election to undergo a test for illegal drugs.

Drug and Alcohol Testing of Hospital Patients

■ *Ferguson v. Charleston,* 532 U.S. 67 (2001)

In a recent case, *Ferguson v. Charleston* (532 U.S. 67 [2001]), the Supreme Court addressed the constitutionality of drug testing of hospital patients. In the fall of 1988, staff at the Charleston, South Carolina, public hospital became concerned over the apparent increase in the use of cocaine by patients who were receiving prenatal treatment. Staff at the hospital approached the city and agreed to cooperate in prosecuting pregnant mothers who tested positive for drugs. A task force was set up, consisting of hospital personnel, police, and other local officials. The task force formulated a policy for how to conduct the tests, preserve the evidence, and use it to prosecute those who tested positive. Several women tested positive for cocaine. The question before the Supreme Court was, Is the Fourth Amendment violated when hospital personnel, working with the police, test pregnant mothers for drug use without their consent? Not surprisingly, the Court answered yes:

> Because the hospital seeks to justify its authority to conduct drug tests and to turn the results over to police without the patients' knowledge or consent, this case differs from the four previous cases in which the Court considered whether comparable drug tests fit within the closely guarded category of constitutionally permissible suspicionless searches. . . . Those cases employed a balancing test weighing the intrusion on the individual's privacy interest against the "special needs" that supported the program. The invasion of privacy here is far more substantial than in those cases. In previous cases, there was no misunderstanding about the purpose of the test or the potential use of the test results, and there were protections against the dissemination of the results to third parties. Moreover, those cases involved disqualification from eligibility for particular benefits, not the unauthorized dissemination of test results. The critical difference, however, lies in the nature of the "special needs" asserted. In each of the prior cases, the "special need" was one divorced from the State's general law enforcement interest. Here, the policy's central and indispensable feature from its inception was the use of law enforcement to coerce patients into substance abuse treatment. (pp. 77–78)

Drug and Alcohol Testing of School Students

The Supreme Court has recently extended its drug testing decisions to include public school students. Specifically, in *Vernonia School District 47J v. Acton* (515 U.S. 646 [1995]), the Court

---

[1]P. T. Bookspan, "Jar Wars: Employee Drug Testing, the Constitution, and the American Drug Problem," *American Criminal Law Review* 26 (1988): 359.

upheld a random drug testing program for school athletes. The program had been instituted because the district had been experiencing significant student drug use. Under the program, all students who wished to play sports were required to be tested at the beginning of the season and then retested randomly later in the season. The Court noted that athletes enjoy a lesser expectation of privacy, given the semipublic nature of locker rooms, which is where the testing took place. Also, athletes are often subject to other intrusions, including physical exams, so drug testing involved a "negligible" privacy intrusion, according to the Court.

DECISION MAKING EXERCISE 7.7

Drug Testing of Students

The school board approved a policy prohibiting a high school student from participating in any extracurricular activities or driving to and from school unless the student and his or her parent or guardian consented to and passed tests for drugs, alcohol, and tobacco in random, unannounced urinalysis examinations. (Extracurricular activities include not only athletic teams but also organizations such as the student council, foreign language clubs, and so on.) When consent for testing had been given and the individuals had taken and passed the tests, then participation in the extracurricular organizations or driving to and from school would be permitted. The testing was to be conducted by Acme Toxicology Services, which would collect the samples, and the local hospital's laboratory services division, which would perform the tests. Can this type of random, suspicionless drug testing be considered an administrative search?

Even more recently, the Supreme Court affirmed *Vernonia School District*. The case of *Board of Education v. Earls* (536 U.S. 822 [2002]) dealt with another student drug testing policy. The Student Activities Drug Testing Policy, implemented by the Board of Education of Independent School District no. 92 of Pottawatomie County, required students who participate in extracurricular activities to submit to random, suspicionless drug tests. Urine tests were intended to detect the use of illegal drugs. Together with their parents, two students, Lindsay Earls and Daniel James, brought a Section 1983 lawsuit against the school district, alleging that the drug testing policy violated the Fourth Amendment, as incorporated to the states through the due process clause of the Fourteenth Amendment. The district court found in favor of the school district, but the Tenth Circuit Court reversed the decision, holding that the policy violated the Fourth Amendment. It concluded that random, suspicionless drug tests would only be permissible if there were some identifiable drug abuse problem. However, the Supreme Court held that random, suspicionless drug testing of students who participate in extracurricular activities "is a reasonable means of furthering the School District's important interest in preventing and deterring drug use among its schoolchildren and does not violate the Fourth Amendment" (p. 822).

■ *Vernonia School District 47J v. Acton*, 515 U.S. 646 (1995)

■ *Board of Education v. Earls*, 536 U.S. 822 (2002)

■ Probation Supervision Searches

A person on probation enjoys a lesser expectation of privacy than the typical citizen. In *Griffin v. Wisconsin* (483 U.S. 868 [1987]), the Court held that a state law or agency rule permitting probation officers to search a probationer's home without a warrant and based on reasonable suspicion was not unconstitutional. The majority (of only five justices) concluded that probation supervision "is a 'special need' of the State permitting a degree of impingement upon privacy that would not be constitutional if applied to the public at large" (p. 875). The same principle almost certainly applies to parolees, but the Supreme Court has not addressed this issue.

The Court has also ruled that evidence seized by parole officers during an illegal search and seizure need not be excluded at a parole revocation hearing (see *Pennsylvania*

■ *Griffin v. Wisconsin*, 483 U.S. 868 (1987)

Board of Probation and Parole v. Scott, 524 U.S. 357 [1998]). This latter decision can be interpreted to mean that the exclusionary rule does not apply in parole revocation hearings. A warrant requirement, the Court noted, "would both hinder the function of state parole systems and alter the traditionally flexible, administrative nature of parole revocation proceedings" (p. 364).

Recently, in *United States v. Knights* (534 U.S. 112 [2001]), the Supreme Court held that warrantless searches of probationers are permissible not only for probation-related purposes (e.g., to ensure that probation conditions are being conformed with) but also for investigative purposes. In that case, a probationer was suspected of vandalizing utility company facilities. A police detective searched the probationer's residence and found incriminating evidence. The Supreme Court held that "[t]he warrantless search of Knights, supported by reasonable suspicion and authorized by a probation condition, satisfied the Fourth Amendment" (p. 112).

Needless to say, all three of the aforementioned decisions do not provide a great deal of guidance to probation officers on the streets. *Griffin,* for example, dealt with the constitutionality of one statute in one state. This means that probation officers are mostly forced to turn to state-level supreme court decisions for guidance. The California Supreme Court has offered some clarification with regard to searches and seizures by probation officers that the Supreme Court has not, but of course, its decisions are limited to California. Some interesting decisions from that state are worth considering, nonetheless.

Searches of Probationers in California

Two weeks after the Supreme Court decided *Griffin,* the California Supreme Court decided *People v. Bravo* (738 P.2d 336 [Cal. 1987]), *cert. denied,* 485 U.S. 904 [1988]). The issue in that case was the constitutionality of a warrantless search conducted in accordance with a probation contract that required the probationer to "submit his person and property to search or seizure at any time of the day or night by any law enforcement officer with or without a warrant" (p. 337, n. 1). Relying on the U.S. Supreme Court's decision in *Schneckloth v. Bustamonte* (412 U.S. 218 [1973]), California's high court ruled that because the search was conducted

A person who is on probation enjoys a lesser expectation of privacy than the average citizen.

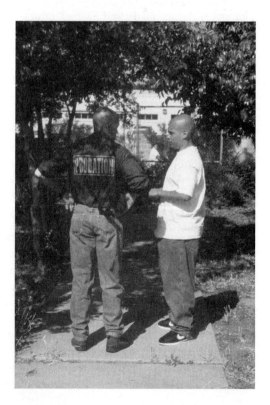

pursuant to the probationer's voluntary consent (i.e., consent given when the probationer agreed to the terms specified in the probation contract), it would violate the Fourth Amendment only if it exceeded the scope of the probationer's consent. The same holds true even for searches of probationers by other peace officers. However, the court also stated that probation searches of the type arising in *Bravo* can only be conducted for "legitimate law enforcement purposes" and not "for harassment or . . . arbitrary and capricious reasons" (p. 342).

Notwithstanding the restrictions just mentioned, the California Supreme Court requires no justification for probation searches. In fact, the California courts have distinguished *Griffin* by arguing that it only applies to searches conducted pursuant to a regulatory scheme, in which the administrative justification balancing act comes into play. For example, in *In re Marcellus L.* (279 Cal. Rptr. 901 [Ct. App. 1991]), the court of appeal for California's first district found that *Griffin* does not apply when the probationer expressly agrees to consent to searches as a condition of probation: "[T]he authority to search [in *Griffin*] existed by way of [Wisconsin's] regulation, not because the defendant specifically agreed to submit to warrantless, unexpected searches" (p. 940).

California's courts have also held that the searching officer need not know of a probationer's consent to search. For example, in *re Tyrell J.* (876 P.2d 519 [Cal. 1994]), the probationer was required to consent to *any* search by *any* law enforcement officer. The California Supreme Court ruled that because the probationer's consent was a valid condition of probation, the constitutionality of any search of him did not hinge on the search officer's knowledge of the probation condition. Of course, if a warrantless, suspicionless search such as that arising in *re Tyrell J.* were conducted on a person who was *not* on probation and who did not consent to searches in this fashion, it would be declared unconstitutional.

In yet another case, *People v. Lilienthal* (22 Cal. 3d 891 [1978]), the California Supreme Court held that a probationer need not be notified that a search is imminent. According to California's high court:

> No persuasive reason appears why a notice requirement should be read into a consent to search condition which contains no such express provision. The condition itself provides general notice to a defendant that he or his belongings may be subjected to warrantless searches. There appears no greater possibility of violence or of violation of innocent third parties' rights than exists with any other search conducted without the knowledge of the owner of the premises or car. (p. 900)

It would appear, based on this review, that probation officers, as well as other peace officers, have great latitude in conducting searches of probationers. However, two federal appellate decisions suggest otherwise. For example, in *United States v. Giannetta* (909 F.2d 571 [1st Cir. 1990]), the First Circuit Court of Appeals held that reasonable suspicion of criminal activity is required for a probation search, regardless of whether consent to search is a condition of probation. And in *United States v. Davis* (932 F.2d 752 [9th Cir. 1991]), the Ninth Circuit (which encompasses California) agreed, stating that reasonable suspicion is required for searches of probationers, regardless of any probation condition. Note, however, that state supreme courts are not bound by the decisions of the federal circuit courts; the federal circuit courts do not have jurisdiction to review state supreme court decisions.

Even so, this conflict between state and federal interpretations on an important Fourth Amendment question suggests that the probationer search issue is ripe for further consideration by the Supreme Court and thus warrants monitoring in the future. To further understand the conflict between the California Supreme Court and the Ninth Circuit Court with regard to probation searches, see Figure 7.2 (pp. 218–219). It contains excerpts from the *California Peace Officers Legal Sourcebook* guidelines for searches of probationers.

Police/Probation Partnerships

A controversial practice closely connected to searches of probationers comes in the form of **police/probation partnerships**, a cutting-edge law enforcement strategy now being

FIGURE 7.2 Example of Guidelines for Searches of Probationers

A. Probation Searches

Even after the U.S. Supreme Court's opinion in *Knights* (2001) 122 S.Ct.587, there remains a substantial conflict between the California Supreme Court and the federal Ninth Circuit Court as to whether "reasonable suspicion" is required before a probation search is lawful under the Fourth Amendment. What follows here is California case law only.

In general, if an adult or juvenile is on searchable probation, California case law permits you to search that person and any property under his control without any particularized suspicion, and without first contacting the probation officer. (*Bravo* (1987) 43 Cal.3d 600,609–610; *Tyrell J.* (1994) 8 Cal.4th 68, 87.)

1. Knowledge of the Search Condition

It is always a good idea to ask or otherwise determine whether the individual whose person or property you wish to search is in fact on searchable probation and, if so, what the terms of that search condition are. This is true because:

- not every person who is on probation has a search condition;
- not all search conditions are the same.

For example, although most conditions permit a search for narcotics, occasionally a condition will limit the search exclusively to some other type of object, such as stolen property or weapons; and you always are entitled to search only for the object(s) specified, and in places where such object(s) might reasonably be located. (Note that if a person tells you that s/he is on searchable probation, you may rely on that statement, even if it turns out to be incorrect.) (*Jeremy G.* (1998) 65 Cal.App.4th 553,556.)

A further example of why it may be important to be aware of the language of the search condition is this: If the condition states that the probationer must submit to a warrantless search only "upon request" or "whenever requested," then you will have to actually contact the probationer

before conducting a search of, for example, his residence. (*Mason* (1971) 5 Cal.3d 759,763; *Lilienthal* (1978) 22 Cal.3d 891,899–900; *Bravo* (1987) 43 Cal.3d 600,609.)

Note, however, that even where such prior contact/notice is required, it is never necessary for the probationer to actually be physically present when you conduct a search of, for example, his residence. (*Lilienthal* (1978) 22 Cal.3d 891,900.)

Despite the foregoing reasons why it is a good idea to be aware of the existence and language of a search condition, the California Supreme Court has ruled that your knowledge of the search condition's existence is not required in order for the search to be valid, at least in most instances (see discussion of *Robles*, below).

In other words, a search will usually be upheld in court as a valid probation search, as long as the prosecutor proves—later, at the suppression hearing—that the suspect was in fact on searchable probation at the time the search took place, even though the officer was not aware of the existence of the condition at the time s/he conducted the search! (*re Tyrell J.* (1994) 8 Cal.4th 68, 83-90; *Marcellus L.* (1991) 229 Cal.App.3d 134, 141; but see *Robles* (2000) 23 Cal.4th 789.) Indeed, this same rationale has been used to "salvage" not only the otherwise-illegal probation search itself, but also (1) the detention which preceded the search (see *Viers* (1991) 1 Cal. App. 4th 990, 993) and (2) the search incident-to-arrest which followed an otherwise illegal arrest (see *Velasquez* (1993) 21 Cal.App.4th 555,558–559.)

2. Contacting the Probation Officer

Under California case law, you do not need to contact the suspect's probation officer before conducting a search pursuant to a probationary search condition, as long as the condition permits a search "by any law enforcement officer" or "any peace officer," which most conditions do. (*Marcellus L.* (1991) 229 Cal.App.3d 134, 141.)

However, in the rare situation where there is no such language in the probationer's search condition, then you do

Source: From *California Peace Officers Legal Sourcebook*, electronic edition, revision 113 (Sacramento, CA: California Department of Justice, Office of the Attorney General), pages 5.5 and 5.6.

experimented with across the country. An example of one such approach is Boston's Operation Night Light. The program began in 1992 as an informal collaboration between probation officers and Boston's Anti–Gang Violence Unit. Teams composed of one probation officer and two police officers serving as backup make surprise visits to the homes, schools, and worksites of high-risk youth probationers, mostly during the hours of 7 p.m. to midnight. The program grew to the extent that 50 police officers and 50 probation officers worked together like this seven nights a week.

Another example of a police/probation partnership in action is the IMPACT project in San Bernardino, California. The program is virtually identical to Boston's. One apparent difference is that the teams consist of one San Bernardino police officer and one San Bernardino County probation officer. (Probation is a county-level function in California.) Also, *all* new probationers are under scrutiny.

have to contact the probation officer first, advise him of the situation, and let him decide whether to conduct a search.

3. Amount of Suspicion Required

If a suspect is on searchable probation, California case law permits you to conduct a search for no reason, that is, without "reasonable suspicion" or any other amount of particularized suspicion, as long as the probation condition permits a search by any law enforcement officer "without a warrant." (*Bravo* (1987) 43 Cal.3d 600, 602, 611; *Brown* (1987) 191 Cal.App.3d 761, 765–766.)

Put another way, because a probationer consents to the condition when he chooses probation over prison and thereby waives his right to privacy (sometimes referred to as a "Fourth waiver"), the only limitations to a valid probation search, according to California state courts, are that (1) you may not undertake a probation search for purposes of harassment or for "arbitrary and capricious" reasons, (2) you may not exceed the permissible scope of the consent, and (3) you may not conduct the search in an unreasonable manner. (*Woods* (1999) 21 Cal.4th 668, 681–682; *Bravo* (1987) 43 Cal.3d 600, 605, 610; *re Tyrell J.* (1994) 8 Cal.4th 68, 87; *Reed* (1994) 23 Cal.App.4th 135, 141.)

"Harassment" exists, for example, if a probation search occurs too often, or at an unreasonable hour, or is unreasonably prolonged, or otherwise demonstrates arbitrary or oppressive police conduct, or if the purpose behind it is personal animosity towards the probationer or something else "unrelated to rehabilitative, reformative, or legitimate law enforcement purposes." (*Clower* (1993) 16 Cal.App.4th 1737, 1742.)

If none of these evils exists, then, as stated, an occasional probation search for "no reason" at all is valid under California law, where the probationer has an "open" or "unrestricted" search condition, i.e., one which includes police

officers and does not specifically require "reasonable cause" or some other level of suspicion. (*Bravo* (1987) 43 Cal.3d 600, 611, 607, fn. 6; *Reed* (1994) 23 Cal.App.4th 135, 139–143.)

Example: Based on an uncorroborated tip from an anonymous informant that an individual appeared to be engaged in drug trafficking from his residence, it was proper to search since he was on probation with a condition which permitted a search "with or without a warrant." (*Bravo* (1987) 43 Cal.3d 600, 607.)

Example: It was legal for Ventura police officers to go to the residence of a juvenile gang member and search for items named in his search condition (stolen property, gang paraphernalia, etc.), even though they had no specific suspicion of criminal activity or of a violation of probation. Such a search is illegal ("arbitrary") only if undertaken "for reasons unrelated to rehabilitative and reformative purposes or legitimate law enforcement purposes." (*Anthony S.* (1992) 4 Cal.App.4th 1000, 1004.)

Example: Reed had been placed on probation in Nevada under what appeared on its face to be an "open" or "unrestricted" search condition. Therefore it was legal for California probation officers to go to Reed's residence to acquaint her with local rules, verify her address, and conduct a search of the premises, which revealed contraband. (*Reed* (1994) 23 Cal.App.4th 135, 139–143.)

Furthermore, there is no such thing as a "pretext" probation search. For example, you may search a probationer's residence, including areas jointly controlled by his roommate (who is not on probation), even where your true purpose is to discover incriminating evidence against the roommate! (*Woods* (1999) 21 Cal.4th 668, 671–672.) Likewise, the search condition permits you to enter, without a warrant, to make an arrest. (*Lewis* (1999) 74 Cal.App.4th 662, 665.) (See discussion and important "Note" under para. C-3 below.)

What makes these and other police/probation partnerships interesting from a Fourth Amendment standpoint are the search and seizure implications. On one hand, these partnerships may be highly effective crime reduction mechanisms. Unfortunately, though, little research is available about their effectiveness. On the other hand, critics of police/probation partnerships claim that they are little more than a method of circumventing the Fourth Amendment's probable cause and warrant requirements. The California Supreme Court's *Bravo* decision (discussed earlier), for example, permits warrantless, suspicionless searches of probationers, even by police officers. And as a result of the in *re Tyrell J.* decision, also discussed earlier, the searching officer need not even know about the probationer's consent to search agreement.

Here again, due process and crime control collide. Police/probation partnerships may effectively reduce crime, but they may also compromise due process. Someday, the constitutionality of these partnerships will be decided in court. Most likely, the U.S. Supreme Court will decide on the matter in the near future. The Fourth Amendment implications are simply too serious to ignore.

■ CONSENT SEARCHES

Technically, most administrative exceptions to having a warrant require no justification. Rather, the courts focus on public safety versus individual privacy. That said, there is one clear-cut situation in which absolutely no justification or balancing act is required in order to decide on the constitutionality of a search. That situation is *consent*. When a person consents to a search, no justification is required. This is known as a **consent search**.

Cases involving consent searches can be placed into three categories. Consent searches must be *voluntary*, so several cases have focused on the meaning of that term. Other cases have defined the *scope* of consent searches, and still others have focused on whether a third-party individual can give consent in order to subject another person's private effects to a search.

■ Voluntariness

■ *Schneckloth v. Bustamonte*, 412 U.S. 218 (1973)

The general rule is that validly obtained consent justifies a warrantless search, with or without probable cause. However, for consent to be valid, it must be voluntary. Consent cannot be "the result of duress or coercion, express or implied" (*Schneckloth v. Bustamonte* 412 U.S. 218 [1973]). When does duress or coercion take place? There is no clear answer to this question. Instead, the Court has opted for a *totality of circumstances* test. This test requires looking at the *surrounding circumstances* of the consent, including whether a show of force was made; whether the person's age, mental condition, or intellectual capacities inhibited understanding; whether the person is or was in custody; and/or whether consent was granted "only after the official conducting the search [had] asserted that he possesses a warrant" (*Bumper v. North Carolina*, 391 U.S. 543 [1968]).

DECISION
MAKING
EXERCISE **7.8**

What Constitutes Voluntary Consent?

Here are some interesting facts from a real-world case: Several undercover police officers went to the apartment where it was believed a robbery suspect was hiding out. They did not have probable cause that the suspect was at that location, and indeed, they did not even know the suspect's name, so no warrant was obtained. Rather, the visit was to be merely investigative, and it was hoped that enough information would be gleaned from the visit so a valid warrant could be obtained. The officers knocked on the apartment door, and the man who answered the door fit the description of the suspect. The officers identified themselves, arrested the man, and conducted a protective sweep of the apartment, fearing that other dangerous individuals may be present. Once the premises had been secured, the officers asked the suspect, who was seated at a table in handcuffs, to sign a "consent to search" form. The suspect said, "You go ahead and search, but I ain't signing nothing." Setting aside the issue of the constitutionality of the arrest and protective sweep, was the suspect's consent voluntary?

Importantly, consent to search may be valid even if the consenting party is unaware of the fact that he or she can refuse consent (*Schneckloth v. Bustamonte*, 412 U.S. 218 [1973]). As the Court stated in *Ohio v. Robinette* (519 U.S. 33 [1996]), "[J]ust as it 'would be thoroughly impractical to impose on the normal consent search the detailed requirements of an effective warning,' so too would it be unrealistic to require police officers to always inform detainees that they are free to go before a consent to search may be deemed involuntary" (pp. 39–40). This view was recently reaffirmed in *United States v. Drayton* (536 U.S. 194 [2002]), a case involving consent searches of bus passengers. Nevertheless, the issue of one's awareness of the right to refuse consent is still factored into the totality of circumstances of analysis (e.g., *United States v. Mendenhall*, 446 U.S. 544 [1980]), although ignorance of the right to refuse is not enough, in and of itself, to render consent involuntary.

FIGURE 7.3 Example of a Consent to Search Form

Crime Report No._____

CONSENT TO SEARCH

I,_____ give the San Bernardino Police Department my consent to search the below listed property.

Address:_____ City_____

County_____

Address:_____ City_____

County_____

Vehicle/s: Make_____ Year_____ Veh. Lic. #_____

Make_____ Year_____ Veh. Lic. #_____

Other:_____

_____

_____

_____

_____

Signed:_____

Date:_____   Time:_____

Witness:_____   Witness:_____

Source: Used courtesy of San Bernardino, California, Police Department.

To err on the side of constitutionality, many police departments have suspects complete "consent to search" forms. An example of one such form, from the San Bernardino, California, Police Department, is shown in Figure 7.3.

■ Scope Limitations

The *scope* of a consent search is limited to the terms of the consent. In other words, the person giving consent delineates the scope. This was the decision reached in the case of *Florida v. Jimeno* (500 U.S. 248 [1991]). For example, if a person tells the police "You may look around," it does not necessarily mean the police can look *anywhere* for evidence of criminal activity.

■ *Florida v. Jimeno,* 500 U.S. 248 (1991)

DECISION MAKING EXERCISE **7.9**

Scope of Consent

Hector Lopez is stopped by the highway patrol for speeding. The officer who approaches his car asks if he will consent to a search of his vehicle. As reinforcements arrive, the officer states that they are concerned about drug smuggling on this stretch of freeway. Lopez gives consent and says, "Yes, you can search my car," and so the officers subject the car to an intensive search. They remove every bag and every moveable item from the vehicle and scrutinize each one carefully. They further check the spare tire compartment, engine compartment, and glove box and even the panels providing access to lighting, electrical, and so on. Have the officers exceeded the scope of Lopez's consent? What if, instead, Lopez stated, "Yes you can search my car, but I'm late for a doctor's appointment, so I have to leave in no more than five minutes"?

Another issue concerning the scope of a consent search is whether consent can be withdrawn once given. In *State v. Brochu* (237 A.2d 418 [Me. 1967]), the Maine Supreme Court held that a defendant's consent to search his house for evidence of his wife's murder did not extend to another search carried out the day after he was arrested as a suspect. Thus, although the man did not expressly request that the search be terminated, the Maine court still decided that consent had been terminated. The Supreme Court has not directly decided whether consent can be withdrawn, however.

Third-Party Consent

A handful of Supreme Court cases have focused on whether a third party can give consent to have another person's property searched (e.g., a landlord consenting to have a tenant's apartment searched; parents consenting to have their child's room searched; etc.). As far as the immediate family is concerned, there are several general rules: (1) Wives and husbands can give consent to have their partners' property searched and (2) parents can give consent to have their children's property searched, but (3) children cannot give consent to have their parents' property searched. The reason children cannot give consent is that they are considered incompetent to give voluntary consent, given their age.

More confusing is the situation of a roommate, former girlfriend, friend, or extended family member. Two important Supreme Court cases are relevant here. First, third-party consent can be given if (1) the third-party individual possesses "common authority" over the area to be searched and (2) the nonconsenting party (e.g., the roommate) is not present (*United States v. Matlock*, 415 U.S. 164 [1974]). According to the Court, **common authority** rests on "mutual use of the property by persons generally having joint access or control for most purposes" (p. 172, n. 7). Thus, a third party could give consent to have a shared bathroom searched but not to have his or her roommate's bedroom searched. What happens, however, if the nonconsenting party is present and affirmatively objects to the search? The courts are divided on this issue.

There are some clear-cut situations, in which two people possess common authority over a particular area, but what happens when it is not clear to officers at the scene whether common authority exists? In response to this question, the Supreme Court has held that the warrantless entry of private premises by police officers is valid if based on the **apparent authority** doctrine. In other words, a warrantless entry of a residence is valid if it is based on the consent of a person whom the police reasonably believe has authority to grant consent, even if their beliefs are ultimately erroneous (*Illinois v. Rodriguez*, 497 U.S. 177 [1990]). The test for reasonableness in this situation, according to the Court, is as follows: "[W]ould the facts available to the officer at the moment [of the entry] . . . warrant a man of reasonable caution in the belief that the consenting party had authority over the premises?" (p. 179). *Rodriguez* involved consent given by a former girlfriend who possessed apparent authority to grant consent because she still had a key to her exboyfriend's apartment.

Still other cases have focused on whether third-party individuals can give consent. Most cannot. For example, a landlord cannot give consent to search property rented to another person (*Stoner v. California*, 376 U.S. 483 [1964]), one lessor cannot give consent to search the premises of another lessor (*United States v. Impink*, 728 F.2d 1228 [9th Cir. 1985]), hotel clerks cannot give consent to search guests' rooms (*Stoner v. California*), and college officials cannot give consent to search students' dormitories (*Piazzola v. Watkins*, 442 F.2d 284 [5th Cir. 1971]). Note, however, that consent given by the driver of a vehicle to search any part of the vehicle is valid, even if the driver is not the owner of the vehicle (*United States v. Morales*, 861 F.2d 396 [3rd Cir. 1988]).

United States v. Matlock, 415 U.S. 164 (1974)

Illinois v. Rodriguez, 497 U.S. 177 (1990)

"Knock and Talk"

So-called **"knock and talk"** consent searches are popular with law enforcement officers because of the difficulty of securing warrants in particular instances. The typical "knock and talk" scenario plays out when police officers approach someone's house, knock on the front door, and request consent to search the home. In *State v. Smith* (488 S.E.2d 210 [N.C. 1997]), the North Carolina Supreme Court described the procedure as follows:

FIGURE 7.4 Questions Often Raised with Regard to "Knock And Talk" Searches

1. *How is it known what was said?* The wording used by the officer to gain consent is of paramount importance.

2. *To what extent was a show of authority relied on by the officer?* A show of authority may diminish voluntariness.

3. *What is the scope of the search?* The scope may be limited by the wording used by the officer or the consenting party.

4. *Can the party that gives consent also terminate consent?* Generally, yes, but who is to be trusted: the officer(s) or the consenting party?

5. *What if the officer threatens to obtain a warrant?* Doing so diminishes voluntariness, if not eliminates it.

6. *What if the officer makes false statements to gain entry?* There is no prohibition against using false statements, but doing so diminishes voluntariness.

7. *Should the consenting party be advised of his or her* Miranda *rights?* Giving the *Miranda* warnings is not necessary unless a custodial interrogation takes place.

8. *Can a third party give consent?* A third party can give consent only if he or she has authority (or apparent authority) to do so.

9. *What if the consenting party is intoxicated?* This factors into the voluntariness determination.

10. *What if, during the course of a "knock and talk" procedure, exigent circumstances develop?* A full search would be permissible under such circumstances.

The "knock and talk" procedure is a tactic used by law enforcement . . . when they get information that a certain person has drugs in a residence but the officers don't have probable cause for a search warrant. The officers then proceed to the residence, knock on the door, and ask to be admitted inside. Thereafter gaining entry, the officers inform the person that they're investigating information that drugs are in the house. The officers then ask for permission to search and apparently are successful in many cases in getting the occupant's "apparent consent." (p. 212)

"Knock and talk" searches are controversial because they are not predicated on warrants, probable cause, or both. Such searches strike at the cardinal Fourth Amendment principle that "physical entrance into the home of another without a warrant is the chief evil the Fourth Amendment has sought to alleviate" (*Payton v. New York*, 445 U.S. 573 [1980], p. 585). What makes "knock and talk" *legal*, in the strictest sense, however, is that the subsequent search is based on consent. Of course, though, the extent to which ordinary people are aware of their right to *refuse* consent is not altogether clear. To date, the Supreme Court has not ruled on the constitutionality of "knock and talk" practices. More than likely, the tactic will continue as long as consent is validly obtained. See Figure 7.4 for a list of questions that are commonly raised during a "knock and talk" situation.

DECISION MAKING EXERCISE 7.10

The Bounds of "Knock and Talk"

In response to a neighbor's complaint, two police officers arrive at a home where there is clearly a loud party taking place. They knock on the door and a person who is visibly intoxicated asks in a slurred manner, "What can I do for you, ocifers?" The officers respond, "We have received a complaint about the noise coming from your house. Would you please tone it down?" The drunk person at the door responds, "Yup, no problem." At that point, the officers ask, "Do you mind if we come in and take a look around?" The drunk responds, "Will you get a search warrant if I refuse?" The officers, in turn, respond, "Yes, we will." The drunk then gives the officers permission to enter. Is doing so acceptable? In particular, assuming the officers do not have probable cause to get a warrant but rather lied in an effort to gain entry, will any contraband that might turn up during the course of the search be considered admissible in a criminal trial?

CONCLUSION

Searches based on administrative justification and consent require neither reasonable suspicion nor probable cause. The term *administrative justification* is something of a euphemism. It is not really *justification* at all. Searches based on administrative justification require that the government's interest in protecting public safety outweighs individual privacy interests. Consent searches need to be predicated on little more than validly given consent.

Searches based on administrative justification are rich in variety. They have been labeled *special needs searches* and *regulatory searches,* but to promote clarity, this chapter has used the language *administrative justification* to refer to all such searches. The most common administrative searches are inventory searches, inspections, checkpoints, school disciplinary searches, searches of government employees' offices, drug and alcohol testing, and searches tied to probation supervision.

Inventory searches come in two varieties: (1) vehicle inventories and (2) person inventories. A vehicle inventory must follow a lawful impoundment, be of a routine nature, follow department policy, and not be used as a pretext concealing an investigative police motive. A person inventory is justified on similar grounds, except that it must be preceded by a lawful arrest.

Four types of inspections have been recognized by the U.S. Supreme Court. First, a general home inspection, such as a code inspection, requires a specific type of warrant, but a welfare inspection, conducted for the purpose of determining compliance with welfare conditions, requires no warrant. Second, an inspection of a closely regulated business is permissible without a warrant if (1) the government has a substantial interest in the activity at stake; (2) the search promotes effective enforcement of the law; and (3) the inspection protocol provides a constitutionally adequate substitute for a warrant. Third, a fire inspection, usually tied to an arson investigation, is permissible without a warrant but must be contemporaneous to the fire. Finally, authorities may open and search international mail without a warrant.

Several types of checkpoints have been challenged on constitutional grounds before the Supreme Court. In general, for a checkpoint to conform to constitutional requirements, it must be minimally intrusive, brief, and not directly tied to a criminal investigation. More specifically, checkpoints at the nation's borders, well inside the borders, at airports, and on the nation's waterways are permissible but mainly for the purpose of identifying incoming individuals. Illegal alien checkpoints are permissible without a warrant or probable cause for the purpose of detecting illegal aliens entering the country but must conform to established policies and procedures. Checkpoints for determining sobriety, as well as license

and safety checkpoints, are constitutionally permissible but must also conform to department policies. Other types of checkpoints, such as airport security checkpoints, have been acknowledged by the Supreme Court and deemed constitutional. Checkpoints intended for the sole purpose of detecting criminal activity are unconstitutional, however.

School disciplinary searches are constitutionally permissible, but they must be reasonable. Random, suspicionless locker searches are permissible but only with ample notice to students. The foregoing applies only to schools for kindergarten through grade 12. A traditional Fourth Amendment approach has been adopted for searches of college students. Drug dog "sniffs" of public school students have not been ruled on by the Supreme Court. For now, it appears that the police have fairly wide latitude in this area.

Searches of government employees' offices are permissible with neither a warrant nor probable cause but must amount to noninvestigatory work-related intrusions or investigatory searches for evidence of suspected work-related employee misconduct. Searches for evidence of non-work-related criminal misconduct require a warrant. None of the foregoing applies to *private* employees. That is, private employees do not enjoy Fourth Amendment protection because their employers are not government actors.

As for drug and alcohol testing, employees and public school students can be screened for substance use but only by properly trained individuals following appropriate policies (e.g., nurses). Hospital patients, however, cannot be subjected to drug and alcohol testing. Probation supervision permits warrantless searches premised on reasonable grounds. Some state supreme court decisions have suggested that no justification is necessary—that such searches are consented to as a result of the probation agreement.

Consent searches are constitutional, but consent must be voluntary, as determined by the totality of circumstances. The scope of a consent search is defined by the person giving consent. Third parties can give consent if they have actual or apparent authority over the premises or property to be searched. A controversial law enforcement practice tied to consent searches is "knock and talk," a strategy in which police seek to gain consent to enter a residence for the purpose of detecting evidence of criminal activity.

This concludes Part II, the section on search and seizure. Figure 7.5 briefly summarizes, in question-and-answer format, the issues discussed in this and the last four chapters. It serves as a helpful guide for determining the constitutionality of searches, seizures, and similar types of law enforcement action.

FIGURE 7.5   Guide to the Fourth Amendment

A. Does the Fourth Amendment apply?

Each of the questions 1–4 must be answered yes for the amendment to apply.

1. Does the person have standing?
2. Is the evidence in question a person, house, paper, or effect?
3. Is the conduct governmental?
4. Has a reasonable expectation of privacy been infringed upon, or has a seizure occurred?

If all of the questions were answered yes, then proceed to B.

B. Was the conduct in question justified?
1. Identify the type of intrusion (e.g., search, stop, arrest, nonsearch, etc.).
2. For the type identified, identify the level of justification required (e.g., probable cause, reasonable suspicion, administrative justification).

If there is a mismatch, between the type and level of justification, then the conduct in question was not justified. If there is not a mismatch, go to C.

C. Was a warrant required?

If yes, answer questions 1–3. If no, move to D.

1. Was it issued by a neutral and detached magistrate?
2. Was it supported by probable cause?
3. Was the particularity requirement satisfied?

All three questions must be answered yes for the warrant to be valid.

D. If a warrant was not required, were the prerequisites met for a warrantless search or seizure?

The answer to this question requires revisiting the material set forth in this and earlier chapters.

E. Any no answers and/or inappropriate justification will result in exclusion of evidence.

REVIEW QUESTIONS

1. In what ways do administrative searches get around the requirements of the Fourth Amendment?
2. What types of inventory searches have been permitted by the Supreme Court? Explain the restrictions on each.
3. What types of inspections have been permitted by the Supreme Court? Explain the restrictions on each.
4. Distinguish between border checkpoints and illegal immigrant checkpoints.
5. Are sobriety and license and safety checkpoints valid? If so, when?
6. At what point do checkpoints become unconstitutional?
7. What are school disciplinary searches? What, if any, justification is required to conduct such searches?
8. Under what circumstances are suspicionless searches of government employees' offices constitutional?
9. Summarize the Supreme Court case law involving drug testing.
10. Explain the Supreme Court's decision in *Griffin v. Wisconsin*. How influential is this case in terms of probation supervision?
11. Considering searches of probationers, how can the tension be reconciled between the decision of the Ninth Circuit Court of Appeals and that of the California Supreme Court?
12. Why are police/probation partnerships controversial?
13. Summarize the requirements for a valid consent search.
14. Under what circumstances can a third party give consent to have another person's property searched?
15. Explain the law enforcement practice known as "knock and talk."

 Answers to the Decision-Making Exercises for this chapter can be found on pages 502–504.

CHAPTER 8

Interrogations and Confessions

OUTLINE

KEY TERMS

fair examination rule
use and derivative use
    immunity
transactional immunity
criminal proceeding
testimonial evidence
physical evidence

confession
admission
due process voluntariness
    approach (to interrogations/
    confessions)
deliberate elicitation
formal criminal proceeding

Miranda warnings
custody
interrogation
functional equivalent of a
    question
18 U.S.C. Section 3501

INTRODUCTION
Getting Suspects to Talk

This chapter turns to the law of confessions and interrogations. The Fifth Amendment is what protects suspects from improper interrogation procedures and from being forced to supply illegally obtained confessions. However, the Fifth Amendment is not the *only* protection offered to suspects in the confession context. Other amendments, such as the Sixth and the Fourteenth, also apply, but the Fifth is most applicable. Accordingly, this chapter begins with an in-depth look at the protections afforded to criminal suspects by the Fifth Amendment.

THE FIFTH AMENDMENT AND SELF-INCRIMINATION

The Fifth Amendment protects against much more than self-incrimination (e.g., it also contains the so-called *eminent domain clause*), but such protections are beyond the scope of a criminal procedures text. Instead, this chapter focuses squarely on what is known as the *self-incrimination clause* of the Fifth Amendment, which states, in relevant part, that no person "shall be compelled in any criminal case to be a witness against himself."

The self-incrimination clause seems straightforward on its face, but it has been litigated extensively in the courts over the years. For ease of exposition, the self-incrimination clause can be broken into four specific components, each of which has come before the U.S. Supreme Court more than once. The four components are what it means to be

KEY CASES

Fifth Amendment in General

- *Brown v. United States*, 356 U.S. 148 (1958)
- *United States v. Sullivan*, 274 U.S. 259 (1927)
- *Garner v. United States*, 424 U.S. 648 (1976)
- *Garrity v. New Jersey*, 385 U.S. 493 (1967)
- *In re Gault*, 387 U.S. 1 (1967)
- *Schmerber v. California*, 384 U.S. 757 (1966)
- *Couch v. United States*, 409 U.S. 322 (1973)

Due Process Voluntariness Approach

- *Brown v. Mississippi*, 297 U.S. 278 (1936)
- *Williams v. United States*, 341 U.S. 97 (1951)
- *Colorado v. Connelly*, 479 U.S. 157 (1986)

Sixth Amendment Approach

- *Massiah v. United States*, 377 U.S. 201 (1964)
- *Brewer v. Williams*, 430 U.S. 387 (1977)
- *United States v. Henry*, 447 U.S. 264 (1980)
- *Kirby v. Illinois*, 406 U.S. 682 (1972)

Miranda

- *Miranda v. Arizona*, 384 U.S. 436 (1966)
- *Berkemer v. McCarty*, 468 U.S. 420 (1984)
- *California v. Beheler*, 463 U.S. 1121 (1983)
- *Rhode Island v. Innis*, 446 U.S. 291 (1980)
- *California v. Prysock*, 453 U.S. 355 (1981)
- *Colorado v. Connelly*, 479 U.S. 157 (1986)
- *Michigan v. Mosley*, 423 U.S. 96 (1975)
- *New York v. Quarles*, 467 U.S. 649 (1984)
- *Dickerson v. United States*, 530 U.S. 428 (2000)

Exclusionary Rule and Confessions

- *Couch v. United States*, 409 U.S. 322 (1973)
- *Harris v. New York*, 401 U.S. 222 (1971)
- *United States v. Bayer*, 331 U.S. 532 (1947)

(1) compelled and (2) in a criminal proceeding as well as what it means (3) to be a witness and (4) a witness against oneself.

■ What It Means to Be *Compelled*

Former Chief Justice Burger once wrote that "absent some officially coerced self-accusation, the Fifth Amendment privilege is not violated by even the most damning admissions" (*United States v. Washington*, 431 U.S.A. 181 [1977]). What Justice Burger meant by this was that voluntary (i.e., noncompelled) admissions are not subject to Fifth Amendment protection. That is, if a person fails to assert Fifth Amendment protection and a waiver is "voluntary and intelligent," then whatever that person says will be admissible (see *Garner v. United States*, 424 U.S. 648 [1976]).

When, then, can a confession or admission be considered *compelled*? According to the Supreme Court, compulsion can occur in a number of formal as well as informal circumstances. As noted in the landmark case of *Miranda v. Arizona* (384 U.S. 436 [1966], discussed at length later in this chapter), if the Fifth Amendment only applied in formal settings, such as during trial, then "all the careful safeguards erected around the giving of testimony, whether by an accused or a witness, would become empty formalities in a procedure where the most compelling possible evidence of guilt, a confession, would have already been obtained at the unsupervised pleasure of the police" (p. 466).

It is useful to distinguish among three types of situations in which compulsion can occur: (1) during questioning, either in or out of court; (2) in written documents; and (3) when a person is threatened with noncriminal sanctions by failing to testify. Grants of immunity by the prosecution also weigh in at this stage. All of these topics will be considered in this section.

Compulsion during Questioning

Whether a person can be compelled to testify against himself or herself, in violation of the Fifth Amendment, requires attention to several distinct varieties of questioning as well as to *whom* is being asked the question: the suspect/defendant or a witness. Specifically, compulsion can occur when certain types of questions are asked of people suspected of being involved in criminal activity. By contrast, compulsion rarely occurs when witnesses are asked questions.

Questioning of Suspects/Defendants. First, if a person is arrested and interrogated after asserting Fifth Amendment protection (and is not provided with counsel), then the Fifth Amendment will be violated. This simple rule stems from the *Miranda* decision, which, as already indicated, is reviewed in depth later in this chapter.

Second, a defendant in a criminal *trial* cannot be compelled to testify under *any* circumstances. The defendant enjoys absolute Fifth Amendment protection from self-incrimination during a criminal proceeding. However, once a defendant takes the stand, he or she can be compelled to answer questions. Indeed, the defendant can be held in contempt for failing to answer questions once he or she has taken the stand. The same rule applies to witnesses. The so-called **fair examination rule** ensures that witnesses at either a trial or a grand jury hearing can be compelled to answer questions once they waive their Fifth Amendment privilege and begin to testify (see, for example, *Brown v. United States*, 356 U.S. 148 [1958]; *Rogers v. United States*, 340 U.S. 367 [1951]).

■ *Brown v. United States*,
356 U.S. 148 (1958)

Questioning of Witnesses. Questioning of witnesses at trial, questioning of witnesses appearing before grand juries, and noncustodial questioning cannot be considered compelled. First, in stark contrast to the *Miranda* decision, which requires officials to notify people of their right to counsel before custodial interrogation, the Supreme Court has held that trial witnesses are not entitled to notification of their right to remain silent.

No assessment as to whether the person's testimony at trial is the product of a voluntary and intelligent waiver is required, either. According to Justice Frankfurter in *United States v. Monia* (317 U.S. 424 [1943]), "[I]f [a witness] desires the protection of the [Fifth Amendment's privilege against self-incrimination], he must claim it or he will not be considered to have been 'compelled' within the meaning of the Amendment" (p. 427).

Trial witnesses do not need to be advised of their privilege against self-incrimination for two reasons. First, it is likely that testimony given at a public trial will be less coercive than any statements made out of view of the court. And second, since a trial witness is not the defendant, the process of questioning will likely be less adversarial; rather, the prosecution will simply question the witness.

Next, witnesses who testify before grand juries are not required to be advised of their privilege against self-incrimination and, as such, cannot be *compelled* in Fifth Amendment terms. This was the decision reached in the case of *United States v. Mandujano* (425 U.S. 564 [1976]), in which the respondent was charged with perjury for making false statements while testifying before a grand jury. He moved to have his false statements suppressed in his criminal trial, but the Supreme Court held that the failure of the state to provide him with *Miranda*-like warnings did not violate the Fifth Amendment (see also *United States v. Wong*, 431 U.S. 174 [1977]; *United States v. Washington*, 431 U.S. 181 [1977]). The reasoning for this rule is simple: Since such testimony takes place before members of the public (i.e., the grand jury itself) and is usually monitored by the court, the potential for coercion is considerably less likely than is possible in a private setting.

Finally, noncustodial questioning of witnesses outside the courtroom contains the potential for coercion, but the courts have held that out-of-court witnesses do not need to be advised of their privilege against self-incrimination. As Justice Scalia noted in *Brogan v. United States* (522 U.S. 398 [1998]), it is "implausible" that people are not aware of their right to remain silent "in the modern age of frequently dramatized '*Miranda*' warnings" (p. 405). In other words, witnesses who are questioned outside court, in noncustodial situations, cannot be considered compelled for Fifth Amendment purposes.

Compulsion via Written Documents

Most states, as well as the federal government, require that citizens fill out documents that can turn out to be incriminating. For example, information supplied in a tax return may serve as a basis for later criminal prosecution. A relevant case is *United States v. Sullivan* (274 U.S. 259 [1927]). There, the Supreme Court upheld a defendant's conviction for failing to file an income tax return. The defendant argued that the return would have been self-incriminating under the Fifth Amendment, but the Court disagreed. In the Court's words, "It would be an extreme if not an extravagant application of the Fifth Amendment to say that it authorized a man to refuse to state the amount of his income because it had been made in a crime" (pp. 263–264).

United States v. Sullivan, 274 U.S. 259 (1927)

In a related case, *Garner v. United States* (424 U.S. 648 [1976]), after being convicted for failure to adequately complete a tax form, the defendant argued that failure to submit a tax return would have led to criminal conviction but that returning an incomplete form would result in punishment under a federal statute that made it criminal to submit incomplete tax documents. In other words, the defendant argued that he had no legal alternative, given the circumstances—a "catch-22," in essence. The Court disagreed that the defendant's statements on his tax form were self-incriminating within the meaning of the Fifth Amendment. In defense of its decision, the Court observed that "a taxpayer, who can complete his return at leisure and with legal assistance, is even less subject to . . . psychological pressures . . . than a witness who has been called to testify in judicial proceedings" (p. 658). That is to say, the argument that the questions on a tax form *compel* incriminating responses is an invalid one.

Garner v. United States, 424 U.S. 648 (1976)

Both *Sullivan* and *Garner* dealt with questions on tax forms that were innocent (i.e., not prosecutorial in nature). In certain situations, however, a person can be compelled to supply *incriminating* information in a written document. This problem arose in the case of *Albertson v. Subversive Activities Control Board* (382 U.S. 70 [1965]). At the heart of that case was a statute that required Communists to register with the government. The petitioners argued that doing so violated the Fifth Amendment's protection against self-incrimination because registering with the Communist party could result in criminal prosecution. The Supreme Court agreed with this reasoning and held that the petitioners were justified in their failure to register:

> In *Sullivan* the questions in the income tax return were neutral on their face and directed at the public at large, but here they are directed at a highly selective group inherently suspect of criminal activities. Petitioners' claims are not asserted in an essentially noncriminal and regulatory area of inquiry, but against an inquiry in an area permeated with criminal statutes, where response to any of the form's questions in context might involve the petitioners in the admission of a crucial element of a crime. (p. 79)

In another case, *Marchetti v. United States* (390 U.S. 39 [1968]), the Court held that tax questions that applied only to gamblers violated the Fifth Amendment because they have the "direct and unmistakable consequence of incriminating" (p. 49) the people who are compelled to answer them (see also *Haynes v. United States*, 390 U.S. 85 [1968]; *Grosso v. United States*, 390 U.S. 62 [1968]).

A third type of written document issue giving rise to self-incrimination concerns the so-called *regulatory purpose doctrine.* The leading case here is *Shapiro v. United States* (335 U.S. 1 [1948]). The question before the Supreme Court in *Shapiro* was whether documents that a business owner was required to keep and provide to the government under the Emergency Price Control Act violated the Fifth Amendment's self-incrimination clause. The Court pointed out that

> first, the purposes of the United States' inquiry must be essentially regulatory; second, information is to be obtained by requiring the preservation of records of a kind which the regulated party has customarily kept; and third, the records themselves must have assumed "public aspects" which render them at least analogous to public documents. (cited in *Grosso v. United States*, 390 U.S. 62 [1968], pp. 67–68)

Interestingly, the Court upheld the business owner's conviction. However, in *California v. Byers* (402 U.S. 424 [1971]), the Court modified its *Shapiro* decision. It held that the required information had to pose "substantial hazards of self-incrimination" (p. 427) before the Fifth Amendment would be violated.

In *Byers*, the defendant left the scene of an accident without reporting his name and was charged with, among other things, failure to stop and identify himself. He argued that had he stopped and identified himself, he would have supplied incriminating information in violation of the Fifth Amendment. But the Court held that such information did "not entail the kind of substantial risk of self-incrimination involved" (p. 431) in cases such as *Grosso* and *Haynes*. The Court noted further that the state's vehicle code (which required Byers to stop and identify himself) was directed at the public at large, rather than an inherently suspect group, such as in *Albertson*.

In summary, then, compulsion can occur via a written document but only in limited circumstances. In particular, if a written document requires a select group to supply incriminating information, a Fifth Amendment violation will most likely occur. In most situations, however, the Fifth Amendment's self-incrimination clause is not violated by written documents. Compulsion via a written document is a relatively rare occurrence.

Threats of Noncriminal Sanctions

■ *Garrity v. New Jersey,*
385 U.S. 493 (1967)

What if a person is threatened with noncriminal sanctions for refusing to supply incriminating information? Just such a question arose in *Garrity v. New Jersey* (385 U.S. 493

[1967]). In that case, police officers were summoned during an investigation of police corruption and told that they would be discharged if they failed to answer questions. The Supreme Court held that such compulsion violated the officers' rights, and it reversed the officers' convictions. Similarly, in *Lefkowitz v. Turley* (414 U.S. 70 [1973]), the Court declared that a New York statute requiring public contractors either to waive immunity or to suffer forfeiture of state contracts was unconstitutional.

In another interesting case, *South Dakota v. Neville* (459 U.S. 553 [1983]), the Supreme Court decided on the constitutionality of a statute that required a suspected drunk driver to take a blood-alcohol test or risk revocation of his or her driver's license. The Court upheld admission of the defendant's refusal to take the test, noting that "the state did not directly compel respondent to refuse the test, for it gave him the choice of submitting to the test or refusing" (p. 562). Furthermore, the Court noted that evidence of refusal to take a blood-alcohol test was admissible because the result of such a test is nontestimonial.

Grants of Immunity

The government is permitted to compel answers from a criminal defendant but only if (1) the nature of the information is irrelevant to any criminal matter; (2) a grant of immunity protects the individual against the future use of any statements resulting from questioning; and/or (3) some other guarantee is provided that the information will not be used against the defendant. Compelled testimony is admissible under these circumstances because it is considered nonincriminating. This section focuses on the second and third of these exceptions, known collectively as the *immunity exception* to the Fifth Amendment's protection against self-incrimination.

Stated simply, a person cannot claim the Fifth Amendment right to be free from compelled self-incrimination if his or her testimony is rendered noncriminal by a grant of immunity. This general rule arose out of the government's need to procure information from criminals about individuals considered more important (i.e., "bigger fish"). By way of example, the immunity exception allows the government to compel answers from a low-level drug dealer in order to facilitate apprehension of a higher-level drug supplier.

Two types of immunity are recognized by the courts: (1) **use and derivative use immunity** and (2) **transactional immunity**. The former immunizes only answers to questions asked. The latter extends immunity to matters discussed that are beyond the scope of the questions asked.

■ Distinguishing between Criminal and Noncriminal Proceedings

The previous section considered several means by which the government can compel people to incriminate themselves. It is now necessary to focus on the definition of **criminal proceeding**, one of the other important elements of the Fifth Amendment's self-incrimination clause. Stated simply, if a statement is compelled but is not used in a criminal proceeding, it cannot have been obtained in violation of the Fifth Amendment's self-incrimination clause. This is because the Fifth Amendment does not apply in noncriminal proceedings.

As a general rule, any criminal defendant has the right to remain silent at grand jury as well as trial proceedings. However, such an individual can also refuse "to answer official questions put to him in any . . . proceeding, civil or criminal, formal or informal, where the answers might incriminate him in *future* criminal proceedings" (*Lefkowitz v. Turley*, 414 U.S. 70 [1973]). Thus, the definition of *criminal proceeding* is not limited to a criminal trial per se.

It is important to note that just because an answer is compelled before a criminal proceeding, it will not necessarily be held in violation of the Fifth Amendment. For example, in *Estelle v. Smith* (451 U.S. 454 [1981]), the Supreme Court held that the state may compel answers from a defendant during pretrial hearings to determine his or her competence to stand trial. Such questioning is not considered criminal, for purposes of the Fifth Amendment.

Some Complications

Outside the criminal trial context (i.e., in civil cases), determining whether a proceeding is criminal for Fifth Amendment purposes is not as easy as one might expect. To deal with this complex determination, the courts usually focus on the issue of *punitive sanctions*. That way, there is no need to distinguish between civil and criminal proceedings. Both types of proceedings possess the potential to hand down punitive sanctions (e.g., forfeiture of one's property or punitive damages in a liability lawsuit).

■ *In re Gault,*
387 U.S. 1 (1967)

That a civil proceeding can be considered criminal for self-incrimination purposes is evidenced in *In re Gault* (387 U.S. 1 [1967]). In that case, the Supreme Court had the opportunity to determine whether a state's *civil* designation of juvenile proceedings diminished the Fifth Amendment's applicability in such proceedings. The Court noted that "our Constitution guarantees that no person shall be 'compelled' to be a witness against himself when he is threatened with deprivation of his liberty" (p. 50). Because juveniles' liberty is often at stake in juvenile trials, even if such trials are designated *civil*, the Fifth Amendment applies.

However, in *Minnesota v. Murphy* (465 U.S. 420 [1984]), the Court noted that questions asked of a probationer that were relevant only to his or her probationary status and "posed no realistic threat of incrimination in a separate criminal proceeding" (p. 435, n. 7) did not violate the Fifth Amendment. That is, the questions did not take place in a criminal proceeding.

In one interesting case, *Allen v. Illinois* (478 U.S. 364 [1986]), the Supreme Court noted that the *Gault* decision's deprivation of liberty criterion was "plainly not good law" (p. 372). Instead, the Court focused on "the traditional aims of punishment—retribution or deterrence" (p. 370). Specifically, the Court considered in *Allen* whether an Illinois statute that provided for the civil commitment of people deemed to be "sexually dangerous" was constitutional. The Court's decision was that civil confinement under the Illinois Sexually Dangerous Persons Act did *not* meet the traditional aims of punishment but was instead rehabilitative. According to the Court, had the civil confinement imposed on the offenders "a regimen which is essentially identical to that imposed upon felons with no need for psychiatric care, this might well be a different case" (p. 373).

So, what exactly is a *criminal proceeding*, for purposes of the Fifth Amendment? It is safe to conclude that a criminal proceeding is one that may result in criminal punishment. This includes criminal trials but also such proceedings as juvenile delinquency hearings, grand jury investigations, capital sentencing hearings, and the like. Civil commitment proceedings and other proceedings intended to serve a rehabilitative or similar purpose (i.e., other than punishment) are not considered criminal for purposes of the Fifth Amendment.

■ What It Means to Be a Witness

Still another issue is relevant concerning the scope of the Fifth Amendment's protection against self-incrimination—namely, the definition of a *witness*. Everyone knows what a witness is in the conventional sense of the term, but in this context, the Supreme Court has declared that the term *witness* can be defined as "one who supplies **testimonial evidence**." That is, the Fifth Amendment protection against compelled self-incrimination is limited to things that people say that are testimonial and communicative in nature. *Testimony* is given at trial; *communicative information* is anything one says while not under oath. So, not only must answers be compelled in a criminal proceeding, but they must also give rise to *testimonial evidence.*

The testimonial evidence requirement does not cover **physical evidence** (e.g., tangible property and the like). In other words, physical evidence is *not* protected by the Fifth Amendment. As Justice Holmes pointed out, "[T]he prohibition of compelling a man in a criminal court to be witness against himself is a prohibition of the use of physical or moral compulsion to extort communications from him, not an exclusion of his body as evidence when it may be material" (*Holt v. United States*, 218 U.S. 245 [1910], pp. 252–253).

More recently, in *Schmerber v. California* (384 U.S. 757 [1966]), the Court held that "the privilege protects an accused only from being compelled to testify against himself, or otherwise provide the State with evidence of a testimonial or communicative nature" (p. 761). As a general rule, then, the government can compel any criminal defendant to supply incriminating *physical* evidence without violating the Fifth Amendment. Indeed, the government can force the accused to wear a particular outfit (e.g., *Holt*), to submit to the extraction of a blood sample (e.g., *Schmerber*), to participate in a lineup (e.g., *United States v. Wade*, 388 U.S. 218 [1967]), or to produce a sample of handwriting (e.g., *Gilbert v. California*, 388 U.S. 263 [1967]; *United States v. Mara*, 410 U.S. 19 [1973]) or a voice exemplar (e.g., *United States v. Dionisio*, 410 U.S. 1 [1973]).

■ *Schmerber v. California,* 384 U.S. 757 (1966)

In addition, the Fifth Amendment "offers no protection against compulsion to submit to fingerprinting, photography, or measurements, . . . to appear in court, to stand, to assume a stance, to walk, or to make a particular gesture" (*United States v. Wade*, 388 U.S. 218 [1967], p. 223). As long as the government does not seek testimonial evidence, the Fifth Amendment cannot be violated, even at trial.

It should be pointed out that *some* verbal responses to questions can be considered noncommunicative and thus exempt from the Fifth Amendment. For example, in *Pennsylvania v. Muniz* (496 U.S. 582 [1990]), the Court held unanimously that the inability to articulate words in a clear manner was not testimonial evidence and could be used against the defendant. In that case, the state introduced the defendant's slurred responses to numerous routine booking questions in order to prove he was guilty of drunk driving.

■ What It Means to Be a Witness against Oneself

The fourth and last element of the Fifth Amendment's self-incrimination clause is that it is limited, not surprisingly, to the person *making* the incriminating statement. That is, the only person who can assert Fifth Amendment protection is the person being compelled to answer a question. According to the Supreme Court, "The Constitution explicitly prohibits compelling an accused to bear witness 'against himself': it necessarily does not proscribe incriminating statements elicited from another. Compulsion upon the person asserting it is an important element of the privilege" (*Couch v. United States*, 409 U.S. 322 [1973], p. 328).

■ *Couch v. United States,* 409 U.S. 322 (1973)

Furthermore, the Court noted that "[w]e cannot cut the Fifth Amendment completely loose from the moorings of its language and make it serve as a general protector of privacy—a word not mentioned in its text and a concept directly addressed in the Fourth Amendment" (*Fisher v. United States*, 425 U.S. 391 [1976], p. 401). Thus, in *Couch*, the Fifth Amendment did not protect a business owner whose accountant turned over documents that incriminated the owner.

There are some exceptions to the rule that only the person being compelled can assert Fifth Amendment privilege. For example, when documents are transferred to an attorney for the purpose of obtaining legal advice, the attorney may assert Fifth Amendment protection in place of his or her client. This exception is not based on the Fifth Amendment, however. (Rather, it is a privileged communication.)

INTERROGATIONS AND CONFESSIONS

As just explained, the Fifth Amendment's self-incrimination clause applies to a variety of forms of compulsion. Now, the focus of discussion will be confessions and admissions. This is not to suggest that incriminating verbal statements are more important than incriminating documents. Instead, it should be emphasized that most of the law concerning confessions and admissions has arisen in the context of police interrogation. The courts have imposed a litany of restrictions on what law enforcement officials can do in order to elicit incriminating statements from suspected criminals.

It is worthwhile, before continuing, to define the terms *confession* and *admission*. A **confession** occurs when a person implicates himself or herself in criminal activity following police questioning and/or interrogation. An **admission**, by contrast, need not be preceded by police questioning; a person can simply admit to involvement in a crime without any police encouragement. Despite these differences, a confession and an admission will be treated synonymously throughout the remainder of this chapter. Toward the end of the chapter, the discussion will turn to what steps law enforcement officials should take to secure a valid, documented confession.

Various Approaches to Confession Law

Confessions and admissions are protected by the Fifth Amendment. The *Miranda* rights, for example, stem from the Fifth Amendment. However, confessions and admissions are also protected by the Fourteenth Amendment's due process clause as well as the Sixth Amendment's right to counsel clause.

The primary focus in this chapter is on the Fifth Amendment, but for the sake of placing Fifth Amendment confession law into context, it is important to briefly consider the extent to which confessions are protected by other constitutional provisions. Indeed, the very fact that *three* amendments place restrictions on what the government can do in order to obtain confessions suggests that the U.S. Constitution places a high degree of value on people's rights to be free from certain forms of questioning.

The Due Process Voluntariness Approach

One approach to confessions and admissions can be termed the **due process voluntariness approach**. In general, when a suspect makes an involuntary statement, his or her statement will not be admissible in a criminal trial (or, as indicated earlier, in any other criminal proceeding) to prove his or her guilt.

At one time, the Fifth and Sixth Amendments did not apply to the states. An illustrative case is *Brown v. Mississippi* (297 U.S. 278 [1936]). There, police officers resorted to whippings and other brutal methods in order to obtain confessions from three African American defendants who were later convicted based on their confessions alone. The Supreme Court analyzed this case under the Fourteenth Amendment's due process clause and found the convictions invalid because the interrogation techniques had been so offensive.

When, then, is a confession involuntary? As decided in *Fikes v. Alabama* (352 U.S. 191 [1957]), the answer is when, under the "totality of circumstances that preceded the confessions," the defendant is deprived of his or her "power of resistance" (p. 198). This answer, unfortunately, does not provide any uniform criteria for determining voluntariness. Instead, the courts take a case-by-case approach to determining voluntariness. Usually, this requires focusing on two issues: (1) the police conduct in question and (2) the characteristics of the suspect.

Brown v. Mississippi, 297 U.S. 278 (1936)

Police Conduct

It has been made patently clear that physical brutality to coerce a confession violates the Fourteenth Amendment. As Justice Douglas stated in *Williams v. United States* (341 U.S. 97 [1951]), "Where police take matters into their own hands, seize victims, and beat them until they confess, they deprive the victims of rights under the Constitution" (p. 101).

 Williams v. United States, 341 U.S. 97 (1951)

In many other situations, however, the police conduct in question may not rise to the level of torture but may still be questionable. For example, in *Rogers v. Richmond* (365 U.S. 534 [1963]), a man confessed after the police told him they were going to take his wife into custody. And in *Lynumm v. Illinois* (372 U.S. 528 [1963]), a defendant confessed after being promised leniency. Both confessions were found to be coerced. This is not to suggest that deception on the part of the police necessarily gives rise to an involuntary confession but only that it is one of several considerations in determining voluntariness.

> **DECISION MAKING EXERCISE 8.1**
>
> ### Police Conduct and Voluntariness
>
> A suspect was interrogated by five officers who, with their guns drawn, stood over him as he lay handcuffed on the ground, semiconscious from a gunshot he had received earlier (a wound that was not inflicted by the officers). The officers did not threaten to shoot the suspect if he failed to confess. Rather, they simply pointed their guns at him. Assuming the suspect confessed, would his confession be considered involuntary under the Fourteenth Amendment?

It is safe to conclude that psychological pressures, promises of leniency, and deception are rarely *by themselves* enough to render a statement involuntary, but two or more such acts (especially if coupled with physical force) will more than likely result in an involuntary confession. Some illustrative cases are worth considering.

For example, in *Spano v. New York* (360 U.S. 315 [1959]), detectives relied on a police officer who was a friend of the accused to question him. The officer falsely stated that his job would be in jeopardy if he did not get a statement from the accused. The Supreme Court concluded that the false statement, including the sympathy thereby obtained, was sufficient to render the accused's statement involuntary.

Next, in *Leyra v. Denno* (347 U.S. 556 [1954]), police relied on a psychiatrist who posed as a doctor in order to give the accused relief from a sinus problem. The psychiatrist used subtle forms of questions and ultimately obtained a statement from the accused. The Court felt that the suspect was unable to resist the psychiatrist's subtle questioning.

Contrast *Spano* and *Denno* with *Frazier v. Cupp* (394 U.S. 731 [1969]). There, the Supreme Court held that a police officer's false statement that a co-defendant implicated the accused was not sufficient to produce an involuntary statement. However, if the accused is questioned far from home and denied access to friends and family for several days, his or her resulting statements will probably be deemed involuntary (see *Fikes v. Alabama*, 352 U.S. 191 [1957]). Similarly, an overly lengthy period of questioning and/or a denial of basic amenities, such as food, may result in a determination of involuntariness (see, e.g., *Crooker v. California*, 357 U.S. 433 [1958]; *Payne v. Arkansas*, 356 U.S. 560 [1958]; *Ashcraft v. Tennessee*, 322 U.S. 143 [1944]; *Chambers v. Florida*, 309 U.S. 227 [1940]).

Characteristics of the Accused

As far as characteristics of the accused are concerned, conditions such as disabilities and immaturity have resulted in excluded confessions. For example, in *Haley v. Ohio*

(332 U.S. 596 [1948]), the Supreme Court reversed a 15-year-old boy's confession. In the Court's words, "Mature men possibly might stand the ordeal from midnight to 5 a.m. but we cannot believe that a lad of tender years is a match for the police in such a contest" (pp. 599–600).[1]

DECISION MAKING EXERCISE 8.2

Suspect Characteristics and Voluntariness

Ed Hornby approached a police officer on the street and said that he had killed someone and wanted to talk about it. He later confessed to an unsolved murder that had occurred several years earlier. Prior to trial, Hornby sought to have his confession excluded, arguing that it was involuntary. At trial, a psychiatrist testified for the defense that Hornby suffered from *command auditory hallucinations*, a condition that rendered him unable to resist what the "voices in his head" told him to do. The court decided that Hornby's confession was not voluntary. The case then went to the Supreme Court. What would it likely decide? What if, instead, Hornby had become hesitant to talk and his confession had been preceded by a lengthy middle-of-the-night interrogation, during which he had been denied food and a desperately needed trip to the restroom?

In some instances, fatigue and pain (e.g., as the result of an injury) can also render an accused's statement involuntary; however, such a result usually requires some questionable conduct on the part of the officials engaged in questioning of the accused (see *Ashcraft v. Tennessee*, 322 U.S. 143 [1944]; *Mincey v. Arizona*, 437 U.S. 385 [1978]; and *Beecher v. Alabama*, 408 U.S. 234 [1972]).

As a general rule, voluntariness is overcome when (1) the police subject the suspect to coercive conduct and (2) the conduct is sufficient to overcome the will of the suspect. The second requirement requires looking at the totality of circumstances to determine if the suspect's vulnerabilities and condition, coupled with the police conduct, led to giving an involuntary confession (see *Colorado v. Connelly*, 479 U.S. 157 [1986]). See Figure 8.1 for a list of factors used to determine whether a confession is voluntary.

■ *Colorado v. Connelly*, 479 U.S. 157 (1986)

FIGURE 8.1   Factors Considered in Determining Voluntariness

Police Behavior	Characteristics of the Suspect
■ Psychological pressure by the police	■ Disability
■ Promises of leniency	■ Immaturity
■ Deception	■ Intoxication
■ Length of detention	■ Fatigue
■ Duration of questioning	■ Pain
■ Intensity of questioning	■ Age
■ Deprivation of access to family, friends, nourishment, and counsel	■ Level of education
■ Whether the suspect was advised of his or her rights	■ Familiarity with the criminal process

---

[1]Note that *Haley* dealt with due process, not *Miranda*. The Court held in *Fare v. Michael C.* (442 U.S. 707 [1979]) that juveniles are not to be treated differently than adults in the *Miranda* context.

The Sixth Amendment Approach

The Sixth Amendment also places restrictions on what the police can do to obtain confessions and admissions from criminal suspects. In particular, the Supreme Court's decision in *Massiah v. United States* (377 U.S. 201 [1964]) led to the rule that the Sixth Amendment's guarantee to counsel in all "formal criminal proceedings" is violated when the government "deliberately elicits" incriminating responses from a person. The two key elements to the Sixth Amendment approach are deliberate elicitation and formal criminal proceedings. The following subsections define each element.

■ *Massiah v. United States,* 377 U.S. 201 (1964)

The Meaning of *Deliberate Elicitation*

In the *Massiah* case, the defendant was released on bail pending a trial for violations of federal narcotics laws and subsequently made an incriminating statement in the car of a friend who had allowed the government to install a radio designed to eavesdrop on the conversation. Justice Stewart, writing for the majority, argued that if the Sixth Amendment's right to counsel is "to have any efficacy it must apply to indirect and surreptitious interrogations as well as those conducted in the jailhouse" (p. 206). Furthermore, "Massiah [the defendant] was more seriously imposed upon . . . because he did not even know that he was under interrogation by a government agent" (p. 206). These are issues of **deliberate elicitation**, in which police officers create a situation likely to induce a suspect into making an incriminating statement.

In another Sixth Amendment case, *Brewer v. Williams* (430 U.S. 387 [1977]), a defendant was suspected of killing a 10-year-old girl. Before he was to be taken by police officers to another city, his attorneys advised him not to make any statements during the trip. The attorneys were also promised by the police officers that they would not question the defendant during the trip. Nevertheless, during the trip, one of the officers suggested that the girl deserved a "Christian burial." The officer further mentioned that an incoming snowstorm would make it difficult to find the girl's body. The officer then stated, "I do not want you to answer me. I don't want to discuss it further. Just think about it as we're riding down the road" (p. 432). Shortly thereafter, the defendant admitted to killing the girl and directed the police to her body. The Court reversed the defendant's conviction, arguing that the officer had "deliberately and designedly set out to elicit information from Williams [the defendant] just as surely as—and perhaps more effectively than—if he had formally interrogated him" (p. 399).

■ *Brewer v. Williams,* 430 U.S. 387 (1977)

In a related case, *United States v. Henry* (447 U.S. 264 [1980]), the Supreme Court focused on whether the officers "intentionally creat[ed] a situation likely to induce Henry [the defendant] to make incriminating statements without the assistance of counsel" (p. 274). In that case, a man named Nichols, who was in jail with Henry, was enlisted by the police to be alert to any statements Henry made concerning a robbery. The police did not ask Nichols to start a *conversation* with Henry, only to be alert to what he said. The Supreme Court found that the officers created a situation likely to elicit an incriminating response but only because Nichols was a paid informant.

■ *United States v. Henry,* 447 U.S. 264 (1980)

However, when law enforcement officers place an informant who is not paid but is working closely with the police in the same cell as the defendant, deliberate elicitation does not necessarily occur. This was the decision reached in *Kuhlmann v. Wilson* (477 U.S. 436 [1986]). Kuhlmann, the informant, did not ask the defendant any questions concerning the crime for which the defendant was charged but instead listened to (and later reported on) the defendant's "spontaneous" and "unsolicited" statements. Clearly, the line between these two cases is thin. The only distinction appears to be that Nichols, the informant in *Henry*, had worked with the police in the past and was being paid.

The Nature of Formal Criminal Proceedings

A case closely related to *Massiah* (and decided shortly after it) is *Escobedo v. Illinois* (378 U.S. 478 [1964]). Escobedo was arrested for murder, questioned, and released. Then, 10 days later, an accomplice implicated Escobedo and he was rearrested. He requested to consult with his attorney, but that request was denied. Escobedo was convicted of murder, based partly on the statement provided by his accomplice. The Supreme Court reversed this decision, however:

> We hold . . . that where, as here, the investigation is no longer a general inquiry into an unsolved crime but has begun to focus on a particular suspect, the suspect has been taken into police custody, the police carry out a process of interrogations that lends itself to eliciting incriminating statements, the suspect has requested and been denied an opportunity to consult with his lawyer, and the police have not effectively warned him of his absolute constitutional right to remain silent, the accused has been denied "the Assistance of Counsel" in violation of the Sixth Amendment . . . and that no statement elicited by the police during the interrogation may be used against him at a criminal trial. (pp. 490–491)

Unfortunately, *Escobedo* was cause for some confusion. In *Massiah*, the Court held that the Sixth Amendment right to counsel applies once formal proceedings have begun (e.g., a preliminary hearing, trial, or anything in between). However, in *Escobedo*, the Court seemed to broaden the scope of the Sixth Amendment by holding that it also applies once the accused becomes the focus of an investigation by the police. This left a significant question unanswered: When does a person become an accused? That is, when do formal criminal proceedings commence?

Massiah was indicted, so many courts have concluded that **formal criminal proceedings** begin with indictment (e.g., *United States ex rel. Forella v. Follette*, 405 F.2d 680 [2nd Cir. 1969]). However, eight years after *Massiah* (and after *Miranda*), the Supreme Court decided *Kirby v. Illinois* (406 U.S. 682 [1972]). In that case, the Court held that the Sixth Amendment is implicated whenever the "adverse positions of the government and defendant have solidified" so that "a defendant finds himself faced with the prosecutorial forces of organized society, and immersed in the intricacies of substantive and procedural criminal law" (p. 689). Fortunately, the Court clarified this statement by noting that the Sixth Amendment applies "whether by way of *formal charge, preliminary hearing, indictment, information, or arraignment*" (p. 689, emphasis added).

Massiah does not apply simply because a suspect or arrestee has retained the services of counsel. In *Moran v. Burbine* (475 U.S. 412 [1986]), the Supreme Court held that what is important in determining whether the Sixth Amendment right to counsel applies is whether "the government's role [has] shift[ed] from investigation to accusation" (p. 430). Similarly, in *Maine v. Moulton* (474 U.S. 159 [1985]), the Court held that "to exclude evidence pertaining to charges as to which the Sixth Amendment right to counsel had not attached at the time the evidence was obtained, simply because other charges were pending at that time, would unnecessarily frustrate the public's interest in the investigation of criminal activities" (p. 180).

It should be noted that the Sixth Amendment approach to interrogations and confessions is offense specific. This was reiterated by the Supreme Court in *Texas v. Cobb* (531 U.S. 162 [2001]), where it held that a man's confession to a crime with which he had not been charged did not violate the Sixth Amendment. In that case, the defendant was indicted for burglary and given access to counsel, which obviously prohibits deliberate elicitation of incriminating information. However, he confessed to murdering the woman and child who lived in the home he allegedly burglarized. He later sought to have his confession excluded, but the Supreme Court disagreed, in essence, finding that the burglary charge did not trigger Sixth Amendment protection for the murder charge.

■ *Kirby v. Illinois*, 406 U.S. 682 (1972)

DECISION MAKING EXERCISE 8.3

Formal Criminal Proceedings

An arrest warrant was issued for Mark Eddie for the crime of burglary, following an indictment for his latest heist. A detective arrested Eddie, brought him to the stationhouse, and then interrogated him at length concerning the burglary without counsel present. The detective also interrogated Eddie about additional burglaries of which he was suspected of being involved. While Eddie refused to talk about the most recent burglary (in which he made off with a substantial amount of money), he did admit to two prior burglaries. Was the questioning constitutional?

The *Miranda* Approach

In a very important yet frequently overlooked case, *Malloy v. Hogan* (378 U.S. 1 [1964]), the Supreme Court held that the Fifth Amendment applies to the *states*. In announcing that ruling some 40 years ago, the Court said that "today the admissibility of a confession in a state criminal prosecution is tested by the same standard applied in federal prosecution since 1897" (p. 7).

Not long after that decision, the Supreme Court moved beyond *Massiah*, *Escobedo*, and the due process voluntariness approaches to interrogation law, focusing instead on the Fifth Amendment. In *Miranda v. Arizona* (384 U.S. 436 [1966]), the Court announced the following important rule: "[T]he prosecution may not use statements, whether exculpatory or inculpatory, stemming from *custodial interrogation* of the defendant unless it demonstrates the use of procedural safeguards effective to secure the privilege against self-incrimination" (p. 444, emphasis added). This wording clearly established that the Fifth Amendment should serve as the basis for determining the constitutionality of a confession.

■ *Miranda v. Arizona,* 384 U.S. 436 (1966)

Importantly, the Sixth and Fourteenth Amendments still apply to interrogations and confessions in certain situations. For example, if the police conduct in question is not a custodial interrogation (as in *Miranda*) but formal charges have been filed, the Sixth Amendment will apply. Similarly, if custody and interrogation do not take place *and* formal charges are not filed, the due process voluntariness test can still be relevant for the purpose of determining the constitutionality of a confession or admission. In fact, think of the Fourteenth Amendment's due process clause, in particular, as being something of a fallback. If no other constitutional protections apply, the guarantee of due process almost always does.

The *Miranda* **warnings**, which are most often read by police to an arrestee, often comprise a series of statements like this: "You have the right to remain silent. Anything you say can and will be used against you in a court of law. You also have the right to an attorney. If you cannot afford an attorney, one will be provided to you at no cost. Do you understand these rights as they have been read to you?"

The discussion will return to some Supreme Court cases addressing the substance and adequacy of these warnings, particularly when they are read differently. But for now, the concepts of custody and interrogation require attention. Since the Supreme Court limited its decision in *Miranda* to custodial interrogations, it is important to understand the definitions of these two important terms: *custody* and *interrogation*.

Custody

Many people believe that *Miranda* rights apply whenever the police begin to question a person. This is not the case; if the person being questioned is not in *custody*, *Miranda* rights do not apply. Simple police questioning, or even a full-blown interrogation, is not enough to trigger the protections afforded by the Fifth Amendment. The person subjected to such questioning must be in police custody.

What is **custody**? The Court announced that *Miranda* applies when "a person has been taken into custody or otherwise deprived of his freedom of action in any significant way." An arrest is a clear-cut case of police custody, but what about a lesser intrusion? Unfortunately, there is no easy answer to this question. Instead, the courts have chosen to focus on the circumstances surrounding each individual case. The Court has stated, however, that "the only relevant inquiry [in analyzing the custody issue] is how a reasonable man in the suspect's position would have understood his situation" (*Berkemer v. McCarty*, 468 U.S. 420 [1984], p. 442).

■ *Berkemer v. McCarty,*
468 U.S. 420 (1984)

In the absence of a full-blown arrest, the courts have focused on four types of police/citizen encounters in determining whether custody exists for purposes of *Miranda*: (1) traffic and field stops; (2) questioning in the home; (3) questioning at the police station or equivalent facility; and (4) questioning for minor crimes.

DECISION MAKING EXERCISE 8.4

The Nature of Custody

Carole Reynolds was being held in jail while awaiting trial on narcotics offenses. The police had been unable to get her to make an incriminating statement, so they decided to place an undercover agent in her cell. The two women eventually struck up a conversation, and the agent asked Reynolds, "What do you do for a living?" She responded, "I'm the head of the West Coast's largest heroin operation." Could Reynolds's statement be used against her at her trial for narcotics offenses?

First, custody does not take place in the typical traffic stop. This was the decision reached in *Berkemer v. McCarty* (468 U.S. 420 [1984]). There, a motorist was stopped for weaving in and out of traffic. After he admitted to drinking and smoking marijuana, the officer arrested him. The motorist argued that he should have been advised of his right to remain silent, but the Supreme Court disagreed, noting that vehicle stops are "presumptively temporary and brief" and sufficiently public to avoid the appearance of being coercive. The Court added, "From all that appears in the stipulation of facts, a single police officer asked [the defendant] a modest number of questions and requested him to perform a simple balancing test at a location visible to passing motorists" (p. 442) and thus did not violate the Fifth Amendment.

The same applies to stops not involving vehicles. *Miranda* permits law enforcement officers to engage in "[g]eneral on-the-scene questioning as to facts surrounding a crime or other general questioning of citizens in the factfinding process" (p. 477). With regard to *Terry* stops in particular, "[t]he comparatively nonthreatening character of [investigative] detentions explains the absence of any suggestion in our opinions that *Terry* stops are subject to the dictates of *Miranda*" (p. 440). But what if an investigative stop becomes more intrusive than a *Terry* stop, say, by taking place over a long period of time and/or in a private setting? Then, the Fifth Amendment's self-incrimination clause, made known to suspects through the *Miranda* warnings, will usually apply.

Next, it is possible for questioning in one's home to rise to the level of custody. In *Orozco v. Texas* (394 U.S. 324 [1969]), the Supreme Court declared that custody existed when four police officers woke a man in his own home and began questioning him. However, in contrast to *Orozco* is *Beckwith v. United States* (425 U.S. 341 [1976]). There, Internal Revenue Service (IRS) agents interviewed a man in his home, an action that the Supreme Court declared noncustodial. The man argued that because he was the focus of a criminal investigation, he should have been advised of his right to remain silent.

However, Chief Justice Burger noted that "*Miranda* specifically defined 'focus,' for its purposes, as 'questioning initiated by law enforcement officers *after* a person has been taken into custody or otherwise deprived of his freedom of action in any significant way'" (p. 347).

Questioning at the police station or an equivalent facility can also rise to the level of custody. However, not all stationhouse questioning can be considered custodial. Consider what the Supreme Court said in *Oregon v. Mathiason* (429 U.S. 492 [1977]), a case involving a man who voluntarily agreed to meet officers at the police station for questioning. He admitted to involvement in a crime but later argued that his visit to the stationhouse was custodial because of its inherently coercive nature. The Court said:

> Any interview of one suspected of a crime by a police officer will have coercive aspects to it, simply by virtue of the fact that the police officer is part of a law enforcement system which may ultimately cause the suspect to be charged with a crime. But police officers are not required to administer *Miranda* warnings to everyone whom they question. Nor is the requirement of warnings to be imposed simply because the questioning takes place in the stationhouse, or because the questioned person is one whom the police suspect. (p. 495)

In a later case, *California v. Beheler* (463 U.S. 1121 [1983]), the Court offered some clarification concerning its decision in *Mathiason*. It pointed out that *Miranda* is not implicated "if the suspect is not placed under arrest, voluntarily comes to the police station, and is allowed to leave unhindered by the police after a brief interview" (p. 1121).

Interestingly, the *Beheler* decision seems to hold even if a person is pressured to come to the police station for questioning (see, e.g., *Yarborough v. Alvarado*, 541 U.S. 652 [2004]). For example, in *Minnesota v. Murphy* (465 U.S. 420 [1984]), a probationer was ordered to meet with his probation officer for questioning. During the meeting, the probationer confessed to a rape and a murder. He later argued that he should have been advised of his *Miranda* rights, but the Court disagreed, holding that Murphy's "freedom of movement [was] not restricted to the degree associated with formal arrest" (p. 430). Furthermore, while "[c]ustodial arrest is said to convey to the suspect a message that he has no choice but to submit to the officers' will and to confess . . . [i]t is unlikely that a probation interview, arranged by appointment at a mutually convenient time, would give rise to a similar impression" (p. 433). The Court commented further in *Murphy*:

> Many of the psychological ploys discussed in *Miranda* capitalize on the suspect's unfamiliarity with the officers and the environment. Murphy's regular meetings with his probation officer should have served to familiarize him with her and her office and to insulate him from psychological intimidation that might overbear his desire to claim the privilege. Finally, the coercion inherent in custodial interrogation derives in large measure from an interrogator's insinuation that the interrogation will continue until a confession is obtained. . . . Since Murphy was not physically restrained and could have left the office, any compulsion he might have felt from the possibility that terminating the meeting would have led to revocation of probation was not comparable to the pressure on a suspect who is painfully aware that he literally cannot escape a persistent custodial interrogator. (p. 433)

Fourth, the Supreme Court has had occasion to determine whether *Miranda* applies—specifically, whether people can be considered in custody for minor offenses. Again, *Berkemer* was a case involving a traffic stop. The second issue before the Court in that case was whether an exception to *Miranda* should exist for relatively minor crimes, such as misdemeanors. The Court declared that no distinction should be drawn between types of crimes as far as *Miranda* is concerned. Instead, the only relevant issue is whether a person is in custody (and, of course, interrogated). Even for a misdemeanor,

■ *California v. Beheler,* 463 U.S. 1121 (1983)

the incentive for police to try to induce the defendant to incriminate himself or herself may well be significant.

DECISION MAKING EXERCISE 8.5

Can Reading *Miranda* Rights Create a Custodial Situation?

Assume that with reasonable suspicion, police officers approach a man whom they suspect of recently robbing the First National Bank. They confront the man, and before initiating any questioning, they immediately read him his *Miranda* rights. Shortly after being read his rights but before questioning, the suspect states, "I'm glad you guys found me. I can't go on like this. I robbed First National." Does the officers' reading of *Miranda* convert a noncustodial situation (the case here) into a custodial one, thus requiring demonstration of a knowing, intelligent, and voluntary waiver?

It should be underscored before moving on that a key component of *Miranda* is that the questioning (and detention) must be conducted by government actors. If the people engaged in questioning cannot be considered government actors, then Fifth Amendment protections do not apply. However, when a private individual conducts a custodial interrogation as an agent of the police (i.e., working for the police), *Miranda* applies (see, e.g., *Wilson v. O'Leary*, 895 F.2d 378 [7th Cir. 1990]). Figure 8.2 provides a list of factors that are used to distinguish custodial from noncustodial encounters.

Interrogation

The second major component of *Miranda* is interrogation. Custody by itself is not enough to require that the *Miranda* warnings be given. For a person to be afforded Fifth Amendment protection—and particularly, to be advised of his or her right to remain silent—then that person must be subjected to interrogation.

DECISION MAKING EXERCISE 8.6

Incriminating Evidence and Interrogation

Police officers lawfully executed a search warrant on Don Cheney's house. Cheney was not at home, but the officers were let into the house by his wife. When Cheney arrived at home, he was immediately arrested. He was then seated on the living room couch, and one of the officers brought in a potted marijuana plant and placed it on the coffee table in front of him. When Cheney saw the plant, he began crying and said, "OK, you got me. The plant is mine. As you probably know, there are plenty more where that came from." At trial, Cheney sought to have his statement suppressed on the grounds that a custodial interrogation without the *Miranda* warnings took place in his living room on the night of the search. How should the court decide?

Rhode Island v. Innis,
446 U.S. 291 (1980)

Miranda defined **interrogation** as "questioning initiated by law enforcement officers." Then, in *Rhode Island v. Innis* (446 U.S. 291 [1980]), the Court noted that interrogation "must reflect a measure of compulsion above and beyond that inherent in custody itself" (p. 300). Thus, any questions that tend to incriminate—that is, those that are directed toward an individual about his or her suspected involvement in a crime—are considered interrogation.

Unfortunately, many *questions* are not readily identifiable as such. In *Innis*, the Supreme Court noted that in addition to "express questioning," the "functional equivalent" of a question is also possible. The **functional equivalent of a question** includes

FIGURE 8.2 Distinguishing between Custodial and Noncustodial Situations

Custodial Situation	Noncustodial Situation
Arrest	Typical traffic stop
Excessively lengthy confrontation	General on-the-scene questioning
Not free to leave	Free to leave
Involuntary encounter	Voluntary encounter
Private place, such as a police station	Public place, where movement not restricted

"any words or actions on the part of the police (other than those normally attendant to arrest and custody) that the police should know are reasonably likely to elicit an incriminating response from the suspect" (p. 302, n. 8).

In *Innis*, while police officers were driving the defendant to the police station after his arrest for armed robbery, they engaged in a conversation about the danger the missing robbery weapon posed to schoolchildren with disabilities. Apparently in response to the conversation, the defendant directed the officers to the location of the weapon. Interestingly, though, the Supreme Court held that the officers' conversation did not constitute interrogation: It was "nothing more than a dialogue between the two officers to which no response from the respondent was invited" (p. 315). The majority assumed implicitly that suspects will not respond to "indirect appeals to . . . humanitarian impulses," but Justice Stevens dissented and argued that such an assumption "is directly contrary to the teachings of police interrogation manuals, which recommend appealing to a suspect's sense of morality as a standard and often successful interrogation technique" (p. 315).

DECISION MAKING EXERCISE 8.7

Another Interrogation?

The police permitted a man who was the suspect in a murder investigation to converse with his wife at the police station where he was being held. Their conversation occurred during the presence of a police officer and was recorded. The man made an incriminating response during the conversation, which was later introduced at his trial for the murder of his child. The man argued that he had been subjected to the functional equivalent of an interrogation when the police officer was present with a tape recorder. Is he correct?

Even though *Innis* did not ultimately involve the functional equivalent of a question, the Court essentially expanded the definition of *questioning*. Namely, a mere conversation between police officers designed to elicit an incriminating response—even if the conversation is not directed toward the suspect—can require giving the *Miranda* warnings. Of course, the person must also be in custody for the *Miranda* warnings to apply. Figure 8.3 lists some of the factors considered when distinguishing between interrogation and general questioning.

FIGURE 8.3 Distinguishing between Interrogation and General Questioning

Interrogation	General Questioning
Guilt-seeking questions	Information-gathering questions
Conversation intended to elicit a response	Conversation not intended to elicit a response

Other *Miranda* Issues

A number of important Supreme Court cases have hinged on (1) the substance and adequacy of the *Miranda* warnings and (2) waivers of *Miranda*. If, for example, the *Miranda* warnings are not given adequately, then the police risk having a confession being thrown out of court. Also, like many rights, those provided by *Miranda* can be waived. That is, suspects can elect *not* to remain silent. Finally, suspects are not required to be advised of their *Miranda* rights when doing so could compromise public safety. These and other *Miranda* issues are considered in the four subsections that follow.

Substance and Adequacy of the Warnings. There is a long line of cases involving people who have sought to have their confessions excluded at trial because all or some of the *Miranda* warnings were not read adequately. For example, in *California v. Prysock* (453 U.S. 355 [1981]), the juvenile defendant was told, "You have the right to talk to a lawyer before you are questioned, have him present with you while you are being questioned, and all during the questioning" (p. 359). The defendant was then told that he had the right to a court-appointed lawyer but not that one would be provided for him if he was indigent.

California v. Prysock, 453 U.S. 355 (1981)

The defendant challenged his conviction, but the Court concluded that the warnings given him were sufficient and that "*Miranda* itself indicates that no talismanic incantation was required to satisfy its strictures" (p. 359).

In another interesting case, *Duckworth v. Eagan* (492 U.S. 192 [1989]), the following warnings were given:

> Before we ask you any questions, you must understand your rights. You have the right to remain silent. Anything you say can be used against you in court. You have the right to talk to a lawyer for advice before we ask you any questions, and to have him with you during questioning. You have this right to the advice and presence of a lawyer even if you cannot afford to hire one. We have no way of giving you a lawyer, but one will be appointed for you, if you wish, if and when you go to court. If you wish to answer questions now without a lawyer present, you have the right to stop answering questions at any time. You also have the right to stop answering at any time until you've talked to a lawyer. (p. 198)

Interestingly, even though the warnings in this version suggested that counsel would only be provided at court, the Supreme Court held, in a 5 to 4 decision, that these warnings

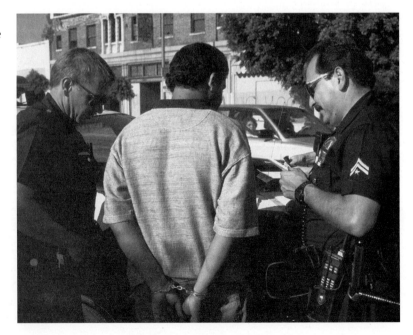

If the police do not read the *Miranda* warnings adequately, they risk having the suspect's confession excluded at trial.

"touched all the bases required by *Miranda*" (p. 203). Thus, as long as all the essential *Miranda* information is communicated, simple departures will not render a confession thereby obtained inadmissible in a criminal trial.

> **DECISION MAKING EXERCISE 8.8**
>
> **Were the *Miranda* Rights Read Properly?**
>
> William Wentworth was interrogated while in police custody. He wore an expensive suit, lavish jewelry, and otherwise exhibited an aura of financial success. Before being interrogated, he was read the following rights: "You have the right to remain silent. Anything you say can and will be used against you in court. You have the right to talk with an attorney, either retained by you or appointed by the court, before giving a statement, and to have your attorney present when answering any questions." Wentworth made an incriminating statement during the interrogation and later moved to suppress it on the grounds that he was not informed that counsel would be provided if he was indigent. How should the court decide? Does it matter that Wentworth, in fact, appeared to be wealthy?

Another factor involving the substance and adequacy of the *Miranda* warnings concerns the role of additional, unnecessary information. If more information than the original *Miranda* warnings is provided to a suspect, will any subsequent confession be inadmissible? For example, must the defendant be advised of the consequences of deciding to answer questions? The case of *Colorado v. Spring* (479 U.S. 564 [1987]) is a useful point of departure. There, the defendant was arrested and questioned on suspicion of transporting stolen firearms. He was also questioned about a homicide. He admitted that he had been given his *Miranda* warnings and that he understood them; however, he argued that the statements he made about the homicide were not admissible because he had not been informed that he was going to be questioned about the homicide (i.e., he was arrested on suspicion of transporting stolen firearms). Unfortunately for the defendant, the majority held that "a suspect's awareness of all the possible subjects of questioning in advance of interrogation is not relevant to determining whether the suspect voluntarily, knowingly, and intelligently waived his Fifth Amendment privilege" (p. 577).

To ensure that the *Miranda* warnings are read properly, most police departments have a policy describing what that should entail. Figure 8.4 provides an example of one such policy, this one from the San Bernardino, California, Police Department.

***Waiver of* Miranda.** In *Miranda*, the Supreme Court stated that if a person talks after he or she has been read the warnings, "a heavy burden rests on the government to demonstrate that the defendant knowingly and intelligently waived his privilege against self-incrimination and his right to retained or appointed counsel" (p. 475). Furthermore, "a valid waiver will not be presumed simply from the silence of the accused after warnings are given or simply from the fact that a confession was in fact eventually obtained" (p. 475). According to the Supreme Court:

> Whatever the testimony of the authorities as to waiver of rights by an accused, the fact of lengthy interrogation or incommunicado incarceration before a statement is made is strong evidence that the accused did not validly waive his rights. In these circumstances the fact that the individual eventually made a statement is consistent with the conclusion that the compelling influence of the interrogation finally forced him to do so. It is inconsistent with any notion of a voluntary relinquishment of the privilege. Moreover, any evidence that the accused was threatened, tricked, or cajoled into a waiver will, of course, show that the defendant did not voluntarily waive his privilege. (p. 476)

FIGURE 8.4 Example of a Miranda Advisement Policy

Purpose

To ensure uniformity when advising persons of their *Miranda* rights.

Procedure

It is *not* necessary that the defendant sign a written waiver of his rights. The law only requires that the waiver be free, intelligent, and voluntary.

The *Miranda* warning should always be *read* to the suspect rather than relying on memory, using the following wording:

1. You have the right to remain silent.

2. Anything you say can and will be used against you in court.

3. You have the right to talk with an attorney and to have an attorney present before and during any questioning.

4. If you cannot afford an attorney, one will be appointed free of charge to represent you before and during any questioning.

After the warning and in order to secure a waiver, the following questions should be asked and an affirmative reply secured to each question. The officer should always make a record of the *exact words* used by the defendant when he answers each of the following questions.

1. Do you understand the rights I have just explained to you?

2. With these rights in mind, do you wish to talk to me/us now?

Source: Chapter 15, Procedure 1, "Procedure for *Miranda* Advisement," from *Standard Operating Procedure,* San Bernardino, California, Police Department (rev. October 26, 1988). Used courtesy of the San Bernardino Police Department.

■ *Colorado v. Connelly,* 479 U.S. 157 (1986)

In recent years, the courts have interpreted this language loosely. That is, whereas *Miranda* declared that a waiver should be viewed with considerable caution, later decisions have suggested that the burden of demonstrating a valid waiver is not difficult to meet. For example, in *Colorado v. Connelly* (479 U.S. 157 [1986]), the Court held that the government need only show the validity of a waiver by a "preponderance of evidence." And in *Fare v. Michael C.* (442 U.S. 707 [1979]), the Court held that the "totality of the circumstances approach is adequate to determine whether there has been a waiver" (p. 725). This latter test is not unlike the due process voluntariness test, discussed earlier in this chapter. It is used to assess juvenile waivers, as well.

Must the waiver be express? That is, must a person affirmatively state something to the effect that "I am willing to answer questions" for a waiver of *Miranda* to take place? The answer to this question is no. In the past, the Court preferred an express waiver. But in *Miranda*, the Court noted that "a valid wavier will not be presumed." Similarly, in *Westover v. United States* (a case joined with *Miranda*), the Court stated that an *articulated waiver* is required before a confession will be considered admissible.

However, in *North Carolina v. Butler* (441 U.S. 369 [1979]), the Court decided otherwise. According to Justice Stewart, "The question [of a waiver] is not one of form, but rather whether the defendant in fact knowingly and voluntarily waived his rights delineated in the *Miranda* case" (p. 373). Further, a "course of conduct indicating waiver" (such as the suspect deciding to converse with the police) is sufficient for a valid waiver to take place. Based on this decision, the current rule is that the government must show a valid waiver based on "the particular facts and circumstances surrounding [the] case, including the background, experience, and conduct of the accused" (pp. 374–375). In other words, the courts now take a case-by-case approach in determining whether *Miranda* waivers are obtained legally.

As was made clear in *Butler*, a valid *Miranda* waiver requires a showing that the waiver was knowing and intelligent. What, then, is a *knowing and intelligent waiver*? There is no clear answer to this question, but the Court has noted that a full and complete understanding of the *Miranda* warnings is not necessary for a valid waiver to take place. This was the decision reached in *Connecticut v. Barrett* (479 U.S. 523 [1987]). In that case, the defendant refused to give the police any written statements before he talked to an attorney. He did state, however, that he had no problem *talking* to the police. As it turned out, the defendant thought that only written statements could be used against him in court. The Court called his actions "illogical" but nonetheless held that his oral statements were admissible.

Another case focusing on the knowing and intelligent requirement was *Wyrick v. Fields* (459 U.S. 42 [1982]). In that case, the defendant expressed some confusion about the duration of a *Miranda* waiver. He had agreed to take a polygraph examination without counsel present. After the examination, he also answered questions from the examiner about his feelings concerning the examination, which led to him supplying incriminating information. When the defendant's statements were used against him, he argued that neither he nor his attorney believed that the polygraph procedure also included post-examination questioning. However, the Supreme Court pointed out that "it would have been unreasonable for Fields [the defendant] and his attorney to assume that Fields would not be informed of the polygraph readings and asked to explain any unfavorable result" (p. 47). In addition, the Court concluded that "the questions put to Fields after the examination would not have caused him to forget the rights of which he had been advised and which he had understood moments before" (p. 49).

Two additional Supreme Court decisions focused on whether the police can use trickery to obtain a *Miranda* waiver and/or statement. In *Colorado v. Spring* (479 U.S. 564 [1987]), the Court held that trickery *had not* taken place when the police failed to advise the defendant that he would be questioned about a different crime than the one for which he was arrested. It did point out, however, that "any evidence that the accused was . . . tricked . . . into a waiver will, of course, show that the defendant did not voluntarily waive his privilege" (p. 575).

In another interesting case, *Moran v. Burbine* (475 U.S. 412 [1986]), the Supreme Court held that a confession was validly obtained even though the police questioned the defendant after assuring his attorney that he would not be questioned until the following day. In a 6 to 3 decision, the Court held that this action did not result in a coerced confession. As Justice O'Connor noted, "[T]he same defendant, armed with the same information and confronted with precisely the same police conduct, would have knowingly waived his *Miranda* rights had a lawyer not telephoned the police station to inquire about his status" (p. 422).

In light of these two cases, it seems somewhat difficult to determine what constitutes trickery. A general rule is this: If officials lead a defendant to believe that he or she has no right to remain silent, then trickery is taking place. However, if the police merely lead a defendant to believe there is no point to remaining silent (as in *Butler*, *Barrett*, *Fields*, *Spring*, and *Burbine*), then any subsequent incriminating statements that are made will probably be viewed as knowing and intelligent.

DECISION MAKING EXERCISE **8.9**

The Circumstances for a Voluntary Waiver

Fred Nicholas was arrested for murder, taken to the police station, and advised of his *Miranda* rights. He stated that he wished his attorney could be present but that he was away on business. Given that, Nicholas said that he "might as well talk." Unknown to Nicholas, his attorney was in town after all, had heard about Nicholas's arrest, and had tried unsuccessfully to contact him. In fact, the police had explicitly refused to let Nicholas meet with his attorney. Nicholas made an incriminating statement. Should it be admissible at trial?

Before moving on, it is worth mentioning that in addition to the requirement that a valid *Miranda* waiver must be knowing and intelligent, it must also be voluntary. The test for voluntariness is similar to the due process voluntariness test discussed earlier in this chapter. Threats, physical force, and the like can lead to defendants issuing involuntary confessions. However, in *Fare v. Michael C.* (442 U.S. 707 [1979]), the Court held that the confession obtained from a 16-year-old was not involuntary. In a strongly worded dissent, Justice Powell argued that the juvenile in this case "was immature, emotional, and uneducated, and therefore was likely to be vulnerable to the skillful, two-on-one, repetitive style of interrogation to which he was subjected" (p. 733). A safe rule is that the police must engage in seriously questionable conduct for the voluntariness requirement of a *Miranda* waiver to be violated.

Again, to be safe, many police departments require that each suspect completes a *Miranda* waiver before interrogation commences. Doing so helps ensure that the waiver is documented. An example of a *Miranda* waiver form, this one from the San Bernardino, California, Police Department, is reprinted in Figure 8.5.

In a recent twist on the notion of *Miranda* waivers (*United States v. Patane*, 542 U.S. 630 [2004]), the Supreme Court considered whether police officers' failure to complete the *Miranda* warnings—after the suspect interrupted midway through by saying, "I understand my rights"—violated the Fifth Amendment. In that case, after the suspect had interrupted the reading of *Miranda* and said he understood his rights, he informed police of the location of a pistol. He was indicted for possession of a firearm by a convicted felon and sought suppression of the pistol, claiming his Fifth Amendment privilege was violated. The Supreme Court disagreed.

Questioning after Assertion of One's Right to Remain Silent. As a general rule, questioning must cease once the accused asserts his or her right to remain silent. According to the Supreme Court in *Miranda*:

FIGURE 8.5 Example of a Miranda Waiver Form

WAIVER

I HAVE BEEN ADVISED THAT:

1. I HAVE THE ABSOLUTE RIGHT TO REMAIN SILENT.

2. ANYTHING I SAY CAN AND WILL BE USED AS EVIDENCE AGAINST ME IN COURT.

3. I HAVE THE RIGHT TO BE REPRESENTED BY AN ATTORNEY AND TO CONSULT WITH HIM BEFORE MAKING ANY STATEMENT OR ANSWERING ANY QUESTIONS AND I HAVE THE RIGHT TO HAVE AN ATTORNEY PRESENT DURING ANY QUESTIONING.

4. IF I CANNOT AFFORD AN ATTORNEY, ONE WILL BE APPOINTED BY THE COURT, FREE OF CHARGE, TO REPRESENT ME BEFORE ANY QUESTIONING, IF I DESIRE.

I UNDERSTAND THESE RIGHTS. THESE RIGHTS HAVE BEEN EXPLAINED TO ME. WITH THESE RIGHTS IN MIND, I AM WILLING TO TALK TO OFFICERS ABOUT THE CHARGES AGAINST ME.

DATE _____ SIGNED_____

WITNESS _____ WITNESS _____

Source: Used courtesy of San Bernardino, California, Police Department.

If the individual indicates in any manner, at any time prior to or during questioning, that he wishes to remain silent, the interrogation must cease. . . . Without the right to cut off questioning, the setting of in-custody interrogation operates on the individual to overcome free choice in producing a statement after the privilege has been once invoked. If the individual states that he wants an attorney, the interrogation must cease until an attorney is present. . . . If the individual cannot obtain an attorney and he indicates that he wants one before speaking to police, they must respect his decision to remain silent. . . . If authorities conclude that they will not provide counsel during a reasonable period of time in which investigation in the field is carried out, they may refrain from doing so without violating the person's Fifth Amendment privilege so long as they do not question him during that time. (pp. 473–474)

However, there is at least one circumstance in which the police can question a suspect after he or she has asserted the *Miranda* rights. In *Michigan v. Mosley* (423 U.S. 96 [1975]), the Supreme Court permitted questioning after an assertion of *Miranda*. In that case, two hours after the defendant had stated that he did not want to talk, a different police officer confronted him in a different room about another crime and read him the *Miranda* rights for a second time. After this, the man made incriminating statements. In a 7 to 2 decision, the Court held that the suspect's *Miranda* rights had been "scrupulously honored." The Court said that the second officer's actions were acceptable because "the police here immediately ceased the interrogation, resumed questioning only after the passage of a significant period of time and the provision of a fresh set of warnings, and restricted the second interrogation to a crime that had not been a subject of the earlier interrogation" (p. 106).

■ *Michigan v. Mosley,*
   423 U.S. 96 (1975)

The key to *Michigan v. Mosley* was that the second set of questions concerned a *separate crime.* Had the police again questioned Mosley about the first crime, which he had stated he did not want to discuss, any inculpatory statements would have been obtained in violation of the Fifth Amendment.

***The Public Safety Exception to* Miranda.** On some occasions, custodial interrogation is permissible without the *Miranda* warnings. Specifically, if public safety is in jeopardy, no warnings are required. This was the decision reached in *New York v. Quarles* (467 U.S. 649 [1984]). There, the Court held that the warnings need not be given if the suspect could have endangered public safety.

■ *New York v. Quarles,*
   467 U.S. 649 (1984)

The facts from *Quarles* are as follows: After receiving information that a man with a gun had just entered a supermarket, Officer Kraft, along with three other officers, entered the store. Kraft spotted the defendant, drew his gun, and ordered the man to stop and put his hands over his head. When the officers frisked the man, they found an empty shoulder holster on him. When they asked where the man had put the gun, he replied, "The gun is over there." Officer Kraft retrieved the revolver and then placed the man under arrest and read him the *Miranda* warnings. The trial court and the lower appellate courts excluded the gun on the grounds that it was obtained in violation of *Miranda* (i.e., the man had not been advised of his right to remain silent at the time the gun was found).

The Supreme Court disagreed. Justice Rehnquist wrote the majority opinion, arguing that rigid application of *Miranda* is not always warranted, particularly when public safety is a concern:

[T]he need for answers to questions in a situation posing a threat to public safety outweighs the need for the prophylactic rule protecting the Fifth Amendment's privilege against self-incrimination. We decline to place officers such as Officer Kraft in the untenable position of having to consider, often in a matter of seconds, whether it best serves society for them to ask the necessary questions without the *Miranda* warnings and render whatever probative evidence they uncover inadmissible, or for them to give the warnings in order to preserve the admissibility of evidence they might uncover but possibly damage or destroy their ability to obtain that evidence and neutralize the volatile situation confronting them. (pp. 657–658)

The Court also made it clear that the appropriate test for determining whether a threat to public safety exists is an objective one—that is, one based on what a reasonable person in the same circumstances would believe: "[W]here spontaneity rather than adherence to a police manual is necessarily the order of the day, the application of the [public safety] exception . . . should not be made to depend on *post hoc* findings at a suppression hearing concerning the subjective motivation of the arresting officer" (p. 656). The majority in *Quarles* apparently believed that an objective threat to public safety existed. Insofar as the officers did not know where the gun was located, not knowing "obviously posed more than one danger to the public safety: an accomplice might make use of it [or] a customer or employee might later come upon it" (p. 657).

The *Quarles* decision is a controversial one. As Justice O'Connor noted in disagreement with the newly issued public safety exception to *Miranda* (though not with the majority's ultimate decision):

> *Miranda* has never been read to prohibit the police from asking questions to secure the public safety. Rather, the critical question *Miranda* addresses is who shall bear the cost of securing the public safety when such questions are asked and answered: the defendant or the state. *Miranda*, for better or worse, found the resolution of that question implicit in the prohibition against compulsory self-incrimination and placed the burden on the State. (p. 664)

Quarles, by contrast, appears to place the burden on the defendant. It does so, in Justice O'Connor's view, not by ensuring that public safety is preserved but by creating a *Miranda* loophole that helps ensure that otherwise inadmissible evidence can be used against the defendant.

The Supreme Court Revisits Miranda. The *Miranda* decision was not without controversy. In 1968, shortly after the decision was announced, Congress passed a Crime Control Act that, among other things, attempted to overrule the *Miranda* decision. The statute, codified as **18 U.S.C. Section 3501**, states that in any federal prosecution, a confession "shall be admissible in evidence if it is voluntarily given." Under the law, suspects are not required to be advised of their right to counsel, their right not to incriminate themselves, and so on.

For several years, Section 3501 remained dormant. The U.S. attorneys general have known that to utilize the statute would be to challenge the authority of the U.S. Supreme Court. But critics of *Miranda* were looking for an opportunity to bring Section 3501 before the Court. That opportunity arose in 2000: Charles Dickerson was indicted for bank robbery and related crimes. He moved to suppress a statement he made to Federal Bureau of Investigation (FBI) agents on the ground that he had not received his *Miranda* warnings. The district court granted Dickerson's motion to suppress but also noted that the confession was voluntary, despite the apparent *Miranda* violation.

Then, the Court of Appeals for the Fourth Circuit held (in a 2 to 1 decision) that "Congress, pursuant to its power to establish the rules of evidence and procedure in the federal courts, acted well within its authority in enacting Section 3501, [and] Section 3501, rather than *Miranda*, governs the admissibility of confession in federal court" (*United States v. Dickerson*, 166 F.3d 667 [4th Cir. 1999], p. 671). The case, *Dickerson v. United States* (530 U.S. 428 [2000]), then went before the Supreme Court. In a 7 to 2 opinion, Chief Justice Rehnquist wrote for the Court:

■ *Dickerson v. United States,*
530 U.S. 428 (2000)

> We hold that *Miranda*, being a constitutional decision of this Court, may not be in effect overruled by an Act of Congress, and we decline to overrule *Miranda* ourselves. We therefore hold that *Miranda* and its progeny in this Court govern the admissibility of statements made during custodial interrogation in both state and federal courts. (p. 431)

The Court further noted:

> Whether or not we would agree with *Miranda's* reasoning and its resulting rule, were we addressing the issue in the first instance, the principles of *stare decisis* weigh heavily against overruling it now. . . . While *stare decisis* is not an inexorable command, particularly when

we are interpreting the Constitution, even in constitutional cases, the doctrine carries such persuasive force that we have always required a departure from precedent to be supported by some special justification.

We do not think there is such justification for overruling *Miranda*. *Miranda* has become embedded in routine police practice to the point where the warnings have become part of our national culture. (p. 443)

The Latest on Miranda. In a recent case (*Chavez v. Martinez*, 538 U.S. 760 [2003]), the Supreme Court seems to have shifted its view on *Miranda*. In that case, a police officer interrogated a man while he was receiving treatment for a gunshot wound. The man was *not* advised of his *Miranda* rights. He was never charged with a crime, but later sued under 42 U.S.C. Section 1983 (see Chapter 2), arguing that his constitutional rights were violated. The Supreme Court disagreed because the man was not compelled to be a "witness" against himself in a "criminal case." This decision would seem to suggest *Miranda* warnings are never required, unless statements obtained without the warnings are actually used against the accused in a criminal case.

In yet another, even more recent case (*Missouri v. Seibert*, 542 U.S. 600 [2004]), the Supreme Court made it clear that *Miranda* warnings must be given *before* interrogation commences. In that case, the accused was interrogated—without *Miranda* warnings having been read—and confessed. She was then advised of her *Miranda* rights and "re-confessed." The Supreme Court declared that the interrogating officer's pre-*Miranda* questioning was improper. The confession was deemed inadmissible at trial.

The Exclusionary Rule and Confession Analysis

It is important to focus on the role of the *exclusionary rule* in the confession analysis. It is often said that the exclusionary rule applies only to the Fourth Amendment. Part of the reason for this is that the Fifth Amendment essentially contains its own exclusionary rule by prohibiting compulsion of testimony. Whatever view one takes, the debate is largely semantic. In the end, evidence obtained in violation of *any* constitutional amendment will not be admissible in a criminal trial.

Generally speaking, a confession obtained in violation of *Miranda* or some constitutional provision will be excluded. However, just because a confession is obtained illegally does not mean that any subsequently obtained evidence will automatically be excluded. In fact, illegally obtained statements are themselves considered admissible in certain instances.

Accordingly, the following subsections focus on three lines of cases involving confessions and the exclusionary rule: (1) standing cases; (2) impeachment cases; and (3) "fruit of the poisonous tree" cases.

Confessions and Standing

For a confession (or evidence thereby obtained) to be excluded, the person arguing for exclusion must have *standing*; that is, one person cannot seek to exclude the confession of another, even if that confession was obtained in violation of *Miranda*. As noted in *Couch v. United States* (409 U.S. 322 [1973]), being advised of *Miranda* is considered a personal right. Thus, a person arguing for exclusion of an (unconstitutionally obtained) incriminating statement must have standing; otherwise, the statement and subsequent evidence will be deemed admissible. (Standing is covered further in Chapter 3.)

■ *Couch v. United States,* 409 U.S. 322 (1973)

Confessions and Impeachment

Another situation in which incriminating statements obtained in violation of *Miranda* are admissible is when such statements are used for purposes of impeachment. A key restriction on this rule, however, is that the statement must be obtained voluntarily in the due process sense.

■ *Harris v. New York,*
401 U.S. 222 (1971)

An illustrative case is *Harris v. New York* (401 U.S. 222 [1971]). In that case, the prosecution sought to introduce an out-of-court statement that was inconsistent with the defendant's in-court testimony, even though the out-of-court statement was obtained in violation of *Miranda*. The Supreme Court held that the out-of-court-statement was admissible. The Court noted further that such a statement must be obtained voluntarily, which it was in Harris's case (see also *Oregon v. Hass*, 420 U.S. 714 [1975]; *New Jersey v. Portash*, 437 U.S. 385 [1978]).

Note that for a statement obtained in violation of *Miranda* to be admissible for impeachment purposes, the statement must, in fact, be an oral communication. The prosecution cannot introduce evidence of an accused's out-of-court *silence* for impeachment purposes. This issue arose in the case of *Doyle v. Ohio* (426 U.S. 610 [1976]), in which after the defendant's in-court exculpatory story, the prosecution sought to introduce evidence that the defendant did not offer the same explanation to the police. The Supreme Court held that the defendant's silence was not admissible for purposes of impeachment (see also *Wainwright v. Greenfield*, 474 U.S. 284 [1986]).

Confessions and "Fruit of the Poisonous Tree"

As noted elsewhere, evidence obtained in flagrant violation of the Fourth Amendment is not admissible under the so-called "fruit of the poisonous tree," or derivative evidence, doctrine. However, the Supreme Court has not been so quick to apply the same rule in the case of illegally obtained confessions. Instead, the Court has held that physical evidence obtained in violation of *Miranda* is admissible, as long as the information supplied by the accused was voluntary in the due process sense.

■ *United States v. Bayer,*
331 U.S. 532 (1947)

The first case of note concerning the derivative evidence doctrine in the confession context was *United States v. Bayer* (331 U.S. 532 [1947]), a case decided well before the *Miranda* decision was handed down. There, the Court held that the Fourth Amendment "fruit of the poisonous tree" doctrine did not control the admissibility of improperly obtained confessions.

DECISION MAKING EXERCISE 8.10

Should the Exclusionary Rule Apply?

Assume the police have Jack Richter in custody and are interrogating him about his suspected involvement in a gruesome murder. They do not advise him of his *Miranda* rights. Further, one of the officers, who is notorious for his aggressive interrogation techniques, holds a .357 revolver (loaded with one round) to Richter's head and plays "Russian roulette" in order to obtain a confession. Richter succumbs to the pressure and admits to the murder. He also points the police to the location of the murder weapon. Obviously, his statement will not be admissible. What about the murder weapon?

Furthermore, in *Michigan v. Tucker* (417 U.S. 433 [1974]), a case decided after *Miranda*, the Court suggested that it had not changed its position. Then, in *Oregon v. Elstad* (470 U.S. 298 [1985]), the Court made it clear that evidence obtained from a violation of *Miranda* is admissible but only if voluntarily obtained.

■ THE IMPORTANCE OF DOCUMENTING A CONFESSION

So far, this chapter has been concerned with the methods by which the police can extract incriminating information from a criminal suspect. Assuming the police are successful in terms of eliciting an incriminating response, it is not enough for the suspect to say "I did

---

FIGURE 8.6   Content of a Typical Interview Log

Interview Log

1. Identity of person interviewed
2. Identity of officers conducting interview
3. Location of interview
4. Date of interview
5. Time of arrest, if applicable
6. Location of arrest
7. Identity of officers making arrest
8. Time interview began
9. Time officers informed subject or suspect of his rights, and if more than one officer, name of officer advising subject or suspect
10. Time subject or suspect waived his rights
11. Time interview concluded
12. Time preparation of statement commenced
13. Identity of person preparing statement
14. Time statement completed
15. Time subject or suspect reviewed statement
16. Time subject or suspect signed written statement
17. A record of requests and complaints of subject and the action taken thereon, such as the time a subject requests permission to call an attorney, the time he made a call to his attorney, the time subject complained of illness, the time and action taken on this complaint, the time subject requested food, the time and action taken on this request, and the details as to how this request was handled.

Source: T. T. Burke, "Documenting and Reporting a Confession with a Signed Statement: A Guide for Law Enforcement," *FBI Law Enforcement Bulletin* (Feb. 2001): 21.

it" or to otherwise offer some form of verbal confession. In fact, if the police hand the suspect a pencil and paper and say, "Write down your confession," this will not be enough, either. Instead, the police need to follow specific procedures for documenting and reporting a confession.

According to one source,[2] the police should document every interrogation and even keep an *interview log*: a document containing information about the individuals involved in the interrogations and actions taken by both sides. A list of topics to be cited in an interview log is shown in Figure 8.6.

Also, a signed statement from the accused should be secured. First, the signed statement should identify the suspect, the investigators, and the crime involved. Second, the statement should describe, in language the suspect can understand, the details of the crime, what the suspect did, and how he or she did it. The statement should then be carefully reviewed with the suspect, even read aloud, so its content is clear. Finally, the statement should be signed by the suspect, the officer who conducted the interrogation, and at least one witness—preferably another officer. Figure 8.7 shows a model statement form for securing a written confession from a criminal suspect.

---

[2]T. T. Burke, "Documenting and Reporting a Confession with a Signed Statement: A Guide for Law Enforcement," *FBI Law Enforcement Bulletin* (Feb. 2001): 17.

FIGURE 8.7 *Sample Form for Securing a Written Confession: White-Collar Crime*

Signed Statement Format
White Collar Crime Sample

I, (*subject's name and address*) hereby make the following free and voluntary statement to (*officer's official name and title*) who has identified himself/herself as a (*title of officer and name of department or agency*). I have been advised that I have been interviewed concerning my involvement in (*phrase describing scheme or nature of crime and victim, such as "the misappropriation and theft of $100,000 from the First National Bank while I was employed there during 1999"*).

I was born on (*subject's date of birth*) at (*subject's place of birth*). I attended (*last school attended*) and completed (*last grade or graduation date*). I read and write the English language.

> Officers should use the next few paragraphs to summarize what the subject did and how the subject did it, in his own words. Because this statement occurs after the subject's confession, officers can assist the subject in formulating the statement, using information previously provided. Officers should include any information the subject provides regarding what happened to the stolen money, how it was spent, items purchased, and other related details.

I knew that what I was doing was wrong, and I regret my actions. I wish to cooperate with the (*name of agency*) investigation and get this matter resolved. (*Optional paragraph, depending on circumstances and subject's remorse*)

I have read this (*number of pages*) page statement, have initialed all corrections, and I am signing it because it is true and correct. (*The subject writes this after reading the statement aloud and accepting its contents.*)

_____
(subject's signature and date)

First witness: _____
(officer taking statement, title, agency, location, and date)

Second witness: _____
(third-party individual, title, agency, location, and date)

(*NOTE: Officers should always have the subject read the statement aloud to them and initial any corrections. Also, they should avoid blank lines between sentences and paragraphs in the statement.*)

Source: T. T. Burke, "Documenting and Reporting a Confession with a Signed Statement: A Guide for Law Enforcement," *FBI Law Enforcement Bulletin* (Feb. 2001): 19.

CONCLUSION

The Fifth Amendment's self-incrimination clause is frequently relied on in challenges to the constitutionality of confessions. However, for the Fifth Amendment to be successfully invoked, several requirements must be met. First, the police must compel a statement that is incriminating as well as testimonial. And, of course, the accused individual is the only one who can assert his or her Fifth Amendment protection against an unconstitutionally obtained confession. Finally, a confession will be thrown out, as was the decision in *Miranda*, if a suspect's incriminating statement is a result of custodial interrogation in which the suspect was not advised of his or her constitutional right to have counsel present.

Confessions are also governed by the Sixth Amendment's right to counsel clause but only when formal

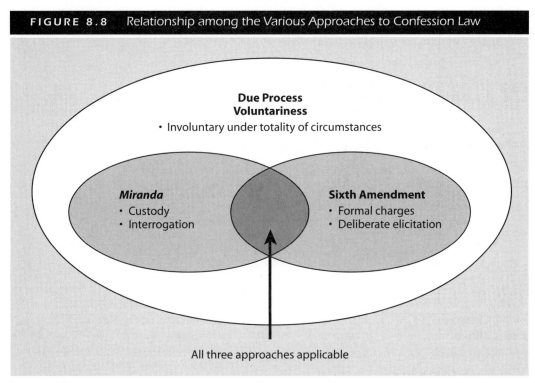

FIGURE 8.8 Relationship among the Various Approaches to Confession Law

All three approaches applicable

Source: Adapted from R. M. Bloom and M. S. Brodin, *Criminal Procedure: Examples and Explanations*, 2nd ed. (New York: Little, Brown, 1996).

charges have been filed. Due process protections also exist—namely, when an incriminating statement is obtained involuntarily. Confessions are afforded more protection than any other form of evidence, such as physical evidence obtained following a search. For example, whereas searches and seizures are governed by only one amendment (the Fourth), law enforcement officials must abide by the Fifth, Sixth, and Fourteenth Amendments when seeking to obtain confessions. The Fourteenth Amendment voluntariness requirement *always* applies,

but the Fifth Amendment only applies when custodial interrogation takes place. The Sixth Amendment only applies once formal charges have been filed.

Figure 8.8 illustrates the relationships among the various constitutional provisions governing police interrogation procedures. The due process/voluntariness approach acts as a fallback and is always applicable. The Sixth and Fifth Amendments, by contrast, apply in specific circumstances, as described. And it is possible (albeit rare) for all three provisions to come into play.

REVIEW QUESTIONS

1. Explain the means by which compulsion can occur, in Fifth Amendment terms.
2. What is the difference between a criminal and a noncriminal proceeding?
3. What does it mean to be a witness, in Fifth Amendment terms?
4. What does it mean, in Fifth Amendment terms, to be a witness against oneself?
5. Summarize the due process voluntariness approach to interrogations and confessions.
6. What factors affect voluntariness?
7. Summarize the Sixth Amendment approach to interrogations and confessions.

8. Explain deliberate elicitation.
9. What are formal criminal proceedings, for purposes of the Sixth Amendment approach to interrogations and confessions?
10. What are the *Miranda* warnings?
11. When does *Miranda* apply?
12. Citing relevant cases, distinguish between custody and interrogation, for *Miranda* purposes.
13. Summarize the requirements for a valid *Miranda* waiver.
14. What is the public safety exception to *Miranda*?
15. How does the exclusionary rule operate in the context of confessions and interrogations?

 Answers to the Decision-Making Exercises for this chapter can be found on pages 505–506.

CHAPTER 9

Identification Procedures and the Role of Witnesses

OUTLINE

KEY TERMS

lineup
showup
photographic array
suggestive lineup
in-court showup
direct examination

cross-examination
specific question
leading question
competence
credibility
accrediting

discrediting
impeachment
rehabilitation
tainted identification

INTRODUCTION
Dealing with Witnesses to Crimes

Identification procedures include those systems and activities that allow witnesses of crimes to identify suspected perpetrators. The three most common types of identification procedures are lineups, showups, and photographic arrays. In a **lineup**, the suspect is placed alongside several other people who resemble him or her and the witness (or victim) picks the suspect out of the lineup. In a **showup**, the suspect is brought before the witness alone, so the witness can be asked whether that person is the perpetrator. Finally, in a **photographic array** (or photographic display), several photographs, including one of the suspect, are shown to a witness or victim and he or she is asked to pick out the perpetrator.

Identification procedures fall into two broad categories: (1) out of court and (2) in court. The three identification procedures just described—lineups, showups, and photographic arrays—occur *out of court* and prior to trial. There are, however, many occasions in which the prosecution may wish to have a witness identify the suspect *in court* and during trial. Of course, not all witnesses recollect accurately and/or can be trusted with regard to a suspect's identification. It is therefore important to consider the *witness examination process* with an eye toward witness identification.

Naturally, it is in the prosecution's interest to introduce evidence that a witness or victim picked the perpetrator out of a lineup. However, it is not as simple as demonstrating that a witness identified the perpetrator. The identification procedure must be fair as well as conform with constitutional requirements. Those constitutional requirements place restrictions on what officials can do in terms of arranging lineups, showups, and photographic arrays. And these restrictions are critical because witnesses to crimes are frequently inaccurate in their descriptions.

KEY CASES

Constitutional Restrictions on Identifications
- *United States v. Wade*, 388 U.S. 218 (1967)
- *Stovall v. Denno*, 388 U.S. 293 (1967)
- *Manson v. Braithwaite*, 432 U.S. 98 (1977)
- *Schmerber v. California*, 384 U.S. 757 (1966)
- *Hayes v. Florida*, 470 U.S. 811 (1985)

Pretrial Identification
- *United States v. Wade*, 388 U.S. 218 (1967)
- *Neil v. Biggers*, 409 U.S. 188 (1972)
- *Moore v. Illinois*, 434 U.S. 220 (1977)

- *Simmons v. United States*, 390 U.S. 377 (1968)
- *Manson v. Brathwaite*, 432 U.S. 98 (1977)

Exclusionary Rule and Identifications
- *Davis v. Mississippi*, 394 U.S. 721 (1969)
- *United States v. Crews*, 445 U.S. 463 (1980)

Accordingly, this chapter begins with a discussion of the constitutional restrictions that govern the identification process. Next, out-of-court identification procedures are considered followed by in-court identification procedures and the witness examination process. The chapter concludes with a look at the role of the exclusionary rule as it applies to in-court and out-of-court identification procedures.

■ CONSTITUTIONAL RESTRICTIONS ON IDENTIFICATION PROCEDURES

Identification procedures have been challenged on several grounds, stemming from the Fourteenth Amendment's due process clause, the Fifth Amendment's self-incrimination clause, and the Sixth Amendment's right to counsel clause. People have also challenged the constitutionality of identification procedures on Fourth Amendment grounds.

■ Right to Counsel

■ *United States v. Wade,*
388 U.S. 218 (1967)

In *United States v. Wade* (388 U.S. 218 [1967]), a defendant was placed in a police lineup, without his attorney present, *after* he had been indicted for a crime. The Supreme Court held that this violated the Sixth Amendment because a postindictment lineup is a "critical stage" in the criminal process. Further, "the presence of counsel [at postindictment lineups] is necessary to preserve the defendant's basic right to a fair trial" (p. 227). Indeed, the right to counsel extends well beyond the identification stage (see Chapter 11).

The key in *Wade* was that the lineup was postindictment—that is, conducted after charges had been filed. Had charges *not* been filed, a different decision would have probably resulted. Another important feature of the *Wade* decision was that it distinguished lineups from "various other preparatory steps, such as systematized or scientific analyzing of the accused's fingerprints, blood sample, clothing, hair and the like" (p. 227). Counsel is not required for these types of activities because

> [k]nowledge of the techniques of science and technology is sufficiently available, and the variables in techniques few enough, that the accused has the opportunity for a meaningful confrontation of the Government's case at trial through the ordinary processes of cross-examination of the Government's expert witnesses and the presentation of the evidence of his own experts. (pp. 227–228)

Recently, the Supreme Court has extended the Sixth Amendment right to counsel to include other hearings, such as preliminary hearings and arraignments (see, e.g., *Kirby v. Illinois,* 406 U.S. 682 [1972]).

■ Due Process

■ *Stovall v. Denno,*
388 U.S. 293 (1967)

The Supreme Court has also clearly stated that the Fourteenth Amendment's due process clause bears on the constitutionality of identification procedures. For example, in *Stovall v. Denno* (388 U.S. 293 [1967]), the Court held that the accused is entitled to protection against procedures "so unnecessarily suggestive and conducive to irreparable mistaken identification" (p. 293) as to amount to a due process violation. In general, for an identification procedure to satisfy the due process clause, it must be (1) reliable and (2) minimally suggestive.

Whether an identification procedure is *reliable* is determined in light of the facts and circumstances surrounding the case. The following factors are used in determining whether an identification procedure is reliable:

The opportunity of the witness to view the criminal at the time of the crime, the witness's degree of attention, the accuracy of the witness's prior description of the criminal, the level of certainty demonstrated by the witness at the confrontation, and the length of time between the crime and the confrontation. (*Neil v. Biggers*, 409 U.S. 188 [1972], p. 199)

Indeed, the Court stated in *Biggers* that reliability is more important than *suggestiveness*. In the Court's words, it is "the likelihood of misidentification which violates a defendant's right to due process" (p. 199). This position was reaffirmed in the case of *Manson v. Braithwaite* (432 U.S. 98 [1977]), where the Court held that the totality of circumstances determines whether an identification procedure is unreliable.

■ *Manson v. Braithwaite,* 432 U.S. 98 (1977)

Suggestiveness has also been important in determining whether an identification procedure violates the due process clause. If the procedure is set up such that the witness or victim is all but guaranteed to pick the perpetrator, it is unnecessarily suggestive. If, for example, an offender is 6 feet tall and placed in a lineup with several others who are considerably shorter, then the procedure will be considered suggestive.

■ The Fifth Amendment

The Fifth Amendment's self-incrimination clause has been invoked with regard to identification procedures. In particular, some defendants have argued that being forced to participate in a lineup or photographic array is itself incriminating and, as such, violates the Fifth Amendment. However, in *United States v. Wade*, the Court held that the privilege against self-incrimination does not limit the use of identification procedures.[1] The reason the Court offered is that even though incriminating information can result from identification procedures, such evidence is physical or real as opposed to testimonial. In *Wade*, the Court decided on the constitutionality of an identification procedure in which the accused was required to utter words that were presumably uttered by the perpetrator. The Court concluded that this type of identification procedure was valid because the defendant's voice was used as an identifying characteristic, not as a means to get him to express his guilt. Thus, the Fifth Amendment does not apply to identification procedures.

■ The Fourth Amendment

Lastly, identification procedures have been challenged on Fourth Amendment grounds. Like the Fifth Amendment, the Fourth Amendment has yet to be successfully invoked with regard to identification procedures. According to the Supreme Court, no one enjoys a reasonable expectation of privacy in characteristics that are exposed to the public. For example, if an offender is viewed by a witness, the witness's identification of the offender will be admissible in court, even though the identification is incriminating. The offender/defendant may argue that the act of being viewed by the witness is incriminating, but the courts consider this sort of knowing exposure as beyond constitutional protection.

One of the leading cases in this area is *Schmerber v. California* (384 U.S. 757 [1966]). There, a sample of the defendant's blood was taken by a doctor in a hospital following the defendant's arrest. The sample was used as evidence in the defendant's trial for drunk driving. The defendant argued that the blood sample was incriminating and should be excluded from trial. The Supreme Court disagreed:

■ *Schmerber v. California,* 384 U.S. 757 (1966)

---

[1]Note that the Fifth Amendment would apply if a defendant in a lineup was forced to answer questions from the police or witnesses.

Particularly in a case such as this, where time had to be taken to bring the accused to a hospital and to investigate the scene of the accident, there was no time to seek out a magistrate and secure a warrant. Given these special facts, we conclude that the attempt to secure evidence of blood-alcohol content in this case was an appropriate incident to petitioner's arrest. (pp. 770–771)

Obviously, if the police want to seize a person so as to obtain fingerprints, a voice exemplar, or some other form of evidence, they are bound by Fourth Amendment restrictions. As noted elsewhere in this book, probable cause is required before the police can seize a person. Assuming a seizure is justified, however, then any real or physical evidence obtained by the arrestee will be admissible.

■ *Hayes v. Florida,*
470 U.S. 811 (1985)

There is at least one exception to the Fourth Amendment's probable cause requirement as it pertains to identification procedures. In *Hayes v. Florida* (470 U.S. 811 [1985]), the Court stated:

> There is . . . support in our cases for the view that the Fourth Amendment would permit seizures for the purpose of fingerprinting, if there is reasonable suspicion that the suspect has committed a criminal act, if there is a reasonable basis for believing that fingerprinting will establish or negate the suspect's connection with that crime, and if the procedure is carried out with dispatch. (p. 817)

However, if conducted in the home, such a seizure must be preceded by judicial authorization.

Summary. Only two constitutional provisions actually place restrictions on identification procedures: the Fourteenth Amendment's due process clause and the Sixth Amendment's right to counsel clause. The Fifth Amendment, while important to confession law, does not come into play when identification procedures are at issue. Similarly, the Fourth Amendment does not apply to identification procedures directly, but it does apply indirectly insofar as probable cause is required if law enforcement officials plan to seize somebody for the purpose of identifying him or her. See Figure 9.1 for a summary of these issues.

FIGURE 9.1 Summary of Constitutional Issues in Identification Procedures

- **Fourth Amendment:** The Fourth Amendment protects from an unlawful search or seizure conducted for the purpose of securing an identification. There is an exception, however: A witness can identify a suspect who is wrongfully seized if the identification is sufficiently independent of the illegal seizure.

- **Fifth Amendment:** Technically, the Fifth Amendment does not apply to identification procedures. This is true even if a suspect is asked to supply a voice exemplar, if this is done for the purpose of identification (and not a confession or admission).

- **Sixth Amendment:** The Sixth Amendment right to counsel exists in the context of making an identification but only in limited circumstances. First, the right to counsel only applies if formal adversarial charges have commenced. Second, a suspect in a photographic array does not enjoy Sixth Amendment protection, regardless of whether charges have been filed.

- **Fourteenth Amendment:** The Fourteenth Amendment's due process clause always applies to identification procedures. In particular, if an identification procedure is too suggestive, it will violate the Fourteenth Amendment.

PRETRIAL IDENTIFICATION TECHNIQUES

As described at the start of this chapter, there are three types of pretrial identification techniques: lineups, showups, and photographic arrays. Each of these identification procedures is described in a following section, with particular focus on how the constitutional restrictions already discussed apply to it.

Lineups

Suspects can be forced to participate in lineups because lineups exhibit physical characteristics, not testimonial evidence. Indeed, suspects placed in lineups can also be required to supply voice exemplars but solely for identification purposes, not as a confession. If a suspect refuses to participate in a lineup, he or she can be cited with contempt (*Doss v. United States*, 431 F.2d 601 [9th Cir. 1970]), and the prosecutor can comment at trial about the suspect's refusal to cooperate (*United States v. Parhms*, 424 F.2d 152 [9th Cir. 1970]).

DECISION MAKING EXERCISE 9.1

Counsel during a Lineup

Sam Linde has been arrested and charged with burglarizing Paul's Appliance Store. Authorities also suspect that Linde has burglarized several other appliance stores in the area, including John's Appliance Store. Suppose the police want to place Linde in a lineup for a witness who saw him leave John's Appliance Store in the middle of the night. Must counsel be present? (You may recall a similar exercise from the previous chapter, which dealt with confessions, but here the issue is a lineup.)

Steps to Minimize Suggestiveness

As noted earlier, the due process clause restricts identification procedures. In particular, an overly **suggestive lineup** violates due process. In *United States v. Wade* (388 U.S. 218 [1967]), the Supreme Court noted that a lineup becomes suggestive when, for instance,

United States v. Wade, 388 U.S. 218 (1967)

> all in the lineup but the suspect were known to the identifying witness, . . . the other participants in a lineup were grossly dissimilar in appearance to the suspect, . . . only the suspect was required to wear distinctive clothing which the culprit allegedly wore, . . . the suspect is pointed out before or during a lineup, and. . . the participants in the lineup are asked to try on an article of clothing which fits only the suspect. (p. 233)

The Project on Law Enforcement Policy and Rulemaking proposes several guidelines for minimizing suggestiveness in a police lineup:

1. The lineup should consist of at least five people, including the suspect.
2. The persons in the lineup should have similar physical characteristics.
3. The suspect should be permitted to choose his or her place in line.
4. Each person in the lineup should be required to take whatever specialized action is required (e.g., to utter certain words).
5. The persons in the lineup should be warned to conduct themselves such that the suspect does not stand out.
6. A lineup should be photographed or videotaped.[2]

[2]From Project on Law Enforcement Policy and Rulemaking, "Eyewitness Identification," *Model Rules for Law Enforcement* series (Tempe, AZ: Arizona State University, 1974).

The International Association of Chiefs of Police (IACP) Legal Center has recommended similar guidelines:

1. A lineup should consist of five to six people.
2. Each participant in the lineup must sign the appropriate waiver form, unless his or her counsel is present.
3. Everyone in the lineup should be of the same sex and race, approximately the same age, and approximately the same height, weight, coloring, build, and so on.
4. Everyone in the lineup should wear approximately the same clothing.
5. The accused should be placed in the lineup at random, so as not to stand out.
6. Persons known to the witness should not be placed in the lineup.
7. Private citizens participating in the lineup (if insufficient numbers of prisoners are available) should sign a written consent form indicating they are aware that no charges have been filed against them, that they are free to leave at any time, and so on.
8. Each witness should view the lineup separately so one witness does not unduly influence another in his or her identification of the perpetrator.
9. Each participant in the lineup should be given the same instructions and should perform the same acts (e.g., supply a voice exemplar).
10. Participants in the lineup should be instructed not to make any statements or comments unless ordered to do so.
11. Frontal and side-profile photographs of the lineup should be taken.
12. A single officer should oversee the lineup procedure.
13. A written waiver of counsel should be obtained if the suspect waives his or her Sixth Amendment right to have counsel present at a *postindictment lineup.*[3]

DECISION MAKING EXERCISE 9.2

Altering the Suspect's Appearance

On December 24, the Toy Emporium was robbed. The suspect escaped before security guards and police could capture him, but store security cameras and several witnesses indicated that the crime was committed by a white male who was 6 feet, 3 inches tall, approximately 270 pounds, between 25 and 30 years of age, wearing a green trench coat, and having long hair. Two hours after the robbery, a man was arrested in a nearby town because he fit the general description of the robber. However, he was *bald* and wearing a *brown* trench coat. A lineup was conducted, in which the suspect was required to wear a wig resembling the long hair of the perpetrator. He was positively identified by several witnesses. Does the act of requiring the suspect to alter his appearance conform to constitutional requirements?

An important restriction concerning lineups is that people cannot be indiscriminately picked off the street for participation. If a person is *not* already in custody, the police must have reasonable suspicion that he or she has committed the crime in question (see *Hayes v. Florida*, 470 U.S. 811 [1985]). However, if the person *is* in custody prior to the lineup, then he or she can be forced to stand in a lineup without any judicial authorization (see *United States v. Anderson*, 490 F.2d 785 [D.C. Cir. 1974]).

■ Showups

A showup is a one-on-one victim/offender confrontation, usually conducted outside the courtroom setting. Specifically, a showup is usually held when the suspect has been apprehended shortly after having committed the crime and the witness is still at or near the scene of the crime. A lineup is always preferable to a showup (because a lineup consists of several potential suspects); however, a showup is necessary under certain circumstances.

[3]International Association of Chiefs of Police, "Eyewitness Identification," in *Legal Points* (Gaithersburg, MD: IACP Legal Center, 1975).

For example, when a witness is immobile and cannot be present at a lineup, a showup is an effective alternative. In *Stovall v. Denno* (388 U.S. 293 [1967]), the Supreme Court noted, "Faced with the responsibility for identifying the attacker, with the need for immediate action and with the knowledge that [the victim] could not visit the jail, the police followed the only feasible procedure and took [the accused] to the hospital room" (p. 295). In a similar vein, a showup is preferable when the *suspect* is immobile (see *Jackson v. United States*, 412 F.2d 149 [D.C. Cir. 1969]).

What Constitutes a Valid Showup?

The police believe that Anna Delgado was involved in a hit-and-run car accident in which a man was killed. They do not have the reasonable suspicion required to seize Delgado for appearance in a lineup, but they do have a witness to the accident. The police decide to take the witness to Delgado's place of work to make an identification. Delgado is identified at her place of employment. Is this type of showup valid?

A showup is sometimes desirable to facilitate prompt identification when time is of the essence. If the witness is required to wait for a lineup, for instance, misidentification is more likely to result. A showup conducted more than 60 minutes after the crime, however, will usually not be upheld (see *United States v. Perry*, 449 F.2d 1026 [D.C. Cir. 1971]). But in at least one case, the Supreme Court upheld a stationhouse showup in which no emergency existed. In *Neil v. Biggers* (409 U.S. 188 [1972]), the Court sanctioned an arranged one-on-one showup, even though it took place well after the point at which the crime in question was committed. The Court noted, given the facts, that there was "no substantial likelihood of misidentification" (p. 201). This was because the witness had an opportunity to view the suspect for almost 30 minutes, under good lighting, prior to the showup.

■ *Neil v. Biggers*, 409 U.S. 188 (1972)

Making a Valid Identification

Wilma Hobbes was unable to identify the man suspected of raping her, even after the police presented her with a photographic array *and* a lineup. Some weeks later, in a chance encounter while walking through the local courthouse, Wilma passed a person whom she believed was her rapist. He was subsequently arrested, and she identified him at the trial. Should this identification be considered valid?

The same constitutional provisions that govern lineups also govern showups. Specifically, the Sixth Amendment right to counsel applies but only after adversarial proceedings have commenced (see *Moore v. Illinois*, 434 U.S. 220 [1977]). Due process protections also exist. If the showup is unnecessarily suggestive under a totality of circumstances analysis, then any identification that comes from it will not be admissible in court.

■ *Moore v. Illinois*, 434 U.S. 220 [1977])

In-Court Showups

What happens when a witness identifies the accused for the first time in *court*? This has happened on occasion and is best described as an **in-court showup**. The key feature of an in-court showup is that the witness has *not* identified the suspect, either in a lineup or related procedure, prior to trial. How do the courts deal with this? The answer is important because an in-court identification is highly suggestive. Namely, the suspect has already been identified by virtue of having been charged with the crime.

The leading case dealing with in-court showups is *Moore v. Illinois* (434 U.S. 220 [1977]), although the focus of the case was on the preliminary hearing, not the trial. The

Court's decision would be expected to apply to criminal trials, as well as other adversarial proceedings, however. Here are the facts from that case, as described by the Supreme Court:

> After petitioner had been arrested for rape and related offenses, he was identified by the complaining witness as her assailant at the ensuing preliminary hearing, during which petitioner was not represented by counsel nor offered appointed counsel. The victim had been asked to make an identification after being told that she was going to view a suspect, after being told his name and having heard it called as he was led before the bench, and after having heard the prosecutor recite the evidence believed to implicate petitioner. Subsequently, petitioner was indicted, and counsel was appointed, who moved to suppress the victim's identification of petitioner. The Illinois trial court denied the motion on the ground that the prosecution had shown an independent basis for the victim's identification. At trial, the victim testified on direct examination by the prosecution that she had identified petitioner as her assailant at the preliminary hearing, and there was certain other evidence linking petitioner to the crimes. He was convicted and the Illinois Supreme Court affirmed. (p. 220)

Notwithstanding the clear violation of the Sixth Amendment in this case (which the Supreme Court also pointed out), the Court pointed to the suggestiveness that occurs when a witness identifies a suspect for the first time at a formal hearing:

> It is difficult to imagine a more suggestive manner in which to present a suspect to a witness for their critical first confrontation than was employed in this case. The victim who had seen her assailant for only 10 to 15 seconds, was asked to make her identification after she was told that she was going to view a suspect, after she was told his name and heard it called as he was led before the bench, and after she heard the prosecutor recite the evidence believed to implicate petitioner. Had petitioner been represented by counsel, some or all of this suggestiveness could have been avoided. (pp. 229–230)

What message is to be gleaned from *Moore v. Illinois*? In general, law enforcement officials should have witnesses identify suspects via lineups, showups, or photographic arrays *prior* to the point at which adversarial proceedings commence. Any of these identification procedures would result in a less suggestive identification than would be likely at trial. Clearly, though, lineups, showups, and photographic arrays can also be suggestive.

■ Photographic Identifications

The last type of identification procedure to be considered in this text is the photographic identification array. It involves displaying a picture of the suspect along with pictures of several other people to a victim or witness for the purpose of identification.

DECISION MAKING EXERCISE 9.5

Creating a Valid Photographic Array

A rapist tells each of his victims that he has already been imprisoned for rape. His latest victim, Sandy, tells the police what he said. The police then show Sandy a single photograph of a rape suspect who was previously imprisoned. Sandy identifies the man in the photo as her rapist. Is this photographic array constitutional? Next, assume that the rapist does not tell his victims he has previously been imprisoned and that the police place his photo in a photographic array with the photos of two other individuals. Is this procedure appropriate? What if five photos are shown: three of the rapist (each from different points in time, with different clothes, etc.) and one each of the other two individuals?

Photographic identification procedures approximate real-life lineups by including several people, but they are not subjected to the same constitutional restrictions that lineups are. In particular, there is no Sixth Amendment right to counsel during a photographic identification. However, due process protections *do* apply.

To minimize due process problems, several photographs of like individuals should be shown to the witness or victim so as to minimize unnecessary suggestiveness. In *Simmons v. United States* (390 U.S. 377 [1968]), the Supreme Court shed some light on the importance of a carefully constructed photographic array:

■ *Simmons v. United States,* 390 U.S. 377 (1968)

> Despite the hazards of initial identification by photograph, this procedure has been used widely and effectively in criminal law enforcement, from the standpoint both of apprehending offenders and of sparing innocent suspects the ignominy of arrest by allowing eyewitnesses to exonerate them through scrutiny of photographs. The danger that use of the technique may result in convictions based on misidentification may be substantially lessened by a course of cross-examination at trial which exposes to the jury the method's potential for error. We are unwilling to prohibit its employment, either in the exercise of our supervisory power or, still less, as a matter of constitutional requirement. Instead, we hold that each case must be considered on its own facts, and that convictions based on eyewitness identification at trial following a pretrial identification by photograph will be set aside on that ground only if the photographic identification procedure was so impermissibly suggestive as to give rise to a very substantial likelihood of irreparable misidentification. (p. 384)

DECISION MAKING EXERCISE 9.6

The Photo Array Revisited

What if for purposes of having several of a suspected rapist's victims identify him in a photographic lineup, the police tell the second witness who the first witness identified, the third witness who the first and second witnesses identified, and so on? What if, instead, the police show five different photographic arrays to a single witness, but the suspected rapist appears once in each array?

As indicated, to conform to due process requirements, multiple photographs of like individuals are ideal for a photographic array. However, in one case, the Supreme Court sanctioned a photographic array consisting of one picture. In *Manson v. Brathwaite* (432 U.S. 98 [1977]), the Court sanctioned an in-court identification based on an earlier identification from a single photograph because it was reliable based on the totality of circumstances. The reasons the Court cited are illustrative. In particular, the Court described how Glover, the witness, who was also a police officer, arrived at his conclusion that the suspect (referred to below as the *vendor* of illegal drugs) in the photograph was, in fact, the perpetrator. Here are the criteria on which the Court focused:

■ *Manson v. Brathwaite,* 432 U.S. 98 (1977)

1. *The opportunity to view.* Glover testified that for two to three minutes he stood at the apartment door, within two feet of the respondent. The door opened twice, and each time the man stood at the door. The moments passed, the conversation took place, and payment was made. Glover looked directly at his vendor. It was near sunset, to be sure, but the sun had not yet set, so it was not dark or even dusk or twilight. Natural light from outside entered the hallway through a window. There was natural light, as well, from inside the apartment.
2. *The degree of attention.* Glover was not a casual or passing observer, as is so often the case with eyewitness identification. Trooper Glover was a trained police officer on duty—and specialized and dangerous duty—when he called at the third

floor of 201 Westland in Hartford on May 5, 1970. . . . It is true that Glover's duty was that of ferreting out narcotics offenders and that he would be expected in his work to produce results. But it is also true that, as a specially trained, assigned, and experienced officer, he could be expected to pay scrupulous attention to detail, for he knew that subsequently he would have to find and arrest his vendor. In addition, he knew that his claimed observations would be subject later to close scrutiny and examination at any trial.

3. *The accuracy of the description.* Glover's description was given to D'Onofrio [a backup officer] within minutes after the transaction. It included the vendor's race, his height, his build, the color and style of his hair, and the high cheekbone facial feature. It also included clothing the vendor wore. No claim has been made that respondent did not possess the physical characteristics so described. D'Onofrio reacted positively at once. Two days later, when Glover was alone, he viewed the photograph D'Onofrio produced and identified its subject as the narcotics seller.

4. *The witness's level of certainty.* There is no dispute that the photograph in question was that of respondent.

5. *The time between the crime and the identification.* Glover's description of his vendor was given to D'Onofrio within minutes of the crime. The photographic identification took place only two days later. We do not have here the passage of weeks or months between the crime and the viewing of the photograph. (pp. 114–116)

Taken together, these five considerations led the Court to this conclusion:

These indicators of Glover's ability to make an accurate identification are hardly outweighed by the corrupting effect of the challenged identification itself. Although identifications arising from single-photograph displays may be viewed in general with suspicion, see *Simmons v. United States*, 390 U.S., at 383, we find in the instant case little pressure on the witness to acquiesce in the suggestion that such a display entails. D'Onofrio had left the photograph at Glover's office and was not present when Glover first viewed it two days after the event. There thus was little urgency and Glover could view the photograph at his leisure. And since Glover examined the photograph alone, there was no coercive pressure to make an identification arising from the presence of another. The identification was made in circumstances allowing care and reflection. (p. 116)

The *Manson* decision suggests that single-photograph arrays are constitutionally permissible, but understand that the witness in this case was a police officer and that the facts were somewhat unusual. It is doubtful that the Supreme Court would uphold a similar identification today. It is always preferable to place multiple pictures of like individuals in a photographic array.

To summarize the points made thus far, see Figure 9.2. It contains the Gallatin, Tennessee, Police Department's policy for the use of showups, lineups, and photographic arrays.

IDENTIFICATION DURING TRIAL

Often, a witness will be called on to identify the perpetrator of a crime (usually, the defendant) *during* the trial. Sometimes, this process is straightforward and subject to little dispute by either party to the case. Other times, an in-court identification can be tainted by an out-of-court identification. (This problem is discussed in the exclusionary rule section toward the end of this chapter.) Accordingly, it is worth considering the witness questioning process.

FIGURE 9.2   Example of a Lineup, Showup, and Photographic Array Policy

9.29 Showup, Lineup, and Photographic Identification

9.29.1 Showup

A showup is the presentation of a suspect to an eyewitness a short time after the commission of a crime. Many courts have suppressed evidence from a showup due to the inherent suggestiveness of the event. Because of this, a lineup is preferred over a showup when possible. However, when exigent circumstances require the use of a showup, the following guidelines will be used:

1. A showup will not be conducted when the suspect is in a cell, restrained, or dressed in jail clothing;

2. A showup will not be conducted with more than one witness present at a time. Witnesses will not be allowed to communicate with each other regarding the identification of the suspect;

3. The same suspect will not be presented to the same witness more than once;

4. The suspect will not be required to put on clothing worn by the perpetrator, speak words uttered by the perpetrator, or perform other actions of the perpetrator; and

5. Officers will not say or do anything that might suggest to the witness that the suspect is or may be the perpetrator.

9.29.2 Photographic Identification

In conducting a photographic identification, an officer must use multiple photographs shown individually to a witness or simultaneoulsy in a book or array. Additionally, an officer will adhere to the following guidelines when conducting a photographic identification:

1. Use at least six photographs of individuals who are reasonably similar in age, height, weight, and general appearance and of the same sex and race;

2. Whenever possible, avoid mixing color and black and white photos, use photos of the same size and basic composition, and never mix mug shots with other snapshots or include more than one photo of the same suspect;

3. Cover any portions of mug shots or other photographs that provide identifying information on the subject, and similarly cover those used in the array;

4. Show the photo array to only one witness at a time;

5. Never make suggestive statements that may influence the judgement or perception of the witness; and

6. Preserve the photo array, together with full information about the identification process, for future reference.

9.29.3 Lineup

A lineup is the live presentation of at least five individuals to a victim. In conducting a lineup, an officer will schedule the lineup on a date and at a time that is convenient for all concerned parties. Additionally, the officer must fulfill necessary legal requirements for the transfer of a subject to the lineup location should he/she be incarcerated at a detention center; make timely notice to the detention center concerning the pickup; and make arrangements for picking up the prisoner. Finally, the officer must make arrangements to have at least four other persons act as "fill ins" at the lineup who are of the same race, sex, and approximate height, weight, age, and physical appearance and who are similarly clothed.

The officer in charge of conducting the lineup will ensure that the following requirements are adhered to:

1. Ensure that the prisoner has been informed of his/her right to counsel if formal charges have been made against him/her, and also ensure that he/she has the opportunity to retain counsel or request that one be provided;

2. Obtain a written waiver on the prescribed departmental form should the prisoner waive his/her right to counsel;

3. Allow counsel representing the accused an opportunity to observe the manner in which the lineup is conducted;

4. Advise the accused that he/she may take any position in the lineup which he/she prefers and may change positions prior to summoning a new witness;

5. Ensure that all persons in the lineup are numbered consecutively and are referred to only by number;

6. Ensure that a complete written, audio, and video record of the lineup proceedings are made and retained when possible;

7. Ensure that witnesses are not permitted to see nor are they to be shown any photographs of the accused immediately prior to the lineup;

8. Ensure that not more than one witness views the lineup at a time and that they are not permitted to speak with one another during lineup proceedings; and

9. Scrupulously avoid using statements, clues, casual comments, or providing unnecessary or irrelevant information that in any manner may influence the witnesses' decision-making process or perception.

Source: From *General Directives Manual*, Gallatin, Tennessee, Police Department (December 28, 1999). Used courtesy of the Gallatin Police Department.

A witness is often called on to identify a suspect at trial.

A criminal trial is a carefully choreographed event, in which each party—the defense and the prosecution—has the right to ask questions as well as attack the credibility or believability of a witness's testimony. By custom, the plaintiff in a *civil case* has the burden of persuasion, so he or she goes first. That is, the plaintiff calls all his or her witnesses and presents the evidence required to build the case. When the plaintiff rests, then the defense has its turn. *Criminal cases* are similarly choreographed. First, the prosecutor presents the state's case, and, then, the defendant presents his or her case. The process of examining witnesses, however, is much more complicated than this simple description. The following subsections are designed to shed light on this often confusing aspect of criminal procedure.

■ Forms of Questions

Witness questioning in a criminal trial proceeds through four stages. The first is **direct examination**, in which the witness is questioned by one party. Next, **cross-examination** takes place. This is where the other party to the case has an opportunity to question the witness. The next two stages are redirect and recross-examination, in which both parties ask further questions of witnesses pursuant to direct and cross-examination.

As a general rule, on direct examination, the questions must be specific but not leading. A **specific question** is one that does not call for a narrative. If the party calling the witness says "Tell us what happened on the day of the incident," the opposing side will probably object. Instead, it is proper to ask something along the lines of "Were you the victim of a burglary on August 6 of this year?"

At the other extreme, it is possible to be too specific, such that a question becomes leading. A **leading question** is, according to the *California Evidence Code*, one "that suggests to the witness the answer that the examining party desires."[4] Leading questions are generally impermissible on direct examination (subject to some exceptions, described later) but permissible on cross-examination. Further, leading questions are permissible on redirect examination but not on recross-examination.

[4]*California Evidence Code*, Section 764. Available online: <www.law.harvard.edu/publications/eviden-ceiii/california.htm>.

Identifying a Leading Question

Determining whether a question is leading is not an easy task. Whether a question is leading is, according to some commentators, a matter of degree. For example, asking a witness to "Tell us anything about anything" is not specific and not leading. At the other extreme, a question such as "You drank one beer per hole when you were golfing, didn't you?" is clearly leading. So, what of the gray area between these extremes? The courts have tried to devise tests for the purpose of determining when questions are leading, but they are not especially helpful.

A safe rule is that a question is leading when it suggests an answer. For example, the question "Is it true that you locked your door when you left the house?" would be leading because it suggests a particular answer—namely, that the door was locked. This question could be rephrased, however, so that it would not be leading. An appropriate question would be "What, if anything, did you do as you left the house?" Another example of a leading question, this time asked by the prosecutor, would be "Isn't that the perpetrator sitting right there at the witness table?"

Leading Questions during Direct Examination

As noted, leading questions are generally not permissible on direct examination, with a few exceptions. As the *California Evidence Code* attests, leading questions on direct examination are permissible "where the interests of justice" require.[5] Similarly, the *Federal Rules of Evidence* permit leading questions on direct examination when it is "necessary to develop testimony."[6]

Leading questions are permissible on direct examination under the following circumstances: (1) in questioning on preliminary or undisputed matters, when the accuracy of the witness's response is more important than the efficiency; (2) when the witness is difficult to control without the use of leading questions (e.g., children, people with mental problems, experts, and others); (3) for the purpose of refreshing the recollection of a forgetful witness (see later for further discussion of the refreshing process); and (4) in eliciting testimony from a hostile witness.

DECISION
MAKING
EXERCISE **9.7**

Identify the Leading Questions

What follows are several hypothetical questions that a prosecutor would ask a witness. Decide whether each is a leading question: (1) "Is the man who assaulted you in the courtroom today?" (2) "Could you point to the man who assaulted you?" (3) "Isn't the man who assaulted you sitting in this courtroom today?" (4) "Isn't that the man who assaulted you?" (5) "Isn't it true that the man who assaulted you is sitting right there?"

The fourth exception requires defining the term *hostile witness*. A hostile witness need not be (and rarely is) a person who is physically hostile. Instead, a witness of this type is considered either *hostile in fact* or *hostile in law*. The former describes a person who is resistant or uncooperative. A witness is hostile in fact when he or she exhibits hostility toward the examiner. For example, a witness who acts as though he or she does not understand a simple question may be considered hostile in fact. A witness who is hostile in law, by contrast, is one who identifies with an adverse party. For example, the widow of a deceased partner is identified with the plaintiff/estate and is so considered hostile in law to the defense (e.g., surviving children, as in a dispute over the deceased's estate).

---

[5]*California Evidence Code*, Section 767.
[6]*Federal Rules of Evidence*, Rule 611(c), issued by the 107th Congress, First Session, December 1, 2001. Available online: <www.house.gov/judiciary/evid2001.pdf>.

Appropriate Questions on Direct Examination

Assume that on direct examination, the prosecutor asks a witness "Can you point to the man who robbed First Security Bank?" The witness points to the defendant. On cross-examination, the defense attorney asks a number of questions designed to impeach the witness: (1) "Isn't it true that you were lying face down on the ground when the bank was robbed?" (2) "Isn't it also true that your glasses were knocked off when you were ordered to lie on the ground?" (3) "And Isn't it true that the robber was wearing a black ski mask, so his facial features were obscured?" What if, in addition to these questions, the defense attorney also asks (4) "Isn't it true that you are legally deaf?" Are these questions appropriate?

Leading Questions during Cross-Examination

Cross-examination is commonly characterized by leading questions. As stated by the *Federal Rules of Evidence*, "Ordinarily leading questions should be permitted on cross-examination."[7]

The use of leading questions during cross-examination serves a number of important purposes. First, it appeals to the conscience and awakens the witness's memory. The hope is to get the witness to tell the truth. Second, leading questions expose inaccuracies or falsehoods expressed during direct examination. Finally, the use of leading questions helps the witness focus on what is important. Considering the issue of witness identification, for instance, the use of leading questions by the defense on cross-examination is intended to demonstrate deficiencies in the prosecution's evidence—specifically, to get the witness to reconsider his or her belief as to who committed the crime in question.

There are a few circumstances in which leading questions are considered *improper* on cross-examination. First, if the questioner goes beyond the scope of direct examination, he or she should not ask leading questions (see, e.g., *MDU Resources Group v. W. R. Grace & Co.*, 14 F.3d 1274 [8th Cir. 1994]). Second, when a party in a civil case calls an adverse party as a witness, the usual method of questioning is reversed. Say, for example, that in a civil asset forfeiture case, the government calls to the stand the defendant's wife, an adverse witness, to testify concerning her husband's marijuana-growing room. In this instance, the direct examination will proceed by asking leading questions (because the questioner is counsel for the adversary) and the cross-examination will proceed by asking nonleading questions. Third, if the calling party is allowed, for some reason, to lead on direct examination (see the exceptions in the previous subsection), then it is likely that cross-examination will be limited to nonleading questions. What if a witness is hostile to both parties? In such a situation, leading questions will probably be permitted on both direct and cross-examination.

Figure 9.3 lists a number of other means for challenging the questions asked of witnesses, which are raised in the form of *objections*. If the judge sustains an objection raised by either party, the witness cannot answer the question. If the witness answers the question anyway, his or her response will be stricken from the record.

Refreshing a Witness's Memory

Witnesses frequently forget the facts to which they are supposed to testify, particularly if a great deal of time has expired between the event witnessed and the date of the in-court testimony. To remedy this problem, the *Federal Rules of Evidence* provide that a witness's prior experience may be *revived* by referral to the witness's prior statements.[8] Of course, if

[7]*Federal Rules of Evidence*, Rule 611(c).
[8]*Federal Rules of Evidence*, Rule 612.

FIGURE 9.3 Common Objections to the Questions Asked of Witnesses

1. *"Asked and answered."* The question simply asked the witness to repeat testimony previously offered in response to a question.
2. *"Assumption of facts not in evidence."* The question asked the witness to comment on information that has not been introduced as evidence.
3. *"Argumentative."* The question was intended to argue with the witness, rather than elicit information from him or her. Such questions are designed to win over the jury.
4. *"Compound."* The question asked more than one question, thus requiring more than one clear-cut answer.
5. *"Misleading."* The question was based on inaccurate evidence or a misinterpretation of events.
6. *"Speculation and conjecture."* The question asked the witness to offer a guess or expectation. Witnesses, especially lay witnesses, are supposed to answer questions based on what they know.
7. *"Uncertain, ambiguous, or unintelligible."* The question has either many meanings or none at all.
8. *"Nonresponsive to the question."* When asked a yes or no question, the witness responded evasively or vaguely.
9. *"Substantive objection."* A rule of evidence has been violated.

---

a witness has no memory whatsoever of the event to which he or she is to testify, then he or she is an incompetent witness. But if a refresher is all that is needed, then the examining party should be able to remind the witness of what he or she said in the past.

The process of refreshing a witness's memory involves two important concepts: (1) present memory revived and (2) past memory recorded. With regard to *present memory revived*, the in-court testimony of the witness is the evidence. By contrast, *past memory recorded* refers to a written account as being the evidence, not the witness's in-court testimony.

A witness's present memory is revived when, for example, he or she is asked to refer to records or other written documents. After the witness views the documents and has his or her memory refreshed, his or her statement to this effect is admitted as evidence. The document(s) shown to the witness is not read or shown to the jury because the *document* is not evidence, only the witness's testimony. Assume, for example, that a witness to a car accident is asked whether she remembers the license plate number of the car that sped away from the scene. She replies that she is uncertain but may be able to recall the number if she can consult some notes she wrote on the day she witnessed the car leaving the scene. If the witness is permitted to rely on her notes and she then remembers the license plate number, then she will be permitted to testify to this effect under a theory of present memory revived.

A somewhat controversial method of refreshing a witness's present memory is *hypnosis*. In the case of *State v. Beachum* (1967 N.M. Lexis 2746 [1967]), a court in New Mexico developed a six-prong test for determining whether the results of a hypnosis session can be used to refresh a witness's memory. The six prongs are as follow:

1. The session must be conducted by a qualified professional.
2. The professional conducting the session should be independent and not regularly employed by the prosecution or defense.
3. Any information given to the hypnotist before the session should be recorded.
4. Before inducing hypnosis, the hypnotist should obtain a detailed description of the facts, as the witness remembers them.

5. All contact between the hypnotist and the person hypnotized should be recorded.
6. Only the hypnotist and the person hypnotized should be present during any stage of the hypnotic session.

When a document is introduced to refresh a witness's present memory, the opposing side is usually entitled to have an opportunity to view it. Under the *Federal Rules of Evidence*, in fact, the adverse party is entitled to see and ask questions about the document used to refresh the witness's memory[9] What of a writing that is consulted by a witness *in advance* of the trial? In such an instance, the document does not necessarily need to be disclosed to the opposing side (see, e.g., *United States v. Blas*, 947 F.2d 1320 [7th Cir. 1991]; *United States v. Williams*, 875 F.2d 846 [11th Cir. 1989]).

There are exceptions, however. In the case of *United States v. Sheffield* (55 F.3d 341 [8th Cir. 1995]), a detective returned a file to the office because he "had trouble keeping up with it on breaks and did not want to carry it with him to the stand" (pp. 343–344); moreover, he did not need it to refresh on any point to which he testified. The defense in that case was not allowed to view the file. Generally, it is within the discretion of the court to decide whether documents viewed prior to trial should be disclosed to the other side.

The second theory of refreshing a witness's memory is, as indicated, *past recollection recorded*. Recall that in such an instance, it is the recording itself that is admitted as evidence. That is, the jury considers the document as opposed to the witness's testimony. The written document essentially becomes a substitute for the witness's memory.

Certain requirements must be met before a past recollection recorded will be admitted into evidence. First, the witness must testify that he or she had personal knowledge of the facts at one time. Second, the witness must testify that the recording was accurate. Third, the witness must testify that he or she does not have adequate recollection of the facts such that he or she could testify to them in court. In addition, the trial judge must be satisfied with the document in order for it to be admissible into evidence. Finally, once a past recollection recorded has been admitted into evidence, the opposing side should have the opportunity to view the document (see *United States v. Kelly*, 349 F.2d 720 [2nd Cir. 1965]; *People v. Banks*, 50 Mich. App. 622 [1974]).

■ Witness Credibility, Impeachment, and Rehabilitation

The topics of credibility and impeachment warrant attention at this juncture. *Credibility*, first off, should be distinguished from *competence*. **Competence** pertains to a witness's ability to remember events, communicate effectively, and understand the importance of telling the truth, as well as the consequences of not doing so. **Credibility** pertains to whether the witness's testimony should be believed. In other words, can the witness's statements be judged as truthful? If the witness is able to remember events, communicate clearly to the jury, and come across as convincing, he or she will probably be regarded as credible.

When discussing competence, courts often refer to the processes of **accrediting** and **discrediting**. A witness can be *discredited* when the prosecution or defense challenges his or her credibility. The process of *accrediting* is the opposite, or when the prosecution or defense attempts to support, bolster, or improve a witness's credibility.

It is important to note that specific rules govern the processes of accrediting and discrediting. First, it is universally agreed on that in absence of an attack on a witness's credibility, no evidence may be introduced to support or bolster his or her credibility. According to the court in *United States v. Price* (722 F.2d 88 [5th Cir. 1983]), "[T]here is no reason why time should be spent in proving that which may be assumed to exist. Every witness must be assumed to be of normal moral character for veracity, just as he is assumed

[9]*Federal Rules of Evidence*, Rule 612.

to be of normal sanity" (p. 90). Simply put, a witness generally cannot be accredited until someone, whether the prosecution or the defense, attempts to *discredit* him or her.

Consider the situation in which a witness is asked to introduce himself or herself and describe his or her background. The prosecution or defense may ask direct questions about the witness's familiarity with the case or, in the case of an expert witness, questions about the witness's occupation, background, and professional accomplishments. This type of questioning would appear to be accrediting, but a certain amount of background information can be supplied by introductory witness questioning without it being considered accreditation. However, there is a point where accrediting must stop, absent an attack on the witness's credibility. Unfortunately, there are few answers as to what amount of accrediting background information is permissible. According to the court in *Government of Virgin Islands v. Grant* (938 F.2d 401 [1985]):

> The jurisprudence of "background" evidence is essentially undeveloped. "Background" or "preliminary" evidence is not mentioned in the evidence codes, nor has it received attention in the treatises. One justification for its admission, at least in terms of the background of a witness qua witness, is that it may establish absence of bias or motive by showing the witness's relationship (or non-relationship) to the parties or to the case. (p. 513)

It is safe to conclude, though, that when the introduction process turns aggrandizing—that is, into more than an introduction—the accrediting of a witness must stop.

In one interesting case, *Pointer v. State* (74 So.2d 615 [Ala. Ct. App. 1954]), the prosecutor, during his closing statement, said that if the prosecution witness had been of bad character, the issue would have been raised by the defense. The court reversed the ensuing conviction, holding that because there was no attack on the witness's credibility during trial, the prosecutor was not permitted to bolster the witness's credibility (see also *Poole v. Commonwealth*, 176 S.E.2d 917 [Va.1970]).

A controversial issue with regard to accrediting concerns what can be done to bolster a witness's credibility when he or she cannot remember important events. If, for example, a witness testifies to a series of events but states that she is unable to remember everything, may another witness be called to offer reasons for the woman's memory lapse? A question similar to this was raised in *United States v. Awkward* (597 F.2d 667 [9th Cir.], *cert. denied*, 444 U.S. 885 [1979]). In that case, the Ninth Circuit Court of Appeals ruled that it was wrong for a prosecution witness to testify that he had been hypnotized and to permit a prosecution expert who had hypnotized that individual to testify about the effects of hypnosis on him or her. As the court observed:

> [U]nless an adverse party attacks the witness's ability to recall by bringing out or exploring the fact of hypnosis, the use of expert testimony to support the efficacy of hypnosis is improper. The party calling a witness should not be permitted to inquire in any way into the witness's ability to recall, or methods of pretrial memory refreshment, until such questions have been raised by the adversary. (p. 679)

In sum, witness accrediting is permissible, but usually "only after the character of the witness for truthfulness has been attacked by opinion or reputation evidence or otherwise" (*Blake v. Cich*, 79 F.R.D. 398 [D. Minn. 1978], p. 403). In legal parlance, accrediting of this sort is also known as *witness rehabilitation*, which is addressed following the discussion of impeachment. Note, however, that this restriction on accrediting is not recognized in most modern evidence statutes, except with regard to character evidence. That is, most modern statutes do not allow accrediting of a witness's character but remain silent as to other types of accrediting.[10]

[10]See Rule 608(a)(2) of the *Federal Rules of Evidence*.

| FIGURE 9.4 | Methods of Witness Impeachment |

1. Establish bias or prejudice.
2. Point to prior convictions.
3. Allege uncharged crimes and immoral acts.
4. Identify contradictions and prior inconsistent statements.
5. Suggest inability to observe events.
6. Challenge reputation.

Impeachment

The formal term for attacking a witness's credibility is **impeachment**. When faced with a witness who is not believed to be telling the truth, the prosecution or defense may decide to challenge the witness's believability before the jury. The jury will then draw its own conclusions as to the witness's truthfulness and believability.

How does impeachment occur? It is most often used by one party to a case against another. Generally, the process begins on cross-examination. The prosecution or the defense can attack a witness's credibility for a number of different, well-established reasons (see Figure 9.4). However, there is little value in attempting to impeach a witness if his or her testimony does not carry much weight or is unpersuasive to the jury. Alternatively, if there is no basis for an attack on a witness's credibility but the opposing side attempts to so do anyway, the impeachment effort could backfire.

Rehabilitation

When the credibility of a witness is attacked, the side that produced the witness can take steps to bolster his or her credibility, either by calling other witnesses or introducing other evidence. This process is known as **rehabilitation**. Rehabilitation occurs during redirect examination, which follows cross-examination. For example, assume the defense calls a witness. The defense attorney will question the witness in an effort to absolve the defendant of guilt. If the prosecution sees fit to impeach the defense witness and succeeds in doing so, the defense attorney will work to rehabilitate its witness during the redirect examination stage.

In discussing the importance of rehabilitation, one court observed that "it is well recognized that once a witness's credibility has been attacked, whether it be by the introduction of evidence of bad reputation, conviction of crime, inconsistent statements, evidence of misconduct, or by incisive cross-examination, the party calling the witness has a right to present evidence designed to rehabilitate the witness's credibility" (*State v. Bowden*, 439 A.2d 263 [R.I. 1982]).

Three common approaches are used to rehabilitate witnesses. The first is to argue that the witness was untruthful in the past but is telling the truth now. Perhaps the witness was once a deceptive miscreant but has been reformed to the extent that he or she can now be trusted. Alternatively, if a witness lies in order to avoid prosecution, it is possible that evidence could be admitted to show that he or she does not have a reputation for telling the truth (*United States v. Lechoco*, 542 F.2d 84 [D.C. Cir. 1976]).

Second, the party seeking to rehabilitate its own witness may argue that a contradictory or inconsistent statement alluded to by the other side was taken out of context. For example, suppose that part of a police report is used to impeach an officer who is giving testimony. The party seeking to rehabilitate the officer may then introduce other portions of the police report that shed light on the part used to impeach the officer (see *Short v. United States*, 271 F.2d 73 [9th Cir. 1959]).

FIGURE 9.5 Tips for Being a Good Witness to Criminal Activity

1. Try to remember the basics:
   a. *Who* was the person?
   b. *What* did he or she do?
   c. *When* and *where* did he or she do this?

2. Was the offender an acquaintance or a stranger? Would you recognize the offender if you saw him or her again?

3. Pay attention to details: Was the offender male or female? What race or ethnicity was he or she? What was his or her approximate age? Height? Weight? Body build? Hair color and length? Any distinguishing features? What clothes was he or she wearing? Was he or she wearing a coat? Hat? Glasses? Did he or she have any weapons? What car was he or she driving, if any? What was the license plate number? What were the make, model, and color of the car? Features of the vehicle?

4. What did the offender say? What did he or she do? How did he or she act? Was anyone injured?

5. Where is the offender, or where did he or she go? How did he or she leave? How long ago did this happen?

Another way to rehabilitate a witness is to introduce other evidence to bolster his or her credibility. For example, suppose that a witness makes a statement *prior* to trial that contradicts his or her statement *at* trial. The other side may then elect to introduce additional pretrial statements supportive of his or her statements at trial. Refer to the infamous O. J. Simpson case and recall that Detective Mark Fuhrman was impeached by the defense because he had made racially discriminatory statements in the past. Had the prosecution called other police witnesses to testify as to Fuhrman's objectivity with regard to race, their testimony may have rehabilitated Fuhrman as a witness.

Given the importance of witness identification, it is useful to know how to be a good witness to criminal activity as well as a good in-court witness. This information is provided in Figure 9.5 and 9.6, respectively.

THE EXCLUSIONARY RULE AND IDENTIFICATIONS

When identification procedures violate constitutional protections, the results from such procedures cannot be considered admissible in a criminal trial. Generally, there are two means by which identifications will be excluded: (1) when an in-court identification is tainted by an out-of-court identification and (2) when a suspect is searched and/or seized improperly and then identified by a witness.

Tainted Identifications

In-court identifications are viewed cautiously. In most such situations, the defendant is sitting in the court room, not surrounded by anyone else matching his or her description (as in a lineup), and sometimes looking sinister or even guilty (e.g., wearing prison coveralls). Furthermore, given the fact that the defendant has been identified—at least, for trial purposes—as the one suspected of having committed a crime, witnesses often jump to the conclusion that the defendant is the one who should be held responsible.

Nevertheless, courts routinely permit in-court identifications. But if an in-court identification is tainted by an out-of-court identification, it may be excluded. This is known as a **tainted identification**.

FIGURE 9.6 Tips for Being a Good In-Court Witness

1. Jurors and other witnesses may be present in the same public areas as you. For that reason, you should not discuss the case with anyone. In addition, jurors may have the opportunity to observe how you act outside of the courtroom. If you see a juror, you are not allowed to speak to the juror, even to say hello.

2. When you are called to testify, you will first be sworn in. You will be asked to raise your right hand and place your left hand on the Bible. When you take the oath, pay attention to the clerk, and say "I do" clearly.

3. When a witness gives testimony, he/she is first asked some questions by the lawyer calling him or her to the stand; in your case, this is an Assistant U.S. Attorney. This is called "direct examination." Then, the witness is questioned by the opposing lawyer (the defense counsel) in "cross-examination." (Sometimes the process is repeated two or three times to help clear up any confusion.) The basic purpose of direct examination is for you to tell the judge and jury what you know about the case. The basic purpose of cross-examination is to explore the accuracy of your testimony. Don't get mad if you feel you are being doubted in cross examination. DO NOT LOSE YOUR TEMPER. An angry or impolite witness will probably not be believed. Always be polite and courteous. In Grand Jury, there is NOT any cross-examination because the defense is not present.

4. Objection is a legal term that means one of the attorneys feels you are being asked an improper question. When you hear a lawyer say "objection," simply stop speaking and wait for the judge to rule on the objection. If the judge decides the question is proper, he/she will overrule the objection. If the judge decides the question is not proper, he/she will sustain the objection. You may not answer the question if it has been sustained. You will be told by the judge or the attorney whether to answer the question if you get confused. In Grand Jury, there are NOT any objections because the defense is not present.

5. Before you testify, try to picture the scene, the objects there, the distances, and exactly what happened so that you can recall the facts more accurately when you are asked. If the question is about distances or time, and if your answer is only an estimate, be sure to say it is only an estimate. Beware of suggestions by attorneys as to distances or times when you do not recall the actual time or distance. Do not agree with their estimate unless you independently arrive at the same estimate.

6. Speak in your own words. Don't try to memorize what you are going to say. Doing so will make your testimony sound rehearsed and unconvincing. Instead, be yourself, and prior to trial go over in your own mind those matters about which you will be questioned.

7. Most important of all, you are sworn to TELL THE TRUTH. Tell it. Every true fact should be readily admitted. Do not stop to figure out whether your answer will help or hurt either side. You are expected to be impartial.

8. The judge and jury are interested in facts that you have observed or personally know about. Do not give your opinion unless asked. Give positive, definite answers when at all possible. Avoid saying, "I think," or "I believe," if you can be positive. If you do not know, say so. Do not make up an answer. Be positive about things you can remember. If you can not remember details, simply say you don't remember.

9. You should only answer the question asked and not volunteer information.

10. The court reporter must be able to hear all your answers, so do not nod your head for a "yes" or "no" answer. Speak loudly and clearly. Also, you will sound best if you do not use words like "yah," "nope," and "uh-huh."

11. Explain your answer if necessary. Give answers in your own words and if the question can not be answered with a yes or no answer, say so and explain.

12. Do not exaggerate. Don't make overly broad statements that you may have to correct. Be particularly careful in responding to a question that begins, "Wouldn't you agree that...?" The explanation should be in your own words. Do not allow an attorney to put words in your mouth.

13. Listen carefully to the whole question you are asked. If you do not understand the question or did not hear it, ask to have it rephrased or repeated.

14. If your answer was not correctly stated, correct it immediately. If your answer was not clear, clarify it immediately. It is better to correct a mistake yourself than to have the attorney discover an error in your testimony. If you realize you have answered incorrectly, say "May I correct something I said earlier?"

15. Sometimes witnesses give inconsistent testimony—something they said before doesn't agree with something they said later. If this happens to you, don't get flustered. Just explain honestly why you were mistaken. The jury, like the rest of us, understands that people make honest mistakes.

16. Sometimes an attorney may ask if you have talked to anybody about the case. It is perfectly proper for you to have talked to people, including the Assistant U.S. Attorney and the case agent before you testified, and you should, of course, respond truthfully to this question.

17. After you have completed testifying, you should not tell other witnesses what was said during your testimony. Thus, do not ask other witnesses about their testimony and do not volunteer information about your own. Once you have been formally excused as a witness, you are free to go.

Source: U.S. Attorney's Office for the Western District of New York, *Tips for Testifying*. Available online:
<www.usdoj.gov/usao/nyw/victim_witness/html/coming_court.htm>.

Unfortunately, it is not always easy to decide whether an in-court identification is "fruit of the poisonous tree." In *United States v. Wade* (388 U.S. 218 [1967]), the Supreme Court held that an illegally conducted lineup does not invalidate later identifications resulting from an "independent source." The independent source in this context does not have to be another person. Instead, if the witness had plenty of time to view the perpetrator prior to the police lineup, showup, or photographic array, then his or her in-court identification may be admissible. Some factors that are considered include

> the prior opportunity to observe the alleged criminal act, the existence of any discrepancy between any pre-lineup description and the defendant's actual description, any identification prior to lineup of another person, the identification by picture of the defendant prior to the lineup, failure to identify the defendant on a prior occasion, and the lapse of time between the alleged act and the lineup identification. (p. 241)

DECISION MAKING EXERCISE 9.9

When Is an In-Court Identification Tainted?

Joan Vines heard noises emanating from Sarah Locklear's apartment and minutes later saw two men, one with black gloves and a brown paper bag, exit from the basement of the building and leave in a green 1956 Plymouth. Vines left her apartment immediately to check on things. She found the door to the Locklear apartment open, and she located a piece of stereo equipment just outside the building. Suddenly, the Plymouth returned, so Vines retreated to her apartment. Through her window, she watched the same two men put the piece of stereo equipment into the car. The men left again in the car, but not before Vines jotted down the license plate number. She later gave it to the police, together with physical descriptions of the two men. Vines was then brought to the station for the purpose of identifying one of the suspects. She was taken to a room in which the suspect was seated. The suspect was requested to stand and turn around, which he did. Vines identified him as one of the two participants in the burglary of Locklear's apartment. Vines later identified the man at his trial for burglary. Will the in-court identification be tainted by the stationhouse identification?

Also, if the witness did not experience intense anxiety or pressure during the criminal act (and thus had plenty of opportunity to absorb what was occurring), it is likely that his or her in-court identification will not be tainted by questionable police conduct during a lineup (see *United States v. Johnson*, 412 F.2d 753 [1st Cir. 1969], *cert. denied*, 397 U.S. 944 [1970]).

■ Identifications Resulting from Illegal Searches and Seizures

What happens if a person is wrongfully arrested—say, based on less than probable cause—and then placed in a lineup and identified by a witness? Can the witness's identification be considered admissible in a criminal trial? What if, further, the lineup is nonsuggestive and otherwise abides by constitutional requirements? Unfortunately, the Supreme Court has offered few answers to these questions.

Davis v. Mississippi (394 U.S. 721 [1969]) is a worthwhile point of departure. In *Davis*, the fingerprint identification of a rape suspect was deemed inadmissible because it was the product of an illegal arrest. However, in *United States v. Crews* (445 U.S. 463 [1980]), the Supreme Court decided otherwise. In that case, Crews was illegally arrested and photographed and then his photograph was shown to a witness, who identified him as the perpetrator. He was tried and convicted based, in part, on the witness's identification.

■ *Davis v. Mississippi*, 394 U.S. 721 (1969)

■ *United States v. Crews*, 445 U.S. 463 (1980)

The Supreme Court agreed with the trial court that the arrest was illegal but still upheld Crews's conviction. Three members of the majority justified this decision by arguing that the "fruit" was gathered at the point of the illegal arrest, as opposed to later, so the derivative evidence doctrine should not apply. The Court further noted that the identification had not "'been come at by exploitation' of the violation of the defendant's Fourth Amendment rights" (p. 471).

DECISION MAKING EXERCISE 9.10

When Is an In-Court Identification Valid?

Valerie DeLuca's house has been burglarized so many times that she has given up all hope that the police will be able to find the perpetrator. She has told them the burglar's *modus operandi* several times and even that he has worn dark clothes and a black ski cap, but the police have still been unable to catch the burglar. Then, one night, the police apprehend a suspicious man, wearing dark clothing and a black ski cap, walking the streets of DeLuca's neighborhood. They don't have probable cause but arrest him anyway. They call DeLuca in to the stationhouse, hoping she can identify the burglar in a lineup. In fact, she is not sure precisely who the burglar is, but she doesn't tell the police she is uncertain. Instead, she is so desperate to put an end to the burglaries that she plays the odds and identifies one of the men in the lineup. That man is then charged with burglary. Later, at trial, DeLuca identifies the man as the one who burglarized her house on several occasions. Will her in-court identification be valid? In other words, even though her testimony would not be truthful, would her in-court identification of the suspect conform to constitutional requirements?

Inasmuch as *Crews* was decided well after *Davis v. Mississippi*, it would seem that an identification resulting from an illegal search and/or seizure would be admissible. Think back, as well, to how the exclusionary rule applies in the *Miranda* context. The Supreme Court held in *United States v. Bayer* (331 U.S. 532 [1947]) that the "fruit of the poisonous tree" doctrine does not control the admissibility of physical evidence obtained from illegal confessions. These decisions, taken together, chip away at the exclusionary rule and reinforce the notion that the "fruit of the poisonous tree" doctrine applies in limited circumstances—primarily, when an illegal search and/or seizure (as opposed to an improper confession or identification) results in the subsequent seizure of tangible evidence.

CONCLUSION

Identification procedures are of three types: (1) lineups; (2) showups; and (3) photographic identifications or arrays. All are bound by the Fourteenth Amendment's due process clause. That is, if they are too suggestive, they will be declared unconstitutional. Lineups and showups are also restricted by the Sixth Amendment's right to counsel clause, but this clause does not apply to photographic identifications. Identification procedures are not protected by the Fifth and Fourth Amendments because an identification is not considered testimony or a seizure.

In addition to pretrial identification, identification during trial is important. As such, it is subject to a number of important restrictions. A criminal trial is a carefully choreographed event, so the order of the questioning proceeds in specific stages. The form of questions, even if simply geared toward having a witness identify the defendant, are also significantly restricted. As a general rule, leading questions are not permissible except on cross-examination. Finally, since some witnesses tend to be untrustworthy, steps can be taken to cast doubt on their credibility. This process is known as impeachment.

An identification, whether occurring during trial or prior to trial, can be excluded as evidence. First, if an in-court identification is tainted by an improper out-of-court identification, it will be inadmissible. Similarly, if an identification takes place following the illegal arrest and/or search of a suspect, it can be excluded, as well.

There are exceptions to these rules, however. Usually, if the identification is sufficiently divorced from any prior illegality, it will be admissible at trial.

REVIEW QUESTIONS

1. Explain how the Sixth Amendment right to counsel applies in the identification context.
2. Explain how due process applies in the identification context.
3. Why are the Fourth and Fifth Amendments not applicable in the identification context?
4. Explain the three types of pretrial identification procedures. How do they differ from one another?
5. What are some methods of reducing the suggestiveness of a lineup?
6. What is an in-court showup?
7. What does a constitutionally valid photographic array look like?
8. Explain how a witness is questioned during trial.

9. What is a leading question? Is it possible for the prosecutor to ask a leading question of a witness who is to identify the suspect in court? If so, how would such a question be phrased?
10. Distinguish between credibility and competence.
11. Distinguish between impeachment and rehabilitation.
12. What is a tainted identification? Why is it important in criminal procedure?
13. Explain the Supreme Court's view on identifications that result from illegal searches and/or seizures.
14. Summarize the tips for being a good witness to criminal activity.
15. Summarize the tips for being a good witness during court.

 Answers to the Decision-Making Exercises for this chapter can be found on pages 507–509.

CHAPTER 10

The Pretrial Process

KEY TERMS

booking
initial appearance
probable cause hearing
pretrial release
bail
bail bonds agents

release on recognizance (ROR)
preventive detention
preliminary hearing
arraignment
guilty
not guilty

nolo contendere
allocution
discovery
nonreciprocal discovery
chain of custody

INTRODUCTION
The Road to Trial

As indicated in Chapter 1, the criminal process begins with one of two events: a warrantless arrest or a criminal complaint. If a person is arrested without a warrant—say, for committing a crime in the presence of a police officer—then the arresting officer will file a criminal complaint against the individual and the formal criminal process will commence. On the other hand, if a warrant is obtained before making an arrest, the warrant must be preceded by a criminal complaint. Basically, the would-be arresting officer needs to convince a judge that a crime has been committed before an arrest warrant will be issued. The complaint serves as a basis for issuing an arrest warrant. The same logic applies if a private party complains as to someone's presumed involvement in criminal activity. In such a situation, an officer will probably investigate the private party's complaint and, if it is meritorious, the officer will apply for a warrant.

Once a person has been arrested, be it with or without a warrant, he or she will be booked at the arresting officer's police station or the sheriff's station (i.e., sheriffs usually run jails). **Booking** consists of filling out paperwork as to who was arrested, the time of the arrest, and the offense involved. Next, the arrestee's personal items will be inventoried. The arrestee may also be photographed and fingerprinted, depending on the offense and the jurisdiction involved. Finally, the arrestee will be placed in a holding cell, jail cell, or similar confinement facility and allowed to contact counsel, family, friends, and other individuals, as needed. (Contrary to popular depictions, more than one phone call is typically allowed.)

KEY CASES

Probable Cause Hearing
- *Gerstein v. Pugh*, 420 U.S. 103 (1975)
- *Riverside County v. McLaughlin*, 500 U.S. 44 (1991)

Pretrial Release
- *Stack v. Boyle*, 342 U.S. 1 (1951)
- *Schall v. Martin*, 467 U.S. 253 (1984)
- *Schilb v. Kuebel*, 404 U.S. 357 (1971)
- *Bell v. Wolfish*, 441 U.S. 520 (1979)

Preliminary Hearing
- *Lem Woon v. Oregon*, 229 U.S. 586 (1913)
- *Coleman v. Alabama*, 399 U.S. 1 (1970)

Discovery
- *Williams v. Florida*, 399 U.S. 78 (1970)
- *United States v. Nobles*, 422 U.S. 225 (1975)
- *Wardius v. Oregon*, 412 U.S. 470 (1973)
- *Brady v. Maryland*, 373 U.S. 83 (1963)
- *Kyles v. Whitley*, 514 U.S. 419 (1995)
- *Arizona v. Youngblood*, 488 U.S. 51 (1988)

THE INITIAL APPEARANCE

Once arrested and booked, the suspect is then brought before a magistrate or judge in what is known as the **initial appearance**. Not all jurisdictions require an initial appearance (also referred to as *presentment*), but for those that do, the suspect must be brought before a judge in a relatively short period of time. Delays of more than six hours are usually unacceptable; they may be necessary on occasion, however, if the time of arrest precludes appearance before a judge (e.g., 1 a.m. on Monday).

The initial appearance is designed to serve a number of purposes. In a misdemeanor case, such as minor in possession, the trial may take place at this stage. In a more serious case, however, the accused will be advised of (1) the reason he or she is being detained (notification of formal charges often comes later at arraignment), (2) his or her protection against self-incrimination, and (3) his or her right to appointed counsel, if need be. The judge may also set bail at the initial appearance, but the bail determination often requires a separate hearing. For ease of exposition, this chapter treats the bail determination as its own hearing, independent of the initial appearance.

The initial appearance is usually swift and subject to few procedural constraints. In fact, there appear to be no Supreme Court cases dealing with constitutional restrictions on the initial hearing. Instead, the probable cause, bail, and preliminary hearings have received much more of the Court's attention. Each will be considered in a later section.

THE PROBABLE CAUSE HEARING

■ *Gerstein v. Pugh,*
  420 U.S. 103 (1975)

In *Gerstein v. Pugh* (420 U.S. 103 [1975], the Supreme Court held that the Fourth Amendment requires a so-called **probable cause hearing** either before or promptly after arrest.[1] A probable cause hearing *before* an arrest usually results in an arrest warrant being issued. Recall that an arrest warrant is issued based on a judge's determination as to whether probable cause is in place. No hearing to determine probable cause after such an arrest is necessary because it would be redundant. However, when an arrest is made *without* a warrant, then a probable cause determination must often be made. The purpose of the probable cause hearing is, in essence, to determine whether there is probable cause to keep a person detained.

The *Gerstein* decision challenged the preliminary hearing system in Florida. Probable cause was determined at preliminary hearings in that state, but those hearings were not required until 30 days after arrest. Basically, a person could be held following a warrantless arrest for 30 days, sometimes longer. The Court held that such a lengthy detention required a judicial determination of probable cause *early on*:

> [W]hile the State's reasons for taking summary action subside, the suspect's need for a neutral determination of probable cause increases significantly. The consequences of prolonged detention may be more serious than the interference occasioned by arrest. Pretrial confinement may imperil the suspect's job, interrupt his source of income, and impair his family's relationship. . . . When the stakes are this high, the detached judgment of a neutral magistrate is essential if the Fourth Amendment is to furnish meaningful protection from unfounded interference with liberty. (p. 114)

The Court decided, in essence, that the prosecutor's decision to charge is not in itself enough to satisfy the probable cause requirement. However, the Court also noted that a probable cause hearing is *not* required after every arrest. An arrest with a warrant, as noted, need not be followed by a probable cause hearing. Likewise, when an arrest is based on a grand jury indictment, a probable cause hearing is not required, either. The

---

[1]Probable cause hearings are not required in certain jurisdictions.

The Probable Cause Hearing

logic for this is that the grand jury performs an investigative function, makes its probable cause determination, and then issues its indictment. Finally, if the detention in question is relatively short, such as when a preliminary hearing follows shortly after arrest, a probable cause hearing will not be required.

DECISION MAKING EXERCISE 10.1

The Probable Cause Hearing

Conner Case was arrested for robbery. He was taken to the police station, booked, and placed in detention. The police department maintains a policy that arrestees may be detained in the city detention facility at the request of an investigatory officer without having formal charges filed against them. Persons who are so detained are said to be "on hold." The main reason for doing so is to stage a lineup in which a witness or a complainant can view and identify the suspect. If the arrestee is suspected of committing multiple offenses, the police department will hold several lineups, extending the period of detention longer than usual. The average time for investigative hold is 26 hours if no charges are filed and 35 hours if charges are filed. Case was held for 35 hours. He is now suing pursuant to 42 U.S.C. Section 1983, claiming that the police violated his Fourth Amendment rights and denied him a prompt probable cause hearing. In particular, he claims that the only valid reasons for delaying a probable cause hearing are those associated with transporting arrestees to the police station, booking them into the jail, and filing charges. How should the court rule?

Procedural Issues Surrounding the Hearing

The lower court's decisions leading up to the Supreme Court's decision in *Gerstein* required that a probable cause hearing resemble an adversarial trial, complete with counsel, compulsory process, and the like. The Supreme Court reversed the lower courts' decisions as to these issues, declaring that the probable cause hearing is a not a "critical stage" of the criminal process. In support of its decision, the Court observed:

> Criminal justice is already overburdened by the volume of cases and the complexities of our system. The processing of misdemeanors, in particular, and the early stages of prosecution generally are marked by delays that can seriously affect the quality of justice. A constitutional doctrine requiring adversary hearings for all persons detained pending trial could exacerbate the problem of pretrial delay. (p. 122, n. 23)

Timing of the Hearing

The Court, in *Gerstein*, required that if it is to be held, the probable cause hearing must take place "promptly after arrest." It did not define what was meant by *promptly*, but in *Riverside County v. McLaughlin* (500 U.S. 44 [1991]), the Court offered some clarification. In a 5 to 4 decision, the Court held that a hearing that takes place within 48 hours of arrest conforms with Fourth Amendment requirements:

■ *Riverside County v. McLaughlin,* 500 U.S. 44 (1991)

> In order to satisfy *Gerstein*'s promptness requirement, a jurisdiction that chooses to combine probable cause determinations with other pretrial proceedings must do so as soon as is reasonably feasible, but in no event later than 48 hours after arrest. Providing a probable cause determination within that time frame will, as a general matter, immunize such a jurisdiction from systemic challenges. Although a hearing within 48 hours may nonetheless violate *Gerstein* if the arrested individual can prove that his or her probable cause determination was delayed unreasonably, courts evaluating the reasonableness of a delay must allow a substantial degree of flexibility, taking into account the practical realities of

pretrial procedures. Where an arrested individual does not receive a probable cause determination within 48 hours, the burden of proof shifts to the government to demonstrate the existence of a bona fide emergency or other extraordinary circumstance, which cannot include intervening weekends or the fact that in a particular case it may take longer to consolidate pretrial proceedings. (p. 44)

Acceptable excuses for delay include "unavoidable delays in transporting arrested persons from one facility to another, handling late-night bookings where no magistrate is readily available, [and] obtaining the presence of an arresting officer who may be busy processing other suspects or securing the premises of an arrest" (p. 57). Unacceptable reasons for delay, by contrast, include the need to gather additional evidence to support the arrest in hindsight and issues of bad faith, such as to inconvenience an individual and make him or her wait for no legitimate reason.

DECISION MAKING EXERCISE 10.2

Timing of the Probable Cause Hearing

With probable cause, Officer Jones arrested three men for impersonating police officers. The men were brought to the police station at 4:30 a.m. and subsequently fingerprinted, photographed, and given breathalyzer tests. The test results showed that all three men were legally intoxicated, with blood-alcohol levels well above the legal limit. The police department maintains a policy that arrestees with blood-alcohol levels of over 0.05 cannot be interviewed until they are sober, so the three men were placed into custody. Eighteen hours later, after sobering up, they were interviewed. All charges against them were dropped following the interviews. The three men sued Officer Jones under Section 1983, arguing that they were denied a prompt probable cause hearing. How should the court rule?

■ PRETRIAL RELEASE

Once a person has been arrested, the question as to whether he or she should be temporarily released (either via bail or on his or her own recognizance) invariably comes up. On the one hand, if the arrestee does not pose a significant risk of flight and has been arrested for a relatively minor offense, **pretrial release** seems a sensible approach. On the other hand, if the arrestee is likely to fail to appear in later proceedings, he or she should probably be jailed pending additional court proceedings.

The Eighth Amendment states, "Excessive bail shall not be required." This simply means that bail cannot be set ridiculously high. Not everyone enjoys a constitutional right to bail, however. In capital cases, for example, bail has always been denied. Consider what the Supreme Court stated in *Carlson v. Landon* (342 U.S. 524 [1952]): "In England, [the Bail] clause has never been thought to accord a right to bail in all cases, but merely to provide that bail shall not be excessive in those cases where it is proper to grant bail. When this clause was carried over into our Bill of Rights, nothing was said that indicated any different concept" (p. 545).

Critics of some courts' decisions to deny bail have argued that because the U.S. criminal justice system presumes innocence, everyone should be released. After all, a defendant cannot be considered guilty until the state proves his or her guilt beyond a reasonable doubt. However, in *Bell v. Wolfish* (441 U.S. 520 [1979]), the Supreme Court stated that the presumption of innocence is merely "a doctrine that allocates the burden of proof in criminal trials" (p. 533).[2]

---

[2]Note that some states have preset bail schedules for low-level offenses. For these states, some of the following discussion is not applicable.

The Pretrial Release Hearing

The Constitution does not specify whether bail should be set in a separate hearing, but numerous Court decisions seem to suggest a separate hearing is warranted. For example, in *Stack v. Boyle* (342 U.S. 1 [1951]), the Court stated that as part of the bail determination, the judge should consider "the nature and circumstances of the offense charged, the weight of the evidence against [the accused], [and] the financial ability of the defendant to give bail and the character of the defendant" (p. 6, n. 3). The Court also stated:

■ *Stack v. Boyle*, 342 U.S. 1 (1951)

> Since the function of bail is limited, the fixing of bail for any individual defendant must be based upon standards relevant to the purpose of assuring the presence of that defendant. The traditional standards as expressed in the Federal Rules of Criminal Procedure . . . are to be applied in each case to each defendant. . . . It is not denied that bail for each petitioner has been fixed in a sum much higher than that usually imposed for offenses with like penalties and yet there has been no factual showing to justify such action in this case. The Government asks the courts to depart from the norm by assuming, without the introduction of evidence, that each petitioner is a pawn in a conspiracy and will, in obedience to a superior, flee the jurisdiction. To infer from the fact of indictment alone a need for bail in an unusually high amount is an arbitrary act. Such conduct would inject into our own system of government the very principles of totalitarianism which Congress was seeking to guard against in passing the statute under which petitioners have been indicted. (pp. 5–6)

Assuming a bail hearing is required, it is also not clear whether a simple probable cause–type hearing is all that is needed or if a more adversarial proceeding is necessary. Since bail is set once charges have already been filed, it would seem that, at a minimum, counsel should be provided. In fact, in *United States v. Salerno* (481 U.S. 739 [1987]), the Court concluded that a federal preventive detention statute that provided for counsel, evidence presentation, and cross-examination was acceptable, but it did not state whether such rights should be afforded to the accused in every bail hearing. Thus, the question of what type of bail hearing is required, if any, remains unanswered. In some situations (and in certain jurisdictions), the bail decision is made during another hearing, such as the initial appearance.

Pretrial Release

The pretrial release decision has traditionally taken one of three forms. The first, and most common, results in release on bail. This is when the court collects a deposit from the individual being released in order to ensure that he or she will appear for later hearings. Second, some arrestees are released on their own recognizance, which means they simply promise to show up when required. Finally, in recent years, the courts have adopted a policy of preventive detention for certain individuals, which involves a calculation as to the arrestee's level of dangerousness and flight risk. Release is denied to those individuals likely to pose a threat to others or not likely to appear at their scheduled hearings.

Bail

Pretrial release with **bail** is a common practice. Indeed, 18 U.S.C. Section 3142 provides that "upon all arrests in criminal cases, bail shall be admitted, except where the punishment may be death." Most states have adopted similar language in their constitutions. California's constitution, for example, provides that "all persons shall be bailable by sufficient sureties, unless for capital offenses when the proof is evidence or the presumption great" (Cal. Const. Art. I, Section 6).

Bail bonds agents sometimes employ bounty hunters to apprehend individuals who have "skipped" bail.

The bail decision is sometimes problematic. More often than not, a judge sets bail according to the nature of the offense in question, not according to the accused's ability to pay.[3] The frequent result of this is that indigent defendants—no matter what they are accused of—languish in jail cells until their court dates because they cannot afford to post bail.

In response to many defendants' inability to post bail, professional **bail bonds agents** have stepped in.[4] These individuals collect a fee from the accused, usually a percentage of bail, and then post a bond so the accused can be released. If the accused shows up at trial, the agent collects his or her fee and gets his or her money back from the court. If the accused fails to show up, then the agent loses the amount posted. In order to avoid such an eventuality, bail bonds agents employ *bounty hunters*, whose job it is to catch the accused and bring him or her before the court. There is a misperception, however, that bail bonds agents can with impunity do whatever it takes to apprehend those who "skip" bail. Indeed, in response to concerns that such agents have been given too much authority, some states have adopted legislation to restrict their activities. Texas is perhaps most restrictive. Figure 10.1 reprints a Texas statute that sets forth the procedures bail bonds agents must follow to rearrest those who skip bail.

DECISION MAKING EXERCISE 10.3

Amount of Bail

Mike Rhodes has been arrested for the crime of robbery, which carries a possible life sentence. The judge sets bail in the amount of $100,000. Rhodes has $12 to his name and no assets. (He rides the bus and lives with his parents.) As such, he cannot even afford the 10 percent deposit typically required to secure a bail bond. His only recourse is to sue under 42 U.S.C. Section 1983, claiming that his Fourteenth Amendment right to equal protection was violated when the judge set bail well beyond his means. Should his lawsuit succeed?

---

[3]See, for example, M. Paulsen, "Pre-Trial Release in the United States," *Columbia Law Review* 66 (1966): 109, 113

[4]Not all states have bail bonds agents.

FIGURE 10.1 Example of Bail Bonds Agent Rearrest Procedures

(a) Any [bail bond agent], desiring to [apprehend] his [bond recipient] and after notifying the [bond recipient's] attorney, if the [bond recipient] is represented by an attorney, in a manner provided by Rule 21a, Texas Rules of Civil Procedure, of the [bail bond agent's] intention to surrender the [bond recipient], may file an affidavit of such intention before the court or magistrate before which the prosecution is pending. The affidavit must state:

(1) the court and cause number of the case;

(2) the name of the defendant;

(3) the offense with which the defendant is charged;

(4) the date of the bond;

(5) the cause for the [apprehension]; and

(6) that notice of the [bail bond agent's] intention to surrender the [bond recipient] has been given as required by this subsection.

(b) If the court or magistrate finds that there is cause for the [bail bond agent] to [apprehend] his [bond recipient], the court shall issue a warrant of arrest for the [bond recipient]. It is an affirmative defense to any liability on the bond that:

(1) the court or magistrate refused to issue a warrant of arrest for the principal; and

(2) after the refusal to issue the warrant the [bond recipient] failed to appear.

(c) If the court or magistrate before whom the prosecution is pending is not available, the [bail bond agent] may deliver the affidavit to any other magistrate in the county and that magistrate, on a finding of cause for the [bail bond agent] to [apprehend] his [bond recipient], shall issue a warrant of arrest for the [bond recipient].

(d) An arrest warrant issued under this article shall be issued to the sheriff of the county in which the case is pending, and a copy of the warrant shall be issued to the [bail bond agent] or his agent.

(e) An arrest warrant issued under this article may be executed by a peace officer, a security officer, or a private investigator licensed in this state.

Source: Texas Code Criminal Procedures, Article 17.19 (2002).

It is important to note an important flaw inherent in the bail bonds agent system. The problem is that the agents, not the courts, gain a certain degree of power. Regardless of what amount the court sets as bail, bonds agents can then decide who gets released or who stays in jail based on the accused's ability to pay. Those who can pay the fee effectively buy their freedom, if only temporarily. Those who cannot pay stay in jail. The courts sit on the sidelines, essentially, while the whole bail bonds process plays out. As described in the decision for *Pannell v. United States* (320 F.2d 698 [D.C.Cir. 1963]):

Certainly the professional bondsman system as used in this District is odious at best. The effect of such a system is that the professional bondsmen hold the keys to the jail in their pockets. They determine for whom they will act as surety—who in their judgment is a good risk. The bad risks, in the bondsmen's judgment, and the ones who are unable to pay the bondsmen's fees, remain in jail. The court and the commissioner are relegated to the relatively unimportant chore of fixing the amount of bail. The result of this system in the District of Columbia is that most defendants, for months on end, languish in jail unable to make bond awaiting disposition of their cases. Instead of being allowed the opportunity of obtaining worthwhile employment to support their families, and perhaps to pay at least in part for their defense, almost 90 per cent of the defendants proceed in forma pauperis, thus casting an unfair burden on the members of the bar of this community who are required to represent these defendants without pay. (p. 699)

Release on One's Own Recognizance

Even though release on bail is the most common form of pretrial release, the courts have experimented with releasing people on their own recognizance. **Release on recognizance (ROR)** means that the accused is released with the assumption that he or she will show up for scheduled court hearings. Naturally, then, this method of pretrial release is reserved for those individuals who pose a minimal risk of flight.

New York City's Manhattan Bail Project was the first significant effort to explore the possibilities of ROR. This program, administered by the Vera Institute, focused on indigent defendants who, according to carefully set criteria, posed a minimal flight risk. Among the criteria considered were previous convictions, the nature of the offense, whether the accused was employed, and whether the accused had roots in the community (e.g., a family to go back to). The program was a resounding success: Only 1.6 percent of those individuals recommended for ROR intentionally failed to appear at court.

The results of the Manhattan Bail Project prompted other cities around the United States to adopt similar programs. And in 1984, Congress passed the federal Bail Reform Act, which provided that any person charged with a noncapital offense "be ordered released pending trial on his personal recognizance or upon the execution of an unsecured appearance bond in an amount specified by the judicial officer, unless the officer determines . . . that such a release will not reasonably assure the appearance of the person as required" (18 U.S.C. Sections 3146–3152).

An important feature of this new legislation was that bail was to be considered only as one of many options to ensure the accused's appearance at trial. Among the other options were restrictions on travel and association, along with other conditions that would ensure the appearance of the accused (see 18 U.S.C. Section 3146[a]). The Bail Reform Act also provided that when bail was to be used, the money should be deposited with the court, not with a bail bonds agent.

The Bail Reform Act further provided that

> the judge shall . . . take into account the available information concerning: the nature and the circumstances of the offense charged, the weight of evidence against the accused, the accused's family ties, employment, financial resources, character and mental condition, the length of his residence in the community, his record of convictions, and his record of appearances at court proceedings or of flight to avoid prosecution or failure to appear at court proceedings. (Section 3146[b])

This is in stark contrast to the notion that judges simply consider the nature of the offense in setting bail.

While the federal government and many states still release people on their own recognizance, this practice is not regularly relied on for serious offenses. In fact, when the offense in question is serious and the accused presents a significant risk of flight, bail may be altogether denied, as the following subsection attests.

Preventive Detention

Growing concern over crimes committed by defendants out on pretrial release prompted some reforms. In 1970, for example, the District of Columbia passed the first **preventive detention** statute, which authorized denial of bail to dangerous persons charged with certain offenses for up to 60 days (D.C. Code 1970 Section 23-1322). Then, Congress passed the federal Bail Reform Act of 1984 (18 U.S.C. Sections 3141–3150), which authorized judges to revoke pretrial release for firearms possession, failure to comply with curfew, and failure to comply with other conditions of release. The act also permitted detention for up to 10 days of an individual who "may flee or pose a danger to any other person or the community" (Section 3142[d]).

Somewhat controversially, the Bail Reform Act of 1984 permitted pretrial detention for *more than* 10 days of certain individuals. Thus, according to the act, if it is deemed that no pretrial release condition "will reasonably assure the appearance of the person as required and the safety of any other person and the community," then indefinite detention is acceptable. For a detention of this nature to conform to Fourth and Eighth Amendment restrictions, a hearing must be held to determine whether the case "involves a serious risk that the person will flee; [or] a serious risk that the person will obstruct or attempt to obstruct justice, or threaten, injure, or intimidate, a prospective witness or jury" (Section 3142[f]).

DECISION MAKING EXERCISE 10.4

Preventive Detention

The Bail Reform Act of 1984 provided that judges can deny bail to certain individuals charged with specific crimes and after finding that "no condition or combination of conditions [attaching to release] will reasonably assure the appearance of the person as required and the safety of any other person and the community" (18 U.S.C. Section 3142[e]). Marty Corelli is a drug kingpin charged with serious narcotics offenses and is presumed to be a significant flight risk. Accordingly, the judge denies bail to Corelli, thereby requiring him to remain in jail until his trial. Is this action constitutional?

Criteria for Release

As indicated already, the Constitution does not guarantee the right to bail. Some people are denied bail, and others are granted bail. What criteria influence a judge's decision? Three factors are typically considered: (1) the accused's flight risk; (2) the level of dangerousness of the accused; and (3) the accused's financial status.

Flight Risk

In *Stack v. Boyle* (342 U.S. 1 [1951]), the Supreme Court declared that the purpose of bail is to ensure the accused's appearance at trial:

> Like the ancient practice of securing the oaths of responsible persons to stand as sureties for the accused, the modern practice of requiring a bail bond or the deposit of a sum of money subject to forfeiture serves as additional assurance of the presence of an accused. . . . Since the function of bail is limited, the fixing of bail for any individual defendant must be based upon standards relevant to the purpose of assuring the presence of that defendant. (p. 5)

This does not mean, though, that a judge can set an unrealistic bail amount, in light of the Eighth Amendment's admonition:

> Admission to bail always involves a risk that the accused will take flight. That is a calculated risk which the law takes as the price of our system of justice. . . . In allowance of bail, the duty of the judge is to reduce the risk by fixing an amount reasonably calculated to hold the accused available for trial and its consequence. But the judge is not free to make the sky the limit, because the Eighth Amendment to the Constitution says: "Excessive bail shall not be required." (p. 8)

In short, a delicate balance needs to be struck to ensure the accused's appearance at trial. Bail should be set at an amount designed to minimize the risk of flight, yet the amount set should not be so much that the accused cannot reasonably afford to pay it, either by cash or by bond.

Dangerousness

Aside from the obvious risk of flight, some defendants are particularly dangerous individuals. Thus, the courts sometimes see fit either to deny bail or to set the amount relatively high because of perceived dangerousness. In *United States v. Salerno* (481 U.S. 739 [1987]), the Supreme Court dealt with a challenge to the Bail Reform Act of 1984 that, among other things, dangerousness cannot be considered. In the Court's words:

> Nothing in the text of the Bail Clause [of the Eighth Amendment] limits permissible government considerations solely to questions of flight. The only arguable substantive limitation of the Bail Clause is that the Government's proposed conditions of release or detention not be "excessive" in light of the perceived evil. . . . [W]hen the government has admitted that its only interest is in preventing flight, bail must be set by a court at a sum designed to ensure that goal, and no more. . . . We believe that when Congress has mandated detention on the basis of a compelling interest other than prevention of flight, as it has here, the Eighth Amendment does not require release on bail. (p. 754)

■ *Schall v. Martin*,
467 U.S. 253 (1984)

The issue of dangerousness, as it pertains to the bail decision, also came up in the case of *Schall v. Martin* (467 U.S. 253 [1984]). There, the Supreme Court upheld a statute that provided for detention of a juvenile who posed a serious risk of committing a crime while on release. The statute was criticized as essentially amounting to punishment without trial, but the Court decided that *punishment* only exists when the government's *intent* is to punish. And since the purpose of the state's detention policy was not to punish but rather to protect the community from a dangerous individual, it was deemed constitutional. Of course, given the problems inherent in predicting criminal behavior, the Court's argument is somewhat specious.

Financial Status

The courts often take into account the accused's financial status in making a bail decision. Surprisingly, bail can be denied simply because the accused is unable to pay it.

■ *Schilb v. Kuebel*,
404 U.S. 357 (1971)

In *Schilb v. Kuebel* (404 U.S. 357 [1971]), the Supreme Court took it upon itself to decide on the constitutionality of a state statute that provided that a criminal defendant who was not released on his or her own recognizance could (1) deposit 10 percent of the amount of set bail with the court, 10 percent of which would be forfeited to the court as *bail bonds costs*, or (2) pay the full amount of bail, all of which would be refunded if the accused showed up at court. The defendant argued that the statute unfairly targeted indigent individuals because they were forced to choose the first option. However, the Supreme Court upheld the statute because "[i]t should be obvious that the poor man's real hope and avenue for relief is the personal recognizance provision" (p. 369). Furthermore, in the words of the Court, "[I]t is by no means clear that [the second option, paying the full amount,] is more attractive to the affluent defendant" (p. 370).

The decision in *Schilb v. Kuebel* was controversial, to say the least, but remember, it focused only on the state statute in question. As a general rule, the courts should take into account the accused's ability to pay in setting bail. Failure to do so may violate the equal protection clause of the Fourteenth Amendment. Setting bail without regard to the accused's financial status also leads to irrational bail determinations, according to one court: Considering the nature of the offense, such a bail determination may lead to the undesired result that "a poor man with strong ties to the community may be more likely to appear than a man with some cash and no community involvement" (*Ackies v. Purdy*, 322 F. Supp. 38 [S.D.Fla.1970], p. 48).

Financial Status and Bail Determination

A prosecution for mail fraud against a postal worker resulted in her conviction. During the trial, the defendant was 30 minutes late in returning after a recess, which the judge had granted so the defendant could go to her office to gather evidence for the defense. Because she was late, the judge ordered her to be held in jail for the balance of the trial. She had not been held in jail prior to the judge's decision. Is this action constitutional?

◾ Treatment of Pretrial Detainees

The Supreme Court has dealt with several cases alleging unconstitutional conditions at pretrial detention facilities. For example, in *Bell v. Wolfish* (441 U.S. 520 [1979]), the Court upheld several of the rules promulgated by New York City's Metropolitan Correctional Center (MCC), including rules prohibiting inmates from receiving books from entities other than publishers, bookstores, and book clubs, as well as outside packages. The Court also upheld unannounced searches of living quarters but was careful to state that when such prohibitions are intended to punish (i.e., instead of to serve some legitimate governmental purpose, such as to ensure the safety and security of inmates), they can violate due process. Quoting the Court:

> [If] a particular condition or restriction of pretrial detention is reasonably related to a legitimate governmental objective, it does not, without more, amount to "punishment." Conversely, if a restriction or condition is not reasonably related to a legitimate goal—if it is arbitrary or purposeless—a court permissibly may infer that the purpose of the governmental action is punishment that may not constitutionally be inflicted upon detainees *qua* detainees. (p. 539)

◾ *Bell v. Wolfish,*
441 U.S. 520 (1979)

Treatment of Pretrial Detainees

Several pretrial detainees at the county jail brought a class action in federal district court against the county sheriff and other officials, claiming that the jail's policy of denying pretrial detainees contact visits with their spouses, relatives, children, and friends violates due process. Should pretrial detainees be constitutionally entitled to contact visits of this nature? If so, why?

In one case, a pretrial detainee argued that unannounced searches of his cell violated the Fourth Amendment. The Court concluded, however, in *Hudson v. Palmer* (468 U.S. 517 [1984]), that prisoners do not enjoy a reasonable expectation of privacy in their cells:

> A prisoner has no reasonable expectation of privacy in his prison cell entitling him to the protection of the Fourth Amendment against unreasonable searches. While prisoners enjoy many protections of the Constitution that are not fundamentally inconsistent with imprisonment itself or incompatible with the objectives of incarceration, imprisonment carries with it the circumscription or loss of many rights as being necessary to accommodate the institutional needs and objectives of prison facilities, particularly internal security and safety. It would be impossible to accomplish the prison objectives of preventing the introduction of weapons, drugs, and other contraband into the premises if inmates retained a right of privacy in their cells. The unpredictability that attends random

searches of cells renders such searches perhaps the most effective weapon of the prison administrator in the fight against the proliferation of weapons, drugs, and other contraband. A requirement that random searches be conducted pursuant to an established plan would seriously undermine the effectiveness of this weapon. (p. 517)

Furthermore, "society would insist that the prisoner's expectation of privacy always yield to what must be considered the paramount interest in institutional security" (p. 528). Prison guards, then, can seize "any articles which, in their view, disserve legitimate institutional interests" (p. 528, n. 8).

THE PRELIMINARY HEARING

The **preliminary hearing** is to be distinguished from the initial appearance, the probable cause hearing, and the pretrial release hearing. It almost always takes place after one of these hearings as well as after the charging decision. According to the decision in *Thies v. State* (178 Wis. 98 [1922]), the preliminary hearing is intended to prevent "hasty, malicious, improvident, and oppressive prosecutions" and to ensure that "there are substantial grounds upon which a prosecution may be based" (p. 103). Finally, the preliminary hearing resembles a criminal trial in that it is usually adversarial.

■ *Lem Woon v. Oregon,* 229 U.S. 586 (1913)

Just as the Constitution does not require a bail hearing, neither is a preliminary hearing required. This was the decision reached in *Lem Woon v. Oregon* (229 U.S. 586 [1913]) and reaffirmed in *Gerstein v. Pugh* (420 U.S. 103 [1975]). Thus, it is up to each state to determine if such a hearing is warranted.

Fortunately, most states, as well as the federal government, require preliminary hearings, at least to a certain extent. Whether a preliminary hearing is required typically depends on a jurisdiction's method of filing criminal charges. In grand jury indictment jurisdictions (i.e., those that *require* that charges be filed in the form of a grand jury indictment), if the prosecutor secures an indictment within a specified time period, no preliminary hearing is required. However, if a prosecutor proceeds by information, then the defendant will usually be entitled to a preliminary hearing before the charges are filed.

Whether a jurisdiction proceeds by indictment or information has important implications concerning the defendant's rights. As discussed further in Chapter 11, the defendant does *not* enjoy the right to counsel during a grand jury proceeding. The defendant does not even enjoy the right to challenge the state's case. In a preliminary hearing, however, both rights exist. Thus, a zealous prosecutor in a jurisdiction that provides for either an indictment or an information-charging decision may opt for indictment because the accused will enjoy fewer rights. Of course, this issue may be moot because accused individuals can and often do waive their right to a preliminary hearing.

DECISION MAKING EXERCISE 10.7

Preliminary Hearings

Assume that a jurisdiction maintains a policy that people charged with misdemeanors will not be given preliminary hearings. Is such a restriction constitutional?

■ The Probable Cause Requirement

Assuming a preliminary hearing is required, the prosecutor has the burden of proving that the case should be *bound over* (i.e., handed over) to a grand jury or go to trial. The standard of proof is *probable cause*. Invariably, this step is confused with the probable cause hearing.

The two hearings can be distinguished as follows: A probable cause hearing dwells on the justification to arrest, whereas a preliminary hearing dwells on whether probable cause exists to proceed with a trial. This is a critical distinction and is often responsible for holding separate probable cause and preliminary hearings in certain states.

The reason for setting probable cause as the appropriate standard for a preliminary hearing is that setting a *higher* standard would essentially make trial pointless. To require proof beyond a reasonable doubt, for example, would make holding a later criminal trial redundant. On the other hand, some people favor having more proof than probable cause because once a probable cause hearing has taken place, the preliminary hearing seems somewhat redundant. To minimize some of the confusion, one court observed that "probable cause to arrest does not automatically mean that the Commonwealth has sufficient competent legal evidence to justify the costs both to the defendant and to the Commonwealth of a full trial" (*Myers v. Commonwealth*, 363 Mass. 843 [1973], p. 849).

Basically, the prosecutor needs to convince the judge that there is enough evidence to proceed with a trial. More specifically, there must be enough evidence to make a judge or jury contemplate which case is more convincing: that of the prosecution or the defense. If it is clear that the state has no case but perhaps had probable cause for arrest, the court will order that the would-be defendant be released.

■ Procedural Issues

Since a preliminary hearing is adversarial in nature, it seems sensible that the right to counsel should apply. According to the Supreme Court, in *Coleman v. Alabama* (399 U.S. 1 [1970]), it does, and the state must provide counsel if the accused is indigent. The Court declared that the preliminary hearing is a critical stage of the criminal process: "Plainly the guiding hand of counsel at the preliminary hearing is essential to protect the indigent accused against an erroneous and improper prosecution" (p. 9).

> ■ *Coleman v. Alabama,* 399 U.S. 1 (1970)

Evidence procedures in a preliminary hearing are markedly different than those in a criminal trial. First, the *Federal Rules of Evidence* state, "The finding of probable cause [in a preliminary hearing] may be based upon hearsay evidence in whole or in part."[5] By contrast, *hearsay evidence* (i.e., what one person previously heard and then repeats while testifying in court) is restricted in a criminal trial. Also, the exclusionary rule does not technically apply in preliminary hearings. Actually, it is not so much that the rule does not apply but rather that the preliminary hearing is an inappropriate stage of the criminal process in which to object to evidence. As the *Federal Rules of Evidence* also state, "Objections to evidence on the ground that it was acquired by unlawful means are not properly made at the preliminary examination."[6] (Note that the *Federal Rules of Evidence* apply to federal courts, not state courts. So some states may maintain different procedures.)

Another procedural matter in the preliminary hearing concerns the right to cross-examine witnesses as well as to use compulsory process to require their appearance. While these rights exist at criminal trials, preliminary hearings restrict them somewhat. In fact, the Supreme Court stated that there is no constitutional right to cross-examine at the preliminary hearing (*Goldsby v. United States*, 160 U.S. 70 [1895]). The court has discretion over the extent of cross-examination, but the bulk of it is reserved for trial.

Some have expressed concern that too much cross-examination at a preliminary hearing may turn it into a full-blown criminal trial. But one court has stated that "past experience indicates that trial strategy usually prevents such a result as both the prosecution and the defense wish to withhold as much of their case as possible" (*Myers v. Commonwealth*). Furthermore, "defense tactics usually mitigate against putting the

---

[5]*Federal Rules of Evidence*, Rule 5.1, issued by the 107th Congress, First Session, December 1, 2001. Available online: <www.house.gov/judiciary/evid2001.pdf>.
[6]*Federal Rules of Evidence*, Rule 5.1.

defendant on the stand or presenting exculpatory testimony at the preliminary hearing unless defense counsel believes this evidence is compelling enough to overcome the prosecution's case" (pp. 856–857).

THE ARRAIGNMENT

Once a person has been formally charged, he or she will be arraigned. The purpose of the **arraignment** is to formally notify the defendant of the charge lodged against him or her. Also at the arraignment, the defendant enters one of three pleas: (1) **guilty**; (2) **not guilty**; or (3) *nolo contendere*. A plea of guilty is an admission by the defendant of every allegation in the indictment or information. Such a plea may be entered for a number of reasons. For example, the defendant may simply elect to be honest and admit responsibility. The defendant may also plead guilty after having made a plea agreement with the prosecution. (Plea bargaining is covered in Chapter 12.)

A plea of not guilty is fairly self-explanatory. The defendant formally contends that he or she did not commit the crime in question. A plea of not guilty will result in a full-blown criminal trial, especially for a serious crime. Finally, a plea of *nolo contendere* means "I do not desire to contest the action." It resembles a guilty plea but is different in the sense that it may not be used against the defendant in any later civil litigation that arises from the acts that led to the criminal charge. Also, in some jurisdictions, if the defendant enters a plea of *nolo contendere*, the court may not ask the defendant whether he or she committed the crime in question. But with a guilty plea, the defendant is required to allocute. **Allocution** is when the defendant explains to the judge exactly what he or she did and why. The allocution is documented in court records and can be used against the defendant in related civil proceedings.

SUMMARY OF PRETRIAL PROCEEDINGS

So far, the discussion has distinguished among five potential pretrial proceedings: (1) the initial appearance; (2) the probable cause hearing; (3) the pretrial release hearing; (4) the preliminary hearing; and (5) the arraignment. The initial appearance usually always takes place, regardless of the method of arrest or even of the charges in question, but it is not constitutionally required. Indeed, for a misdemeanor, the trial may take place at this stage.

The probable cause hearing is also not *required* by the Constitution. Nevertheless, a probable cause determination needs to be made at some stage of the criminal process. If the arrest is by warrant, the hearing is not necessary. If the arrest is warrantless, then a probable cause hearing is necessary but only if a preliminary hearing is not set to take place immediately. Also, if the arrest is premised on a grand jury indictment, a probable cause hearing will not be necessary. In short, the purpose of the probable cause hearing is to avoid unnecessarily lengthy detention unsupported by probable cause.

A few court decisions seem to suggest that a separate pretrial release hearing is required, but the Supreme Court has offered no clarification on this matter. And as a practical matter, it is sometimes worthwhile to make the bail decision in another hearing, such as the initial appearance. Today, whether a bail hearing is required hinges on the jurisdiction in question and the nature of the offense.

Finally, the preliminary hearing is required but only in limited circumstances and for certain offenses—usually felonies. If a prosecutor obtains a grand jury indictment within a short period of time, a preliminary hearing may not be necessary. On the other hand, if the prosecutor proceeds with information, then a preliminary hearing may be required. Once a person has been charged with a crime, he or she will be arraigned.

At the arraignment, the defendant will be notified of the charges against him or her and be allowed to enter a formal plea of guilty, not guilty, or *nolo contendere.*

DISCOVERY

If one learned of the criminal process only by watching courtroom dramas on prime-time television, his or her understanding of the process would be sorely limited. It is rarely the case that prosecutors and defense attorneys are mortal enemies or that one side springs surprise evidence on the other side. Instead, criminal (as well as civil) trials in the United States are carefully choreographed events with few unpredictable twists and turns. In fact, as many a litigator will attest, criminal trials are relatively boring and predictable. Even the most celebrated criminal trial of the 1990s, the O. J. Simpson trial, put the most attentive of observers to sleep at times.

Trials in this country are rarely exciting for several reasons. First, most prosecutors and defense attorneys are not great orators. And second, given the process of *discovery*, each side *knows* what evidence the other side will present, with few exceptions.

Discovery is the process by which each party to a case learns of the evidence that the opposition will present. The *Federal Rules of Evidence* provide that the defendant may, upon request, *discover* from the prosecution (1) any written statements or transcriptions of oral statements made by the defendant that are in the prosecution's possession; (2) the defendant's prior criminal record; and (3) documents, photographs, tangible items, results from physical and mental evaluations, and other forms of real evidence considered *material* to the prosecution's case.[7] Evidence is considered *material* if it is consequential to the case or, more simply, capable of influencing the outcome of the case. If the defense requests items in the second or third categories, then the prosecution will be granted *reciprocal discovery*, where it learns of the defense's evidence. Relevant portions of Rule 16 are reprinted in Figure 10.2 (pages 296–297).

Rule 16 of the *Federal Rules of Evidence* seems to permit a great deal of discovery, but it is actually restrictive. Several states permit even more discovery, such as the names and addresses of all persons known to have any information concerning the case. This means that the prosecution must provide the defense with a list of *all* individuals likely to give testimony at trial—and vice versa.

Discovery ends where strategy begins. That is, while both sides are given great latitude in terms of learning what evidence the opposition intends to use, strategy does not need to be shared. For example, the method of argument that the prosecution wishes to use in order to convince the jury of a particular fact is not subject to discovery. Similarly, the order in which the defense seeks to call witnesses need not be communicated to the prosecution. Strategy is also referred to as *work product.* Work product is not part of the discovery process.

The sections that follow focus on discovery by the prosecution, discovery by the defense, and constitutional issues raised in the discovery process. Be reminded that, consistent with the title of this chapter, discovery is part of the *pretrial process.* It takes place in the hours and days leading up to the criminal trial. But if, for example, a new witness becomes available during the course of a trial, then discovery can take place later in the criminal process, as well.

Discovery by the Prosecution

Discovery by the prosecution is relatively limited because of the constitutional rights enjoyed by criminal defendants. For example, the defense cannot be compelled to provide the prosecution with incriminating information, particularly in the form of statements and

---

[7]*Federal Rules of Evidence*, Rule 16.

FIGURE 10.2 Types of Discovery under Rule 16

(a) Governmental Disclosure of Evidence.

(1) Information Subject to Disclosure.

(A) *Statement of Defendant.* Upon request of a defendant the government must disclose to the defendant and make available for inspection, copying, or photographing: any relevant written or recorded statements made by the defendant, or copies thereof, within the possession, custody, or control of the government, the existence of which is known, or by the exercise of due diligence may become known, to the attorney for the government; that portion of any written record containing the substance of any relevant oral statement made by the defendant whether before or after arrest in response to interrogation by any person then known to the defendant to be a government agent; and recorded testimony of the defendant before a grand jury which relates to the offense charged. The government must also disclose to the defendant the substance of any other relevant oral statement made by the defendant whether before or after arrest in response to interrogation by any person then known by the defendant to be a government agent if the government intends to use that statement at trial. Upon request of a defendant which is an organization such as a corporation, partnership, association or labor union, the government must disclose to the defendant any of the foregoing statements made by a person who the government contends (1) was, at the time of making the statement, so situated as a director, officer, employee, or agent as to have been able legally to bind the defendant in respect to the subject of the statement, or (2) was, at the time of the offense, personally involved in the alleged conduct constituting the offense and so situated as a director, officer, employee, or agent as to have been able legally to bind the defendant in respect to that alleged conduct in which the person was involved.

(B) *Defendant's Prior Record.* Upon request of the defendant, the government shall furnish to the defendant such copy of the defendant's prior criminal record, if any, as is within the possession, custody, or control of the government, the existence of which is known, or by the exercise of due diligence may become known, to the attorney for the government.

(C) *Documents and Tangible Objects.* Upon request of the defendant the government shall permit the defendant to inspect and copy or photograph books, papers, documents, photographs, tangible objects, buildings or places, or copies or portions thereof, which are within the possession, custody or control of the government, and which are material to the preparation of the defendant's defense or are intended for use by the government as evidence in chief at the trial, or were obtained from or belong to the defendant.

(D) *Reports of Examinations and Tests.* Upon request of a defendant the government shall permit the defendant to inspect and copy or photograph any results or reports of physical or mental examinations, and of scientific tests or experiments, or copies thereof, which are within the possession, custody, or control of the government, the existence of which is known, or by the exercise of due diligence may become known, to the attorney for the government, and which are material to the preparation of the defense or are intended for use by the government as evidence in chief at the trial. (E) Expert Witnesses. At the defendant's request, the government shall disclose to the defendant a written summary of testimony the government intends to use under Rules 702, 703, or 705 of the *Federal Rules of Evidence* during its case in chief at trial. If the government requests discovery under subdivision (b)(1)(C)(ii) of this rule and the defendant complies, the government shall, at the defendant's request, disclose to the defendant a written summary of testimony

Source: Federal Rules of Evidence, Rule 16, issued by the 107th Congress, First Session, December 1, 2001. Available online: <www.house.gov/judiciary/evid2001.pdf>.

admissions. The scope of prosecutorial discovery has been addressed repeatedly in the courts via the Fifth and Sixth Amendments.

Fifth Amendment Restrictions

■ *Williams v. Florida,* 399 U.S. 78 (1970)

What if the defense wishes to present an alibi at trial or to assert a defense to criminal liability? Should the prosecutor be permitted to discover this information? The Supreme Court faced the alibi issue in *Williams v. Florida* (399 U.S. 78 [1970]). Florida had a *notice of alibi statute,* which provided that the defendant had to permit discovery of alibi the government intends to use under Rules 702, 703, or 705 as evidence at trial on the issue of the defendant's mental condition. The summary provided under this subdivision shall describe the witnesses' opinions, the bases and the reasons for those opinions, and the witnesses' qualifications.

(2) Information Not Subject to Disclosure.

Except as provided in paragraphs (A), (B), (D), and (E) of subdivision (a)(1), this rule does not authorize the discovery or inspection of reports, memoranda, or other internal government documents made by the attorney for the government or any other government agent investigating or prosecuting the case. Nor does the rule authorize the discovery or inspection of statements made by government witnesses or prospective government witnesses except as provided in *18 U.S.C. Sec. 3500.*

(3) Grand Jury Transcripts.

Except as provided in Rules *6, 12(i)* and *26.2,* and subdivision (a)(1)(A) of this rule, these rules do not relate to discovery or inspection of recorded proceedings of a grand jury.

[(4) Failure to Call Witness. Deleted Dec. 12, 1975]

(b) The Defendant's Disclosure of Evidence.

(1) Information Subject to Disclosure.

(A) *Documents and Tangible Objects.* If the defendant requests disclosure under subdivision (a)(1)(C) or (D) of this rule, upon compliance with such request by the government, the defendant, on request of the government, shall permit the government to inspect and copy or photograph books, papers, documents, photographs, tangible objects, or copies or portions thereof, which are within the possession, custody, or control of the defendant and which the defendant intends to introduce as evidence in chief at the trial.

(B) *Reports of Examinations and Tests.* If the defendant requests disclosure under subdivision (a)(1)(C) or (D) of this rule, upon compliance with such request by the government, the defendant, on request of the government, shall permit the government to inspect and copy or photograph any results or reports of physical or mental examinations and of scientific tests or experiments made in connection with the particular case, or copies thereof, within the possession or control of the defendant, which the defendant intends to introduce as evidence in chief at the trial or which were prepared by a witness whom the defendant intends to call at the trial when the results or reports relate to that witness' testimony.

(C) *Expert Witnesses.* Under the following circumstances, the defendant shall, at the government's request, disclose to the government a written summary of testimony that the defendant intends to use under Rules 702, 703, or 705 of the *Federal Rules of Evidence* as evidence at trial: (i) if the defendant requests disclosure under subdivision (a)(1)(E) of this rule and the government complies, or (ii) if the defendant has given notice under Rule 12.2(b) of an intent to present expert testimony on the defendant's mental condition. This summary shall describe the witnesses' opinions, the bases and reasons for those opinions, and the witnesses' qualifications.

(2) Information Not Subject to Disclosure.

Except as to scientific or medical reports, this subdivision does not authorize the discovery or inspection of reports, memoranda, or other internal defense documents made by the defendant, or the defendant's attorneys or agents in connection with the investigation or defense of the case, or of statements made by the defendant, or by government or defense witnesses, or by prospective government or defense witnesses, to the defendant, the defendant's agents or attorneys.

defenses coupled with a list of witnesses who would support them. The Court found that this type of discovery does not violate the Fifth Amendment because it is not self-incriminating. In fact, the purpose of an alibi defense is to exculpate (i.e., clear) the defendant. According to the Court, "Nothing in the Fifth Amendment privilege entitles a defendant as a matter of constitutional right to await the end of the State's case before announcing the nature of his defense, any more than it entitles him to await the jury's verdict on the State's case-in-chief before deciding whether or not to take the stand himself" (p. 85).

The *Williams* decision extends to other defenses, as well. For example, if the defense intends to argue that the defendant is not guilty by reason of insanity, then the prosecutor needs to be notified in advance of this intention. Alternatively, if the defense intends to argue that the defendant acted in self-defense, then the prosecution should be notified. The reason for requiring this notification is that it provides the prosecutor with an opportunity to plan its argument to the contrary.

The defense often has to supply the prosecution with a witness list, also, and it must contain, at a minimum, the names of all the witnesses. Often, the defense also must provide the prosecution with information about how the witnesses will be testifying. Some people believe that compelling the defense to supply a witness list to the prosecution is incriminatory, but in fact, the prosecution would eventually discover the names and identities of the witnesses, as well as their testimony, at trial anyway.

One item concerning witnesses that the defense is *not* required to share with the prosecutor is whether the defendant will testify. In *Brooks v. Tennessee* (406 U.S. 605 [1972]), the Supreme Court declared unconstitutional a state statute that required the defendant, if he or she was to testify, to do so immediately after the prosecution rested its case. The Court held that the statute violated the Fifth Amendment's privilege against self-incrimination and diminished the defense counsel's ability to make such determinations as to when certain witnesses will testify. In reaching its decision, the Court cited *United States v. Shipp* (359 F.2d 185 [1966]):

> If the man charged with a crime takes the witness stand in his own behalf, any and every arrest and conviction, even for lesser felonies, can be brought before the jury by the prosecutor, and such evidence may have devastating and deadly effect, although unrelated to the offense charged. The decision as to whether the defendant in a criminal case shall take the stand is, therefore, often of utmost importance, and counsel must, in many cases, meticulously balance the advantages and disadvantages of the prisoner's becoming a witness in his own behalf. Why, then, should a court insist that the accused must testify before any other evidence is introduced in his behalf, or be completely foreclosed from testifying thereafter? . . . This savors of judicial whim, even though sanctioned by some authorities; and the cause of justice and a fair trial cannot be subjected to such a whimsicality of criminal procedure. (pp. 190–191)

It may prove useful, for example, to let the defendant take the stand at the *end* of the defense case if it is believed (1) that the defense's case was not particularly persuasive and (2) the defendant can offer testimony likely to sway the jury to support his or her version of events.

DECISION MAKING EXERCISE 10.8

Prosecutorial Discovery

Anne Tator, the local prosecutor, learns from defendant Fred Lyons that he has a list of potential witnesses who will testify on his behalf. Tator learns further that Lyons will not call at least half of the potential witnesses. Nevertheless, Tator demands that Lyons supply her with the full names of everyone on the list, even the names of those who will not testify. Is Tator constitutionally entitled to discover the identities of witnesses whom the defense will not call to testify?

So far, the discussion has focused on Fifth Amendment restrictions to discovery in terms of defenses and witnesses. Of course, discovery extends beyond these areas to real evidence (e.g., a murder weapon) as well as documentary evidence (e.g., a falsified tax return). In general, the Fifth Amendment is not violated when the defense is compelled to disclose real and documentary evidence that will be introduced at trial. The reason for this should, by now, be clear: The Fifth Amendment's protection against self-incrimination is a personal right—that is, it applies to *people*, not to real or documentary evidence. However, the defense *cannot* be compelled to disclose evidence that will *not* be used at trial because of attorney/client privilege.

In summary, the Fifth Amendment is *not* violated when the defense is forced to provide the prosecution, in advance of trial, any of the following: (1) an alibi or other affirmative defense that will be raised at trial; (2) notice of witnesses who are to testify, including their statements; or (3) real or documentary evidence concerning the crime in question. By contrast, the Fifth Amendment *is* violated when the defense is compelled to (1) notify the prosecution as to whether the defendant intends to testify; (2) identify witnesses who will not testify at trial; or (3) disclose evidence that will not be introduced at trial.

Sixth Amendment Restrictions

The Sixth Amendment provides, in relevant part, that the accused enjoys the right "to have compulsory process for obtaining witnesses in his favor." As such, some constitutional challenges to the discovery process have been raised on these grounds.

For example, in *United States v. Nobles* (422 U.S. 225 [1975]), the defense attempted to call a private investigator to the stand whose testimony would have cast doubt on the prosecution's case. The trial judge ruled that the investigator could not testify until the prosecution received portions of the investigator's pretrial investigative report. The Supreme Court upheld this decision. The defense argued that this decision infringed on the accused's right to compulsory process—namely, to call the investigator to the stand. But according to the Court, "The Sixth Amendment does not confer the right to present testimony free from the legitimate demands of the adversarial system; one cannot invoke the Sixth Amendment as a justification for presenting what might have been a half-truth" (p. 241). The defense further argued that being forced to supply information from the investigator's report violated attorney/client privilege, but the Court countered by concluding that attorney/client privilege was basically waived when the defense decided to have the investigator testify about the contents of his report.

■ *United States v. Nobles, 422 U.S. 225 (1975)*

A second Sixth Amendment issue that has been raised with regard to discovery is whether the testimony can be excluded of a witness whom the defense does not inform the prosecution will testify. In *Taylor v. Illinois* (484 U.S. 400 [1988]), the defense called a witness who had not been on a witness list supplied to the prosecution before trial. The trial court excluded the witness's testimony, citing a violation of discovery procedure. The defendant appealed, arguing that exclusion of the witness's testimony violated the compulsory process clause of the Sixth Amendment. However, the Supreme Court ruled that exclusion of the testimony was appropriate and did not violate the Sixth Amendment. The purpose of discovery, the Court noted, is to "minimize the risk that fabricated testimony will be believed" (p. 413). (Also see *Michigan v. Lucas*, 500 U.S. 145 [1991], for further attention to the relationship between certain Sixth Amendment rights and the discovery process.)

In summary, *Nobles* and *Taylor* suggest that it is relatively difficult to infringe on a defendant's Sixth Amendment rights, as far as discovery is concerned. If the defense takes steps to secure a tactical advantage over the prosecution, either by failing to supply a complete list of witnesses or the documents about which witnesses will testify, then the Sixth Amendment right to compulsory process will not be violated. Thus, this particular Sixth Amendment right is a qualified one. Compulsory process must be preceded by granting the prosecution appropriate discovery.

■ Discovery by the Defense

Naturally, discovery should benefit the *defense* more than the *prosecution*. After all, the prosecution presents the state's case against the defendant; it is only sensible that the defense should learn the nature of the prosecution's case. Generally, though, the prosecution has the most information of both parties because it has to prove *beyond* a reasonable doubt that the defendant committed the crime. The defense, by contrast, only needs to raise reasonable doubt in the minds of the jurors that the defendant did *not* commit the crime.

As indicated in the previous section, the Fifth and Sixth Amendments limit what the prosecution can discover concerning the defense's case. The Fifth and Sixth Amendments do not limit defense discovery. This is because the Bill of Rights notifies criminal defendants of their constitutional rights in the justice process. Accordingly, the next few sections focus on the relatively few restrictions to defense discovery and then on discovery permitted by the defense but not the prosecution.

Cases Dealing with Discovery by the Defense

It was already pointed out that in *Williams v. Florida* (399 U.S. 78 [1970]), the Supreme Court required the defense to notify the prosecution as to any defenses, alibi or otherwise, it would assert as well as a list of witnesses who would testify in support of those defenses. In *Wardius v. Oregon* (412 U.S. 470 [1973]), the Court declared that this type of discovery must be *reciprocal.* That is, the Court held that the prosecution must provide the defense with a list of witnesses who will testify in rebuttal to the defendant's alibi or defense:

■ *Wardius v. Oregon,* 412 U.S. 470 (1973)

> [I]n the absence of a strong showing of state interests to the contrary, discovery must be a two-way street. The State may not insist that trial be run as a "search for truth" so far as defense witnesses are concerned, while maintaining "poker game" secrecy for its own witnesses. It is fundamentally unfair to require a defendant to divulge the details of his own case while at the same time subjecting him to the hazard of surprise concerning refutation of the very pieces of evidence which he disclosed to the State. (pp. 475–476)

A key feature of the *Wardius* decision is that it applies only to evidence that is truly reciprocal. More specifically, if the defense supplies the prosecution with a list of witnesses who will testify, the prosecution is not necessarily required to supply the defense with something wholly disconnected from a witness list. This was the decision reached in *United States v. Armstrong* (517 U.S. 456 [1996]), in which the Supreme Court held that the prosecution need only supply the defense with evidence that is "material to the preparation of the defendant's case" (p. 462).

Basically, if the evidence the defense wants to discover is a "shield," or used to refute the state's case, access will be granted. If, by contrast, the evidence is a "sword," or intended to challenge prosecutorial conduct, access will not be granted.

In *State v. Eads* (166 N.W.2d 766 [Iowa 1969]), one court summarized the restrictions on defense discovery even for "shield" purposes. If a *state interest* is likely to be compromised, then the prosecution is not required to disclose evidence to the defense, even if such evidence is intended to be used by the defense to challenge or refute the state's case. State interest precludes discovery by the defense under these circumstances:

> (1) It would afford the defendant increased opportunity to produce perjured testimony and to fabricate evidence to meet the State's case; (2) witnesses would be subject to bribe, threat and intimidation; (3) since the State cannot compel the defendant to disclose . . . evidence [protected by the Fifth Amendment], disclosure by the State would afford the defendant an unreasonable advantage at trial; and (4) disclosure is unnecessary in any event because of the other sources of information which defendant has under existing law. (p. 769)

In the wake of *Eads,* several states have imposed restrictions on defense discovery when certain state interests have been called into question. For example, many states prohibit discovery of the identities of prosecution witnesses until after they have testified so as to prevent defense tampering with (or threatening of) prosecution witnesses.

Defense Discovery

The so-called Jencks Act (18 U.S.C. § 3500 [1976]) provides, in part, that "[i]n any criminal prosecution brought by the United States, no statement or report in the possession of the United States which was made by a Government witness or prospective Government witness (other than the defendant) shall be the subject of subpoena, discovery, or inspection until said witness has testified on direct examination in the trial of the case." Assume that a defendant wishes to obtain a written statement made by one of the prosecution's witnesses *prior* to the witness's testimony. Clearly, the Jencks Act prohibits this. Thus, the defendant claims that the act seriously restricts his ability to conduct an effective defense. If you represented the appellate court charged with deciding on the constitutionality of this section of the Jencks Act, how would you decide?

■ Nonreciprocal Discovery

With few exceptions, discovery is a two-way-street: The defense must supply the prose-cution with certain information and vice versa. For example, as already indicated, when the defense wants to assert an alibi, it must supply the prosecution with that alibi; the prosecution must, in turn, supply the defense with a list of witnesses who will testify in rebuttal to the alibi.

The restrictions on discovery discussed in the previous section, although controversial, do not leave the defense at a disadvantage. In fact, in some circumstances, the prosecution is required to supply information to the defense but *not* vice versa. Specifically, the prosecution has a constitutional duty to disclose exculpatory evidence to the defense. This is significant because, typically, the prosecution is interested in gaining a conviction. A requirement to disclose exculpatory evidence—evidence that would otherwise not be admitted at trial—would seem to damage the state's case, especially since the defense is not required to disclose evidence that *it* will not use at trial. But the Supreme Court disagrees with this position.

Second, the prosecution has a constitutional duty to preserve evidence, but the defense does not. These two methods of so-called **nonreciprocal discovery** are discussed in the two subsections that follow.

The Prosecution's Duty to Disclose Exculpatory Evidence

As a matter of due process, the prosecution has a constitutional duty to reveal exculpatory evidence to the defense. Simply put, if the prosecution obtains evidence suggesting that the defendant is not guilty, it needs to inform the defense of this fact either before or well into the trial (*United States v. Baxter*, 492 F.2d 150 [9th Cir. 1973]; *United States v. Harris*, 498 F.2d 1164 [3rd Cir. 1974]). Numerous Supreme Court cases have supported this important requirement. However, if the evidence clearly establishes factual innocence, it should be disclosed before the trial (*Unites States v. Ruiz*, 536 U.S. 622 [2002]).

First, in *Mooney v. Holohan* (294 U.S. 103 [1935]), the prosecution allegedly used perjured testimony to convict the defendant. The Court held that due process is violated when the prosecution "has contrived a conviction through the pretense of a trial which in truth is but used as a means of depriving a defendant of liberty through a deliberate deception of court and jury by the presentation of testimony known to be perjured" (p. 112). The key in *Mooney* was that the prosecution *arranged* to have a witness give false testimony. If perjured testimony is *not* arranged by the prosecution but, rather, given by a witness on his or her own volition, and if the prosecution learns of this, it will still be bound to notify the defense (*Alcorta v. Texas*, 355 U.S. 28 [1957]).

Next, in *Napue v. Illinois* (360 U.S. 264 [1959]), the Supreme Court held that falsification concerning the credibility of a witness constitutes a due process violation. In that case, a witness testified falsely that the prosecution had not promised him leniency for his willingness to cooperate. Since the prosecutor knew the witness's testimony was false and did nothing to correct it, the defendant's conviction was reversed, since "[t]he jury's estimate of the truthfulness and reliability of a given witness may well be determinative of guilt or innocence, and it is upon such subtle factors as the possible interest of the witness in testifying falsely that a defendant's life or liberty may depend" (p. 269). In a related case, *Giglio v. United States* (405 U.S. 150 [1972]), the promise of leniency was offered by a different prosecutor but the Court still required reversal, citing a due process violation.

■ *Brady v. Maryland,*
373 U.S. 83 (1963)

In *Brady v. Maryland* (373 U.S. 83 [1963]), the Supreme Court drastically altered its previous decisions concerning the prosecution's duty to disclose exculpatory evidence. The Court held that "the suppression by the prosecution of evidence favorable to an accused upon request violates due process where the evidence is *material either to guilt or to punishment*, irrespective of the good faith or bad faith of the prosecution" (p. 87; emphasis added). The Court also eloquently stated:

> Society wins not only when the guilty are convicted but when criminal trials are fair; our system of the administration of justice suffers when any accused is treated unfairly. An inscription on the walls of the Department of Justice states the proposition candidly for the federal domain: "The United States wins its point whenever justice is done its citizens in the courts." . . . A prosecution that withholds evidence on demand of an accused which, if made available, would tend to exculpate him or reduce the penalty helps shape a trial that bears heavily on the defendant. That casts the prosecutor in the role of an architect of a proceeding that does not comport with standards of justice, even though, as in the present case, his action is not "the result of guile." (pp. 87–88)

Whether evidence is *material* is not entirely clear, but in *United States v. Agurs* (427 U.S. 97 [1976]), the Supreme Court offered some clarification. In that case, the defendant stabbed and killed another man with the man's knife. She claimed self-defense but was nevertheless found guilty. The defense argued that because the prosecution had not disclosed that the victim had a prior criminal record, the conviction should be reversed. The Court disagreed, stating that the victim's prior criminal record was not material enough to the question of guilt or innocence. Important to this decision is the fact that the defense did not request information about the victim's prior criminal record at trial, only on appeal. Had the defense explicitly requested such information at trial, a different decision probably would have resulted.

An obvious problem is posed by the *Agurs* decision: If the defense does not know what exculpatory evidence the prosecution has, it cannot request that evidence. Does this mean that the defense should be denied access to exculpatory evidence if it does not request it? In *United States v. Bagley* (473 U.S. 667 [1985]), the Court sought to answer this question but, unfortunately, offered little clarification. In that case, the defense posed a broad request to the prosecution for discovery of "any deals, promises or inducements made to [prosecution] witnesses in exchange for their testimony" (pp. 669–670). The prosecution failed to disclose some of the requested information, but on appeal, the Supreme Court held that this action did not constitute a due process violation. According to the Court, there was no "reasonable probability" that the exculpatory evidence would have influenced the outcome of the case.

■ *Kyles v. Whitley,*
514 U.S. 419 (1995)

What amounts to a *reasonable probability* that the outcome of the case may be altered by failure to disclose exculpatory evidence? In *Kyles v. Whitley* (514 U.S. 419 [1995]), the Court sought to answer this question. Justice Souter's opinion in that case cited four elements of the reasonable probability standard that should be considered. First, reasonable probability does not mean a preponderance of evidence but something less. Second, when exculpatory evidence is included, the reasonable probability standard does not require the defense to show that the other evidence presented by the prosecution is insufficient to prove guilt. Third, once the defense demonstrates a reasonable probability of a different outcome, its job is done. Moreover, the appellate court cannot decide that the prosecution's failure to disclose evidence amounted to a harmless error. Finally, while the prosecution is not required to present every shred of evidence that may prove helpful to the defense, it "must be assigned the consequent responsibility to gauge the likely net effect of all such evidence and make disclosure when the point of 'reasonable probability' is reached" (p. 437).

DECISION MAKING EXERCISE 10.10

Disclosure of Exculpatory Evidence

Leonard Baum was convicted of first-degree murder and sentenced to death. In preparing an appeal, Baum's attorney learned that the state never disclosed certain evidence favorable to Baum. That evidence included eyewitness statements taken by the police following the murder; statements made to the police by an informant, who was never called to testify; and a list of the license numbers of cars parked at the crime scene on the night of the murder, which did not include Baum's car. Baum argues that had this evidence been disclosed at his trial, there would have been a reasonable probability that he would not have been found guilty. Should Baum be granted a new trial?

In summary, the prosecution's constitutional duty to disclose exculpatory evidence hinges on whether such evidence would have a reasonable probability of changing the outcome of the case. The *Brady* decision, which created the reasonable probability standard, suggests that some of the Court's previous decisions in this area may have been altered. For example, it is possible that failure on the part of the prosecution to disclose that a witness presented perjured testimony (i.e., as in *Mooney*) may not amount to a due process violation if the exculpatory evidence does not have a reasonable probability of influencing the jury's decision. Thus, the purpose of *Brady*, *Kyles*, and the cases that followed is not to correct or deter prosecutorial misconduct but only to ensure that due process protections are not violated (see, e.g., *Smith v. Phillips*, 455 U.S. 209 [1982]).

Who makes the decision as to what constitutes a reasonable probability that the outcome of a case will be changed if exculpatory evidence is not disclosed? Depending on the case, it is usually the judge (i.e., court) or prosecutor who makes the decision. If the defense can show that the prosecution possesses exculpatory evidence, then a hearing to determine the reasonable probability issue may be required (see *DeMarco v. United States*, 415 U.S. 449 [1974]). However, if the defense has no knowledge of specific evidence possessed by the prosecution that may prove exculpatory, the prosecution can make the decision. In *Pennsylvania v. Ritchie* (480 U.S. 39 [1987]), for example, the Supreme Court held that the "defendant's right to discover exculpatory evidence does not include the unsupervised authority to search through the Commonwealth's files" (p. 59).

The Prosecution's Duty to Preserve Evidence

The prosecution is also constitutionally bound to *preserve* evidence. Simply put, the prosecution cannot destroy exculpatory evidence in an effort to gain a conviction. To do so would be a violation of due process. For the defense to convince the court that the prosecution has destroyed exculpatory evidence, it must demonstrate three facts: (1) that the evidence was expected to "play a significant role in the suspect's defense"; (2) that the evidence was of "such a nature that the defendant would be unable to obtain

FIGURE 10.3   Example of a Chain of Custody Policy

9.30.2 Statutory Authority and Departmental Authorization

Any property used in commission or furtherance of certain crimes or used for the transportation of stolen property may be confiscated and forfeited as per TCA 40-33-101 through TCA 40-33-204.

Any time an officer wishes to seize or confiscate property under these circumstances (i.e. seizure of vehicle driven by an individual whose license is revoked), the officer will contact his/her shift supervisor for authorization. The shift supervisor will in turn notify the Field Operations Commander and/or the Chief of Police, or his/her designee, for authorization prior to the vehicle being seized by the requesting officer.

9.30.3 Processing Evidence

An officer that has evidence to be placed in the evidence room will make an inventory of the evidence at the location it was found or recovered. The seizing officer will properly handle, mark, and package all evidence, and place the evidence in the collection box in the processing room, if practical, or directly to the evidence room as soon as practical. The seizing officer must turn in evidence no later than the end of his/her tour of duty.

Evidence that cannot be marked directly for identification will be placed in a sealed container or package and the package will be marked for identification. Items will be placed in separate packages when the possibility of contamination exists. Items requiring lab analysis or processing must be placed in separate packages. Money and controlled substances will be counted or weighed by two officers, placed in envelopes

separate from other evidence, and then sealed. Both officers will sign the envelopes.

Evidence of a hazardous nature will be appropriately packaged and stored in accordance with necessary safety precautions. Such substances include, but are not limited to, items that may have been exposed to or contaminated by communicable diseases, hazardous chemicals or waste products, or explosive or highly combustible products. When appropriate, the Property Officer will make arrangements and assume responsibility for storage and control of such items outside the evidence room.

An evidence envelope will be filled out and sealed for all evidence. If the items or evidence is too large to be placed into an envelope, only the evidence control form will be placed with the item. The chain of custody form will be forwarded with all required reports.

The reporting officer will document all evidence on the evidence control form. The reporting officer will fill out a chain of custody form. The departmental case number will be placed on all evidence forms.

If an officer needs a particular piece of property processed, the officer may request Investigations to make arrangements or assist in making arrangements, or may process the property himself/herself. Vehicles are to be processed at the scene, the impound lot, or other appropriate location.

9.30.4 Impounding Evidence

The Property Officer will be responsible for receiving, storing, maintaining, releasing, and accounting for all evidence in compliance with this policy. When evidence is deposited with

Source: From *General Directives Manual*, Gallatin, Tennessee, Police Department (December 28, 1999). Used courtesy of the Gallatin Police Department.

comparable evidence by other reasonably available means"; and (3) that the destruction of the evidence was a result of "official animus toward [the defendant] or . . . a conscious effort to suppress exculpatory evidence" (*California v. Trombetta*, 467 U.S. 479 [1984]). Note that the third requirement departs from the *Brady* decision discussed in the previous section. *Brady* did not consider the prosecution's state of mind relevant.

A case that offers some clarification concerning these three requirements is *Arizona v. Youngblood* (488 U.S. 51 [1988]). There, the Supreme Court stated that "unless a criminal defendant can show bad faith on the part of the police [or prosecution], failure to preserve potentially useful evidence does not constitute due process of law" (p. 58).

■ *Arizona v. Youngblood,* 488 U.S. 51 (1988)

Not only must prosecutors preserve evidence but so, too, must police. Without a proper **chain of custody** (and sometimes even with one), the defense will allege that the evidence was tampered with or tainted in such away that it cannot prove the defendant's involvement in a crime. As such, prosecutors' offices and police departments are very concerned with maintaining a proper chain of custody. Figure 10.3 presents portions of the Gallatin, Tennessee, Police Department's policy for processing and preserving evidence.

the Property Officer or in an approved holding facility, an evidence receipt will be completed by the seizing officer. The evidence receipt will include all information necessary to both document and ensure the integrity or the chain of custody. All drugs will be weighed and monies counted by the Property Officer and recorded on the evidence receipt. The Property Officer will be responsible for developing and maintaining a master file of all evidence invoices and evidence tags completed. This file will be cross-indexed with the chain of custody file.

9.30.5 Storage of Evidence

The Property Officer will assign a storage location for each item of evidence and record this information on the evidence receipt and evidence tag. Evidence requiring added security, including money, precious metals, jewelry, gemstones, weapons, narcotics, and dangerous drugs, will be stored in a separate secured area. Perishable items will be stored in a refrigerator or other suitable container.

9.30.6 Access to the Evidence Room

Only employees authorized by the Chief may enter the evidence room. A log will be kept by the Property Officer to identify each authorized employee entering the evidence room.

9.30.7 Inspections of the Evidence Room

On a monthly basis, the Staff Services Commander will make an inspection of the evidence room to ensure adherence to appropriate policies and procedures. Unannounced inspections of the evidence room will be conducted semiannually as directed by the Chief. An annual inventory of evidence held by the Department will be conducted by a commanding officer, appointed by the Chief, not routinely or directly connected with evidence control.

9.30.8 Recording Transfers of Custody

The Property Officer will be responsible for developing and maintaining a file that documents all changes in custody of physical evidence. The file will be capable of readily identifying the individual or organization currently maintaining custody of all evidence. A written record of all transfers of physical evidence will be made. Officers who assume custody of evidence from the evidence room bear full responsibility for ensuring its security, proper storage, and maintenance, and for the ready retrieval of such evidence upon demand.

9.30.16 Removing Evidence from Storage

When evidence is needed for court, it may be obtained from the Property Room. This will be done during the Property Room hours. The officer will sign the Chain of Custody Form and assume full responsibility for the evidence. The Property Room Officer will note the officer's name and reason for removing the evidence on the appropriate log. All evidence will be returned at the end of the day's proceedings. If the Property Room Officer is not on-duty at the time the evidence is returned, the officer will have his/her supervisor place the evidence in the Evidence Locker. This will be noted on the Chain of Custody Form. If the evidence is in a sealed container or envelope, it will not be opened unless directed by the court or is needed for processing.

CONCLUSION

Before recapping what occurs at each stage of the pretrial process, it is important to underscore the fact that this process differs substantially across the United States. Some jurisdictions follow the procedures outlined in this chapter, in the order presented (see Figure 10.4). Others follow the same basic procedures but in a different order. Still others combine various hearings into a single hearing or do not require them at all. Readers are advised to familiarize themselves with the procedures followed where they reside.

That said, the pretrial process always begins with an initial appearance. This is where, at a minimum, the accused is advised of the charges against him or her. In a misdemeanor case, the trial may take place at this stage. Also, the accused may be advised of his or her privilege against self-incrimination as well as the right to appointed counsel, if he or she is indigent.

Next, a probable cause hearing may be required. In particular, if the defendant is arrested without a warrant, a separate court hearing may be held to determine whether probable cause to arrest existed. This determination can be made independent of any other hearing. The probable cause hearing, if required, needs to be held promptly after arrest, usually within 48 hours.

After the probable cause hearing is the pretrial release determination. The accused may be released on bail, in which case he or she deposits a certain amount of money with the court (possibly through a bail bonds agent) as an incentive to show up for later hearings. Failure to show up will result in, among other things,

FIGURE 10.4 Summary of the Pretrial Process

Initial Appearance

a. Not required in all jurisdictions
b. Trial may take place at this stage for a misdemeanor
c. Accused informed of complaint against him or her, of protection against self-incrimination, of right to appointed counsel if need be

Probable Cause Hearing

a. Only required if arrest is warrantless
b. Must be held within 48 hours, but clear time limit has not been set

Pretrial Release/Bail Determination

a. Methods of ensuring defendant's return are bail, release on recognizance, preventive detention
b. Bail cannot be excessive

Preliminary Hearing

a. Serves as check on charging decision and is not same as probable cause hearing
b. May not be held if defendant waives it or prosecution proceeds by indictment

Arraignment

a. Suspect advised of formal charges filed against him or her
b. Suspect enters plea of guilty, not guilty, or *nolo contendere*

Discovery

a. Prosecution advises defense of evidence to be used in securing conviction
b. Defense advises prosecution of evidence to be used in securing acquittal
c. Prosecution must disclose exculpatory evidence and preserve it

Note: There are several variations to this order of events throughout the United States.

forfeiture of the bail money. A defendant can also be released on his or her own recognizance (ROR). At the other extreme, a defendant who is presumed to pose a significant risk of flight may be held without bail. This tactic is known as preventive detention. Three different criteria are considered in making the pretrial release determination: the accused's (1) flight risk; (2) level of dangerousness; and (3) financial status.

The preliminary hearing is the next stage in the pretrial process. The preliminary hearing differs from the other hearings already discussed in that it is intended to be a check on the prosecution's charging decision.

A preliminary hearing is generally not required, however, if (1) the defendant waives it or (2) the prosecutor proceeds by indictment. In the latter instance, the grand jury essentially serves as an appropriate check on the charging decision.

Next, the arraignment is held. At this stage, the defendant is notified of the charges against him or her. In addition, he or she enters a plea of guilty, not guilty, or *nolo contendere*.

The last stage of the pretrial process discussed in this chapter is discovery. In actuality, however, discovery can take place early on, perhaps prior to a preliminary hearing, or well into a trial. Discovery is the process whereby the prosecution advises the defense of the evidence it will use to secure a conviction. The defense must also disclose the evidence it intends to use to exonerate the defendant. The prosecution has a duty to disclose the defendant's statements in its possession, tangible evidence that will be introduced at trial, test results that are material to the case, and a list of witnesses who will testify for the prosecution as well as the substance of their testimony. The defense, by contrast, must supply the defense with its intended alibi or other defense as well as a list of witnesses (and their statements) who will testify in support of the defense. Finally, the due process clause of the Fourteenth Amendment requires the prosecution to disclose exculpatory evidence to the defense *and* to preserve said evidence while in its custody.

REVIEW QUESTIONS

1. What is booking?
2. What is the initial appearance? What is its purpose?
3. What is the probable cause hearing? What is its purpose? When is it required?
4. How soon after arrest must the probable cause hearing be held?
5. What methods of pretrial release are available? Define each.
6. What are the criteria for pretrial release? How have they been used in court decisions?
7. Summarize the key cases dealing with the treatment of pretrial detainees.
8. What is the preliminary hearing? What is its purpose? When is it required?
9. What rights does the defendant enjoy during the preliminary hearing?
10. What is discovery?
11. Citing cases, what are the restrictions on discovery by the prosecution?
12. Citing cases, what are the restrictions on discovery by the defense?
13. What is nonreciprocal discovery?
14. Explain what it means to require the prosecution to disclose exculpatory evidence. What are the consequences if the prosecution fails to do so?
15. Is the prosecution bound to preserve evidence? The police? If so, how?

 Answers to the Decision-Making Exercises for this chapter can be found on pages 509–512.

CHAPTER 11

Prosecutors, Grand Juries, and Defense Attorneys

KEY TERMS

prosecutor
prosecutorial discretion
selective prosecution
pretextual prosecution
vindictive prosecution
joinder

severance
grand jury
true bill
subpoena *ad testificandum*
subpoena *duces tecum*
transactional immunity

use and derivative use immunity
contempt power
variance
pro se defense
effective assistance of counsel
courtroom work group

INTRODUCTION
Bringing Charges and Mounting a Defense

This chapter turns attention to the roles of the prosecutor, grand jury, and defense attorney. In a way, this chapter does not flow directly from the preceding chapter; for example, the right to counsel attaches to varying degrees well before the pretrial process is set into motion. Similarly, when the services of the grand jury are required, it can perform an investigative function well before the arrest stage of the criminal process. Prosecutors, too, perform a great deal of work before the pretrial process. Nevertheless, the functions of all three parties will be considered here for the sake of an orderly presentation. Just understand that the prosecutor, grand jury, and defense attorney do not necessarily enter the picture *after* the pretrial process has commenced.

This chapter begins by focusing on the prosecutor and, in particular, the decision whether or not to charge. In this vein, this chapter also introduces restrictions on the prosecutor's charging decision as well as the notion of *joinder.* Most of the discussion will be limited to the prosecutor's role leading up to a criminal trial. To delve into the prosecutor's role at trial (e.g., the order and method by which the state's case is presented) would take the discussion into another area. The prosecutor's role at trial is best understood in terms of the law of evidence, a topic not typically taken up in criminal procedure class.

Next, this chapter turns attention to the grand jury. The function of the grand jury is a source of some confusion to criminal procedure students. As such, the role of the grand jury is considered in detail, particularly when a grand jury is required and what roles it performs. This chapter also discusses the secrecy of grand juries, the rights of witnesses testifying before grand juries, and the various methods for challenging indictments. As with the section on the prosecutor, the grand jury section of this chapter is pretrial in nature. Indeed, the grand jury's function ceases once the charging decision has been made.

KEY CASES

Prosecutor

- *Oyler v. Boles*, 368 U.S. 448 (1968)
- *Blackledge v. Perry*, 417 U.S. 21 (1974)
- *United States v. Batchelder*, 442 U.S. 114 (1979)
- *United States v. Lane*, 474 U.S. 438 (1986)

Grand Jury

- *Hurtado v. California*, 110 U.S. 516 (1884)
- *Taylor v. Louisiana*, 419 U.S. 522 (1975)
- *Rose v. Mitchell*, 443 U.S. 545 (1979)
- *Butterworth v. Smith*, 494 U.S. 624 (1990)
- *United States v. Mandujano*, 425 U.S. 564 (1976)

- *United States v. Calandra*, 414 U.S. 338 (1974)
- *United States v. Dioniso*, 410 U.S. 1 (1973)
- *Hale v. Henkel*, 201 U.S. 43 (1906)
- *United States v. Miller*, 471 U.S. 130 (1985)

Defense Attorney

- *Gideon v. Wainwright*, 372 U.S. 335 (1963)
- *Powell v. Alabama*, 287 U.S. 45 (1932)
- *United States v. Wade*, 388 U.S. 218 (1967)
- *Kirby v. Illinois*, 406 U.S. 682 (1972)
- *Johnson v. Zerbst*, 304 U.S. 458 (1938)
- *Strickland v. Washington*, 466 U.S. 668 (1984)

Finally, this chapter turns to the role of the defense attorney in criminal procedure. The Fourth Amendment and interrogation sections of this text have already discussed the function of defense counsel at various stages of the criminal process. Those functions are revisited briefly in this chapter, but the focus is primarily on the defense attorney's role at trial. The bulk of the defense attorney section of this chapter concerns the accused's right to effective assistance of counsel. This chapter also discusses the waiver of counsel and the distinctions between privately retained counsel and public defenders. It concludes with some attention to the so-called courtroom work group.

THE PROSECUTOR

The **prosecutor** performs a valuable function in reinforcing the notion that a crime is an offense against the state. In fact, Article II, Section 3, of the U.S. Constitution states that the executive branch of the federal government "shall take Care that the Laws be faithfully executed." This constitutionally mandated duty to execute the law usually falls on prosecutors. Of course, police officers, as part of the executive branch, do their part to execute the laws, but a strong argument can be made that prosecutors possess even more authority because of their ability to decide whether to bring formal charges against suspected criminals.

Just as police officers have the discretion to decide whether to make an arrest, so, too, do prosecutors have enormous discretion. As the Supreme Court noted in *Bordenkircher v. Hayes* (434 U.S. 357 [1978]), "[S]o long as the prosecutor has probable cause to believe that the accused committed an offense defined by statute, the decision whether or not to prosecute, and what charge to file or bring before a grand jury, generally rests entirely on his discretion" (p. 364). Figure 11.1 presents a sample prosecutor's charging document.

Prosecutors do not have *unlimited* discretion, however. There are important restrictions on their decision to charge. Some stem from the Constitution, while others stem from statutes and other related sources.

The Charging Decision

The prosecutor generally has the authority to decide whether to proceed with charges. This is known as **prosecutorial discretion**. He or she can elect not to charge for a number of reasons, even over strenuous objection on the part of the complainant or victim. The prosecutor's discretion can be further manifested by the act of *plea bargaining* (see Chapter 12); that is, he or she can accept a guilty plea for a lesser offense than the one charged. Finally, prosecutors sometimes have to answer to authorities that mandate, or at least strongly encourage, prosecution.

Deciding Not to Prosecute

The most obvious reason for nonprosecution is lack of evidence. The prosecutor may determine that, based on the evidence presented to him or her by the police, the suspect is innocent. In such an event, there would be no point in proceeding to trial on the slight

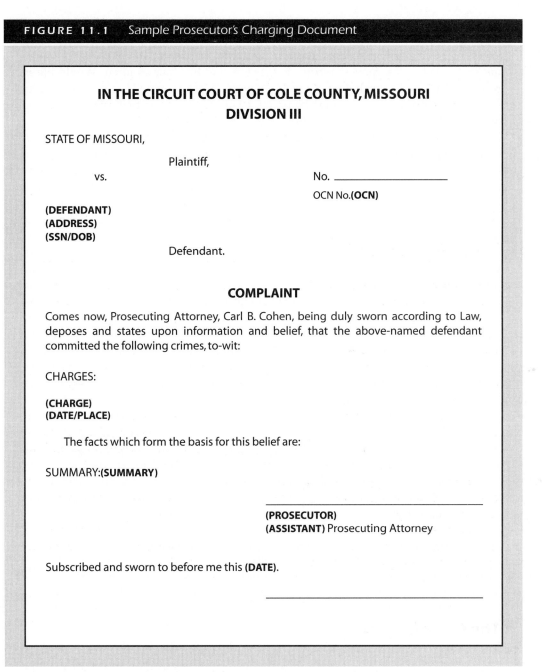

FIGURE 11.1 Sample Prosecutor's Charging Document

IN THE CIRCUIT COURT OF COLE COUNTY, MISSOURI
DIVISION III

STATE OF MISSOURI,

        Plaintiff,

   vs.   No. _____

                                 OCN No.**(OCN)**

(DEFENDANT)
(ADDRESS)
(SSN/DOB)

        Defendant.

COMPLAINT

Comes now, Prosecuting Attorney, Carl B. Cohen, being duly sworn according to Law, deposes and states upon information and belief, that the above-named defendant committed the following crimes, to-wit:

CHARGES:

(CHARGE)
(DATE/PLACE)

    The facts which form the basis for this belief are:

SUMMARY:**(SUMMARY)**

                            _____
                            (PROSECUTOR)
                            (ASSISTANT) Prosecuting Attorney

Subscribed and sworn to before me this **(DATE)**.

                            _____

Source: Used courtesy of Cole County, Missouri.

chance that a conviction would be obtained. Even if the prosecutor *believes* the suspect is guilty, if there is not enough *evidence* to obtain a conviction, then he or she will likely elect not to prosecute.

    There are other reasons not to prosecute, as well. For example, even if the state's case is strong, there may be an incentive not to prosecute. In particular, if it appears the defense's case is *stronger*, then it may behoove the prosecutor to proceed with charges against a different individual.

Nonetheless, prosecutors are human and, as such, can be influenced by the facts of a particular case. Say, for instance, that a law mandates life in prison for growing in excess of 1,000 marijuana plants. Assume further that a suspect apprehended for violating such a law has a spotless record, is married, and has four children. Would life in prison be the best punishment for such an individual, or would a fine, community service, or other sanction be more appropriate? This decision is up to the prosecutor, and depending on the nature of the case, he or she may elect not to proceed with charges.

As another example, California's "three strikes" law requires life in prison for third-time felons. The first two felonies that qualify as "strikeable" under California's law can only be of certain varieties; typically, they are serious offenses. However, the third felony can be of *any* type. Critics of California's "three strikes" law often point to the man who was sentenced to prison for life for stealing a slice of pizza. Had the prosecutor that charged this individual been more sensible in exercising his or her discretion, then public outcry may not have been so significant.

Another reason for not charging traces to economic concerns. Simply put, it is not possible, given the resource restrictions that exist in most public agencies (prosecutors' offices included), to proceed with charges against every suspect. Not having the time to build a case because of a high caseload may effectively force a prosecutor to be lenient with certain individuals.

DECISION MAKING EXERCISE 11.1

Reasons for Nonprosecution

Another controversial reason for nonprosecution is a byproduct of the United States' so-called war on drugs. Civil asset forfeiture statutes permit the forfeiture of money and property tied to criminal activity—most frequently, the illicit drug trade. Many asset forfeiture statutes permit forfeited proceeds to go to the executive branch, which usually means the police but sometimes prosecutors. Some have argued that when there is not enough evidence to proceed with a criminal case, prosecutors can opt to pursue civil forfeiture, for which the burden of proof is generally lower. And as an added bonus, if a forfeiture action succeeds and a person's property is forfeited to the state, then the prosecutor may reap a financial reward for selecting a civil proceeding instead of a criminal one. Is the possibility of civil asset forfeiture a legitimate reason not to prosecute? That is, if a prosecutor chooses not to press criminal charges against someone, instead opting for forfeiture, should the decision be considered constitutional?

Challenging the Decision Not to Prosecute

A prosecutor's decision not to press charges is rarely challenged, but on occasion, higher authorities may get involved when they disagree with a prosecutor's decision. Failure to press charges can sometimes be questioned by a court, which can provide relief to individuals who disagree with the prosecutor's decision (e.g., *NAACP v. Levi*, 418 F.Supp. 1109 [D.D.C. 1976]). Other times, a prosecutor's supervisor or other high-ranking official may step in. According to one source, "Many states by statute confer upon the attorney general the power to initiate prosecution in cases where the local prosecutor has failed to act. In practice, however, attorneys general have seldom exercised much control over local prosecuting attorneys."[1]

---

[1]Y. Kamisar, W. LaFave, and J. Israel, *Modern Criminal Procedure*, 9th ed. (St. Paul, MN: West, 1999), p. 894.

The Decision Not to Charge

Following are the facts reported by the U.S. District Court for the District of Columbia in *NAACP v. Levi* (418 F. Supp. 1109 [D.D.C. 1976]), discussed on the previous page:

> On May 31, 1971, Carnell Russ, a 24-year-old black, while operating his motor vehicle on an Arkansas highway, was arrested for an alleged speeding violation by Jerry Mac Green, a white state trooper. Russ was accompanied by his wife, their minor children and an adult cousin. The trooper directed him to the County Courthouse. Russ complied and upon arrival, parked his vehicle and was escorted into the Courthouse by the arresting trooper and two other white law enforcement officers, Charles Ratliff and Norman Draper. Minutes later, Russ returned to the vehicle where his family awaited. He requested and received from his wife sufficient money to post the necessary collateral. He then joined the three officers who were close by observing his actions. The four retraced their steps with Russ again in custody. A short time thereafter, Mrs. Russ first observed two of the officers leave and minutes later an ambulance depart from the rear of the Courthouse area where her husband had just entered in the officers' custody. She later learned that Mr. Russ, while under detention, had been shot in the center of his forehead by Ratliff and then transported to a hospital. Green and Draper were the sole witnesses to the shooting. Her husband died from the gunshot wound within hours. (p. 1112)

Ratliff was indicted and found not guilty of voluntary manslaughter pursuant to an investigation by the state police. Criminal charges were not brought against the other two officers, and the case was closed. Does the prosecutor's decision not to pursue charges against the other officers seem reasonable?

Another way of preventing prosecutors from abusing their discretion (i.e., by failing to act) is to require them to abide by standards of conduct. These standards help prosecutors decide which cases are worthy of prosecution as well as what charges to pursue, all the while ensuring that they act in accordance with the law. Figure 11.2 (pages 314–315) presents portions of the "Code of Conduct for Judicial Employees," published by the Administrative Office of the U.S. Courts.

Some U.S. jurisdictions require court approval of a prosecutor's decision not to pursue charges. The prosecutor is typically required to explain to the court in writing his or her reasons for failing to prosecute. While this approach may seem sensible on its face, the Supreme Court has been somewhat critical of judicial review of prosecutorial decisions. In *Wayte v. United States* (470 U.S. 598 [1985]), the Court gave this reason for avoiding judicial oversight: "Such factors as the strength of the case, the prosecution's general deterrence value, the Government's overall enforcement plan are not readily susceptible to the kind of analysis the courts are competent to make" (p. 606).

In general, if the prosecutor's decision not to press charges stems from legitimate factors, such as lack of evidence or case backlog, then the decision should be honored. The prosecutor's decision should be honored even if he or she agrees to dismiss criminal charges if the defendant agrees not to file a civil suit.

Another Decision Not to Charge

Chief Lord, of the Springfield Police Department, arrested Nancy Simpson for tampering with a witness, Terri Flanders, the alleged victim of an assault by a friend of Simpson's. Simpson hired an attorney, and discussions with the local prosecutor ensued. Simpson agreed to sign a written release—in which she promised not to sue the city, its officials, or the alleged victim of the assault—if the prosecutor dismissed the criminal charges. The criminal charges were dropped. Is fear of being sued a valid reason not to prosecute?

FIGURE 11.2   Code of Conduct for Judicial Employees

A. Code of Conduct for Judicial Employees.

CANON 1: A JUDICIAL EMPLOYEE SHOULD UPHOLD THE INTEGRITY AND INDEPENDENCE OF THE JUDICIARY AND OF THE JUDICIAL EMPLOYEE'S OFFICE

An independent and honorable Judiciary is indispensable to justice in our society. A judicial employee should personally observe high standards of conduct so that the integrity and independence of the Judiciary are preserved and the judicial employee's office reflects a devotion to serving the public. Judicial employees should require adherence to such standards by personnel subject to their direction and control. The provisions of this code should be construed and applied to further these objectives. The standards of this code shall not affect or preclude other more stringent standards required by law, by court order, or by the appointing authority.

CANON 2: A JUDICIAL EMPLOYEE SHOULD AVOID IMPROPRIETY AND THE APPEARANCE OF IMPROPRIETY IN ALL ACTIVITIES

A judicial employee should not engage in any activities that would put into question the propriety of the judicial employee's conduct in carrying out the duties of the office. A judicial employee should not allow family, social, or other relationships to influence official conduct or judgment. A judicial employee should not lend the prestige of the office to advance or to appear to advance the private interests of others. A judicial employee should not use public office for private gain.

CANON 3: A JUDICIAL EMPLOYEE SHOULD ADHERE TO APPROPRIATE STANDARDS IN PERFORMING THE DUTIES OF THE OFFICE

In performing the duties prescribed by law, by resolution of the Judicial Conference of the United States, by court order, or by the judicial employee's appointing authority, the following standards apply:

A. A judicial employee should respect and comply with the law and these canons. A judicial employee should report to the appropriate supervising authority any attempt to induce the judicial employee to violate these canons.

Note: A number of criminal statutes of general applicability govern federal employees' performance of official duties. These include:

18 U.S.C. § 201 (bribery of public officials and witnesses);

18 U.S.C. § 211 (acceptance or solicitation to obtain appointive public office);

18 U.S.C. § 285 (taking or using papers relating to government claims);

18 U.S.C. § 287 (false, fictitious, or fraudulent claims against the government);

18 U.S.C. § 508 (counterfeiting or forging transportation requests);

18 U.S.C. § 641 (embezzlement or conversion of government money, property, or records);

18 U.S.C. § 643 (failing to account for public money);

18 U.S.C. § 798 and 50 U.S.C. § 783 (disclosure of classified information);

18 U.S.C. § 1001 (fraud or false statements in a government matter);

18 U.S.C. § 1719 (misuse of franking privilege);

18 U.S.C. § 2071 (concealing, removing, or mutilating a public record);

31 U.S.C. § 1344 (misuse of government vehicle);

31 U.S.C. § 3729 (false claims against the government).

In addition, provisions of specific applicability to court officers include:

18 U.S.C. § § 153,154 (court officers embezzling or purchasing property from bankruptcy estate);

18 U.S.C. § 645 (embezzlement and theft by court officers);

18 U.S.C. § 646 (court officers failing to deposit registry moneys);

18 U.S.C. § 647 (receiving loans from registry moneys from court officer).

This is not a comprehensive listing but sets forth some of the more significant provisions with which judicial employees should be familiar.

B. A judicial employee should be faithful to professional standards and maintain competence in the judicial employee's profession.

C. A judicial employee should be patient, dignified, respectful, and courteous to all persons with whom the judicial employee deals in an official capacity, including the general public, and should require similar conduct of personnel subject to the judicial employee's direction and control. A judicial employee should diligently discharge the responsibilities of the office in a prompt, efficient, nondiscriminatory, fair, and professional manner. A judicial employee should never influence or attempt to influence the assignment of cases, or

Source: From Chapter 2, "Code of Conduct for Judicial Employees," in *Guide to Judiciary Policies and Procedures,* vol. 2 (Washington, DC: Administrative Office of the U.S. Courts, September 19, 1995). Available online:<www.uscourts.gov/guide/vol2/ch2a.html>.Accessed July 30, 2002.

perform any discretionary or ministerial function of the court in a manner that improperly favors any litigant or attorney, nor should a judicial employee imply that he or she is in a position to do so.

D. A judicial employee should avoid making public comment on the merits of a pending or impending action and should require similar restraint by personnel subject to the judicial employee's direction and control. This proscription does not extend to public statements made in the course of official duties or to the explanation of court procedures. A judicial employee should never disclose any confidential information received in the course of official duties except as required in the performance of such duties, nor should a judicial employee employ such information for personal gain. A former judicial employee should observe the same restrictions on disclosure of confidential information that apply to a current judicial employee, except as modified by the appointing authority.

E. A judicial employee should not engage in nepotism prohibited by law.

Note: See also 5 U.S.C. § 3110 (employment of relatives); 28 U.S.C. § 458 (employment of judges' relatives).

F. Conflicts of Interest.

> (1) A judicial employee should avoid conflicts of interest in the performance of official duties. A conflict of interest arises when a judicial employee knows that he or she (or the spouse, minor child residing in the judicial employee's household, or other close relative of the judicial employee) might be so personally or financially affected by a matter that a reasonable person with knowledge of the relevant facts would question the judicial employee's ability properly to perform official duties in an impartial manner. . . .

CANON 4: IN ENGAGING IN OUTSIDE ACTIVITIES, A JUDICIAL EMPLOYEE SHOULD AVOID THE RISK OF CONFLICT WITH OFFICIAL DUTIES, SHOULD AVOID THE APPEARANCE OF IMPROPRIETY, AND SHOULD COMPLY WITH DISCLOSURE REQUIREMENTS

A. *Outside Activities.* A judicial employee's activities outside of official duties should not detract from the dignity of the court, interfere with the performance of official duties, or adversely reflect on the operation and dignity of the court or office the judicial employee serves. Subject to the foregoing standards and the other provisions of this code, a judicial employee may engage in such activities as civic, charitable, religious, professional, educational, cultural, avocational,

social, fraternal, and recreational activities, and may speak, write, lecture, and teach. If such outside activities concern the law, the legal system, or the administration of justice, the judicial employee should first consult with the appointing authority to determine whether the proposed activities are consistent with the foregoing standards and the other provisions of this code. . . .

CANON 5: A JUDICIAL EMPLOYEE SHOULD REFRAIN FROM INAPPROPRIATE POLITICAL ACTIVITY

A. *Partisan Political Activity.* A judicial employee should refrain from partisan political activity; should not act as a leader or hold any office in a partisan political organization; should not make speeches for or publicly endorse or oppose a partisan political organization or candidate; should not solicit funds for or contribute to a partisan political organization, candidate, or event; should not become a candidate for partisan political office; and should not otherwise actively engage in partisan political activities.

B. *Nonpartisan Political Activity.* A member of a judge's personal staff, clerk of court, chief probation officer, chief pretrial services officer, circuit executive, and district court executive should refrain from nonpartisan political activity such as campaigning for or publicly endorsing or opposing a nonpartisan political candidate; soliciting funds for or contributing to a nonpartisan political candidate or event; and becoming a candidate for nonpartisan political office. Other judicial employees may engage in nonpartisan political activity only if such activity does not tend to reflect adversely on the dignity or impartiality of the court or office and does not interfere with the proper performance of official duties. A judicial employee may not engage in such activity while on duty or in the judicial employee's workplace and may not utilize any federal resources in connection with any such activity.

Note: See also 18 U.S.C. chapter 29 (elections and political activities).

■ Restrictions on Bringing Charges

This section turns to situations in which charges are filed but for inappropriate reasons. In other words, whereas the previous sections considered situations in which the prosecutor *fails* to bring charges, this section considers situations in which the prosecutor *cannot* bring charges.

There are three basic reasons a prosecutor cannot bring charges against an accused individual: (1) if the prosecution is unfair and selective (i.e., targets a certain individual unfairly); (2) if the prosecution is pursued for vindictive reasons; and (3) if the prosecution is pursued in disregard of statutory intent. The following subsections focus in detail on these situations.

Before going ahead, it is important to point out that prosecutors may occasionally bring charges, say, for vindictive reasons. Assuming such conduct comes to the attention of someone in a higher position of authority, the prosecuting decision will essentially be overruled. That is, the charges against the accused will be dropped or, in the event that the person is charged and convicted, his or her conviction will be overturned. However, if a prosecutor brings charges for inappropriate reasons and this decision goes uncontested, then the charges will most likely stand.

Unfair and Selective Prosecution

If the prosecutor's decision to press charges is *discriminatory* in nature, the Fourteenth Amendment's equal protection clause can be violated. For example, in *Yick Wo. v. Hopkins* (118 U.S. 356 [1886]), the Supreme Court stated:

> Though the law itself be fair on its face and impartial in appearance, yet, if it is applied and administered by public authority with an evil eye and an unequal hand, so as practically to make unjust and illegal discriminations between persons in similar circumstances, material to their rights, the denial of equal justice is still within the prohibition of the Constitution. (pp. 373–374)

Simply put, if an individual is targeted for prosecution merely because he or she falls into a certain group (e.g., a minority group), then his or her constitutional rights will be violated. This is known as **selective prosecution**.

■ *Oyler v. Boles,*
368 U.S. 448 (1968)

Since *Yick Wo*, the Court has become more specific as to what constitutes selective prosecution. In *Oyler v. Boles* (368 U.S. 448 [1968]), the Court held that prosecution becomes selective and in violation of the equal protection clause only when it is intentional and is intended to target "a certain class of cases . . . or specific persons." In that case, the defendant presented evidence that he was the only individual of six sentenced under a particular statute. The Court held that this was not discriminatory because the defendant was unable to demonstrate intent by the prosecutor or provide evidence that he fit the group targeted for prosecution. In fact, the Court noted:

> The conscious exercise of some selectivity in enforcement is not in itself a federal constitutional violation. Even though the statistics in this case might imply a policy of selective enforcement, it was not stated that the selection was deliberately based upon an unjustifiable standard such as race, religion, or other arbitrary classification. (p. 456)

Since the *Oyler* decision, the courts have imposed a three-pronged test for determining whether prosecution violates equal protection. It must be shown that (1) similarly situated individuals were not prosecuted, (2) the prosecutor intended for this to happen, and (3) the decision resulted from an arbitrary, rather than rational, classification scheme. An *arbitrary* classification scheme would be based on, for example, race or sex.

A *rational* classification scheme would be one that considers the evidence against each individual without regard to the color of his or her skin, country of origin, religious preference, sex, or other such criterion.

Filing charges for discriminatory reasons is not the only type of unfair prosecution. Sometimes, prosecutors aggressively pursue *conspicuous individuals* and open themselves to criticism. This is not to say that highly public lawbreakers cannot be charged, however. Indeed, the courts have justified prosecution on the highest charge of certain individuals for the sole purpose of discouraging other people from committing the same offense. As one court noted, "Selective enforcement may . . . be justified when a striking example or a few examples are sought in order to deter other violators" (*People v. Utica Daw's Drug Co.*, 16 A.D.2d 12 [1962], p. 21).

What Is Selective Treatment?

Donnerville instituted a zero-tolerance policy for speeding. Anyone who exceeded the posted speed limit by five or more miles per hour would receive a minimum $100 fine. The policy seemed to be working: Speeding was down, and revenue was up. However, one driver, Carol Wise, who had received a $1,000 ticket, claimed that she had been fined significantly more than other drivers. Moreover, she was prepared to present evidence that the reason for this was that she had said to the citing officer, "You are a moron. The police force would be better off without the likes of you." Assuming Wise can present evidence that she was fined significantly more than other motorists, should she succeed with her claim that she was unfairly and selectively targeted?

In addition to being criticized for prosecuting high-profile offenders, prosecutors can also get into trouble for targeting the most *significant offender* in a group of offenders. To clarify, think of the conspicuous person cases discussed in the previous paragraphs, in which prosecutors opted to charge one offender instead of another, even though both were suspected of having committed the same offense. When a group of individuals is suspected of having committed various degrees of the same offense, why does the prosecutor only pursue the individual suspected of having committed the most serious offense?

An example of a case illustrating this practice is *State v. McCollum* (159 Wis.2d 184 [App. 1990]). In that case, the court dismissed prostitution charges against nude female dancers. In its decision, the court pointed out that the male patrons of these dancers were not charged, even though Wisconsin law criminalized their behavior, as well.

A fourth method by which prosecutors can open themselves to allegations of unfair and selective prosecution is through what is known as **pretextual prosecution**. This occurs when the prosecutor lacks the evidence to charge someone with a particular crime and so charges him or her with a lesser crime. However, prosecutors are rarely chastised for this type of conduct. For example, in *United States v. Sacco* (428 F.2d 164 [9th Cir. 1970]), a court noted that allowing a prosecutor to pursue lesser charges when the evidence to mount a more serious charge does not exist is perfectly acceptable.

The Supreme Court recently decided a case dealing with alleged discriminatory prosecution. Specifically, in *United States v. Bass* (536 U.S. 862 [2002]), the Court considered a defendant's request for discovery of the Department of Justice's charging practices in capital cases. He alleged that blacks were disproportionately charged in such cases and that he was charged because of his race. His argument did not succeed, however.

What Is Pretextual Prosecution?

The district attorney (D.A.) suspects that Corinne Dwyer is running a call-girl service out of her suburban home. The D.A. does not have enough evidence to prosecute Dwyer for her prostitution activities, but he does have sufficient evidence to prosecute Dwyer for abandoning an appliance. Dwyer had put a refrigerator at the end of her driveway with a "Free" sign on it, in violation of a statute that provides that "any person who discards or abandons or leaves in any place accessible to children, any refrigerator, icebox, deep freeze locker, . . . which is no longer in use, and which has not had the door removed or the hinges and such portion of the latch mechanism removed to prevent latching or locking of the door, is guilty of a misdemeanor." (This is an actual offense under the California Penal Code, Section 402b.) Dwyer is thus charged and argues that she has been unfairly targeted for pretextual prosecution, in violation of her Fourteenth Amendment right to equal protection. What should the court decide?

Vindictive Prosecution

If a prosecutor's charging decision is motivated by revenge, then the resulting charge violates the due process clause of the Fourteenth Amendment. Specifically, if a prosecutor charges an individual simply because he or she is exercising his or her constitutional rights, such charges will not be allowed. This is known as **vindictive prosecution.**

Blackledge v. Perry,
417 U.S. 21 (1974)

This was the decision reached in *Blackledge v. Perry* (417 U.S. 21 [1974]). In that case, the defendant was convicted in a lower court for misdemeanor assault with a deadly weapon. After the defendant filed an appeal with the county superior court, the prosecutor obtained an indictment charging the offender with *felony* assault for the same conduct. The defendant pled guilty to this offense and was sentenced to five to seven years. Notwithstanding the obvious double-jeopardy concerns (covered further in Chapter 14) raised by the prosecutor's conduct in this case, the Supreme Court concluded that "vindictiveness against a defendant for having successfully attacked his first conviction must play no part in the sentence he receives after a new trial" (p. 33). The Court concluded further that such punishment after the fact must be overturned, unless the prosecutor can explain the increase in charges.

The Supreme Court's decision in *Blackledge* applies only in limited contexts, a point that cannot be overemphasized. Namely, it applies only after (1) the charged individual exercises his or her legal rights and (2) the prosecutor increases the charges after the first trial. With regard to the latter restriction, this means that if the prosecutor threatens the defendant with more serious charges during the pretrial phase, the Fourteenth Amendment will not be violated. New evidence could come along during this phase, which may legitimately warrant a more serious charge.

However, in *United States v. Goodwin* (457 U.S. 368 [1982]), the Supreme Court noted that it is possible for a prosecutor to act vengefully during the pretrial phase. It is possible, the Court noted, that "a defendant in an appropriate case might prove objectively that the prosecutor's [pretrial] charging decision was motivated by a desire to punish him for doing something that the law plainly allowed him to do" (p. 384). Furthermore, while "the defendant is free to tender evidence to the court to support a claim that enhanced charges are a direct and unjustifiable penalty for the exercise of a procedural right . . . only in rare cases [will] a defendant be able to overcome the presumptive validity of the prosecutor's actions through such a demonstration" (p. 384). In other words, if the more serious charging decision is made prior to trial, it is presumed that the prosecutor is not acting in a vindictive fashion, and the defendant must prove otherwise.

What Is Vindictive Prosecution?

Cesar Fresco was arrested for uttering (i.e., giving, offering, cashing, or passing or attempting to pass) a forged document, which is a felony punishable by a prison term of 2 to 10 years. He has an extensive criminal history and has committed forgery in the past. The prosecutor offers a plea bargain to Fresco, giving him two choices: (1) He can plead guilty to the crime and the prosecutor will recommend a 5-year sentence, or (2) he can reject the plea, be prosecuted under the habitual offender statute, and face a potential life term. The prosecutor tells Fresco, "If you do not accept this agreement, I will prosecute you as a habitual offender and you will go to prison for the rest of your life." Fresco rejects the plea and is convicted. Later, he sues, claiming that the prosecution was vindictive. Will he succeed?

Prosecution in Disregard of Legislative Intent

Legislators sometimes pass new laws without realizing that identical laws are already on the books. In doing so, they have been known to penalize the same conduct differently under the new law compared to the old law. Prosecutors are then faced with deciding which law to invoke when pressing charges.

Such was the issue raised in *United States v. Batchelder* (442 U.S. 114 [1979]). There, a man was sentenced to five years in prison for a firearms offense. The court of appeals reversed this decision, noting that another statute provided a maximum penalty of only two years for the same conduct. The court concluded that the intent of the legislature was to limit the prison term to the two-year term, not the five-year term. The case then went to the Supreme Court, which concluded that the legislature did not intend for one or the other statute to be used. Specifically, it found "no appreciable difference between the discretion a prosecutor exercises when deciding whether to charge under one or two statutes with different elements and the discretion he exercises when choosing one of two statutes with identical elements" (p. 125).

The Court's decision in *Batchelder* makes it nearly impossible for an individual to challenge his or her conviction based on the fact that two statutes mandate different punishments for the same conduct. Indeed, the Court concluded that neither a due process nor an equal protection claim would be successful in such a situation.

■ *United States v. Batchelder,*
442 U.S. 114 (1979)

Summary. Thus, there are two clear situations in which it is inappropriate for a prosecutor to bring charges: (1) when such prosecution is unfair or biased and (2) when it is vindictive. A third possible situation is when the charging decision is in disregard of legislative intent, but based on the Supreme Court's decision in *Batchelder*, it would seem that prosecution under a harsher statute that penalizes the same conduct as a milder statute is not problematic. Fortunately, such prosecutions are rare.

■ Joinder

Joinder refers to a situation in which the prosecutor either (1) brings multiple charges against the same individual in the same trial or (2) brings charges against multiple individuals in the same trial. In determining whether either is appropriate, two questions must be asked: First, based on the jurisdiction in question, is joinder appropriate? Second, if joinder is appropriate, will it be unfairly prejudicial? An answer of no to the first question and yes to the second requires what is known as a **severance**.

The question of whether joinder is appropriate is best resolved prior to trial, but sometimes joinder is not addressed until *after* trial. Assume, for example, that a single

■ *United States v. Lane,*
  474 U.S. 438 (1986)

defendant is charged in the same trial for assault and robbery. Assume further that he is convicted on both counts. If he later claims that joinder was inappropriate (which, incidentally, means the burden of proof falls on him) and succeeds with this argument, what will the result be? According to the Supreme Court in *United States v. Lane* (474 U.S. 438 [1986]), if this joinder has "a substantial and injurious effect or influence in determining the jury's verdict" (p. 449), then new and separate trials must be held.

Multiple Charges against the Same Individual

According to the *Federal Rules of Criminal Procedure,* multiple charges can be brought against the same individual under the following circumstances: when the charges arise out of (1) the same criminal event (e.g., robbery of a convenience store and assault when fleeing the scene); (2) two separate criminal acts that are tied together in some fashion (e.g., a convenience store robbery to obtain cash to buy and sell illegal drugs); or (3) two criminal acts that are the same or similar in character.[2] This latter circumstance is somewhat vague, but an example should clarify: If a serial killer uses the same *modus operandi* against his victims, he may be tried for several homicides in the same criminal trial.

When the defense argues against joinder, there are a number of motivating concerns. First, there is the concern that the jury (or the judge, if a bench trial is held) will not consider the criminal acts for which the accused is charged separately. Another concern is that the jury will view all the evidence against the accused in a cumulative, rather than separate, fashion. Say, for example, that the prosecution presents eyewitness testimony against a defendant accused of robbery. Also assume that the prosecution presents a murder weapon allegedly used by the defendant on the victim of the robbery. The jury may consider together the eyewitness testimony and the murder weapon and arrive at the conclusion that the accused is guilty. But if the robbery and homicide were tried separately, the jury may not arrive at this conclusion so easily. Finally, another defense argument against joinder is that by trying an individual on several charges in the same trial, he or she will have difficulty asserting separate defenses to the criminal acts at issue.

An obvious problem with joinder is the possibility of double jeopardy. When a prosecutor tries a person on several related crimes in the same trial, he or she must do so carefully. In short, the criminal acts alleged must be similar but not identical. Double jeopardy is considered in Chapter 14, but for now, an example may prove helpful: If the prosecutor charges an individual for first-degree as well as second-degree murder of the same victim in the same trial and the individual is convicted of both offenses, then it will be deemed unconstitutional.

Charges against Multiple Defendants

The second form of joinder is when multiple defendants are charged in the same criminal trial. The *Federal Rules of Criminal Procedure* state, "Two or more defendants may be charged in the same indictment or information if they are alleged to have participated in the same act or transaction or in the same series of acts or transactions constituting an offense or offenses."[3] In other words, joinder of defendants is reserved in most instances for crimes of conspiracy (i.e., crimes where two or more individuals plot during a criminal act).

As with joinder of *charges,* joinder of *defendants* raises a number of concerns. For instance, the jury may get confused as to who, if anyone, is guilty and simply convict all of the defendants. Or the jury may convict one defendant who is perhaps less guilty than

---

[2] *Federal Rules of Criminal Procedure,* Rule 8, issued by the 107th Congress, First Session, December 1, 2001. Available online: <www.house.gov/judiciary/crim2001.pdf>. ➡

[3] *Federal Rules of Criminal Procedure,* Rule 8[b].

another defendant who is clearly guilty simply because they associated together. Also, it is conceivable that one defendant may testify against another but then refuse to answer questions on cross-examination, citing self-incrimination concerns.

There are clearly arguments against joinder, concerning both charges and defendants. However, there is one clear argument in favor of joinder—namely, efficiency. Allowing prosecutors to join charges and defendants reduces court backlog and speeds up the administration of justice.

THE GRAND JURY

According to the Fifth Amendment, "No person shall be held to answer for a capital, or otherwise infamous crime, unless on a presentment or indictment of a grand jury." This part of the Fifth Amendment cannot be fully appreciated without considering the time in which it was written. The framers favored **grand jury** indictments in certain situations for fear that the prosecutor, a representative of government, could become too powerful in terms of making charging decisions. Indeed, the framers shared a clear sentiment that government should be kept in check, and the grand jury was one method of ensuring this.

Despite that intent, the grand jury is no longer so independent. Instead, the grand jury is now highly dependent on the actions of the prosecutor. Grand juries still perform important investigative functions, and they are quite powerful in terms of, for instance, being able to subpoena witnesses and records. But their role today is tied closely to the prosecutor. In fact, almost every state makes the prosecutor the main legal adviser of the grand jury and requires him or her to be present during all grand jury sessions. However, in some states, the grand jury functions independently of the prosecutor.

Even though the Fifth Amendment suggests that indictment by grand jury is guaranteed for certain offenses, this right has not been incorporated. In the 1884 decision of *Hurtado v. California* (110 U.S. 516 [1884]), the Supreme Court stated that indictment by a grand jury is not a right guaranteed by the due process clause of the Fourteenth Amendment. The Court stated:

■ *Hurtado v. California,* 110 U.S. 516 (1884)

[W]e are unable to say that the substitution for a presentment or indictment by a grand jury of [a] proceeding by information after examination and commitment by a magistrate, certifying to the probable guilt of the defendant, with the right on his part to the aid of counsel, and to the cross-examination of the witnesses produced for the prosecution, is not due process of law. (p. 538)

It should be emphasized that just because the right to grand jury indictment has not been incorporated to the states, this does not mean that states do not require this method of prosecution. Several states do require that, for the most part, felonies are to be prosecuted only by grand jury indictment. The same is true for the federal system. Most states, however, permit prosecution by indictment or information. See Figure 11.3 for an overview of the mechanisms for filing serious charges in each state.

So, since most states permit indictment or information, under what circumstances is one or the other method used? Typically, grand jury indictment will be the charging mechanism of choice when (1) the case is of great public and/or political significance; (2) the investigative power of the grand jury is useful; (3) the grand jury may be able to issue an indictment more quickly compared to holding a preliminary hearing and then issuing an information indictment; or (4) one or more witnesses is hesitant to speak in open court, preferring the secrecy surrounding grand jury proceedings.

FIGURE 11.3 Charging Methods for Serious Crimes by State

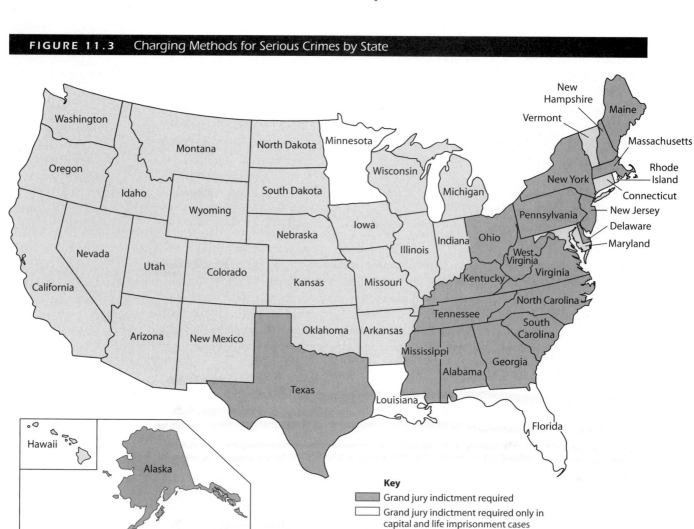

Key
- ■ Grand jury indictment required
- □ Grand jury indictment required only in capital and life imprisonment cases
- ▣ Grand jury indictment not required

Source: Based on S. S. Beale et al., *Grand Jury Law and Practice,* 2nd ed. (St. Paul, MN: West Publishing, 2001).

■ How a Grand Jury Is Constructed

A grand jury can be *impaneled* either by the court or the prosecutor. Usually, the court has this responsibility, but prosecutors are becoming increasingly able to decide whether a grand jury is necessary.

The term *grand jury* should not be construed as singular; in larger jurisdictions, several grand juries may be acting at the same time. One or more could be performing investigative functions, and one or more others could be working on specific cases.

Duration

Once a grand jury has been convened, its members serve for a specified period of time. A term can last from one to three months but sometimes less, if the court or prosecutor believes that further deliberation is unnecessary. Under the *Federal Rules of Criminal Procedure,* a regular grand jury cannot serve for a period longer than 18 months, unless the court extends the service "upon a determination that such extension is in the public interest."[4] Fortunately, people selected for grand juries do not have to meet every day; usually, a grand jury meets several days a month.

[4]*Federal Rules of Criminal Procedure,* Rule 6[g].

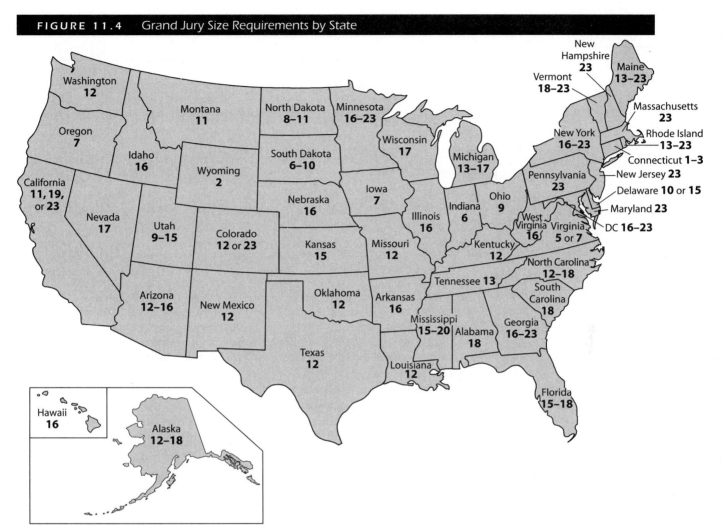

FIGURE 11.4 Grand Jury Size Requirements by State

Source: Data available online:<www.udayton.edu/~grandjur/stategj/sizegj.htm>.

Size

Grand juries are larger than ordinary trial juries. In the past, grand juries consisting of 24 or so people were not uncommon. Today, grand juries are usually smaller, or in the neighborhood of 16 to 20 people. One state, Tennessee, permits a grand jury of 13 individuals, but the voting requirements in that state are fairly restrictive. See Figure 11.4 for an illustration of grand jury size requirements by state.

Voting Requirements

Grand jury voting requirements also vary by state. The most common voting requirement is that 12 grand jury members must agree on an indictment. However, one state, Virginia, requires only four votes for issuance of a **true bill**, which is the endorsement made by a grand jury when it finds sufficient evidence to warrant a criminal charge. As with a *petit jury* (i.e., that used in criminal trials), a grand jury is headed by a foreperson, who is charged with, among other duties, signing the indictment and keeping track of the votes of each member. Figure 11.5 (page 324) presents a sample grand jury indictment.

Selection of Members

People are selected for a grand jury in the same way they are selected for an ordinary trial (i.e., petit) jury. They are subpoenaed. In some states, grand jury members are selected

FIGURE 11.5 *Sample Grand Jury Indictment*

IN THE CIRCUIT COURT OF COLE COUNTY, MISSOURI

STATE OF MISSOURI,   )
                         Plaintiff,   )
)
         vs.   )   Case No.
)   OCN No.
JOHN DOE,   )
                         Defendant.   )

INDICTMENT

The Grand Jurors of the County of Lewis, State of Missouri, charge that the defendant, John Doe, in violation of Section *575.030,*RSMo, committed the class D felony of hindering prosecutions punishable upon conviction under Section 558.011.1(4) and 560.011 RSMo, in that on or about March 5, 2003, in the County of Cole, State of Missouri, the defendant, for the purpose of preventing the apprehension of Lawrence Green for conduct constituting the crime of a felony of murder in the first degree and robbery in the first degree on or about March 4, 2003, by providing Lawrence Green transportation.

Defendant is a prior offender under Sections 558.016 and *557.036* RSMo, in that he has pleaded guilty to or has been found guilty of a felony as follows:

1. On or about November 2, 1998, defendant pleaded guilty to; was convicted of or was found guilty of the felony of property damage first degree in the Circuit Court of Cole County, Missouri.

A true bill

_____
    Foreman

                              _____
                              Carl B. Cohen #24290
                              Prosecuting Attorney

Received and filed this ___ day of March, 2003, and bail set at $_____.

                              _____
                              Circuit Judge

                    WITNESSES FOR STATE

Source: Used courtesy of Cole County, Missouri.

from a list of eligible voters. In others, they are selected from a list of licensed drivers. Still other states select grand jury members from a list of tax returns, telephone directories, and so on. Most people do not get the opportunity to serve on a grand jury because grand juries are not convened that frequently.

The grand jury selection process usually involves two stages. First, a list of potential grand jury members is compiled by any of the methods (or others) just described. This

The pool from which a grand jury is selected must be a fair cross-section of the community.

list of grand jury members is known as the *venire.* Next, people are selected from the list to serve on the grand jury. At both stages, constitutional complications can arise.

First, special steps need to be taken to ensure that the list of potential grand jurors, like that for a typical petit jury, is fair and impartial. In particular, the defendant can raise constitutional challenges to the grand jury selection process if it is *not* fair and impartial. One such challenge is based on the *equal protection clause.* This requires showing that there is a significant disparity between a group's representation in the community and its representation on the grand jury (see *Casteneda v. Partida,* 430 U.S. 482 [1977]).

Another constitutional challenge against the composition of the grand jury pool stems from the *fair cross-section requirement* announced in *Taylor v. Louisiana* (419 U.S. 522 [1975]). There, the Court held that "systematic exclusion" of a "large distinct group" from the pool from which the (petit) jury is chosen violates the Sixth Amendment. The same logic carries over to the grand jury. If, for example, a grand jury consists of all white members and 40 percent of the community is black, the fair cross-section requirement will have been violated. By contrast, if the grand jury does not contain a snake handler, a militant feminist, a rabbi, or some such specific type of individual, the fair cross-section requirement will not have been violated because these and other individuals do not constitute large, distinct groups.

Taylor v. Louisiana, 419 U.S. 522 (1975)

As for the selection of grand jury members from the pool, similar constitutional concerns can be raised. If, for instance, the grand jury pool is representative of a fair cross-section of the community, it is still possible that people could be excluded from the jury on a systematic basis. In *Rose v. Mitchell* (443 U.S. 545 [1979]), the Court held that the "right to equal protection of the laws [is] denied when [the defendant] is indicted from a grand jury from which members of a racial group purposefully have been excluded" (p. 556). The final composition of the grand jury can also be challenged on due process grounds (see *Beck v. Washington,* 369 U.S. 541 [1962]).

Rose v. Mitchell, 443 U.S. 545 (1979)

Secrecy of Grand Jury Proceedings

Grand jury proceedings are intensely secretive. In *United States v. Rose* (215 F.2d 617 [1954]), the Third Circuit Court of Appeals announced several reasons for this:

(1) to prevent the escape of those whose indictment may be contemplated; (2) to insure the utmost freedom to the grand jury in its deliberations, and to prevent persons subject to indictment or their friends from importuning the grand jurors; (3) to prevent subornation of perjury or tampering with the witnesses who may testify before the grand jury and later appear at the trial of those indicted by it; (4) to encourage free and untrammeled disclosures by persons who have information with respect to the commission of crimes; [and] (5) to protect the innocent accused who is exonerated from disclosure of the fact that he has been under investigation, and from the expense of standing trial where there was no probability of guilt. (pp. 628–629)

Notwithstanding these concerns, there are two categories of case law concerning grand jury secrecy: (1) cases addressing whether grand jury witness testimony should be supplied to the defense and (2) cases addressing the extent to which grand jury witnesses can share their testimony with other parties, such as other government officials.

Disclosure of Witness Testimony to the Defense

According to the *Federal Rules of Criminal Procedure*, grand jury proceedings can be shared with the defense when the defendant makes "a showing that grounds may exist for a motion to dismiss the indictment because of matters occurring before the grand jury."[5] This type of disclosure is exceedingly rare and generally limited to situations in which there is evidence that prosecutorial misconduct occurred before the grand jury proceedings commenced.

Disclosure of Witness Testimony to Other Parties

- *Butterworth v. Smith,*
  494 U.S. 624 (1990)

In *Butterworth v. Smith* (494 U.S. 624 [1990]), the Supreme Court declared that the First Amendment may provide an exception to the grand jury secrecy requirement. In that case, the Court held that a Florida statute that prohibited grand jury witnesses from recounting their own testimony violated freedom of speech.

Butterworth dealt with a defendant who wanted to share his testimony with third parties. However, many more cases deal with the issue of whether other third parties (i.e., besides the defense) should be able to access the records of grand jury proceedings. One such case is *Douglas Oil Co. of California v. Petrol Stops Northwest* (441 U.S. 211 [1979]). In that case, the Supreme Court held that parties seeking access to grand jury records "must show that the material they seek is needed to avoid a possible injustice to another judicial proceeding, that the need for disclosure is greater than the need for continued secrecy, and that their request is structured to cover only material so needed" (p. 222).

A third party that has traditionally been given greater latitude in terms of access to grand jury proceedings is the government. In fact, the *Federal Rules of Criminal Procedure* provide that no showing of "particularized need" is necessary in order to disclose information to other government attorneys who are assisting in prosecution.[6] However, when disclosure is sought by government officials who are *not* assisting in the prosecution, the Supreme Court has held that a showing of need *does* have to be made (see *United States v. Sells Engineering, Inc.*, 463 U.S. 418 [1983]).

Enter the Patriot Act

Section 203(a) of the Patriot Act, passed in late 2001 (see Chapter 1 for an introduction), amends Rule 6 of the *Federal Rules of Criminal Procedure*, drastically altering the historic secrecy of grand jury proceedings. Specifically, the new version of Rule 6 allows the disclosure of foreign intelligence, counterintelligence, and foreign intelligence information that

---

[5]*Federal Rules of Criminal Procedure*, Rule 6.
[6]*Ibid.*

has arisen from a grand jury's investigation to a variety of federal officials "in order to assist the official in receiving that information in the performance of his official duties" (U.S. Patriot Act, Pub. L. No. 107-56, 203a, 115 Stat. 272 [2001], p. 280). Prior to the Patriot Act, the records of all grand jury proceedings were closely guarded unless, for example, the defense could show a substantial need for such records to be disclosed.

What is controversial about the portion of the Patriot Act addressing grand jury secrecy is the definition of the term *foreign intelligence information.* It includes the following:

> (A) information, whether or not concerning a United States person, that relates to the ability of the United States to protect against (i) actual or potential attack or other grave hostile acts of a foreign power or an agent of a foreign power; (ii) sabotage or international terrorism by a foreign power or an agent of a foreign power; or (iii) clandestine intelligence activities by an intelligence service or network of a foreign power or by an agent of foreign power; or (B) information, whether or not concerning a United States person, with respect to a foreign power or foreign territory that relates to (i) the national defense or the security of the United States; or (ii) the conduct of the foreign affairs of the United States. (p. 281)

Note the *whether or not* language. Interpreted literally, this means that even information relating to U.S. citizens that results from grand jury investigations can be shared between law enforcement agencies. This provision of the Patriot Act seems to chip away substantially at the historical secrecy of grand jury investigations.

◼ Rights of Witnesses Testifying before Grand Juries

Grand juries rely heavily on witness testimony. However, the rights afforded to grand jury witnesses differ significantly from those afforded to witnesses in other settings (e.g., at trial). Also, the rights afforded to the individuals targeted by grand jury investigations differ from those afforded to criminal defendants.

The cases in this area revolve around three issues: (1) the right of the individual targeted by a grand jury investigation to testify; (2) whether grand jury witnesses are required to be advised of their right not to testify; and (3) the right to counsel as applied in grand jury proceedings.

Right to Testify

It is well known that the defendant in a criminal trial has a constitutional right to testify or not testify in his or her own defense. In contrast, someone who is the target of a grand jury investigation usually *does not* enjoy the right to testify. Indeed, several states do not even grant the target of a grand jury investigation the right to be present. This restriction is justified on the same secrecy grounds discussed earlier. Also, since many grand jury proceedings are investigative, there may not be a specific target until the proceedings have reached a close. In such a situation, it would be cumbersome to allow all potential targets to be present in order to give testimony in their defense.

Being Advised of the Right Not to Testify

When witnesses appear before grand juries, they enjoy the Fifth Amendment's privilege against self-incrimination. This is no different than in a criminal trial. However, a question has arisen in the courts over whether grand jury witnesses must be *told* that they can remain silent. In other words, the courts have grappled with whether the *Miranda* warnings should apply in the grand jury context.

As noted earlier in this book, the *Miranda* warnings are only required during custodial interrogation. Therefore, the question must be asked, Are grand jury proceedings akin to custodial interrogations? At least one decision suggests that *Miranda* does not apply in the grand jury context because the proceedings are not as "inherently coercive" as traditional custodial interrogations (e.g., *Gollaher v. United States*, 419 F.2d 520 [9th Cir. 1969]). However, some states require by law that the targets of grand jury investigations, as well as grand jury witnesses, be advised of their right not to testify. The Supreme Court has yet to rule on this issue.

Right to Counsel

Should grand jury witnesses and the targets of grand jury investigations be provided with counsel? The Supreme Court has answered no to this question in at least two cases: *In re Groban's Petition* (352 U.S. 330 [1957]) and *United States v. Mandujano* (425 U.S. 564 [1976]). A person who has already been charged may have a right to counsel before a grand jury proceeding, but such an individual is rarely the target of such a proceeding (see, e.g., *Kirby v. Illinois*, 406 U.S. 682 [1972]).

■ *United States v. Mandujano,* 425 U.S. 564 (1976)

The Supreme Court has stated that grand jury proceedings take place before the initiation of adversarial criminal proceedings and, as such, are outside the scope of the Sixth Amendment's right to counsel. There are also several additional reasons for not allowing counsel to be present during grand jury proceedings: (1) the investigation could be delayed if the witness repeatedly confers with his or her attorney; (2) the investigation could be disrupted if the witness raises objections and arguments; and, of course, (3) secrecy could be compromised.

■ Investigative Powers of the Grand Jury

One of the main duties of a grand jury is to investigate alleged wrongdoing in order to determine whether an indictment should be issued. Because of this function, a grand jury has a great deal of investigative power. For example, as decided in *United States v. Calandra* (414 U.S. 338 [1974]), a grand jury "may compel the production of evidence or the testimony of witnesses as it considers appropriate, and its operation generally is unrestrained by the technical procedural and evidentiary rules governing the conduct of criminal trials" (p. 343). In this vein, a grand jury can subpoena witnesses and evidence. However, it can also extend grants of immunity to certain individuals in exchange for their testimony, and it can find people in contempt for failing to cooperate with an investigation.

■ *United States v. Calandra,* 414 U.S. 338 (1974)

Subpoenas

Two types of subpoenas are available to grand juries: (1) a **subpoena** *ad testificandum* and (2) a **subpoena** *duces tecum.* The former compels a witness to appear before the grand jury, and the latter compels the production of tangible evidence (e.g., a suspected murder weapon). The power of the grand jury to utilize both of these mechanisms is virtually unrestricted; however, there have been a few constitutional objections to their use.

First, some have argued that a subpoena to appear before the grand jury amounts to a seizure within the meaning of the Fourth Amendment. The Supreme Court acknowledged in *United States v. Dioniso* (410 U.S. 1 [1973]) that being forced to appear before a grand jury may be inconvenient but not in comparison to the "historically grounded obligation of every person to appear and give his evidence before the grand jury" (pp. 9–10). Furthermore, Fourth Amendment restrictions on the grand jury's subpoena power "would assuredly impede its investigation and frustrate the public's interest in the fair and expeditious administration of the laws" (p. 17).

■ *United States v. Dioniso,* 410 U.S. 1 (1973)

As for tangible evidence, the Supreme Court has likewise held that a subpoena *duces tecum* does not amount to a Fourth Amendment seizure. However, according to the Court in *Hale v. Henkel* (201 U.S. 43 [1906]), such a subpoena must comport with the

■ *Hale v. Henkel,* 201 U.S. 43 (1906)

Fourth Amendment's particularity requirement. In *United States v. Gurule* (437 F.2d 239 [10th Cir. 1970]), the Tenth Circuit announced a three-prong test for ensuring that a grand jury subpoena satisfies the Fourth Amendment's reasonableness requirement: "(1) the subpoena may command only the production of things relevant to the investigation being pursued; (2) specification of things to be produced must be made with reasonable particularity; and (3) production of records covering only a reasonable period of time may be required" (p. 241).

DECISION
MAKING
EXERCISE **11.7**

Grand Jury Investigations

Assume that the grand jury is investigating a major case of corporate fraud. Assume further that the grand jury issues a subpoena *duces tecum*, calling for "all understandings, contracts or correspondence between the Fabulous Widgets Company and all of its business partners, as well as all reports made and accounts rendered by such companies from the date of the organization of the Fabulous Widgets Company, as well as all letters received by that company since its organization from all of its business partners." Can this subpoena be considered sufficiently particular?

It has already been noted that grand jury witnesses enjoy the Fifth Amendment privilege, but could being forced to appear before a grand jury itself be incriminating? Not surprisingly, people have objected to grand jury subpoenas for this reason. Few, if any, have succeeded, however. Why? Someone who is appearing before a grand jury does not know in advance what questions will be asked and, as such, cannot assert the Fifth Amendment privilege prior to his or her appearance.

Grants of Immunity

Even though witnesses appearing before the grand jury enjoy the Fifth Amendment privilege against self-incrimination, the grand jury can get around this. In particular, the grand jury can extend *grants of immunity* to witnesses in exchange for their testimony. A grant of **transactional immunity** prohibits future prosecution on the acts for which the witness testifies. However, **use and derivative use immunity** only bars the use of the witness's testimony against him or her in the future. If evidence is obtained after the fact, independent of the witness's testimony before the grand jury, then he or she can be charged (see *Kastigar v. United States*, 406 U.S. 441 [1972]).

Findings of Contempt

When someone is subpoenaed to appear before the grand jury but does not show up, the jury's **contempt power** can be utilized. That is, the grand jury can impose civil and criminal sanctions on the individual. For example, an individual who refuses to appear before the grand jury can be jailed until which point he or she agrees to appear. Note that the grand jury's contempt power is limited to compelling the presence of the witness, not his or her testimony. The witness who *does* appear can still invoke the Fifth Amendment privilege and not make a statement.

◾ Challenging a Grand Jury Indictment

Restrictions on prosecutors' charging decisions were discussed earlier in this chapter. Restrictions are also placed on grand jury indictments. That is, it is possible to challenge a grand jury indictment on constitutional and similar grounds, including (1) lack of evidence; (2) misconduct by the prosecutor as the adviser of the grand jury; (3) unfair selection of grand jury members; and (4) use of different evidence at trial from that presented to the grand jury. When any of these circumstances exists, a grand jury indictment will be *quashed*, or declared invalid.

There is considerable variation among the states as to what amount of evidence is necessary to secure a valid indictment. Some states hold to the probable cause standard. Others state that the grand jury can only issue an indictment when all the evidence before it would, if unexplained, warrant a conviction at trial. In Utah, an indictment can only be issued on clear and convincing evidence that a crime was committed and that the person charged committed it. In either case, a grand jury indictment can be quashed if the evidence relied on to obtain the indictment is insufficient. Also, if the evidence used to obtain an indictment is obtained in an unconstitutional fashion, the indictment can be quashed by essentially invoking the exclusionary rule.

Flagrant prosecutorial misconduct can also lead to an indictment being quashed. If, for instance, the prosecutor fails to supply the grand jury with exculpatory evidence, a subsequent indictment *may* be quashed but only if such misconduct violates existing law. There is, surprisingly, very little existing case law in this area. Indeed, the Supreme Court held in *United States v. Williams* (504 U.S. 36 [1992]) that federal courts cannot easily dismiss an indictment because of prosecutorial misconduct. "Because the grand jury is an institution separate from the courts, over whose functioning the courts do not preside, we think it clear that, as a general matter at least, no such 'supervisory' judicial authority exists" (p. 47).

While the courts have been hesitant to quash indictments based on insufficient evidence and prosecutorial misconduct, discrimination in the selection of grand jury members is taken very seriously. As indicated earlier in this chapter, the composition of the grand jury must comply with the due process and equal protection requirements. When it does not, subsequent indictments can be quashed. The Court noted in *United States v. Mechanik* (475 U.S. 66 [1986]) that "racial discrimination in the selection of grand jurors is so pernicious and other remedies so impractical, that the remedy of automatic reversal [may be] necessary as a prophylactic means of deterring grand jury discrimination in the future" (p. 70).

DECISION MAKING EXERCISE 11.8

Deciding on Variance

A grand jury returned an indictment against two women, charging them both with conspiracy to commit murder. Typically, a criminal *conspiracy* exists when two or more persons agree to commit a crime and then commit some sort of overt act in furtherance of that agreement (e.g., *People v. Cockrell*, 63 Cal. 2d 779). The grand jury was presented with a recorded telephone call between the two women, in which they agreed to murder their husbands. The grand jury was *not* presented with evidence that the women bought handguns for themselves. That evidence was introduced by the prosecutor at trial, however. The women were convicted and are now appealing their convictions, claiming that there was a variance between their indictment and the prosecutor's case. Will they succeed?

■ *United States v. Miller,* 471 U.S. 130 (1985)

Finally, if the prosecutor presents evidence at trial that departs significantly from that relied on by the grand jury for the purpose of issuing an indictment, sanctions will be imposed. If this **variance** between the trial evidence and the grand jury evidence is minimal, the indictment will probably not be quashed. Interpreted differently, if the evidence presented by the prosecutor to secure an indictment is "in no way essential to the offense on which the jury convicted," the indictment will probably not be quashed (see *United States v. Miller,* 471 U.S. 130 [1985]).

THE DEFENSE ATTORNEY

The Sixth Amendment to the U.S. Constitution provides "in all criminal prosecutions, the accused shall enjoy the right . . . to have the Assistance of Counsel for his defense." This right was applied to the states in the landmark decision of *Gideon v. Wainwright* (372 U.S. 335 [1963]). While on its face, this portion of the Sixth Amendment seems straightforward, it has actually given rise to two important questions: (1) What constitutes a *criminal prosecution*? and (2) what does *assistance of counsel* mean?

■ *Gideon v. Wainwright,* 372 U.S. 335 (1963)

Answers to these two questions are provided in the subsections that follow. The right to counsel as applied at other stages of the criminal process and waiver of counsel and the right to counsel of one's own choice are also addressed.

The Right to Counsel in a Criminal Prosecution

Due Process Origins

Prior to *Gideon*, the right to counsel did not exist for all individuals. Usually, counsel was provided only for defendants who could afford it. There were occasions prior to the 1960s, however, in which counsel was provided to criminal defendants who could *not* afford it. For example, the constitutional right of an indigent defendant to be represented by counsel was first announced in *Powell v. Alabama* (287 U.S. 45 [1932]). In that case, the Supreme Court reversed the convictions of several indigent defendants who were not represented by counsel at trial. Significantly, though, the Court based its decision on the Fifth Amendment's due process clause, not the Sixth Amendment. In the Court's words:

■ *Powell v. Alabama,* 287 U.S. 45 (1932)

> The right to be heard would be, in many cases, of little avail if it did not comprehend the right to be heard by counsel. Even the intelligent and educated layman has small and sometimes no skill in the science of law. If charged with crimes, he is incapable, generally, of determining for himself whether the indictment is good or bad. He is unfamiliar with the rules of evidence. Left without aid of counsel he may be put on trial without a proper charge, and convicted upon incompetent evidence, or evidence irrelevant to the issue or otherwise inadmissible. He lacks both the skill and knowledge adequately to prepare his defense, even though he may have a perfect one. He requires the guiding hand of counsel at every step in the proceedings against him. Without it, though he be not guilty, he faces the danger of conviction because he does not know how to establish his innocence. (pp. 68–69)

However, the right to counsel announced in *Powell* was not without limitations. It applied only to "capital case[s], where the defendant is unable to employ counsel, and is incapable adequately of making his own defense because of ignorance, feeble-mindedness, illiteracy, or the like" (p. 71).

The Contemporary Sixth Amendment Approach

In *Johnson v. Zerbst* (304 U.S. 458 [1938]), the Court recognized a Sixth Amendment right to counsel in all federal prosecutions, stating that the Sixth Amendment "embodies a realistic recognition of the obvious truth that the average defendant does not have the professional legal skill to protect himself" (pp. 462–463).

But the Sixth Amendment's right to counsel was still not extended to the states. In *Johnson*, the Court refused to apply its decision to the states, and this holding was reaffirmed a few years later in the case of *Betts v. Brady* (316 U.S. 455 [1942]). There, the Court held that "[t]he Due Process Clause of the Fourteenth Amendment does not incorporate, as such, the specific guarantees found in the Sixth Amendment" (pp. 461–462). It would not be until the 1963 decision in *Gideon v. Wainwright* that the Sixth Amendment right to counsel became incorporated. In that case, the Court recognized that "lawyers in criminal courts are necessities, not luxuries" (p. 344).

Gideon dealt with a felony, which led the Supreme Court to conclude that the Sixth Amendment right to counsel applies only in felony proceedings. However, in *Argersinger v. Hamlin* (407 U.S. 25 [1972]), the Court held that the right to counsel applies in misdemeanor cases, also. According to the Court, "The requirement of counsel may well be necessary for a fair trial even in petty-offense prosecution. We are by no means convinced that legal and constitutional questions involved in a case that actually leads to imprisonment even for a brief period are any less complex than when a person can be sent off for six months or more" (p. 33).

This decision was then clarified in *Scott v. Illinois* (440 U.S. 367 [1979]), in which the Court held that the right to counsel does not apply where loss of liberty is merely a *possibility*. In short, when there is no possibility of confinement, the Sixth Amendment right to counsel does not apply. A twist on the *Scott* decision was recently handed down in *Alabama v. Shelton* (535 U.S. 654 [2002]), in which the Court held that "[a] suspended sentence that may 'end up in the actual deprivation of a person's liberty' may not be imposed unless the defendant was accorded 'the guiding hand of counsel' in the prosecution for the crime charged" (p. 654). *Shelton* differed from *Scott* because Shelton was placed on probation; Scott was not.

■ The Right to Counsel at Other Stages of the Criminal Process

Until the Supreme Court's 1963 decision in *Gideon*, its cases on the right to counsel had addressed this right primarily in the context of trials. After *Gideon*, however, the Court began to turn its attention to the right to counsel at other stages of the criminal process. This right can be tied to the Sixth Amendment, but the Court has also defended it (i.e., to the extent it exists) on grounds of self-incrimination, due process, and equal protection.

The Sixth Amendment Approach

In order to determine whether the Sixth Amendment right to counsel applies outside the trial context, the Court once held that a *critical stage* analysis was necessary. In *United States v. Wade* (388 U.S. 218 [1967]), the Supreme Court announced a two-prong test for determining when counsel is required under the Sixth Amendment: (1) "whether potential substantial prejudice to the defendant's rights inheres in the particular confrontation;" and (2) whether counsel can "help avoid that prejudice" (p. 227). In support of its decision, the Court stated, "The trial which might determine the accused's fate may well not be that in the courtroom but that at the pretrial confrontation, with the State aligned against the accused, the witness the sole jury, and the accused unprotected against the overreaching, intentional or unintentional, [influence of the government]" (p. 235).

What, then, was considered a *critical stage?* The Court stated that the period from arraignment to trial was arguably the most critical period of the proceedings. Preliminary hearings and sentencing hearings were also considered critical stages in the criminal process (see *Mempa v. Rhay*, 389 U.S. 128 [1967]; *Coleman v. Alabama*, 399 U.S. 1 [1970]).

In the 1973 decision *United States v. Ash* (413 U.S. 300 [1973]), the Court abandoned the critical stage analysis and focused instead on whether "trial-like confrontations" necessitate counsel. The Court was unsatisfied with the open-endedness of the critical stage analysis. *Trial-like confrontations*, according to the Court, were proceedings that confronted the accused with the "intricacies of the law and the advocacy of the public prosecutor" (p. 309). Cases in which this definition was applied include but are not limited to *Gerstein v. Pugh* (420 U.S. 103 [1975]) and *Estelle v. Smith* (451 U.S. 454 [1981]). But since this definition is equally vague, the Court abandoned it for a third and final approach to the Sixth Amendment right to counsel outside trial.

In *Kirby v. Illinois* (406 U.S. 682 [1972]), the Court became even more specific and held, once and for all, that the right to counsel applies not only in criminal prosecutions

United States v. Wade, 388 U.S. 218 (1967)

Kirby v. Illinois, 406 U.S. 682 (1972)

but at the "initiation of adversary proceedings." This means that the Sixth Amendment right to counsel applies after indictment, formal charging, and on through sentencing. According to the Court's most recent decisions, then, the Sixth Amendment right to counsel is limited; prior to indictment or formal charges, it does not apply.

DECISION MAKING EXERCISE 11.9

Right to Counsel in the Pretrial Phase

A man was arrested without a warrant when a police officer caught him robbing the First Street branch of American Bank. Four hours later, the man was brought before a judge for a probable cause hearing. The judge decided that the officer had probable cause to arrest. The man was convicted of the crime and sentenced to prison. He is now appealing his conviction, claiming that he should have been given access to counsel at the probable cause hearing. Is he right?

The Fifth Amendment Approach

As was already noted in Chapter 8, the right to counsel has also been applied through the Fifth Amendment. In *Miranda v. Arizona* (384 U.S. 436 [1966]), the Court held that the Fifth Amendment's privilege against self-incrimination grants suspects the right to counsel during custodial interrogations because of the "inherent coerciveness" of such activities. Furthermore, the right to counsel during custodial interrogations applies before or after commencement of formal adversary proceedings.

The Due Process/Equal Protection Approach

The right to counsel also stems from the equal protection and due process clauses to the Fourteenth Amendment but only in certain circumstances. The Fourteenth Amendment has been used to justify the right to counsel primarily in criminal appeals and probation/parole revocation hearings. For example, in *Douglas v. California* (372 U.S. 353 [1963], the Court held that the right to counsel extends to convicted indigents for appeals as of right (i.e., appeals to which the individual is legally entitled). And in *Gagnon v. Scarpelli* (411 U.S. 778 [1973]), the Court held that as a matter of due process, indigents are entitled to counsel at probation and parole revocation hearings but only on a case-by-case basis (e.g., whether the complexity of the issues at stake is significant).

In contrast, the right to counsel does not necessarily exist so that indigent convicts can prepare petitions for *discretionary* appeals (i.e., those that the reviewing court gets to decide it wants to hear) (see *Ross v. Moffitt*, 417 U.S. 600 [1974]). The Court noted that the government "does not automatically . . . act . . . unfairly by refusing to provide counsel to indigent defendants at every stage of the [appellate process]" (p. 611). Similarly, in *Pennsylvania v. Finley* (481 U.S. 551 [1987]), the Court announced that the right to counsel does not exist so that convicted criminals can prepare *habeas corpus* petitions. The reason offered by the Court is that "[post-]conviction relief is even further removed from the criminal trial than is discretionary direct review" (pp. 556–557).

Criminal Procedure in Post–September 11 America

The Patriot Act, passed in the wake of the September 11 attacks, changed criminal procedure in several ways. It is important to note, however, that the changes discussed in this subsection are not actually found in the Patriot Act. Rather, they are changes to federal administrative procedures, as outlined in the *Federal Register.* They are discussed here in the context of the Patriot Act only to show that they are closely tied to the new antiterrorism legislation.

First, on October 30, 2001, the U.S. Department of Justice imposed a new requirement on federal correctional facilities that permits the correspondence between prisoners and their attorneys to be monitored. This requirement effectively abandons the time-honored respect for attorney/client confidentiality. This rule was put into effect without notice and without public comment. In fact, the rule was posted in the *Federal Register* the *day after* it went into effect. More importantly, the new requirement that attorney/client communications be monitored in certain situations is not limited to terrorism investigations. Rather, it appears to apply to all individuals incarcerated in federal correctional facilities.[7] Under the new rule, communications between prisoners and their attorneys may be monitored if the attorney general "has certified that reasonable suspicion exists to believe that an inmate may use communications with attorneys or their agents to further or facilitate acts of violence or terrorism."[8] Clearly, this new rule has implications for the Sixth Amendment right to counsel. As such, it will almost certainly be litigated in the courts at some point.

■ Waiver of the Right to Counsel

Though the Sixth Amendment provides for the right to counsel, accused individuals sometimes prefer to represent themselves. Indeed, according to the Supreme Court, criminal defendants have a constitutional right to represent themselves at trial (*Faretta v. California*, 422 U.S. 806 [1975]). This is known as a *pro se* **defense**. In reaching this decision, the Court noted that the Sixth Amendment only guarantees the *assistance* of counsel, not necessarily *representation* by counsel:

> The language and spirit of the Sixth Amendment contemplate that counsel, like the other defense tools guaranteed by the Amendment, shall be an aid to a willing defendant—not an organ of State interposed between an unwilling defendant and his right to defend himself personally. . . . An unwanted counsel "represents" the defendant only through a tenuous and unacceptable legal fiction. Unless the accused has acquiesced in such representation, the defense presented is not the defense guaranteed him by the Constitution, for in a very real sense, it is not his defense. (pp. 820–821)

The Court also emphasized in *Faretta* that the framers viewed the "inestimable worth of free choice" as more important than the right to counsel. Also, "[t]o force a lawyer on a defendant can only lead [the defendant] to believe that the law contrives against him" (p. 834).

■ *Johnson v. Zerbst,* 304 U.S. 458 (1938)

Not every defendant who wishes to proceed without counsel is allowed to do so, however. In *Johnson v. Zerbst* (304 U.S. 458 [1938]), the Supreme Court stated that a defendant may only waive counsel if the waiver is "competent and intelligent." According to the Court in *Carnley v. Cochran* (369 U.S. 506 [1962]), "the record must show, or there must be an allegation and evidence must show, that an accused was offered counsel but intelligently and understandingly rejected the offer. Anything less is not a waiver" (p. 516). The Court elaborated further in *Von Moltke v. Gillies* (332 U.S. 708 [1948]):

> To be valid such waiver must be made with an apprehension of the nature of the charges, the statutory offenses included within them, the range of allowable punishments thereunder, possible defenses to the charges and circumstances in mitigation thereof, and all other facts essential to a broad understanding of the whole matter. A judge can make certain that an accused's professed waiver of counsel is understandingly and wisely made only from a penetrating and comprehensive examination of all the circumstances. (p. 724)

What constitutes a knowing and intelligent waiver is not always clear. However, in *Massey v. Moore* (348 U.S. 105 [1954]), the Court offered clarification by stating that "[o]ne might not be insane in the sense of being incapable of standing trial and yet lack the capacity to stand trial without benefit of counsel" (p. 108). But in *Godinez v. Moran*

---

[7]See *Federal Register* 66 (31 October 2001): 55,061 and 55,063.
[8]*Federal Register*, 55,063.

(509 U.S. 389 [1993]), a case decided some years later, the Court held that a person who is competent to stand trial is also competent to waive counsel at trial and for pleading purposes. This decision all but reversed an earlier decision in which the Court held that competence to stand trial could be interpreted as competence to waive counsel (see *Westbrook v. Arizona*, 384 U.S. 150 [1966]).

In certain circumstances, while permitting waiver of counsel, the court can require that *standby counsel* be available to the defendant—that is, an attorney who is standing by in order to assist the accused, if necessary. This was the decision reached in *McKaskle v. Wiggins* (465 U.S. 168 [1984]), in which the Court held that a judge can appoint standby counsel "to relieve the judge of the need to explain and enforce basic rules of courtroom protocol or to assist the defendant in overcoming routine obstacles that stand in the way of the defendant's achievement of his own clearly indicated goals" (p. 184). When waiver of counsel is knowing and intelligent, a judge's decision to appoint standby counsel will not be unconstitutional as long as (1) the defendant retains control over the case and (2) the jury understands that the defendant represents himself or herself.

In 2004, the Supreme Court decided that waiver of the right to counsel is one that the defendant takes, potentially, at his or her own peril. In *Iowa v. Tovar* (541 U.S. 77 [2004]), the Court decided that a trial court was not required to warn the accused that waiving the right to counsel at a plea hearing involves two risks: (1) the possibility that valid defenses will be overlooked and (2) the accused will be deprived of advice as to whether a guilty plea is warranted.

Indigent versus Nonindigent Defendants' Right to Counsel of Their Choice

Clearly, the defendant who is not indigent can hire counsel of his or her choosing. What's more, the wealthier the defendant, the better counsel he or she can afford. Unfortunately, the indigent defendant does not have such a choice. The Sixth Amendment right to counsel does not guarantee the indigent defendant permission to *choose* counsel; rather, counsel will be *provided*. Usually, counsel will be a public defender. If, however, an indigent can show good cause that the attorney appointed to represent him or her is not doing so adequately, another attorney can be appointed. What constitutes *inadequate representation* is discussed in the next section.

Surprisingly, there are situations in which defendants, if they can afford representation, cannot hire counsel of their choice. If, for example, the defendant's choice of an attorney poses serious conflict-of-interest problems, the defendant may be forced to hire another attorney (e.g., *Wheat v. United States*, 486 U.S. 153 [1988]). Or if the defendant's attorney is not qualified to practice law, then another attorney may be required (e.g., cf. *Leis v. Flynt*, 439 U.S. 438 [1979]). And somewhat controversially, if a defendant's assets are frozen pursuant to a civil forfeiture statute and he or she cannot afford counsel of his or her choosing, then a less expensive attorney may be required or a public defender may be appointed (see *Caplin v. Drysdale v. United States*, 491 U.S. 617 [1989]).

An issue related to counsel of one's choice is whether indigent defendants can retain expert witnesses of their own choosing. In *Ake v. Oklahoma* (470 U.S. 68 [1985]), the Supreme Court held that an indigent defendant enjoys a constitutional right to an expert witness when his or her sanity is at issue. However, the Court limited its holding to provide for only one expert and one who is state employed. Experts in other fields besides psychiatry are generally not provided to indigent defendants. At a point, it becomes necessary to assume that the state's experts (e.g., ballistics experts) present objective and accurate testimony that is not prejudicial to the accused.

Effective Assistance of Counsel

If the Sixth Amendment's right to counsel provision was extended to indigent defendants with a blind eye, then some defendants would be convicted and others acquitted because

FIGURE 11.6 Code of Conduct for Federal Public Defender Employees

B. Code of Conduct for Federal Public Defender Employees

CANON 1: A FEDERAL PUBLIC DEFENDER EMPLOYEE SHOULD UPHOLD THE INTEGRITY AND INDEPENDENCE OF THE OFFICE

An independent and honorable defender system is indispensable to justice in our society. A defender employee should personally observe high standards of conduct so that the integrity and independence of the office are preserved and so that the defender office reflects a devotion to serving the public defender's clients and the principle of equal justice under law. Defender employees should require adherence to such standards by personnel subject to their direction and control. The provisions of this code should be construed and applied to further these objectives. The standards of this code shall not affect or preclude other more stringent standards required by law, by applicable codes of professional responsibility, by court order, or by the federal public defender.

CANON 2: A FEDERAL PUBLIC DEFENDER EMPLOYEE SHOULD AVOID IMPROPRIETY AND THE APPEARANCE OF IMPROPRIETY IN ALL ACTIVITIES

A defender employee should not engage in any activities that would put into question the propriety of the defender employee's conduct in carrying out the duties of the office. A defender employee should not use public office for private gain.

CANON 3: A FEDERAL PUBLIC DEFENDER EMPLOYEE SHOULD ADHERE TO APPROPRIATE STANDARDS IN PERFORMING THE DUTIES OF THE OFFICE

In performing the duties prescribed by law, by resolution of the Judicial Conference of the United States, by court order, or by the federal public defender, the following standards apply:

A. A defender employee should respect and comply with the law and these canons. A defender employee should report to the appropriate supervising authority any attempt to induce the defender employee to violate these canons.

> *Note:* A number of criminal statutes of general applicability govern defender employees' performance of official duties. These include:

> 18 U.S.C. § 201 (bribery of public officials and witnesses);

> 18 U.S.C. § 211 (acceptance or solicitation to obtain appointive public office);

> 18 U.S.C. § 285 (taking or using papers relating to government claims);

> 18 U.S.C. § 287 (false, fictitious, or fraudulent claims against the government);

> 18 U.S.C. § 508 (counterfeiting or forging transportation requests);

> 18 U.S.C. § 641 (embezzlement or conversion of government money, property, or records);

> 18 U.S.C. § 643 (failing to account for public money);

> 18 U.S.C. § 798 and 50 U.S.C. § 783 (disclosure of classified information);

> 18 U.S.C. § 1001 (fraud or false statements in a government matter);

> 18 U.S.C. § 1719 (misuse of franking privilege);

> 18 U.S.C. § 2071 (concealing, removing, or mutilating a public record);

> 31 U.S.C. § 1344 (misuse of government vehicle);

> 31 U.S.C. § 3729 (false claims against the government).

This is not a comprehensive listing but sets forth some of the more significant provisions with which defender employees should be familiar.

B. A defender employee should be faithful to professional standards and maintain competence in the defender employee's profession.

C. A defender employee should be patient, dignified, respectful, and courteous to all persons with whom the defender employee deals in an official capacity, and should require similar conduct of personnel subject to the defender employee's direction and control. A defender employee should diligently discharge the responsibilities of the office in a nondiscriminatory fashion.

D. A defender employee should not solicit or accept a payment of money or anything of value from a client, except that a defender employee may accept an appropriate memento or token that is neither money nor of commercial value. A defender employee should never disclose any confidential communications from a client, or any other confidential information received in the course of official duties, except as authorized by law. A former defender employee should observe the same restrictions on disclosure of confidential information that apply to a current defender employee.

E. A defender employee should not engage in nepotism prohibited by law.

Note: See also 5 U.S.C. § 3110 (employment of relatives); 28 U.S.C. § 458 (employment of judges' relatives).

F. *Conflicts of Interest.*

> (1) In providing legal representation to clients, a public defender should observe applicable rules of professional conduct governing the disclosure and avoidance of conflicts of interest. . . .

CANON 4: A FEDERAL PUBLIC DEFENDER EMPLOYEE MAY ENGAGE IN ACTIVITIES TO IMPROVE THE LAW, THE LEGAL SYSTEM, AND THE ADMINISTRATION OF JUSTICE

A defender employee, subject to the proper performance of official duties, may engage in the law-related activities enumerated below.

A. A defender employee may speak, write, lecture, teach, and participate in other activities concerning defender services, the legal system, and the administration of justice.

Source: From Chapter 2, "Code of Conduct for Judicial Employees," in *Guide to Judiciary Policies and Procedures,* vol. 2 (Washington, DC: Administrative Office of the U.S. Courts, September 19, 1995). Available online:<www.uscourts.gov/guide/vol2/ch2b.html>. Accessed July 30, 2002.

B. A defender employee may serve as a member, officer, or director of an organization or governmental agency devoted to the improvement of the law, the legal system, or the administration of justice. A defender employee may assist such an organization in raising funds and may participate in the management and investment of such funds. A defender employee may make recommendations to public and private fund-granting agencies on projects and programs concerning the law, the legal profession, and the administration of justice. A defender employee may solicit funds for law-related activities, subject to the following limitations:

(1) A defender employee should not use or permit the use of the prestige of the office in the solicitation of funds.

(2) A defender employee should not solicit subordinates to contribute funds to any such activity but may provide information to them about a general fund-raising campaign.

(3) A defender employee should not solicit or accept funds from lawyers, clients, or other persons likely to have official business with the federal public defender office, except as an incident to a general fund-raising activity.

C. A defender employee may promote the development of professional organizations and foster the interchange of information and experience with others in the profession. A defender employee may make himself or herself available to the public at large for speaking engagements and public appearances designed to enhance the public's knowledge of the operation of defender services and the criminal justice system.

CANON 5: A FEDERAL PUBLIC DEFENDER EMPLOYEE SHOULD REGULATE EXTRA-OFFICIAL ACTIVITIES TO MINIMIZE THE RISK OF CONFLICT WITH OFFICIAL DUTIES

A. *Avocational Activities.* A defender employee may write, lecture, teach, and speak on subjects unrelated to the profession, and may engage in the arts, sports, and other social and recreational activities, if such avocational activities do not detract from the dignity of the office, interfere with the performance of official duties, or adversely reflect on the public defender's role as an advocate. A defender employee may solicit funds for avocational activities, subject to the limitations set forth in canon 4B.

B. *Civic and Charitable Activities.* A defender employee may participate in civic and charitable activities that do not detract from the dignity of the office, interfere with the performance of official duties, or adversely reflect on the public defender's role as an advocate. A defender employee may serve as an officer, director, trustee or advisor of an educational, religious, charitable, fraternal, or civic organization, and may solicit funds for any such organization subject to the limitations set forth in canon 4B.

C. *Financial Activities.*

(1) A defender employee should refrain from financial and business dealings that tend to detract from the dignity of the office or interfere with the performance of official duties. . . .

CANON 6: A FEDERAL PUBLIC DEFENDER EMPLOYEE SHOULD REGULARLY FILE REPORTS OF COMPENSATION RECEIVED FOR ALL EXTRA-OFFICIAL ACTIVITIES

A defender employee may receive compensation and reimbursement of expenses for outside activities provided that receipt of such compensation or reimbursement is not prohibited or restricted by this code, the Ethics Reform Act, and other applicable law, and provided that the source or amount of such payments does not influence or give the appearance of influencing the defender employee in the performance of official duties or otherwise give the appearance of impropriety. Expense reimbursement should be limited to the actual cost of travel, food, and lodging reasonably incurred by a defender employee and, where appropriate to the occasion, by the defender employee's spouse or relative. Any payment in excess of such an amount is compensation. A defender employee should make and file reports of compensation and reimbursement for outside activities to the extent prescribed by the Ethics Reform Act, other applicable law, or the Judicial Conference of the United States.

Notwithstanding the above, a defender employee (other than a defender employee serving without compensation) should not receive any salary, or any supplementation of salary, as compensation for official government services from any source other than the United States.

Note: See 5 U.S.C. App. § § 101 to 111 (Ethics Reform Act financial disclosure provisions). See also 5 U.S.C. App. § § 501 to 505 (outside earned income and employment).

CANON 7: A FEDERAL PUBLIC DEFENDER EMPLOYEE SHOULD REFRAIN FROM INAPPROPRIATE POLITICAL ACTIVITY

A. A defender employee should not be a candidate for or hold partisan elective office and should not solicit partisan political contributions. A defender employee should not engage in any political activity while on duty or in the defender employee's workplace and may not utilize any federal resources in any such activity. Political activity includes, but is not limited to, displaying campaign literature, badges, stickers, signs or other items of political advertising on behalf of any party, political committee, or candidate for political office and soliciting signatures for political candidacy or membership in a political party.

B. A defender employee may engage in political activity not otherwise prohibited, provided that such activity does not detract from the dignity of the office or interfere with the proper performance of official duties. A defender employee who participates in political activity should not use his or her position or title in connection with such activity.

Note: See also 18 U.S.C. Chapter 29 (elections and political activities).

of varying levels of competence among attorneys. All attorneys are not the same. Some, while authorized to practice law, prove to be totally ineffective in their duties. As such, the courts have grappled with what constitutes **effective assistance of counsel**.

When the Right Applies

The Sixth Amendment does not explicitly state that effective assistance of counsel is required, but the Supreme Court has interpreted it in this way. However, the right to *effective assistance* only applies when the right to *counsel* applies. For example, the Supreme Court has held that a defense attorney's failure to file a timely discretionary appeal is not ineffective because the right to counsel does not extend to such appeals (*Wainwright v. Torna*, 455 U.S. 586 [1982]). Only when counsel is required can an ineffective assistance claim be made out.

It is important to realize that claims of ineffective assistance can be filed against both retained and appointed counsel. For a time, the Supreme Court held that a nonindigent defendant who retained his or her own attorney was bound by that attorney's representation, for better or worse, because there was no state action responsible for the ineffective representation. However, in *Cuyler v. Sullivan* (446 U.S. 335 [1980]), the Court held that privately retained counsel can be ineffective in the same way a public defender can:

> The vital guarantee of the Sixth Amendment would stand for little if the often uninformed decision to retain a particular lawyer could reduce or forfeit the defendant's entitlement to constitutional protection. Since the State's conduct of a criminal trial itself implicates the State in the defendant's conviction, we see no basis for drawing a distinction between retained and appointed counsel that would deny equal justice to defendants who must choose their own lawyers. (p. 344)

The Meaning of *Effective Assistance*

So, what constitutes effective assistance of counsel? The lower courts are somewhat divided in terms of how to answer this question, so it is necessary to focus on the Supreme Court's standard for deciding whether defense counsel's assistance is or is not effective. Before getting to the cases, however, Figure 11.6 (pages 336–337) reprints portions of the "Code of Conduct for Federal Public Defender Employees," published by the Administrative Office of the U.S. Courts. Public defenders are defense attorneys for indigent individuals, but the Code is informative nevertheless.

In the first case, *McMann v. Richardson* (397 U.S. 759 [1970]), the Court held that counsel is effective when his or her legal advice is "within the range of competence demanded of attorneys in criminal cases" (p. 771). This is something of a vague standard, so the Court created a new test in *Strickland v. Washington* (466 U.S. 668 [1984]). There, the Court held that a two-prong test must be applied in order to determine whether counsel is ineffective:

■ *Strickland v. Washington,* 466 U.S. 668 (1984)

> First, the defendant must show that counsel's performance was deficient. This requires showing that counsel made errors so serious that counsel was not functioning as the "counsel" guaranteed the defendant by the Sixth Amendment. Second, the defendant must show that the deficient performance prejudiced the defense. This requires showing that counsel's errors were so serious as to deprive the defendant of a fair trial, a trial whose result is unreliable. (p. 687)

The two prongs announced in this case are now known as the *performance* prong and the *prejudice* prong. With regard to the former, "The proper measure of attorney performance remains simply reasonableness under prevailing professional norms" (p. 688). Defense counsel's performance will be considered adequate if he or she avoids conflicts of interest, serves as an advocate for the defendant's case, and brings to bear "such skill and knowledge as will render the trial a reliable adversarial testing process" (p. 688). Furthermore, defense counsel "has a duty to make reasonable investigations or to make a reasonable decision that makes particular investigations unnecessary" (p. 691).

For example, in *Strickland*, the Court stated that "[a]ctual or constructive denial of the assistance of counsel" and "various kinds of state interference with counsel's assistance" are "legally presumed to result in prejudice" (p. 692). State interference of this sort can occur when the defendant is either denied counsel or provided with counsel too late. Also, if the state blocks counsel's performance to some degree or otherwise interferes with the attorney/client relationship, an ineffective assistance of counsel claim is likely to succeed.

With regard to conflict of interest, this form of ineffective assistance can be manifested in several ways. For example, ineffective assistance is likely if the attorney (1) tries to represent more than one defendant in the same trial; (2) has represented one of the prosecution's witnesses in a previous trial; (3) is being paid by a third party; or (4) is contracted with a publishing company to write the defendant's story. Numerous other conflict-of-interest scenarios are possible, as well. Recently, in *Mickens v. Taylor* (535 U.S. 162 [2002]), the Supreme Court considered the question of whether a defense attorney's conflict of interest violates the defendant's Sixth Amendment rights. The defendant in this case claimed his conviction should be overturned because the judge should have inquired about the conflict of interest at trial and did not. However, the Supreme Court held that the judge's failure to do so did not entitle the defendant to an automatic reversal. Instead, the Court held that the defendant had to establish that the potential conflict of interest adversely affected the trial attorney's performance.

In another case involving the ineffective assistance of counsel, *Bell v. Cone* (535 U.S. 685 [2002]), the Supreme Court held that defense counsel's failure to present any mitigating evidence or to make a closing statement at the defendant's capital sentencing hearing was not ineffective. Among the reasons for the Court's decision was that the mitigating evidence that was *not* presented during the sentencing hearing *was* presented at trial, so the jury did have an opportunity to review it.

In *Rompilla v. Beard* (125 S.Ct. 2456 [2005]), the Court declared that defense counsel is bound to make reasonable efforts to obtain and review material that it knows the prosecution will probably rely on as part of its case, something the defense attorney did not do. But, contrast *Beard* with the Court's decision in *Florida v. Nixon* (543 U.S. 175 [2004]). There, the defense attorney acknowledged—in open court—his client's guilt and instead focused his defense on reasons why the defendant's life should be spared. The evidence was so clearly indicative of the defendant's guilt, that the Supreme Court did not feel the defense attorney's strategy was ineffective.

Even without state interference or conflict of interest, there are countless other means by which counsel can be considered ineffective. Attorneys' errors can come in several varieties. Generally, though, the defendant must point to a specific error or set of errors, not the overall performance of his or her counsel. If defense counsel makes a specific error and can offer no explanation for the error, then the defendant will have a good chance in succeeding with a claim of ineffective assistance of counsel. This chance hinges, however, on the second prong announced in *Strickland*: prejudice.

DECISION MAKING EXERCISE 11.10

Effective Assistance of Counsel

A woman has been convicted of check fraud. On appeal, she claims that she was denied access to effective counsel. She argues that her attorney, a young public defender, had never tried a jury case and did not have enough time to prepare an adequate defense. Will her appeal succeed?

Proving defense counsel's ineffective assistance is not enough to ensure a conviction will be overturned. In addition, the defendant must prove that "there is a reasonable probability that, but for counsel's unprofessional errors, the result of the proceeding would have been different" (*Strickland*, p. 694). In other words, the burden falls on the defendant to show that the outcome of the case hinged on the ineffective assistance provided by his or her defense attorney. If defense counsel acted ineffectively but such actions did not influence the outcome of the case, then a *Strickland* claim cannot succeed. The Supreme Court has not elaborated extensively on these issues, but they have been touched on extensively in the lower courts.

■ THE COURTROOM WORK GROUP

It is fitting at this juncture to point out that prosecutors and defense attorneys do not always work independently of each other. In contrast, most prosecutors and defense attorneys see each other on a regular basis. Moreover, they often appear before the same judges. This leads to a great deal of familiarity among the three parties. Researchers have used the term **courtroom work group** to describe this relationship. Walker has described the process in this way:

> Working together every day, members of the courtroom work group reach a general consensus about how different kinds of cases should be handled. This involves shared understanding about how much cases are "worth." There are "heavy" cases (that is, serious violent crimes) and "garbage" cases (relatively minor theft). This valuation allows them to move cases along quickly. . . . Conflict between prosecution and defense is the exception rather than the rule. Although in theory we have an *adversarial* process, in which truth is to be determined through conflict between prosecution and defense, the reality is that an *administrative* system is in effect, with a high degree of consensus and cooperation.[9]

Thus, even though this chapter has treated the prosecution and defense as distinctly separate, in reality this is not the case. Indeed, the general perception is that criminal procedure in the United States is combative and adversarial. On the whole, this is not true, either. It is in the interest of prosecutors and defense attorneys, especially public defenders, to work together, and also with the judge, to speed up the administration of justice. A lengthy, drawn-out adversarial process would contribute to delay.

CONCLUSION

A prosecutor's decision whether to charge is rarely challenged. Reasons for nonprosecution include a lack of evidence and too much court backlog. However, a prosecutor's decision not to press charges *can* be challenged. On rare occasions, a court can effectively overrule a prosecutor's decision not to charge someone. Also, a prosecutor's superior can demand that charges be brought.

Prosecutors' charging decisions are subject to certain constitutional restrictions. Unfair and selective prosecutions are inappropriate and violate the equal protection clause of the Fourteenth Amendment. Prosecutions based on one of two duplicative statutes can also violate equal protection. Finally, vindictive prosecutions violate due process.

Joinder refers either to (1) bringing several charges against the same individual in the same trial or (2) bringing charges against multiple defendants in the same trial. Both methods of joinder are generally considered appropriate, but if the crimes (or defendants) in question are

only tied together because they are similar, separate trials may be warranted. Assuming the court permits joinder, then for separate trials to be held, the defendant must prove that his or her interests will be prejudiced in some fashion by a joint trial.

Approximately one-third of all states and the federal system require that prosecution in felony cases proceed by grand jury indictment. In the remaining states, prosecution can proceed by indictment or information. Grand juries are closely related to prosecutors in terms of their charging decisions. Frequently, the grand jury serves as a means of formalizing the prosecutor's decision to charge. A grand jury is useful when the case in question is of great public and/or political significance, when its extensive investigative powers are helpful, when time is of the essence, and when one or more witnesses is hesitant to speak in open court, preferring the secrecy that surrounds grand jury proceedings.

The size of a grand jury varies, depending on location. Typically, the smaller the grand jury, the higher the

---

[9]S. Walker, *Sense and Nonsense about Crime and Drugs*, 5th ed. (San Francisco: Wadsworth, 2001), p. 53.

voting requirement. Grand jury selection pools must be representative in terms of race and gender. That is, a grand jury selection procedure that purposefully discriminates on the basis of race and/or gender will be unconstitutional. Indeed, if the selection procedure systematically excludes an identifiable segment of society, then it is inappropriate. The final grand jury itself does not need to be representative of the community.

Grand jury proceedings are typically held in secret. Thus, there are significant restrictions on what information from grand jury proceedings can be shared with the defense as well as other parties. There are several reasons for secrecy: (1) to prevent the escape of possible indictees; (2) to ensure freedom to the grand jury in its deliberations; (3) to prevent tampering with the witnesses who may testify; (4) to encourage persons who have information with respect to the commission of crimes to come forward; and (5) to protect the innocence of those who are ultimately exonerated by grand jury investigations.

An individual who is the target of a grand jury investigation does not have the right (1) to appear in front of the grand jury; (2) to have the assistance of counsel during the grand jury's investigation; (3) to be told he or she is the target of the investigation; or (4) to be reminded that he or she has the right to remain silent. In short, many of the constitutional rights that apply in the context of a criminal trial do not apply during the course of a grand jury investigation.

Grand juries possess extensive investigative powers. They can issue subpoenas *ad testificandum*, which require witnesses to appear and testify, and subpoenas *duces tecum,* which compel the production of evidence. Unlike subpoenas to elicit testimony, subpoenas to compel the production of tangible evidence must be sufficiently particular, relevant to the investigation, and not overly burdensome. As part of their investigative powers, grand juries can also grant immunity and hold people in contempt.

Just as there are constraints on prosecutors' charging decisions, there are restrictions on grand juries' indictment decisions; however, a grand jury indictment is rarely quashed. Only when there is evidence of serious prosecutorial tampering, discrimination in the composition of the grand jury pool, or variance between the evidence presented during the grand jury investigation and that presented at trial will a grand jury indictment possibly be quashed.

Criminal defendants enjoy the Sixth Amendment right to counsel once adversarial criminal proceedings have commenced; this usually means once charges have been filed. Otherwise, when there is no possibility of confinement, the right to counsel does not apply. Like many constitutional rights, the right to counsel can be waived, but the court can appoint standby counsel in certain circumstances. Finally, the Supreme Court has interpreted the right to counsel to mean the right to effective counsel. Counsel is ineffective when specific errors are made that are prejudicial to the defendant's case.

REVIEW QUESTIONS

1. What is the role of the prosecutor?
2. What are some reasons for nonprosecution? What can be done to challenge a prosecutor's decision not to pursue charges?
3. What types of restrictions exist on the ability of the prosecutor to bring charges? Cite relevant cases.
4. What is joinder? Explain the differences between joinder of charges and joinder of defendants.
5. Referring to Figure 11.4 (page 323), what is the size of the grand jury in your state? Investigate the voting requirements and selection methods of grand juries in your state.
6. Explain some significant Supreme Court decisions with regard to the secrecy of grand jury proceedings.
7. Explain the rights of witnesses testifying before grand juries.

8. Distinguish among three types of investigative powers that grand juries possess.
9. Can a grand jury indictment be challenged? If so, how? If not, why not?
10. What two constitutional provisions does the right to counsel in a criminal prosecution come from?
11. Explain how the right to counsel applies at other stages of the criminal process.
12. Can the Sixth Amendment right to counsel be waived? If so, what are the requirements for a valid waiver? Also, can a judge overrule a defendant's decision to waive counsel?
13. When might a defendant not be able to hire counsel of his or her choice?
14. Explain the meaning of *effective assistance of counsel.*
15. What must a defendant show in order to succeed with an ineffective assistance of counsel claim?

 Answers to the Decision-Making Exercises for this chapter can be found on pages 513–515.

CHAPTER 12

Plea Bargaining and Guilty Pleas

OUTLINE

KEY TERMS

plea bargaining
prosecutorial inducements

ad hoc plea bargaining
statutory inducements

judicial inducements
guilty plea

INTRODUCTION
Methods of Avoiding Trial

Obtaining a guilty plea as the result of plea bargaining is the most common method of securing a conviction. The overwhelming majority—90 percent, by some estimates—of criminal convictions in the United States result from guilty pleas, rather than trials. Moreover, these pleas usually derive from some bargaining between the defense attorney and the prosecutor. Both parties stand to gain something from a guilty plea: The prosecutor obtains a conviction, and the defense attorney usually succeeds in getting lenient treatment for his or her client.

Plea bargaining is essential to the administration of justice. If every defendant demanded his or her right to a jury trial and succeeded in such a demand, the criminal justice system would literally collapse. In this vein, arguments against plea bargaining are really like thought exercises; nothing can be done to eliminate plea bargaining because there are just too many criminals and not enough prosecutors, courts, and prisons.

At the same time, though, critics' views should not be dismissed. Consistent with what Americans are all taught, many people believe that judges and juries should determine guilt and that prosecutors and defense attorneys should only play a secondary role in this process. Plea bargaining essentially permits attorneys to decide the outcome of a case without ever going to trial. And it is well known that when two defendants face the same charge, the one who plea bargains invariably receives a lesser sentence than the one who does not.

KEY CASES

Supreme Court's View on Plea Bargaining
- *Brady v. United States*, 397 U.S. 742 (1970)

Plea-Bargaining Process
- *Bordenkircher v. Hayes*, 434 U.S. 357 (1978)
- *United States v. Goodwin*, 457 U.S. 368 (1982)
- *Corbitt v. New Jersey*, 439 U.S. 212 (1978)

Effects of Plea Bargaining
- *Mabry v. Johnson*, 467 U.S. 504 (1984)
- *Santobello v. New York*, 404 U.S. 257 (1971)

- *United States v. Benchimol*, 471 U.S. 453 (1985)
- *Ricketts v. Adamson*, 483 U.S. 1 (1987)

Valid Guilty Pleas
- *Henderson v. Morgan*, 426 U.S. 637 (1976)
- *Boykin v. Alabama*, 395 U.S. 238 (1969)
- *McCarthy v. United States*, 394 U.S. 459 (1969)

Understand, though, that plea bargaining is not the only way to arrive at a guilty plea. Many defendants plead guilty to the charges against them even when no bargaining takes place. The bulk of this chapter focuses on plea bargaining; however, the section Elements of a Valid Guilty Plea is especially important for both types of guilty pleas: those that follow bargaining and those that do not. A sample of the plea form that is submitted to the court is presented in Figure 12.1.

FIGURE 12.1 Sample Plea Form

Plea Form

STATE OF TEXAS   IN THE MUNICIPAL COURT
                                                  CITY OF FRISCO
          VS   WEST COUNTY, TEXAS

_____
(Full Name)

CASE/CITATION NO. _____

☐ **PLEA OF GUILTY**

I, the undersigned, do hereby enter my appearance on the complaint of the offense as filed in municipal court. I have been informed of my right to a jury trial and that my signature to this plea of guilty will have the same force and effect as a judgment of the court. I do hereby plead guilty to the offense as charged, waive my right to a jury trial or hearing by the court and agree to pay the fine and costs the judge assesses.

☐ **PLEA OF NOLO CONTENEDRE**

I, the undersigned, do hereby enter my appearance on the complaint of the offense as filed in municipal court. I do hereby plead nolo contendere to said offense as charged, waive my right to a jury trial or hearing by the court and agree to pay the fine and costs the judge assesses.

☐ **NOT GUILTY**

I, the undersigned, do hereby enter my plea of not guilty and waive my right to a jury trial, and request a trial date for trial before the Judge.

_____   _____
Date   Defendant's Signature

                                        _____
                                        Address

                                        _____
                                        City/State/Zip

_____
Judge's Signature

_____
Date

Source: Used courtesy of Frisco, Texas.

PLEA BARGAINING

Definitions of *Plea Bargaining*

There is no agreed upon definition of **plea bargaining**, so the following subsections consider two definitions. The first is a specific definition found in *Black's Law Dictionary*, and the second is a more general definition.

A Specific Definition

Black's Law Dictionary provides a specific definition of *plea bargaining*. Namely, it is "the process whereby the accused and the prosecutor in a criminal case work out a mutually satisfactory disposition of the case subject to court approval. It usually involves the defendant's pleading guilty to a lesser offense or to only some of the counts of a multi-count indictment in return for a lighter sentence than the possible sentence for the graver charge."[1]

It is useful to distinguish between charge bargaining and sentence bargaining. *Charge bargaining* refers to the prosecutor's ability to negotiate with the defendant in terms of the charges that could be filed. *Sentence bargaining*, by contrast, is when the defendant agrees to plead guilty in exchange for a less serious sentence. Charge bargaining is largely carried out between the prosecution and the defense. Sentence bargaining requires getting the judge involved because he or she usually hands down the sentence. In fact, there is even such a thing as *count bargaining*, in which the defense negotiates to have the defendant charged with fewer counts of a certain offense.

Black's definition first states that a plea bargain results in "a mutually satisfactory disposition." It is true, as will be noted later, that a plea bargain must be intelligent and voluntary, but it is not always satisfactory to both parties. For example, the prosecutor may simply be *forced* to present a favorable offer to the defendant because of procedural errors that would make it difficult to prove the state's case. Or the prosecutor may present the defendant with equally unfavorable choices. As one researcher observed, "[T]he right to reject the proposed plea bargain is largely chimerical. Fear of heavier sentence after trial and deference to advice of defense counsel might lead defendants to accept virtually all plea agreements."[2]

Black's definition of plea bargaining also states that each bargain must be "subject to court approval." While this is usually true, the plea-bargaining process is mostly carried on between the defense and the prosecution with little judicial review. For example, prosecutors can do a great deal to drop or alter charges against an individual prior to bringing any subsequent agreement to the attention of the trial judge.

Finally, the foregoing definition of plea bargaining states that it "usually involves the defendant's pleading guilty to a lesser offense . . . in return for a lighter sentence." While this statement is true, it also obscures the reality that many concessions (i.e., besides a lighter sentence) can be offered to the defendant in exchange for a guilty plea. For example, sentence-bargaining concessions may include, but are not limited to, (1) the judge agreeing to impose certain probation conditions; (2) the prosecutor recommending a certain sentence to the judge; (3) the prosecutor agreeing not to invoke certain sentencing provisions, say, for multiple offenders; and (4) an agreement that the defendant will serve his or her sentence in a certain institution.[3]

A General Definition

In light of some of the shortcomings of the *Black's Law Dictionary* definition of plea bargaining, at least one authority has offered a more general definition: *Plea bargaining* is

---

[1]*Black's Law Dictionary*, 6th ed. (1990), p. 1152.
[2]"Plea Bargaining and the Transformation of the Criminal Process," *Harvard Law Review* 90 (1977): 564, 579.
[3]For a review of other such concessions, see H. S. Miller et al., *Plea Bargaining in the United States* (Ann Arbor, MI: Inter University Consortium for Political and Social Research, 1978), p. 17.

"the defendant's agreement to plead guilty to a criminal charge with the reasonable expectation of receiving some consideration from the state."[4] This definition is far more inclusive in that it recognizes that several varieties of bargaining can actually take place. Several of these are considered throughout the remainder of this chapter.[5]

■ The History and Rise of Plea Bargaining

Article II, Section 2, of the U.S. Constitution provides that "the trial of all Crimes, except in Cases of Impeachment, shall be by Jury." Obviously, plea bargaining supplants trial by jury. An interesting historical question is, therefore, At what point did this provision of the Constitution lose its significance? That is, at what point in history did the practice of plea bargaining gain acceptance?

Historical Origins

One of the earliest reported cases addressing plea bargaining was decided in the early 1800s. In that case, *Commonwealth v. Battis* (1 Mass. 95 [1804]), a court was hesitant to permit a guilty plea by a defendant charged with a capital crime. The court gave the defendant time to contemplate his plea and even "examined, under oath, the sheriff, the jailer and justice (before whom the examination of the prisoner was had [sic] previous to commitment), as to the sanity of the prisoner; and whether there had been tampering with him, either by promises, persuasions, or hopes of pardon if he would plead guilty" (p. 96).

Following *Battis*, other cases involving some degree of plea bargaining were reported. One court's opinion focused on a Michigan statute that set forth specific requirements necessary for a valid guilty plea. The court expressed concern that some of what could be called *plea bargaining* was taking place without the approval of the courts (*Edwards v. People*, 39 Mich. 760 [1878]). The court observed that Michigan passed the statute "for the protection of prisoners and of the public" in response "to serious abuses caused by [prosecutors] procuring prisoners to plead guilty when a fair trial might show they were not guilty, or might show other facts important to be known" (p. 761). The court also found it "easy to see that the Legislature thought there was danger that prosecuting attorneys . . . would procure prisoners to plead guilty by assurances [that] they have no power to make[,] of influence in lowering the sentence, or by bringing some other unjust influence to bear on them" (p. 762). These claims suggest that plea bargaining was a somewhat common practice by the second half of the nineteenth century.

Plea bargaining became even more common in the early to mid 1900s. Many states had, by then, impaneled commissions to study the workings of their criminal justice systems. An example of one such commission was the New York State Crime Commission, which was impaneled in 1927. The studies published by these commissions reported an increase in the practice of plea bargaining. For example, the Georgia Department of Public Welfare reported that the rate of pleading guilty increased 70 percent from 1916 to 1921.[6] Similarly, statistics in New York revealed that between 1839 and 1920, the guilty plea rate rose to some 90 percent of all cases.[7]

Reasons for the Rise

Why the apparent rise in plea bargaining? Historical accounts show that in the early days of English criminal justice, a jury would hear 12 to 20 felony cases in a single day.[8]

[4]Miller, pp. 1–2.
[5]Much of the discussion that follows is based on D. D. Guidorizzi, "Should We Really 'Ban' Plea Bargaining? The Core Concerns of Plea Bargaining Critics," *Emory Law Journal* 47 (1998): 753.
[6]Georgia Department of Public Welfare, "Crime and the Georgia Courts," *Journal of the American Institute of Criminal Law and Criminology* 16 (1924): 16.
[7]R. Moley, "The Vanishing Jury," *Southern California Law Review* 2 (1928): 97, 107.
[8]J. H. Langbein, "The Criminal Trial before Lawyers," *University of Chicago Law Review* 45 (1978): 263, 277.

Trials played out in a similar fashion in U.S. courts during the 1800s. One historian points out that many early trials in the United States were carried out without lawyers for the defendant and even, in some cases, for the government.[9] As the U.S. legal system began to mature and lawyers became regular participants, trials slowed down and guilty plea rates increased out of necessity. According to one source, "[P]lea bargaining should be viewed as a natural outgrowth of a progressively adversarial criminal justice system."[10]

Despite its apparent necessity, plea bargaining was criticized extensively by early commentators. Some called it an "incompetent, inefficient, and lazy method of administering justice."[11] Others suggested that plea bargaining was just a means of avoiding trials for individuals charged with committing criminal acts. The following section considers some of these criticisms in further depth.

■ Arguments in Support of Plea Bargaining

There are several arguments in support of plea bargaining. And given that plea bargaining is a widely accepted practice in the U.S. justice system, these arguments have clearly won out. Plea bargaining is widely accepted because, despite certain drawbacks (discussed later), it benefits all members of the courtroom work group: the judge, the prosecutor, and the defense attorney (not to mention the defendant). Thus, the arguments in support of plea bargaining are really arguments concerning the *benefits* of reaching plea agreements. Each of these arguments needs to be viewed in context, however. In some situations, such as highly celebrated cases, the costs of plea bargaining may outweigh the benefits.

Plea bargaining benefits the prosecutor because it provides him or her with a greater ability to dispose of a busy case load. District attorneys are often faced with limited resources and, as such, cannot prosecute every case that comes before them. Specifically, a district attorney may opt to pursue charges on cases that have a highly public element and/or are likely to result in guilty convictions. Cases that do not look promising may be prime candidates for plea bargaining. And according to one observer, plea bargaining may be favored by the prosecution simply because it allows the courtroom work group to further its "mutual interest in avoiding conflict, reducing uncertainty, and maintaining group cohesion."[12]

Defense attorneys also benefit from plea bargaining. Public defenders, who are the most common type of counsel in criminal trials, face resource constraints similar to those of prosecutors. Thus, plea bargaining benefits public defenders by allowing quick disposition of cases. It also allows them to focus on cases that they perceive as being worthy of trial. Bargaining also benefits privately retained counsel because it speeds up the process, which translates into "more money for less work." This is not to suggest, however, that this is the prime motivation of defense attorneys. Many zealously guard the interests of their clients.

On one level, plea bargaining benefits the defendant perhaps more than the prosecutor or the defense attorney. The obvious reason for this is that the defendant generally receives a lesser sentence (or charge, which also affects the ultimate punishment) as a result of plea bargaining. On another level, as will be discussed later, the defendant loses his or her chance at an acquittal and, sometimes, important rights, including the right to a trial by jury. But the Supreme Court has said that these costs may be outweighed by the benefits of "avoiding the anxieties and uncertainties of trial" (*Blackledge v. Allison*, 431 U.S. 63 [1977], p. 71).

[9]L. M. Friedman, *Crime and Punishment in American History* (New York: Basic Books, 1993), p. 235.
[10]Guidorizzi, pp. 753, 760.
[11]A. W. Alschuler, "Plea Bargaining and Its History," *Law and Society Review* 13 (1979): 211 (quoting the *Chicago Tribune*, April 27, 1928, p. 1).
[12]R. A. Weninger, "The Abolition of Plea Bargaining: A Case Study of El Paso County, Texas," *UCLA Law Review* 35 (1987): 265, 267, n. 5.

FIGURE 12.2   Arguments For and Against Plea Bargaining

Arguments For	Arguments Against
Contributes to cohesion in the courtroom work group	Behooves the prosecutor to choose the most serious charge from which to begin bargaining
Helps the prosecutor dispose of a busy case load	Contributes to inefficiency
Helps the public defender dispose of a busy case load	Wastes time; most defendants plead guilty anyway
Benefits the defendant by providing a reduction in charges and/or a favorable sentencing recommendation	Undermines the integrity of the justice system
Saves on judicial resources by avoiding the costs of going to trial	Decides the defendant's guilt without having a trial
May give the victim the satisfaction of having a prompt resolution of the case	Allows the criminal to get away with his or her crime
May benefit the victim who does not wish to testify at trial	An innocent individual may be coerced to plead guilty (i.e., legal versus factual guilt)

The court also benefits from plea bargaining. The prompt disposition of cases saves judicial resources, as researching a plea bargain takes less time than holding a full-blown trial. In fact, to the chagrin of many, the victims of crime may even benefit from plea bargaining. A quickly reached plea bargain may give the victim the satisfaction of having the case closed sooner rather than later. Moreover, the victim may also not want to testify or risk the possibility that the prosecution will not succeed in obtaining a conviction.[13] Figure 12.2 summarizes the arguments for and against plea bargaining.

Criticisms of Plea Bargaining

Apart from the obvious concern with the prosecutor and defense attorney effectively deciding a defendant's guilt, there are other problems posed by plea bargaining. One is that in an effort to secure a conviction, the prosecutor will start with the most serious charge and work down. That is, the prosecutor may *overcharge* as a first step in the bargaining process. This negotiation process is much like that of buying a used car at a dealership, in which the dealer usually starts with a ridiculously high price but is willing to negotiate. In the end, however, few buyers end up purchasing a car for its fair market value. The concern with plea bargaining, then, is that the defendant will be encouraged to plead guilty to an offense that is more serious than that for which he or she would be convicted at trial.

Again, according to many commentators, plea bargaining is a method of streamlining the adjudication process; it is prized on efficiency grounds. However, some critics of plea bargaining claim that the practice actually contributes to *inefficiency*. As one researcher observed, "[D]efense attorneys commonly devise strategies whose only utility lies in the threat they pose to the court's and prosecutor's time."[14]

Critics further contend that not only is plea bargaining inefficient, but it also wastes time. They claim that plea bargaining is not necessary to obtain guilty pleas and that

[13]C. E. Demarest, "Plea Bargaining Can Often Protect the Victim," *New York Times*, April 15, 1994, p. A30.
[14]A. W. Alschuler, "The Prosecutor's Role in Plea Bargaining," *Chicago Law Review* 36 (1968): 50, 54.

most defendants plead guilty anyway, if they think it is highly likely that going to trial will result in a verdict of guilty.[15]

Perhaps one of the most well-known criticisms of plea bargaining is that it undermines the integrity of the criminal justice system. Throughout this book, discussion has examined the complex rules of criminal procedure set forth by the U.S. Constitution and interpreted by the Supreme Court. Critics of plea bargaining claim that the practice circumvents these "rigorous standards of due process and proof imposed during trials."[16]

Another reason that plea bargaining may undermine the criminal process is that it effectively decides the defendant's guilt without having a trial, an exhaustive investigation, or the presentation of evidence and witness testimony. As mentioned earlier in this section, the defendant's guilt is effectively decided by the prosecutor. One critic has argued that plea-bargaining decisions result from improper considerations:

> One mark of a just legal system is that it minimizes the effect of tactical choices upon the outcome of its processes. In criminal cases, the extent of an offender's punishment ought to turn primarily upon what he did and, perhaps, upon his personal characteristics rather than upon a postcrime, postarrest decision to exercise or not to exercise some procedural option.[17]

Yet another argument against plea bargaining is that it allows criminals to get away with their crimes—or at least to receive lenient sentences. Further, critics claim that providing reduced sentences may reduce the deterrent effect of harsh punishment. In both cases, plea bargaining may give the impression that defendants can negotiate their way out of being adequately punished for their crimes.

At the other extreme, critics of plea bargaining also claim that innocent individuals may be coerced to plead guilty. In such a situation, a plea bargain amounts to an admission of legal guilt, when, in fact, the defendant may not be factually guilty. An example of the pressure on innocent defendants to plead guilty can be found in *North Carolina v. Alford* (400 U.S. 25 [1970]). In that decision, the Court reprinted this statement made by the defendant: "I pleaded guilty on second degree murder because they said there is too much evidence, but I ain't shot no man, but I take the fault for the other man. We never had an argument in our life and I just pleaded guilty because they said if I didn't they would gas me for it, and that is all" (p. 28).

■ Attempts to Restrict Plea Bargaining

Concerns over plea bargaining have led some jurisdictions to abandon the practice. In fact, at one point, the whole criminal justice system of Alaska banned plea bargaining, which led researchers to conclude that "the efficient operation of Alaska's criminal justice system did not depend upon plea bargaining."[18]

Several other jurisdictions have experimented with restricting the practice of plea bargaining, and their experience is perhaps more illustrative than the Alaska experience. (Alaska is not representative of the overall U.S. crime problem.) Methods of restricting plea bargaining have ranged from outright bans to bans on bargaining in certain types of crimes.

One method by which some jurisdictions have restricted plea bargaining is to impose a cutoff date, which prohibits plea bargaining after a case has been in process for

---

[15]P. Arenella, "Rethinking the Functions of Criminal Procedure: The Warren and Burger Courts' Competing Ideologies," *Georgia Law Journal* 72 (1983): 185, 216–219.

[16]A. P. Worden, "Policymaking by Prosecutors: The Uses of Discretion in Regulating Plea Bargaining," *Judicature* 73 (1990): 335, 336.

[17]A. W. Alschuler, "The Changing Plea Bargaining Debate," *California Law Review* 69 (1981): 652.

[18]M. L. Rubenstein and T. J. White, "Alaska's Ban on Plea Bargaining," *Law and Society Review* 13 (1979): 367.

a certain amount of time. For example, the Brooklyn (New York) District Attorney has adopted a cutoff date of 74 days after indictment.[19] Plea bargaining is acceptable prior to the deadline. And if a case goes all the way to trial within the cutoff period, plea bargaining could conceivably take place all the way through jury deliberations.

Another method of restricting plea bargaining has been to ban the practice in some or all types of plea agreements. Alaska is, of course, the most notable example of a total ban. In 1975, the Alaska Attorney General banned all forms of plea bargaining in an effort to increase convictions and restore public confidence in the justice system.[20] In a study on the ban, the Alaska Judicial Council concluded the following:

> Plea bargaining as an institution was clearly curtailed. The routine expectation of a negotiated settlement was removed; for most practitioners justifiable reliance on negotiation to settle criminal cases greatly diminished in importance. There is less face-to-face discussion between adversaries, and when meetings do occur, they are not usually as productive as they used to be.[21]

It is important to understand that Alaska banned plea bargaining but not the entering of guilty pleas. Defendants could still plead guilty to the crimes for which they were charged. In fact, the Judicial Council also found that the rate of guilty pleas remained essentially the same after the ban, suggesting that perhaps some degree of behind-the-scenes plea bargaining was still taking place. Also, in Alaska, the attorney general can hire and fire the district attorneys, which gives him or her substantial leverage to ban plea bargaining. (In most jurisdictions around the United States, district attorneys are elected officials and do not serve at the desire of the state attorney general.)

Some jurisdictions have also experimented with banning plea bargaining for certain offenses. For example, the Bronx County (New York) District Attorney enacted a ban on plea bargaining whenever a grand jury returned a felony indictment. This move was seriously criticized, as are most attempts to restrict plea bargaining, but the district attorney stated that the ban "means that society has ceded control to those it has accused of violating its laws; and it means that our system is running us, instead of the other way around."[22] Critics challenged the Bronx County District Attorney's ban on postfelony indictment plea bargaining for at least two reasons: (1) it did not eliminate plea bargaining, and (2) it encouraged plea bargaining prior to indictment.[23]

Another approach tried in Philadelphia was the *jury waiver*, which gives the defendant the opportunity to engage in plea negotiations in exchange for giving up his or her right to a jury trial. Actually, this approach is not plea bargaining in the traditional sense. Instead, the defendant gets his or her day in court, but to receive concessions from the state, he or she must not demand a jury trial. This process has come to be known as the *slow plea of guilty*, insofar as it does not result in the disposition of a case prior to trial. One researcher described the process in more detail:

> Slow pleas are informal and abbreviated, and consist largely of the defense's presentation of statements concerning the defendant's allegedly favorable personal characteristics. . . . The defense presentation is not concerned with guilt or innocence since it usually is implicitly assumed by all parties involved in the process that the defendant is guilty of at least some wrongdoing.[24]

---

[19]C. Mirsky, "Plea Reform Is No Bargain," *New York Newsday*, March 4, 1994, p. 70.
[20]T. W. Carns and J. A. Kruse, "Alaska's Ban on Plea Bargaining Reevaluated," *Judicature* 75 (1992): 310, 317
[21]Guidorizzi, pp. 753, 775.
[22]Press release, statement from R. T. Johnson, District Attorney, Office of the District Attorney of Bronx County, New York, November 24, 1992.
[23]Guidorizzi, pp. 753, 778.
[24]M. A. Levin, *Urban Politics and the Criminal Courts* (Chicago: University of Chicago Press, 1977), p. 80.

Still other attempts to restrict or ban plea bargaining have occurred. California attempted to abandon plea bargaining by popular referendum in 1982. The voters passed the referendum and the resulting statute (Cal. Penal Code 1192.7) imposed the following restrictions: No plea bargaining in any case involving (1) a serious felony, (2) a felony in which a firearm was used, or (3) the offense of driving under the influence. Plea bargaining is permissible, however, if the prosecution's evidence is weak, witnesses are unavailable, or a plea agreement does not result in a significantly reduced sentence. Despite the statute, plea bargaining continues almost unabated in the state of California (*People v. Brown*, 223 Cal. Rptr. 66 [Ct. App. 1986], p. 72, n. 11).

El Paso County, Texas, also experimented with plea-bargaining restrictions. In 1987, two state district judges adopted a policy of prohibiting all plea negotiations in their courts as a method of ensuring equal treatment for similarly situated defendants.[25] Maricopa County, Arizona, adopted a similar approach in 1995. Five Maricopa County Superior Court judges adopted a policy that prohibited plea agreements based on stipulated (i.e., agreed upon) sentences. In other words, the judges refused to accept any plea agreement that included a negotiated sentence, believing that sentencing should be a decision left to the trial courts (*Espinoza v. Martin*, 894 P.2d. 688 [Ariz. 1995]).

The Supreme Court's View on Plea Bargaining

Notwithstanding the competing views on plea bargaining, the Supreme Court has essentially laid the debate to rest by upholding the validity of the practice. In *Brady v. United States* (397 U.S. 742 [1970]), for example, the Court stated, "Of course, that the prevalence of guilty pleas is explainable does not necessarily validate those pleas or the system which produces them. But we cannot hold that it is unconstitutional for the State to extend a benefit to a defendant who in turn extends a substantial benefit to the State" (pp. 752–753). Next, in the case of *Santobello v. New York* (404 U.S. 257 [1971]), the Court offered the following argument in support of plea bargaining: "The disposition of criminal charges by agreement between the prosecutor and the accused, sometimes loosely called 'plea bargaining,' is an essential component of the administration of justice. Properly administered, it is to be encouraged" (p. 260).

■ *Brady v. United States,* 397 U.S. 742 (1970)

How, then, is plea bargaining to be properly administered? The following sections seek to answer this question. First, the plea-bargaining process is described, and then the effects of plea bargaining, the rules concerning plea bargaining, and situations in which guilty pleas can be challenged are all discussed. The reader will develop an understanding of the complex practice of plea bargaining as it has been interpreted through the courts—most notably, the U.S. Supreme Court.

THE PLEA-BARGAINING PROCESS

The prosecutor can make several different offers in order to secure a guilty plea. The most straightforward and common method is to reduce the charge or charges against the defendant. Other alternatives include dismissing other pending charges, promising to recommend a particular sentence, and promising not to contest a point made by the defense.

Assuming that what is offered by the prosecution is acceptable to the defendant, then he or she can make one of two pleas: a simple plea of guilty or a plea of *nolo contendere*. The former is akin to saying "I am guilty," and the latter is akin to saying "I do not contest this." Both pleas are effectively the same. The only difference is that the *nolo* plea cannot be used as an admission of guilt in a subsequent civil case.

[25]R. A. Weninger, "The Abolition of Plea Bargaining: A Case Study of El Paso County, Texas," *UCLA Law Review* 35 (1987): 265, 275.

Constitutional Rights during Plea Bargaining

Plea bargaining is a method of circumventing criminal trial, so not surprisingly, the rights available to the defendant during bargaining are not the same as those available at trial. There are, however, important rights that the defendant still enjoys during the plea-bargaining process, including the rights to effective assistance of counsel and to be informed of exculpatory evidence. The defendant does not have the right to be present at important stages of the bargaining process, however.

The Sixth Amendment right to counsel applies during plea bargaining because charges have already been filed before bargaining commences. According to the Supreme Court in *Kirby v. Illinois* (406 U.S. 682 [1972]), the right to counsel attaches when, after charges have been filed, the "defendant finds himself faced with the prosecutorial forces of organized society, and immersed in the intricacies of substantive and procedural criminal law" (p. 689). This means that the prosecutor cannot bargain directly with the defendant unless counsel has been waived.

The Sixth Amendment also requires that defense counsel be effective during the plea-negotiation process. This means that the defense attorney must, at a minimum, investigate the case so as to make an informed decision with regard to what sentences and charges are offered by the prosecution. To be effective, counsel must also ensure that his or her client understands the consequences of the plea-bargaining process. This is not to suggest that the defendant can easily succeed in claiming ineffective assistance of counsel during negotiation, however. According to the Court in *Hill v. Lockhart* (474 U.S. 52 [1985]), the defendant must show "a reasonable probability that, but for counsel's errors, he would not have pleaded guilty and would have insisted on going to trial" (p. 58).

Next, the defendant enjoys the right to be informed of exculpatory evidence in possession of the prosecution. That is, if the prosecutor has evidence that casts doubt on the accused's guilt, he or she must inform the defense of that evidence. For evidence to be considered *exculpatory*, it must have a reasonable probability of affecting the outcome of the case. Evidence that is inconsequential to the question of guilt, which is clearly rare, need not be provided to the defense (*United States v. Bagley*, 473 U.S. 667 [1985]).

Finally, as will be considered in an upcoming chapter, the defendant enjoys the right to be present at his or her own trial. However, this right does not apply in the context of plea bargaining. That is to say, no court has required that a criminal defendant be provided a constitutional right to be present during plea bargaining. This could change, but for now, all that is required is that the defense effectively communicates to his or her client the nature of the sentence or charges offered by the prosecution.

Recently, in *United States v. Ruiz* (536 U.S. 622 [2002]), the Supreme Court decided that the defendant *does not* have the right to impeachment information relating to informants and other witnesses nor does he or she have the right to information supporting any affirmative defense that he or she might raise if the case went to trial. Thus, there are limitations to the defendant's rights during the plea-bargaining process.

Acceptable Inducements by the Prosecution

The Constitution places few restrictions on offers the prosecution may make during the bargaining process, which are known as **prosecutorial inducements**. Since *Brady v. United States* (397 U.S. 742 [1970]) was the first Supreme Court case to condone plea bargaining, it is a fitting point of departure before considering the offers prosecutors can make. The defendant in *Brady* was charged with kidnapping under a statute that permitted (1) a jury to recommend the death penalty if it saw fit *or* (2) a judge to sentence the defendant to life in prison, if guilt was determined via a bench trial. The defendant opted for a jury trial but then changed his plea to guilty and was sentenced to 30 years. He then argued that the statute effectively compelled him to plead guilty because of fear of the death penalty. The Supreme Court rejected this claim.

The reasoning the Court offered for its decision is somewhat complicated but important. Justice White emphasized that the statute in *Brady caused* the guilty plea but did not *coerce* it. He then emphasized that coercion is possible only when physical force or mental pressure is applied. This means that if "Brady was so gripped by fear of the death penalty or hope of leniency that he did not or could not, with the help of counsel, rationally weigh the advantages of going to trial against the advantages of pleading guilty" (p. 750), then his argument would have succeeded. However, Justice White found that the statute at most *influenced* Brady and that the coercion argument was exaggerated. In further support of his opinion, Justice White quoted an appellate court decision dealing with plea bargaining, *Shelton v. United States* (246 F.2d 571 [5th Cir. 1957]):

> [A] plea of guilty entered by one fully aware of the direct consequences, including the actual value of any commitments made to him by the court, prosecutor, or his own counsel, must stand unless induced by threats (or promises to discontinue improper harassment), misrepresentation (including unfulfilled or unfulfillable promises), or perhaps by promises that are by their nature improper as having no proper relationship to the prosecutor's business (e.g., bribes). (p. 572)

In short, a guilty plea resulting from an inducement from the prosecution, like a confession obtained in a police interrogation room, should not be involuntary. A guilty plea will be considered involuntary when it results from prosecutorial coercion (e.g., physical force or strong psychological pressuring). If, by contrast, the prosecutor causes a guilty plea simply because the accused thinks that pleading as such is his or her best way of avoiding a long prison term, then the defendant cannot succeed by claiming such a plea is involuntary.

DECISION MAKING EXERCISE 12.1

What Constitutes Coercion?

The prosecutor approaches the defendant and his attorney and says, "I am prepared to charge you with petty larceny in lieu of grand larceny. If you plead guilty to the petty larceny charge, you will avoid being prosecuted under the state's 'three strikes' statute. If you don't plead guilty, I will charge you under the 'three strikes' law and I will make sure that you will go to prison for the rest of your natural life." The defendant accepts the plea agreement but later appeals it, claiming that it was coerced by the prosecution. How should the court rule?

What, then, offers/inducements can the prosecution properly make? *Brady* answered this question only insofar as the Court held that the prosecutor cannot coerce a guilty plea. In *Bordenkircher v. Hayes* (434 U.S. 357 [1978]), the Court attempted to offer a clearer answer. In that case, the defendant was indicted by a grand jury for forging a check for $88.30. The range of punishment was 2 to 10 years in prison. The prosecutor offered to recommend a 5-year sentence but threatened to seek an indictment under a habitual criminal statute if the defendant did not accept the offer. Since the defendant had two prior felony convictions, a conviction under the habitual criminal statute could have resulted in life in prison.

Bordenkircher v. Hayes, 434 U.S. 357 (1978)

Somewhat controversially, in a 5 to 4 decision, the Supreme Court upheld the defendant's conviction under the habitual criminal statute on the theory that it resulted from a choice among known alternatives. Basically, the Court said that the defendant had the choice to accept 5 years in prison and neglected to take the opportunity. The defendant argued that his second conviction was vindictive, citing *North Carolina v. Pierce* (395 U.S. 711 [1969]; see Chapter 11). But the Court countered by stating that "the imposition of these difficult choices [is] an inevitable—'and permissible'—attribute of any legitimate system which tolerates and encourages the negotiation of pleas" (*Bordenkircher v. Hayes*, p. 364).

Reduced to its most fundamental elements, the Court's opinion in *Bordenkircher* thus implies that the prosecution has great latitude in terms of being able to persuade the defendant to accept a plea, as long as the higher charges are authorized by law and are openly presented to the defense. This suggests, as well, that the prosecution may offer a charge or sentencing concession in exchange for the defendant agreeing not to appeal or claim that some constitutional right has been violated. The Court stated further:

> There is no doubt that the breadth of discretion that our country's legal system vests in prosecuting attorneys carries with it the potential for both individual and institutional abuse. And broad though that discretion may be, there are undoubtedly constitutional limits upon its exercise. We hold only that the course of conduct engaged in by the prosecutor in this case, which no more than openly presented the defendant with the unpleasant alternatives of forgoing trial or facing charges on which he was plainly subject to prosecution, did not violate the Due Process Clause of the Fourteenth Amendment. (p. 365)

■ *United States v. Goodwin,*
457 U.S. 368 (1982)

In a related case, *United States v. Goodwin* (457 U.S. 368 [1982]), the Court reached a similar decision. There, the defendant was indicted on additional charges after plea negotiations broke down. The Court held that the prosecutor could file additional charges if an initial expectation that the defendant would plead guilty to a lesser charge proved unfounded. The Court refused to accept the defendant's argument that this prosecution was vindictive and, once again, gave broad authority to prosecutors in the plea-bargaining process.

Nonetheless, certain prosecutorial inducements are *not* permissible. For example, the Supreme Court has stated that "a prosecutor's offer during plea bargaining of adverse or lenient treatment for some person *other* than the accused . . . might pose a greater danger of inducing a false guilty plea by skewing the assessment of the risks a defendant must consider" (*Bordenkircher v. Hayes*, p. 365, n. 8). Also, if the prosecutor flagrantly deceives the accused or fabricates evidence and/or starts rumors concerning the accused's level of involvement in the offense, a resulting guilty plea will be deemed unconstitutional.

DECISION MAKING EXERCISE 12.2

Prosecutorial Deception

Assume that a prosecutor and defendant are negotiating a plea agreement. In the negotiation, the prosecutor lies to the defendant, saying, "We have a videotape recording of you engaged in the crime. If you do not plead guilty, this evidence will be used against you at trial. No jury in its right mind would acquit you based on the recording. However, if you plead guilty to petty larceny, then you will be out of jail in no time flat." The defendant pleads guilty but later appeals his conviction, claiming that his plea was the result of prosecutorial deception. What should the court decide?

■ Questionable Inducements

Colquitt has recently used the term **ad hoc plea bargaining** to refer to some of the strange concessions that defendants agree to make as part of prosecutors' decisions to secure guilty pleas. He states:

> Ad hoc bargains exist in at least five forms: (1) the court may impose an extraordinary condition of probation following a guilty plea, (2) the defendant may offer or be required to perform some act as a quid pro quo for a dismissal or more lenient sentence, (3) the court may impose an unauthorized form of punishment as a substitute for a statutorily established method of punishment, (4) the State may offer some unauthorized benefit in

---

FIGURE 12.3   Examples of Ad Hoc Plea-Bargaining Concessions

1. Charitable contributions in lieu of fines or jail terms: *State v. Stellato* (523 A.2d 1345 [Conn. App. Ct. 1987]); *Ratliff v. State* (596 N.E.2d 241 [Ind. Ct. App. 1992])

2. Relinquished property ownership: *United States v. Thao Dinh Lee* (173 F.3d 1258 [10th Cir. 1999])

3. Agreement to surrender a professional license or not work in a particular profession: *United States v. Hoffer* (129 F.3d 1196 [11th Cir. 1997])

4. Voluntary agreement to undergo sterilization: *State v. Pasicznyk* (1997 WL 79501 [Wash. Ct. App. Feb. 25, 1997])

5. Voluntary agreement to undergo surgical castration: *ACLU v. State* (5 S.W.2d 418 [Ark. 1999])

6. Agreement to enter the army on a four-year enlistment: *State v. Hamrick* (595 N.W.2d 492 [Iowa 1999])

7. Agreement not to appeal: *People v. Collier* (641 N.Y.S.2d 181 [App. Div. 1996])

8. Shaming punishments, such as bumper stickers for convicted DUI offenders: *Ballenger v. State* (436 S.E.2d 793 [Ga. Ct. App. 1993])

9. Agreement to seal the records of a case: *State v. Campbell* (21 Media L. Rep. 1895 [Wash. Super. Ct. 1993])

10. Ordering offenders to surrender profits, such as from books written about their crimes: *Rolling v. State ex rel. Butterworth* (741 So. 2d 627 [Fla. Dist. Ct. App. 1999])

11. Banishment to another location: *State v. Culp* (226 S.E.2d 841 [N.C. Ct. App. 1976]); *Phillips v. State* (512 S.E.2d 32 [Ga. Ct. App. 1999])

12. Pleading guilty to nonexistent crimes (i.e., crimes that are not prohibited by law): *Bassin v. Isreal* (335 N.E.2d 53 [Ill. App. Ct. 1975])

Source: Adapted from J. A. Colquitt, "Ad Hoc Plea Bargaining," *Tulane Law Review* 75 (2001): 69. See Colquitt's article for a *thorough* discussion of various, sometimes stranger concessions made as a result of ad hoc plea bargaining (i.e., note 26).

---

return for a plea of guilty, or (5) the defendant may be permitted to plead guilty to an unauthorized offense, such as a 'hypothetical' or nonexistent charge, a nonapplicable lesser-included offense, or a nonrelated charge.[26]

Colquitt also states that ad hoc plea bargaining "may involve neither a plea nor a sentence. For example, if a defendant charged with public intoxication seeks to avoid a statutorily mandated minimum sentence of ten days in the county jail, the prosecutor might agree to dismiss the charges if the defendant agrees to make a monetary contribution to a local driver's education program" (p. 711).

Judges can even get involved in ad hoc plea bargaining. Colquitt points to one shocking example of this method of bargaining run amok. The case, *Ryan v. Comm'n on Judicial Performance* (754 P.2d 724 [Cal. 1988]), involved a woman who was required to participate in a drug treatment program as a result of several narcotics convictions. The probation officer asked to have the woman removed from the program because she supposedly failed to follow program guidelines. At a hearing to decide on the matter, the woman, "who was wearing a low-cut sweater, bent over several times to remove documents from her purse. Thereafter the judge dismissed all criminal charges against her. When his clerk asked why the charges had been dropped, [the judge] replied, 'she showed me her boobs'" (p. 734). The judge was subsequently removed from the bench. Some less extreme examples of ad hoc plea concessions, as well as some relevant cases, are described in Figure 12.3 (this page).

[26]J. A. Colquitt, "Ad Hoc Plea Bargaining," *Tulane Law Review* 75 (2001): 695.

An Inducment of Banishment

Carl Moore was arrested for sodomy and other crimes. With the assistance of his counsel, Moore negotiated a guilty plea to three counts of sodomy, one count of violating the Controlled Substances Act, and one count of sexual exploitation of children. The trial judge accepted the guilty plea and followed the state's recommendation to impose (1) a 20-year sentence (i.e., 3 years to serve and 17 years on probation); (2) banishment from the state; and (3) a $10,000 fine. Is banishment an acceptable inducement by the prosecution?

■ Statutory and Judicial Inducements

So far, the discussion has considered only what the prosecution can and cannot do as far as inducing the defendant to plead guilty. There have also been some interesting cases dealing with statutory and judicial inducements. **Statutory inducements** refer to laws that provide lenient sentences in exchange for guilty pleas. **Judicial inducements** include actions by judges that influence the bargaining process.

Statutory Inducements

■ *Corbitt v. New Jersey,* 439 U.S. 212 (1978)

With regard to statutory inducements, an illustrative case is *Corbitt v. New Jersey* (439 U.S. 212 [1978]). In that case, the defendant was convicted of first-degree murder and sentenced to life in prison, as required by the state statute with which he was charged. However, the statute provided that if he decided to plead guilty to the crime, he could be sentenced either to life imprisonment or to a term of 30 years. The defendant claimed that the statute violated due process, but the Supreme Court upheld it in the spirit of consistency. That is, the Court stated that it could not permit prosecutorial bargaining as in *Bordenkircher* "and yet hold that the legislature may not openly provide for the possibility of leniency in return for a plea" (p. 221). Further, the Court stated:

> It cannot be said that defendants found guilty by a jury are "penalized" for exercising the right to a jury trial any more than defendants who plead guilty are penalized because they give up the chance of acquittal at trial. In each instance, the defendant faces a multitude of possible outcomes and freely makes his choice. Equal protection does not free those who made a bad assessment of risks or a bad choice from the consequences of their decision. (p. 226)

The Court also noted, though, that plea bargaining should be an *executive*, as opposed to *legislative*, function. That is, legislatures should not be permitted to decide "that the penalty for every criminal offense to which a defendant pleads guilty is to be one-half the penalty to be imposed upon a defendant convicted of the same offense after a not guilty plea" (p. 227).

Judicial Inducements

Traditionally, plea bargaining results from the prosecution and the defense reaching an agreement; the judge is usually not part of the negotiation process. Today, however, certain jurisdictions permit a degree of judicial involvement in the plea-bargaining process. For example, the American Bar Association standards regarding guilty pleas permit judicial participation when it is requested but only for the purpose of clarifying acceptable charges and sentences. The judge cannot at any point, "either directly or indirectly, [communicate] to the defendant or defense counsel that a plea agreement should be accepted or that a guilty plea should be entered."[27]

[27]American Bar Association, Standard 14-3.3[d], from *Standards for Criminal Justice*, 2nd ed., supp., vol. 3 (Washington, DC: Author, 1986).

Judicial Inducements

Judge Dubois has before her the prosecutor, defense attorney, and defendant in one of the cases slated to be heard in her court. The defense attorney and prosecutor tell the judge that they have reached a plea agreement and that Charles Down, the defendant, has agreed to plead guilty to manslaughter instead of first-degree murder. Judge Dubois then questions Down to ensure that the plea is voluntary, intelligent, and based in fact. During the questioning, Down begins to express reservations about the plea agreement and says, "On second thought, I don't want to plead guilty." Judge Dubois then looks at Down and says, "You should really plead guilty, because from the looks of things, you're going to get the chair if you don't." Down agrees to plead guilty but later appeals, arguing that his plea was not voluntary. How should the court rule?

In order to summarize the plea-bargaining process, Figure 12.4 (page 358) presents relevant portions of Rule 11 of the *Federal Rules of Criminal Procedure*. The procedures outlined are those by which the federal courts must abide.

EFFECTS OF PLEA BARGAINING

A plea bargain ultimately affects three separate parties: (1) the court; (2) the prosecutor; and (3) the defendant (the latter, most often through the defense attorney). How plea bargaining affects these individual parties is discussed in the subsections that follow.

Effects on the Court

The court is not directly bound by a plea agreement. The federal courts permit a plea "only after due consideration of the views of the parties *and* the interest of the public in the effective administration of justice."[28] Thus, if accepting a plea agreement poses a significant risk to the public—say, because a dangerous criminal will be spared prison and placed on probation (an unlikely event)—then the court has the discretion to deny it.

An illustrative case is *United States v. Bean* (564 F.2d 700 [5th Cir. 1977). The facts were as follow: Bean was charged on October 22, 1976, with theft of property (i.e., a car) and with burglary of a habitation, in violation of state law. At the initial arraignment, Bean pleaded not guilty to both counts. On November 30, another arraignment was held on Bean's request. At this time, the court was informed that a plea bargain had been reached between the government prosecutor and Bean and his counsel. Bean would plead guilty to the theft count and cooperate with the prosecutor in investigating others involved in the burglary. In return, the prosecutor would move for a dismissal of the burglary charge. Judge Spears rejected the plea because the offense of entering a home at night where people were sleeping was a much more serious offense than the theft of an automobile. The Fifth Circuit Court of Appeals upheld Judge Spears's decision, stating:

> Without deciding what unusual circumstances may result in the refusal of a plea bargain being an abuse of discretion, we find that Judge Spears' action in this case was well within the scope of his discretion. A decision that a plea bargain will result in the defendant's receiving too light a sentence under the circumstances of the case is a sound

[28] *Federal Rules of Criminal Procedure*, Rule 11, issued by the 107th Congress, First Session, December 1, 2001. Available online: <www.house.gov/judiciary/crim2001.pdf>.

FIGURE 12.4 Plea-Bargaining Procedure

(e) Plea Agreement Procedure.

(1) *In General.* The attorney for the government and the attorney for the defendant—or the defendant when acting pro se—may agree that, upon the defendant's entering a plea of guilty or nolo contendere to a charged offense or to a lesser or related offense, the attorney for the government will:

    (A) move to dismiss other charges; or

    (B) recommend, or agree not to oppose the defendant's request, for a particular sentence, or sentencing range, or that a particular provision of the Sentencing Guidelines, or policy statement, or sentencing factor is or is not applicable to the case. Any such recommendation or request is not binding on the court; or

    (C) agree that a specific sentence or sentencing range is the appropriate disposition of the case, or that a particular provision of the Sentencing Guidelines, or policy statement, or sentencing factor is or is not applicable to the case. Such a plea agreement is binding on the court once it is accepted by the court.

The court shall not participate in any discussions between the parties concerning any such plea agreement.

(2) *Notice of Such Agreement.* If a plea agreement has been reached by the parties, the court shall, on the record, require the disclosure of the agreement in open court or, on a showing of good cause, in camera, at the time the plea is offered. If the agreement is of the type specified in subdivision (e)(1)(A) or (C), the court may accept or reject the agreement, or may defer its decision as to the acceptance or rejection until there has been an opportunity to consider the presentence report. If the agreement is of the type specified in subdivision (e)(1)(B), the court shall advise the defendant that if the court does not accept the recommendation or request the defendant nevertheless has no right to withdraw the plea.

(3) *Acceptance of a Plea Agreement.* If the court accepts the plea agreement, the court shall inform the defendant that it will embody in the judgment and sentence the disposition provided for in the plea agreement.

(4) *Rejection of a Plea Agreement.* If the court rejects the plea agreement, the court shall, on the record, inform the parties of this fact, advise the defendant personally in open court or, on a showing of good cause, in camera, that the court is not bound by the plea agreement, afford the defendant the opportunity to then withdraw the plea, and advise the defendant that if the defendant persists in a guilty plea or plea of nolo contendere the disposition of the case may be less favorable to the defendant than that contemplated by the plea agreement.

(5) *Time of Plea Agreement Procedure.* Except for good cause shown, notification to the court of the existence of a plea agreement shall be given at the arraignment or at such other time, prior to trial, as may be fixed by the court.

(6) *Inadmissibility of Pleas, Plea Discussions, and Related Statements.* Except as otherwise provided in this paragraph, evidence of the following is not, in any civil or criminal proceeding, admissible against the defendant who made the plea or was a participant in the plea discussions:

    (A) a plea of guilty which was later withdrawn;

    (B) a plea of nolo contendere;

    (C) any statement made in the course of any proceedings under this rule regarding either of the foregoing pleas; or

    (D) any statement made in the course of plea discussions with an attorney for the government which do not result in a plea of guilty or which result in a plea of guilty later withdrawn.

However, such a statement is admissible (i) in any proceeding wherein another statement made in the course of the same plea or plea discussions has been introduced and the statement ought in fairness be considered contemporaneously with it, or (ii) in a criminal proceeding for perjury or false statement if the statement was made by the defendant under oath, on the record, and in the presence of counsel.

Source: Federal Rules of Criminal Procedure, Rule 11, issued by the 107th Congress, First Session, December 1, 2001. Available online:<www.house.gov/judiciary/crim2001.pdf>.

reason for a judge's refusing to accept the agreement. . . . In this case, Judge Spears was faced with a man who was charged with burglarizing at night a home on Fort Sam Houston in Texas, while Lieutenant Colonel Robert W. Oppenlander, his wife, two daughters and one son were asleep inside. In addition, the presentence report indicated that Bean had previously been committed to four years in the Texas Department of Corrections for state charges of burglary and theft of a business at nighttime. Bean had also served twenty days for unlawfully carrying a weapon in San Antonio. Given this information Judge Spears was reluctant to accept a plea bargain that would allow Bean to plead guilty to only the theft of an automobile. (p. 704)

Judicial Rejections

Roger Moss has been arrested for and charged with intentionally and with premeditation killing his wife. He reaches an agreement with Terry Stand, the local district attorney, to plead guilty to negligent manslaughter. Stand has a poor track record in the district attorney's office and has lost countless cases to shrewd defense attorneys. He figures entering into this plea agreement is his best shot at finally obtaining a guilty verdict. When Stand and Moss's defense attorney present the plea agreement to the judge, she rejects it on the ground that is unduly lenient. Can the judge reject the plea for this reason?

■ Effects on the Prosecutor

The consequences of plea bargaining are of far greater magnitude for the prosecutor than for the court. Assuming the court accepts a plea bargain, whether it is a charge or sentence reduction, then the prosecutor must fulfill his or her part of the agreement. Note, however, that the prosecutor is not strictly obligated to fulfill his or her promises early in the plea-bargaining process. More specifically, the prosecutor is not bound by the plea bargain prior to the point at which it is accepted by the court.

Prosecutorial Obligations before the Court Accepts the Bargain

The prosecutor has a considerable amount of latitude with regard to fulfilling a plea bargain before it is accepted by the court. This should not be particularly surprising because before the court accepts (or rejects) the bargain, it is not formalized. When the court accepts the bargain, it becomes formalized, at which point the prosecutor must fulfill his or her promises.

A case dealing with the extent to which a prosecutor must uphold his or her end of the bargain prior to the point at which the court accepts it is *Mabry v. Johnson* (467 U.S. 504 [1984]). In that case, the defense attorney called the prosecutor to accept a plea offer, but the prosecutor told him that the offer was a mistake and withdrew it. The prosecutor then offered a more harsh offer in its place, one that would have resulted in a longer prison term. The Supreme Court upheld this practice, arguing that the plea agreement was reached with full awareness on the part of the defendant and "was thus in no sense the product of governmental deception; it rested on no 'unfulfilled promise' and fully satisfied the test for voluntariness and intelligence" (p. 510).

■ *Mabry v. Johnson,* 467 U.S. 504 (1984)

The Prosecutor's Duty to Fulfill the Bargain

Connor Leaves was charged with armed robbery and with possession of a firearm during the commission of a felony. A plea agreement was reached wherein Leaves would plead guilty to attempted armed robbery and to the possession charge. In exchange for this reduction in charges, Leaves would assist the police and prosecution in investigating an unrelated crime. Leaves proceeded to fulfill his end of the agreement and told authorities that his friend, Bill Wright, was the man they were looking for. The prosecutor then withdrew the plea offer, stating that it was contrary to his office's policy. Leaves moved to reinstate the negotiated plea agreement, and the motion was granted. The prosecution has now appealed this decision. How should the appellate court rule?

Prosecutorial Obligations after the Court Accepts the Bargain

■ *Santobello v. New York*, 404 U.S. 257 (1971)

In general, the prosecution is bound to its plea-bargaining promises after the court accepts the bargain. An illustrative case is *Santobello v. New York* (404 U.S. 257 [1971]). In that case, the defendant was indicted for two felonies. He first entered a plea of not guilty on each count. After subsequent negotiations, however, the prosecutor agreed to allow the defendant to plead guilty to a lesser offense. The defendant then withdrew his pleas of not guilty and agreed to plead guilty to the lesser offense. The court accepted the plea. At sentencing, however, a new prosecutor, who was unaware of what had transpired earlier, requested the maximum sentence. The defense objected on the grounds that the previous prosecutor promised not to make any particular sentencing recommendation. The judge then stated that he was not influenced by the second prosecutor's sentencing recommendation and imposed the maximum sentence.

In response to this turn of events, the Supreme Court declared that the sentence should be declared unconstitutional as a matter of due process. The Court stated that "when a plea rests in any significant degree on a promise or agreement of the prosecutor, so that it can be said to be part of the inducement or consideration, such promise must be fulfilled" (p. 262).

Unfortunately, though, the Court was not altogether clear in terms of what remedy is preferable when the prosecutor breaches his or her agreement. In *Santobello*, the Court voided the defendant's conviction, but the Justices seemed mixed on the appropriate remedy for future cases. Some agreed that if the prosecution breaches its promise after the court has accepted the bargain, then it must be forced to uphold the bargain or the defendant should be able to withdraw the guilty plea. Others felt that the trial court should decide what remedy is necessary. The issue remains unresolved.

■ *United States v. Benchimol*, 471 U.S. 453 (1985)

Some years after *Santobello*, in the case of *United States v. Benchimol* (471 U.S. 453 [1985]), the Supreme Court seemed to change its opinion with regard to a prosecutor's breach of a plea agreement after the court has accepted it. In *Benchimol*, the prosecutor agreed to recommend a sentence of probation with restitution, but the presentence report mentioned nothing of the agreement. The defense attorney pointed out the error, and the prosecution agreed that an agreement had been reached. Even so, the court sentenced the defendant to six years. The defendant then sought to have his sentence vacated, and the court of appeals agreed. However, the Supreme Court reversed, holding that unless the prosecution supports a recommendation "enthusiastically" or sets forth its reasons for a lenient recommendation, the court is under no obligation to honor the agreement. According to the Supreme Court:

> It may well be that the Government in a particular case might commit itself to "enthusiastically" make a particular recommendation to the court, and it may be that the Government in a particular case might agree to explain to the court the reasons for the Government's making a particular recommendation. But respondent does not contend, nor did the Court of Appeals find, that the Government had in fact undertaken to do either of these things here. The Court of Appeals simply held that as a matter of law such an undertaking was to be implied from the Government's agreement to recommend a particular sentence. But our view of Rule 11(e) [of the *Federal Rules of Evidence*, which sets forth procedures for plea bargaining] is that it speaks in terms of what the parties in fact agree to, and does not suggest that such implied-in-law terms as were read into this agreement by the Court of Appeals have any place under the Rule. (p. 455)

DECISION MAKING EXERCISE **12.7**

Two Prosecutors, One Bargain

A plea bargain was reached between Prosecutor 1 and the defendant, in which the defendant agreed to plead guilty to less serious charges. Three months later, at the defendant's sentencing hearing, a different prosecutor, Prosecutor 2, represented the state. The following exchange took place between the judge and Prosecutor 2:

> *Prosecutor 2*: At this time, Your Honor, the government calls for sentencing the case of the *United States of America v. Defendant*.
>
> *Judge*: Anything you wish to say, Mr. Prosecutor 2?
>
> *Prosecutor 2*: Well, Your Honor, in light of the plea-bargaining agreement, the government, at this time, is recommending three years' incarceration. We also recommend that, if possible, the defendant be incarcerated at a minimum security prison.
>
> *Judge*: Why?
>
> *Prosecutor 2*: Well, Your Honor, that was part of the plea bargain.
>
> *Judge*: Not because you believe in it?
>
> *Prosecutor 2*: Well, Your Honor, I do have some problems with that, but this is the way I understand it.
>
> *Judge*: Anything else?
>
> *Prosecutor 2*: Nothing further.

The defendant was then sentenced to four years in prison at a different institution. He has appealed his sentence. How should the appellate court rule?

■ Effects on the Defendant

The defendant who accepts an offer to plead guilty often faces consequences besides a reduced sentence or charge. For instance, the defendant can be required to waive his or her right to appeal a guilty plea. Also, if the defendant supplies inaccurate information during the course of plea negotiations, he or she may not benefit from lenient treatment. Furthermore, in exchange for pleading guilty, the prosecution may require that the defendant testifies against a co-defendant.

DECISION MAKING EXERCISE **12.8**

Waiving Rights as a Consequence of Plea Bargaining

Here are the facts from an actual case, *United States v. Black* (201 F.3d 1296 [10th Cir. 2000]):

> On November 20, 1997, a grand jury charged Mr. Black with five federal firearms offenses. . . . On April 15, 1998, Mr. Black entered into a plea agreement with the government. . . . Under the agreement, Mr. Black agreed to plead guilty to count three of the indictment. . . . He also agreed to waive his right to appeal his sentence. . . . The agreement stated that "the defendant agrees to waive his right to appeal the sentence he receives as a result of this Plea Agreement." . . . The government agreed to dismiss the remaining counts of the indictment and to recommend that Mr. Black receive a three-level downward adjustment in his offense level for acceptance of responsibility. It also agreed that if it appealed the district court's sentencing decision, Mr. Black would be released from the waiver of his right to appeal. (p. 1298)

Should a defendant be required to give up his or her right to appeal pursuant to a plea agreement?

■ *Ricketts v. Adamson,*
   483 U.S. 1 (1987)

A significant Supreme Court case dealing with the latter consequence—that is, possible testimony against a co-defendant—is *Ricketts v. Adamson* (483 U.S. 1 [1987]). In that case, the defendant testified against both of his co-defendants in exchange for a reduction in the charge he was facing. He was then sentenced on the reduced charge. After that, the co-defendants' convictions were overturned on appeal. The prosecution then retried the co-defendants, but the original defendant refused to testify at the second trial, claiming that his duty had been fulfilled. The prosecution then filed on information charging him with first-degree murder. The Supreme Court did not bar the first-degree murder prosecution because the original agreement contained a clause to the effect that the agreement would be void if the defendant refused to testify against his co-defendants. Justice Brennan did acknowledge, however, that the defendant could have construed the plea agreement only to require his testimony at the first trial. The Court noted that the proper procedure, if such a situation would arise in the future, would be to submit a disagreement over the plea to the court that accepted the plea. That way, the expense of a further trial and appeals could be avoided.

At the other extreme, the defendant can sometimes *preserve* certain rights following a plea agreement. These types of arrangements are known as *conditional guilty pleas.* For example, New York law provides that an order denying a motion to suppress evidence alleged to have been obtained as a result of unlawful search and seizure "may be reviewed on appeal from a judgment of conviction notwithstanding the fact that such judgment of conviction is predicated upon a plea of guilty" (N.Y. Crim. Proc. Law §§ 710.20 [1], 710.70 [2]). These types of agreements are rare, however. In *Tollett v. Henderson* (411 U.S. 258 [1973]), the Supreme Court stated that "[w]hen a criminal defendant has solemnly admitted in open court that he is in fact guilty of the offense with which he is charged, he may not thereafter raise independent claims relating to the deprivation of constitutional rights that occurred prior to the entry of the guilty plea" (p. 267).

■ ELEMENTS OF A VALID GUILTY PLEA

Assuming the prosecutor offers an acceptable inducement to the defendant and assuming the defendant agrees to plead guilty in exchange for leniency, the judge still must determine that the defendant understands the plea. This is in addition to the need to determine that the plea conforms to statutory and other requirements, as discussed earlier. In *Boykin v. Alabama* (395 U.S. 238 [1969]), the Supreme Court held that it would be unconstitutional "for the trial judge to accept [a] guilty plea without an affirmative showing that it is intelligent and voluntary" (p. 242). In order to determine that the plea is voluntary, the judge usually questions the defendant. As the Court noted in *McCarthy v. United States* (394 U.S. 459 [1969]):

> By personally interrogating the defendant, not only will the judge be better able to ascertain the plea's voluntariness, but he also will develop a more complete record to support his determination in a subsequent post-conviction attack. . . . Both of these goals are undermined in proportion to the degree the district court judge resorts to "assumptions" not based upon recorded responses to his inquiries. (p. 468)

For a **guilty plea** to be valid, it must conform to three requirements: (1) it must be intelligent; (2) it must be voluntary, not coerced; and (3) it must be based in fact. That is, if the defendant pleads guilty to a crime he or she did not commit, then technically, the plea will be invalid. The following subsections consider the case law regarding these three important requirements.

■ Intelligence and Understanding

In general, for a plea to be *intelligent* (i.e., understood), it must conform to specific requirements. The defendant must understand (1) the nature of the charge or charges of

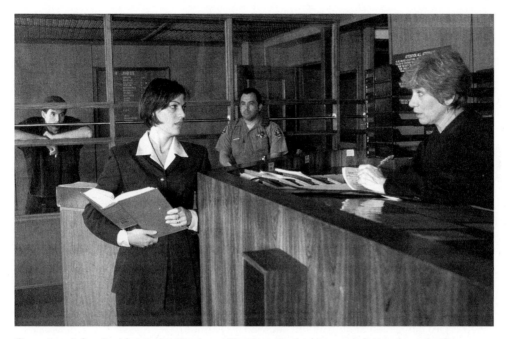

Once the defendant has submitted a guilty plea, the judge must determine whether the defendant understands the plea, whether it was made voluntarily, and whether it is based in fact.

which he or she is accused; (2) the possible sentence or sentences associated with the charges; and (3) the rights he or she may waive if a guilty plea is entered. A person whose mental capacity is called into question may be declared incompetent at a pretrial hearing and treated in order to restore his or her competency. (The issue of competency is discussed further in Chapter 14.)

Understanding the Charge

In *Henderson v. Morgan* (426 U.S. 637 [1976]), the defendant was charged with first-degree murder. However, he pleaded guilty to second-degree murder following an offer by the prosecution. Several years later, he sought to have his conviction voided on the grounds that at the time he entered his plea, he did not understand that one of the elements of second-degree murder was intent to cause death. The Supreme Court held that "since respondent did not receive adequate notice of the offense to which he pleaded guilty, his plea was involuntary and the judgment of conviction was entered without due process of law" (p. 647). The element of intent in second-degree murder (i.e., the *mens rea*) was viewed as critical, which meant it should have been explained to the defendant.

■ *Henderson v. Morgan,* 426 U.S. 637 (1976)

It is not clear based on *Henderson* whether the *judge* must explain the elements of the offense to the defendant or whether this is the job of *counsel*. The Court intimated that if defense counsel explains the offense to the accused, then little else is needed: "[I]t may be appropriate to presume that in most cases defense counsel routinely explain the nature of the offense in sufficient detail to give the accused notice of what he is being asked to admit" (p. 647). Nevertheless, the judge should at least inquire as to whether the defendant understands the charge.

Understanding Possible Sentences

There are virtually no Supreme Court cases dealing with the defendant's understanding of the possible sentences that could result from a plea bargain. However, the *Federal Rules of Criminal Procedure* require that the defendant understand "the consequences of the plea."[29] This includes an understanding of the minimum and maximum sentences as well as applicable sentencing guidelines that the judge might be required to abide by.

Other consequences attendant to plea bargaining and sentencing do not have to be explained, however. For instance, at least one lower court has held that the defendant does not need to be informed of the loss of the right to vote (e.g., *People v. Thomas*, 41 Ill.2d 122 [1968]). Whether failure to inform the defendant of the consequences associated with sentencing rises to the level of a constitutional violation has yet to be determined, however.

DECISION MAKING EXERCISE 12.9

A Valid Guilty Plea?

Bill Dover, a federal prisoner, filed a *habeas corpus* petition (i.e., a method of challenging his confinement; see Chapter 15), claiming that his guilty plea was not knowing and intelligent because of ineffective assistance of counsel. Specifically, Dover claimed that his attorney mistakenly advised him that if he pleaded guilty, he would become eligible for parole after serving one-third of his prison sentence. In actuality, because Dover was as a second-time offender, he was required under state law to serve *one-half* of his sentence before being eligible for parole. In other words, Dover claimed that he was not advised of the actual sentence that would result from his plea bargaining. Should he succeed with his petition?

Understanding of Rights Waived as a Result of Pleading Guilty

The rights *waived* as a result of plea bargaining are different than the rights *denied* as a result of plea bargaining. For example, loss of the right to vote is not a loss due to voluntary waiver; it is a consequence tied to being convicted (even if by guilty plea) of a serious crime. The rights *waived* are those the defendant would otherwise be granted by the Constitution but are essentially given up in exchange for lenient treatment.

The constitutional rights typically waived through plea bargaining are the right to trial by jury, the privilege against self-incrimination, and the right to confront adverse witnesses. By pleading guilty, the defendant forgoes having a trial, which is when these rights are frequently applicable. The privilege against self-incrimination, however, still applies outside the trial context, such as in pretrial custodial interrogations. Regardless, the defendant must be clearly informed of the constitutional rights that are waived as a result of plea bargaining. According to the Supreme Court in *Boykin v. Alabama* (395 U.S. 238 [1969]), there can be no presumption of "a waiver of these three important federal rights from a silent record" (p. 243).

■ *Boykin v. Alabama,* 395 U.S. 238 (1969)

DECISION MAKING EXERCISE 12.10

Another Valid Guilty Plea?

Caroline Wynn pleaded guilty to federal drug charges and was sentenced to 247 months in prison by the U.S. District Court. At sentencing, the court neglected to inform Wynn of her right to appeal her sentence. Several months later, while Wynn was in prison, she filed a *habeas corpus* petition, alleging that the district court's failure to advise her of her right to appeal her sentence violated the express terms of Rule 32(a)(2) of the *Federal Rules of Criminal Procedure*, which provides that "[t]here shall be no duty on the court to advise the defendant of any right of appeal after sentence is imposed following a plea of guilty or *nolo contendere*, except that the court shall advise the defendant of any right to appeal the sentence." Wynn knew of her right to appeal at the time of sentencing but did not file an appeal. Now, she seeks postconviction relief. How should the court decide?

[29] *Federal Rules of Criminal Procedure*, Rule 11.

Voluntariness

In addition to the requirement that a plea be understood, it also must be voluntary. Even though a plea may be understood, it may have resulted from coercion, threats, physical abuse, or the like. Thus, the *Federal Rules of Criminal Procedure* require that a plea be "voluntary and not the result of force or threats or of promises apart from a plea agreement."[30]

Factual Basis

For a plea bargain to be valid, the plea must result from conduct that has a basis in fact. In other words, a defendant cannot (i.e., according to the courts anyway) plead guilty to a crime he or she did not commit. This means that the court should inquire about the crime in question by, perhaps, having the accused describe the conduct giving rise to his or her guilty plea. This does not always occur, but according to the Supreme Court in *McCarthy v. United States* (394 U.S. 459 [1969]):

■ *McCarthy v. United States*, 394 U.S. 459 (1969)

> Requiring this examination of the relation between the law and the acts the defendant admits having committed is designed to "protect a defendant who is in the position of pleading voluntarily with an understanding of the nature of the charge but without realizing that his conduct does not actually fall within the charge." (p. 467)

Importantly, the Court in *McCarthy* did not state that a factual basis for the plea bargain is a *constitutional* requirement, only that there should be one.

The Court elaborated on this matter in a similar case, in which the defendant pleaded guilty but insisted on his innocence. The Court stated that "an express admission of guilt . . . is not a constitutional requisite to the imposition of a prison sentence even if he is unwilling or unable to admit his participation in the acts constituting the crime" (*North Carolina v. Alford*, 400 U.S. 25 [1970]). The Court upheld the man's plea but also pointed out the following:

> Because of the importance of protecting the innocent and of insuring that guilty pleas are a product of free and intelligent choice, various state and federal court decisions properly caution that pleas coupled with claims of innocence should not be accepted unless there is a factual basis for the plea . . . and until the judge taking the plea has inquired into and sought to resolve the conflict between the waiver of trial and the claim of innocence. (p. 38, n. 10)

Thus, while there appears to be no constitutional basis for requiring that a guilty plea be tied to specific criminal acts, the courts—including the Supreme Court—prefer to avoid guilty pleas accepted from otherwise innocent defendants. Unfortunately, it would be purely conjecture to estimate how many innocent criminal defendants plead guilty in order to "play the odds" and avoid potentially lengthy prison terms.

In summary, a valid guilty plea must consist of several elements: knowledge, intelligence, voluntariness, and factual basis. Figure 12.5 presents relevant portions of Rule 11 of the *Federal Rules of Criminal Procedure*, which succinctly summarizes the elements of a valid guilty plea from a perspective other than that of the Supreme Court.

[30]*Federal Rules of Criminal Procedure*, Rule 11[d].

FIGURE 12.5 Elements of a Valid Guilty Plea

(a) [*Types of Pleas*]

(1) *In General.* A defendant may plead guilty, not guilty, or nolo contendere. If a defendant refuses to plead or if a defendant organization, as defined in 18 U.S.C. sec. 18, fails to appear, the court shall enter a plea of not guilty.

(2) *Conditional Pleas.* With the approval of the court and the consent of the government, a defendant may enter a conditional plea of guilty or nolo contendere, reserving in writing the right, on appeal from the judgment, to review of the adverse determination of any specified pretrial motion. A defendant who prevails on appeal shall be allowed to withdraw the plea.

(b) *Nolo Contendere.* A defendant may plead nolo contendere only with the consent of the court. Such a plea shall be accepted by the court only after due consideration of the views of the parties and the interest of the public in the effective administration of justice.

(c) *Advice to Defendant.* Before accepting a plea of guilty or nolo contendere, the court must address the defendant personally in open court and inform the defendant of, and determine that the defendant understands, the following:

(1) the nature of the charge to which the plea is offered, the mandatory minimum penalty provided by law, if any, and the maximum possible penalty provided by law, including the effect of any special parole or supervised release term, the fact that the court is required to consider any applicable sentencing guidelines but may depart from those guidelines under some circumstances, and, when applicable, that the court may also order the defendant to make restitution to any victim of the offense; and

(2) if the defendant is not represented by an attorney, that the defendant has the right to be represented by an attorney at every stage of the proceeding and, if necessary, one will be appointed to represent the defendant; and

(3) that the defendant has the right to plead not guilty or to persist in that plea if it has already been made, the right to be tried by a jury and at that trial the right to the assistance of counsel, the right to confront and cross-examine adverse witnesses, and the right against compelled self-incrimination; and

(4) that if a plea of guilty or nolo contendere is accepted by the court there will not be a further trial of any kind, so that by pleading guilty or nolo contendere the defendant waives the right to a trial; and

(5) if the court intends to question the defendant under oath, on the record, and in the presence of counsel about the offense to which the defendant has pleaded, that the defendant's answers may later be used against the defendant in a prosecution for perjury or false statement; and:

(6) the terms of any provision in a plea agreement waiving the right to appeal or to collaterally attack the sentence.

(d) *Insuring That the Plea Is Voluntary.* The court shall not accept a plea of guilty or nolo contendere without first, by addressing the defendant personally in open court, determining that the plea is voluntary and not the result of force or threats or of promises apart from a plea agreement. The court shall also inquire as to whether the defendant's willingness to plead guilty or nolo contendere results from prior discussions between the attorney for the government and the defendant or the defendant's attorney.

Source: Federal Rules of Criminal Procedure, Rule 11, issued by the 107th Congress, First Session, December 1, 2001. Available online:<www.house.gov/judiciary/crim2001.pdf>.

CONTESTING A GUILTY PLEA

The defendant may wish to contest the guilty plea he or she enters, for several reasons, including the following: (1) if the plea was the product of coercion by the prosecution; (2) if the prosecution has failed to fulfill its end of the bargain; and (3) if other problems emerge, such as unconstitutional conduct on the part of law enforcement officials. A defendant who challenges his or her guilty plea does so in several ways, which include withdrawal of the plea and appeal.[31] Each mechanism is considered in a following subsection.

---

[31] A *habeas corpus* review of a guilty plea is also possible (see Chapter 15).

■ Withdrawing a Guilty Plea

Anytime the court refuses to accept a plea agreement reached by the prosecution and the defense, the defendant can usually withdraw the plea. Similarly, if the defendant pleads guilty even when there has been no plea bargaining, he or she can seek to withdraw his or her plea. However, if the prosecution disagrees with the court's decision to refuse the plea, then the defendant might *not* be able to withdraw his or her plea.

Once a plea has been accepted by the court, then it can only be withdrawn in limited circumstances. The *Federal Rules of Criminal Procedure* provide that a plea can be withdrawn prior to sentencing if the defendant shows a "fair and just" reason for overturning the plea.[32] Fair and just reasons are the same as those mentioned at the outset of this section: involuntary pleas, prosecutorial breaches, and lack of evidence or similar deficiency. Once a sentence has been entered, however, the only methods to challenge a plea are to appeal and, to a lesser extent, to have a *habeas corpus* review (see Chapter 15). Also, many jurisdictions place a time limit on plea withdrawals; usually, withdrawal is not permitted once a sentence has been imposed.

■ Appealing a Guilty Plea

If the defendant moves to withdraw his or her plea and is denied this request, then an appeal is appropriate. However, if the withdrawal period has passed, then the only other method of appealing a guilty plea is through *direct* appeal. This creates something of a difficult situation for the defense. Since an appeal is mostly considered based on the trial court record, then the defendant has limited resources with which to prepare an argument. Namely, there is no transcript of a trial because by entering a guilty plea, the defendant elected to forgo trial. Thus, the only record left may be that from the arraignment or a similar pretrial proceeding. In sum, it is *very difficult* to succeed with a direct appeal of a guilty plea.

Fortunately, some states and the federal government permit appeals based on specific pretrial motions, such as a motion to exclude evidence on constitutional grounds. This is the case in New York and in other jurisdictions that maintain conditional plea mechanisms, as mentioned earlier. These issues aside, there are few Supreme Court precedents addressing appeals of guilty pleas. In *McCarthy v. United States*, the Supreme Court held that the trial court's failure to abide by proper arraignment procedure required reversal of a guilty plea on appeal. This is because the arraignment procedure—especially when there is no trial—"is designed to assist the district judge in making the constitutionally required determination that a defendant's guilty plea is truly voluntary" (p. 465).

Note that the decision to appeal a court's denial of a motion to withdraw a guilty plea is not necessarily the same as an appeal of one's conviction. The former may go to the voluntariness of the plea. The latter may concern some other procedural matter, such as an improper search or seizure, and may be appealable, provided the defendant has not waived his or her right to appeal as a result of plea bargaining.

Finally, note that *plea bargaining* and *pleading guilty* are not the same. Plea bargaining often results in a guilty plea, but a defendant does not have to engage in bargaining to plead guilty. Regardless of how the guilty plea is arrived at, the defendant can still seek to withdraw the plea. By contrast, a guilty plea that is entered *without* plea bargaining is more appealable than one reached as a result of bargaining. In the latter instance, the accused often gives up important rights, such as the right to appeal.

---

[32]*Federal Rules of Criminal Procedure*, Rule 11.

CONCLUSION

Plea bargaining occurs when the prosecution offers some concession to the defendant in exchange for a guilty plea. Two common forms of plea bargaining can be discerned. The first, charge bargaining, occurs when the prosecutor offers to charge the accused with a less serious offense in exchange for a guilty plea. The second, sentence bargaining, occurs when the prosecutor promises the defendant a favorable sentencing recommendation.

Plea bargaining is how most cases in the U.S. criminal justice system are disposed of. By some estimates, 90 percent of all criminal cases are plea bargained. Supporters of the practice claim that bargaining is necessary to ensure the orderly and prompt flow of criminal cases. Critics claim, among other things, that defendants are forced to give up important constitutional rights as a result of the plea-bargaining process. In response to criticism, some jurisdictions have experimented with banning or restricting plea bargaining. Despite these attempts, plea bargaining flourishes today. One of the reasons for this is that the Supreme Court condones the practice.

Despite the Supreme Court's support for plea bargaining, it still requires that certain procedures be followed. First, the defendant must be represented by counsel and that counsel must be effective. Second, the defendant has the right to be informed by the prosecution of exculpatory evidence in the state's possession. Third, the prosecution can offer a wide range of inducements to the defense in order to secure a guilty plea, but those inducements cannot be coercive in nature. Further, there is some question about the propriety of so-called ad hoc plea bargaining: the practice of offering inducements to the defendant other than charge reductions and sentencing recommendations. Finally, statutory and judicial inducements for the defendant to plead guilty should be kept to a minimum.

Plea bargaining affects three parties: (1) the court; (2) the prosecutor; and (3) the defendant (most often through the defense attorney). It affects the court only insofar as the court has to decide whether to accept the plea. A plea agreement that is excessively lenient is likely to be rejected by the court. The prosecutor is affected by plea bargaining only after the agreement has been accepted by the court. That is, the prosecutor must honor the agreement after the judge has accepted it but is under no obligation to do so beforehand. The defendant is perhaps most affected by plea bargaining. He or she often gives up certain rights by pleading guilty but can preserve certain rights pursuant to conditional plea agreement statutes.

Not just any plea agreement suffices. All plea agreements must be valid; that is, they must be knowing and intelligent, voluntary, and based in fact. A knowing and intelligent waiver is one in which the defendant understands the charge, the possible sentences, and the rights waived as a result of bargaining. A voluntary plea is one that is not coerced by the state. Finally, a plea agreement should be based in fact—that is, premised on conduct that actually took place. In other words, the defendant should not plead guilty to a crime he or she did not commit, although this clearly happens from time to time.

A guilty plea can be contested in at least two ways. First, the defendant can seek to withdraw his or her guilty plea. Doing so is fairly difficult once the court has accepted the plea. The defendant must show, for example, that the plea was involuntary to have it withdrawn after the court accepts it. Next, if the defendant is denied a request to withdraw his or her guilty plea, he or she can appeal that decision. Also, the defendant can sometimes appeal his or her conviction (i.e., as opposed to a court's decision to reject a motion to withdraw a guilty plea). The latter is increasingly rare because the defendant often agrees to waive his or her right to appeal as a result of plea bargaining.

REVIEW QUESTIONS

1. What is plea bargaining? Can a defendant plead guilty without plea bargaining?
2. Explain the historical origins of plea bargaining.
3. What are the reasons for the popularity of plea bargaining?
4. Summarize the arguments against plea bargaining.
5. What has been done in response to criticisms of plea bargaining?
6. Summarize the arguments in support of plea bargaining.
7. Explain the accused's constitutional rights during plea bargaining.

8. What are some examples of acceptable inducements by the prosecution?

9. Explain ad hoc plea bargaining. Cite some examples.

10. Explain how judges and statutes can induce guilty pleas.

11. Summarize the effects of plea bargaining on the court.

12. What are the prosecutor's duties before and after the court accepts a plea bargain?

13. In what ways does plea bargaining affect the defendant?

14. Explain the elements of a valid guilty plea.

15. How can a plea of guilty be contested, if at all?

 Answers to the Decision-Making Exercises for this chapter can be found on pages 515–517.

CHAPTER 13

Rights at Trial

OUTLINE

KEY TERMS

INTRODUCTION
Ensuring an Expeditious and Fair Trial

At this point, the discussion turns to the defendant's rights at trial. Assuming a defendant does not plea bargain, a trial will probably result. Thus, it is important to focus on constitutional rights during the trial stage. The three rights considered in this chapter are (1) the right to a speedy trial, (2) the right to an impartial judge, and (3) the right to an impartial jury. Additional rights afforded to the defendant at trial are covered in Chapter 14.

THE RIGHT TO A SPEEDY TRIAL

The Sixth Amendment provides, in part, "In all criminal prosecutions, the accused shall enjoy the right to a **speedy trial.**" What constitutes a *speedy trial*? Unfortunately, there are no easy answers to this question.

Somewhat surprisingly, it was not until 1966 that the Supreme Court addressed the Sixth Amendment's speedy trial provision. In *United States v. Ewell* (383 U.S. 116 [1966]), the Court identified three advantages associated with having a speedy trial: (1) it prevents excessive incarceration; (2) it minimizes anxiety experienced by the accused as a result of a publicized accusation; and (3) it prevents damage to the defendant's case resulting from too much delay.

In *Barker v. Wingo* (407 U.S. 514 [1972]), the Court elaborated on these points:

> If an accused cannot make bail, he is generally confined, as was Barker [the defendant] for 10 months, in a local jail. This contributes to the overcrowding and generally deplorable state of those institutions. Lengthy exposure to these conditions "has a destructive effect on human character and makes the rehabilitation of the individual offender much more difficult." At times the result may even be violent rioting. Finally,

KEY CASES

Speedy Trial
- *United States v. Marion*, 404 U.S. 307 (1971)
- *Doggett v. United States*, 505 U.S. 647 (1992)
- *United States v. Lovasco*, 431 U.S. 783 (1977)
- *Barker v. Wingo*, 407 U.S. 514 (1972)
- *United States v. Loud Hawk*, 474 U.S. 302 (1986)
- *Strunk v. United States*, 412 U.S. 434 (1973)

Impartial Judge
- *Tumey v. Ohio*, 273 U.S. 510 (1927)
- *Ward v. Monroeville*, 409 U.S. 57 (1972)

Impartial Jury
- *McKeiver v. Pennsylvania*, 403 U.S. 528 (1971)
- *Baldwin v. New York*, 399 U.S. 66 (1970)
- *Johnson v. Louisiana*, 406 U.S. 356 (1972)
- *Duren v. Missouri*, 439 U.S. 357 (1979)
- *Smith v. Phillips*, 455 U.S. 209 (1982)
- *Witherspoon v. Illinois*, 391 U.S. 510 (1968)
- *Batson v. Kentucky*, 476 U.S. 79 (1986)
- *Gray v. Mississippi*, 481 U.S. 648 (1987)

lengthy pretrial detention is costly. The cost of maintaining a prisoner in jail varies from $3 to $9 per day, and this amounts to millions across the Nation. In addition, society loses wages which might have been earned, and it must often support families of incarcerated breadwinners. (pp. 520–521)

Not only does the defense benefit from a speedy trial, but so do the government and even society at large. First, having a speedy trial provides the opportunity for a guilty verdict to be secured quickly (assuming, of course, that the defendant is guilty). Also, having a speedy trial minimizes the opportunity for an individual out on bail to commit additional crimes while awaiting trial. However, if the accused is kept in detention prior to trial, too much delay can take a financial toll on the government.

For the reasons just set forth, having a speedy trial can prove advantageous. However, this can be a double-edged sword. Having a speedy trial may promote efficiency, but too much efficiency may damage the defense's case. That is, if the defense is not given adequate time to prepare, then an erroneous guilty verdict could result. In *Ewell*, the Court stated that "[t]he essential ingredient is orderly expedition and not mere speed" (p. 120).

■ When the Right to a Speedy Trial Applies

A fair amount of case law addresses when the right to a speedy trial applies. First, the right generally applies once a person has been *accused* of a crime. The timing of the accusation and the number of accusations can complicate matters, however. The accusation rule will be addressed next and then cases that have tested the limits of the rule. Note that this section focuses on *when* the right to a speedy trial applies, not *whether* the right has been violated. The violation issue is taken up later.

The Accusation Rule

■ *United States v. Marion,*
404 U.S. 307 (1971)

In *United States v. Marion* (404 U.S. 307 [1971]), the defendants sought to dismiss the indictment against them by arguing that the government had known of their identities for three years prior to the indictment. More specifically, they argued that their Sixth Amendment right to a speedy trial had been violated because the government had known of them prior to the point at which they had been indicted. Their argument failed miserably; the Court held that the Sixth Amendment's guarantee to a speedy trial attaches only *after* the person (or persons) has been accused of a crime. The Court further stated that being accused of a crime did not necessarily mean that formal charges had to be filed. Namely, "[T]he actual restraints imposed by arrest and holding to answer on a criminal charge" (pp. 327–328) can be sufficient to amount to an accusation. This has since come to be known as the **accusation rule**.

DECISION
MAKING
EXERCISE **13.1**

Putting Charges on Hold

A prosecutor can sometimes use what is known as a *nolle prosequi* device, which involves charging a person with a crime but deciding, for the time being, not to prosecute the matter any further. The charges are not dismissed; rather, they are put on hold. The suspect can essentially be prosecuted thereafter at the whim of the prosecutor. Assume that a prosecutorial *nolle prosequi* is issued in Rick O'Shea's case. O'Shea has been charged with aggravated assault, but the primary witness against him is in a coma. Assume further that the witness does not come out of the coma for an entire year. O'Shea is then convicted and later appeals, claiming his Sixth Amendment right to a speedy trial was implicated once the *nolle prosequi* commenced. What should the court decide?

Charged and Charged Again

What if a person is charged, has the charges against him or her dropped, and is then charged again at some point in the future? In *United States v. MacDonald* (456 U.S. 1 [1982]), the Court held that the right to a speedy trial does not apply until the second set of charges is filed. In *MacDonald*, there were four years of delay between the dismissal of charges against the accused and a re-indictment on the same charges. According to the Court, "Following dismissal of charges, any restraint on liberty, disruption of employment, strain on financial resources, and exposure to public obloquy, stress and anxiety is no greater than it is upon anyone openly subject to a criminal investigation" (p. 9). The Court also observed that MacDonald had been "free to go about his affairs, to practice his profession, and to continue his life" (p. 10) in the period between the two sets of charges, so the right to a speedy trial did not apply until the second set of charges was filed.

An interesting twist on *MacDonald* was presented in *United States v. Loud Hawk* (474 U.S. 302 [1986]). There, charges against the accused were dismissed but the prosecution appealed the dismissal. This action distinguished *Loud Hawk* from *MacDonald* because it suggested that the prosecution was not done accusing Loud Hawk. Even so, the Court still held that the defendant's right to a speedy trial was not implicated because he was granted unconditional release while the prosecution continued to mount its case. Thus, if an individual is accused but then released to go about his or her business *with no charges pending*, any attempt to claim a violation of the Sixth Amendment's speedy trial provision could prove difficult. However, if a person is released *while* charges are pending, a speedy trial argument could be successfully raised.

Ignorance of Charges

It is often said that ignorance is not a defense, but in the context of speedy trial, it can be. In *Doggett v. United States* (505 U.S. 647 [1992]), the defendant did not know that he had been charged with a crime and was not restrained in any way. Doggett left the United States just prior to the government's attempt to arrest him and, still unaware of the charges against him, returned over two years later. Doggett was eventually found (although he never *evaded* authorities) and arrested over eight years after he was indicted.

Doggett v. United States,
505 U.S. 647 (1992)

The Supreme Court held in *Doggett* that the speedy trial clause of the Sixth Amendment was implicated. This was a surprising decision because Doggett was never detained nor could he claim any anxiety associated with the charges being filed against him (since he failed to learn of them until some eight years later). Also, Doggett carried on a law-abiding life, so he was not a threat to society. The Court was then forced to fall back on the argument that the ability of the defendant to mount an effective defense was undermined by the delay. Despite the Court's somewhat controversial decision in this case, *Doggett* has probably had little influence on subsequent defendants' speedy trial claims. The simple reason is that most defendants *know* when they are charged.

Violation of Due Process

What if a person commits a crime and is not charged for some time thereafter? Usually, most jurisdictions do not have statutes of limitations for serious offenses (i.e., laws that place restrictions on when charges can be brought against someone). For not-so-serious offenses, however, failure to bring charges in a speedy fashion can amount to a due process violation. Indeed, even if the time period for bringing charges has lapsed, failure to bring charges quickly can rise to the level of a constitutional violation.

United States v. Lovasco (431 U.S. 783 [1977]) is an illustrative case. There, the Supreme Court held that even when the statute of limitations period has not expired, the due process clause is violated if the delay exceeds "the community's sense of fair play and decency." In that case, two witnesses died during an 18-month delay between the crime and the indictment. The Court developed an *either/or* rule for determining whether

United States v. Lovasco,
431 U.S. 783 (1977)

this type of delay is unconstitutional: The delay must be for the purpose of gaining "a tactical advantage over the accused" or "in reckless disregard of circumstances . . . suggesting that there existed an appreciable risk that delay would impair the ability to mount an effective defense" (p. 796, n. 17).

Summary. This section has focused on when the right to a speedy trial applies, not whether it is violated under various factual scenarios. The next section turns attention to *when* the right to speedy trial is violated. To this point, then, the right to a speedy trial applies when a person is accused of a crime. This usually occurs when charges have been filed but not always. If a person is charged, let go, and later recharged, the right to a speedy trial does not apply until the latter charge is made. Due process can also be violated if charges are not brought in a timely fashion. This is sometimes true even if charges are not brought against a person before the statute of limitations, if applicable, expires.

■ Violations of the Right to a Speedy Trial

So far, the right to a speedy trial has been shown to apply in two contexts: (1) when a person has been accused and (2) when too much time has elapsed between the criminal act and the point at which charges are made. The only remedy in either instance is to dismiss the charges. An important question has not yet been answered: Assuming the right to a speedy trial applies, when is the right violated?

■ *Barker v. Wingo,* 407 U.S. 514 (1972)

The Supreme Court sought to answer this question in *Barker v. Wingo* (407 U.S. 514 [1972]). In that case, the defendant did not assert his Sixth Amendment right until after the prosecution had sought 16 continuances, which lasted over five years. The Supreme Court announced a four-element test to assist in determining when the right to a speedy trial is violated: "(1) Length of delay; (2) the reason for the delay; (3) the defendant's assertion of his right; and (4) prejudice to the defendant" (p. 530). According to the Court, none of these four criteria is, by itself, determinative. Instead, the courts must balance one against the others in deciding whether a Sixth Amendment violation has taken place. Each of these four criteria will now be considered in depth.

When Too Much Time Has Elapsed

In *Doggett v. United States,* introduced earlier, the Supreme Court suggested that a delay of one year could be "presumptively prejudicial"—that is, in violation of the Sixth Amendment. However, in *Loud Hawk,* also discussed earlier, the delay was longer than seven years and the Court found no violation of the right to a speedy trial. In another case, *United States v. Eight Thousand Eight Hundred & Fifty Dollars* (461 U.S. 555 [1983]), the Court held that 18 months of delay prior to an asset forfeiture proceeding was "quite significant" but still not of constitutional magnitude.

These decisions seem controversial, but in light of the other three criteria announced in *Barker,* the delay was insufficient to cause any prejudice to the defendant. That is, a violation of one of the four criteria is not, in itself, determinative.

When the Delay Is Intentional

Barker also suggested that the reason or reasons for the delay can be important:

> A deliberate attempt to delay the trial in order to hamper the defense should be weighted heavily against the government. A more neutral reason such as negligence or overcrowded courts should be weighted less heavily but nevertheless should be considered since the ultimate responsibility for such circumstances must rest with government rather than the defendant. [Finally,] a valid reason, such as a missing witness . . . should serve to justify appropriate delay. (p. 531)

A key element of this quote is that the delay should be deliberate. An accidental delay, or one that is beyond the control of the prosecution, would probably be constitutional. But even if the prosecution deliberately seeks to delay the case, it must be shown that the delay is prejudicial to the defense's case. A nonprejudicial delay is unlikely to violate the Sixth Amendment.

To clarify, consider what the Supreme Court stated in *United States v. Loud Hawk* (474 U.S. 302 [1986], mentioned earlier. In that case, part of the reason for the delay was that the prosecution sought numerous appeals with regard to the trial court's decision. The Supreme Court then stated that courts should focus on "the strength of the Government's position on the appealed issue, the importance of the issue in the posture of the case, and—in some cases—the seriousness of the crime" (pp. 315–316). As to the seriousness of the crime, the Court also stated, "[T]he charged offense usually must be sufficiently serious to justify restraints that may be imposed on the defendant pending the outcome of the appeal" (p. 316). In other words, if the government delays a trial by appealing, for instance, a decision on a motion to suppress, its position must be persuasive and the case serious. Frivolous delays for the purpose of weakening the defense should be avoided.

When delay is a result of prosecutorial negligence (i.e., as opposed to unavailable witnesses, court backlog, etc.), the Supreme Court has been considerably more strict. Recall that in *Doggett*, six years elapsed between the defendant's return to the United States and his arrest. The Supreme Court pointed out that this delay occurred because the government failed to continue tracking Doggett once he left the country. In their words:

> Although negligence is obviously to be weighted more lightly than a deliberate intent to harm the accused's defense, it still falls on the wrong side of the divide between acceptable and unacceptable reasons for delaying a criminal prosecution once it has begun. And such is the nature of the prejudice presumed that the weight we assign to official negligence compounds over time as the presumption of evidentiary prejudice grows. Thus, our toleration of such negligence varies inversely with its protractedness, and its consequent threat to the fairness of the accused's trial. (p. 657)

■ *United States v. Loud Hawk*, 474 U.S. 302 (1986)

DECISION MAKING EXERCISE 13.2

When the Defendant Is Responsible for the Delay

Charles Pitt escaped from jail while awaiting his trial on narcotics offenses. He was apprehended by the police nine months later. He was then tried, convicted, and sentenced to prison for 10 years. He has appealed his conviction, claiming that his Sixth Amendment right to a speedy trial was denied because of the nine-month delay. How should the appellate court rule?

When the Defendant Asserts the Right

Obviously, if the defendant does not assert his or her right to a speedy trial, then the courts should view any subsequent appeals with skepticism. However, if the defendant does not *formally* assert his or her right, can the courts then infer a waiver? That is, just because a defendant does not expressly state that his or her right to a speedy trial has been violated, does this mean the defendant should not be able to claim the right was denied in a subsequent appeal?

Referring back to *Barker v. Wingo*, the Supreme Court stated that "failure to assert the [speedy trial] right will make it difficult for a defendant to prove that he was denied a speedy trial" (p. 532). The Court also stated that the "frequency and force of the [defense] objections [to delay]" need to be taken into account. This means that formally asserting the right to a speedy trial may not be enough; the defendant should be sincere in his or her claims that the right was violated.

Recall from the *Miranda* discussion in Chapter 8 that silence cannot be construed as a waiver of the right to remain silent. The same does not hold true, then, with regard to the right to a speedy trial. That is, total silence by the defense concerning the Sixth Amendment right to counsel means that, for all practical purposes, the defendant has waived the right.

DECISION MAKING EXERCISE 13.3

Court Backlog

Lorna Bath robbed the First Street branch of State Bank because she believed the bank did not care about its customers and needed to be "hit where it hurts." Unfortunately, she was caught and indicted for first-degree robbery. However, because the court had a significant case backlog, Bath was not tried until 15 months after the robbery. During that time, she never asserted her right to a speedy trial. She was tried, convicted, and later appealed. The appeal, which is before the court now, claims that Bath's Sixth Amendment right to a speedy trial was delayed because of the 15-month delay. How should the court decide?

When the Delay Is Prejudicial to the Defendant

The fourth and final requirement for a defendant to succeed in raising a speedy trial claim is that the delay actually caused prejudice to him or her. In other words, an important question needs to be answered: Did the delay impair the ability of the defendant to mount an adequate defense? If the answer is yes and the three aforementioned requirements have been met, the Sixth Amendment right to a speedy trial may have been violated.

What exactly constitutes *prejudice* to the defendant? The Supreme Court *almost* answered this question in *Dickey v. Florida* (398 U.S. 30 [1970]), where it held that a seven-year delay, during which time two defense witnesses died and another became unavailable, warranted dismissal of charges. And as noted in the *Doggett* case, a longer delay that resulted from government negligence was reason for dismissal. Thus, it would seem that an excessively lengthy delay can cause prejudice to the defense.

The Supreme Court *almost* answered the question as to what constitutes prejudice because its decision in *Barker* seems to suggest that a lengthy delay is not always prejudicial. In that case, the Court held that a delay of over five years was insufficient to be considered prejudicial. In that case, though, the question of prejudice hinged on the ability of a witness to remember certain events. The Court said that it would be difficult to show a memory lapse and, consequently, that such a memory lapse hurt the defense. More concrete reasons for prejudice—such as deceased defense witnesses, as in *Dickey*—would seem more acceptable.

In summary, then, the defense must show clear and substantial damage to its case for a prejudice claim to succeed. The mere possibility that prejudice occurred is not enough. Coupled with the three other requirements announced in *Barker*, this points to a clear message: Succeeding in a claim that one's constitutional right to a speedy trial has been violated is exceedingly difficult.

DECISION MAKING EXERCISE 13.4

Deceased Witnesses

To continue the case from Decision-Making Exercise 13.3, suppose that Lorna Bath is prepared to file another appeal. This time, she argues that during the 15-month time lapse, the lead defense witness—who was prepared to testify that Bath was nowhere near the scene of the crime on the day of the robbery—died of a massive heart attack. Bath argues this time that the delay was prejudicial to her case and that her conviction should be overturned. Will she succeed with this appeal?

FIGURE 13.1   Methods of Ensuring a Speedy Trial by State

Alabama: Section 6, Alabama Constitution

Alaska: Rule 45, Alaska Rules of Criminal Procedure

Arizona: Article III, Section 24, Arizona Constitution; Rule 8, Arizona Rules of Criminal Procedure

Arkansas: Rule 28, Arkansas Rules of Criminal Procedure

California: Article I, Section 5, California Constitution; Section 1382, California Penal Code

Colorado: Article II, Section 16, Colorado Constitution; Colo. Rev. Stat Section 18-1-405; Rule 48(b), Colorado Rules of Criminal Procedure

Connecticut: Article I, Section 8, Connecticut Constitution

Delaware: Article I, Section 7, Delaware Constitution

Florida: Rule 3.191, Florida Rules of Criminal Procedure; Article I, Section 16, Florida Constitution

Georgia: Article I, Section 1, Georgia Constitution; Ga. Code Ann. Section 27-1901

Hawaii: Rule 48(b), Hawaii Rules of Criminal Procedure

Idaho: Article 1, Section 13, Idaho Constitution; Idaho Code Section 19-3501

Illinois: Ill. Rev. Stat. ch. 38, Section 103-5

Indiana: Article I, Section 12, Indiana Constitution; Ind. Code Ann. Section 35-34-1-4(a); Rule 4, Indiana Rules of Criminal Procedure

Iowa: Article I, Section 10, Iowa Constitution; Iowa Code Ann. ch. 813.2

Kansas: Kan. Stat. Ann. Section 22-3401

Kentucky: Article 1, Section 11, Kentucky Constitution; Kentucky Rules of Criminal Procedure Section 9.02; Ky. Rev. State Section 440.450

Louisiana: Articles 578, 579, Louisiana Code of Criminal Procedure; Article I, Section 16, Louisiana Constitution

Maine: Article I, Section VI, Maine Constitution; Rule 48(b), Maine Rules of Criminal Procedure

Maryland: Article 21, Maryland Declaration of Rights; Md. Ann. Code art. 27 Section 591

Massachusetts: Rule 36, Massachusetts Rules of Criminal Procedure

Michigan: Article I, Section 20, Michigan Constitution; Mich. Stat. Ann. Section 28.1024

Minnesota: Rules 6.06, 11.10, Minnesota Rules of Criminal Procedure; Minnesota Constitution, Section 6

Mississippi: Article 3, Section 26, Mississippi Constitution; Miss. Code Ann. Section 99-17-1

Missouri: Article 1, Section 14, Missouri Constitution; Mo. Ann. Stat. Section 545.780

Montana: Article II, Section 246, Montana Constitution; Mont. Code Ann. Section 46-13-201

Nebraska: Article 1, Section 11, Nebraska Constitution; Neb. Rev. Stat. Section 29-1205

Nevada: Nev. Rev. Stat. Section 169.025; Nev. Rev. Stat. Section 178.495

New Hampshire: New Hampshire Constitution pt. 1 art. 14; N.H. Rev. Stat. Ann Section 606-A:1

New Jersey: Article I, Section 10, New Jersey Constitution; N.J. Ct. R. 3:25-2 & 3.25-3

New Mexico: Rule 37(b), New Mexico Rules of Criminal Procedure; Article II, Section 14, New Mexico Constitution

New York: N.Y. Crim. Proc. Section 30.30

North Carolina: N.C. Gen. Stat. Section 15A-701 to Section 15A-704

North Dakota: Article I, Section 12, North Dakota Constitution; Rule 48(b), North Dakota Rules of Criminal Procedure; N.D. Cent. Code Section 29-33-01 to 29-33-08

Ohio: Article I, Section 10, Ohio Constitution; Ohio Rev. Code Ann. Sections 2945.71-2945.73

Oklahoma: Article II, Section 20, Oklahoma Constitution; Okla. Stat. Ann. tit. 22 Sections 1345-1349

Oregon: Or. Rev. Stat. Sections 135.745 & 135.775

Pennsylvania: Article I, Section 9, Pennsylvania Constitution; 42 Pa. Cons. Stat. Ann. Section 9101; Rule 1100, Pennsylvania Rules of Criminal Procedure

Rhode Island: Article 1, Section 10, Rhode Island Declaration of Rights; Rule 48(b), Rhode Island Rules of Criminal Procedure; R.I. Gen. Laws Section 12-13-7

South Carolina: S.C. Code Section 17-23-90

South Dakota: Article IV, Section 7, South Dakota Constitution

Tennessee: Article 1, Section IX, Tennessee Constitution; Tenn. Code. Ann. Section 40-14-101

Texas: Article 1, Section 10, Texas Constitution; Tex. Code Crim. Proc. Ann. art. 32A.02

Utah: Article I, Section XII, Utah Constitution; Utah Code Ann. Section 77-65-2

Vermont: Article X, Vermont Constitution; Vt. Stat. Ann. tit. 4, Section 3

Virginia: Article I, Section VIII, Virginia Constitution; Va. Code Section 19.2-243

Washington: Article 1, Section 22, Washington Constitution; Wash. Rev. Code Section 10.46.010; Rule 3.3, Superior Court Criminal Rules

West Virginia: Article 3, Section 14, West Virginia Constitution; W.Va. Code Section 62-3-1

Wisconsin: Wis. Stat. Section 971.10; Article I, Section 7, Wisconsin Constitution

Wyoming: Article I, Section 10, Wyoming Constitution; Wyo. Stat. Sections 7-11-207 and 7-11-208; Rule 45, Wyoming Rules of Criminal Procedure

Note: These state-level methods are in addition to the provisions of the U.S. Constitution's Sixth Amendment. Most states also have other statutes addressing the right to a speedy trial besides those listed here.

Source: R. L. Misner, *Speedy Trial: Federal and State Practice* (Charlottesville, VA: Michie Company, 1983).

Consequences of Violating the Right to a Speedy Trial

■ *Strunk v. United States,*
412 U.S. 434 (1973)

Assuming prosecution is delayed to an unconstitutional degree, what is the appropriate remedy? This question was answered in *Strunk v. United States* (412 U.S. 434 [1973]). In that case, the defendant was found guilty of a crime in a federal district court after a 10-month delay between indictment and arraignment. The Seventh Circuit Court of Appeals held that the defendant was denied a speedy trial but only remanded the case for a reduction in the defendant's sentence. The U.S. Supreme Court reversed, holding that dismissal is the *only* remedy. Thus, any time a defendant's right to a speedy trial is denied, the charges against him or her will be dismissed altogether. This is in contrast to the plea-bargaining discussion in Chapter 12; in that context, if the prosecution fails to fulfill its end of a plea bargain, the accused does not necessarily go free.

Statutory Clarification

At this point, the reader is likely somewhat uncertain as to *precisely* when the Sixth Amendment's speedy trial provision has been violated. In fact, the Supreme Court has been quite vague on this matter, as the previous decisions attest. Part of the reason for this is that it is not the Court's responsibility to establish law. Legislatures are charged with establishing law.

Fortunately, there is some legislation that provides answers to lingering questions. Many states have enacted so-called *speedy trial laws*; Figure 13.1 (page 377) lists the most common methods of enforcing the right to a speedy trial at the state level. In the interest of consistency, however, the focus here will be on some important federal legislation—namely, the federal **Speedy Trial Act**. This legislation was codified into law as 18 U.S.C. Section 3161 and signed into law in 1974.

It is important to note that the act's provisions do not replace protections afforded by the Sixth Amendment. Indeed, Section 3173 of the act states, "No provision of this chapter shall be interpreted as a bar to any claim of denial of speedy trial as required by Amendment VI of the Constitution." Thus, if the defendant does not succeed in arguing that his or her statutory right (i.e., as established by the Speedy Trial Act) was violated, then he or she could proceed with a Sixth Amendment claim.

The act has a number of specific provisions. First, it requires that all federal courts create a plan for trying criminal cases within 100 days of an arrest or receipt of a summons. This does not mean that a trial must take place within 100 days, only that a *plan* for trial be established within that period. Beyond this, the act established other important deadlines, as follows:

1. Charges must be filed within 30 days from arrest or service of summons. If no grand jury is in session, a delay can be granted. Also, according to the act, the right to a speedy trial only applies once charges have been filed, not at the time of arrest.
2. Trial must take place within 70 days from the point at which charges are filed or from the date on which the defendant appears before a judge, whichever is later. And in a jury trial, the act provides that the trial is said to have commenced once the *voir dire* process has been set in motion. (*Voir dire* is discussed later in this chapter.)
3. Trial cannot take place *less* than 30 days from when the defendant first appears, unless the defendant agrees to an earlier trial. This restriction exists so that the defense can build an adequate case.

The federal Speedy Trial Act also provides some exceptions to the time restrictions just discussed. Eight different delays can be sanctioned:

1. Delays caused by the defendant, such as competency hearings, hearings on motions, trials on other charges, and interlocutory appeals (i.e., appeals filed before final adjudication; see Chapter 15)
2. Delays resulting from deferred (i.e., delayed) prosecution but only with agreement of all parties involved (i.e., the defense, prosecution, and court)
3. Delays caused by the unavailability of the defendant or important witnesses for either the prosecution or defense
4. Delays resulting from the defendant's mental incompetence or physical unfitness to stand trial
5. Delays resulting from treatment of the defendant pursuant to the Narcotics Addict Rehabilitation Act
6. Delays between the dropping of original charges and the filing of new charges for the same or a related offense
7. Reasonable periods of delay because of the joinder of defendants (i.e., two defendants are to be tried in the same trial)
8. Any other delay granted by the court with justice cited as the main reason

This last delay is the catchall category; for example, the defense can agree with the prosecution to set a trial date beyond the specified limit (e.g., *New York v. Hill*, 528 U.S. 110 [2000]). Even so, the court must set forth in the record the precise reason for granting a continuance. The act requires that several factors be taken into account before a continuance can be granted:

1. Whether failure to grant a delay would result in a miscarriage of justice
2. Whether the case is so unusual or complex that it is unreasonable to expect adequate preparation during the time limits established by the act
3. Whether when a defendant is arrested and later indicted the grand jury would have a difficult time determining whether charges should be filed (e.g., again, the case is so unusual or complex)
4. Whether a delay would deny the defendant (or either party) the ability to mount an effective case
5. Whether the continuance was granted for an inappropriate reason, such as court backlog or government negligence

Consequences of Violating the Act

If any of the time limits set forth by the federal Speedy Trial Act is violated, and assuming that no exceptions/exemptions apply, then the remedy is dismissal of charges. However, the judge can decide whether to dismiss with or *without prejudice*. A dismissal without prejudice means that there remains an avenue for appeal. A dismissal *with prejudice* is akin to a final disposition, which bars any future action.

THE RIGHT TO AN IMPARTIAL JUDGE

It is important to note that the Sixth Amendment speaks only of juries (in addition to other important provisions), not judges. But the Supreme Court has held that the due process clause of the Fourteenth Amendment guarantees a criminal defendant the right to trial by an **impartial judge**. This right applies in two situations: (1) a *bench trial*, in which the judge decides the defendant's fate instead of a jury; and (2) a *jury trial*, in which the judge acts solely as a trier of law (i.e., makes legal decisions, not factual ones). The discussion begins with the right to an impartial judge and then moves into the more complicated issue of the right to trial by an impartial jury.

The Supreme Court first decided on the matter of an impartial judge in *Tumey v. Ohio* (273 U.S. 510 [1927]). In that case, the judge of a municipal court was also the city

■ *Tumey v. Ohio*, 273 U.S. 510 (1927)

mayor. In addition, he received the fines and fees that he levied against those convicted in his courtroom. The Supreme Court concluded that due process is violated when the judge "has a direct, personal, substantial pecuniary interest in reaching a conclusion against him in his case" (p. 523). This decision should sound somewhat familiar; recall from Chapter 4 that judges are not considered impartial when issuing warrants if they seek to gain financially from doing so.

■ *Ward v. Monroeville,*
409 U.S. 57 (1972)

Another impartial judge case was *Ward v. Monroeville* (409 U.S. 57 [1972]), in which the fees/fines collected by the judge did not go to the mayor/judge but instead to the town's budget. The amount of money collected was apparently substantial. The Court concluded, again, that due process was violated, this time stating that "the mayor's executive responsibilities for village finances may make him partisan to maintain the high level of contribution from the mayor's court" (p. 59). Contrast this decision with that of *Dugan v. Ohio* (277 U.S. 61 [1928]). There, the Supreme Court held that due process was *not* violated because the mayor/judge was one of several members of a city commission and, as such, did not have substantial control over the city's funding sources.

DECISION MAKING EXERCISE 13.5

An Impartial Judge?

During Beau Archer's criminal trial for assault, Archer, who represented himself, engaged in disruptive conduct and made insulting and slanderous remarks to the judge, calling him a "dirty, tyrannical old dog," "stumbling dog," and "fool" and further charged him with running a "Spanish Inquisition" and telling him to "Keep your mouth shut." Archer was found guilty of assault by a jury. At a subsequent sentencing hearing, the trial judge also pronounced Archer guilty of criminal contempt arising from his conduct during the trial. The judge further sentenced Archer to an extra 11 to 22 years in prison on the contempt accounts. Archer appealed, claiming that he was denied an impartial judge. What should the court decide?

■ Methods of Removing a Judge Who Is Not Impartial

In most jurisdictions, either the defense or the prosecution can seek to have a judge removed *for cause.* That is, the individual seeking the judge's removal will argue that the judge is biased for or against a particular party to the case. Strangely, though, the only person who can remove such a judge is usually the judge himself or herself.

The second method of removing a biased judge is fairly rare. Some jurisdictions allow either party to a case to *peremptorily* remove a judge. This is akin to the jury selection process, which will be covered at length later in this chapter. Basically, the judge can be removed without any reason whatsoever. The number of peremptory removals, if permitted, is very small—usually one per case. If one judge has been removed, then the parties can only seek to remove the second judge with cause.

In most situations, the judge does not need to be removed at the request of another party. Responsible judges remove themselves when conflicts of interest exist. Indeed, most judicial codes of ethics require that a judge *recuse* (i.e., disqualify) himself or herself if, among other things, he or she has a personal bias or prejudice concerning a party, personal knowledge of disputed evidentiary facts concerning the proceeding, or some conflict of interest in the case (see, e.g., American Bar Association, Code of Judicial

Conduct, Canon 3-C). Figure 13.2 (pages 382–385) presents relevant ethical canons from the Code of Judicial Conduct utilized in the state of Texas.

THE RIGHT TO AN IMPARTIAL JURY

As noted in the previous section, it is fairly easy to determine when a judge is impartial. After all, a judge is one person. Deciding on what constitutes an **impartial jury** is far more difficult and complex. For this reason, the remainder of this chapter focuses on the right to trial by an impartial jury.

Referring again to the previous section, it is important to note that the due process right to an impartial judge applies in *all* proceedings, whether petty or serious, pretrial or otherwise. By contrast, the right to a trial by jury is *qualified*; that is, it does not *always* apply, even though the Sixth Amendment seems to suggest otherwise. First, the process of plea bargaining can eliminate the need to have a trial altogether. But even if the defendant opts not to plea bargain, the right to a jury trial may not exist. To begin, the discussion will focus on when the right to trial by an impartial jury applies.

When the Right to a Jury Trial Applies

The right to a jury trial has always been recognized in the federal courts, but this right was not extended to the states until 1968 in the case of *Duncan v. Louisiana* (391 U.S. 145 [1968]). The Court noted in that case that the right to a jury trial is "an inestimable safeguard against the corrupt or overzealous prosecutor and against the compliant, biased, or eccentric judge" (p. 156). The right to a jury trial has therefore been incorporated, but subsequent decisions have restricted this right. The following subsections describe how.

The Noncriminal Proceeding Rule

First, there is no Sixth Amendment constitutional right to a jury trial in noncriminal proceedings. This has come to be known as the **noncriminal proceeding rule**. The reason for this should be fairly obvious: The Sixth Amendment states, "In all *criminal prosecutions*, the accused shall enjoy the right to a . . . trial, by an impartial jury" (emphasis added). Unfortunately, it is not always clear what constitutes a noncriminal proceeding. An example is a juvenile delinquency hearing. In *McKeiver v. Pennsylvania* (403 U.S. 528 [1971]), the Court held that juveniles charged with delinquent acts do not enjoy a right to a jury trial. Also, civil commitment hearings do not need to be conducted before a jury (e.g., *Lynch v. Baxley*, 386 F. Supp. 378 [M.D. Ala. 1974]).

■ *McKeiver v. Pennsylvania*, 403 U.S. 528 (1971)

Note that the Seventh Amendment states, "In Suits at common law, where the value in controversy shall exceed twenty dollars, the right of trial by jury shall be preserved." Jury trials clearly take place in the realm of civil litigation. The noncriminal proceeding rule, however, is only concerned with criminal procedure. Civil procedure is another matter altogether.

The Petty Crime Exception

The Supreme Court has carved out a *petty crime exception* to the Sixth Amendment right to a jury trial. In *Duncan*, mentioned earlier, the Court expressly forbade jury trials for petty offenses, and in *Baldwin v. New York* (399 U.S. 66 [1970]), the Court announced its reasoning for this. It argued that the "disadvantages, onerous though they may be," of denying a jury trial for a petty crime are "outweighed by the benefits that result from speedy and inexpensive nonjury adjudication" (p. 73).

■ *Baldwin v. New York*, 399 U.S. 66 (1970)

FIGURE 13.2 Example of a Code of Judicial Conduct

CANON 1
Upholding the Integrity and Independence of the Judiciary

An independent and honorable judiciary is indispensable to justice in our society. A judge should participate in establishing, maintaining and enforcing high standards of conduct, and should personally observe those standards so that the integrity and independence of the judiciary is preserved. The provisions of this Code are to be construed and applied to further that objective.

CANON 2
Avoiding Impropriety and the Appearance of Impropriety In All of the Judge's Activities

A. A judge shall comply with the law and should act at all times in a manner that promotes public confidence in the integrity and impartiality of the judiciary.

B. A judge shall not allow any relationship to influence judicial conduct or judgment. A judge shall not lend the prestige of judicial office to advance the private interests of the judge or others; nor shall a judge convey or permit others to convey the impression that they are in a special position to influence the judge. A judge shall not testify voluntarily as a character witness.

C. A judge shall not knowingly hold membership in any organization that practices discrimination prohibited by law.

CANON 3
Performing the Duties of Judicial Office Impartially and Diligently

A. Judicial Duties in General. The judicial duties of a judge take precedence over all the judge's other activities. Judicial duties include all the duties of the judge's office prescribed by law. In the performance of these duties, the following standards apply:

B. Adjudicative Responsibilities.

(1) A judge shall hear and decide matters assigned to the judge except those in which disqualification is required or recusal is appropriate.

(2) A judge should be faithful to the law and shall maintain professional competence in it. A judge shall not be swayed by partisan interests, public clamor, or fear of criticism.

(3) A judge shall require order and decorum in proceedings before the judge.

(4) A judge shall be patient, dignified and courteous to litigants, jurors, witnesses, lawyers and others with whom the judge deals in an official capacity, and should require similar conduct of lawyers, and of staff, court officials and others subject to the judge's direction and control.

(5) A judge shall perform judicial duties without bias or prejudice.

(6) A judge shall not, in the performance of judicial duties, by words or conduct manifest bias or prejudice, including but not limited to bias or prejudice based upon race, sex, religion, national origin, disability, age, sexual orientation or socioeconomic status, and shall not knowingly permit staff, court officials and others subject to the judge's direction and control to do so.

(7) A judge shall require lawyers in proceedings before the court to refrain from manifesting, by words or conduct, bias or prejudice based on race, sex, religion, national origin, disability, age, sexual orientation or socioeconomic status against parties, witnesses, counsel or others. This requirement does not preclude legitimate advocacy when any of these factors is an issue in the proceeding.

(8) A judge shall accord to every person who has a legal interest in a proceeding, or that person's lawyer, the right to be heard according to law. A judge shall not initiate, permit, or consider *ex parte* communications or other communications made to the judge outside the presence of the parties between the judge and a party, an attorney, a guardian or attorney ad litem, an alternative dispute resolution neutral, or any other court appointee concerning the merits of a pending or impending judicial proceeding. A judge shall require compliance with this subsection by court personnel subject to the judge's direction and control. This subsection does not prohibit:

(a) communications concerning uncontested administrative or uncontested procedural matters;

(b) conferring separately with the parties and/or their lawyers in an effort to mediate or settle matters, provided, however, that the judge shall first give notice to all parties and not thereafter hear any contested matters between the parties except with the consent of all parties;

(c) obtaining the advice of a disinterested expert on the law applicable to a proceeding before the judge if the judge gives notice to the parties of the person consulted and the substance of the advice, and affords the parties reasonable opportunity to respond;

(d) consulting with other judges or with court personnel;

(e) considering an *ex parte* communication expressly authorized by law.

(9) A judge should dispose of all judicial matters promptly, efficiently and fairly.

(10) A judge shall abstain from public comment about a pending or impending proceeding which may come before the judge's court in a manner which suggests to a reasonable person the judge's probable decision on any particular case. The judge shall require similar abstention on the part of court personnel subject to the judge's direction and control. This section does not prohibit judges from making public statements in the course of their official duties or from explaining for public information the procedures of the court. This section does not apply to

proceedings in which the judge is a litigant in a personal capacity.

(11) A judge shall not disclose or use, for any purpose unrelated to judicial duties, nonpublic information acquired in a judicial capacity. The discussions, votes, positions taken, and writings of appellate judges and court personnel about causes are confidences of the court and shall be revealed only through a court's judgment, a written opinion or in accordance with Supreme Court guidelines for a court approved history project.

C. Administrative Responsibilities.

(1) A judge should diligently and promptly discharge the judge's administrative responsibilities without bias or prejudice and maintain professional competence in judicial administration, and should cooperate with other judges and court officials in the administration of court business.

(2) A judge should require staff, court officials and others subject to the judge's direction and control to observe the standards of fidelity and diligence that apply to the judge and to refrain from manifesting bias or prejudice in the performance of their official duties.

(3) A judge with supervisory authority for the judicial performance of other judges should take reasonable measures to assure the prompt disposition of matters before them and the proper performance of their other judicial responsibilities.

(4) A judge shall not make unnecessary appointments. A judge shall exercise the power of appointment impartially and on the basis of merit. A judge shall avoid nepotism and favoritism. A judge shall not approve compensation of appointees beyond the fair value of services rendered.

(5) A judge shall not fail to comply with Rule 12 of the Rules of Judicial Administration, knowing that the failure to comply is in violation of the rule.

D. Disciplinary Responsibilities.

(1) A judge who receives information clearly establishing that another judge has committed a violation of this Code should take appropriate action. A judge having knowledge that another judge has committed a violation of this Code that raises a substantial question as to the other judge's fitness for office shall inform the State Commission on Judicial Conduct or take other appropriate action.

(2) A judge who receives information clearly establishing that a lawyer has committed a violation of the Texas Disciplinary Rules of Professional Conduct should take appropriate action. A judge having knowledge that a lawyer has committed a violation of the Texas Disciplinary Rules of Professional Conduct that raises a substantial question as to the lawyer's honesty, trustworthiness or fitness as a lawyer in other respects shall inform the Office of the General Counsel of the State Bar of Texas or take other appropriate action.

CANON 4
Conducting the Judge's Extra-Judicial Activities to Minimize the Risk of Conflict with Judicial Obligations

A. Extra-Judicial Activities in General. A judge shall conduct all of the judge's extra-judicial activities so that they do not:

(1) cast reasonable doubt on the judge's capacity to act impartially as a judge; or

(2) interfere with the proper performance of judicial duties.

B. Activities to Improve the Law. A judge may:

(1) speak, write, lecture, teach and participate in extra-judicial activities concerning the law, the legal system, the administration of justice and non-legal subjects, subject to the requirements of this Code; and,

(2) serve as a member, officer, or director of an organization or governmental agency devoted to the improvement of the law, the legal system, or the administration of justice. A judge may assist such an organization in raising funds and may participate in their management and investment, but should not personally participate in public fund raising activities. He or she may make recommendations to public and private fund-granting agencies on projects and programs concerning the law, the legal system and the administration of justice.

C. Civic or Charitable Activities. A judge may participate in civic and charitable activities that do not reflect adversely upon the judge's impartiality or interfere with the performance of judicial duties. A judge may serve as an officer, director, trustee or non-legal advisor of an educational, religious, charitable, fraternal, or civic organization not conducted for the profit of its members, subject to the following limitations:

(1) A judge should not serve if it is likely that the organization will be engaged in proceedings that would ordinarily come before the judge or will be regularly or frequently engaged in adversary proceedings in any court.

(2) A judge shall not solicit funds for any educational, religious, charitable, fraternal or civic organization, but may be listed as an officer, director, delegate, or trustee of such an organization, and may be a speaker or a guest of honor at an organization's fund raising events.

(3) A judge should not give investment advice to such an organization, but may serve on its board of directors or trustees even though it has the responsibility for approving investment decisions.

D. Financial Activities.

(1) A judge shall refrain from financial and business dealings that tend to reflect adversely on the judge's

Figure 13.2   Continued

impartiality, interfere with the proper performance of the judicial duties, exploit his or her judicial position, or involve the judge in frequent transactions with lawyers or persons likely to come before the court on which the judge serves. This limitation does not prohibit either a judge or candidate from soliciting funds for appropriate campaign or officeholder expenses as permitted by state law.

(2) Subject to the requirements of subsection (1), a judge may hold and manage investments, including real estate, and engage in other remunerative activity including the operation of a business. A judge shall not be an officer, director or manager of a publicly owned business. For purposes of this Canon, a "publicly owned business" is a business having more than ten owners who are not related to the judge by consanguinity or affinity within the third degree of relationship.

(3) A judge should manage any investments and other economic interests to minimize the number of cases in which the judge is disqualified. As soon as the judge can do so without serious financial detriment, the judge should divest himself or herself of investments and other economic interests that might require frequent disqualification. A judge shall be informed about the judge's personal and fiduciary economic interests, and make a reasonable effort to be informed about the personal economic interests of any family member residing in the judge's household.

(4) Neither a judge nor a family member residing in the judge's household shall accept a gift, bequest, favor, or loan from anyone except as follows:

(a) a judge may accept a gift incident to a public testimonial to the judge; books and other resource materials supplied by publishers on a complimentary basis for official use; or an invitation to the judge and spouse to attend a bar-related function or activity devoted to the improvement of the law, the legal system, or the administration of justice;

(b) a judge or a family member residing in the judge's household may accept ordinary social hospitality; a gift, bequest, favor, or loan from a relative; a gift from a friend for a special occasion such as a wedding, engagement, anniversary, or birthday, if the gift is fairly commensurate with the occasion and the relationship; a loan from a lending institution in its regular course of business on the same terms generally available to persons who are not judges; or a scholarship or fellowship awarded on the same terms applied to other applicants;

(c) a judge or a family member residing in the judge's household may accept any other gift, bequest, favor, or loan only if the donor is not a party or person whose interests have come or are likely to come before the judge;

(d) a gift, award or benefit incident to the business, profession or other separate activity of a spouse or other family member residing in the judge's household, including gifts, awards and benefits for the use of both the spouse or other family member and the judge (as spouse or family member), provided the gift, award or benefit could not reasonably be perceived as intended to influence the judge in the performance of judicial duties.

E. Fiduciary Activities.

(1) A judge shall not serve as executor, administrator or other personal representative, trustee, guardian, attorney in fact or other fiduciary, except for the estate, trust or person of a member of the judge's family, and then only if such service will not interfere with the proper performance of judicial duties.

(2) A judge shall not serve as a fiduciary if it is likely that the judge as a fiduciary will be engaged in proceedings that would ordinarily come before the judge, or if the estate, trust, or ward becomes involved in adversary proceedings in the court on which the judge serves or one under its appellate jurisdiction.

(3) The same restrictions on financial activities that apply to a judge personally also apply to the judge while acting in a fiduciary capacity.

Source: Used courtesy the State of Texas. Available online: <www.courts.state.tx.us/Judethics/canons.htm>. Accessed August 10, 2002.

What exactly is a *petty crime?* Unfortunately, there are no easy answers to this question, either. *Duncan* failed to define a *petty* offense, but in *Baldwin*, the Court concluded that any crime that can bring punishment of more than six months is no longer a petty one. This has come to be known as the **six-month imprisonment rule**; thus, defendants do not enjoy a right to jury trial when the punishment they face is less than six months in jail or prison.

What if a person is charged with several crimes for which the combined term of imprisonment exceeds six months? Surprisingly, in *Lewis v. United States* (518 U.S. 322 [1996]), the Court announced that a defendant charged in a single proceeding with several petty crimes does not have a right to jury trial even if the maximum penalty for *all* offenses could exceed six months in prison.

F. Service as Arbitrator or Mediator. An active full-time judge shall not act as an arbitrator or mediator for compensation outside the judicial system, but a judge may encourage settlement in the performance of official duties.

G. Practice of Law. A judge shall not practice law except as permitted by statute or this Code. Notwithstanding this prohibition, a judge may act pro se and may, without compensation, give legal advice to and draft or review documents for a member of the judge's family.

H. Extra-Judicial Appointments. Except as otherwise provided by constitution and statute, a judge should not accept appointment to a governmental committee, commission, or other position that is concerned with issues of fact or policy on matters other than the improvement of the law, the legal system, or the administration of justice. A judge, however, may represent his or her country, state, or locality on ceremonial occasions or in connection with historical, educational, and cultural activities.

I. Compensation, Reimbursement and Reporting.

(1) Compensation and Reimbursement. A judge may receive compensation and reimbursement of expenses for the extra-judicial activities permitted by this Code, if the source of such payments does not give the appearance of influencing the judge's performance of judicial duties or otherwise give the appearance of impropriety.

(a) Compensation shall not exceed a reasonable amount nor shall it exceed what a person who is not a judge would receive for the same activity.

(b) Expense reimbursement shall be limited to the actual cost of travel, food, and lodging reasonably incurred by the judge and, where appropriate to the occasion, by the judge's family. Any payment in excess of such an amount is compensation.

(2) Public Reports. A judge shall file financial and other reports as required by law.

CANON 5
Refraining From Inappropriate Political Activity

(1) A judge or judicial candidate shall not make statements that indicate an opinion on any issue that may be subject to judicial interpretation by the office which is being sought or held, except that discussion of an individual's judicial philosophy is appropriate if conducted in a manner which does not suggest to a reasonable person a probable decision on any particular case.

(2) A judge or judicial candidate shall not:

(i) make pledges or promises of conduct in office regarding judicial duties other than the faithful and impartial performance of the duties of the office, but may state a position regarding the conduct of administrative duties;

(ii) knowingly or recklessly misrepresent the identity, qualifications, present position, or other fact concerning the candidate or an opponent.

(3) A judge or judicial candidate shall not authorize the public use of his or her name endorsing another candidate for any public office, except that either may indicate support for a political party. A judge or judicial candidate may attend political events and express his or her views on political matters in accord with this Canon and Canon 3B(10).

(4) A judge shall resign from judicial office upon becoming a candidate in a contested election for a non-judicial office either in a primary or in a general or in a special election. A judge may continue to hold judicial office while being a candidate for election to or serving as a delegate in a state constitutional convention or while being a candidate for election to any judicial office.

(5) A judge or judicial candidate subject to the Judicial Campaign Fairness Act, Tex. Elec. Code § 253.151, *et seq.* (the "Act"), shall not knowingly commit an act for which he or she knows the Act imposes a penalty. Contributions returned in accordance with Sections 253.155(e), 253.157(b) or 253.160(b) of the Act are not a violation of this paragraph.

DECISION
MAKING
EXERCISE **13.6**

A Twist on the Six-Month Rule

During their criminal trial for auto theft, defendants Ray Katz and Jacob Apple committed various disrespectful and disruptive acts. After a verdict of guilty was returned on the theft charge, the judge sentenced Katz and Apple on contempt charges, as well. The combined sentence for Katz was three years, and that for Apple was two years and eight months. Both have appealed their contempt convictions, claiming that they were denied a jury trial because their individual sentences exceeded six months. Is it conceivable that they could succeed in light of *Lewis v. United States* (518 U.S. 322 [1996])?

Finally, what if a person is charged with a crime with a possible six-month imprisonment term and is sanctioned in some other manner, as well? This question was answered in *Blanton v. City of North Las Vegas* (489 U.S. 538 [1989]). The Court announced in that case that the right to a jury trial in such a situation applies "only if [the defendant] can demonstrate that any additional statutory penalties, viewed in conjunction with the maximum authorized period of incarceration, are so severe that they clearly reflect a legislative determination that the offense in question is a 'serious' one" (p. 543). The defendant was charged with drunk driving, a crime that carried a penalty of, at most, six months as well as a 90-day suspension of his driver's license. The Court stated, "[W]e cannot say that a 90-day suspension is that significant as a Sixth Amendment matter, particularly when a restricted license may be obtained after only 45 days" (p. 544, n. 9). In another case, *Muniz v. Hoffman* (422 U.S. 454 [1975]), the Court stated that a potential sentence of six months coupled with a *fine* does not require a jury trial.

In summary, the right to a jury trial applies in a criminal proceeding when the penalty for a single offense exceeds six months. In no other situation does the Sixth Amendment right to a jury trial apply, even if multiple charges for petty offenses could result in a lengthy prison term.

Criminal Procedure in Post–September 11 America

On November 13, 2001, President Bush issued an executive order that suspended the rights of grand jury indictment, trial by jury, appeals, and *habeas corpus* for noncitizens accused of aiding and abetting terrorists.[1] The order was meant not only to target al Qaida and its members but also anyone who has "engaged in, aided or abetted, or conspired to commit, acts of international terrorism, or acts in preparation therefore, that have caused, threaten to cause, or have as their aim to cause, injury to or adverse effects on the United States, its citizens, national security, foreign policy, or the economy" and anyone who has harbored any such individuals.[2]

The order was issued pursuant to President Bush's authority as commander in chief of the U.S. armed forces. He stated that the September 11, 2001, attacks amounted to war on the United States and created an armed conflict between the United States and terrorists, necessitating the use of the military to quell future threats. The order states, in relevant part, that in order to "protect the United States and its citizens, and for the effective conduct of military operations and prevention of terrorist attacks, it is necessary for individuals subject to this Order . . . to be detained, and, when tried, to be tried for violations of the laws of war and other applicable laws."[3]

Additionally, President Bush called for the use of so-called **military tribunals** to serve this purpose. Specifically, the order directed the secretary of defense, Donald Rumsfeld, to institute regulations for the appointment of military commissions that would try suspected terrorists in military tribunals. Perhaps more important, the order explicitly stated that given the threat posed by terrorism, the tribunals would not "apply the principles of law or the rules of evidence that are used in normal criminal cases."[4] In other words, the traditional rules of criminal procedure do not apply. A tribunal can impose the death penalty, and reaching a unanimous verdict is not necessary.

This development is not without its critics. For instance, Whitehead and Aden write, "The military tribunal Order, by abolishing the right to trial by jury and reserving the power to the Executive Branch to determine when, where, and under what conditions such tribunals will be conducted, represents arguably the most drastic

---

[1] *Federal Register* 66 (13 November 2001): 57,833.
[2] *Federal Register*, p. 57,834.
[3] *Federal Register*, p. 57,833.
[4] *Federal Register*, p. 57,835.

curtailment of the Sixth Amendment rights of the criminally accused since the Second World War."[5]

The rules and guidelines by which military tribunals are to be conducted have not been finalized, and until they are, President Bush's executive order will serve as the guiding force. In closing this section, it is worth pointing out that the courts have held that the authority of Congress, as specified in Article II of the U.S. Constitution, "to make rules for the government and regulation of the land and naval forces" does not give it authority to create military tribunals for trying civilians (see *Reid v. Covert*, 354 U.S. 1 [1957]). President Bush has effectively circumvented this restriction by giving the order for the implementation of military tribunals himself. The last time something similar happened was on July 2, 1942, when President Franklin Delano Roosevelt appointed a military commission to try eight German citizens.

■ Jury Size and Voting Requirements

Many juries consist of 12 members, but the Supreme Court has stated that this is not a requirement. In *Williams v. Florida* (399 U.S. 78 [1970]), the Court stated that the 12-member jury was a "historical accident" and "unnecessary to effect the purposes of the jury system" (p. 102). The Court noted that a 6-member jury would even provide "a fair possibility for obtaining a representative cross-section of the community, . . . [a]s long as arbitrary exclusions of a particular class from the jury rolls are forbidden" (p. 102).

However, in *Ballew v. Georgia* (435 U.S. 223 [1978]), the Court concluded that a 5-member jury was unconstitutional and found it unlikely that such a small group could engage "in meaningful deliberation, . . . remember all the facts and arguments, and truly represent the common sense of the entire community" (p. 241). Thus, the appropriate size for a jury is anywhere between 6 and 12 members.

Jury size differs by state. See Figure 13.3 (page 388) for a listing of jury sizes by state, specifically for courts of general jurisdiction (i.e., those with jurisdiction to try several types of cases, including more serious criminal cases).

As for voting requirements, a unanimous decision is not always required. In two companion cases, *Johnson v. Louisiana* (406 U.S. 356 [1972]) and *Apodaca v. Oregon* (406 U.S. 404 [1972]), the Court upheld a Louisiana statute that permitted 9 to 3 jury verdicts as well as an Oregon statute permitting 10 to 2 decisions. According to the Court:

■ *Johnson v. Louisiana,*
406 U.S. 356 (1972)

> In our view, disagreement of three jurors does not alone establish reasonable doubt, particularly when such a heavy majority of the jury, after having considered the dissenters' views, remained convinced of guilt. . . . That want of jury unanimity is not to be equated with the existence of reasonable doubt emerges even more clearly from the fact that when a jury in a federal court, which operates under the unanimity rule and is instructed to acquit a defendant if it has a reasonable doubt, . . . cannot agree unanimously upon a verdict, the defendant is not acquitted, but is merely given a new trial. (p. 363)

In short, guilt can be determined by less than a unanimous jury in certain jurisdictions. This is somewhat controversial, however, because according to the dissent in *Johnson* and *Apodaca*, permitting a less than unanimous decision diminishes reliability. Namely, jurors may not debate as fully as they may if a unanimous decision is required; that is, people may succumb to group pressure. See Figure 13.4 (page 389) for a listing of jury voting requirements by state, again for courts of general jurisdiction.

---

[5]J. W. Whitehead and S. H. Aden, "Forfeiting 'Enduring Freedom' for 'Homeland Security': A Constitutional Analysis of the USA Patriot Act and the Justice Department's Anti-Terrorism Initiatives," *American University Law Review* 51 (2002): 1120.

FIGURE 13.3	Jury Sizes by State for Courts of General Jurisdiction		

| | | **Trial Type** | |
State	*Felony*	*Misdemeanor*	*Civil*
Alabama	12	12	12
Alaska	12	12	12
Arizona	12/8	6	8
Arkansas	12	12	12
California	12	12	12
Colorado	12	6	6
Connecticut	6	6	6
Delaware	12	12	12
Florida	6	6	6
Georgia	12	6	12
Hawaii	12	12	12
Idaho	12	6	12/6
Illinois	12	12	12/6
Indiana	12/6	6	6
Iowa	12	12/6	8
Kansas	12	6	6/12
Kentucky	12	12	12
Louisiana	12	6	12
Maine	12	12	8
Maryland	12	12	6
Massachusetts	12	12	12
Michigan	12	12	6
Minnesota	12	6	6
Mississippi	12	6	12
Missouri	12	12	12
Montana	12	12	12
Nebraska	12	12	12
Nevada	12	12	12
New Hampshire	12	6	12
New Jersey	12	12	6/12
New Mexico	12	12	12
New York	12	12	6
North Carolina	12	12	12
North Dakota	12	12/6	6/9
Ohio	12	8	12/8
Oklahoma	12	6	6/12
Oregon	12	6	6/12
Pennsylvania	12	12	12
Rhode Island	12	12	12
South Carolina	12	12	12
South Dakota	12	12	12
Tennessee	12	12	12
Texas	12	12	12
Utah	8/12	6/4	8
Vermont	12	12	12
Virginia	12	7	5/7
Washington	12	12	6
West Virginia	12	12	6
Wisconsin	12	6	6
Wyoming	12	6	6

Note: There are exceptions to these size requirements in each state. Also, where two numbers are listed, the jury size requirement differs depending on the crime or the nature of the case.
Source: Bureau of Justice Statistics, U.S. Department of Justice, *State Court Organization, 1998* (Washington, DC: Department of Justice, 2000).

FIGURE 13.4 Jury Voting Requirements by State for Courts of General Jurisdiction

State	Trial Type		
	Felony	*Misdemeanor*	*Civil*
Alabama	U	U	U
Alaska	U	U	5/6
Arizona	U	U	3/4
Arkansas	U	U	3/4
California	U	U	3/4
Colorado	U	U	U
Connecticut	U	U	U
Delaware	U	U	U
Florida	U	U	U
Georgia	U	U	U
Hawaii	U	U	5/6
Idaho	U	U	3/4
Illinois	U	U	U
Indiana	U	U	U
Iowa	U	U	7/8 or U
Kansas	U	U	5/6 or U
Kentucky	U	U	3/4
Louisiana	10/12*	U	5/6
Maine	U	U	3/4
Maryland	U	U	U
Massachusetts	U	U	5/6
Michigan	U	U	5/6
Minnesota	U	U	5/6 or U
Mississippi	U	U	3/4
Missouri	U	U	3/4
Montana	U	U	2/3
Nebraska	U	U	5/6 or U
Nevada	U	U	3/4
New Hampshire	U	U	U
New Jersey	U	U	5/6
New Mexico	U	U	5/6
New York	U	U	5/6
North Carolina	U	U	U
North Dakota	U	U	U
Ohio	U	U	3/4
Oklahoma	U	U	U
Oregon	5/6**	5/6	3/4
Pennsylvania	U	U	5/6
Rhode Island	U	U	U
South Carolina	U	U	U
South Dakota	U	U	5/6
Tennessee	U	U	U
Texas	U	U	5/6
Utah	U	U	3/4 or majority
Vermont	U	U	U
Virginia	U	U	U
Washington	U	U	5/6
West Virginia	U	U	U
Wisconsin	U	U	5/6
Wyoming	U	U	U

Key: U = Unanimous; 5/6 = 5 out of 6 jurors must agree (3/4, 7/8, etc., interpreted similarly)

*Some sentences.

**Not capital cases.

Note: There are exceptions to these size requirements in each state. Also, where two voting requirements are listed, the voting requirement differs depending on the crime or the nature of the case.

Source: Bureau of Justice Statistics, U.S. Department of Justice, *State Court Organization, 1998* (Washington, DC: Department of Justice, 2000).

Small-Jury Voting Requirements

A man was charged with the offense of obscenity and convicted in a state trial court before a six-person jury. A poll of the jury after the verdict indicated that the jury had voted 5 to 1 to convict. The man appealed his conviction, claiming that his right to trial by jury under the Sixth Amendment was violated when the State permitted a less than unanimous verdict by a six-member jury. How should the appellate court decide?

■ Waiving the Right to a Jury Trial

Based on the discussion thus far, it appears that the Supreme Court has somewhat reduced the Sixth Amendment right to a jury trial. This may seem somewhat unfair to those concerned with the defendant's civil liberties. Nevertheless, there are occasions on which the defendant wishes to waive his or her right to a jury trial. If the case is particularly inflammatory or one with which the community is intimately familiar, then obtaining a fair jury may be difficult. In such a situation, the defendant may opt for a *bench trial*, in which the judge decides the question of guilt.

The leading case dealing with waiver of the right to a jury trial is *Patton v. United States* (281 U.S. 276 [1930]). In that case, the defendants argued that their decision to waive the right to a jury trial was invalid because they lacked the authority to do so. The Supreme Court disagreed and stated that the right to a jury trial can be waived at the request of the defendant. The waiver must, however, be "express and intelligent." The waiver must also be voluntary, not a product of government coercion (see *United States v. Jackson*, 390 U.S. 570 [1968]).

It is important to note that waiver of the right to a jury trial can be vetoed. That is, the judge can *require* a jury trial, even if the defendant desires otherwise. Often, such a

Jury size differs by state and trial type but is between six and twelve members.

veto comes at the request of the prosecutor. In *Singer v. United States* (380 U.S. 24 [1965]), the Court upheld a federal statute permitting vetoes of this nature. According to the Court, refusal to grant the defendant a waiver merely subjects the defendant to "the very thing that the Constitution guarantees him" (p. 36)—namely, a jury trial. In describing some reasons for a veto, the Court stated further, "The Constitution recognizes an adversary system as the proper method of determining guilt, and the Government, as a litigant, has a legitimate interest in seeing that cases in which it believes a conviction is warranted are tried before the tribunal which the Constitution regards as most likely to produce a fair result" (p. 36). Thus, if the government feels that a jury trial is preferable, in the sense that it will produce a fairer result than a bench trial, then a veto of the defendant's waiver of a jury trial is constitutionally permissible.

■ Selection of Potential Jurors

The process behind selecting an impartial jury is rather complicated. To begin, a list of potential, or prospective, jurors must be compiled. The creation of this list is critical, for without an impartial list, the final jury will not reflect a fair cross-section of the community. Once a list has been put together, then a panel of jurors is selected. This is when individuals are selected, usually randomly, for *jury duty.*

Thus, think of jury selection as a three-stage process: (1) a list of potential jurors is compiled; (2) potential jurors are selected from that list; and then (3) the jury itself is chosen. This section addresses the first and second stages; the third stage, *voir dire*, is addressed later.

The list of potential jury members can be called the *jury pool, master jury wheel,* or *jury list.* For simplicity, the term **jury list** will be used here. The jury list can be compiled from a number of sources. One of the most common methods is to draw from voter registration lists. The federal courts, the state of Washington, and several other states rely on this method. Another method of compiling the list is via driver's license registration lists. California currently uses this method. Some states even use telephone directory lists. Still other states rely on jury commissioners: individuals appointed by a judge who are responsible for compiling jury lists.

To be on the jury list, potential jurors usually have to possess important traits. For example, they must be of a certain age—usually, over 18. They must also be U.S. citizens and free of felony convictions. The requirements to serve on a jury vary considerably from one state to the next.

Once the jury list has been compiled, people are selected from the list for service. Individuals selected from the jury list are called a *panel* or *venire.* The term **jury panel** will be used here.

Anyone who has been called on for jury duty has, at one time, been part of a jury panel. And as most people know, there are several means by which one can be excused from a jury panel. Examples of people typically exempted from jury service are aliens, individuals unable to speak English, those under 18, those charged with a felony or who are serving a sentence, and those for whom jury service could cause severe hardship. People in law enforcement positions or who work in so-called critical occupations, such as the military and government, are typically exempted, as well.

Once the jury panel has been chosen, then *voir dire* commences. Before turning to *voir dire*, however, it is important to consider constitutional challenges to the jury selection process described thus far. Many defendants have appealed their convictions on the grounds that the jury list or panel was biased in some fashion. These challenges generally fall into two camps: (1) equal protection challenges and (2) fair cross-section challenges.

Both types of challenges can be made when the defendant examines the jury list for evidence of problems. Indeed, *Test v. United States* (420 U.S. 28 [1975]) grants federal defendants the right to inspect and copy jury lists in order to mount equal protection and/or fair cross-section challenges. Unfortunately, the jury list provides little more than individuals' names; sex and race must be inferred.

Note that an unbiased jury list or panel and an unbiased jury are *not* always the same. While the jury list or panel may be unbiased and highly representative of the community at large, the final jury may not be. Clearly, it is difficult to represent the community with 12 or fewer people. It is much easier to do so via the jury panel, however. Thus, the constitutional challenges discussed in the following sections apply to the selection of jury *lists* and *panels*, not to juries themselves. Jury selection is considered in the *voir dire* section.

Equal Protection Challenges

Before the Sixth Amendment was incorporated to the states, the only method of challenging the fairness of a jury pool or panel was based on the equal protection clause of the Fourteenth Amendment. In one case, *Strauder v. Virginia* (100 U.S. 303 [1879]), the Supreme Court declared unconstitutional a statute that explicitly excluded African Americans from jury service. The statute was a violation of equal protection, according to the Court.

Strauder was a fairly easy and predictable decision, given the nature of the statute involved. But what about exclusion of a particular group for other than statutory reasons? In *Whitus v. Georgia* (385 U.S. 545 [1967]), the Court held that an equal protection challenge will succeed when there is a significant disparity between, in that case, the proportion of African Americans on the jury panel and the proportion in the community. In another case, *Castaneda v. Partida* (430 U.S. 482 [1977]), the Supreme Court used the equal protection argument again. There, it held that systematic exclusion of people with Spanish surnames violated equal protection. In both cases, a *significant disparity* was deemed one that cannot be attributed to chance.

In summary, an equal protection challenge against the composition of a jury list or panel succeeded when (1) there was purposeful discrimination against certain individuals and (2) that discrimination was significant. The past tense is used here because the equal protection approach was abandoned in the 1975 case of *Taylor v. Louisiana* (419 U.S. 522 [1975]). That and some similar cases are considered next.

Fair Cross-Section Challenges

Prior to 1975, the Supreme Court noted that the Sixth Amendment required that jury selection procedures be based on "the concept of the jury as a cross-section of the community" (*Glasser v. United States*, 315 U.S. 60 [1942], p. 86). That decision, however, only applied to the federal courts. It was not until 1975 and the case of *Taylor v. Louisiana* (419 U.S. 522 [1975]) that the Supreme Court stated, "We accept the fair cross-section requirements as fundamental to the jury trial guaranteed by the Sixth Amendment." *Taylor* was therefore significant because (1) it abandoned the equal protection approach and (2) it applied the Sixth Amendment's fair cross-section requirement to the state courts through the due process clause of the Fourteenth Amendment.

Taylor was also significant because it abandoned the requirement of significant exclusion, replacing it with the lower standard of **systematic exclusion**. That is, in order to succeed with a fair cross-section challenge, the defendant need only show systematic exclusion of a distinctive group, not necessarily significant exclusion. *Taylor* also permitted fair cross-section challenges with regard to *any* distinctive group, not just racial and ethnic minorities, which were the only groups discussed in the equal protection cases from the previous section.

■ *Duren v. Missouri,*
439 U.S. 357 (1979)

In a later case, *Duren v. Missouri* (439 U.S. 357 [1979]), the Court clarified the *Taylor* language. Specifically, the Court required that the defendant prove three elements to succeed with a fair cross-section challenge:

(1) that the group alleged to be excluded is a *"distinctive"* group in the community; (2) that the representation of this group in venires from which juries are selected is not fair and reasonable in relation to the number of such persons in the community; and (3) that this *underrepresentation* is due to *systematic exclusion* of the group in the jury-selection process. (p. 364, emphasis added)

The following paragraphs focus on these three elements: the distinctive group requirement, underrepresentation, and systematic exclusion.

First, what is a **distinctive group**? Generally, the group must be large and identifiable. The group must also meet with the spirit of the Sixth Amendment, which is to guarantee a fair cross-section of the community. In *Lockhart v. McCree* (476 U.S. 162 [1986]), the Court noted that the distinctive group requirement

(1) "guards against the exercise of arbitrary power" and [ensures] that the "common-sense judgment of the community" will act as a "hedge against the overzealous or mistaken prosecutor;" (2) [preserves] "public confidence in the fairness of the criminal justice system;" and (3) [implements] our belief that "sharing in the administration of justice is a phase of civic responsibility." (pp. 174–175)

Examples of distinctive groups are, therefore, racial and ethnic minorities, including African Americans, Hispanic Americans, Native Americans, Jews, and others. Women are also considered a distinctive group. *Nondistinctive* groups include blue-collar workers (e.g., *Anaya v. Hansen*, 781 F.2d 1 [1st Cir. 1986]) and young adults (e.g., *Ford v. Seabold*, 841 F.2d 677 [6th Cir. 1988]). Basically, any group that has received protection via legislation and the equal protection clause (i.e., most notably, women and minorities) is considered distinctive for jury purposes.

DECISION MAKING EXERCISE 13.8

What Composes a Distinctive Group?

Tanya Oki, a resident of an elite suburban neighborhood, was charged with burglary. She was tried and convicted by a 12-member jury and later sentenced to five years in prison. While in prison, she acquired a copy of the jury list (which, incidentally, is now permitted following the Supreme Court's decision in *Test v. United States*, 420 U.S. 28 [1975]) and decided, based on the addresses in the list, that none of the jurors who convicted her were "yuppies." As such, she had her privately retained attorney draft an appeal, claiming that her Sixth Amendment right to an impartial jury was violated. In particular, she claimed that "yuppies" are a distinctive group and should be more adequately represented in the jury list. How should the appellate court decide?

Next, what is **underrepresentation**? This can be difficult to determine, but most Supreme Court cases to date have not dealt with difficult determinations. For example, in *Taylor*, the Court concluded that women were underrepresented in the jury panel because while they made by 53 percent of the population of people eligible for jury service, only 10 percent of the people in the jury panel were women. Similarly, in *Duren*, 54 percent of the adults in the county were women, but only 15 percent of the people on the jury panel were women.

It was easy for the Court to determine underrepresentation based on these startling percentages. When the discrepancies are not this apparent, however, determining underrepresentation can be quite difficult. It appears that a discrepancy of 10 percent or more between the jury panel and the distribution of a particular group in the community is unacceptable (*United States v. Rodriguez*, 776 F.2d 1509 [11th Cir. 1985]).

The last requirement for a fair cross-section challenge to succeed is whether the exclusion in question is a systematic exclusion or an accidental one. The only guidance the Supreme Court has offered with regard to this matter was announced in *Duren v. Missouri* (439 U.S. 357 [1979]): "[I]n Sixth Amendment fair-cross-section cases, systematic disproportion itself demonstrates an infringement of the defendant's interest in a jury chosen from a fair cross-section" (p. 368).

The *Voir Dire* Process

Thus far, the focus has been on the composition of jury lists (i.e., consisting of all possible jurors) and jury panels (i.e., those called for jury duty). If either excludes a particular group of people to the extent that the defendant's equal protection rights are violated or the Sixth Amendment's fair cross-section requirement is violated, then any resulting conviction could be reversed. Next, the focus turns to *voir dire*, which is the process of selecting a jury from a jury panel.

It is important to understand that once *voir dire* commences, the concern is *not* to ensure that the jury represents a fair cross-section of the community. Instead, *voir dire* is concerned with the selection of jury members who can be *impartial*, as the Sixth Amendment requires. The term *voir dire* means "to see what is said." Thus, at this stage, the judge, prosecutor, and defense have an opportunity to review potential jurors for evidence of bias.

Voir dire can be simple or complicated. In some jurisdictions, the judge decides who will serve on the jury. The prosecution and defense merely suggest questions to the judge in these jurisdictions. Doing so speeds up the process and also helps ensure that jurors do not develop preconceived ideas about the case in question.

Usually, however, it is the attorneys who do the questioning. This process can take anything from a few hours to a few weeks. *Voir dire* at O. J. Simpson's criminal trial took several weeks. *Voir dire* can also take time because nothing precludes the attorneys from investigating jurors' backgrounds, interviewing their acquaintances, and even hiring social scientists who are experts in anticipating prospective jurors' probable decisions.

Most readers are familiar with the basic elements of the *voir dire* process. Each side, the defense and prosecution, has an unlimited number of so-called *challenges for cause*. A challenge for cause is when one or the other attorney argues that a particular person should be excluded from service on the jury because of bias or a similar reason. Each side is also given a certain number of *peremptory challenges*, which permit the attorney to exclude members of the jury panel without giving any reason. Before either challenge is used, however, the judge usually opens by asking questions of the jurors. Each of these three methods is considered in a following subsection. But before moving on, see Figure 13.5 for a summary of the *voir dire* process by state, including who conducts *voir dire* and the number of peremptory challenges allocated by specific crime type.

Questioning by the Judge

Voir dire usually begins with the judge asking questions—for instance, dealing with potential jurors' familiarity with the case, attitudes toward one or the other party to the case, demographic information, and so on. This is often done to guide the attorneys in their *voir dire* questioning. The Supreme Court has upheld this type of questioning, noting that it is perfectly acceptable for the judge to question jurors about their knowledge and opinions concerning the case (*Mu'Min v. Virginia*, 500 U.S. 415 [1991]).

Note that the reverse is also true: The judge is not required to ask any questions in certain types of cases. In an obscenity case, the Supreme Court noted that the judge is not required to ask questions as to "whether the jurors' educational, political, and religious beliefs might affect their views on the question of obscenity" (*Hamling v. United States*, 418 U.S. 87 [1974]).

State	Who Conducts Voir Dire?	Number of Peremptory Challenges					
		Capital: State	Capital: Defense	Felony: State	Felony: Defense	Misdemeanor: State	Misdemeanor: Defense
Alabama	Attorneys & Judge	12	12	6	6	3	3
Alaska	Attorneys &/or Judge	N/A	N/A	10	10	3	3
Arizona	Judge	10	10	6	6	6	6
Arkansas	Attorneys & Judge	10	12	6	8	3	3
California	Judge with some Attorney questions	20	20	20/10	20/10	10/6	10/6
Colorado	Attorneys & Judge	10	10	5	5	3	3
Connecticut	Attorneys	25	25	15/6	15/6	3	3
Delaware	Judge	12	20	6	6	6	6
Florida	Attorneys & Judge	10	10	6/10	6/10	3	3
Georgia	Attorneys & Judge	10	20	6	12	2	4
Hawaii	Attorneys & Judge	N/A	N/A	3/12	3/12	3	3
Idaho	Attorneys & Judge	10	10	6	6	4	4
Illinois	Judge with some Attorney questions	20	20	10	10	5	5
Indiana	Attorneys & Judge	20	20	10	10	5	5
Iowa	Attorneys & Judge	10	N/A	10/6	10/6	4	4
Kansas	Attorneys & Judge	12	12	12/8/6	12/8/6	3	3
Kentucky	Attorneys & Judge	8	8	8	8	N/A	N/A
Louisiana	Attorneys & Judge	12	12	12/6	12/6	6	6
Maine	Attorneys & Judge	N/A	N/A	8/10	8/10	4	4
Maryland	Attorneys & Judge	10	20	5	10	4	4
Massachusetts	Judge	12	12	4	4	4	4
Michigan	Attorneys & Judge	12	N/A	5/12	5/12	N/A	N/A
Minnesota	Attorneys & Judge	9	N/A	9/3	15/5	N/A	N/A
Mississippi	Attorneys & Judge	12	12	6	6	6	6
Missouri	Attorneys & Judge	9	9	6	6	2	2
Montana	Attorneys & Judge	8	8	6/3	6/3	6/3	6/3
Nebraska	Attorneys & Judge	12	12	6	6	3	3
Nevada	Attorneys & Judge	8	8	4	4	4	4
New Hampshire	Judge	10	20	15/3	15/3	3	3
New Jersey	Judge	12	20	12	20	10	10
New Mexico	Attorneys & Judge	8	12	3	5	3	5
New York	Attorneys & Judge	20	20	20/15/10	20/15/10	10	10
North Carolina	Attorneys	14	14	6	6	6	6
North Dakota	Attorneys & Judge	N/A	N/A	6/4	6/4	6/4	6/4
Ohio	Attorneys & Judge	6	6	4	4	3	3
Oklahoma	Attorneys & Judge	9	9	5	5	3	3
Oregon	Attorneys & Judge	12	12	6	6	6	6
Pennsylvania	Attorneys &/or Judge	20	20	7	7	5	5
Rhode Island	Attorneys & Judge	N/A	N/A	6	6	3	3
South Carolina	Attorneys & Judge	5	10	5	10	5	5
South Dakota	Attorneys & Judge	20	20	20/10	20/10	3	3
Tennessee	Attorneys & Judge	15	15	8	8	3	3
Texas	Attorneys	15	15	10	10	5	5
Utah	Attorneys & Judge	10	10	4	4	3	3
Vermont	Attorneys & Judge	N/A	N/A	6	6	6	6
Virginia	Attorneys & Judge	4	4	4	4	3	3
Washington	Attorneys & Judge	12	12	6	6	3	3
West Virginia	Attorneys & Judge	N/A	N/A	2	6	4	4
Wisconsin	Attorneys & Judge	N/A	N/A	6/4	6/4	4	4
Wyoming	Attorneys	12	12	8	8	4	4

Key: N/A = not applicable.
Note: Cells with more than one number indicate states with different numbers of peremptories based on the type of offense: capital, felony, or misdemeanor.
Source: Bureau of Justice Statistics, U.S. Department of Justice, *State Court Organization, 1998* (Washington, DC: Department of Justice, 2000).

However, the Supreme Court has required that in certain types of cases—notably, those dealing with racial prejudice and capital punishment—judges must ask certain types of questions. For instance, in *Ham v. South Carolina* (409 U.S. 524 [1973]), the Court noted that questions about racial prejudice must be asked if racial issues are closely tied to the criminal conduct at issue. *Ham* was a case in which an African American defendant was tried for marijuana possession. The defendant claimed that because he was a well-known civil rights activist, the police had framed him on the narcotics charge. The Supreme Court stated that the general introductory questions asked by the judge were insufficient and that special attention should have been given to the race issue.

In another case, *Ristaino v. Ross* (424 U.S. 589 [1976]), a black defendant was convicted of a violent crime committed against a white security guard. The trial judge denied the defendant's motion that specific questions about racial prejudice be asked of potential jurors. Instead, the judge just asked basic questions about *general* prejudice, not any directed at the facts of the case in question. Surprisingly, the Supreme Court upheld the trial judge's decision. This decision seems contradictory to *Ham*, but the Court noted that in this case, racial issues did not permeate. Instead, the fact that the defendant was black and the victim was white was secondary to the question of guilt.

The Supreme Court has also decided whether judges should ask detailed questions of potential jurors who serve on *death-qualified juries*—that is, juries that may recommend a death sentence.[6] The Court has actually been more emphatic with regard to death penalty cases than with those involving racial issues. It has stated that the judge *must*, at the request of either party and only in cases in which capital punishment is a possible outcome, ask specific questions of jurors so as to assess their attitudes toward capital punishment. This rule was announced in *Morgan v. Illinois* (504 U.S. 719 [1992]). There, the Court held that defendants in capital cases may require potential jurors to state whether they would automatically impose the death penalty on conviction.

In summary, there are few constitutional restrictions on judges' questioning of potential jurors. With the exceptions of capital cases and those in which racial and ethnic matters permeate the trial, judges are under no obligation to ask questions of potential jurors. By the same token, judges are given considerable latitude in terms of asking almost any questions they desire. Detailed questions, however, are mostly asked by the attorneys in the case.

Challenges for Cause

The prosecution and defense are given unlimited opportunities to make **challenges for cause**. Convincing reasons can be found for the exclusion of potential jurors, some of which even have statutory origins. For example, if a member of the jury panel is related to the defendant, a challenge for cause will almost certainly succeed. Also, if the potential juror served on a past jury in a case dealing with a similar crime, a challenge for cause will probably succeed. If a potential juror stands to benefit financially from the outcome of the case, he or she will probably be excused based on a challenge for cause. While the list goes on, only two challenges have been dealt with by the Supreme Court: (1) those based on bias and (2) those based on attitudes toward capital punishment.

Challenges Based on Bias. Generally, if a juror is unable or unwilling to hear the case fairly and impartially, he or she may be excluded in a challenge for cause. However, as Supreme Court precedent seems to attest, challenges for cause dealing with alleged bias rarely succeed. That is, in situations in which a person *appears* biased but does not state anything to this effect, it is difficult to succeed with a challenge for cause.

---

[6]A *death-qualified jury* is one in which each juror is at least open to the idea of sentencing someone to death. Death-qualified jurors are selected after being asked questions about whether they support the death penalty and would hand down a sentence of death, if the need arose.

In fact, there is only one case in which the Supreme Court sanctioned exclusion of a potential juror because of alleged bias. In *Leonard v. United States* (378 U.S. 544 [1964]), the Court held that jury panel members who had heard the guilty verdict at the defendant's previous trial should have been excluded from serving on the jury in the present trial. The Court believed that the previous verdict may have influenced jurors in the second trial.

Leonard stands alone, though. In *Dennis v. United States* (339 U.S. 162 [1950]), the Court required a showing of *actual* bias, not *alleged* bias. In that case, the defendant claimed that his conviction on contempt charges for failure to appear before the Committee on Un-American Activities was tainted because the jury consisted mostly of federal employees, who were all subject to discharge if they were not loyal to the government. The Court disagreed with Dennis's argument, stating that "[p]reservation of the opportunity to prove actual bias is a guarantee of a defendant's right to an impartial jury" (pp. 171–172).

In a more recent case, *Smith v. Phillips* (455 U.S. 209 [1982]), the Court held once again that actual bias must be shown for a challenge for cause to succeed. In that case, the Court did not infer bias from the fact that a potential juror had been seeking employment from the prosecutor's office. However, this decision and the one before it should not be construed to suggest that actual bias must *always* be shown over alleged bias. Alleged, or implied, bias may be sufficient in certain limited circumstances for exclusion of a potential juror based on a challenge for cause.

■ *Smith v. Phillips,*
455 U.S. 209 (1982)

Challenges in Death Penalty Cases. Defendants in capital trials have the right to exclude jurors who have certain preconceived ideas about the death penalty. In *Witherspoon v. Illinois* (391 U.S. 510 [1968]), the Court decided on the constitutionality of a statute that provided for exclusion of all potential jurors who "expressed scruples" against the death penalty. The Court held that a death sentence returned from such a jury would be unconstitutional because the jury resulting from the statute would be "organized to return a verdict of death" (p. 521). Importantly, in *Witherspoon*, it was only the defendant's death sentence that was invalidated, not his conviction. Also, note that nothing prohibits a prosecutor from excluding a juror who would *never* return a verdict of death.

■ *Witherspoon v. Illinois,*
391 U.S. 510 (1968)

DECISION MAKING EXERCISE **13.9**

Strong Opinions on the Death Penalty

Assume that during *voir dire,* the following exchange takes place between a defense attorney and a potential juror:

Defense Attorney: Do you have any reservations against the death penalty?

Potential Juror: No, of course not. I firmly support capital punishment. I think we should execute all criminals.

Defense Attorney: Do you think you can set aside your personal convictions for the purposes of this trial and make an objective decision based on the evidence?

Potential Juror: I suppose so. I think I could probably keep an open mind.

Now, assume that the defense attorney seeks to exercise one of her challenges for cause and asks the judge to exclude this juror. The judge denies the request. Assuming that the remaining jurors are not as opinionated, do you think the resulting jury will conform to the Sixth Amendment requirements discussed thus far?

In short, challenges for cause in death penalty cases usually come in two varieties. If the defendant can show that a potential juror is predisposed to return a verdict of death, such a juror will probably be excluded. Similarly, if the prosecution can show that a potential juror is all but certain to oppose capital punishment, that juror will probably be excluded, as well.

Peremptory Challenges

The foregoing section showed that challenges for cause come in several varieties, but the only ones previously dealt with by the Supreme Court concerned bias as well as attitudes toward the death penalty. In either case, one of the parties to the case presented its argument to the judge as to why a potential juror should be excluded. **Peremptory challenges**, by contrast, call for removal of potential jurors *without* any type of argument.

Think of a peremptory challenge as a fallback measure. If, say, the defense fails with a challenge for cause to exclude a potential juror who it believes will be biased against the defendant, a peremptory challenge can be used. In fact, a peremptory challenge can be used to exclude a potential juror for any reason. As the Supreme Court stated in *Swain v. Alabama* (380 U.S. 202 [1965]), the peremptory challenge "is often exercised upon the 'sudden impressions and unaccountable prejudices we are apt to conceive upon the bare looks and gestures of another,' upon a juror's 'habits and associations,' or upon the felling that the 'bare questioning [of a juror's] indifference may sometimes provoke a resentment'" (pp. 242–243).

Because peremptory challenges need not be predicated on any type of argument, there are not many Supreme Court cases dealing with them. Of the few relevant cases, however, some deal with peremptory challenges by the prosecution. The rest deal with challenges by the defense.

Challenges by the Prosecution. It is generally unacceptable for the prosecution (and the defense) to exclude a juror based on race or ethnicity. A *challenge for cause* arguing that a person's race or ethnicity will cause him or her to be biased will never succeed. But what if a *peremptory challenge* is used to exclude a juror based on race or ethnicity? This question was addressed in *Swain v. Alabama*, cited earlier. In that case, the defendant argued that the prosecutor excluded all minority jurors through peremptory challenges and, as such, violated the equal protection clause of the Fourteenth Amendment. The Court rejected this argument, as follows:

> [The peremptory challenge] is often exercised upon the "sudden impressions and unaccountable prejudices we are apt to conceive upon the bare looks and gestures of another," . . . upon a juror's "habits and associations," . . . or upon the feeling that "the bare questioning [a juror's] indifference may sometimes provoke a resentment." . . . It is no less frequently exercised on grounds normally thought irrelevant to legal proceedings or official action, namely, the race, religion, nationality, occupation or affiliations of people summoned for jury duty. For the question a prosecutor or defense counsel must decide is not whether a juror of a particular race or nationality is in fact partial, but whether one from a different group is less likely to be. (pp. 220–221)

The Court continued:

> Hence veniremen are not always judged solely as individuals for the purpose of exercising peremptory challenges. Rather they are challenged in light of the limited knowledge counsel has of them, which may include their group affiliations, in the context of the case to be tried. (p. 221)

Had the prosecutor in this case sought to exclude minorities from all juries and had this come to light, a successful equal protection challenge probably could have been mounted.

Several years after *Swain*, the Supreme Court revisited the issue of using peremptory challenges for excluding racial and ethnic minorities. In *Batson v. Kentucky* (476 U.S. 79 [1986]), the Court decided that prosecutors can be called on to explain their use of peremptory challenges to exclude minorities but only if the defense shows that the challenges were used for this purpose. This showing requires that the people excluded

■ *Batson v. Kentucky,*
476 U.S. 79 (1986)

through the peremptory challenges constitute a distinct group, that these people were excluded by the prosecution through the use of peremptory challenges, and that "these facts and any other relevant circumstances raise an inference that the prosecutor used [peremptories] to exclude the veniremen from the petit jury on account of their race" (p. 124); for some recent California-specific attention to *Batson*, see *Johnson v. California* (125 S.Ct. 2410 [2005]); also see *Miller El v. Dretke* (125 S.Ct. 2317 [2005]).

If the defense makes the showing, then the prosecutor will be required to explain his or her reasons for excluding jurors based on race and ethnicity. However, this explanation does not need to be as convincing as one that would accompany a challenge for cause. It simply needs to be what the Court calls *race neutral.*

What is a race-neutral explanation? In *Hernandez v. New York* (500 U.S. 352 [1991]), the prosecutor sought to use peremptory challenges to exclude four potential jurors of Hispanic descent. They were the only three people on the panel with apparent Hispanic origins. The prosecutor argued that the jurors were excluded for two reasons: (1) that two of the panel members were involved in criminal activity and (2) that the other two "looked away" from him during questioning. The Court declared that this explanation was race neutral. Had the prosecution argued that the excluded jurors would likely decide a case in a certain way, given their Hispanic descent, the Court would have decided differently. Thus, a race-neutral argument is one that really has nothing to do with race or ethnicity.

Appropriate Use of the Peremptory Challenge

An African American defendant, who was charged in a state trial court with robbery, objected to the prosecutor's use of peremptory challenges to excuse two black men from the jury panel. The prosecutor explained that he excused the first juror because the juror had long unkempt hair, a mustache, and a beard. The prosecutor then said that he excluded the second juror because the juror had a mustache and a beard. The trial court overruled the defendant's objection, impaneled the jury, and convicted the defendant of robbery. The defendant filed an interlocutory appeal (i.e., one filed before final adjudication), raising the same argument as in his trial motion. If the appellate court decides the hear this argument, how should it rule?

In summary, peremptory challenges used to exclude racial and ethnic minorities are constitutionally valid only when (1) the prosecutor offers a race-neutral explanation for doing so and (2) the judge believes the reason is genuine. These two requirements only matter, however, if the defendant raises the argument that race or ethnicity was a motivating factor behind the prosecutor's use of peremptory challenges. In other words, the defense has the initial burden of showing racial or ethnic bias in the peremptory challenge stage. These guidelines apply not only to peremptory exclusion of racial and ethnic minorities (e.g., related cases include *Powers v. Ohio*, 499 U.S. 400 [1991]; *Holland v. Illinois*, 493 U.S. 474 [1990]) but also to gender-based exclusion (see *J.E.B. v. Alabama*, 511 U.S. 127 [1994]).

Challenges by the Defense. The defense also cannot exclude potential jurors through peremptory challenges based on race and ethnicity. For example, in *Georgia v. McCollum* (502 U.S. 1056 [1992]), the Court refused to sanction the exclusion of black panel members in the trial of white defendants charged with assaulting black individuals. At the same time, though, the defense cannot be forced to use a peremptory challenge to excuse a juror he or she argues should have been excused for cause. (See *United States v. Martinez-Salazar*, 528 U.S. 304 [2000], for a further explanation.)

■ *Gray v. Mississippi,*
481 U.S. 648 (1987)

Remaining Supreme Court cases concerning peremptory challenges by the defense have revolved around the question of how many, if any, peremptory challenges should be constitutionally permissible. In response, the Court stated in *Gray v. Mississippi* (481 U.S. 648 [1987]) that peremptory challenges are not constitutionally guaranteed. And in *Stilson v. United States* (250 U.S. 583 [1919]), the Court held that in trials of co-defendants, the number of peremptories should be reduced to the number each defendant would have if tried separately. Other cases suggest that the defense can be required to exercise its peremptory challenges before the government does (*Pointer v. United States*, 151 U.S. 396 [1894]) and that the defense can be required to exclude, through use of its peremptory challenges, jurors that the judge should have excused for cause (*Ross v. Oklahoma*, 487 U.S. 81 [1988]).

■ When Judges Preempt Juries

Recently, the Supreme Court gave some attention to what the jury must consider during its deliberations—and to what extent judges can preempt juries. In *Blakely v. Washington* (542 U.S. 296 [2004]), a man was convicted of kidnapping his estranged wife. After the jury returned its verdict, the judge decided that the man acted with "deliberate cruelty" and he handed down a harsher sentence than would have otherwise been authorized had he not identified such aggravating factors. The Supreme Court declared that the defendant's right to a jury trial was violated because the facts supporting the judge's finding of "deliberate cruelty" were not admitted by the accused *or* found by a jury. In other words, the judge could not preempt the jury's fact-finding role (see also *United States v. Booker*, 543 U.S. 220 [2005]).

CONCLUSION

The defendant has three important rights at trial: (1) the right to a speedy trial; (2) the right to an impartial judge; and (3) the right to an impartial jury. The first and third rights have constitutional (i.e., Sixth Amendment) origins. The right to an impartial judge does not; it is a right created by the Supreme Court, in much the same way the exclusionary rule is a judicial creation.

The right to a speedy trial applies once a person has been accused of a crime. If the defendant is charged, let go, and then charged again, the right does not apply until the second set of charges has been filed. Even if the defendant does not know he or she has been accused of and/or charged with a crime, the right to speedy trial can apply. This right sometimes extends beyond the Sixth Amendment and, according to the Supreme Court, can have a due process component.

Four criteria are used to determine when the right to a speedy trial has been *violated*: (1) too much delay between accusation and trial; (2) intentional delay; (3) whether the defendant asserts the right to a speedy trial; and (4) whether the delay is prejudicial. No criterion by itself is necessarily enough for the right to be violated, however. If, for instance, the delay is too long, intentional, prejudicial, and accompanied by the defendant's demand for a speedy

trial, the right will almost certainly be violated. The consequence of violating the right to a speedy trial is dismissal of charges. Finally, the federal Speedy Trial Act attempted to clarify important Supreme Court decisions regarding the Sixth Amendment right to a speedy trial.

The defendant also enjoys the right to trial by an impartial judge. A judge cannot be considered impartial if he or she has a pecuniary interest in the outcome of a case. Usually, judges will remove themselves if they deem themselves less than impartial, but some jurisdictions permit the peremptory removal of judges. This allows counsel to remove one judge and request a second one. This method is extreme, however.

Finally, the defendant enjoys the right to trial by an impartial jury. However, the Supreme Court has held that this right applies only to criminal proceedings in which the possible punishment exceeds six months' detention. Jury size and voting requirements vary by jurisdiction, but as a general rule, the smaller the jury, the more unanimous the required verdict. Like many constitutional rights, the right to a jury trial can be waived, in which case the defendant opts for a so-called bench trial.

Jury selection occurs in three stages. First, a list of potential jurors, known as the jury list, is compiled.

From that list, potential jurors are selected for jury service. Those selected for jury service are part of a jury panel. From the jury panel, some people are selected and required to go to a courtroom, where *voir dire* commences. *Voir dire* begins with the judge asking questions, some of which he or she is required to ask. Next, the attorneys on both sides will exercise their peremptory challenges and challenges for cause. The former are almost unrestricted but limited in number. The latter must be argued before the judge and are not limited in number.

It is important to understand that the jury list and panel must be representative of the community at large but not the final jury. The only way for a defendant to succeed in arguing that the jury itself is not representative is if he or she can show that the prosecution used its peremptory challenges to exclude individuals from distinctive groups and engages in this practice during the *voir dire* process for *all* juries. If the prosecution uses its peremptory challenges to occasionally excuse a juror based on race or ethnicity, the Sixth Amendment will not be violated. Finally, judges cannot preempt the jury's role.

REVIEW QUESTIONS

1. Explain when the right to a speedy trial applies.
2. What criteria are used to determine when the right to a speedy trial has been violated?
3. Summarize the consequences of violating the accused's right to a speedy trial.
4. Briefly outline important provisions of the federal Speedy Trial Act, including the consequences of violating it.
5. Under what circumstances could a judge be considered *not* impartial (i.e., biased)? Cite relevant cases.
6. What methods are available for removing a judge who cannot be consider impartial?
7. When does the right to a jury trial apply?

8. Explain the jury size and voting requirements in your state.
9. Can the right to a jury trial be waived? If so, what are the requirements for doing so?
10. Identify the methods used for creating a jury list.
11. What are the three stages of jury selection?
12. What are the requirements for a successful fair cross-section challenge of a jury panel?
13. Summarize the *voir dire* process.
14. What questions has the Supreme Court required judges to ask during *voir dire*?
15. Under what circumstances has the Supreme Court imposed restrictions on the use of peremptory challenges?

 Answers to the Decision-Making Exercises for this chapter can be found on pages 517–519.

CHAPTER 14

More Rights at Trial

KEY TERMS

public trial
change of venue
jury sequestration
gag order
confrontation
physical presence
mental competence

live testimony
unavailable witness
hearsay exceptions
direct examination
cross-examination
redirect examination
recross-examination

compulsory process
double jeopardy
same offense
Blockburger rule
entrapment defense

INTRODUCTION
More Protections for the Accused

In addition to guaranteeing the right to counsel, the Sixth Amendment provides that "[i]n all criminal prosecutions, the accused shall enjoy the right to . . . [a] public trial[,] to be confronted with the witnesses against him [and] to have compulsory process for obtaining witnesses in his favor." These rights are intended to assist the accused in mounting an effective defense. Without them, a criminal prosecution would be largely one sided; that is, it would favor the prosecution.

In addition to the rights to a public trial, confrontation, and compulsory process, criminal defendants in the United States also enjoy other important rights at trial. One such right, known as protection from *double jeopardy*, is found in the Fifth Amendment: "[N]or shall any person be subject for the same offence to be twice put in jeopardy of life or limb." This means that an accused person cannot be convicted of or punished for the same offense twice. Finally, a defendant can assert the well-known *entrapment defense*. This defense is considered here, as well, even though it is not a constitutional guarantee, as the other rights are.

KEY CASES

Public Trial

- *In re Oliver*, 333 U.S. 257 (1948)
- *Waller v. Georgia*, 467 U.S. 39 (1984)
- *Sheppard v. Maxwell*, 384 U.S. 333 (1966)
- *Rideau v. Louisiana*, 373 U.S. 723 (1963)
- *Nebraska Press Ass'n v. Stuart*, 427 U.S. 539 (1976)

Confrontation

- *Illinois v. Allen*, 397 U.S. 337 (1970)
- *Taylor v. Illinois*, 484 U.S. 400 (1988)
- *Dusky v. United States*, 362 U.S. 402 (1960)
- *Mattox v. United States*, 156 U.S. 237 (1895)
- *Motes v. United States*, 178 U.S. 458 (1900)
- *White v. Illinois*, 502 U.S. 346 (1992)
- *Coy v. Iowa*, 487 U.S. 1012 (1988)
- *Chambers v. Mississippi*, 410 U.S. 284 (1973)

Compulsory Process

- *Washington v. Texas*, 388 U.S. 14 (1967)
- *Crane v. Kentucky*, 476 U.S. 683 (1986)
- *United States v. Scheffer*, 523 U.S. 303 (1998)

Double Jeopardy

- *Benton v. Maryland*, 395 U.S. 784 (1969)
- *Kansas v. Hendricks*, 521 U.S. 346 (1997)
- *Blockburger v. United States*, 284 U.S. 299 (1932)

Entrapment

- *Sorrells v. United States*, 287 U.S. 435 (1932)
- *Sherman v. United States*, 356 U.S. 369 (1958)
- *United States v. Russell*, 411 U.S. 423 (1973)
- *Hampton v. United States*, 425 U.S. 484 (1976)

THE RIGHT TO A PUBLIC TRIAL

■ *In re Oliver,*
333 U.S. 257 (1948)

In *In re Oliver* (333 U.S. 257 [1948]), the Supreme Court stated, "The knowledge that every criminal trial is subject to contemporaneous review in the forum of public opinion is an effective restraint on possible abuse of power. . . . Without publicity, all other checks are insufficient; in comparison of publicity, all other checks are of small account" (p. 271). Furthermore, "the presence of interested spectators may keep [the defendant's] triers keenly alive to a sense of their responsibility and to the importance of their functions" (p. 271, n. 25). This is what is meant by a **public trial**: It is one that is open to the public.

Oliver dealt expressly with criminal trials, but the Supreme Court has suggested that openness also applies to other hearings. For example, suppression hearings should be open to the public (*Waller v. Georgia*, 467 U.S. 39 [1984]). By extension, most other hearings—with the exception of grand jury proceedings, which are traditionally carried out in secret—should be considered public, as well.

When the Right May Not Apply

Most trials are open to the public but not all of them. Indeed, the defendant, whose interest is frequently served by openness, may want the trial closed to the public. This could be in an effort to minimize negative publicity, especially when the trial is for a heinous crime. In this way, the defendant's Sixth Amendment rights can be waived, just like many other constitutional rights can. The government can also seek to close a trial to the public. Each method of closure is touched on in a following subsection.

Government-Sought Closure

■ *Waller v. Georgia,*
467 U.S. 39 (1984)

In *Waller v. Georgia* (467 U.S. 39 [1984]), the Supreme Court created a test for determining when the government will succeed in closing a trial to the public. The government must show (1) that there is an overriding interest, such as protection of certain witnesses; (2) that the closure is no broader than absolutely necessary; and (3) that reasonable alternatives have been considered.

Waller dealt with the closure of a suppression hearing in which a video of people not yet indicted was played. The Court held that closure of the hearing was unconstitutional because the government did not identify "whose privacy interests might be infringed, how they would be infringed, what portions of the tape might infringe on them, and what portion of the evidence consisted of the tapes" (p. 48). At present, the threat of terrorism is being used as justification by the government for the closure of certain judicial hearings.

Defense-Sought Closure

■ *Sheppard v. Maxwell,*
384 U.S. 333 (1966)

Sheppard v. Maxwell (384 U.S. 333 [1966]) illustrates the occasional conflict that can arise with the negative effects of trial publicity. In that case, the courtroom was packed with members of the public and media for all nine weeks of the trial. This made if difficult for people to hear one another. The press also handled and took pictures of evidentiary exhibits. The Supreme Court reversed the defendant's conviction, citing the "carnival atmosphere" of the trial in its decision.[1]

In another case, *Estes v. Texas* (381 U.S. 532 [1965]), the Court also reversed the defendant's conviction, noting that the presence of television cameras distracted

---

[1] While the defense in *Sheppard* did not directly seek closure of the trial, it did make requests for a continuance, a change of venue, and a mistrial.

parties to the case in addition to the witnesses who gave testimony. This ruling does not provide a blanket prohibition of television cameras in courtrooms, however. In *Chandler v. Florida* (449 U.S. 560 [1981]), the Supreme Court upheld Florida's rule permitting the use of still photography and television cameras in court. Cameras are impermissible only if the defendant can show that "the media's coverage of his case—be it printed or broadcast—[compromises] the ability of the . . . jury . . . to adjudicate fairly" (p. 575).

■ The First Amendment and Public Trials

The First Amendment guarantees freedom of speech and of the press. Thus, any effort to close a trial or pretrial hearing to the public—be it by the government or the defense—may cause the press to rally in opposition. Supreme Court precedent suggests that unless the government or the defense can demonstrate that significant prejudice is likely to result from a public trial, closure of a trial is unlikely.

Gannett Co., Inc. v. DePasquale (443 U.S. 368 [1979]) is an illustrative case. There, the Supreme Court held that the trial judge may, at the defendant's request, close a pretrial suppression hearing in an effort to avoid the "reasonable probability of prejudice." The Supreme Court sanctioned closure of this nature because it was at the defendant's request and because the media did not oppose closure.

In *Richmond Newspapers, Inc. v. Virginia* (448 U.S. 555 [1980]), however, the Court indicated that closure will seldom be allowed if the media asserts an interest in having access to the hearing. The defendant in *Richmond Newspapers* sought closure of his trial because he had been through four previous mistrials, one of which stemmed from a juror telling other jurors about press reports of the case. The Court rejected the defendant's argument, noting that "the right to attend criminal trials is implicit in the guarantees of the First Amendment; without the freedom to attend such trials, which people have exercised for centuries, important aspects of freedom of speech and of the press could be eviscerated" (p. 580). And in another case, *Globe Newspaper Co. v. Superior Court* (457 U.S. 596 [1982]), the Court noted that the First Amendment serves "to ensure that the individual citizen can effectively participate in and contribute to our republican system of self-government" and "fosters an appearance of fairness, thereby heightening public respect for the judicial process" (p. 606).

DECISION MAKING EXERCISE 14.1

The Right to a Public Trial

A nurse was charged with murdering 12 patients by administering massive doses of the heart drug Lidocaine. The judge granted her motion to exclude the public from her preliminary hearing under a state statute that requires such proceedings to be open unless "exclusion of the public is necessary in order to protect the defendant's right to a fair and impartial trial." Following the conclusion of the preliminary hearing, the judge refused a local newspaper's request to release the transcript of the proceedings. The matter went all the way to the state supreme court, which denied the newspaper's request, holding that there is no general First Amendment right of access to preliminary hearings and that under the state statute, if the defendant establishes a "reasonable likelihood of substantial prejudice," then the transcript does not need to be released. Assuming this case goes the U.S. Supreme Court, how should it decide?

In summary, with regard to the First Amendment and the defendant's interest in a fair trial, closure of a criminal trial is highly unlikely. None of the Supreme Court cases reviewed thus far have permitted outright closure. By contrast, closure of a pretrial hearing is more likely to be sanctioned. In either case, difficulty will only be encountered if the press raises a First Amendment objection to the proposed closure.

Dealing with Media Influence

The media can seemingly influence the fairness of a criminal trial in two ways: (1) by its pretrial coverage and (2) by being present in the courtroom, as just discussed. However, if either form of coverage is prejudicial, this does not necessarily mean the media should be excluded and the hearing closed to the public.

In response to this problem, the Supreme Court has addressed several alternatives to the closure of pretrial hearings and/or the trial itself. Each is aimed at ensuring a fair trial for the accused. The alternatives are (1) *voir dire* with special attention to pretrial publicity; (2) a change of venue; (3) jury sequestration; (4) a gag order on the media; and (5) a gag order on other parties.

As explained in Chapter 13, *voir dire* is the process by which jury members are selected from a panel of potential jurors. The judge can ask several questions, and the attorneys can exclude jurors for cause and by use of peremptory challenges. When media coverage of a crime is extensive and presumed to have influenced members of the jury panel, *voir dire* can be used to detect that bias.

In *Marshall v. United States* (360 U.S. 310 [1959]), the Supreme Court held that potential jurors who have learned from news coverage of a defendant's prior record are presumed to be prejudiced. Similarly, in *Irvin v. Dowd* (366 U.S. 717 [1961]), the Court decided that pretrial publicity can be so influential that jurors' statements about being willing to make impartial decisions can be discounted. But in two later cases, *Murphy v. Florida* (421 U.S. 794 [1975]) and *Patton v. Yount* (467 U.S. 1025 [1984]), the Court indicated that unless a juror candidly admits bias due to pretrial publicity, a defendant's constitutional challenge to jury impartiality is unlikely to succeed.

As a second method of addressing bias induced by press coverage, a **change of venue** can be sought. In *Rideau v. Louisiana* (373 U.S. 723 [1963]), the Court overturned a defendant's death sentence because the trial court refused to grant the defendant's motion for a change of venue. In that case, Rideau's confession had been broadcast all over local television. The Court stated that "due process of law in this case required a trial before a jury drawn from a community of people who had not seen and heard Rideau's interview" (p. 727). Of course, a change of venue is not a realistic option when pretrial publicity has influenced potential jurors in multiple jurisdictions. A change of venue rarely succeeds, then, in the trial of someone whose crime is well known over a wide geographical area.

A third method of dealing with the influence of the press is **jury sequestration**. This method is mostly used to minimize the influence of press coverage *during* the trial. Sequestration is basically jury isolation. Members are usually put up in a hotel and denied access to television and print media coverage of the trial. Sequestration is an extreme method but necessary in certain cases. After all, judges' warnings to jury members to avoid media accounts while at home are probably naïve. The Supreme Court has recognized that jury sequestration is a valid option in certain extreme circumstances (see *Sheppard v. Maxwell*, 384 U.S. 333 [1966]).

A **gag order** on the media can be used, as well. A gag order is a judge's order to keep the media quiet concerning a particular matter. In *Nebraska Press Ass'n v. Stuart* (427 U.S. 539 [1976]), the trial judge prohibited the media from reporting information regarding the defendant. While the Supreme Court disagreed, it did indicate that a gag order would be permissible given "(a) the nature and extent of pretrial coverage; (b) whether other measures [i.e., changes of venue, continuances, *voir dire*, sequestration, and/or instructions to jury to ignore press coverage] would be likely to mitigate the effects of unrestrained pretrial publicity; and (c) how effectively a restraining order would operate to prevent the threatened danger" (p. 562).

■ *Rideau v. Louisiana,* 373 U.S. 723 (1963)

■ *Nebraska Press Ass'n v. Stuart,* 427 U.S. 539 (1976)

DECISION
MAKING
EXERCISE 14.2

Gag Orders on the Media

Following are the facts from an actual case:

> After they had published articles identifying by name a 14-year-old youth who had been arrested for allegedly killing another youth, two newspapers which had learned the juvenile's identity through the use of routine reporting techniques—the monitoring of the police band radio frequency and the questioning of witnesses, the police, and an assistant prosecuting attorney at the scene of the killing—were indicted by a state grand jury in West Virginia for having violated a West Virginia law making it a crime for a newspaper to publish, without the written approval of a juvenile court, the name of any youth charged as a juvenile offender . . .. [T]he newspapers alleged that their indictment had been based on a statute violative of the First and Fourteenth Amendments to the United States Constitution. (1979 U.S. LEXIS 139 [1979])

The statute was not a gag order per se, but it acted as such. Does the statute violate the First Amendment?

Finally, the courts have experimented with gag orders on trial participants. This is an indirect method of reducing media coverage of a trial because it seeks to quiet the media's sources. This practice appears to have met with greater approval by the Supreme Court. In *Sheppard v. Maxwell*, for instance, the Court suggested that under certain circumstances, the judge has a constitutional obligation "to control the release of leads, information, and gossip to the press by police officers, witnesses and the counsel for both sides" (p. 333). For a gag order of this nature to succeed, it should be clear that the absence of a gag order presents a "clear and present danger" to the impartiality of the trial.

It is worth mentioning that with regard to attorneys, professional codes of ethics restrict them from making certain statements. For example, the *Annotated Model Rules of Professional Conduct* of the American Bar Association (ABA) prohibit lawyers from making "extrajudicial statements" that "will have a substantial likelihood of materially prejudicing an adjudicative proceeding." This includes statements as to "the character, credibility, reputation or criminal record of a party, suspect, . . . or witness, . . . the expected testimony of a party or witness, . . . [or the] . . . possibility of a plea of guilty, . . . the performance or results of any examination or test, [and] . . . any opinion as to . . . guilt or innocence."[2] The Supreme Court later held that state bars can reprimand attorneys for making statements that cause "a substantial likelihood of material prejudice" to the case, apparently expanding on the ABA's *Annotated Model Rules of Professional Conduct* (see *Gentile v. Nevada State Bar*, 501 U.S. 1030 [1991]).

THE RIGHT TO CONFRONTATION

The Sixth Amendment's provision that an accused person enjoys the right to be "confronted with the witnesses against him" is manifested in three ways. The first method of **confrontation** is to allow the defendant to appear at his or her own trial. In fact, in *Illinois v. Allen* (397 U.S. 337 [1970]), the Supreme Court expressly stated that "[o]ne of the most basic of rights guaranteed by the Confrontation Clause is the accused's right to be present in the courtroom at every state of his trial" (p. 338). The other two methods of confrontation extended to the defendant are to require the live testimony of witnesses before the defendant and to permit him or her to challenge

■ *Illinois v. Allen,*
397 U.S. 337 (1970)

[2]American Bar Association, *Annotated Model Rules of Professional Conduct* (Washington, DC: Center for Professional Responsibility, 2002), Rule 3.6.[a][b].

witnesses' statements in open court. Each of these methods of confrontation is considered in a following section.

◼ The Defendant's Right to Be Present

The Supreme Court's opinion in *Illinois v. Allen* seems eminently sensible. Certainly, the defendant would be seriously hampered in his or her ability to confront adverse witnesses if he or she was not allowed to attend the trial. But allowing the defendant to be physically present in the courtroom may not be enough to satisfy the Sixth Amendment's confrontation clause. In particular, if the accused is not competent and is unable to understand what is taking place so as to be able to challenge the opposition, the Sixth Amendment may be violated. Given this, some Supreme Court cases have dealt with physical confrontation, and some have dealt with defendants' mental competence as it pertains to confrontation. Before considering these types of cases, however, refer to Figure 14.1, which presents Rule 43 of the *Federal Rules of Criminal Procedure*. It succinctly summarizes the discussion that follows.

Physical Presence

Even though the Supreme Court's opinion in *Illinois v. Allen* suggests that the accused enjoys an unqualified right to **physical presence**, nothing could be further from the truth. In the cases decided after *Allen*, the Court placed significant restrictions on when the defendant is permitted to be physically present. By way of preview, the Court's decisions have indicated that the accused can only be present during critical proceedings. Also, the defendant's physical presence can be voluntarily waived or forfeited by failing to appear or by acting improperly.

First, even though *Allen* spoke of the right to be present "at every stage of [the] trial," the Court changed course in *United States v. Gagnon* (470 U.S. 522 [1985]) and *Kentucky v. Stincer* (479 U.S. 1028 [1987]). In the former case, the defendant was denied physical presence at a meeting between a judge and juror, while in the latter, the defendant was not allowed to attend a pretrial determination of a child witness's competence. The

The right to confrontation provides that an accused person can appear at his or her own trial, face the live testimony of witnesses, and challenge witness testimony.

FIGURE 14.1   Policy on Presence of the Defendant

Rule 43. Presence of the Defendant

(a) *Presence Required.* The defendant shall be present at the arraignment, at the time of the plea, at every stage of the trial including the impaneling of the jury and the return of the verdict, and at the imposition of sentence, except as otherwise provided by this rule.

(b) *Continued Presence Not Required.* The further progress of the trial to and including the return of the verdict, and the imposition of sentence, will not be prevented and the defendant will be considered to have waived the right to be present whenever a defendant, initially present at trial, or having pleaded guilty or nolo contendere,

    (1) is voluntarily absent after the trial has commenced (whether or not the defendant has been informed by the court of the obligation to remain during the trial),

    (2) in a noncapital case, is voluntarily absent at the imposition of sentence, or

    (3) after being warned by the court that disruptive conduct will cause the removal of the defendant from the courtroom, persists in conduct which is such as to justify exclusion from the courtroom.

(c) *Presence Not Required.* A defendant need not be present:

    (1) when represented by counsel and the defendant is an organization, as defined in *18 U.S.C. Sec. 18;*

    (2) when the offense is punishable by fine or by imprisonment for not more than one year or both, and the court, with the written consent of the defendant, permits arraignment, plea, trial, and imposition of sentence in the defendant's absence;

    (3) when the proceeding involves only a conference or hearing upon a question of law; or

    (4) when the proceeding involves a reduction or correction of sentence under *Rule 35*(b) or (c) or *18 U.S.C. sec. 3582(c).*

Source: Federal Rules of Criminal Procedure, Rule 43, issued by the 107th Congress, First Session, December 1, 2001. Available online:<www.house.gov/judiciary/crim2001.pdf>.

Court sanctioned the trial courts' actions in both cases. Generally, however, whether the defendant can be denied the right to be physically present at certain supposedly noncritical stages of the trial process depends on the nature of the communication in question and the hearing at issue.

Second, the defendant may not be physically present through waiver. That is, the defendant can waive his or her Sixth Amendment right to confrontation. Only the defendant can make this determination. In *Taylor v. Illinois* (484 U.S. 400 [1988]), the Court held that the defense attorney cannot waive the defendant's right to be physically present without his or her consent. The defendant can waive his or her right to be present through an express request (*Diaz v. United States*, 223 U.S. 442 [1912]) or by implying waiver. As an example of an implied waiver, in *Taylor v. United States* (414 U.S. 17 [1973]), the Court decided that the defendant's refusal to return to the courtroom after a lunch recess, even though it was not an intentional waiver, could have amounted to a violation of his Sixth Amendment right:

■ *Taylor v. Illinois,*
484 U.S. 400 (1988)

> It is wholly incredible to suggest that [Taylor, the defendant,] . . . entertained any doubts about his right to be present at every stage of the trial. It seems equally incredible to us, as it did to the Court of appeals, "that a defendant who flees from a courtroom in the midst of a trial—where judge, jury, witnesses and lawyers are present and ready to continue—would not know that as a consequence the trial could continue in his absence." (p. 20)

Indigence and the Right to be Present

Adam Fish was a soldier in the U.S. Army and stationed in Arizona. He was arrested and charged with the sale of marijuana, in violation of state law. Prior to his trial on this charge, Fish was discharged from the army and voluntarily left Arizona for New York. When the trial date was set, Fish's court-appointed attorney requested that he return to Arizona. However, because Fish lacked the funds necessary to travel from New York to Arizona, he did not appear in Arizona on the date set for trial. The trial proceeded without Fish's presence, and the jury returned a guilty verdict. After the verdict was rendered, Fish obtained the necessary travel funds and returned to Arizona in time for his sentencing. He was sentenced to not less than five or more than five-and-one-half years in prison. He is now appealing his conviction, claiming that his Sixth Amendment right to confrontation was violated. What should the court decide?

Finally, the defendant may not be permitted to be physically present at his or her own trial for reasons related to conduct. In *Illinois v. Allen*, for instance, the defendant was removed from his trial following repeated warnings by the judge to cease his disruptive behavior. The Supreme Court sanctioned the trial court judge's decision, holding that the right to be physically present can be waived if, after several warnings, the defendant acts "in a manner so disorderly, disruptive, and disrespectful of the court that his trial cannot be carried on with him in the courtroom" (p. 343). The Court also noted, however, that the defendant can reappear in the courtroom when he is "willing to conduct himself consistently with the decorum and respect inherent in the concept of courts and judicial proceedings" (p. 343).

Mental Competence

The Supreme Court has also held that the defendant must demonstrate **mental competence**. In other words, the conviction of an incompetent person is unconstitutional (*Pate v. Robinson*, 383 U.S. 375 [1966]). Specifically, due process—and by implication, the right to confrontation—is violated when the defendant cannot understand what is happening to him or her in a criminal trial.

The question of whether a defendant is mentally competent to stand trial was answered by a test announced by the Supreme Court in *Dusky v. United States* (362 U.S. 402 [1960]). The test assesses whether the defendant "has sufficient present ability to consult with his lawyer with a reasonable degree of rational understanding—and whether he has a rational as well as factual understanding of the proceedings against him" (p. 402). The burden of proving *incompetence* falls on the defendant (*Medina v. California*, 505 U.S. 437 [1992]).

It is important to understand that this test for competency is different from the insanity defense often discussed in criminal law texts. *Competency to stand trial*—the type of competency considered here—deals with the defendant's ability to understand what is happening at trial (as well as at pretrial hearings, etc.). The *insanity defense* deals with the defendant's competence at the time he or she committed the crime. The competency to stand trial issue is narrowly concerned with the defendant's ability to understand what is happening and communicate with counsel.

The defendant's competency is usually considered in a separate pretrial hearing. This was the rule announced in *Pate v. Robinson* (383 U.S. 375 [1966]), a case dealing with an Illinois trial judge's decision not to hold a hearing on the question of the defendant's mental condition, even though he had a long history of mental problems. The Supreme Court held that a hearing was necessary, noting that "[the Illinois court's] reasoning offers no justification for ignoring the uncontradicted testimony of Robinson's [the

Dusky v. United States,
362 U.S. 402 (1960)

defendant's] history of pronounced irrational behavior. While Robinson's demeanor at trial might be relevant to the ultimate decision as to his [present] sanity, it cannot be relied upon to dispense with a hearing on that very issue" (p. 385).

What happens to the defendant if he or she is declared incompetent to stand trial? Usually, the defendant will be hospitalized until his or her competency is restored, if it ever is. However, in *Jackson v. Indiana* (406 U.S. 715 [1972]), the Supreme Court held that there are constitutional limitations on how long a defendant can be hospitalized for the purpose of restoring competency. That case dealt with a 27-year-old deaf-mute individual with the mental level of a preschooler, who was being hospitalized until the staff determined him sane. The Court concluded that it was likely the defendant's condition would *never* improve. Thus, the Court said:

> We hold . . . that a person charged by a State with a criminal offense who is committed [to an institution] solely on account of his incapacity to proceed to trial cannot be held more than the reasonable period of time necessary to determine whether there is a substantial probability that he will attain that capacity in the foreseeable future. If it is determined that this is not the case, then the State must either institute the customary civil commitment proceeding that would be required to commit indefinitely any other citizen, or release the defendant. (p. 738)

Drawbacks of Being Present

Guaranteeing the defendant the right to be present at trial could be prejudicial—that is, it could be harmful. First, if the defendant is present but refuses to take the stand and testify (exercising a right guaranteed by the Fifth Amendment), the jury may conclude that he or she has something to hide. The Supreme Court has been so concerned with this possibility that it has prohibited the prosecution from calling attention to the defendant's refusal to testify (*Griffin v. California*, 380 U.S. 609 [1965]) and even required judges to advise jury members that no adverse inferences can be drawn from a defendant's refusal to testify (*Carter v. Kentucky*, 450 U.S. 288 [1981]).

The defendant's presence may also be prejudicial because by virtue of being in the courtroom, the defendant may remind jurors about the crime. It is often thought, in fact, that a defendant who is dressed in prison attire is not viewed the same, in the eyes of a jury, as someone dressed in a suit. An illustrative case concerning this matter is *Estelle v. Williams* (425 U.S. 501 [1976]). There, the Supreme Court held that a state may not compel the defendant to wear jail attire in the courtroom. The Court concluded that a "constant reminder of the accused's condition implicit in such distinctive, identifiable attire may affect a juror's judgment" (p. 504). Another recent case addressing possible negative consequences for the defense by the defendant's physical presence is *Portuondo v. Agard* (529 U.S. 61 [2000]).

■ The Defendant's Right to Live Testimony

As mentioned earlier, the Sixth Amendment's mention of confrontation includes, according to the Supreme Court, the defendant's right to **live testimony**. That is, he or she enjoys the right to have witnesses physically appear in the courtroom to give their testimony. Even so, this right may be qualified for certain reasons. In fact, over 100 years ago, the Supreme Court stated in *Mattox v. United States* (156 U.S. 237 [1895]) that the defendant's right to live testimony is "subject to exceptions, recognized long before the adoption of the Constitution" (p. 243). The Court stated further:

■ *Mattox v. United States*, 156 U.S. 237 (1895)

> Such exceptions were obviously intended to be respected. A technical adherence to the letter of a constitutional provision may occasionally be carried farther than is necessary to the

just protection of the accused, and farther than the safety of the public will warrant. For instance, there could be nothing more directly contrary to the letter of the provision in question than the admission of dying declarations. They are rarely made in the presence of the accused; they are made without any opportunity for examination or cross-examination; nor is the witness brought face to face with the jury; yet from time immemorial they have been treated as competent testimony, and no one would have the hardihood at this day to question their admissibility. They are admitted not in conformity with any general rule regarding the admission of testimony, but as an exception to such rules, simply from the necessities of the case, and to prevent a manifest failure of justice. (pp. 243–244)

The Supreme Court has considered several situations in which witness testimony can be admitted at trial without the physical appearance of the witness. First, if the witness, also known as the *declarant*, is unavailable because he or she is dead (as described in the previous paragraph), then an exception to the defendant's right to live testimony will be made. Similar exceptions are made when a witness is unavailable for other reasons, such as being in the hospital. Also, a witness may not be required to give live testimony if his or her statements fall under one of the established hearsay exceptions, permitting introduction of those statements by a third party. Each of these exceptions to the defendant's right to live testimony is considered in a following section.

Deceased Witnesses

In *Mattox*, already mentioned, the Supreme Court upheld the admissibility of a witness's past testimony from the defendant's first trial in the defendant's second trial because the witness died between the two trials. According to the Court, "To say that a criminal, after having once been convicted by the testimony of a certain witness, should go scot free simply because death has closed the mouth of that witness, would be carrying his constitutional protection to an unwarrantable extent" (p. 243). The Court also stated, in relevant part:

> The primary object of the [confrontation clause of the Sixth Amendment] was to prevent depositions or ex parte affidavits, such as were sometimes admitted in civil cases, being used against the prisoner in lieu of a personal examination and cross-examination of the witness in which the accused has an opportunity, not only of testing the recollection and sifting the conscience of the witness, but of compelling him to stand and face the jury in order that they may look at him, and judge by his demeanor upon the stand and the manner in which he gives his testimony whether he is worthy of belief. (p. 259)

Unavailable Witnesses

The Supreme Court has held that an **unavailable witness**, for purposes of the confrontation clause, is one who permanently moves to another country (e.g., *Mancusi v. Stubbs*, 408 U.S. 204 [1972]), cannot be located after a careful search by the prosecution (e.g., *Ohio v. Roberts*, 448 U.S. 56 [1980]), or suffers from a lapse in memory (e.g., *California v. Green*, 399 U.S. 149 [1970]).

DECISION
MAKING
EXERCISE 14.4

An Unavailable Witness

In the space of six months, the prosecution sent five subpoenas to a person it wished to testify at four separate trials. All five subpoenas were sent to the witness's residence, but the witness never appeared at trial. Can the witness be considered unavailable for confrontation purposes?

In *Motes v. United States* (178 U.S. 458 [1900]), the Court stated that it would violate the Sixth Amendment "to permit the deposition or statement of an absent witness . . . to be read at the final trial when it does not appear that the witness was absent by the suggestion, connivance, or procurement of the accused, but does appear that this absence was due to the negligence of the prosecution" (p. 474). In other words, if the prosecution fails to conduct a careful search for a certain witness and then claims that the witness is unavailable, then the defendant's right to live testimony will be violated.

■ *Motes v. United States*, 178 U.S. 458 (1900)

In another case, *Barber v. Page* (390 U.S. 719 [1968]), the Court considered whether statements by a witness who was not physically present at a preliminary hearing conformed to constitutional requirements, even though the witness was later found to be available and could have given testimony at the hearing. The Court stated that "a witness is not 'unavailable' for purposes of the exception to the confrontation requirement unless the prosecutorial authorities have made a good-faith effort to obtain his presence at trial" (pp. 724–725).

The state of Washington recognized a privilege that barred one spouse from testifying against the other without the other's consent. As a result, a wife did not testify in court at her husband's domestic violence trial. Instead, a tape-recorded statement to the effect that she was stabbed by her husband was admitted in court. In *Crawford v. Washington* (541 U.S. 36 [2004]), the Supreme Court declared that the victim could not be considered unavailable. Consequently, it held that the accused's Sixth Amendment right to confrontation was violated. Some have argued that this case may deal a blow to the prosecution of domestic violence cases because it requires that victims must testify in person.

Statements under Hearsay Exceptions

The death or unavailability of a witness is considered an exception to the defendant's right to live testimony. In either situation, the witness's statements are introduced by a third party. This is known as *hearsay*. Hearsay is testimony about what a declarant who is not in court has previously said. It is often introduced by someone who *hears* and then *says* (hence, the term *hearsay*) what the declarant said.

Hearsay is generally not admissible in a criminal trial. It is regarded skeptically because if the declarant is not available to be confronted by the defense, then there is no opportunity to question the truthfulness of his or her statements. The possibility also exists that the person communicating the declarant's statements may have misunderstood his or her intentions or forgotten exactly what he or she said.

Even so, there are several **hearsay exceptions**, which permit out-of-court statements made by declarants to be admitted at trial. On the surface, these exceptions seem to violate the defendant's right to live testimony. But the Supreme Court, nevertheless, permits hearsay in limited circumstances. The reader is encouraged to consult an evidence textbook for a full review of specific exceptions to the hearsay rule. The following cases consider only two such exceptions.

One pertinent case is *White v. Illinois* (502 U.S. 346 [1992]), which dealt with the admissibility of out-of-court statements made by a 4-year-old girl. The prosecution argued that the statements should be admissible because of the "spontaneous declaration" and "seeking medical treatment" exceptions to the hearsay rule. The former admits statements made in the "heat of the moment," while the latter admits statements made while an individual is seeking medical treatment from a doctor. The Court held that the confrontation clause was not violated in this instance:

■ *White v. Illinois*, 502 U.S. 346 (1992)

> A statement that has been offered in a moment of excitement—without the opportunity to reflect on the consequences of one's exclamation—may justifiably carry more weight with a trier of fact than a similar statement made in the course of procuring medical services, where the declarant knows that a false statement may cause misdiagnosis or mistreatment, carries special guarantees of credibility that a trier of fact may not think replicated by courtroom testimony. (p. 356)

In another case, *United States v. Inadi* (475 U.S. 387 [1986]), the Court decided on the admissibility of out-of-court statements from a co-conspirator. The Court admitted the statements, claiming that they "derive much of their value from the fact that they are made in a context very different from trial, and therefore are usually irreplaceable as substantive evidence" (p. 406). Stated differently, the Court thought that the out-of-court statements made by one co-conspirator to another should be admitted at trial because it would be difficult to replicate the conversation in a courtroom.

As indicated in Figure 14.2, numerous other hearsay exceptions exist, as well. Indeed, even if a relevant exception does not exist, a court may still admit the hearsay. Generally, if other *indicia of reliability* exist such that the accuracy and truthfulness of a hearsay statement can be judged, then it may be admissible (see *Idaho v. Wright*, 497 U.S. 805 [1990]). These indicia must, according to the Court, be "particularized guarantees of trustworthiness" (p. 816).

DECISION
MAKING
EXERCISE **14.5**

A Hearsay Exception?

Following are the actual facts from another Supreme Court case:

> Wright was charged under Idaho law with two counts of lewd conduct with a minor—specifically, her 5½- and 2½-year-old daughters. At the trial, it was agreed that the younger daughter was not "capable of communicating to the jury." However, the court admitted, under Idaho's residual hearsay exception, certain statements she had made to a pediatrician having extensive experience in child abuse cases. The doctor testified that the child had reluctantly answered questions about her own abuse but had spontaneously volunteered information about her sister's abuse. Wright was convicted on both counts but appealed only the conviction involving the younger child. The state supreme court reversed, finding that the admission of the doctor's testimony under the residual hearsay exception violated Wright's rights under the confrontation clause. The court noted that the child's statements did not fall within the traditional hearsay exception and lacked "particularized guarantees of trustworthiness" because the doctor had conducted the interview without procedural safeguards: He failed to videotape the interview, asked leading questions, and had a preconceived idea of what the child should be disclosing. (*Idaho v. Wright*, 497 U.S. 805 [1990])

How should the Supreme Court decide?

■ The Defendant's Right to Challenge Witness Testimony

Part of the defendant's right to confrontation is the ability to challenge witnesses in the courtroom. This ability is manifested when each witness physically appears in court before the defendant. This type of confrontation permits questioning by the defense and is intended to submit the witness's account to relevant scrutiny. Interestingly, though, the Supreme Court has identified at least one situation in which the defendant's right to challenge witness testimony is not compromised by the witness's absence.

Also, the Court has held that the defendant can be limited in terms of the nature of the confrontation, which is usually accomplished through questioning—specifically, *cross-examination*. Each of these limitations is discussed in a following subsection. First, the order of questioning in a typical criminal trial is considered. Then, the focus moves to when face-to-face contact is required and what Supreme Court case law addresses the defendant's right to cross-examine witnesses.

FIGURE 14.2   Common Hearsay Exceptions

■ *Present-sense impressions:* For example, Lisa sues Nicole for negligence following an automobile accident, alleging that Nicole ran a stop sign. Witness Brian testifies for Lisa that he was standing next to Jay just before the collision and heard Jay say, "Wow! That car blew through the stop sign!" Jay's statement is hearsay, but it is admissible because it was a present-sense impression, or a description of the event that sparked the lawsuit.

■ *Excited utterances:* Assume that Steve was severely injured by a hit-and-run driver. While he was being treated in the hospital emergency room, he saw Mary walk in. He started to shake and then shouted, "That's the woman who ran me down and nearly killed me!" Assume further that the nurse who was treating Steve later testifies at trial as to Steve's emergency room statement. Steve's statement is admissible (through the nurse) as an excited utterance because it relates to a startling event and was made while the declarant, Steve, was under stress and excitement.

■ *Then-existing mental, emotional, or physical condition:* Suppose that Sally testifies that she heard Lewis say "John looks really tired" just before John fell asleep at the wheel of his 18-wheeler and jumped the median, killing a motorist traveling in the opposite direction. Sally's testimony is admissible because it is in reference to John's state of mind at the time of the crash (i.e., he was tired). The same applies to statements concerning physical condition. Had Lewis said, "Look, John is wearing a cast. I don't know how he thinks he can drive," the statement would also be admissible. In short, this exception covers statements about what a person was feeling at the time he or she spoke.

■ *Statements for medical diagnosis/treatment:* A statement made for the purpose of medical diagnosis of the declarant or some other person is admissible, regardless of whether the declarant is available as a witness.

■ *Past recollection recorded:* Assume, for example, that a woman witnessed a mugging at a bus stop. At the time of the crime, she jotted some notes down to herself concerning the description of the perpetrator. She later testifies at trial that she cannot remember what the perpetrator looks like but that she has written notes describing the defendant. Her written statements are admissible.

■ *Business records:* Statements recorded, whether in writing or by audio, as a matter of routine in the records of a regularly conducted business (or business-like) activity are admissible, without regard to the availability of the declarant.

■ *Official (public) records:* A writing, statement, report, data compilation, or other record by a government agency (known as either *official* or *public*) is admissible if it records (1) acts of the agency; (2) matters the agency is required to observe and report; and/or (3) factual findings of an investigation.

■ *Vital statistics:* Public records of vital statistics—including births, deaths, and marriages—are the subject of two separate hearsay exceptions in the *Federal Rules of Evidence.** These documents are usually made by people with an obligation to report and with no motive to lie.

■ *Former testimony:* When a person is unavailable as a witness, his or her previous testimony can be admitted into evidence in the present trial, subject to the following restrictions: (1) it was made under oath and subject to direct or cross-examination, and (2) it was given in a prior trial, deposition, or similar judicial hearing.

■ *Dying declarations:* Under common law, the dying declaration of a homicide victim was admissible against the murderer in a criminal prosecution. The rationale for the present-day version of this exception is reliability: There is no motive to lie right before one is about to die.

■ *Declarations against interest:* For example, assume a man is on trial for selling drugs to high school students. When a witness testifies at trial that she has seen the man sell drugs in the cafeteria, he cries out in the courtroom, "You liar! It was in the gym!" Assume further that the gym teacher is fired for failing to intervene. If the gym teacher sues to challenge the firing, then the drug dealer's statement will be admissible in the civil trial. The rationale for permitting this is reliability: A reasonable person would not make such a statement unless he or she believed it was true.

■ *Statements of family history:* Assume that Susan claims that her late father, Don, was the son of Claude. Margie testifies that she was once told by Don that he was Claude's son. Don's statement, though hearsay, is admissible for the truth of its assertion. The rationale for this exception is reliability: One is unlikely to be mistaken about his or her own history or about that of persons or families with whom he or she is associated.

■ *Forfeiture by wrongdoing:* Assume, for example, that Jean knew about certain crimes committed by Larry, who had been charged with multiple counts of burglary. She also told her friend Cody all the details of Larry's criminal activities. Jean was planning to testify against Larry at his criminal trial, but he promptly had her killed when he learned of her intent. Unfortunately for Larry, Cody can testify about everything that Jean told him. Jean's statements are admissible not only because she is unavailable but because her death was the result of Larry's wrongdoing.

Federal Rules of Evidence, Rules 803(9) and 803(12), issued by the 107th Congress, First Session, December 1, 2001. Available online: <www.house.gov/judiciary/evid2001.pdf>.

Order and Scope of Questions

Witness testimony proceeds in several stages. That testimony is examined at each stage by a particular party to the case: the state or the defendant in a criminal case and the plaintiff or the defendant in a civil case. And each examination is subject to limitations in terms of scope. In other words, the stages must occur sequentially, and only certain types of questions are permissible.

The four stages of witness examination, as introduced in Chapter 9, are (1) direct; (2) cross; (3) redirect; and (4) recross. Every witness called to the stand in either a criminal or civil case is questioned four separate times. However, because the focus here is on constitutional rights at trial, after the four types of questioning have been introduced, the focus will be mainly on the defendant's rights during cross- and recross-examination.

Direct Examination. The first examination of a witness is called **direct examination**, and it is usually conducted by the party calling the witness. The scope of direct examination is broad. In general, questions are permitted about any consequential facts that may prove or disprove a certain point.

Cross-Examination. The next step in examining a witness is **cross-examination**. It is conducted by a party other than the one who called the witness. For example, the state may call a witness in a criminal trial. Once the state's direct examination has concluded, the defense will have an opportunity to cross-examine the state's witness.

Whereas the scope of questioning in a direct examination is broad, the scope of questioning on cross is restricted. In particular, cross-examination is limited to matters covered on direct examination. Inquiries into the credibility of the witness are also permissible. Together, these two restrictions constitute the *scope of direct rule*. This helps ensure that the opposing party (i.e., the party conducting the cross-examination) cannot use cross-examination of the witness to direct the jury's attention to other issues not raised by the party calling the witness. For example, assume that in a robbery trial, a defense witness testifies about the defendant's whereabouts on the day of the robbery. Assume further that on cross-examination, the prosecutor asks that witness whether the defendant expressed the desire to rob a bank on the day *before* the robbery. The prosecutor's question will not be permissible on cross-examination because it is beyond the scope of the original defense questioning (assuming, of course, that the defense did not ask its witness about the defendant's feelings the day before the robbery).

Redirect Examination. The party calling the witness conducts the **redirect examination** and does so *after* the cross-examination. Thus, the scope of questioning on redirect is limited to the scope of questioning on cross-examination. Again, new issues cannot be raised.

Consider another example: Suppose that on cross-examination, a burglary victim is asked about what persons have permission to enter his residence while he is away. Assume further that on redirect, the prosecutor asks the burglary victim about an incident that occurred several days prior to the burglary, in which he saw the defendant "casing" the neighborhood. The prosecutor's question is not permissible because it is beyond the scope of the cross-examination (assuming, again, that the prior incident did not come to light during the defense's cross-examination).

Recross-Examination. The last stage in witness questioning is known as **recross-examination**. This includes any subsequent examination of a witness by a party who has previously cross-examined him or her. Recross-examination is also limited in scope to the subject matter of the examination that preceded it. That is, the party engaged in recross-examination cannot probe issues not raised during redirect examination.

Assume that an eyewitness to an accident is testifying for the plaintiff and is asked on cross-examination if she was wearing her prescription glasses at the time of the accident. If, during redirect examination, it is determined that the witness could see fine *without* her glasses, then the defense cannot question her on recross-examination about her relation to the plaintiff.

Taken together, the four stages of witness examination follow a pattern of *progressive narrowing.* That is, each subsequent examination has an increasingly narrow focus, such that there is less and less to ask the witness. In other words, the four stages of examination should clarify, rather than confuse, the witness's testimony.

Face-to-Face Contact

In *Coy v. Iowa* (487 U.S. 1012 [1988]), the Supreme Court considered the constitutionality of a state law that permitted the placement of a large opaque screen between the defendant and two young girls who testified that he had sexually assaulted them. The Court declared that the statute was unconstitutional because "the Confrontation Clause guarantees the defendant a face-to-face meeting with witnesses appearing before the trier of fact" (p. 1016).

In another case, *Maryland v. Craig* (497 U.S. 836 [1990]), the Court considered whether a statute permitting a witness's testimony via closed-circuit television was constitutional. The statute provided for such a procedure in cases in which the judge determined that face-to-face testimony would "result in the child suffering serious emotional distress such that the child cannot reasonably communicate" (p. 836). The Court upheld the procedure, claiming that it did not violate the confrontation clause. It stated that a central concern of the confrontation clause "is to ensure the reliability of the evidence against a criminal defendant by subjecting it to rigorous testing in the context of an adversary proceeding before the trier of fact" (p. 845). Further, it held that the statute in question did "not impinge upon the truth-seeking or symbolic purposes of the Confrontation Clause" (p. 852).

Coy v. Iowa, 487 U.S. 1012 (1988)

Cross-Examining and Obtaining Evidence

The Supreme Court has considered, more than once, the constitutionality of state- and court-imposed restrictions on the defendant's right to cross-examine (and by extension, to engage in recross-examination). For instance, in *Smith v. Illinois* (390 U.S. 129 [1968]), the Court considered whether the prosecution can conceal the identity of a witness who is a police informant. The Court held that the witness's identity must be revealed because such information "opens countless avenues of in-court examination and out-of-court investigation" (p. 131).

In another case, *Davis v. Alaska* (415 U.S. 308 [1974]), the Court considered whether the identity of a juvenile who testifies at a criminal trial can be disguised. There, the state's lead witness in the defendant's burglary trial was a juvenile. The Court held that the juvenile's identity should have been revealed and that "the right of confrontation is paramount to the State's policy of protecting a juvenile offender" (p. 319).

In still another case, *Chambers v. Mississippi* (410 U.S. 284 [1973]), the Court considered the constitutionality of a state statute that barred *any* cross-examination by the defense. In that case, the defendant sought to cross-examine a witness who, on three previous occasions, had confessed to the murder with which the defendant was charged. The state did not call the witness, so the defense was forced to. However, the judge prohibited cross-examination based on the *voucher rule*, which provides that the party calling the witness vouches for (i.e., attests to) his or her credibility. According to

Chambers v. Mississippi, 410 U.S. 284 (1973)

this rule, cross-examination would be pointless because that is not typically the job of the party calling the witness. But since this case placed something of a unique twist on the voucher rule, the Supreme Court unanimously reversed the defendant's conviction. According to the Court, "The availability of the right to confront and cross-examine those who give damaging testimony against the accused has never been held to depend on whether the witness was initially put on the stand by the accused or by the state" (pp. 297–298).

Finally, the Court has also considered whether the confrontation clause is violated when the prosecution withholds from the defense documentation of a witness's out-of-court statements. In *United States v. Bagley* (473 U.S. 667 [1985]), the Court held that the prosecution is not obligated to provide the defense with such information, unless it is exculpatory, in which case the due process clause requires disclosure. According to the Court, "[F]ailure [on the part of the prosecution] to assist the defense by disclosing information that might have been helpful in conducting . . . cross-examination . . . amounts to a constitutional violation . . . only if the evidence is material in the sense that its suppression undermines confidence in the outcome of the trial" (p. 678).

DECISION MAKING EXERCISE 14.6

The Defendant's Right to Obtain Evidence

Vance Lester was charged with sexual offenses against his 4-year-old daughter. The matter was referred to Children's Services, the state agency charged with investigating cases of suspected child abuse. During pretrial discovery, Lester served Children's Services with a subpoena, seeking access to its records related to his alleged crime as well as earlier records related to a previous investigation into another sexual offense against his daughter. Children's Services refused to supply the requested records, claiming that they were privileged under a statute that provides that the agency's records are confidential, subject to certain exceptions. One of the exceptions specified by the statute was that Children's Services may disclose reports to a "court of competent jurisdiction pursuant to a court order." At a hearing on the matter, Lester argued that he was entitled to the information because the file might contain the names of favorable witnesses and/or exculpatory evidence. Should his argument succeed?

In summary, the defense is given wide latitude in terms of its authority to cross-examine. Courts and states cannot conceal the identity of a witness testifying against the defendant, nor can they bar cross-examination simply because the defense is calling the witness it wishes to cross-examine. Finally, the defendant's right to cross-examine rarely is violated if the prosecution fails to produce documentation of witness's out-of-court statements when they are not at all exculpatory.

■ THE RIGHT TO COMPULSORY PROCESS

The compulsory process clause of the Sixth Amendment provides that the defendant can use subpoenas to obtain witnesses, documents, and other objects that are helpful to his or her defense. The right to **compulsory process** was incorporated to the states in *Washington v. Texas* (388 U.S. 14 [1967]), in which the Supreme Court stated that compulsory process protects "[t]he right to offer the testimony of witnesses, and to compel their attendance" (p. 19). Further, the Court stated:

■ *Washington v. Texas,* 388 U.S. 14 (1967)

We hold that the petitioner in this case was denied his right to have compulsory process for obtaining witnesses in his favor because the State arbitrarily denied him the right to put on the stand a witness who was physically and mentally capable of testifying to events that he had personally observed, and whose testimony would have been relevant and material to the defense. The Framers of the Constitution did not intend to commit the futile act of giving to a defendant the right to secure the attendance of witnesses whose testimony he had no right to use. The judgment of conviction must be reversed. (p. 23)

Several state and federal statutes govern compulsory process, as do the *Federal Rules of Criminal Procedure.* Relevant portions of Rule 17 of the *Federal Rules* are reprinted in Figure 14.3 (this page). And Figure 14.4 (pages 420–421) is an example of a subpoena typically used in a criminal case.

FIGURE 14.3   Policy on Subpoenas

Rule 17. Subpoenas

(a) *For Attendance of Witnesses; Form; Issuance.* A subpoena shall be issued by the clerk under the seal of the court. It shall state the name of the court and the title, if any, of the proceeding, and shall command each person to whom it is directed to attend and give testimony at the time and place specified therein. The clerk shall issue a subpoena, signed and sealed but otherwise in blank to a party requesting it, who shall fill in the blanks before it is served. A subpoena shall be issued by a United States magistrate judge in a proceeding before that magistrate judge, but it need not be under the seal of the court.

(b) *Defendants Unable to Pay.* The court shall order at any time that a subpoena be issued for service on a named witness upon an ex parte application of a defendant upon a satisfactory showing that the defendant is financially unable to pay the fees of the witness and that the presence of the witness is necessary to an adequate defense. If the court orders the subpoena to be issued the costs incurred by the process and the fees of the witness so subpoenaed shall be paid in the same manner in which similar costs and fees are paid in case of a witness subpoenaed in behalf of the government.

(c) *For Production of Documentary Evidence and of Objects.* A subpoena may also command the person to whom it is directed to produce the books, papers, documents or other objects designated therein. The court on motion made promptly may quash or modify the subpoena if compliance would be unreasonable or oppressive. The court may direct that books, papers, documents or objects designated in the subpoena be produced before the court at a time prior to the trial or prior to the time when they are to be offered in evidence and may upon their production permit the books, papers, documents or objects or portions thereof to be inspected by the parties and their attorneys.

(d) *Service.* A subpoena may be served by the marshal, by a deputy marshal or by any other person who is not a party and who is not less than 18 years of age. Service of a subpoena shall be made by delivering a copy thereof to the person named and by tendering to that person the fee for 1 day's attendance and the mileage allowed by law. Fees and mileage need not be tendered to the witness upon service of a subpoena issued in behalf of the United States or an officer or agency thereof.

(e) *Place of Service.*

(1) *In United States.* A subpoena requiring the attendance of a witness at a hearing or trial may be served at any place within the United States.

(2) *Abroad.* A subpoena directed to a witness in a foreign country shall issue under the circumstances and in the manner and be served as provided in *Title 28, U.S.C., Sec. 1783.*

(f) *For Taking Deposition; Place of Examination.*

(1) *Issuance.* An order to take a deposition authorizes the issuance by the clerk of the court for the district in which the deposition is to be taken of subpoenas for the persons named or described therein.

(2) *Place.* The witness whose deposition is to be taken may be required by subpoena to attend at any place designated by the trial court, taking into account the convenience of the witness and the parties.

(g) *Contempt.* Failure by any person without adequate excuse to obey a subpoena served upon that person may be deemed a contempt of the court from which the subpoena issued or of the court for the district in which it issued if it was issued by a United States magistrate judge. . . .

Source: Federal Rules of Criminal Procedure, Rule 17, issued by the 107th Congress, First Session, December 1, 2001. Available online:<www.house.gov/judiciary/crim2001.pdf>.

FIGURE 14.4 Subpoena in a Criminal Case

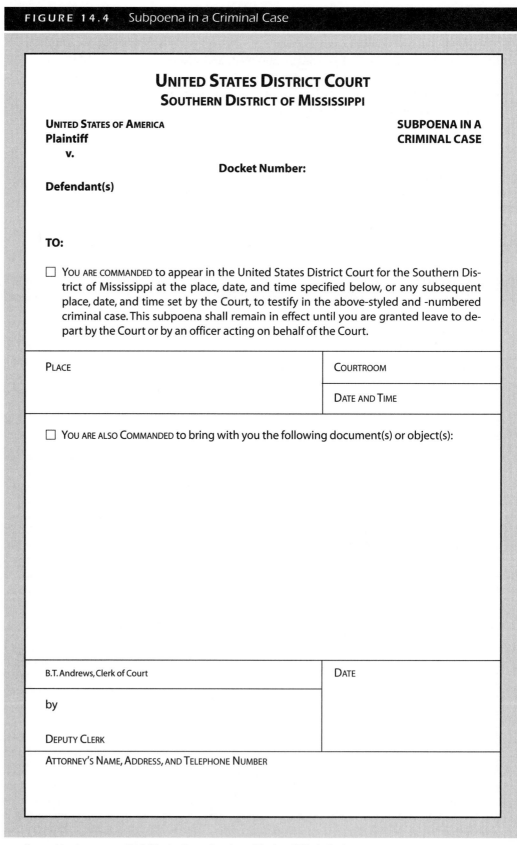

PROOF OF SERVICE

RECEIVED BY SERVER	DATE	PLACE
SERVED	DATE	PLACE
SERVED ON (PRINT NAME)		FEES AND MILEAGE TENDERED TO WITNESS ☐ YES AMOUNT:$ _____ ☐ NO
SERVED BY (PRINT NAME)		TITLE

DECLARATION OF SERVER

I declare under penalty of perjury under the laws of the United States of America that the foregoing information contained in the Proof of Service is true and correct.

Executed on _____
              DATE   SIGNATURE OF SERVER

_____
SERVER'S ADDRESS

_____

ADDITIONAL INFORMATION:

Statutes and formal rules aside, at least two Supreme Court cases have considered aspects of the defendant's right to compulsory process. In particular, questions as to constitutional rights violations have been posed in instances in which the defense has been denied the right to subpoena a witness.

For example, in *Roviaro v. United States* (353 U.S. 53 [1957]), the prosecution refused to provide the defense with the identity of a police informant. The Court recognized that the government had a significant interest in concealing the identity of the informant, mainly to further its efforts in combating the trafficking of illicit drugs. But the Court also found that the defendant's right to confrontation was denied by the prosecution's refusal to release the witness's identity. The informant was the only witness to the drug transaction for which the defendant was charged, so the defense clearly would have had a difficult time mounting an effective case without this witness.

Next, in *United States v. Valenzuela-Bernal* (458 U.S. 858 [1982]), the defendant was charged with transporting illegal narcotics. He was arrested along with three other individuals who were unlawfully in the United States. Immigration officials concluded that two of the three aliens were not needed for the prosecution, so it deported them. The defendant then argued that his right to compulsory process was violated by the deportation. Surprisingly, the Court held that the government's interest in deporting illegal aliens and minimizing overcrowding in detention facilities outweighed the defendant's interest in mounting an effective defense. The Court concluded that the defendant did not offer a valid reason why the two deported witnesses were necessary for his defense.

The Right to Present Evidence

The Sixth Amendment's compulsory process clause appears only to grant the defendant the right to subpoena and question witnesses. However, in *Washington v. Texas*, the Supreme Court modified the definition of compulsory process to include the right of the *defense* to present evidence. The Court stated that compulsory process also guarantees "the right to present the defendant's version of the facts as well as the prosecution's to the jury so that it may decide where the truth lies" (p. 19). Given this interpretation, the Court has more than once considered the constitutionality of restrictions placed on the defense's ability to present its case.

Decisions in Favor of the Defense

For example, in *Washington*, the Court decided on the constitutionality of a statute that prevented accomplices from testifying for each other. The statute was enacted out of fear that accomplices would give false testimony in order to benefit one another. The Court struck down the statute, stating that the defendant must be allowed to present the testimony of any witness who is capable of testifying.

In another case, *Chambers v. Mississippi* (410 U.S. 284 [1973]), the Court overturned the conviction of a defendant who was not allowed to put three witnesses on the stand. The defendant, Chambers, had attempted to prove that another person, MacDonald, committed the murder for which he was charged. The three people Chambers wanted to put on the stand were those to whom MacDonald had allegedly confessed. The Court felt the witnesses' testimony should have been admissible, even though it would have been considered hearsay, because MacDonald "spontaneously" confessed to each person, making it likely that these individuals' testimony would be truthful and accurate. The Court felt that "the exclusion of this critical evidence, coupled with the State's refusal to permit Chambers to cross-examine MacDonald, denied him a trial in accord with traditional and fundamental standards of due process" (p. 302).

Threatening a Witness

A man was convicted of burglary and sentenced to prison for 12 years. He appealed his conviction, claiming that the trial judge violated his Fifth Ammendment constitutional right by harassing the only defense witness. Following is what the judge said to the witness in *Webb v. Texas* (409 U.S. 95 [1972]), the actual case on which this exercise is based:

> Now you have been called down as a witness in this case by the Defendant. It is the Court's duty to admonish you that you don't have to testify, that anything you say can and will be used against you. If you take the witness stand and lie under oath, the Court will personally see that your case goes to the grand jury and you will be indicted for perjury and the likelihood is that you would get convicted of perjury and that it would be stacked onto what you have already got, so that is the matter you have got to make up your mind on. If you get on the witness stand and lie, it is probably going to mean several years and at least more time that you are going to have to serve. It will also be held against you in the penitentiary when you're up for parole and the Court wants you to thoroughly understand the chances you're taking by getting on that witness stand under oath. You may tell the truth and if you do, that is all right, but if you lie you can get into real trouble. The court wants you to know that. You don't owe anybody anything to testify and it must be done freely and voluntarily and with the thorough understanding that you know the hazard you are taking. (p. 96)

Did the judge violate the defendant's right to due process?

In *Crane v. Kentucky* (476 U.S. 683 [1986]), another related case, the defendant sought to present evidence that his confession was unreliable because it had been obtained when he was young and uneducated and had been interrogated at great length. The trial court excluded this evidence and the defendant was convicted. The Supreme Court reversed that decision, however, declaring that a state may not exclude "competent, reliable evidence bearing on the credibility of a confession when such evidence is central to the defendant's claim of innocence" because "[w]hether rooted directly in the Due Process Clause . . . or in the Compulsory Process or Confrontation Clause . . . the Constitution guarantees criminal defendants a 'meaningful opportunity' to present a complete defense" (p. 690).

■ *Crane v. Kentucky,*
476 U.S. 683 (1986)

Decisions against the Defense

On a few occasions, the Court *has* sanctioned exclusion of certain defense evidence. For example, in *United States v. Scheffer* (523 U.S. 303 [1998]), the Court upheld a trial court's decision to exclude polygraph evidence presented by the defense. The Court stated, "There is simply no consensus that polygraph evidence is reliable. To this day, the scientific community remains extremely polarized about the reliability of polygraph evidence" (p. 309). Thus, the defense's ability to present its case can be restricted if the evidence it seeks to present cannot be considered reliable (see also *United States v. Salerno*, 505 U.S. 317 [1992]).

■ *United States v. Scheffer,*
523 U.S. 303 (1998)

Another important example of Court-sanctioned restrictions on the ability of the defense to present a case is *Michigan v. Lucas* (500 U.S. 145 [1991]). There, the Court held that the defendant can be prevented from presenting evidence because of his or her attorney's misconduct. In this case, the trial judge in the defendant's rape trial excluded evidence about the victim's sexual history because the defendant failed to give notice of this to the prosecution within 10 days of the trial, in violation of discovery rules. A similar decision was reached in *Taylor v. Illinois* (484 U.S. 400 [1988]), in which the Court sanctioned a lower court's decision to deny a defense witness's testimony because of providing short notice to the prosecution, again in violation of discovery rules.

■ THE RIGHT TO DOUBLE-JEOPARDY PROTECTION

The constitutionally guaranteed protection against **double jeopardy** is designed to ensure that a person who has been convicted or acquitted of a crime is not tried or punished for the same offense twice. Double jeopardy occurs when, for the same offense, a person is (1) reprosecuted after acquittal; (2) reprosecuted after conviction; or (3) subjected to separate punishments for the same offense. Double jeopardy does not apply, however, to prosecutions brought by separate sovereigns. The federal government, each state government, and each Native American tribe is considered a separate sovereign.

Early English common law contains the foundations of the modern-day protection against double jeopardy. The rule of *autrefois acquit* prohibited the retrial of a defendant who was found not guilty. The rule of *autrefois convict*, on the other hand, prohibited the retrial of a defendant who *was* found guilty. These rules were adopted by the American colonies.

■ *Benton v. Maryland,*
395 U.S. 784 (1969)

Today, every state provides double-jeopardy protection because of the Supreme Court's decision in *Benton v. Maryland* (395 U.S. 784 [1969]), in which the Court declared that the Fifth Amendment's protection against double jeopardy is a fundamental right:

> The fundamental nature of the guarantee against double jeopardy can hardly be doubted. Its origins can be traced to Greek and Roman times, and it became established in the common law of England long before this Nation's independence. . . . As with many other elements of the common law, it was carried into the jurisprudence of this Country through the medium of Blackstone, who codified the doctrine in his Commentaries. "The plea of *autrefoits acquit*, or a former acquittal," he wrote, "is grounded on this universal maxim of the common law of England, that no man is to be brought into jeopardy of his life more than once for the same offence." . . . Today, every State incorporates some form of the prohibition in its constitution or common law. As this Court put it in *Green v. United States*, 355 U.S. 184, 187–188 (1957), "the underlying idea, one that is deeply ingrained in at least the Anglo-American system of jurisprudence, is that the State with all its resources and power should not be allowed to make repeated attempts to convict an individual for an alleged offense, thereby subjecting him to embarrassment, expense and ordeal and compelling him to live in a continuing state of anxiety and insecurity, as well as enhancing the possibility that even though innocent he may be found guilty." This underlying notion has from the very beginning been part of our constitutional tradition. Like the right to trial by jury, it is clearly "fundamental to the American scheme of justice." (pp. 795–796)

Before discussing the case law surrounding double jeopardy, it is worth mentioning the popular misconceptions that abound on this issue. Students of criminal procedure, in particular, ask about the presentation of legal issues in movies such as *Double Jeopardy*. In response to these students' many thoughtful inquiries, Figure 14.5 summarizes the movie and the legal flaws in the story.

■ When Double-Jeopardy Protection Applies

The Fifth Amendment suggests that double jeopardy occurs when a person's "life or limb" is threatened. This language has been taken to mean that double jeopardy applies in all criminal proceedings. Determining whether a proceeding is criminal, however, is

FIGURE 14.5 An Anaylsis of the Movie *Double Jeopardy*

The Plot

Libby Parsons has a young son and a successful husband. After spending a passionate night with her husband aboard their boat, she wakes up to find him missing and herself accused of killing him. She is convicted of the murder and sent to prison. While in prison, Parsons finds out that her husband is still alive. Two "jailhouse lawyers" tell her that when she gets out of prison, she can kill her husband. Further, they inform her, she cannot be convicted of his murder because she has already been convicted of that crime—hence, the movie's title. When she gets out on parole six years later, she sets out to find her husband, kill him, and get back her son. She eventually succeeds.

The Basic Legal Flaws

1. Parsons did not really kill her husband the first time. So, if she kills him for real, double jeopardy will not apply because the murder would not be the same offense. In other words, the second killing would be a separate act because the first killing never took place.

2. Parsons is initially convicted in Washington State. If she locates her husband in another state and kills him there, she will also be tried there, since the two states are separate sovereigns.

3. Even if Parsons succeeds in killing her husband pursuant to some belief that the Fifth Amendment's double-jeopardy provision will protect her, she will likely be sued in court for any number of civil violations. (The civil case filed against O. J. Simpson after his criminal acquittal illustrates this point.)

4. In the end, Parsons kills her husband in self-defense, making the title of the movie something of a misnomer.

Note: *Double Jeopardy* was released in 1999. It was directed by Bruce Beresford and distributed by Paramount Pictures.

not always easy. Courts will often look to the legislature's intent in writing the statute that is the basis for prosecution. For example, in *Kansas v. Hendricks* (521 U.S. 346 [1997]), the Supreme Court found that a statute providing for a "sexual predator" proceeding, in addition to a criminal proceeding, did not place the defendant in double jeopardy because it provided for *civil* confinement. The Court stated:

Kansas v. Hendricks, 521 U.S. 346 (1997)

> Because we have determined that the Kansas Act is civil in nature, initiation of its commitment proceedings does not constitute a second prosecution. Cf. *Jones v. United States*, 463 U.S. 354, 77 L. Ed. 2d 694, 103 S. Ct. 3043 (1984) (permitting involuntary civil commitment after verdict of not guilty by reason of insanity). Moreover, as commitment under the Act is not tantamount to "punishment," Hendricks' involuntary detention does not violate the Double Jeopardy Clause, even though that confinement may follow a prison term. Indeed, in *Baxstrom v. Herold*, 383 U.S. 107, 15 L. Ed. 2d 620, 86 S. Ct. 760 (1966), we expressly recognized that civil commitment could follow the expiration of a prison term without offending double jeopardy principles. We reasoned that "there is no conceivable basis for distinguishing the commitment of a person who is nearing the end of a penal term from all other civil commitments." *Id.*, at 111–112. If an individual otherwise meets the requirements for involuntary civil commitment, the State is under no obligation to release that individual simply because the detention would follow a period of incarceration. (pp. 369–370)

The courts will also examine the punitiveness of the sanctions involved in determining whether a proceeding is criminal. In *Helvering v. Mitchell* (303 U.S. 391 [1938]), the Supreme Court upheld the constitutionality of a tax proceeding that was used to recover back taxes from a person *after* the person was acquitted on criminal charges. The Court declared that the proceeding was designed as a remedial sanction to reimburse the government. Because it was not considered punitive, double jeopardy did not apply. In the Court's words:

> The doctrine of double jeopardy is inapplicable because the 50% addition to tax provided by § 293 (b) is not primarily punitive but is a remedial sanction imposed as a safeguard for protection of the revenue and to reimburse the Government for expense and loss resulting from the taxpayer's fraud. As such it may be enforced by a civil procedure to which the accepted rules and constitutional guaranties governing the trial of criminal prosecutions do not apply. (p. 398)

DECISION MAKING EXERCISE **14.8**

A Case of Double Jeopardy?

In *United States v. Ursery* (518 U.S. 267 [1996]), an actual Supreme Court case, the issue was asset forfeiture. Police had found marijuana and growing equipment when they searched the defendant's house. He was prosecuted criminally, but the federal government also sought civil forfeiture of his house, pursuant to a federal law. The defendant filed a Section 1983 lawsuit against the government, claiming that the proposed forfeiture of his house would amount to double jeopardy, a violation of the Fifth Amendment. Does civil asset forfeiture in addition to criminal prosecution place a person in double jeopardy?

The *Blockburger* Rule

■ *Blockburger v. United States,* 284 U.S. 299 (1932)

A rather complicated issue in double-jeopardy jurisprudence concerns the definition of same offense. In *Blockburger v. United States* (284 U.S. 299 [1932]), the Supreme Court developed a test that states that "[w]here the same act or transaction constitutes a violation of two distinct statutory provisions, the test to be applied to determine whether there are two offenses or only one, is whether each requires proof of an additional fact which the other does not" (p. 304). This test came to be known as the *Blockburger* rule.

According to the *Blockburger* rule, an offense is considered the same offense if two separate statutes that define the offense both contain elements A, B, and C. Moreover, if one crime contains elements A, B, and C and the other has elements A and B, both are considered the same offense because neither statute requires proof of a fact that the other does not. For example, assume that the offense of first-degree murder contains elements A (premeditated), B (deliberate), and C (killing) and that the offense of second-degree murder contains elements B (deliberate) and C (killing). Both offenses are considered the same for double-jeopardy purposes because second-degree murder does not require proof of another element that first-degree murder does not. If a person is convicted of first-degree murder, then, according to this example, he or she cannot be charged with second-degree murder.

Separate offenses can be identified when, for example, one crime contains elements A, B, and C and the other contains elements A, B, and D. Both crimes require proof of an additional element that the other does not. For example, assume the offense of joyriding contains elements A (unlawful taking), B (of an automobile), and C (the intent to *temporarily* deprive the owner of possession). Assume also that the offense of car theft contains elements A (unlawful taking), B (of an automobile), and D (the intent to *permanently* deprive the owner of possession). These are considered separate offenses because each offense requires proof of an element that the other does not. Thus, a person who is found guilty of joyriding can also be charged with the crime of car theft (see *Brown v. Ohio*, 432 U.S. 161 [1977]).

■ When Double-Jeopardy Protection Does Not Apply

There are four exceptions to the *Blockburger* rule, which means that there are four situations in which double-jeopardy protection does not apply. First, double jeopardy does not apply if the second prosecution is based on conduct committed after the first prosecution. This was the decision reached in *Diaz v. United States* (223 U.S. 442 [1912]). There, the defendant was convicted of assault and battery. When the victim later died, the defendant was charged with homicide. The Court stated, "The death of the injured person was the principal element of the homicide, but was no part of the assault and battery. At the time of the trial for the latter the death had not ensued, and not until it did ensue was the homicide committed. Then, and not before, was it possible to put the accused in jeopardy for that offense" (p. 449).

Second, if the defendant is responsible for the second prosecution, double jeopardy does not apply. In *Jeffers v. United States* (432 U.S. 137 [1977]), the defendant was indicted twice for two offenses. The state sought joinder on the charges, but the defendant successfully moved to have the charges tried separately. He was convicted in both trials but claimed that the latter conviction amounted to double jeopardy, in violation of the Fifth Amendment. The Court stated:

> In this case, trial together of the conspiracy and continuing-criminal-enterprise charges could have taken place without undue prejudice to petitioner's Sixth Amendment right to a fair trial. . . . If the two charges had been tried in one proceeding, it appears that petitioner would have been entitled to a lesser-included-offense instruction. . . . If such an instruction had been denied on the ground that § 846 was not a lesser included offense of § 848, petitioner could have preserved his point by proper objection. Nevertheless, petitioner did not adopt that course. Instead, he was solely responsible for the successive prosecutions for the conspiracy offense and the continuing-criminal-enterprise offense. Under the circumstances, we hold that his action deprived him of any right that he might have had against consecutive trials. It follows, therefore, that the Government was entitled to prosecute petitioner for the § 848 offense, and the only issue remaining is that of cumulative punishments upon such prosecution and conviction. (p. 153)

Third, double jeopardy does not apply when the court hearing the first offense lacks jurisdiction to try the second offense. This exception came from the Supreme Court's decision in *Fugate v. New Mexico* (471 U.S. 1112 [1985]). There, the Court held that a defendant's conviction on drunk-driving charges in municipal court did not bar prosecution in a higher court for vehicular homicide tied to the same incident. The Court noted that the municipal court did not have jurisdiction to try a homicide case, so double-jeopardy protections did not apply.

Fourth, if the defense plea bargains over the prosecution's objection, double-jeopardy protections do not apply. In *Ohio v. Johnson* (467 U.S. 493 [1984]), the defendant succeeded in convincing the judge to dismiss certain charges against him, over the prosecution's objection. The defendant was later tried on the dismissed charges, and the Court held that double-jeopardy protections did not apply. Had the prosecution acquiesced to the dismissal, the result would have been different. Indeed, it is unlikely the defendant would have been prosecuted on the dismissed charges if the prosecution had agreed with the judge's decision.

There are still other exceptions in which reprosecution for the same offense is permissible. First, if a defendant successfully appeals a criminal conviction or otherwise succeeds in overturning a conviction, he or she may be reprosecuted. In *United States v. Tateo* (377 U.S. 463 [1964]), the Court held:

> It would be a high price indeed for society to pay were every accused granted immunity from punishment because of any defect sufficient to constitute reversible error in the proceedings leading to conviction. From the standpoint of a defendant, it is at least doubtful that appellate courts would be as zealous as they now are in protecting against the effects of improprieties at the trial or pretrial stage if they knew that reversal of a conviction would put the accused irrevocably beyond the reach of further prosecution. In reality, therefore, the practice of retrial serves defendants' rights as well as society's interest. The underlying purpose of permitting retrial is as much furthered by application of the rule to this case as it has been in cases previously decided. (p. 466)

Second, if a case is dismissed by the judge but the defendant is not acquitted, he or she may be reprosecuted. In *United States v. Scott* (437 U.S. 82 [1978]), the Court held, in part, that "where a *defendant* successfully seeks to avoid his trial prior to its conclusion by a motion for a [dismissal], the Double Jeopardy Clause is not offended by a second prosecution. Such a motion by the defendant is deemed to be a deliberate election on his part to forgo his valued right to have his guilt or innocence determined by the first trier of fact" (p. 92).

Finally, reprosecution is permissible if a *mistrial* occurs over the defendant's objections and is a "manifest necessity." That is, reprosecution is permissible following a mistrial "when the defendant's interest in proceeding to verdict is outweighed by the competing and equally legitimate demand for public justice" (*Illinois v. Somerville*, 410 U.S. 458 [1973]). Also, the defendant may be reprosecuted if the judge declares a mistrial with the defendant's consent or by the defendant's motion, provided that the prosecution does not agree to the defendant's consent or motion in bad faith (e.g., by intending to pursue a subsequent retrial for the purpose of subjecting the defendant to the harassment of multiple trials) (see, e.g., *Lee v. United States*, 432 U.S. 23 [1977]; *Oregon v. Kennedy*, 456 U.S. 667 [1982]).

DECISION MAKING EXERCISE 14.9

Reprosecution after a Mistrial

In another actual Supreme Court case, *Lee v. United States* (432 U.S. 23 [1977]), the facts were as follow:

> After the prosecutor's opening statement in petitioner's bench trial for theft in violation of the Assimilative Crimes Act and the applicable Indiana statute, petitioner's counsel moved to dismiss the information on the ground that it did not allege specific intent as required by the Indiana statute. The court tentatively denied the motion subject to further study, whereupon petitioner's counsel outlined the defense and did not object to going forward with the trial. At the close of the evidence the court, though observing that petitioner's guilt had been proved beyond any reasonable doubt, granted petitioner's motion to dismiss. Thereafter, petitioner was indicted for the same crime and convicted.

The defendant in this case claimed that the double-jeopardy clause should have barred the second trial. Is he right?

■ Double Jeopardy and Sentencing

Double-jeopardy protection also extends to sentencing increases. First, the Supreme Court has considered whether double jeopardy is violated with the use of *consecutive punishments* (i.e., back-to-back punishments)—say, when the defendant is sentenced to a total of 10 years for convictions on two counts that each carry a 5-year sentence. The Court has held that this determination depends on legislative intent (see, e.g., *Albernaz v. United States*, 450 U.S. 333 [1981]). That is, provided the consecutive punishment is not for two of the same offenses, if the criminal law permits such punishment, double jeopardy is not violated.

Questions about double jeopardy have also been raised when a defendant is resentenced following some important development in the case. Increasing the sentence for the same charge (i.e., as opposed to increasing the sentence for separate charges, as in the case of cumulative punishments) after it has been imposed is permissible (1) when a conviction is reversed by an appeal (*North Carolina v. Pierce*, 395 U.S. 711 [1969]); (2) after the prosecution has appealed a sentence, provided there is legal authorization to do so (a rare occurrence, as Chapter 15 attests) (*United States v. DiFrancesco*, 449 U.S. 117 [1980]); and (3) after discovery of a legal defect in the first sentence (e.g., *In re Bradley*, 318 U.S. 50 [1943]).

In a recent—and controversial—case (*Sattazahn v. Pennsylvania*, 537 U.S. 101 [2003]), an individual was charged with capital murder, but the jury could not unanimously conclude that the death penalty was warranted. As required by a Pennsylvania statute, the judge then sentenced the offender to life in prison. The defendant was then retried and sentenced to death. He argued that the Fifth Amendment's double-jeopardy clause was violated, but the Supreme Court disagreed. The Court argued that the deadlocked jury did not amount to a "death penalty acquittal," so it saw no constitutional problems with retrying the offender.

■ THE RIGHT TO ASSERT AN ENTRAPMENT DEFENSE

A person tried for a crime can assert any of numerous defenses to criminal liability, including self-defense, insanity, involuntary intoxication, and others. Criminal law texts cover these in detail. One defense that straddles the line between criminal law and criminal procedure is the *entrapment defense*. It is a defense, in the criminal law sense, but it is one of the only defenses that calls into question law enforcement's role in the instigation of a crime. Hence, it is almost always brought up in the realm of criminal procedure. The defendant can assert entrapment prior to trial, but for simplicity's sake, it will be discussed here. Entrapment is an affirmative defense, which means it can easily be raised at trial.

The heading of this section suggests that the defendant enjoys the *right* to assert an entrapment defense. It is important to note, however, that the Constitution does not provide this right. It is a right only in the sense that the Supreme Court has decided that an accused person can assert an entrapment defense.

The **entrapment defense** is based on the belief that someone should not be convicted of a crime that the government instigated. In its simplest form, the entrapment defense arises when government officials "plant the seeds" of criminal intent. That is, if a person commits a crime that he or she otherwise would not have committed but for the government's conduct, he or she will probably succeed with an entrapment defense.

The first Supreme Court case recognizing the entrapment defense was *Sorrells v. United States* (287 U.S. 435 [1932]). In that case, Chief Justice Hughes stated, "We are

■ *Sorrells v. United States,* 287 U.S. 435 (1932)

unable to conclude that . . . [the] . . . processes of detection or enforcement should be abused by the instigation by government officials of an act on the part of persons otherwise innocent in order to lure them to its commission and to punish them" (p. 448). This reasoning underlies the treatment of the entrapment defense in U.S. courts to this day. The Court further stated:

> The appropriate object of this permitted activity, frequently essential to the enforcement of the law, is to reveal the criminal design; to expose the illicit traffic, the prohibited publication, the fraudulent use of the mails, the illegal conspiracy, or other offenses, and thus to disclose the would-be violators of the law. A different question is presented when the criminal design originates with the officials of the Government, and they implant in the mind of an innocent person the disposition to commit the alleged offense and induce its commission in order that they may prosecute. (pp. 441–442)

Despite its apparent simplicity, the entrapment defense has been a contentious one. In particular, there has been some disagreement in the courts over the relevance of the offender's predisposition and how far the government can go in order to lure a person into criminal activity. When an entrapment decision is based on the offender's predisposition, this is known as a *subjective inquiry.* By contrast, a focus on the government conduct presumably responsible for someone's decision to commit a crime is known as an *objective inquiry.*

The American Law Institute's *Model Penal Code* takes an objective approach with regard to the entrapment defense: If the government "employ[ed] methods of persuasion or inducement which create a substantial risk that such an offense will be committed by persons other than those who are ready to commit it,"[3] then the defense is available regardless of the offender's initial willingness to offend. The Supreme Court, however, has opted to focus on the subjective predisposition of the offender instead the government's role in instigating the crime in question (e.g., *Hampton v. United States,* 425 U.S. 484 [1976]).

In *Sorrells,* which was decided in 1932, the defendant was charged with violating the National Prohibition Act.[4] After two unsuccessful attempts, a law enforcement agent convinced the defendant to sell him whiskey. Chief Justice Hughes noted that "artifice and stratagem" are permissible methods of catching criminals, so entrapment did not occur. Instead, it was the defendant's predisposition to offend that was important.

Sherman v. United States, 356 U.S. 369 (1958)

In the next leading entrapment case, *Sherman v. United States* (356 U.S. 369 [1958]), the Supreme Court reached the opposite conclusion but still adhered to the predisposition test. In that case, a government informant met the defendant at a doctor's office, where both were being treated for narcotics addiction. After repeated requests by the informant, the defendant provided him with illegal narcotics. The Supreme Court reversed the defendant's conviction, noting that entrapment was "patently clear" as a matter of law. Even so, the Court also pointed out that it is difficult to judge the conduct of an informant without knowing how predisposed the offender was to act before the crime was committed.

United States v. Russell, 411 U.S. 423 (1973)

In *United States v. Russell* (411 U.S. 423 [1973]), the Court continued to focus on the defendant's predisposition. In *Russell,* a narcotics agent posed as a narcotics manufacturer and offered the defendant a difficult to obtain ingredient used to manufacture a drug. The defendant accepted and was convicted. Justice Rehnquist, author of the

[3]American Law Institute, *Model Penal Code* 2.13(1)(b) (1985).
[4]Recall that during the Prohibition era, from 1920 to 1933, it was illegal to produce and sell alcohol in the United States.

majority opinion, observed that there was sufficient predisposition on the part of the defendant, so the entrapment defense did not apply.

In *Hampton v. United States* (425 U.S. 484 [1976]), the Supreme Court once again focused on the defendant's predisposition. In that case, the defendant was convicted of distributing heroin supplied to the defendant by a government informant. The Court stated that "[i]f the police engage in illegal activity in concert with a defendant beyond the scope of their duties the remedy lies, not in freeing the equally culpable defendant, but in prosecuting the police under the applicable provisions of state or federal law" (p. 490). In other words, it is the defendant's predisposition that matters in the context of the entrapment defense, not the government's conduct.

To suggest that the Supreme Court has ignored the role of government conduct is not entirely true. In a concurring opinion cited in *Hampton*, Justices Powell and Blackmun argued that government behavior that "shocks the conscience" could conceivably violate due process. In their words, "[T]here is certainly a limit to allowing governmental involvement in crime. . . . It would be unthinkable . . . to permit government agents to instigate robberies and beatings merely to gather evidence to convict other members of a gang of hoodlums" (p. 493, n. 4).

The Supreme Court has yet to affirmatively recognize a due process–based defense to government entrapment, but some lower courts have. Generally, if government officials use violence, supply contraband that is wholly unobtainable, or engage in a criminal enterprise, then the defendant in such a case will often succeed with the entrapment defense based on a due process argument.

■ *Hampton v. United States*, 425 U.S. 484 (1976)

DECISION MAKING EXERCISE 14.10

Outrageous Government Conduct

In an actual case, Drug Enforcement Agency (DEA) agents sought out a convicted felon, Kubica, and offered to reduce the severity of his sentence if he agreed to cooperate with them. At the request of the DEA, Kubica contacted another man, Neville, and suggested that they set up a lab to manufacture "speed." Neville agreed, and the government supplied Kubica with glassware and a difficult to obtain ingredient used in the manufacture of speed. The government also made arrangements for purchasing the chemicals and even supplied an isolated farmhouse to serve as the laboratory. The laboratory was set up at the farmhouse and operated for one week. The men produced approximately six pounds of methamphetamine hydrochloride (i.e., speed). Kubica was completely in charge of the entire laboratory. At the end of the first week of lab operations, Neville left the farmhouse with the drugs in a suitcase. Kubica notified the DEA agents, who arrested Neville driving down the road. A search of the car revealed, in addition to the suitcase containing six pounds of methamphetamine hydrochloride, a Lysol can containing cocaine and some more speed. Neville was arrested, charged, and convicted. He appealed his conviction not on entrapment grounds but by arguing that the government's outrageous conduct had violated the due process clause of the Fourteenth Amendment. What should the court decide?

CONCLUSION

This chapter concludes the focus on constitutional rights at trial. The first right is that of a public trial—one that is open to the public. This right has been expanded to cover several pretrial proceedings, such as suppression hearings. Sometimes, the right to a public trial does not apply. First,

the government may seek closure, but to do so, it must show (1) that there is an overriding interest, such as the protection of certain witnesses; (2) that the closure is no broader than absolutely necessary; and (3) that reasonable alternatives were considered. Second, the accused may seek closure of a trial but only if an open proceeding will compromise the ability of the jury to make a fair decision.

Attempts to close trials (and related proceedings) to the public often meet with resistance on First Amendment grounds. In response to this problem, the courts have recognized that there may be other ways to ensure an open trial that remains fair, despite media coverage. Some of these methods include (1) *voir dire* with special attention to pretrial publicity; (2) a change of venue; (3) jury sequestration; (4) gag orders on the media; and (5) gag orders on other parties.

The right to confrontation refers to the ability of the defendant to face his or her accusers. This right is manifested in three ways: (1) by permitting the defendant to be present at trial; (2) by requiring live testimony; and (3) by allowing the defendant to challenge the government's witnesses through cross-examination.

The defendant enjoys not only the right to be physically present but also to be mentally competent. Deciding competence hinges on whether the defendant is able to consult with his or her lawyer with a reasonable degree of understanding. Physical presence can be damaging to the defense, however, in cases in which the defendant does not testify or his or her being in court reminds jurors of the crime.

The defendant's right to live testimony requires that witnesses appear in person. Recordings and the like are generally not permissible, but there are exceptions: (1) if the witness is unavailable because he or she is dead; (2) if the witness is unavailable for other reasons, such as by being hospitalized or confined to an institution; and (3) if the statement made by a witness who will not provide live testimony falls under one of the established hearsay exceptions, permitting introduction of those statements by a third party.

Finally, the defendant's third guarantee for confrontation concerns the right to challenge witness testimony. The defendant can challenge witness testimony by engaging in cross-examination and recross-examination. Both forms of examination follow prosecutorial questioning and are intended to cast doubt on the witness's testimony. The Supreme Court has restricted as well as enhanced the defendant's right to challenge witness testimony. It has restricted the right insofar as witnesses are not always required to testify before the defendant, and it has enhanced the right because the defense is given wide latitude in terms of its authority to cross-examine. Further, courts and states cannot conceal the identity of a witness testifying against the defense, nor can they bar cross-examination simply because the defense is calling the witness it wishes to cross-examine.

Compulsory process is another right enjoyed by a criminal defendant in the United States. It means that the defendant is legally entitled to compel the production of witnesses. This can be accomplished via a subpoena, if the witness will not voluntarily come forward. Compulsory process also extends to the production of physical evidence. However, there are restrictions that stem from the rules of evidence.

The defendant further enjoys the right to double-jeopardy protection. In general, a defendant cannot, by the same sovereign, be reprosecuted after acquittal, reprosecuted after conviction, or subjected to separate punishments for the same offense. Several exceptions exist to the Fifth Amendment's double-jeopardy clause. First, double jeopardy does not apply if the second prosecution is based on conduct committed after the first prosecution. Second, double jeopardy does not apply if the defendant is responsible for the second prosecution. Third, double jeopardy does not apply when the court hearing the first offense lacks jurisdiction to try the second offense. Fourth, if the defense plea bargains over the prosecution's objection, double-jeopardy protection does not apply. Fifth, if a defendant successfully appeals a criminal conviction or otherwise succeeds in overturning a conviction, he or she may be reprosecuted. Sixth, if a case is dismissed by the judge but the defendant is not acquitted, the defendant may be reprosecuted. Finally, reprosecution is permissible if the dismissal occurs over the defendant's objections and is a "manifest necessity."

The defendant also enjoys the right to assert an entrapment defense. While this is not a constitutional right, it has, nevertheless, been given a high degree of protection by the Supreme Court. This defense can be asserted prior to trial—say, in a probable cause hearing or a preliminary hearing—but entrapment is also a common-law defense that can be affirmatively asserted at trial. An entrapment defense will succeed if the defendant can show, in general, that government officials "planted the seeds" of criminal intent and induced him or her into committing the crime in question.

REVIEW QUESTIONS

1. Explain the term *public trial.*
2. When may the right to a public trial not apply?
3. Why is the First Amendment relevant when discussing the right to a public trial?
4. What methods are available to deal with media influence on a criminal trial?
5. In what three ways is the defendant's right to confrontation manifested?

6. Explain both elements of the defendant's right to be present. Cite pertinent cases.

7. How might the defendant's right to be present do more harm than good?

8. Explain the exceptions to the defendant's right to live testimony.

9. Explain the order and scope of questions in a criminal trial.

10. Explain both elements of the right to compulsory process.

11. Summarize two Supreme Court decisions that address compulsory process: one in favor of the defense and another against.

12. When does double-jeopardy protection apply?

13. What is the *same offense* for double-jeopardy purposes?

14. When can a defendant not assert double-jeopardy protection?

15. What is the entrapment defense? When can it succeed? Can entrapment rise to the level of a due process violation? If so, how?

 Answers to the Decision-Making Exercises for this chapter can be found on pages 520–523.

CHAPTER 15

Sentencing, Appeals, and *Habeas Corpus*

KEY TERMS

sentencing
rehabilitation
retribution
incapacitation
deterrence
specific deterrence
general deterrence
indeterminate sentencing

determinate sentencing
mandatory sentencing
sentencing guidelines
bifurcated trial
appeal
appeal of right
direct appeal
discretionary appeal

trial *de novo*
interlocutory appeal
harmless error
retroactivity
habeas corpus
Antiterrorism and Effective
Death Penalty Act

INTRODUCTION
Closing the Door on the Criminal Process

The criminal process typically ends when the defendant is found *not guilty*. It does not end when the accused is found *guilty*, for three reasons. First, the accused must be sentenced, which is usually accomplished in a posttrial hearing. Second, the accused can appeal his or her conviction. Finally, if the accused's appeal fails to succeed, the U.S. Constitution provides the right to *habeas corpus*, a method of challenging the constitutionality of one's confinement.

SENTENCING

Once a person has been convicted at trial, he or she must be sentenced. **Sentencing** occurs at a separate, posttrial hearing but rarely for misdemeanor convictions. Individuals charged with misdemeanors are often tried and sentenced in the same hearing.

When sentencing is carried out in a separate hearing, however, it is usually preceded by the judge requesting a *presentence report*. This report provides the judge with information concerning the defendant's pretrial record, financial characteristics, family status, employment status, and other factors that can be relevant in deciding on the appropriate sentence. The time needed to complete this report is the main reason for the time lapse between trial and sentencing. The report is intended to assist the judge in reaching his or her decision and is usually completed by a probation officer retained by the court.

KEY CASES

Sentencing

- *Roberts v. United States*, 445 U.S. 552 (1980)
- *Furman v. Georgia*, 408 U.S. 238 (1972)
- *Gregg v. Georgia*, 428 U.S. 153 (1976)
- *Roberts v. Louisiana*, 97 S.Ct. 1993 (1977)
- *United States v. Tucker*, 404 U.S. 443 (1972)

Appeals

- *Griffin v. Illinois*, 351 U.S. 12 (1956)
- *Douglas v. California*, 372 U.S. 353 (1963)
- *North Carolina v. Pierce*, 395 U.S. 711 (1969)
- *Cohen v. Beneficial Industrial Loan Corp.*, 337 U.S. 541 (1949)
- *Carroll v. United States*, 354 U.S. 394 (1957)

- *Cobbledick v. United States*, 309 U.S. 323 (1940)
- *Kotteakos v. United States*, 328 U.S. 750 (1946)
- *Chapman v. California*, 386 U.S. 18 (1967)
- *Stovall v. Denno*, 388 U.S. 293 (1967)

Habeas Corpus

- *Sanders v. United States*, 373 U.S. 1 (1963)
- *Stone v. Powell*, 428 U.S. 465 (1976)
- *Teague v. Lane*, 489 U.S. 288 (1989)
- *Herrera v. Collins*, 506 U.S. 390 (1993)
- *Hill v. United States*, 368 U.S. 424 (1962)
- *Kuhlmann v. Wilson*, 477 U.S. 436 (1986)
- *Fay v. Noia*, 372 U.S. 391 (1963)

Several sentencing options are available to the judge. The judge may impose a sentence and then suspend it, pending good behavior on the part of the defendant. The judge may also require the defendant to pay a fine or, in more extreme cases, to serve a term in prison. Probation or another method of supervised release is a possibility, as well. In any case, the type of sentence can hinge on the judge's own goal of sentencing—that is, his or her view as to the most important purpose of sentencing. The following section considers leading goals of criminal sentencing.

■ Goals of Sentencing

Four broad goals of sentencing can be identified: (1) **rehabilitation**, or reformation; (2) **retribution**; (3) **incapacitation**; and (4) **deterrence**, either general or specific. **Specific deterrence** refers to what it takes to discourage the offender from committing additional crimes. **General deterrence** refers to what it takes to discourage all would-be offenders from committing crimes.

The differences among these four goals of punishment have been well described in a famous case heard by the Pennsylvania Supreme Court, *Commonwealth v. Ritter* 13 (Pa. D. & C. 285 [1930]):

> 1. As far as the principle of reformation is concerned, however important it may be in the general run of cases, it obviously has little or no application to such a case as the present. Whichever be the penalty here inflicted, the defendant will not again be in contact with society, and since secular law is concerned with one's relation to the community and not primarily with his inward moral development, the spiritual regeneration of a defendant is not, in such a case as this, a dominant factor. In other words, it would not be a practical consideration weighing in favor of life imprisonment that thereby the defendant might be susceptible of moral reformation, whereas the opportunity for this would be denied to him if the death penalty were inflicted.

> 2. The second theory which has been urged as a basis for the imposition of penalties is that of retribution. This may be regarded as the doctrine of legal revenge, or punishment merely for the sake of punishment. It is to pay back the wrong-doer for his wrongdoing, to make him suffer by way of retaliation even if no benefit result thereby to himself or to others. This theory of punishment looks to the past and not to the future, and rests solely upon the foundation of vindictive justice. It is this idea of punishment that generally prevails, even though those who entertain it may not be fully aware of their so doing. Historically, it may be said that the origin of all legal punishments had its root in the natural impulse of revenge. At first this instinct was gratified by retaliatory measures on the part of the individual who suffered by the crime committed, or, in the case of murder, by his relatives. Later, the state took away the right of retaliation from individuals, and its own assumption of the function of revenge really constituted the beginning of criminal law. The entire course, however, of the refinement and humanizing of society has been in the direction of dispelling from penology any such theory. Indeed, even in classical times moralists and philosophers rejected the idea entirely. Plato puts into the mouth of Protagoras the words: "No one punishes those who have been guilty of injustice solely because they have committed injustice, unless indeed he punishes in a brutal and unreasonable manner. When any one makes use of his reason in inflicting punishment, he punishes, not on account of the fault that is past, for no one can bring it about that what has been done may not have been done, but on account of a fault to come, in order that the person punished may not again commit the fault and that his punishment may restrain from similar acts those persons who witness the punishment." . . .

> 3. Rejecting, therefore, the theory of retribution as a proper basis upon which to impose the penalty of law, we come to the third principle which has been advocated,

namely, the restraint of the wrong-doer in order to make it impossible for him to commit further crime. Here we arrive not only at a justifiable basis for action but at one which is vital to the protection of society. To permit a man of dangerous criminal tendencies to be in a position where he can give indulgence to such propensities would be a folly which no community should suffer itself to commit, any more than it should allow a wild animal to range at will in the city streets. If, therefore, there is danger that a defendant may again commit crime, society should restrain his liberty until such danger be past, and, in cases similar to the present, if reasonably necessary for that purpose, to terminate his life. Admittedly, restraint by imprisonment can never be as wholly effectual as execution, and there are, from time to time, cases where imprisonment may not be sufficient for the protection of society. It is on this ground that it is pertinent to take testimony in regard to the history of a defendant and of the circumstances attending his commission of crime. If his record shows that he is of a dangerous type, or that he habitually commits grave crimes, or that he has a homicidal tendency, or that he is hopelessly depraved, or that he has a savage nature, or that he has committed murder under circumstances of such atrocity and inhuman brutality as to make his continued existence one of likely danger to society, then, in my opinion, the sentence of death is both justifiable and advisable. The community may not be safe with such a man in existence even though he be serving a term of life imprisonment; he may again commit murder within the prison walls, or may escape and again make innocent victims his prey, or may even, by cunning simulation of repentance, obtain a pardon from governmental authorities. . . .

4. This brings us to the final and what must be fairly regarded as one of the most important objectives of punishment, namely, the element of deterrence—the theory which regards the penalty as being not an end in itself but the means of attaining an end, namely, the frightening of others who might be tempted to imitate the criminal. From this angle a penalty is a cautionary measure, aimed at the prevention of further crime in the community. There has been much controversy and an enormous amount of literature on the subject as to whether the death penalty does or does not act as a deterrent. With that controversy we have nothing to do. As before stated, the law of Pennsylvania retains the death penalty as an optional alternative. The real question is not as to whether the death penalty is in general a deterrent, but as to the particular kinds of murder cases in which execution would or would not be most likely to effect deterrence. It becomes a problem of determining the basis upon which to make such classification. (pp. 15–21)

■ Types of Sentences

At least four types of sentences can be identified, some of which are closely related to one another. **Indeterminate sentencing** gives the judge the authority to set the sentence. This form of sentencing empowers the judge to set the maximum sentence—that is, up to what the legislature will allow—or the minimum sentence for the offender to serve in prison. Under this system, a parole board usually ends up deciding the actual amount of time the offender will spend in prison.

In the second type of sentencing, **determinate sentencing**, the judge is permitted to hand down a fixed sentence that cannot later be altered by a parole board. Determinate sentencing has the effect of treating all offenders similarly. It also has the effect of ensuring that criminals will be incarcerated for longer periods of time than may be permissible under indeterminate sentencing.

The third type of sentencing is **mandatory sentencing**. It is a form of determinate sentencing but differs insofar as it takes discretion away from the judge. "Three strikes" laws require mandatory sentencing. For example, under California's "three strikes" law, if a person who has two "strikeable" felonies on his or her record commits a third felony of any type, he or she will go to prison for life. Critics of mandatory sentencing say such laws transfer discretion from the judge to the prosecutor.

Finally, **sentencing guidelines** can be used to determine the appropriate sentence. They constitute the middle ground between indeterminate and determinate methods of sentencing. As such, they serve to reduce disparities in sentencing by recommending a certain term of imprisonment for a certain type of offender. Sentencing guidelines can be voluntary or involuntary, depending on state or federal law. Sentencing guidelines that must be followed exactly are known as *presumptive guidelines.*

The U.S. Sentencing Commission was created in 1984 to deal with sentencing problems in the federal courts. It put together a *sentencing grid* that federal judges use to determine appropriate sentences (see Figure 15.1). Both criminal history (i.e., horizontal axis) and offense level (i.e., vertical axis) are taken into account, such that a judge can set the appropriate sentence in months. Readers are encouraged to visit the U.S. Sentencing Commission's Web site to learn more about these guidelines.[1]

Determining the Appropriate Sentence

Determining the appropriate sentence almost always involves considering both the seriousness of the offense and the offender's prior record. Other factors that are considered include the defendant's possible threat to the community and his or her degree of remorse for committing the crime. Even age, family ties, employment status, and other demographic factors can come into play. Moreover, the defendant who pleads guilty may receive a different sentence than the defendant who is found guilty in a trial. A guilty plea suggests that the defendant is willing to admit what he or she did and, as such, should be treated more leniently.

Sentencing can also be determined by the number of separate crimes growing out of a single criminal act. If, for instance, a defendant is convicted of killing another person with a handgun, he or she may be sentenced for the killing as well as for unlawful possession of a handgun, if the law permits the latter. In such a situation, the judge may sentence the defendant to consecutive or concurrent sentences. With a *concurrent sentence,* the defendant serves time for both crimes at once. *Consecutive sentences,* by contrast, are served separately, one after another. In the murder example, the defendant would serve time in prison for the killing, and then when that term was completed, he or she would begin serving the sentence for possession.

■ *Roberts v. United States,* 445 U.S. 552 (1980)

Indeed, sentencing can be influenced by the defendant's degree of cooperation with the police. In *Roberts v. United States* (445 U.S. 552 [1980]), the Court held that the sentencing judge was permitted to consider the defendant's refusal to cooperate with the police in investigating his crime. Still other factors, such as the offender's mental status, can be considered. In fact, it has been held that a mentally ill individual can be held in custody, such as in a mental institution, for a longer term than a traditional prison sentence for the crime charged (e.g., *Jones v. United States,* 103 S.Ct. 3043 [1983]). This often happens following an insanity plea.

Most jurisdictions have what is known as the "going rate" for a criminal offense.[2] Usually, this is an unwritten, informal agreement between members of a courtroom work group (i.e., a judge, defense attorney, and prosecutor) as to what sentence a typical case merits. Usually, if the seriousness of the offense and the offender's background characteristics are known, one can predict with a fair degree of accuracy what sentence will be imposed.

A judge's sentencing decisions can also be influenced by *victim impact statements.* For example, Proposition 8, adopted by California voters in 1982, provides that "the vic-

---

[1]U.S. Sentencing Commission: <www.ussc.gov>.
[2]See S. Walker, *Sense and Nonsense about Crime and Drugs,* 5th ed. (San Francisco: Wadsworth, 2001), p. 41.

FIGURE 15.1   Federal Sentencing Guidelines

	Offense Level	Criminal History Category (Criminal History Points)					
		I (0 or 1)	II (2 or 3)	III (4, 5, 6)	IV (7, 8, 9)	V (10, 11, 12)	VI (13 or more)
Zone A	1	0–6	0–6	0–6	0–6	0–6	0–6
	2	0–6	0–6	0–6	0–6	0–6	1–7
	3	0–6	0–6	0–6	0–6	2–8	3–9
	4	0–6	0–6	0–6	2–8	4–10	6–12
	5	0–6	0–6	1–7	4–10	6–12	9–15
	6	0–6	1–7	2–8	6–12	9–15	12–18
	7	0–6	2–8	4–10	8–14	12–18	15–21
	8	0–6	4–10	6–12	10–16	15–21	18–24
Zone B	9	4–10	6–12	8–14	12–18	18–24	21–27
	10	6–12	8–14	10–16	15–21	21–27	24–30
Zone C	11	8–14	10–16	12–18	18–24	24–30	27–33
	12	10–16	12–18	15–21	21–27	27–33	30–37
	13	12–18	15–21	18–24	24–30	30–37	33–41
	14	15–21	18–24	21–27	27–33	33–41	37–46
	15	18–24	21–27	24–30	30–37	37–46	41–51
	16	21–27	24–30	27–33	33–41	41–51	46–57
	17	24–30	27–33	30–37	37–46	46–57	51–63
	18	27–33	30–37	33–41	41–51	51–63	57–71
	19	30–37	33–41	37–46	46–57	57–71	63–78
	20	33–41	37–46	41–51	51–63	63–78	70–87
	21	37–46	41–51	46–57	57–71	70–87	77–96
	22	41–51	46–57	51–63	63–78	77–96	84–105
	23	46–57	51–63	57–71	70–87	84–105	92–115
	24	51–63	57–71	63–78	77–96	92–115	100–125
	25	57–71	63–78	70–87	84–105	100–125	110–137
	26	63–78	70–87	78–97	92–115	110–137	120–150
Zone D	27	70–87	78–97	87–108	100–125	120–150	130–162
	28	78–97	87–108	97–121	110–137	130–162	140–175
	29	87–108	97–121	108–135	121–151	140–175	151–188
	30	97–121	108–135	121–151	135–168	151–188	168–210
	31	108–135	121–151	135–168	151–188	168–210	188–235
	32	121–151	135–168	151–188	168–210	188–235	210–262
	33	135–168	151–188	168–210	188–235	210–262	235–293
	34	151–188	168–210	188–235	210–262	235–293	262–327
	35	168–210	188–235	210–262	235–293	262–327	292–365
	36	188–235	210–262	235–293	262–327	292–365	324–405
	37	210–262	235–293	262–327	292–365	324–405	360–life
	38	235–293	262–327	292–365	324–405	360–life	360–life
	39	262–327	292–365	324–405	360–life	360–life	360–life
	40	292–365	324–405	360–life	360–life	360–life	360–life
	41	324–405	360–life	360–life	360–life	360–life	360–life
	42	360–life	360–life	360–life	360–life	360–life	360–life
	43	life	life	life	life	life	life

Commentary to Sentencing Table

Application Notes:

1. The Offense Level (1–43) forms the vertical axis of the Sentencing Table. The Criminal History Category (I–VI) forms the horizontal axis of the Table. The intersection of the Offense Level and Criminal History Category displays the Guideline Range in months of imprisonment. "Life" means life imprisonment. For example, the guideline range applicable to a defendant with an Offense Level of 15 and a Criminal History Category of III is 24–30 months of imprisonment.

2. In rare cases, a total offense level of less than 1 or more than 43 may result from application of the guidelines. A total offense level of less than 1 is to be treated as an offense level of 1. An offense level of more than 43 is to be treated as an offense level of 43.

3. The Criminal History Category is determined by the total criminal history points from Chapter Four, Part A, except as provided in §§4B1.1 (Career Offender) and 4B1.4 (Armed Career Criminal). The total criminal history points associated with each Criminal History Category are shown under each Criminal History Category in the Sentencing Table.

Historical Note: Effective November 1, 1987. Amended effective November 1, 1989 (see Appendix C, amendment 270); November 1, 1991 (see Appendix C, amendment 418); November 1, 1992 (see Appendix C, amendment 462).

Source: U.S. Sentencing Commission, *2002 Federal Sentencing Guidelines Manual,* Chapter 1. Available online: <www.ussc.gov/2002guid/5a.htm>. Accessed December 12, 2002.

tim of any crime, or the next kin of the victim, . . . has the right to attend all sentencing proceedings . . . [and] to reasonably express his or her views concerning the crime, the person responsible, and the need for restitution."[3]

The judge is then required to take the victim's or next of kin's statement into account when deciding on a sentence for the offender.

Death Penalty Sentencing

■ *Furman v. Georgia,*
408 U.S. 238 (1972)

■ *Gregg v. Georgia,*
428 U.S. 153 (1976)

■ *Roberts v. Louisiana,*
97 S.Ct. 1993 (1977)

The most serious punishment that can be imposed is *capital punishment,* or the death penalty. Prior to the 1970s, several executions were carried out each year. However, in 1972, the Supreme Court decided the landmark case *Furman v. Georgia* (408 U.S. 238 [1972]). In that case, the Court held that the death penalty was carried out in the United States in a way that amounted to cruel and unusual punishment, in violation of the Eighth Amendment. Then, in 1976, the Court reinstated the death penalty in *Gregg v. Georgia* (428 U.S. 153 [1976]), holding that death is an acceptable sentence, provided the sentencing process is reasonable.

Determining whether death should be imposed is now frequently in the hands of a jury. Most state statutes call for, in essence, two trials. In legal parlance, this is called a **bifurcated trial**. In the first trial, the defendant's guilt or lack of involvement in the crime is determined. This is the traditional trial. Then, the jury sits for what is basically another trial to determine whether a death sentence should be handed down. The importance of such a procedure is that it allows a jury of the defendant's peers, not just a judge, to determine whether capital punishment is appropriate. Further, the jury must take into account aggravating and mitigating circumstances. As decided in *Roberts v. Louisiana* (97 S.Ct. 1993 [1977]), failure to do so is unconstitutional.

In *Stebbing v. Maryland* (469 U.S. 900 [1984]), Justice Marshall described one state's approach to death penalty sentencing that relies on a jury's decision:

> Like most death penalty statutes, the Maryland statute begins by requiring the sentencing authority—either a judge or a jury—first to consider whether the prosecutor has proved, beyond a reasonable doubt, the existence of any of 10 statutory aggravating circumstances. . . . If the sentencer does not find at least one aggravating factor, the sentence must be life imprisonment. . . . If the sentencer finds that one or more aggravating factors exist, it then must determine whether the defendant has proven, by a preponderance of the evidence, that any of eight statutory mitigating factors exist. . . . If no mitigating factors are found, the sentencer must impose death. If, instead, the sentencer has found at least one mitigating factor, it must determine, by a preponderance of the evidence, whether the proven mitigating factors outweigh the aggravating circumstances. If they do, the sentencer must impose a life sentence. If the mitigating factors do not outweigh aggravating factors, the jury must impose a death sentence. (p. 902)

Whereas a jury must take aggravating and mitigating factors into consideration when determining whether a death sentence is appropriate, it is not appropriate for a judge to do so. Such was the decision in *Ring v. Arizona* (122 S.Ct. 2428 [2002]). There, the Supreme Court held that allowing a sentencing judge, without a jury, to find aggravating circumstances necessary for imposition of the death penalty violated the Sixth Amendment's jury trial provision.

[3]California Penal Code, Section 1191.1 (1996).

DECISION MAKING EXERCISE 15.1

Death Penalty Sentencing

Assume that a state law gives the trial judge authority to sentence to death a defendant convicted of a capital crime but also requires the judge to consider the jury's recommendation as to whether the death penalty should be imposed. Assume further that a man has been sentenced to death by the judge in his trial, even though the jury that convicted him recommended life in prison. The man appeals, claiming that the statute is unconstitutional because it does not specify the weight the judge must give to the jury's sentencing recommendation and thus permits the arbitrary imposition of the death penalty. He further claims that the judge should be forced to give "great weight" to the jury's recommendation. How should the appellate court rule?

The death penalty is most commonly handed down for first-degree, premeditated murder. But whether death is the appropriate sentence for less serious offenses has raised some questions. The Supreme Court has answered these questions to some extent. For example, in *Coker v. Georgia* (433 U.S. 584 [1977]), the Court held that a sentence of death for the crime of rape against an adult woman was grossly disproportionate and in violation of the Eighth and Fourteenth Amendments to the U.S. Constitution.

Other Important Sentencing Decisions

Several other recent decisions have sought to clarify the circumstances in which death and/or other types of sentences can be imposed. A handful of the cases and their holdings are as follow:

Woodson v. North Carolina (428 U.S. 280 [1976]). Decided on the same day as *Gregg*, the Court held that mandatory death penalty laws—that is, those that do not take aggravating and mitigating circumstances into account—are unconstitutional.

Enmund v. Florida (458 U.S. 782 [1982]). It is unconstitutional to impose death on a person who participates in a felony that results in murder without considering the participant's level of intent.

Cabana v. Bullock (474 U.S. 376 [1986]). The death penalty cannot be imposed on a mere accomplice, unless there is clear finding that the accomplice killed, attempted to kill, or intended to kill.

Ford v. Wainwright (477 U.S. 399 [1986]). The execution of someone who is insane violates the Eighth Amendment.

Tison v. Arizona (107 S.Ct. 1714 [1987]). The death penalty can be imposed in the absence of intent to kill if the defendant substantially participated in a felony likely to result in a loss of life.

Harmelin v. Michigan (501 U.S. 957 [1991]). A life sentence without the possibility of parole for a first-time, nonviolent drug offender does not constitute cruel and unusual punishment.

Kansas v. Hendricks (521 U.S. 346 [1997]). Civil commitment was upheld for convicted child molesters who have served their sentences under the state's Sexually Violent Predators Act.

Atkins v. Virginia (122 S. Ct. 2242 [2002]). The execution of a mentally retarded person violates the Eighth Amendment.

Kansas v. Crane (534 U.S. 407 [2002]). Concerning the civil commitment of sexual offenders under Kansas's Sexually Violent Predators Act, such offenders cannot be civilly committed without having proof that they have serious difficulty in controlling their behavior.

Roper v. Simmons (543 U.S. 551 [2005]). The execution of offenders who committed their capital crime under the age of 18 violates the Eighth Amendment.

Deck v. Missouri (125 S.Ct. 2007 [2005]). The constitution forbids the use of visible shackles during a capital trial's penalty phase.

■ Constitutional Rights during Sentencing

A convicted criminal enjoys several important constitutional rights during the sentencing process. First, the double-jeopardy provision of the Fifth Amendment, as discussed in the last chapter, applies. Further, the defendant is entitled to a reasonable punishment for his or her crime. Namely, the punishment should reflect the seriousness of the crime. For example, in *Solem v. Helm* (463 U.S. 277 [1983]), the Court held that a life sentence for the defendant's seventh nonviolent offense was unconstitutional. The Court prohibited the sentence, stating that the defendant "received the penultimate sentence for relatively minor criminal conduct" (p. 305).

The defendant also has the right to participate in the sentencing process. With the possible exception of misdemeanor sentencing, which may take place out of the presence of the defendant, the defendant has the right to be present during sentencing. Also, the defendant should be advised of his or her right to appeal. The defendant also has the right to have counsel present at the sentencing hearing to argue on his or her behalf. The Sixth Amendment right to counsel operates essentially the same way at sentencing as it does at trial.

■ *United States v. Tucker,*
404 U.S. 443 (1972)

The defendant also has the right to ask the sentencing judge to ignore past convictions that were obtained in violation of the right to counsel. For example, in *United States v. Tucker* (404 U.S. 443 [1972]), the Supreme Court invalidated an individual's 25-year sentence because the sentencing judge arrived at the sentence by considering the defendant's past convictions, for which he was not afforded counsel. The Court stated:

> The government is . . . on solid ground in asserting that a sentence imposed by a federal district judge, if within statutory limits, is generally not subject to review. . . . But these general propositions do not decide the case before us. For we deal here not with a sentence imposed in the informed discretion of a trial judge, but with a sentence founded at least in part upon misinformation of constitutional magnitude. As in *Townsend v. Burke*, 334 U.S. 736 (1690), "this prisoner was sentenced on the basis of assumptions concerning his criminal record which were materially untrue." The record in the present case makes evident that the sentencing judge gave specific consideration to the respondent's previous convictions before imposing sentence upon him. Yet it is now clear that two of those convictions were wholly unconstitutional under *Gideon v. Wainwright*, 372 U.S. 335 (1963). (p. 446)

In summary, a defendant enjoys at least three important constitutional rights during the sentencing process: (1) the right not to be put twice in jeopardy; (2) the right to a sentence that conforms with the Eighth Amendment's proscription against cruel and unusual punishment; and (3) the right to counsel at sentencing-related hearings, regardless of his or her ability to afford representation.

■ APPEALS

An **appeal** occurs when an appellate court, such as one of the federal courts of appeal, examines a lower court's decision in order to determine whether the proper procedure was followed or the correct law was applied. In other words, when a defendant appeals, he or she is claiming that the court made an error. Thus, the appeal guarantees that a defendant who is found guilty can challenge his or her conviction. Further, the appeal guarantees that another judge or panel of judges, disconnected from the initial trial, will make the relevant decision.

Although appealing convictions is an important part of the criminal process, the Supreme Court has never held that doing so is constitutionally permissible. That is, nowhere does the U.S. Constitution specify that a certain number of appeals will be granted to each convicted criminal. In *McKane v. Durston* (153 U.S. 684 [1894]), the Supreme Court stated, "A review by an appellate court of the final judgment in a criminal case, however grave the offense of which the accused is convicted, was not at common law, and is not now, a necessary element of due process of law" (p. 687).

Most appeals are posttrial in nature and filed by the defense, which is why this topic is being discussed at the end of this book. However, in some situations, the defense appeals a court's decision, such as on a motion to suppress evidence, during the trial. And in some instances, the prosecution can even file an appeal. Thus, this chapter will consider three types of appeals: (1) appeals by the defense prior to adjudication; (2) appeals by the defense after adjudication; and (3) appeals by the prosecution. First, however, it is important to review the common types of appeals and their consequences and the important Supreme Court cases dealing with the appellate process (i.e., the procedures courts are required to follow).

Types and Effects of Appeals

Despite the Supreme Court's view that appealing one's conviction is not constitutionally guaranteed, every state and the federal government each has rules providing a certain number of appeals to a convicted criminal. At both the state and federal levels, a convicted criminal is usually granted at least one **appeal of right**, also known as a **direct appeal**, and at least one **discretionary appeal**.

An appeal of right, or a direct appeal, is automatically granted to the defendant by law. That is, an appeal of right *must* be heard by an appellate court. It is not up to the appellate court to decide whether to hear such an appeal. By contrast, the appellate court can decide, at its own discretion, whether to hear a discretionary appeal. Also, appeals of right are limited, but discretionary appeals can be filed several times, provided they are not redundant.

When a defendant appeals a decision, there are a number of possible consequences. In the typical appeal, the defendant seeks to correct a decision by the lower court that he or she perceives to be in error. In such an instance, the appellate court will either affirm or reverse the lower court's decision. It may also remand (i.e., send back) the case for further proceedings, consistent with its opinion.

The federal government and every state each has rules that provide a certain number of appeals to someone who has been convicted of a crime.

Another consequence of an appeal can be a **trial *de novo***. When the defendant appeals for a trial *de novo*, he or she is essentially requesting a new, independent trial at the appellate level. Trials *de novo* are rare. Further, they are usually limited to appeals of decisions arising from misdemeanor courts of limited jurisdiction. Rarely, if ever, will a convicted felon succeed in obtaining a trial *de novo* in an appellate court. The primary reason for this is that an appellate court interprets the *law*, not the *facts*. It is the job of the trial court to determine guilt based on the facts.

Whether the defendant seeks a new trial or simply a review of the trial court's decision on some matter, he or she will not necessarily go free if a decision is returned in his or her favor. If, for example, the appellate court considers a lower court's decision not to exclude evidence and decides that the lower court's decision should be reversed, this means the evidence should have been excluded, not that the defendant should be acquitted. For example, in the famous *Miranda* case (*Miranda v. Arizona*, 384 U.S. 436 [1966]), the Supreme Court did not free Ernesto Miranda. Instead, it remanded his case for a new trial. He was subsequently found guilty and sentenced to more than 20 years in prison. It is, therefore, important when reading cases to understand precisely what the reviewing court is deciding. Rarely does an appellate court decide guilt; its job is to interpret the law and review the conduct of the trial court.

What happens to convicted defendants while they are appealing? In almost all cases, they serve out the conditions of their sentences. Assume, for example, that a defendant appeals his guilty conviction on the grounds that he was denied counsel at trial. Assume further that the defendant's appeal has merit. If he was sentenced to prison following trial, he will remain there until the appeal is heard, if it ever is. However, for a select few convicts, the judge will issue a *stay*, which means the convicted individual will not serve time before the appeal is heard. This is a rare situation and usually involves an individual who poses a low flight risk. The fact that most convicted criminals are considered flight risks further explains why stays of imprisonment are rarely granted.

■ The Appellate Process

Even though the Supreme Court has held that appealing one's conviction is not constitutionally required, it has held, on a number of occasions, that when an appeal is permissible, the government must follow certain procedures. Specifically, the government must ensure that the defendant has (1) access to trial transcripts; (2) the right to counsel; and (3) the right to be free from government retaliation for a successful appeal. Before these procedural issues can be considered, though, the defendant must file *notice of an appeal*. An example of such a notice, from the U.S. District Court for the Southern District of California, is presented in Figure 15.2.

Ensuring That the Defendant Has Access to Trial Transcripts

■ *Griffin v. Illinois*,
351 U.S. 12 (1956)

In *Griffin v. Illinois* (351 U.S. 12 [1956]), the Supreme Court considered whether an Illinois appellate procedure that required the defendant to produce transcripts of the trial—even if he or she could not afford to do so—violated the Constitution. The Court struck down the procedure, claiming that the government cannot impose a restriction on the right to appeal "in a way that discriminates against some convicted defendants on account of their poverty" (p. 18). In a related case, *Entsminger v. Iowa* (386 U.S. 748 [1967]), decided some time later, the Court invalidated a state procedure that allowed defense counsel, rather than an indigent defendant, to decide whether an appeal could continue with an incomplete trial transcript. An actual trial transcript order form, from the Tenth Circuit Court of Appeals, is presented in Figure 15.3.

FIGURE 15.2 Example of a Notice of Appeal

NAME AND ADDRESS OF ATTORNEY

_____

_____

_____

PHONE: _____

_____ RETAINED _____ APPOINTED

IN THE UNITED STATES DISTRICT COURT
SOUTHERN DISTRICT OF CALIFORNIA

TRIAL JUDGE_____   COURT REPORTER _____

)

)

UNITED STATES OF AMERICA   )

(Appellant/Appellee)   )

)   NOTICE OF APPEAL   (Criminal)

vs.   )

)

)

(Appellant/Appellee)   )

_____)

Notice is hereby given that _____,
defendant/plaintiff above names, hereby appeals to the United States Court of Appeals
for the Ninth Circuit from the: (check one)

( ) Final Judgment

( ) Sentence Only (sentence imposed) _____

( ) Order (describe) _____

entered in this proceeding on the _____ day of _____, 20 _____

If government appeal: Was the filing of this appeal approved in accordance with 18 U.S.C.
3742(b)(4)? _____ Yes _____ No

Date: _____   _____
                                          Signature

Transcripts required*   _____ Yes   _____ No

Date   ( ) Indictment   ( ) Information Filed: _____

Bail status_____

Will there be a request to expedite the appeal?   _____ Yes   _____ No

(Note: This does not alleviate the requirement of filing a motion to expedite which must
be done in accordance with FRAP 27).

*If transcript(s) required, a transcript designation and ordering form must be completed and the court
reporter(s) contacted to make arrangements for transcription.

Source: Used courtesy of U.S. District Court, Southern District of California.

FIGURE 15.3 Example of a Trial Transcript Order Form

PART I — To be completed by appellant within ten days of filing the notice of appeal

Short Title: _____ District: _____

District Court Number: _____ Circuit Court Number: _____

Name of Attorney: _____

Name of Law Firm: _____

Address of Firm: _____

Telephone of Firm: _____ Attorneys for: _____

Name of Court Reporter: _____ Telephone of Reporter: _____

PART II — COMPLETE SECTION A OR SECTION B

SECTION A — I HAVE NOT ORDERED A TRANSCRIPT BECAUSE

    ☐ A transcript is not necessary for this appeal, or

    ☐ The necessary transcript is already on file in District Court

    ☐ The necessary transcript was ordered previously in appeal number

---

SECTION B — I HEREBY ORDER THE FOLLOWING TRANSCRIPT:

(Specify the date and proceeding in the space below)

Voir Dire: _____; Opening Statements:; _____;

Trial Proceedings: _____; Instruction Cnf: _____;

Jury Instructions: _____; Closing Arguments: _____;

Post Trial Motions: _____; Other Proceedings: _____.

(Attach additional pages if necessary)

    ☐ Appellant will pay the cost of the transcript.

My signature on this form is my agreement to pay for the transcript ordered on this form.

    ☐ This case is proceeding under the Criminal Justice Act.

NOTE: Leave to proceed *in forma pauperis* does not entitle appellant to a free transcript. An order of the district court allowing payment for the transcript at government expense must be obtained. *See* 28 U.S.C. §753(f).

CERTIFICATE OF COMPLIANCE

I certify that I have read the instructions on the reverse of this form and that copies of this transcript order form have been served on the court reporter (if transcript ordered), the Clerk of U.S. District Court, all counsel of record or pro se parties, and the Clerk of the U.S. Court of Appeals for the Tenth Circuit. I further certify that satisfactory arrangements for payment for any transcript ordered have been made with the court reporter(s).

Signature of Attorney/Pro Se: _____ Date: _____

PART III — TO BE COMPLETED BY THE COURT REPORTER

Upon completion, please file one copy with the Clerk of the U.S. Court of Appeals and one copy with the Clerk of the U.S. District Court.

Date arrangements for payment completed: _____

Estimated completion date: _____

Estimated number of pages: _____

I certify that I have read the instructions on the reverse side and that adequate arrangements for payment have been made.

Signature of Court Reporter: _____ Date: _____

Source: Used courtesy of U.S. Court of Appeals, Tenth Circuit.

DECISION
MAKING
EXERCISE **15.2**

Constitutional Rights during the Appeals Process

Judge Lawson has before him two convicted criminals who are giving notice of their intent to appeal their convictions for robbery. The two are indigent and thus pursuing their appeals without the assistance of counsel. They request access to the trial transcripts, but Judge Lawson rules against them, claiming that because, in his view, their appeals are frivolous, it would be a waste of taxpayer funds to supply them with the trial transcripts. Is this action constitutional?

Ensuring the Defendant's Right to Counsel during Appeals

As has been discussed at some length in this text, criminal defendants enjoy the Sixth Amendment right to counsel under a number of circumstances. However, the Sixth Amendment expressly states that this right only applies in *criminal prosecutions.* Even so, the Supreme Court has required that counsel be provided to indigent defendants *on appeal* as a matter of either equal protection or due process. Interestingly, though, the Court has also said that there is no right to self-representation at the appellate stage (see *Martinez v. Court of Appeal*, 528 U.S. 152 [2000]).

The first case discussing the right to counsel during the appellate stage was *Douglas v. California* 372 U.S. 353 [1963]). There, the Court concluded that the government must provide an indigent defendant with counsel to assist in his or her appeals of right. The Court stated that "where the merits of the *one and only* appeal an indigent has as of right are decided without benefit of counsel . . . an unconstitutional line has been drawn between rich and poor" (p. 357). The Court has also held that the Constitution requires counsel—particularly, effective counsel—for a nonindigent defendant in his or her appeals of right (see *Evitts v. Lucey*, 469 U.S. 387 [1985]).

Both *Douglas* and *Evitts* dealt with the right to counsel in appeals of right. By contrast, the Supreme Court has held that counsel is not constitutionally guaranteed in *discretionary appeals.* Specifically, in *Ross v. Moffitt* (417 U.S. 600 [1974]), the Court held:

> A defendant in respondent's circumstances is not denied meaningful access to the State Supreme Court simply because the State does not appoint counsel to aid him in seeking review in that court, since at that stage, under North Carolina's multitiered appellate system, he will have, at the very least, a transcript or other record of the trial proceedings, a brief in the Court of Appeals setting forth his claims of error, and frequently an opinion by that court disposing of his case, materials which, when supplemented by any *pro se* submission that might be made, would provide the Supreme Court with an adequate basis for its decision to grant or deny review under its standards of whether the case has "significant public interest," involves "legal principles of major significance," or likely conflicts with a previous Supreme Court decision. (pp. 614–615)

■ *Douglas v. California,* 372 U.S. 353 (1963)

DECISION
MAKING
EXERCISE **15.3**

Effective Assistance of Counsel during the Appeals Process

June Gale was convicted in state court on several felony counts, and her convictions were affirmed by the intermediate appellate court. Gale then appealed to the state supreme court, but the court dismissed her application for a *writ of certiorari* because the application was not filed within the proper time frame as specified by state law. Gale then sought to have her appeal heard by the U.S. Supreme Court, claiming that she was denied effective assistance of counsel when her attorney missed the deadline for filing a discretionary appeal. Assuming the Supreme Court grants review, how should it decide?

Government Retaliation for Successful Defense Appeals

■ *North Carolina v. Pierce*, 395 U.S. 711 (1969)

Several times, the Supreme Court has dealt with retaliation by the prosecution for a successful defense appeal. The first noteworthy case in this regard was *North Carolina v. Pierce* (395 U.S. 711 [1969]). There, the defendant was reconvicted after a successful appeal and was actually punished more harshly the second time around. The Court concluded that due process required that the "defendant be freed of apprehension of such a retaliatory motivation on the part of the sentencing judge" (p. 725).

In another case, *Blackledge v. Perry* (417 U.S. 21 [1974]), the Court decided against a prosecutor's decision to increase the charge against a defendant who was convicted but appealed to a higher court for a trial *de novo*. The Court held that "upping the ante" in this fashion, simply because the defendant had exercised his right to appeal, was unconstitutional.

By contrast, there have been a few cases in which the Supreme Court has held that vindictiveness cannot be inferred from the judge's or jury's decision to increase a defendant's *sentence* following appeal. For instance, in *Colten v. Kentucky* (407 U.S. 104 [1972]), the Court held that a judge did not act vindictively by increasing the defendant's sentence following his trial *de novo*. And in a similar case, *Chaffin v. Stynchcombe* (412 U.S. 17 [1973]), the Court held that a jury's decision to increase the defendant's sentence in his trial *de novo* was constitutional.

In both *Colten* and *Chaffin*, the sentencing authority was disconnected from the first trial. That is, a different judge sentenced Colten the second time, and a second jury convicted the defendant in *Chaffin* following his trial *de novo*. What if, by contrast, the same judge who presided over the defendant's first trial then decided the defendant's sentence following an appeal? This question was answered in *Texas v. McCullough* (475 U.S. 134 [1986]), in which the Court held that the trial judge had no motivation to be vindictive. Importantly, the defendant's first sentence was decided by a jury. The judge only *presided* over the first trial. Had the judge actually handed down the defendant's sentences in both trials, the second, increased sentence probably would have been considered vindictive.

DECISION MAKING EXERCISE 15.4

Retaliation for a Successful Appeal

Here are the facts from an actual case, *Thigpen v. Roberts* (468 U.S. 27 [1984]), as reported by the Supreme Court:

> Following an accident in which he lost control of his car and collided with a pickup truck, killing a passenger in the truck, respondent was charged with four misdemeanors—reckless driving, driving while his license was revoked, driving on the wrong side of the road, and driving while intoxicated. Upon being convicted of these charges in a Mississippi Justice of the Peace Court, he appealed, and the case was transferred to the Circuit Court for a trial de novo. While the appeal was pending, he was indicted for manslaughter based on the same accident, and was convicted.

Note that the convictions were obtained by different prosecutors. Can the second prosecution be considered retaliatory?

Summary. In order to make appealing meaningful for a criminal defendant, the Supreme Court has required that three important rights be observed during this process. First, the defendant must be given access to the trial transcripts, even if he or she cannot afford them, in order to make an appeal. Second, the defendant must be given counsel during the appellate process, regardless of whether he or she can afford representation. Finally, neither the judge nor the prosecutor can act in a retaliatory fashion when the defendant decides to appeal. It is not always easy to determine what constitutes retaliation, but it is safe to say that when the judge or prosecutor has an interest in the outcome of a defendant's appeal and, consequently, increases the charge or sentence following the appeal, that action will be considered unconstitutional.

Timing of Defense Appeals

The defense can file an appeal at one of two stages: (1) prior to the reading of the verdict—that is, prior to adjudication; or (2) following adjudication. The typical appeal is filed after adjudication, but there can be reasons to file an appeal prior to adjudication, as well. Both types of appeals are considered in the sections that follow. However, the bulk of the discussion will focus on appeals prior to adjudication because the Supreme Court has imposed far more restrictions on these.

Appeals prior to Adjudication

An appeal filed prior to adjudication is known as an **interlocutory appeal**. This type of appeal is governed by a complex and confusing body of case law. In simple terms, though, an interlocutory appeal will only succeed if it is important and unrelated to the cause of action. That is, it must deal with a critical constitutional question and have nothing to do with determining the defendant's guilt. Otherwise, the defendant will face what is known as the *final judgment rule*, which generally limits appeals until the court hands down its final judgment as to the defendant's guilt.

Cohen v. Beneficial Industrial Loan Corp. (337 U.S. 541 [1949]) is perhaps the first noteworthy case in which the Supreme Court upheld certain interlocutory appeals: namely, "a small class [of preadjudication decisions] which finally determine claims of right separable from, and collateral to, rights asserted in the action, too important to be denied review and too independent of the cause itself to required that appellate consideration be deferred until the whole case is adjudicated" (p. 546). This quote does not lend itself to easy interpretation, unfortunately. But clarification can be provided by considering some examples of cases in which the Court applied its ruling in *Cohen*. The following two cases illustrate *successful* appeals prior to adjudication, while the subsequent cases focus on *unsuccessful* appeals.

In *Stack v. Boyle* (342 U.S. 1 [1951]), the Court held that the defendant could appeal a judge's decision rejecting his argument that bail was excessive, in apparent violation of the Eighth Amendment. The Court believed that the trial judge's decision on this matter was more or less independent of deciding the defendant's guilt. It also felt that delaying appeal until after adjudication would make it pointless; a bail determination after a guilty verdict would have virtually no bearing on anything.

In another case, *Abney v. United States* (431 U.S. 651 [1977]), the Court held that a defendant could appeal a preadjudication order denying dismissal of his indictment on double-jeopardy grounds. The reason for this decision should be fairly obvious: If the protection against double jeopardy is to have any meaning, then a defendant who claims double jeopardy must be able to appeal before the second conviction is handed down. Otherwise, the appellate court would have to consider whether a defendant's Fifth Amendment protection was denied in *hindsight*, which is not a preferable approach.

An example of a preadjudication appeal that did *not* succeed can be found in *Carroll v. United States* 354 U.S. 394 [1957]). There, the Court held that a defendant cannot appeal a decision on a preadjudication search-and-seizure motion until after final adjudication has taken place. In other words, the Court felt that an appeal of a decision addressing evidence critical to the defendant's case is not sufficiently independent of the trial.

In another case, *DiBella v. United States* (369 U.S. 121 [1962]), the Court held that a judge's preadjudication decision not to suppress evidence following the defendant's assertion that his Fourth Amendment rights were violated was not appealable until after trial. The Court felt that "appellate intervention makes for truncated presentation of the issue of admissibility, because the legality of the search too often cannot truly be determined until the evidence at the trial has brought all circumstances to light" (p. 129).

- *Cohen v. Beneficial Industrial Loan Corp.*, 337 U.S. 541 (1949)

- *Carroll v. United States*, 354 U.S. 394 (1957)

An Appeal prior to Adjudication

Federal agents executed a warrant to search the offices of Standard Drywall, Inc., and seized several books and records for presentation to a grand jury that was investigating crimes allegedly committed by the company. Shortly after the search and prior to final adjudication, Standard Drywall filed a motion for the return of all property seized pursuant to the search warrant. Should the company succeed? (Note that this is an interlocutory appeal but does not concern what is taking place at trial. Rather, the appellant is seeking return of its property, which is before the grand jury for investigation.)

Why does all this matter? Uninformed readers of Supreme Court cases often wonder why some cases are appealed after final adjudication and others before. Understanding the restrictions imposed by the Supreme Court on preadjudication appeals is important because it helps readers trace the progress of particular cases. But because preadjudication appeals can impose serious delays, they are usually the exception, rather than the rule.

Despite the obvious time- and resource-saving benefits of restricting preadjudication appeals, requiring that most appeals be filed after trial can have serious consequences for defendants. Many defendants who are found guilty on serious charges go to prison and are forced to pursue their appeals from there. Given that most appeals—especially those that raise constitutional questions and ultimately reach the Supreme Court—take several years, people who are wrongfully convicted can languish in prison. This is one of the weaknesses of the U.S. system of justice.

Appeals after Adjudication

Appeals filed after adjudication are subject to few restrictions. Indeed, there appear to be few Supreme Court cases addressing postadjudication appeals. Nonetheless, it is important to understand that postadjudication appeals are almost limitless in terms of their possible substance. Anything from the trial (i.e., as recorded in the transcripts) that the defense perceives to be in error can be appealed.

The constitutional rights violations that most commonly serve as the basis for an appeal (or appeals) involve convictions obtained by any of these means:

1. A plea of guilty that was unlawfully induced or not made voluntarily with understanding of the nature of the charge and the consequences of the plea
2. The use of a coerced confession
3. The use of evidence gained pursuant to an unconstitutional search or seizure
4. The use of evidence obtained pursuant to an unlawful arrest
5. A violation of the privilege against self-incrimination
6. The unconstitutional failure of the prosecution to disclose to the defendant evidence favorable to him or her
7. A violation of the Fifth Amendment's double-jeopardy clause
8. Action of a grand jury or petit jury that was unconstitutionally selected and impaneled
9. The denial of effective assistance of counsel
10. Denial of the rights to a speedy trial and appeal

■ Appeals by Parties Other Than the Defense

Most commonly, an appeal is filed by the defense because the defendant arguably has the most to lose in a criminal trial (i.e., his or her liberty). However, in some limited circumstances, the prosecution or a third party can appeal a judge's decision. The following subsections briefly digress from the focus on the defendant and consider appeals by the prosecution and third parties.

Prosecution Appeals

As indicated in Chapter 14, the prosecution is usually barred from appealing a defendant's conviction because of the double-jeopardy clause of the Fifth Amendment. Trial court rulings besides those deciding the issue of guilt, however, can sometimes be appealed by the prosecution. As the Supreme Court stated in *Carroll v. United States* (354 U.S. 394 [1957]), "[A]ppeals by the government in criminal cases are something unusual, exceptional, not favored. The history shows resistance of the Court to the opening of an appellate route for the Government until it was plainly provided by the Congress, and after that a close restriction of its uses to those authorized by statute" (p. 400). In other words, appeals by the prosecution are possible in certain situations but only as authorized by state or federal law.

One statute that permits appeal by the prosecution can be found at the federal level. It is found in 18 U.S.C. Section 3731 and provides for interlocutory prosecution appeal of a district court's decision to suppress or exclude evidence from trial. This type of appeal is permissible because if the defendant is acquitted at trial, the prosecution will not likely appeal the defendant's conviction because of the double-jeopardy clause. The defendants cannot assert double-jeopardy protection at a preadjudication hearing, which is why it behooves the prosecution to appeal before the end of the trial. Indeed, many of the Supreme Court cases encountered in this book and elsewhere came before the Court because the prosecution disagreed with a trial judge's decision to exclude or suppress evidence.

Other prosecution appeals, besides those addressing decisions to exclude or suppress evidence, are severely restricted because of double jeopardy. These restrictions were discussed in the previous chapter. The most common type of prosecution appeal, however, is one addressing a judge's decision on whether to permit or exclude evidence that the prosecution wants to use against the accused. In criminal procedure, when a judge excludes or suppresses evidence, it is because the police acted in violation of some constitutional provision. Note, however, that evidence may not be admissible because it is irrelevant, incompetent, immaterial, or otherwise limited.

A Prosecution Appeal

Martin Katt, who was indicted for federal drug charges, moved twice before trial and once during trial to dismiss the charges, claiming that the pre-indictment delay was unconstitutional. Once the government finished presenting its case, the court decided in Katt's favor and granted his motion for a dismissal. The government appealed the judge's decision to dismiss Katt's case. Should the prosecution's appeal be heard?

Third-Party Appeals

Third parties—that is, individuals besides the prosecution and the defense—are sometimes permitted to appeal. For example, in *Cobbledick v. United States* (309 U.S. 323 [1940]), the Supreme Court held that a person can appeal a court order, such as a subpoena, but only if he or she has been found in contempt of court for failing to abide by that order. The Court said that a decision to the contrary "would forever preclude review of the witness' claim, for his alternatives are to abandon the claim or languish in jail" (p. 328).

Cobbledick v. United States, 309 U.S. 323 (1940)

Other varieties of third-party appeals are conceivable but rare. Only when a trial judge's decision impinges on another person's rights will a third-party appeal succeed. An appeal by the media to overturn a judge's gag order may be permissible on First

Amendment grounds, but there appear to be no Supreme Court cases addressing this possibility. The number of third-party appeals pales in comparison to the number filed by defendants, either prior to or after adjudication.

■ When Appeals Do Not Succeed

As indicated already, an appeal may not succeed simply because the appellate court is unwilling to hear it, as is the case with many discretionary appeals. However, even when the appellate court agrees to hear an appeal and even when the court agrees with the defendant's position, it may decide that the defendant should remain in prison or otherwise receive the same sentence. In such an instance, the appellate court is saying that the trial court's decision is a **harmless error**: a mistake at the trial level that has little practical consequence in terms of deciding whether the defendant is guilty or innocent.

Constitutional versus Nonconstitutional Errors

Deciding what constitutes harmless error requires first determining what type of error is alleged. Two types of errors can be discerned: (1) constitutional and (2) nonconstitutional. *Constitutional errors* result from constitutional rights violations, such as denying the accused the right to confront adverse witnesses at trial. *Nonconstitutional errors* do not have constitutional implications. An example of a nonconstitutional error is a trial court's decision to admit hearsay evidence; there is no constitutional prohibition against hearsay evidence in the courtroom.

■ *Kotteakos v. United States,* 328 U.S. 750 (1946)

■ *Chapman v. California,* 386 U.S. 18 (1967)

Once a decision has been made as to the type of harmless error alleged, then the appropriate test for determining whether the error is harmless must be used. Two Supreme Court cases are helpful in this regard. The first, *Kotteakos v. United States* (328 U.S. 750 [1946]), set the test for deciding what constitutes a nonconstitutional error. The second case, *Chapman v. California* (386 U.S. 18 [1967]), set the test for constitutional error.

In *Kotteakos,* the Supreme Court held that a nonconstitutional harmless error occurs when it does not influence the jury but instead has a "very slight effect" on the outcome of the trial. In other words, "[I]f one cannot say, with fair assurance, after pondering all that happened without stripping the erroneous action from the whole, that the judgment was not substantially swayed by the error, it is impossible to conclude that substantial rights were not affected" (p. 765).

In *Chapman v. California,* discussed earlier, the Court concluded that the test for a constitutional harmless error is requiring the state to prove "beyond a reasonable doubt that the error complained of did not contribute to the verdict obtained" (p. 24). This test is reserved for what could be termed *modest* violations of constitutional rights. However, in situations in which a fundamental constitutional right has been violated, no harmless error test is required. Each scenario is considered in the next two subsections.

A Review of Relevant Cases

Since this book is geared toward constitutional criminal procedure, this section considers only cases in which the Supreme Court has applied the so-called *Chapman* test for determining constitutional harmless error. First, two cases are considered in which the Court held that the error *was not* harmless, and then one case is considered in which the Court held that the error *was* harmless.

In *Chapman v. California,* the Court considered whether a harmless error resulted when the prosecutor's closing argument repeatedly referred to the defendant's refusal to take the stand and testify. (As discussed earlier in this text, a jury cannot draw adverse inferences from a defendant's refusal to testify.) The Court reversed the defendant's conviction, reasoning that "though the case in which this occurred presented a reasonably strong 'circumstantial web of evidence' against petitioners, it was also a case in which, absent the constitutionally forbidden comments, honest fair-minded jurors might very well have brought in not-guilty verdicts" (pp. 25–26).

Similarly, in *Connecticut v. Johnson* (460 U.S. 73 [1983]), the Court refused to conclude that the judge's flawed instructions to the jury could be considered harmless. In that case, the judge instructed the jury that it could presume intent on the part of the defendant for a specific intent crime (i.e., a crime that requires the state to prove a specific type of intent). This error was considered so serious that, according to the Court, it "permitted the jury to convict respondent without ever examining the evidence concerning an element of the crime charged" (p. 88).

By contrast, an example of a harmless error can be seen in *Milton v. Wainwright* (407 U.S. 371 [1972]). There, the defendant claimed that his confession should not have been admissible because it was obtained following a conversation with an undercover police officer who was posing as the defendant's fellow prisoner. The prosecution was able to prove beyond a reasonable doubt that the confession did not constitute error because three other confessions made by the defendant were admissible. In other words, the Court concluded that the confession resulting from the prison conversation was a harmless error.

DECISION MAKING EXERCISE 15.7

A Harmless Error?

At Pat Warren's trial on charges of kidnapping and transporting women across state lines for immoral purposes, the victims testified that he repeatedly raped and sodomized them. The defense attorney argued that the women consented and that they had possibly misidentified Warren. Warren did not testify. During the prosecutor's closing argument, the defense attorney objected when the prosecutor began to comment on the fact that Warren never challenged the kidnapping, the interstate transportation of the victims, or the sexual acts. The defense then moved for a mistrial, claiming that Warren's Fifth Amendment protection against self-incrimination was violated when the prosecutor said what he did to the jury. How should the appellate court decide?

Serious Constitutional Error

In some cases, the Supreme Court has concluded that an error was so serious as to require automatic reversal of the defendant's conviction. In such a case, the prosecution is not required to prove beyond a reasonable doubt that the error is harmless. Instead, the error is automatically presumed to be harmful because of its serious nature. In fact, in *Chapman v. California*, the Court concluded that some errors may involve "rights so basic to a fair trial that their infraction can never be treated as harmless error" (p. 23).

The Court has stated that serious constitutional errors—those that cannot be considered harmless—arise in the following specific circumstances:

1. The defendant's confession was coerced (*Payne v. Arkansas*, 356 U.S. 560 [1958]).
2. The right to counsel at trial was violated (*Gideon v. Wainwright*, 372 U.S. 335 [1963]).
3. The right to an impartial judge was violated (*Tumey v. Ohio*, 273 U.S. 510 [1927]).
4. The right to a speedy trial was violated (*Strunk v. United States*, 412 U.S. 434 [1973]).
5. The defendant was put in double jeopardy (*Price v. Georgia*, 398 U.S. 323 [1970]).
6. The right to a representative jury was violated (*Taylor v. Louisiana*, 419 U.S. 522 [1975]).

▪ Retroactivity of Decisions from Appeals

A successful appeal clearly benefits the party who filed it. But what about third parties? In particular, should third parties who have been convicted be allowed to benefit from a successful appeal by another defendant? This question has been posed because at times, several defendants are filing similar appeals. The Supreme Court has been forced to decide to what extent its decision on one defendant's appeal should apply only to that person or have a more sweeping effect and benefit several defendants. This issue, **retroactivity**, is concerned with the extent to which a decision should be applied to each defendant in a similar predicament.

On one level, it seems fair to treat all defendants with similar appeals the same. However, the consequences of doing so could be enormous. Multiple reversals, for example, could require many new trials for several defendants, imposing a serious cost on the justice system. In light of this concern, the Court has handed down several important decisions. First, in *Linkletter v. Walker* (381 U.S. 618 [1965]), the Court held that whether a constitutional ruling on a defendant's appeal should be considered retroactive depends on the nature of the appeal. Next, in *United States v. Johnson* (457 U.S. 537 [1982]), the Court held that retroactivity depends on the *timing* of all appeals in question; in other words, all defendants who have appeals on file at the same time should benefit.

▪ *Stovall v. Denno,*
388 U.S. 293 (1967)

Third, in *Stovall v. Denno* (388 U.S. 293 [1967]), the Court handed down a specific test for determining whether a decision of constitutional magnitude should be retroactive. It requires determining "(a) the purpose to be served by the new standards, (b) the extent of the reliance by law enforcement authorities on the old standards, and (c) the effect on the administration of justice of a retroactive application of the new standards" (p. 297). This has come to be known as the *Linkletter-Stovall test,* and an example of it in application can be found in the *Stovall* case itself. There, the Court considered whether its decision in *United States v. Wade* (388 U.S. 218 [1967]), which required counsel at postindictment, pretrial lineups, should be retroactive to other defendants appealing violations of that decision. Surprisingly, the Court held that *Wade* should *not* be retroactive because even though such a decision would benefit certain defendants, it would mean that lineups could be challenged on due process grounds. In other words, according to the second element of the *Linkletter-Stovall* test, law enforcement was not heavily reliant on the *Wade* decision; lineups are governed by other constitutional provisions.

The Supreme Court also felt that making *Wade* retroactive would bog down the courts with many new trials, which corresponds to the third element of the *Linkletter-Stovall* test. Finally, the Court felt that the purpose of *Wade* was to ensure fairness at lineups, but it also felt that its decision was not *necessary* to ensure fairness; that is, a fair lineup can be held without the assistance of counsel. In short, the Court felt that its decision in *Wade* did not serve a purpose quite as lofty as, say, guaranteeing the right to counsel at trial, was not heavily relied on by the police, and would have a significant impact on the administration of justice if applied retroactively.

The Supreme Court has also refused to apply its decisions retroactively in other important cases already discussed in this text, including but not limited to *Mapp v. Ohio* (367 U.S. 643 [1961]), which requires that the exclusionary rule be recognized by the states, and *Katz v. United States* (389 U.S. 347 [1967]), which prohibits nonconsensual electronic eavesdropping without probable cause and a warrant. By contrast, the Court *has* held that the failure to provide counsel in misdemeanor trials (see *Berry v. Cincinnati,* 414 U.S. 29 [1973]) and also to require unanimous verdicts in six-member juries (see *Brown v. Louisiana,* 447 U.S. 323 [1980]), among other errors, *should* be retroactive.

In *Griffith v. Kentucky* (479 U.S. 314 [1987]), the Supreme Court finally clarified retroactivity in the appeals context. There, it held that any new rule it announces (i.e., one that does not involve applying precedent to a particular situation) should be retroactive to all other cases pending review at the time. The reasoning offered by the Court in this case was far more straightforward and sensible than that applied in *Linkletter, Johnson,* and

Stovall: Failure to apply new constitutional decisions retroactively to other pending appeals would have the unfair consequence of benefiting the one individual whose appeal was selected for review by the Supreme Court. In other words, failure to retroactively apply new rules would be "unfair," because it would benefit only one individual, not others similarly situated.

It is important to note that *Griffith* applied to cases "pending review at that time." Contrast that with final judgments. Final judgments are those in which "a judgment of conviction has been rendered, the availability of appeal exhausted, and the time for a petition for *certiorari* elapsed or a petition for *certiorari* finally denied" (*Griffith*, p. 321). In contrast, pending review means that an appeal has not yet been heard. Why should retroactivity not apply to final judgments? There are two answers. One is that *habeas corpus* petitions can be filed (the topic of the next section). Another is that allowing new rules to be retroactive to final judgments opens the proverbial can of worms. Justice Harlan expressed this point eloquently in *Mackey v. United States* (401 U.S. 667 [1971], p. 690):

> It is, I believe, a matter of fundamental import that there be a visible end to the litigable aspect of the criminal process. Finality in the criminal law is an end which must always be kept in plain view.

HABEAS CORPUS

As already noted in this chapter, the most common method of challenging one's conviction is to appeal. However, filing an appeal or several appeals is not the only avenue of redress for a person who is wrongfully convicted. Another avenue is by means of a **habeas corpus** petition filed with the federal courts. This is known as a *collateral attack* and is a constitutional right.[4]

Habeas corpus plays out as follows: First, the accused individual petitions one of the federal district courts and asks the court to issue a *writ of habeas corpus*, which literally means "you have the body." Portions of an actual petition for *habeas corpus* form, from the U.S. District Court for the Southern District of California, are reprinted in Figure 15.4 (pages 456–460). Then, if the court decides to issue the writ, the petitioner is brought before the court so the constitutionality of his or her confinement can be reviewed.

Given that the Supreme Court hears a limited number of cases each term, it is unlikely that it will issue a writ. This leaves the defendant with the option of petitioning the federal district court. Also, it is important to remember that a *habeas corpus* petition must be limited to a constitutional claim. Finally, it is totally within the discretion of the court that is petitioned to decide whether the writ will be issued. The Constitution provides that the "privilege of the Writ of Habeas Corpus shall not be suspended," but this has been interpreted to mean that a defendant can *submit habeas petitions*, not that the defendant will necessarily get his or her day in court.

On several occasions, the Supreme Court has emphasized the importance of the writ. For example, in *Sanders v. United States* (373 U.S. 1 [1963]), the Court emphasized that "[c]onventional notions of finality of litigation have no place where life or liberty is at stake and infringement of constitutional rights is alleged" (p. 8). Similarly, in *Kaufman v. United States* (394 U.S. 217 [1969]), the Court held that the writ is necessary to provide "adequate protection of constitutional rights" (p. 226).

However, more recently, the Court has intimated that a *habeas corpus* review should be qualified. In particular, it has held that writs should not be liberally issued for claims arising from state courts. As the Court stated in *Stone v. Powell* (428 U.S. 465 [1976]), "Despite differences in institutional environment and the unsympathetic attitude to

■ *Sanders v. United States*, 373 U.S. 1 (1963)

■ *Stone v. Powell*, 428 U.S. 465 (1976)

[4]See the U.S. Constitution, art. 1, sect. 9, cl. 2.

federal constitutional claims of some state judges in years past, we are unwilling to assume that there now exists a general lack of appropriate sensitivity to constitutional rights in the trial and appellate courts of the several States" (p. 494, n. 35).

These conflicting perspectives have influenced a number of important Supreme Court cases addressing the constitutional right to *habeas corpus*. Recently, the Court has placed limitations on the scope of the writ. Also, the Antiterrorism and Effective Death Penalty Act of 1996 has had important effects on *habeas corpus*. The following sections focus on some of these restrictions and modifications.

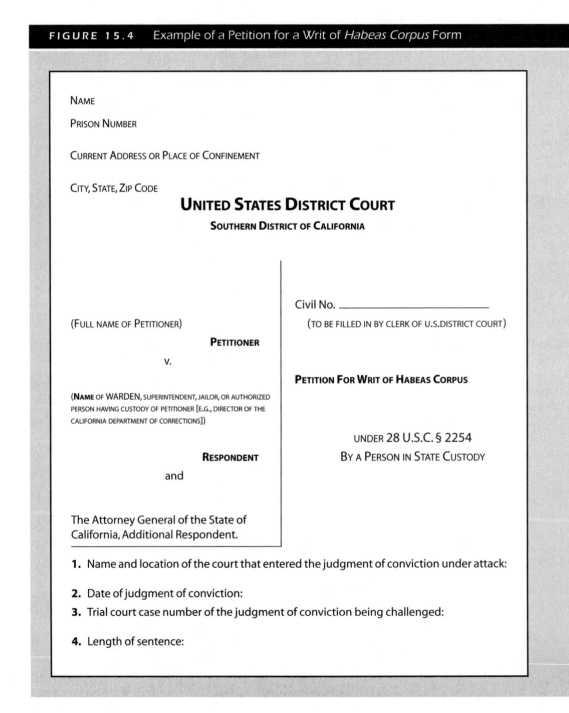

FIGURE 15.4 Example of a Petition for a Writ of *Habeas Corpus* Form

NAME

PRISON NUMBER

CURRENT ADDRESS OR PLACE OF CONFINEMENT

CITY, STATE, ZIP CODE

UNITED STATES DISTRICT COURT
SOUTHERN DISTRICT OF CALIFORNIA

Civil No. _____

(FULL NAME OF PETITIONER)   (TO BE FILLED IN BY CLERK OF U.S. DISTRICT COURT)

PETITIONER

v.

PETITION FOR WRIT OF HABEAS CORPUS

(**NAME** OF WARDEN, SUPERINTENDENT, JAILOR, OR AUTHORIZED PERSON HAVING CUSTODY OF PETITIONER [E.G., DIRECTOR OF THE CALIFORNIA DEPARTMENT OF CORRECTIONS])

RESPONDENT

and

UNDER 28 U.S.C. § 2254
BY A PERSON IN STATE CUSTODY

The Attorney General of the State of California, Additional Respondent.

1. Name and location of the court that entered the judgment of conviction under attack:

2. Date of judgment of conviction:

3. Trial court case number of the judgment of conviction being challenged:

4. Length of sentence:

Restrictions on the Right to *Habeas Corpus*

The Supreme Court has restricted the right to *habeas corpus* in a number of ways. First, it has limited the types of claims that can succeed. Second, the Court has held that *habeas* review may not be granted if the petitioner fails to submit a claim within the time frame specified by state law. Third, it is generally necessary for a convicted individual to exhaust all state remedies before a federal *habeas* review will be granted. Finally, restrictions have been imposed in situations in which a prisoner filed multiple *habeas* petitions.

---

5. Sentence start date and projected release date:

6. Offense(s) for which you were convicted or pleaded guilty (all counts):

7. What was your plea? (CHECK ONE)

   (a) Not guilty   ☐

   (b) Guilty   ☐

   (c) Nolo contendere   ☐

8. If you pleaded not guilty, what kind of trial did you have? (CHECK ONE)

   (a) Jury   ☐

   (b) Judge only   ☐

9. Did you testify at the trial?

   ☐ Yes   ☐ No

DIRECT APPEAL

10. Did you appeal from the judgment of conviction in the **California Court of Appeal?**

   ☐ Yes   ☐ No

11. If you appealed in the California Court of Appeal, answer the following:

   (a) Result:

   (b) Date of result, case number and citation, if known:

   (c) Grounds raised on direct appeal:

12. If you sought further direct review of the decision on appeal by the California Supreme Court (e.g., a Petition for Review), please answer the following:

   (a) Result:

   (b) Date of result, case number and citation, if known:

   (c) Grounds raised:

(continued)

Types of Claims for Which Writs Will Not Be Issued

Five types of *habeas corpus* petitions will not succeed, according to the Supreme Court. The first was announced in *Stone v. Powell*, discussed earlier. In that case, the Court held that "where the State has provided an opportunity for full and fair litigation of a Fourth Amendment claim," a federal court should not issue a writ of *habeas corpus.* Unfortunately, the Court has not been entirely clear as to how this first rule should be applied. For example, in *Jackson v. Virginia* (443 U.S. 307 [1979]), the Court granted *habeas* review of a claim alleging that the defendant's conviction was not based on proof beyond a reasonable doubt—mainly because it was not a Fourth Amendment claim. However, in *Kimmelman*

FIGURE 15.4 Continued

13. If you filed a petition for certiorari in the United States Supreme Court, please answer the following with respect to that petition:

(a) Result:

(b) Date of result, case number and citation, if known:

(c) Grounds raised:

COLLATERAL REVIEW IN STATE COURT

14. Other than a direct appeal from the judgment of conviction and sentence, have you previously filed any petitions, applications, or motions (e.g., a Petition for Writ of *Habeas Corpus*) with respect to this judgment in the **California Superior Court?**

☐ Yes   ☐ No

15. If your answer to #14 was "Yes," give the following information:

(a) **California Superior Court** Case Number:

(b) Nature of proceeding:

(c) Grounds raised:

(d) Did you receive an evidentiary hearing on your petition, application or motion?
☐ Yes   ☐ No

(e) Result:

(f) Date of result:

16. Other than a direct appeal from the judgment of conviction and sentence, have you previously filed any petitions, applications, or motions (e.g., a Petition for Writ of *Habeas Corpus*) with respect to this judgment in the **California Court of Appeal?**

☐ Yes   ☐ No

v. Morrison (477 U.S. 365 [1986]), the Court did grant review of a Sixth Amendment claim of ineffective assistance of counsel.

Second, the Court held in *Teague v. Lane* (489 U.S. 288 [1989]) that unless a claim is dictated by precedent, it cannot be heard on *habeas* review. In other words, if *habeas* review would result in a new rule, then review is impermissible. Only claims based on existing case law should be granted review. The Court did announce two exceptions to this rule, however. If the claim questions the jurisdiction of the trial court or is central to the accused's guilt or innocence, then it can be granted review in federal court.

■ *Teague v. Lane*, 489 U.S. 288 (1989)

---

17. If your answer to #16 was "Yes," give the following information:

(a) **California Court of Appeal** Case Number:

(b) Nature of proceeding:

(c) Grounds raised:

(d) Did you receive an evidentiary hearing on your petition, application or motion?
☐ Yes   ☐ No

(e) Result:

(f) Date of result:

18. Other than a direct appeal from the judgment of conviction and sentence, have you previously filed any petitions, applications, or motions (e.g., a Petition for Writ of *Habeas Corpus*) with respect to this judgment in the **California Supreme Court?**
☐ Yes   ☐ No

19. If your answer to #18 was "Yes," give the following information:

(a) **California Supreme Court** Case Number:

(b) Nature of proceeding:

(c) Grounds raised:

(d) Did you receive an evidentiary hearing on your petition, application or motion?
☐ Yes   ☐ No

(e) Result:

(f) Date of result:

(continued)

■ *Herrera v. Collins,* 506 U.S. 390 (1993)

Next, *habeas* review will only be granted if it raises a federal constitutional question. In other words, review will only be granted to cases in much the same way the Supreme Court decides to hear a case: It must raise a constitutional question. This ruling was applied in *Herrera v. Collins* (506 U.S. 390 [1993]), in which the petitioner claimed that his death sentence should be vacated because new evidence pointed to his innocence. The Court held that the claim could not be heard on *habeas* review because it did not raise a constitutional question. The Court explained that "[i]n light of the historical availability of new trials . . . and the contemporary practice in the States, we cannot say that Texas' refusal to entertain petitioner's newly discovered evidence eight years after his convictions transgresses a principle of fundamental fairness" (p. 411).

FIGURE 15.4 Continued

20. If you did *not* file a petition, application or motion (e.g., a Petition for Review or a Petition for Writ of *Habeas Corpus*) with the **California Supreme Court,** containing the grounds raised in this federal Petition, explain briefly why you did not:

COLLATERAL REVIEW IN FEDERAL COURT

21. Is this your **first** federal petition for writ of *habeas corpus* challenging this conviction?

☐ Yes   ☐ No   (IF "YES" SKIP TO #22)

(a) If no, in what federal court was the prior action filed?

    (i)   What was the prior case number?

    (ii) Was the prior action (CHECK ONE):

        ☐ Denied on the merits?

        ☐ Dismissed for procedural reasons?

    (iii) Date of decision:

(b) Were any of the issues in this current petition also raised in the prior federal petition?

    ☐ Yes   ☐ No

(c) If the prior case was denied on the merits, has the Ninth Circuit Court of Appeals given you permission to file this second or successive petition?

    ☐ Yes   ☐ No

CAUTION:

☐ **Exhaustion of State Court Remedies:** In order to proceed in federal court you must ordinarily first exhaust your state court remedies as to each ground on which you request action by the federal court. This means that even if you have exhausted some grounds by raising them before the California Supreme Court, you must first present **all** other grounds to the California Supreme Court before raising them in your federal Petition.

☐ **Single Petition:** If you fail to set forth all grounds in this Petition challenging a specific judgment, you may be barred from presenting additional grounds challenging the same judgment at a later date.

☐ **Factual Specificity:** You must state facts, not conclusions, in support of your grounds. For example, if you are claiming incompetence of counsel you must state facts specifically setting forth what your attorney did or failed to do. A rule of thumb to follow is — state who did exactly what to violate your federal constitutional rights at what time or place.

Source: Used courtesy of U.S. District Court, Southern District of California.

A Constitutional Question?

Ling Yu was convicted of first-degree murder and sentenced to death. The evidence against her consisted of the body of the victim, the murder weapon, and testimony from several witnesses that Yu spoke openly about wanting to kill the victim. Three years after her conviction, while she was awaiting execution on death row, new evidence was discovered, suggesting that Yu may not have committed the murder. The new evidence came in the form of a witness who was prepared to testify that Yu was with her in a different city on the night of the murder. Assume that Yu exhausts all state-level appellate mechanisms, to no avail, and decides to petition a federal district court for a writ of *habeas corpus*. Will her petition be heard?

A *habeas corpus* review will sometimes be granted to a nonconstitutional claim but not if it fails to point to "an omission inconsistent with the rudimentary demands of fair procedure." That was the Court's decision in *Hill v. United States* (368 U.S. 424 [1962]). This is therefore the fourth limitation on *habeas* review; a nonconstitutional claim that does not allege that a fundamental defect took place at trial will not succeed. Admittedly, this ruling is something of a double negative, but it is stated in this fashion deliberately. That is, the ruling is intended to emphasize that nonconstitutional claims rarely succeed. The ones that *do* succeed must argue that a serious miscarriage of justice took place at trial.

■ *Hill v. United States,*
368 U.S. 424 (1962)

The fifth type of petition that will not be granted review is similar, in several respects, to the one just described. It is the *harmless error exception*—the same one encountered in the previous discussion of appeals. Recall that the appropriate test for determining whether a constitutional error is harmless is whether it is "harmless beyond a reasonable doubt" (*Chapman v. California*, 386 U.S. 18 [1967]). By contrast, the test for nonconstitutional error is whether it has a "substantial and injurious effect or influence in determining the jury's verdict" (*Kotteakos v. United States*, 328 U.S. 750 [1946]). The Court has since held that the test announced in *Kotteakos* should be applied to *habeas corpus* petitions, as well. Such was the decision reached in *Brecht v. Abrahamson* (507 U.S. 619 [1993]).

Restrictions Based on the Timing of a Claim

A *habeas corpus* petition typically must be filed within a certain specified time period after the trial or sentencing hearing. When a defendant fails to appeal or file a *habeas* petition within that period, he or she is said to have *defaulted*, or given up the right to appeal or to petition for *habeas* review. For a time, when the Supreme Court was trying to decide whether *habeas* review should be granted following default, it focused on the state rule or statute that imposed the time restriction (see, e.g., *Daniels v. Allen*, 344 U.S. 443 [1953]). If the statute was problematic, then review could be granted. Not satisfied with this approach, the Court then turned its attention to whether the defendant's default was intentional or accidental (*Fay v. Noia*, 372 U.S. 391 [1963]). Later cases required the defendant to demonstrate why a lack of *habeas* review, due to default, would be prejudicial to his or her case (e.g., *Davis v. United States*, 411 U.S. 233 [1973]).

The current standard for determining whether *habeas* review should be granted is known as the *actual innocence standard*. It was first referenced in *Murray v. Carrier* (477 U.S. 478 [1986]) and then again in *Sawyer v. Whitley* (505 U.S. 333 [1992]). In *Kuhlmann v. Wilson* (477 U.S. 436 [1986]), the Court set a specific standard: "[T]he prisoner must show a fair probability that, in light of all the evidence, including that alleged to have been illegally admitted (but with due regard to any unreliability of it) and evidence tenably claimed to have been wrongly excluded or to have become available only after the

■ *Kuhlmann v. Wilson,*
477 U.S. 436 (1986)

trial, the trier of the facts would have entertained a reasonable doubt of his guilt" (p. 454, n. 17). In other words, when a prisoner has failed to file a *habeas* petition in a timely manner, he or she may still succeed in doing so provided that the petition sets forth sufficient facts as to his or her actual innocence.

Importantly, the appropriate standard of proof for granting review under this new rule is that there be a *fair probability* of the prisoner's innocence (see *Kuhlmann v. Wilson*). A different standard has been imposed in death penalty cases, however. Specifically, in *Schlup v. Delo* (513 U.S. 298 [1995]), the Court held that in order to be granted a *habeas* review, an individual convicted of a capital crime must show that "it is more likely than not that no reasonable juror would have convicted [the petitioner]" (p. 327).

DECISION MAKING EXERCISE 15.9

Timing of a *Habeas Corpus* Petition

A man was convicted of the murder of a fellow prison inmate and sentenced to death. He claimed in a *habeas corpus* petition that a constitutional error had been committed at his trial and thus deprived the jury of critical evidence that would have established his innocence. In particular, he claimed that his defense attorney had acted ineffectively by failing to call witnesses who could testify to his innocence. The district court refused to consider the man's claim, holding that he could not satisfy the threshold showing of actual innocence. Was the district court correct in requiring this?

Summary. When a person is convicted of a crime, he or she is generally given a limited amount of time in which to file an appeal and/or a *habeas corpus* petition. Failure to do so in the required time period is known as *default*. In almost all cases, once a convicted individual has defaulted, he or she has no other means by which to challenge conviction. However, the Supreme Court has held that when a *habeas* petition goes to a prisoner's innocence and he or she can show a fair probability of innocence, review can be granted. (See the Appeals section for similar restrictions on appeals.) The higher standard of "more likely than not" is required for death penalty *habeas* petitions.

Importance of Exhausting State Remedies

Before *habeas corpus* becomes an option, a convicted criminal typically must exhaust all available state-level appeals. As the Supreme Court stated in *Ex parte Hawk* (321 U.S. 114 [1944]), "[O]rdinarily an application for habeas corpus by one detained ˙under a state court judgment of conviction will be entertained . . . only after all state remedies available, including all appellate remedies in the state courts and in this Court by appeal or writ of certiorari, have been exhausted" (pp. 116–117).

Most prisoners are denied *habeas* review until they have exhausted state-level remedies because imposing such a restriction ensures that the states can correct federal constitutional violations. However, if a federal court sees fit to grant a *habeas* petition before a prisoner has exhausted all available state-level appeals, that is its prerogative (see *Granberry v. Greer*, 481 U.S. 129 [1987]).

There is even a federal statute addressing *habeas corpus*. It states that *habeas corpus* is not available to state prisoners "unless it appears that the applicant has exhausted the remedies available in the courts of the State, or that there is either an absence of available State corrective process or the existence of circumstances rendering such process ineffective to protect the rights of the prisoner" (28 U.S.C. Section 2254[b]). Unfortunately, the meanings of some of the terms in this statute are not entirely clear. Thus, it is useful to consider the Supreme Court's response to some pertinent questions stemming from Section 2254(b).

First, what is the meaning of *available State corrective process*? The Court answered this question in *Fay v. Noia* (372 U.S. 391 [1963]), in which it held that prisoners must pursue appeals through all state-level appellate courts. Further, it held that prisoners do not necessarily have to appeal all the way to a state supreme court to satisfy the exhaustion requirement. In other words, a prisoner *can* be said to have exhausted state-level remedies even if he or she does not appeal all the way to the state supreme court. However, the Supreme Court has held that a prisoner must pursue direct as well as discretionary appeals (see previous discussion). The case from which this conclusion emerged was *O'Sullivan v. Boerckel* (526 U.S. 838 [1999]).

Section 2254(b) also mentions that state-level remedies must be pursued unless they are ineffective. What is an *ineffective* state-level remedy? In *Duckworth v. Serrano* (454 U.S. 1 [1981]), the Court held that exhaustion is not necessary if there is "no opportunity to obtain redress in state court or if the corrective process is so clearly deficient as to render futile any effort to obtain relief" (p. 3). What does this mean, precisely? For example, if a state prohibits all appeals of criminal cases (which is clearly unlikely), then that state's remedy can be considered ineffective because it is effectively absent.

■ *Fay v. Noia*, 372 U.S. 391 (1963)

DECISION MAKING EXERCISE 15.10

Were All State Remedies Exhausted?

A man was convicted of murder in a trial court and appealed his conviction to the court of appeals, claiming that the trial judge's instructions to the jury were erroneous. The court of appeals affirmed the lower court's ruling. The man then appealed to the state supreme court. It, too, affirmed the man's conviction. He then petitioned the federal district court for a writ of *habeas corpus*, claiming that his constitutional right to due process was violated by the judge's erroneous instructions. He did not, however, raise the due process issue in any of the state-level appeals. Should his petition be heard?

Restrictions on Filing Multiple *Habeas Corpus* Petitions

Prisoners often file several *habeas corpus* petitions. (Arguably, some prisoners do not have much else to do while in custody.) Thus, the issue of filing multiple petitions has come before the Supreme Court more than once. In one of the more important cases, however, *Sanders v. United States* (373 U.S. 1 [1963]), the Court permitted successive petitions in which the same issues were raised. To do so, though, the petitioner must show that he or she was not given a "full or fair" hearing on the petition the first time around or that there has been "an intervening change in the law or some other justification for having failed to raise a crucial point or argument in the prior application" (p. 17). Later, in *Kuhlmann v. Wilson*, the Court held that successive petitions raising the same issues must be supplemented with a "colorable showing of factual innocence" (p. 436) (i.e., a fairly clear indication that the petitioner is possibly innocent).

The Supreme Court has also decided to seriously restrict successive petitions making *different* claims. For instance, if a prisoner accidentally fails to raise a claim the first time around, it will probably not be permitted the second time. Also, a successive petition that raises different issues from the previous one should be dismissed if "the applicant has . . . on the earlier application deliberately withheld the newly asserted ground *or* otherwise abused the writ" (*McCleskey v. Zant*, 499 U.S. 467 [1991], p. 486; see also *Slack v. McDaniel*, 529 U.S. 473 [2000]).

■ When a *Habeas Corpus* Proceeding Resembles a Trial

To reiterate, an appellate court cannot decide issues of fact. Instead, it is to focus on the extent to which proper rules and procedures were followed at the trial court level. If, as indicated earlier, an appellate court was permitted to be a fact-finder, like a trial court, then its decisions would raise double-jeopardy problems. For example, if an appellate court acquitted a defendant because of an improperly obtained confession, then the prosecution's attempt to retry the defendant using other evidence (e.g., eyewitness testimony) would be tantamount to trying the defendant twice for the same crime. By contrast, an appellate court reviewing a *habeas corpus* petition *can* engage in fact-finding under certain limited circumstances. That is, a *habeas* court can effectively become a trial court when reviewing a prisoner's constitutional challenge to his or her confinement.

The leading case in this area is *Townsend v. Sain* (372 U.S. 293 [1963]). In that case, the Supreme Court identified six specific events that can permit a *habeas* court to engage in independent fact-finding. The Court held that a fact-finding hearing should take place on *habeas* review only when

> (1) the merits of the factual dispute were not resolved in the state hearing; (2) the state factual determination is not fairly supported by the record as a whole; (3) the fact-finding procedure employed by the state court was not adequate to afford a full and fair hearing; (4) there is a substantial allegation of newly discovered evidence; (5) material facts were not adequately developed at the state court hearing; or (6) for any reason it appears that the state trier of fact did not afford the habeas applicant a full and fair hearing. (p. 314)

Importantly, a *habeas* court cannot engage in independent fact-finding if the petitioner deliberately bypasses state-level appellate mechanisms (*Keeney v. Tamayo-Reyes*, 504 U.S. 1 [1992]). In other words, the petitioner must exhaust state-level remedies before fact-finding can take place at a *habeas* proceeding. Taken together, *Townsend* and *Keeney* suggest that it is exceedingly difficult for a prisoner to succeed in having his or her guilt or innocence determined on *habeas* review.

The Right to Counsel in the *Habeas Corpus* Context

Earlier in this chapter, it was shown that the Supreme Court has guaranteed the right to counsel in direct appeals of right but not in discretionary appeals. Since *habeas corpus* is purely discretionary, the Supreme Court has held that no right to counsel exists, unless, of course, the prisoner can afford representation (see *Ross v. Moffitt*, 417 U.S. 600 [1974]). The Court has held, however, that federal prisoners have a "constitutional right of access to the courts" (*Bounds v. Smith*, 430 U.S. 817 [1977]).

The Supreme Court has also held that a state cannot prohibit prisoners from helping each other prepare and submit *habeas corpus* petitions (*Johnson v. Avery*, 393 U.S. 483 [1969]). Moreover, the Court has held that an indigent *habeas corpus* petitioner is entitled to a free transcript of his or her trial to assist in preparing the appropriate paperwork (see *Griffin v. Illinois*, 351 U.S. 12 [1956]).

Retroactivity in the *Habeas Corpus* Context

Retroactivity in the *habeas corpus* context is different than it is in the appeals context. Specifically, *habeas corpus* decisions are less often made retroactive than appeals decisions. In *Teague v. Lane* (489 U.S. 288 [1989]), the Court decided that only those appellate decisions that are dictated by precedent should be retroactive; that is, new rules should not be retroactive, unless one of two exceptions is in place.

Before getting to the exceptions, decisions that are *dictated by precedent* are those to which the reviewing court has applied a previous decision. Assume, for example, that a prisoner files a *habeas* petition claiming that he was denied counsel at trial (which is highly unlikely). Relief will almost certainly be granted because precedent (i.e., *Gideon*) requires having counsel at trial. When the reviewing court hands down a new constitutional rule, however, there is no precedent. An example of a new constitutional rule would be that the Sixth Amendment requires counsel to be present at all *pre*-indictment lineups; such a rule is not in place at present.

In *Teague*, the petitioner claimed that *Taylor v. Louisiana*'s (419 U.S. 522 [1975]) requirement that a jury list represent a cross-section of the community should be applied to the jury itself. In essence, the petitioner was asking the Court to hand down a new rule because the Court also held in *Taylor* that the final jury does not need to represent a fair cross-section of the community. The Court found that neither of two exceptions applied to petitioner Teague's claim.

To backtrack, new rules are not retroactive on *habeas corpus* review unless one of two exceptions is in place. First, in *Teague*, the Court held that a new rule should not be retroactive unless it places certain types of private individual conduct "beyond the power of the criminal law-making authority to proscribe" (p. 307). Needless to say, this language is a little cryptic. An example of it in application can be found in *Bousley v. United States* (523 U.S. 614 [1998]). There, the petitioner claimed that his guilty plea was involuntary because it was based on a flawed interpretation of the statute he was charged with violating. Specifically, the petitioner pled guilty to a firearms offense because he was under the impression that the statute prohibited mere *possession* of a firearm when, in fact, it prohibited *active use* of the firearm. The Court held that the claim could be heard because the petitioner was essentially convicted (through a guilty plea) for an act the statute did not define as criminal. In other words, the act in question was one that was "beyond the power of the criminal law-making authority to proscribe" (*Teague*, p. 307).

Second, a "new rule" will not be retroactive to other cases pending review unless it is "implicit in the concept of ordered liberty" (p. 307). To clarify this, the Court stated in *Sawyer v. Smith* (497 U.S. 227 [1990]) that a new rule is "implicit" to "ordered liberty" if it "alter[s] our understanding of the bedrock procedural elements essential to the fairness of a proceeding" (p. 242). The Court has yet to find a new rule that falls under this second exception, and much the same can be said of the first exception. Even so, the Court has cited *Gideon* as a case that would fall under the second exception.

A recent Supreme Court case may shed some additional light on the notion of retroactivity in the *habeas corpus* context. In *Beard v. Banks* (542 U.S. 406 [2004]), the Court decided that its ruling in *Mills v. Maryland* (486 U.S. 367 [1988]), a case dealing with mitigating factors in capital sentencing, was a new one and therefore could not be applied retroactively. The *Mills* rule was one to the effect that the Constitution's Eighth Amendment forbids states from imposing a requirement that the jury *unanimously* identify mitigating factors before such factors could figure into their death penalty decisions. The Court further noted that *Mills* did not meet either of *Teague*'s exceptions, which would have been necessary for the decision to be applied retroactively (see also *Schriro v. Summerlin*, 542 U.S. 348 [2004]).

The Antiterrorism and Effective Death Penalty Act (AEDPA) of 1996

To be sure, the *habeas corpus* process is fairly complex and difficult to understand. It has become even more clouded in light of the **Antiterrorism and Effective Death Penalty Act (AEDPA) of 1996**, which was passed in the wake of the infamous Oklahoma City bombing.

The Oklahoma City bombing was arguably Americans' first real experience with terrorism. Even though it was *domestic* terrorism, as opposed to *international*, this event alerted policymakers to the fact that people can inflict catastrophic damage with relatively crude weaponry. The bombing led to numerous proposals in Congress for how to address terrorism. Early proposals called for drastic, controversial measures designed to curb the new terrorist threat. Several months after the bombing, however, the legislation agreed to by both the House and the Senate was significantly less forceful. It was signed into law by President Clinton in April 1996.

The AEDPA's supporters heralded it as a significant bipartisan achievement that would help root out terrorism. Critics of the new law claimed that it was so "watered

FIGURE 15.5 Overview of the Antiterrorism and Effective Death Penalty Act (AEDPA) of 1996 (Unrelated to *Habeas Corpus*)

Mandatory Victim Restitution

The mandatory victim restitution provisions of the bill require a federal court to impose mandatory restitution, without consideration of the defendant's ability to pay. This applies in any case in which an identifiable victim or victims suffered physical or pecuniary loss from an offense that is a crime of violence, an offense against property (including any offense committed by fraud or deceit), or a crime related to tampering with consumer products. Last year, Judge Maryanne Trump Barry (D. N.J.), chair of the Judicial Conference Committee on Criminal Law, testified before Congress on the issue of mandatory restitution, pointing out that such legislation would replace a flexible system, based on common sense and judicial discretion, with an inflexible, mandatory system that would be extremely expensive to implement.

Closed Circuit Televised Proceedings for Victims of Crime

Another provision in the bill requires a federal trial court, in any criminal trial where the venue is changed from the state in which the case was originally brought and more than 350 miles from the location in which those proceedings originally would have taken place, to order closed circuit televising of the proceedings back to the original location. The televised coverage is to be provided for such persons the court determines have a compelling interest and who are otherwise—because of inconvenience or expense—unable to attend the trial.

The provision takes effect notwithstanding any contrary provision of the Federal Rules of Criminal Procedure, although there is a sunset mechanism. The Judicial Conference may promulgate and issue rules, or amend existing rules, to "effectuate the policy addressed by this section." Upon implementation of such rules, the closed circuit tele-

vision provision ceases to be effective. The cost of such closed circuit proceedings will be paid for by appropriated funds and/or through donations.

Other Provisions

Among other provisions in the bill are those that:

- Create an Alien Terrorist Removal Court composed of five sitting U.S. district judges designated by the Chief Justice;

- Expand the definition of an aggravated felony under which aliens may be deported, and streamline the deportation of criminal aliens after they serve their sentences;

- Create a five-member Commission on the Advancement of Federal Law Enforcement to study criminal law enforcement, the chair of which will be appointed by the Chief Justice;

- Authorize appropriations for the Judiciary of $41 million from the Crime Trust Fund from fiscal year 1997 to FY 2000 to help meet the increased demands for judicial branch activities resulting from enactment of the bill;

- Set compensation for court-appointed attorneys in capital cases at a rate of not more than $125 per hour for in-court and out-of-court time, but also authorize the Judicial Conference to increase the rate of compensation in the future under a "CPI escalator" mechanism;

- Cap fees and expenses paid for investigative and expert services in capital cases at $7,500, but provide for a waiver mechanism whereby such expenses can exceed that cap if the excess payment is certified by the court as necessary to provide fair compensation for services of an unusual character or duration and if the amount of the excess payment is approved by the chief judge of the circuit.

Source: "New Antiterrorism Law Contains Habeas Reform and Victim Restitution," *The Third Branch: The Newsletter of the Federal Courts* (Washington, DC: Administrative Office of the U.S. Courts, April 1996).

down" that it had virtually nothing to do with combating terrorism. To an extent, the critics are correct. One of the most significant components of the AEDPA places restrictions on *habeas corpus* petitions for death row inmates. The reader can draw his or her own conclusion as to the relationship between *habeas corpus* and domestic terrorism. Even so, it is worth considering the AEDPA's effects at this point because it has altered the *habeas corpus* landscape in several unmistakable ways. The AEDPA also goes beyond restricting *habeas corpus*. Figure 15.5 briefly outlines the matters covered by the legislation.

Restrictions on *Habeas Corpus* Petitions Resulting from the AEDPA

The first change to *habeas corpus* procedure resulting from the AEDPA is that review is permitted only when the state-level decision "(1) resulted in a decision that was contrary to, or involved an unreasonable application of, clearly established Federal law, as determined by the Supreme Court of the United States"; or (2) "resulted in a decision that was based on an unreasonable determination of the facts in light of the evidence presented in the State court proceeding" (28 U.S.C. Section 2254[d]). This is in contrast to *Stone v. Powell* (428 U.S. 465 [1976]), cited earlier, in which the Supreme Court held that *habeas* review should not be granted when "the State has provided an opportunity for full and fair litigation of a Fourth Amendment claim" (p. 465). The AEDPA limits this decision (see also *Williams v. Taylor*, 529 U.S. 362 [2000]; *Ramdass v. Angelone*, 530 U.S. 156 [2000]; and *Penry v. Johnson*, 121 S.Ct. 1910 [2001]). This new AEDPA provision was adhered to in *Bell v. Cone* (535 U.S. 685 [2002]).

Second, the AEDPA alters *habeas* review in capital cases (i.e., in which the accused is on death row). The act provides that if a prisoner defaults and fails to submit a petition in a timely fashion, then review will only be granted when his or her failure to file a petition is "(1) the result of State action in violation of the Constitution or laws of the United States"; (2) "the result of the Supreme Court's recognition of a new Federal right that is made retroactively applicable"; or (3) "based on a factual predicate that could not have been discovered through the exercise of due diligence in time to present the claim for State or Federal post-conviction review" (28 U.S.C. Section 2264[a]). These new default rules are significantly more restrictive than those discussed earlier.

The AEDPA also places restrictions on filing successive *habeas corpus* petitions. It states that a "claim presented in a second or successive *habeas corpus* application shall be dismissed" (28 U.S.C. Section 2244[b][1]). Indeed, there has already been one challenge to this part of the legislation, but the Supreme Court held that the new restriction was well within constitutional guidelines (*Felker v. Turpin*, 518 U.S. 651 [1996]).

The AEDPA further restricts filing successive petitions that raise different claims. Specifically, the legislation restricts a prisoner's successive and different claim to one that (1) "relies on a new rule of constitutional law, made retroactive to cases on collateral review by the Supreme Court, that was previously unavailable" or one for which (2) "the factual predicate could not have been discovered previously through the exercise of due diligence" and which "would be sufficient to establish by clear and convincing evidence that, but for constitutional error no reasonable factfinder would have found the applicant guilty of the underlying offense" (28 U.S.C. Section 2244[b][2]). The Court interpreted some of this confusing language in *Tyler v. Cain* (533 U.S. 656 [2001]).

Next, the AEDPA imposes strict filing deadlines for *habeas corpus* petitions. Namely, most *habeas corpus* petitions must be filed within one year from the date of the final state-level appellate judgment. For a death penalty case, the legislation is even more restrictive. It requires that a death row petition be filed within six months from the "final state court affirmance of the conviction and sentence on direct review or the expiration of the time for seeking review" (28 U.S.C. Sections 2244[d][1][A] & 2263). Both restrictions are intended to reduce the opportunities prisoners have to challenge their confinement and, in the case of death row inmates, to speed up execution.

Another AEDPA restriction on *habeas corpus*, though certainly not the last, addresses the *habeas* court's ability to engage in independent fact-finding. The legislation prohibits a *habeas* court from holding hearings to determine questions of fact unless the petitioner can make a showing why it is necessary. The Supreme Court recently interpreted this requirement, making it even more restrictive (see *Williams v. Taylor*, 529 U.S. 420 [2000]).

The AEDPA imposes several other restrictions on *habeas* review that need not be addressed in depth here, although the Supreme Court is starting to address them on a fairly regular basis (see, e.g., *Gonzalez v. Crosby*, 125 S.Ct. 2641 [2005]; *Pace v. DiGuglielmo*, 125 S.Ct. 1807 [2005]; *Rhines v. Weber*, 125 S.Ct. 1528 [2005]; *Pliler v. Ford*, 542 U.S. 225 [2004]; *Woodford v. Garceau*, 538 U.S. 202 [2003]; *Mayle v. Felix*, 125 S.Ct. 2562 [2005]). It is just important to know that the AEDPA has altered *habeas corpus* procedure in a significant way. The implications of the AEDPA have been considered separately from the Supreme Court's decisions on *habeas corpus* because the act relies significantly on previous Court decisions, rather than replaces them. To an extent, then, many of the Supreme Court's *habeas* decisions still stand.

To conclude the *habeas corpus* discussion, it is useful to consider the Supreme Court's opinion in *Sanders v. United States* (373 U.S. 1 [1963]). In that case, Justice Brennan announced the logic underlying *habeas corpus*: "Conventional notions of finality of litigation have no place where life or liberty is at stake and infringement of constitutional rights is alleged. If 'government [is] always [to] be accountable to the judiciary for a man's imprisonment, access to the courts on habeas must not be thus impeded'" (p. 8).

There is a tendency among many criminal justice critics to claim that criminals enjoy too many appeals. And while the Antiterrorism and Effective Death Penalty Act of 1996, not to mention a long line of Supreme Court cases, places significant restrictions on *habeas* review, the appellate and *habeas corpus* processes are still fundamental to the U.S. system of justice. Without them, the potential for mistakes would loom large.

CONCLUSION

The criminal process concludes with sentencing, appeals, and *habeas corpus*. Every convicted criminal needs to be sentenced. A sentence can range from a modest fine or supervised probation to life in prison or even death. Once a defendant has been sentenced, if not before, he or she frequently appeals his or her conviction. Filing an appeal is often followed by filing a *habeas corpus* petition. If the defendant fails in his or her appeals and *habeas corpus* petitions, he or she will be forced to serve out his or her term.

Sentencing in the United States is carried out with one or more of four sentencing objectives in mind: deterrence, incapacitation, retribution, and rehabilitation. If a judge favors rehabilitation, he or she will probably be inclined to hand down a sentence of probation rather than imprisonment. Many judges and criminal justice commentators also believe rehabilitation is possible in a traditional prison environment. The aim of deterrence is to discourage others from committing crime by punishing the offender harshly. Finally, incapacitation and retribution simply remove the offender from society and give him or her what is deserved.

While a judge's goal or objective of punishment may guide his or her sentencing practices, other factors are considered, as well. Some of these factors include, but are not limited to, the crime in question, the defendant's prior record, his or her ties to the community and family, the defendant's employment history, whether he or she was convicted for several different crimes as opposed to one specific crime, the degree of the defendant's cooperation with authorities during the investigative stage, the defendant's mental status, his or her feelings of remorse, if any, and several other pertinent factors.

Death penalty sentencing must be carried out with special care. The preferred method is to have a jury, not a

judge, decide whether death is appropriate and to take into account aggravating and mitigating circumstances (see *Ring v. Arizona*, 122 S.Ct. 2428 [2002]). The death penalty is inappropriate for young offenders but *is* sometimes appropriate for offenses other than first-degree murder. The Supreme Court has also handed down other important restrictions concerning death penalty sentencing. Excessive punishments can violate the Eighth Amendment's cruel and unusual punishment clause.

Once a sentence has been handed down, the convicted person can appeal. An appeal can also be sought prior to sentencing. This type of appeal is known as an interlocutory appeal. Most jurisdictions favor appeals after final adjudication, but sometimes it is necessary to appeal prior to conviction. An appeal filed prior to adjudication must be unrelated to the cause of action. One filed after adjudication can be any of many varieties. Typically, the defendant is granted one appeal of right. Subsequent appeals are called discretionary appeals. They are discretionary because the appellate court decides if it wants to hear the appeal.

An appeal rarely results in the defendant going free. This point cannot be overemphasized. What happens, in most cases, is one of two things: (1) the appellate court agrees with the trial court, in which case it affirms the lower court's decision; or (2) the appellate court reverses the trial court's decision. A reversal typically results in a new trial for the defendant, or a remand. Sometimes, a trial *de novo* is held at the appellate level, but usually only for a misdemeanor appeal.

The appellate process must be carried out such that the defendant's constitutional rights are respected. According to the Supreme Court, this means that the defendant (1) must have access to the trial transcripts; (2)

must have access to counsel for appeals of right, though not necessarily for discretionary appeals; and (3) must not be retaliated against for exercising his or her right to appeal.

An appeal can also be filed by a party other than the defense, or a third party. For example, the prosecution can appeal the court's decision to exclude evidence. Another party, such as a witness, can appeal a subpoena requiring him or her to show up at court, but only if he or she is held in contempt for failing to appear.

Some appeals, though meritorious, may not succeed according to the harmless error doctrine. When a non-constitutional harmless error occurs, it does not influence the jury but has a very slight effect on the outcome of the trial. By contrast, to show a constitutional error, the state must prove beyond a reasonable doubt that the error did not affect the verdict of the trial. However, in some cases, the Supreme Court has concluded that an error was so serious as to require automatic reversal of the defendant's conviction.

The last appeals issue considered in this chapter was that of retroactivity. To what extent should appellate court decisions benefit other defendants with similar appeals? The case law surrounding the issue of retroactivity is complex and confusing. But in sum, the retroactivity doctrine says that every new constitutional rule announced on direct review must be applied retroactively to other cases pending review that raise the same issue.

Habeas corpus is another method challenging one's conviction. It is also known as a collateral attack. The Supreme Court has restricted the right to *habeas* review in a number of ways. First, it has limited the types of claims that can succeed. Second, the Court has held that a *habeas corpus* review may not be granted if the petitioner fails to submit a claim within the time frame specified by state law. Third, it is generally necessary for a convicted individual to exhaust all state remedies before a federal *habeas* review will be granted. Finally, restrictions have been imposed in situations in which prisoners have filed multiple *habeas* petitions.

A *habeas corpus* proceeding can resemble a criminal trial in certain situations. In particular, a *habeas* court can engage in fact-finding (which is typically the province of the trial court). This is permissible when, for example, a factual dispute was not resolved at the state level or there is a substantial allegation of newly discovered evidence. Other such conditions have also been identified by the Supreme Court.

The Supreme Court has held that prisoners are not strictly entitled to counsel to assist in preparing their *habeas* petitions. They do, however, have constitutional access to the courts. In other words, the right to counsel is virtually nonexistent in the *habeas corpus* process, exists somewhat more so in the appellate process (i.e., mainly for direct appeals), and exists completely at trial.

Retroactivity is rare with regard to *habeas corpus* petitioners. Petitions that *do not* ask the reviewing court to hand down a new rule are retroactive. Those that *do* ask for a new rule are not retroactive unless (1) the new rule is one that involves individual conduct that cannot be prohibited by law or (2) the new rule is closely tied to the fairness of a criminal proceeding.

Finally, the Antiterrorism and Effective Death Penalty Act (AEDPA) of 1996, passed in the wake of the Oklahoma City bombing, places significant restrictions on *habeas corpus*. The act does not completely supplant Supreme Court precedent pertaining to *habeas corpus* because the new restrictions imposed in the act rely heavily on past Supreme Court decisions.

REVIEW QUESTIONS

1. Explain the goals of sentencing.
2. Identify several criteria used in determining the appropriate sentence.
3. What constitutional rights exist during sentencing?
4. What guidelines has the Supreme Court imposed on the appellate process?
5. Summarize the relevant rules governing an appeal before adjudication as well as after.
6. Who else besides the defendant can appeal? For what reasons?
7. Explain the harmless error doctrine.
8. Explain the differences between constitutional and nonconstitutional errors.

9. What is retroactivity? How does it differ in the appeals process versus the *habeas corpus* process?
10. What is *habeas corpus*? From where does this right stem?
11. Summarize four restrictions on *habeas corpus* petitions.
12. When can a *habeas corpus* proceeding resemble a criminal trial?
13. Summarize the right to counsel as it applies (or does not apply) in the *habeas corpus* context.
14. Summarize the leading provisions of the Antiterrorism and Effective Death Penalty Act (AEDPA) of 1996.
15. How does the AEDPA place restrictions on *habeas corpus*?

 Answers to the Decision-Making Exercises for this chapter can be found on pages 523–525.

The Constitution of the United States of America

We the people of the United States, in order to form a more perfect union, establish justice, insure domestic tranquility, provide for the common defense, promote the general welfare, and secure the blessings of liberty to ourselves and our posterity, do ordain and establish this Constitution for the United States of America.

■ Article I

Section 1.

All legislative powers herein granted shall be vested in a Congress of the United States, which shall consist of a Senate and House of Representatives.

Section 2.

The House of Representatives shall be composed of members chosen every second year by the people of the several states, and the electors in each state shall have the qualifications requisite for electors of the most numerous branch of the state legislature.

No person shall be a Representative who shall not have attained to the age of twenty-five years, and been seven years a citizen of the United States, and who shall not, when elected, be an inhabitant of that state in which he shall be chosen.

Representatives and direct taxes shall be apportioned among the several states which may be included within this union, according to their respective numbers, which shall be determined by adding to the whole number of free persons, including those bound to service for a term of years, and excluding Indians not taxed, three-fifths of all other Persons. The actual Enumeration shall be made within three years after the first meeting of the Congress of the United States, and within every subsequent term of ten years, in such manner as they shall by law direct. The number of Representatives shall not exceed one for every thirty thousand, but each state shall have at least one Representative; and until such enumeration shall be made, the state of New Hampshire shall be entitled to choose three, Massachusetts eight, Rhode Island and Providence Plantations one, Connecticut five, New York six, New Jersey four, Pennsylvania eight, Delaware one, Maryland six, Virginia ten, North Carolina five, South Carolina five, and Georgia three.

When vacancies happen in the Representation from any state, the executive authority thereof shall issue writs of election to fill such vacancies.

The House of Representatives shall choose their speaker and other officers; and shall have the sole power of impeachment.

Source: Available online: <www.midnightbeach.com/jon/US-Constitution.htm>. Accessed December 12, 2002.

Section 3.

The Senate of the United States shall be composed of two Senators from each state, chosen by the legislature thereof, for six years; and each Senator shall have one vote.

Immediately after they shall be assembled in consequence of the first election, they shall be divided as equally as may be into three classes. The seats of the Senators of the first class shall be vacated at the expiration of the second year, of the second class at the expiration of the fourth year, and the third class at the expiration of the sixth year, so that one third may be chosen every second year; and if vacancies happen by resignation, or otherwise, during the recess of the legislature of any state, the executive thereof may make temporary appointments until the next meeting of the legislature, which shall then fill such vacancies.

No person shall be a Senator who shall not have attained to the age of thirty years, and been nine years a citizen of the United States and who shall not, when elected, be an inhabitant of that state for which he shall be chosen.

The Vice President of the United States shall be President of the Senate, but shall have no vote, unless they be equally divided.

The Senate shall choose their other officers, and also a President pro tempore, in the absence of the Vice President, or when he shall exercise the office of President of the United States.

The Senate shall have the sole power to try all impeachments. When sitting for that purpose, they shall be on oath or affirmation. When the President of the United States is tried, the Chief Justice shall preside: And no person shall be convicted without the concurrence of two thirds of the members present.

Judgment in cases of impeachment shall not extend further than to removal from office, and disqualification to hold and enjoy any office of honor, trust or profit under the United States: but the party convicted shall nevertheless be liable and subject to indictment, trial, judgment and punishment, according to law.

Section 4.

The times, places and manner of holding elections for Senators and Representatives, shall be prescribed in each state by the legislature thereof; but the Congress may at any time by law make or alter such regulations, except as to the places of choosing Senators.

The Congress shall assemble at least once in every year, and such meeting shall be on the first Monday in December, unless they shall by law appoint a different day.

Section 5.

Each House shall be the judge of the elections, returns and qualifications of its own members, and a majority of each shall constitute a quorum to do business; but a smaller number may adjourn from day to day, and may be authorized to compel the attendance of absent members, in such manner, and under such penalties as each House may provide.

Each House may determine the rules of its proceedings, punish its members for disorderly behavior, and, with the concurrence of two thirds, expel a member.

Each House shall keep a journal of its proceedings, and from time to time publish the same, excepting such parts as may in their judgment require secrecy; and the yeas and nays of the members of either House on any question shall, at the desire of one fifth of those present, be entered on the journal.

Neither House, during the session of Congress, shall, without the consent of the other, adjourn for more than three days, nor to any other place than that in which the two Houses shall be sitting.

Section 6.

The Senators and Representatives shall receive a compensation for their services, to be ascertained by law, and paid out of the treasury of the United States. They shall in all cases, except treason, felony and breach of the peace, be privileged from arrest during their attendance at the session of their respective Houses, and in going to and returning from the same; and for any speech or debate in either House, they shall not be questioned in any other place.

No Senator or Representative shall, during the time for which he was elected, be appointed to any civil office under the authority of the United States, which shall have been created, or the emoluments whereof shall have been increased during such time: and no person holding any office under the United States, shall be a member of either House during his continuance in office.

Section 7.

All bills for raising revenue shall originate in the House of Representatives; but the Senate may propose or concur with amendments as on other Bills.

Every bill which shall have passed the House of Representatives and the Senate, shall, before it become a law, be presented to the President of the United States; if he approve he shall sign it, but if not he shall return it, with his objections to that House in which it shall have originated, who shall enter the objections at large on their journal, and proceed to reconsider it. If after such reconsideration two thirds of that House shall agree to pass the bill, it shall be sent, together with the objections, to the other House, by which it shall likewise be reconsidered, and if approved by two thirds of that House, it shall become a law. But in all such cases the votes of both Houses shall be determined by yeas and nays, and the names of the persons voting for and against the bill shall be entered on the journal of each House respectively. If any bill shall not be returned by the President within ten days (Sundays excepted) after it shall have been presented to him, the same shall be a law, in like manner as if he had signed it, unless the Congress by their adjournment prevent its return, in which case it shall not be a law.

Every order, resolution, or vote to which the concurrence of the Senate and House of Representatives may be necessary (except on a question of adjournment) shall be presented to the President of the United States; and before the same shall take effect, shall be approved by him, or being disapproved by him, shall be repassed by two thirds of the Senate and House of Representatives, according to the rules and limitations prescribed in the case of a bill.

Section 8.

The Congress shall have power to lay and collect taxes, duties, imposts and excises, to pay the debts and provide for the common defense and general welfare of the United States; but all duties, imposts and excises shall be uniform throughout the United States;

To borrow money on the credit of the United States;

To regulate commerce with foreign nations, and among the several states, and with the Indian tribes;

To establish a uniform rule of naturalization, and uniform laws on the subject of bankruptcies throughout the United States;

To coin money, regulate the value thereof, and of foreign coin, and fix the standard of weights and measures;

To provide for the punishment of counterfeiting the securities and current coin of the United States;

To establish post offices and post roads;

To promote the progress of science and useful arts, by securing for limited times to authors and inventors the exclusive right to their respective writings and discoveries;

To constitute tribunals inferior to the Supreme Court;

To define and punish piracies and felonies committed on the high seas, and offenses against the law of nations;

To declare war, grant letters of marque and reprisal, and make rules concerning captures on land and water;

To raise and support armies, but no appropriation of money to that use shall be for a longer term than two years;

To provide and maintain a navy;

To make rules for the government and regulation of the land and naval forces;

To provide for calling forth the militia to execute the laws of the union, suppress insurrections and repel invasions;

To provide for organizing, arming, and disciplining, the militia, and for governing such part of them as may be employed in the service of the United States, reserving to the states respectively, the appointment of the officers, and the authority of training the militia according to the discipline prescribed by Congress;

To exercise exclusive legislation in all cases whatsoever, over such District (not exceeding ten miles square) as may, by cession of particular states, and the acceptance of Congress, become the seat of the government of the United States, and to exercise like authority over all places purchased by the consent of the legislature of the state in which the same shall be, for the erection of forts, magazines, arsenals, dockyards, and other needful buildings;—And

To make all laws which shall be necessary and proper for carrying into execution the foregoing powers, and all other powers vested by this Constitution in the government of the United States, or in any department or officer thereof.

Section 9.

The migration or importation of such persons as any of the states now existing shall think proper to admit, shall not be prohibited by the Congress prior to the year one thousand eight hundred and eight, but a tax or duty may be imposed on such importation, not exceeding ten dollars for each person.

The privilege of the writ of habeas corpus shall not be suspended, unless when in cases of rebellion or invasion the public safety may require it.

No bill of attainder or ex post facto Law shall be passed.

No capitation, or other direct, tax shall be laid, unless in proportion to the census or enumeration herein before directed to be taken.

No tax or duty shall be laid on articles exported from any state.

No preference shall be given by any regulation of commerce or revenue to the ports of one state over those of another: nor shall vessels bound to, or from, one state, be obliged to enter, clear or pay duties in another.

No money shall be drawn from the treasury, but in consequence of appropriations made by law; and a regular statement and account of receipts and expenditures of all public money shall be published from time to time.

No title of nobility shall be granted by the United States: and no person holding any office of profit or trust under them, shall, without the consent of the Congress, accept of any present, emolument, office, or title, of any kind whatever, from any king, prince, or foreign state.

Section 10.

No state shall enter into any treaty, alliance, or confederation; grant letters of marque and reprisal; coin money; emit bills of credit; make anything but gold and silver coin a tender in payment of debts; pass any bill of attainder, ex post facto law, or law impairing the obligation of contracts, or grant any title of nobility.

No state shall, without the consent of the Congress, lay any imposts or duties on imports or exports, except what may be absolutely necessary for executing its inspection laws: and the net produce of all duties and imposts, laid by any state on imports or exports, shall be for the use of the treasury of the United States; and all such laws shall be subject to the revision and control of the Congress.

No state shall, without the consent of Congress, lay any duty of tonnage, keep troops, or ships of war in time of peace, enter into any agreement or compact with another state, or with a foreign power, or engage in war, unless actually invaded, or in such imminent danger as will not admit of delay.

Article II

Section 1.

The executive power shall be vested in a President of the United States of America. He shall hold his office during the term of four years, and, together with the Vice President, chosen for the same term, be elected, as follows:

Each state shall appoint, in such manner as the Legislature thereof may direct, a number of electors, equal to the whole number of Senators and Representatives to which the State may be entitled in the Congress: but no Senator or Representative, or person holding an office of trust or profit under the United States, shall be appointed an elector.

The electors shall meet in their respective states, and vote by ballot for two persons, of whom one at least shall not be an inhabitant of the same state with themselves. And they shall make a list of all the persons voted for, and of the number of votes for each; which list they shall sign and certify, and transmit sealed to the seat of the government of the United States, directed to the President of the Senate. The President of the Senate shall, in the presence of the Senate and House of Representatives, open all the certificates, and the votes shall then be counted. The person having the greatest number of votes shall be the President, if such number be a majority of the whole number of electors appointed; and if there be more than one who have such majority, and have an equal number of votes, then the House of Representatives shall immediately choose by ballot one of them for President; and if no person have a majority, then from the five highest on the list the said House shall in like manner choose the President. But in choosing the President, the votes shall be taken by States, the representation from each state having one vote; A quorum for this purpose shall consist of a member or members from two thirds of the states, and a majority of all the states shall be necessary to a choice. In every case, after the choice of the President, the person having the greatest number of votes of the electors shall be the Vice President. But if there should remain two or more who have equal votes, the Senate shall choose from them by ballot the Vice President.

The Congress may determine the time of choosing the electors, and the day on which they shall give their votes; which day shall be the same throughout the United States.

No person except a natural born citizen, or a citizen of the United States, at the time of the adoption of this Constitution, shall be eligible to the office of President; neither shall any person be eligible to that office who shall not have attained to the age of thirty-five years, and been fourteen Years a resident within the United States.

In case of the removal of the President from office, or of his death, resignation, or inability to discharge the powers and duties of the said office, the same shall devolve on the

Vice President, and the Congress may by law provide for the case of removal, death, resignation or inability, both of the President and Vice President, declaring what officer shall then act as President, and such officer shall act accordingly, until the disability be removed, or a President shall be elected.

The President shall, at stated times, receive for his services, a compensation, which shall neither be increased nor diminished during the period for which he shall have been elected, and he shall not receive within that period any other emolument from the United States, or any of them.

Before he enter on the execution of his office, he shall take the following oath or affirmation:—"I do solemnly swear (or affirm) that I will faithfully execute the office of President of the United States, and will to the best of my ability, preserve, protect and defend the Constitution of the United States."

Section 2.

The President shall be commander in chief of the Army and Navy of the United States, and of the militia of the several states, when called into the actual service of the United States; he may require the opinion, in writing, of the principal officer in each of the executive departments, upon any subject relating to the duties of their respective offices, and he shall have power to grant reprieves and pardons for offenses against the United States, except in cases of impeachment.

He shall have power, by and with the advice and consent of the Senate, to make treaties, provided two thirds of the Senators present concur; and he shall nominate, and by and with the advice and consent of the Senate, shall appoint ambassadors, other public ministers and consuls, judges of the Supreme Court, and all other officers of the United States, whose appointments are not herein otherwise provided for, and which shall be established by law: but the Congress may by law vest the appointment of such inferior officers, as they think proper, in the President alone, in the courts of law, or in the heads of departments.

The President shall have power to fill up all vacancies that may happen during the recess of the Senate, by granting commissions which shall expire at the end of their next session.

Section 3.

He shall from time to time give to the Congress information of the state of the union, and recommend to their consideration such measures as he shall judge necessary and expedient; he may, on extraordinary occasions, convene both Houses, or either of them, and in case of disagreement between them, with respect to the time of adjournment, he may adjourn them to such time as he shall think proper; he shall receive ambassadors and other public ministers; he shall take care that the laws be faithfully executed, and shall commission all the officers of the United States.

Section 4.

The President, Vice President and all civil officers of the United States, shall be removed from office on impeachment for, and conviction of, treason, bribery, or other high crimes and misdemeanors.

Article III

Section 1.

The judicial power of the United States, shall be vested in one Supreme Court, and in such inferior courts as the Congress may from time to time ordain and establish. The judges, both of the supreme and inferior courts, shall hold their offices during good behaviour, and shall, at stated times, receive for their services, a compensation, which shall not be diminished during their continuance in office.

Section 2.

The judicial power shall extend to all cases, in law and equity, arising under this Constitution, the laws of the United States, and treaties made, or which shall be made, under their authority;—to all cases affecting ambassadors, other public ministers and consuls;—to all cases of admiralty and maritime jurisdiction;—to controversies to which the United States shall be a party;—to controversies between two or more states;—between a state and citizens of another state;—between citizens of different states;—between citizens of the same state claiming lands under grants of different states, and between a state, or the citizens thereof, and foreign states, citizens or subjects.

In all cases affecting ambassadors, other public ministers and consuls, and those in which a state shall be party, the Supreme Court shall have original jurisdiction. In all the other cases before mentioned, the Supreme Court shall have appellate jurisdiction, both as to law and fact, with such exceptions, and under such regulations as the Congress shall make.

The trial of all crimes, except in cases of impeachment, shall be by jury; and such trial shall be held in the state where the said crimes shall have been committed; but when not committed within any state, the trial shall be at such place or places as the Congress may by law have directed.

Section 3.

Treason against the United States, shall consist only in levying war against them, or in adhering to their enemies, giving them aid and comfort. No person shall be convicted of treason unless on the testimony of two witnesses to the same overt act, or on confession in open court.

The Congress shall have power to declare the punishment of treason, but no attainder of treason shall work corruption of blood, or forfeiture except during the life of the person attainted.

Article IV

Section 1.

Full faith and credit shall be given in each state to the public acts, records, and judicial proceedings of every other state. And the Congress may by general laws prescribe the manner in which such acts, records, and proceedings shall be proved, and the effect thereof.

Section 2.

The citizens of each state shall be entitled to all privileges and immunities of citizens in the several states.

A person charged in any state with treason, felony, or other crime, who shall flee from justice, and be found in another state, shall on demand of the executive authority of the state from which he fled, be delivered up, to be removed to the state having jurisdiction of the crime.

No person held to service or labor in one state, under the laws thereof, escaping into another, shall, in consequence of any law or regulation therein, be discharged from such service or labor, but shall be delivered up on claim of the party to whom such service or labor may be due.

Section 3.

New states may be admitted by the Congress into this union; but no new states shall be formed or erected within the jurisdiction of any other state; nor any state be formed by the junction of two or more states, or parts of states, without the consent of the legislatures of the states concerned as well as of the Congress.

The Congress shall have power to dispose of and make all needful rules and regulations respecting the territory or other property belonging to the United States; and nothing in this Constitution shall be so construed as to prejudice any claims of the United States, or of any particular state.

Section 4.

The United States shall guarantee to every state in this union a republican form of government, and shall protect each of them against invasion; and on application of the legislature, or of the executive (when the legislature cannot be convened) against domestic violence.

Article V

The Congress, whenever two thirds of both houses shall deem it necessary, shall propose amendments to this Constitution, or, on the application of the legislatures of two thirds of the several states, shall call a convention for proposing amendments, which, in either case, shall be valid to all intents and purposes, as part of this Constitution, when ratified by the legislatures of three fourths of the several states, or by conventions in three fourths thereof, as the one or the other mode of ratification may be proposed by the Congress; provided that no amendment which may be made prior to the year one thousand eight hundred and eight shall in any manner affect the first and fourth clauses in the ninth section of the first article; and that no state, without its consent, shall be deprived of its equal suffrage in the Senate.

Article VI

All debts contracted and engagements entered into, before the adoption of this Constitution, shall be as valid against the United States under this Constitution, as under the Confederation.

This Constitution, and the laws of the United States which shall be made in pursuance thereof; and all treaties made, or which shall be made, under the authority of the United States, shall be the supreme law of the land; and the judges in every state shall be bound thereby, anything in the Constitution or laws of any State to the contrary notwithstanding.

The Senators and Representatives before mentioned, and the members of the several state legislatures, and all executive and judicial officers, both of the United States and of the several states, shall be bound by oath or affirmation, to support this Constitution; but no religious test shall ever be required as a qualification to any office or public trust under the United States.

Article VII

The ratification of the conventions of nine states, shall be sufficient for the establishment of this Constitution between the states so ratifying the same.

Done in convention by the unanimous consent of the states present the seventeenth day of September in the year of our Lord one thousand seven hundred and eighty seven and of the independence of the United States of America the twelfth. In witness whereof We have hereunto subscribed our Names,

G. Washington:	Presidt. and deputy from Virginia
New Hampshire:	John Langdon, Nicholas Gilman
Massachusetts:	Nathaniel Gorham, Rufus King
Connecticut:	Wm. Saml. Johnson, Roger Sherman
New York:	Alexander Hamilton
New Jersey:	Wil. Livingston, David Brearly, Wm. Paterson, Jona. Dayton
Pennsylvania:	B. Franklin, Thomas Mifflin, Robt. Morris, Geo. Clymer, Thos. FitzSimons, Jared Ingersoll, James Wilson, Gouv Morris
Delaware:	Geo. Read, Gunning Bedford jr, John Dickinson, Richard Bassett, Jaco. Broom
Maryland:	James McHenry, Dan of St Thos. Jenifer, Danl Carroll
Virginia:	John Blair, James Madison Jr.
North Carolina:	Wm. Blount, Richd. Dobbs Spaight, Hu Williamson
South Carolina:	J. Rutledge, Charles Cotesworth Pinckney, Charles Pinckney, Pierce Butler
Georgia:	William Few, Abr Baldwin

AMENDMENTS TO THE CONSTITUTION OF THE UNITED STATES

Amendment I (1791)

Congress shall make no law respecting an establishment of religion, or prohibiting the free exercise thereof; or abridging the freedom of speech, or of the press; or the right of the people peaceably to assemble, and to petition the government for a redress of grievances.

Amendment II (1791)

A well regulated militia, being necessary to the security of a free state, the right of the people to keep and bear arms, shall not be infringed.

Amendment III (1791)

No soldier shall, in time of peace be quartered in any house, without the consent of the owner, nor in time of war, but in a manner to be prescribed by law.

Amendment IV (1791)

The right of the people to be secure in their persons, houses, papers, and effects, against unreasonable searches and seizures, shall not be violated, and no warrants shall issue, but upon probable cause, supported by oath or affirmation, and particularly describing the place to be searched, and the persons or things to be seized.

Amendment V (1791)

No person shall be held to answer for a capital, or otherwise infamous crime, unless on a presentment or indictment of a grand jury, except in cases arising in the land or naval forces, or in the militia, when in actual service in time of war or public danger; nor shall any person be subject for the same offense to be twice put in jeopardy of life or limb; nor shall be compelled in any criminal case to be a witness against himself, nor be deprived of life, liberty, or property, without due process of law; nor shall private property be taken for public use, without just compensation.

Amendment VI (1791)

In all criminal prosecutions, the accused shall enjoy the right to a speedy and public trial, by an impartial jury of the state and district wherein the crime shall have been committed, which district shall have been previously ascertained by law, and to be informed of the nature and cause of the accusation; to be confronted with the witnesses against him; to have compulsory process for obtaining witnesses in his favor, and to have the assistance of counsel for his defense.

Amendment VII (1791)

In suits at common law, where the value in controversy shall exceed twenty dollars, the right of trial by jury shall be preserved, and no fact tried by a jury, shall be otherwise reexamined in any court of the United States, than according to the rules of the common law.

Amendment VIII (1791)

Excessive bail shall not be required, nor excessive fines imposed, nor cruel and unusual punishments inflicted.

Amendment IX (1791)

The enumeration in the Constitution, of certain rights, shall not be construed to deny or disparage others retained by the people.

Amendment X (1791)

The powers not delegated to the United States by the Constitution, nor prohibited by it to the states, are reserved to the states respectively, or to the people.

Amendment XI (1798)

The judicial power of the United States shall not be construed to extend to any suit in law or equity, commenced or prosecuted against one of the United States by citizens of another state, or by citizens or subjects of any foreign state.

Amendment XII (1804)

The electors shall meet in their respective states and vote by ballot for President and Vice-President, one of whom, at least, shall not be an inhabitant of the same state with themselves; they shall name in their ballots the person voted for as President, and in distinct ballots the person voted for as Vice-President, and they shall make distinct lists of all persons voted for as President, and of all persons voted for as Vice-President, and of the number of votes for each, which lists they shall sign and certify, and transmit sealed to the seat of the government of the United States, directed to the President of the Senate;—The President of the Senate shall, in the presence of the Senate and House of Representatives, open all the certificates and the votes shall then be counted;—the person having the greatest number of votes for President, shall be the President, if such number be a majority of the whole number of electors appointed; and if no person have such majority, then from the persons having the highest numbers not exceeding three on the list of those voted for as President, the House of Representatives shall choose immediately, by ballot, the President. But in choosing the President, the votes shall be taken by states, the representation from each state having one vote; a quorum for this purpose shall consist of a member or members from two-thirds of the states, and a majority of all the states shall be necessary to a choice. And if the House of Representatives shall not choose a President whenever the right of choice shall devolve upon them, before the fourth day of March next following, then the Vice-President shall act as President, as in the case of the death or other constitutional disability of the President. The person having the greatest number of votes as Vice-President, shall be the Vice-President, if such number be a majority of the whole number of electors appointed, and if no person have a majority, then from the two highest numbers on the list, the Senate shall choose the Vice-President; a quorum for the purpose shall consist of two-thirds of the whole number of Senators, and a majority of the whole number shall be necessary to a choice. But no person constitutionally ineligible to the office of President shall be eligible to that of Vice-President of the United States.

Amendment XIII (1865)

Section 1.

Neither slavery nor involuntary servitude, except as a punishment for crime whereof the party shall have been duly convicted, shall exist within the United States, or any place subject to their jurisdiction.

Section 2.

Congress shall have power to enforce this article by appropriate legislation.

Amendment XIV (1868)

Section 1.

All persons born or naturalized in the United States, and subject to the jurisdiction thereof, are citizens of the United States and of the state wherein they reside. No state shall make or enforce any law which shall abridge the privileges or immunities of citizens of the United States; nor shall any state deprive any person of life, liberty, or property, without due process of law; nor deny to any person within its jurisdiction the equal protection of the laws.

Section 2.

Representatives shall be apportioned among the several states according to their respective numbers, counting the whole number of persons in each state, excluding Indians not taxed. But when the right to vote at any election for the choice of electors for President and Vice President of the United States, Representatives in Congress, the executive and judicial officers of a state, or the members of the legislature thereof, is denied to any of the male inhabitants of such state, being twenty-one years of age, and citizens of the United States, or in any way abridged, except for participation in rebellion, or other crime, the basis of representation therein shall be reduced in the proportion which the number of such male citizens shall bear to the whole number of male citizens twenty-one years of age in such state.

Section 3.

No person shall be a Senator or Representative in Congress, or elector of President and Vice President, or hold any office, civil or military, under the United States, or under any state, who, having previously taken an oath, as a member of Congress, or as an officer of the United States, or as a member of any state legislature, or as an executive or judicial officer of any state, to support the Constitution of the United States, shall have engaged in insurrection or rebellion against the same, or given aid or comfort to the enemies thereof. But Congress may by a vote of two-thirds of each House, remove such disability.

Section 4.

The validity of the public debt of the United States, authorized by law, including debts incurred for payment of pensions and bounties for services in suppressing insurrection or rebellion, shall not be questioned. But neither the United States nor any state shall assume or pay any debt or obligation incurred in aid of insurrection or rebellion against the United States, or any claim for the loss or emancipation of any slave; but all such debts, obligations and claims shall be held illegal and void.

Section 5.

The Congress shall have power to enforce, by appropriate legislation, the provisions of this article.

Amendment XV (1870)

Section 1.

The right of citizens of the United States to vote shall not be denied or abridged by the United States or by any state on account of race, color, or previous condition of servitude.

Section 2.

The Congress shall have power to enforce this article by appropriate legislation.

Amendment XVI (1913)

The Congress shall have power to lay and collect taxes on incomes, from whatever source derived, without apportionment among the several states, and without regard to any census of enumeration.

Amendment XVII (1913)

The Senate of the United States shall be composed of two Senators from each state, elected by the people thereof, for six years; and each Senator shall have one vote. The electors in each state shall have the qualifications requisite for electors of the most numerous branch of the state legislatures.

When vacancies happen in the representation of any state in the Senate, the executive authority of such state shall issue writs of election to fill such vacancies: Provided, that the legislature of any state may empower the executive thereof to make temporary appointments until the people fill the vacancies by election as the legislature may direct.

This amendment shall not be so construed as to affect the election or term of any Senator chosen before it becomes valid as part of the Constitution.

Amendment XVIII (1919)

Section 1.

After one year from the ratification of this article the manufacture, sale, or transportation of intoxicating liquors within, the importation thereof into, or the exportation thereof from the United States and all territory subject to the jurisdiction thereof for beverage purposes is hereby prohibited.

Section 2.

The Congress and the several states shall have concurrent power to enforce this article by appropriate legislation.

Section 3.

This article shall be inoperative unless it shall have been ratified as an amendment to the Constitution by the legislatures of the several states, as provided in the Constitution, within seven years from the date of the submission hereof to the states by the Congress.

Amendment XIX (1920)

The right of citizens of the United States to vote shall not be denied or abridged by the United States or by any state on account of sex.

Congress shall have power to enforce this article by appropriate legislation.

Amendment XX (1933)

Section 1.

The terms of the President and Vice President shall end at noon on the 20th day of January, and the terms of Senators and Representatives at noon on the 3d day of January, of the years in which such terms would have ended if this article had not been ratified; and the terms of their successors shall then begin.

Section 2.

The Congress shall assemble at least once in every year, and such meeting shall begin at noon on the 3d day of January, unless they shall by law appoint a different day.

Section 3.

If, at the time fixed for the beginning of the term of the President, the President elect shall have died, the Vice President elect shall become President. If a President shall not have been chosen before the time fixed for the beginning of his term, or if the President elect shall have failed to qualify, then the Vice President elect shall act as President until a President shall have qualified; and the Congress may by law provide for the case wherein neither a President elect nor a Vice President elect shall have qualified, declaring who shall then act as President, or the manner in which one who is to act shall be selected, and such person shall act accordingly until a President or Vice President shall have qualified.

Section 4.

The Congress may by law provide for the case of the death of any of the persons from whom the House of Representatives may choose a President whenever the right of choice shall have devolved upon them, and for the case of the death of any of the persons from whom the Senate may choose a Vice President whenever the right of choice shall have devolved upon them.

Section 5.

Sections 1 and 2 shall take effect on the 15th day of October following the ratification of this article.

Section 6.

This article shall be inoperative unless it shall have been ratified as an amendment to the Constitution by the legislatures of three-fourths of the several states within seven years from the date of its submission.

Amendment XXI (1933)

Section 1.

The eighteenth article of amendment to the Constitution of the United States is hereby repealed.

Section 2.

The transportation or importation into any state, territory, or possession of the United States for delivery or use therein of intoxicating liquors, in violation of the laws thereof, is hereby prohibited.

Section 3.

This article shall be inoperative unless it shall have been ratified as an amendment to the Constitution by conventions in the several states, as provided in the Constitution, within seven years from the date of the submission hereof to the states by the Congress.

Amendment XXII (1951)

Section 1.

No person shall be elected to the office of the President more than twice, and no person who has held the office of President, or acted as President, for more than two years of a term to which some other person was elected President shall be elected to the office of the President more than once. But this article shall not apply to any person holding the office of President when this article was proposed by the Congress, and shall not prevent any person who may be holding the office of President, or acting as President, during the term within which this article becomes operative from holding the office of President or acting as President during the remainder of such term.

Section 2.

This article shall be inoperative unless it shall have been ratified as an amendment to the Constitution by the legislatures of three-fourths of the several states within seven years from the date of its submission to the states by the Congress.

Amendment XXIII (1961)

Section 1.

The District constituting the seat of government of the United States shall appoint in such manner as the Congress may direct:

A number of electors of President and Vice President equal to the whole number of Senators and Representatives in Congress to which the District would be entitled if it were a state, but in no event more than the least populous state; they shall be in addition to those appointed by the states, but they shall be considered, for the purposes of the election of President and Vice President, to be electors appointed by a state; and they shall meet in the District and perform such duties as provided by the twelfth article of amendment.

Section 2.

The Congress shall have power to enforce this article by appropriate legislation.

■ Amendment XXIV (1964)

Section 1.

The right of citizens of the United States to vote in any primary or other election for President or Vice President, for electors for President or Vice President, or for Senator or Representative in Congress, shall not be denied or abridged by the United States or any state by reason of failure to pay any poll tax or other tax.

Section 2.

The Congress shall have power to enforce this article by appropriate legislation.

■ Amendment XXV (1967)

Section 1.

In case of the removal of the President from office or of his death or resignation, the Vice President shall become President.

Section 2.

Whenever there is a vacancy in the office of the Vice President, the President shall nominate a Vice President who shall take office upon confirmation by a majority vote of both Houses of Congress.

Section 3.

Whenever the President transmits to the President pro tempore of the Senate and the Speaker of the House of Representatives his written declaration that he is unable to discharge the powers and duties of his office, and until he transmits to them a written declaration to the contrary, such powers and duties shall be discharged by the Vice President as Acting President.

Section 4.

Whenever the Vice President and a majority of either the principal officers of the executive departments or of such other body as Congress may by law provide, transmit to the President pro tempore of the Senate and the Speaker of the House of Representatives their written declaration that the President is unable to discharge the powers and duties of his office, the Vice President shall immediately assume the powers and duties of the office as Acting President.

Thereafter, when the President transmits to the President pro tempore of the Senate and the Speaker of the House of Representatives his written declaration that no inability exists, he shall resume the powers and duties of his office unless the Vice President and a majority of either the principal officers of the executive department or of such other body as Congress may by law provide, transmit within four days to the President pro tempore of the Senate and the Speaker of the House of Representatives their written declaration that the President is unable to discharge the powers and duties of his office. Thereupon

Congress shall decide the issue, assembling within forty-eight hours for that purpose if not in session. If the Congress, within twenty-one days after receipt of the latter written declaration, or, if Congress is not in session, within twenty-one days after Congress is required to assemble, determines by two-thirds vote of both Houses that the President is unable to discharge the powers and duties of his office, the Vice President shall continue to discharge the same as Acting President; otherwise, the President shall resume the powers and duties of his office.

Amendment XXVI (1971)

Section 1.

The right of citizens of the United States, who are 18 years of age or older, to vote, shall not be denied or abridged by the United States or any state on account of age.

Section 2.

The Congress shall have the power to enforce this article by appropriate legislation.

Amendment XXVII (1992)

No law varying the compensation for the services of the Senators and Representatives shall take effect until an election of Representatives shall have intervened.

■ CHAPTER 1 Introduction to Criminal Procedure

1.1 The First Amendment and Criminal Procedure In general, no. The First Amendment is not very relevant to criminal procedure because it does not address how criminal justice officials are required to confront, handle, and process criminal suspects. More important, a police officer could easily violate someone's First Amendment rights, but as will be discussed in Chapter 2, unless criminal evidence is somehow obtained when the person's First Amendment rights are violated, very little can be done to remedy such a violation. That is, the police could completely ignore someone's First Amendment rights, but there would be little or no available recourse in the criminal process. Rather, a civil lawsuit would need to be filed (see Chapter 2). The First Amendment matters in criminal procedure only when (1) criminal charges are filed against a person for exercising his or her First Amendment rights or (2) the press is not allowed to attend important court hearings as well as the trial (a point to be addressed later).

1.2 Traditional Legal Doctrine Meets High-Tech Crime The Court of Appeals for the Armed Forces said it should not. That is, the court concluded that "good faith" does not apply in this case because, as is required to assert good faith, there must be reliance on the language of a search warrant. This did not occur because AOL employees compiled the records requested by the agent before the warrant was actually obtained. The reasoning for this will become more clear in Chapter 2 (and the reader is advised to consult the *Maxwell* case for further clarification), but for now, this case illustrates the difficulty in applying existing case law to new search-and-seizure questions. Several other issues were raised in this case, as well, including the expectation of privacy, specificity, plain view, inevitable discovery, and "fruit of the poisonous tree," all of which will be covered in this text, most notably in the Fourth Amendment section (Part II).

1.3 Theory and Reality Collide No. This exercise illustrates the difference between theory and reality. The Supreme Court's decision prohibits the police from interrogating people who are in custody and not advised of their *Miranda* rights. However, a little creative police work can get around the Supreme Court's decision. Since the police did not interrogate the suspect, which is one of the *Miranda* requirements, they did not violate his Fifth Amendment rights. Countless other Supreme Court decisions like *Miranda* may have little or no bearing in reality. And even if such decisions are relevant and influential, the police (and other criminal justice officials) can often bend the rules without breaking them.

1.4 Due Process or Crime Control? Both cases reflect a due process orientation. Indeed, *Miranda* is loathed by many in the law enforcement community because it requires informing suspects of their Fifth Amendment rights. The same holds for *Kyllo*, which prohibits thermal imaging scans without a warrant supported by probable cause. Clearly, this decision places restrictions on what the police can do when investigating crime. Further, it reinforces the importance of people's privacy interests in their homes.

1.5 Due Process or Crime Control? The answer should be fairly clear: Both decisions emphasize crime control because they give greater authority to the police. The Supreme Court basically stated in *Leon* and in *Sheppard* that violations of people's rights are permissible if based on reasonable mistakes. Prior to these decisions, if a police officer violated someone's rights because of a mistake, the court would return a decision in favor of the suspect, not the police. The "good faith" exception to the exclusionary rule changed this. Significantly, both decisions were handed down during the 1980s, a period in which the Supreme Court sided with the law enforcement community in many important decisions (most of which are discussed throughout the remainder of this book).

1.6 Interpreting a Supreme Court Holding The U.S. Supreme Court's reversal in this case has one clear consequence: The search of Smith was not unconstitutional. So, in plain English, the Supreme Court said that what the police did in this case was acceptable. The search of Smith did not violate any constitutional provision because it did not need to be supported by probable cause. Importantly, the Supreme Court's reversal in this hypothetical case was not a reversal of *Smith's conviction.* Rather, it was a reversal of the U.S. Court of Appeals' decision that the search needed to be supported by probable cause. And what is the moral of the story? It is important to pay attention to what issue each individual appellate court is deciding.

1.7 Would the Supreme Court Hear This Case? The answer to the first question is almost certainly no. It is highly unlikely that the U.S. Supreme Court would hear this case, for several reasons. First of all, of the thousands of petitions for a *writ of certiorari* presented to the Court every year, only a handful (some 5 percent) are granted review. This case would not likely be one of them because it does not appear to raise a federal question. Instead, it deals with rules of evidence at the state level. Importantly, the Supreme Court has no jurisdiction over matters of state law—cases based *exclusively* on state laws and constitutions. It is conceivable, however, that if the judge's decision violated due process, the Supreme Court would hear the case. A federal question can arise in state court when a criminal suspect or defendant claims that an action taken by the authorities violated a right protected by the Bill of Rights, as applied to the states through the due process clause of the Fourteenth Amendment. I am not aware, however, of any such case being decided by the nation's highest court. As for the second question, it is possible that the Supreme Court would grant review in this situation. The prosecutor's comment about the defendant's refusal to testify appears to violate the Fifth Amendment's protection against compelled self-incrimination.

1.8 A Bright-Line Rule or Case-by-Case Adjudication? It's somewhat difficult to say. *Garner* is a bright-line decision insofar as the Supreme Court said that deadly force is permissible only under specific circumstances. However, the *Garner* decision is also somewhat vague because it is not always clear what constitutes probable cause in deciding whether the suspect poses a serious threat of death or physical injury. In other words, the probable cause analysis requires looking at the facts and circumstances of each case. The *Garner* decision therefore cannot be easily characterized as bright line or otherwise.

1.9 Subjective or Objective? The answer is *objective* reasonableness. A police officer who is sued can benefit from qualified immunity even for violating someone's clearly established constitutional rights, provided that the officer's mistaken belief is objectively reasonable (see *Anderson v. Creighton*, 483 U.S. 635 [1987], and *Malley v. Briggs*, 475 U.S. 335 [1988]). Had a *subjective* reasonableness test been used, the Supreme Court would have rephrased its *Harlow* decision, stating that qualified immunity will be granted if the individual police officer who is being sued *thinks* he or she did not violate someone's clearly established rights.

1.10 The Issue of Personal Privacy This case appears to decrease personal privacy. One of the reasons that the police are allowed to search a person and his or her grabbing area following an arrest is to promote officer safety. In *Belton*, the Supreme Court authorized a search of the passenger compartment even when safety is no longer an issue. Obviously, a person who is arrested, handcuffed, and placed in a patrol car presents no threat to officer safety, but the Court permitted a search of the passenger compartment regardless. This is clearly a decision that favors law enforcement. Furthermore, it is fairly clear that it erodes personal privacy. This is not surprising, however, because people do not enjoy quite the same expectation of privacy in their cars as they do in their houses. This issue, too, will be revisited in the Fourth Amendment section (particularly Chapter 5).

■ CHAPTER 2 Remedies for Constitutional Violations

2.1 Section 1983 Civil Liability   In *Costa v. Frye* (138 Pa. Commw. 388 [1991]), the case on which this example is based, the plaintiffs' lawsuit against the city did not succeed. Here is what the court said:

> Frye [the real name of the defendant officer] participated in a private argument over the use of a poker machine. The fact that the argument escalated to the point where Frye believed it was necessary to draw his gun does not transform the incident into a police matter. Frye's involvement in the fight and response to violence were not an exercise of some power bestowed upon him by the City. Clearly, Frye's conduct cannot be characterized as actions which were made possible only because Frye was a police officer. The City did not require Frye to carry his gun while off-duty and he did not properly assert any authority as a police officer during the altercation. The evidence presented at trial demonstrates that Frye was engaged in a purely private incident which cannot be fairly attributed to the City. We conclude that Frye was not acting under the color of state law while participating in a barroom brawl. (p. 393)

2.2 Municipal Liability   No. First, no police agency would adopt a formal policy permitting the use of excessive force. Thus, the real issue is the frequency with which events like the one in question have taken place. In fact, the beating was an isolated incident. But even if the plaintiffs could show that this was a common practice, the city would not necessarily be held liable. For that to happen, the practice must have been sanctioned by those high-ranking officials responsible for policymaking. As one court noted, official policy is

> [1] A policy statement, ordinance, regulation, or decision that is officially adopted and promulgated by the municipality's lawmaking officers or by an official to whom the lawmakers have delegated policy-making authority; or [2] A persistent, widespread practice of city officials or employees, which, although not authorized by officially adopted and promulgated policy, is so common and well settled as to constitute a custom that fairly represents municipal policy. Actual or constructive knowledge of such custom must be attributable to the governing body of the municipality or to an official to whom that body had delegated policy-making authority. Actions of officers or employees of a municipality do not render the municipality liable under § 1983 unless they execute official policy as above defined. (*Webster v. Houston*, 735 F.2d 838 [5th Cir. 1984], p. 841)

2.3 Culpability under Section 1983   If you read the section on deliberate indifference carefully, you know that it is not the appropriate standard on which to decide the case. The Supreme Court would apply a "shocks the conscience" standard to a substantive due process claim. In the case on which this example is based, *County of Sacramento v. Lewis* (323 U.S. 833 [1998]), the Court stated that "in the circumstances of a high-speed chase aimed at apprehending a suspected offender, where unforeseen circumstances demand an instant judgment on the part of an officer who feels the pulls of competing obligations, only a purpose to cause harm unrelated to the legitimate object of arrest will satisfy the shocks-the-conscience test" (p. 857). In other words, it is now very difficult to succeed with a Section 1983 lawsuit alleging a violation of substantive due process. Had another amendment been invoked by the plaintiffs, the relevant culpability standards would have been lower.

2.4 The Fourth Amendment and Qualified Immunity   At first, this may seem to be a reasonable decision. But at second glance, after paying special attention to what tests are used to determine Fourth Amendment reasonableness (as well as whether qualified immunity should be granted), a paradox seems evident. The Court basically stated that the officers in this case acted unreasonably with regard to the Fourth Amendment, but because the law in this area was not clearly established, given the limited number of guiding precedents, the officers acted reasonably. Reading between the lines, the Supreme Court sees nothing wrong with declaring certain police conduct to be "reasonably unreasonable."[1]

2.5 Use of Deadly Force   The answer is obviously no. The Supreme Court (not to mention police department policy) expressly forbids shootings of this nature. Interestingly, the facts

[1]See J. L Worrall, "The Reasonably Unreasonable Police Officer: A Paradox in Police Civil Liability Jurisprudence," *Policing* 24 (2001): 449–469.

presented here closely resemble a real-world case, in which a police officer was sued for shooting a suspect in the back during a foot chase in a Louisiana swamp. The events surrounding the shooting were in dispute, but according to the plaintiff, they were exactly as depicted in this exercise. Not in dispute were the facts that (1) the plaintiff, whose real name was Snyder, was shot in the back (and paralyzed from the waste down but not killed) and (2) no weapon belonging to Snyder was ever found at the scene. The Fifth Circuit declared, somewhat surprisingly, "We reverse the portion of the judgment holding the city liable under Section 1983 and render judgment for the city. We affirm the portion of the judgment granting Trepagnier [the defendant officer] qualified immunity and affirm the refusal to find liability for assault and battery" (*Snyder v. Trepagnier*, 142 F.3d 791 [5th Cir. 1998], p. 801). In other words, the officer, Trepagnier, was granted qualified immunity. There was no dispute over whether the Fourth Amendment was violated (and it clearly was), only over the qualified immunity issue. The reader is encouraged to learn more about this case in order to develop an informed opinion about the Fifth Circuit Court's decision. For now, this case illustrates that while the Supreme Court has set clear guidelines with respect to the use of deadly force, qualified immunity can be granted, sometimes weakening the Fourth Amendment's grasp on law enforcement personnel.

2.6 When Does the Exclusionary Rule Not Apply? In the case on which this exercise is based, *One 1958 Plymouth Sedan v. Pennsylvania* (380 U.S. 693 [1965]), the Supreme Court stated, "[W]e hold that the constitutional exclusionary rule *does* apply to such forfeiture proceedings" (p. 696, emphasis added). As the Court reasoned:

> There is nothing even remotely criminal in possessing an automobile. It is only the alleged use to which this particular automobile was put that subjects Mr. McGonigle to its possible loss. And it is conceded here that the Commonwealth could not establish an illegal use without using the evidence resulting from the search which is challenged as having been in violation of the Constitution. Furthermore, the return of the automobile to the owner would not subject him to any possible criminal penalties for possession or frustrate any public policy concerning automobiles. . . . This distinction between what has been described as contraband *per se* and only derivative contraband has indeed been recognized by Pennsylvania itself in its requirement of mandatory forfeiture of illegal liquor, and stills, and only discretionary forfeiture of such things as automobiles illegally used. (p. 699)

2.7 An Act of "Good Faith"? This exercise places something of a twist on the "good faith" exception announced in *Arizona v. Evans* in that it deals with reliance on information provided by other police officers. The Supreme Court has been hesitant to permit a "good faith" defense in such situations. Instead, the Court has favored first determining whether the information that leads to the warrant, and ultimately the police bulletin, withstands Fourth Amendment scrutiny. In *Whiteley v. Warden* (401 U.S. 560 [1971]), the case on which this example is based, the Court held that "[t]he complaint, which did not mention that the sheriff acted on an informer's tip, and which consisted of no more than the sheriff's conclusion that the individuals named committed the offense, could not support the independent judgment of a disinterested magistrate" (p. 560). In other words, all the evidence should have been excluded at trial.

2.8 The Impeachment Exception The T-shirt would be admissible under the impeachment exception to the exclusionary rule. As the Supreme Court noted in *United States v. Havens* (446 U.S. 620 [1980]):

> It is essential . . . to the proper functioning of the adversary system . . . that when a defendant takes the stand, the government be permitted proper and effective cross-examination in an attempt to elicit the truth. (pp. 626–627)

Furthermore,

> We also think that the policies of the exclusionary rule no more bar impeachment here than they did in *Walder, Harris,* and *Hass.* In those cases, the ends of the exclusionary rules were thought adequately implemented by denying the government the use of the challenged evidence to make out its case in chief. The incremental furthering of those ends by forbidding impeachment of the defendant who testifies was deemed insufficient to permit or require that false testimony go unchallenged, with the resulting impairment of the integrity of the factfinding goals of the criminal trial. We reaffirm this assessment of the competing interests,

and hold that a defendant's statements made in response to proper cross-examination reasonably suggested by the defendant's direct examination are subject to otherwise proper impeachment by the government, albeit by evidence that has been illegally obtained and that is inadmissible on the government's direct case, or otherwise, as substantive evidence of guilt. (pp. 627–628)

2.9 The "Purged Taint" Exception The Supreme Court considered a question very much like this in *United States v. Ceccolini* (435 U.S. 268 [1978]). Specifically, it considered whether a *witness* (such as the employee) who was discovered as a result of an illegal search was considered "fruit of the poisonous tree." Significantly, a four-month period elapsed between the illegal search and the questioning of a witness whose identity was discovered because of the illegal search. The Court admitted the witness's testimony because of the "length of the road" between the search and the testimony. A decision to the contrary, according to the Court, would have opened the door to illegal searches designed to discover witnesses who can supply incriminating testimony against criminal defendants:

> Witnesses are not like guns or documents which remain hidden from view until one turns over a sofa or opens a filing cabinet. Witnesses can, and often do, come forward and offer evidence entirely of their own volition. And, evaluated properly, the degree of free will necessary to dissipate the taint will very likely be found more often in the case of live-witness testimony than other kinds of evidence. (pp. 276–277)

2.10 The Independent Source Exception It depends on whether probable cause to obtain a warrant existed prior to and independent of the initial warrantless entry. According to the Supreme Court in *Murray v. United States* (487 U.S. 533 [1988]), the case on which this example is based:

> Although the federal agents' knowledge that marijuana was in the warehouse was assuredly acquired at the time of the unlawful entry, it was also acquired at the time of entry pursuant to the warrant, and if that later acquisition was not the result of the earlier entry, the independent source doctrine allows the admission of testimony as to that knowledge. This same analysis applies to the tangible evidence, the bales of marijuana. . . . The ultimate question is whether the search pursuant to warrant was in fact a genuinely independent source of the information and tangible evidence at issue. This would not have been the case if the agents' decision to seek the warrant was prompted by what they had seen during the initial entry or if information obtained during that entry was presented to the Magistrate and affected his decision to issue the warrant. (p. 533)

Incidentally, this case was remanded to the district court to determine whether the independent source exception should be applied.

■ CHAPTER 3 Introduction to the Fourth Ammendment

3.1 A "Moonlighting" Scenario Generally, private security guards are not restricted by the Fourth Amendment, but this is true only if they act independently of the police (see *United States v. Francoeur*, 547 F.2d 891 [5th Cir. 1977]). Also, the extent to which the private security guard *replaces* the police may be important (see *People v. Mangiefico*, 25 Cal.App.3d 1041 [1972]). Some courts have held that private security guards are constrained by the Fourth Amendment, particularly when they take on quasi–law enforcement functions (*People v. Zelinski*, 155 Cal.Rptr. 575 [1979]). In the present case, however, the fact that Clark is an off-duty police officer is determinative. In the case of *Commonwealth v. Leone* (386 Mass. 329 [1982]), the court ruled that an off-duty police officer "moonlighting" as a security guard was bound by the Fourth Amendment.

3.2 A Private or Government Search? If law enforcement officials become involved in an otherwise private search, then the Fourth Amendment is implicated. For example, had police officers *asked* the meter reader to peer through the window, her actions would have amounted to a search (see *Raymond v. Superior Court*, 19 Cal. App. 3d 321 [1971]). In the present case, the meter reader was acting independently, which is the important factor. She cannot be considered a government actor based on the information presented here. What would happen, though, if the electrical company were owned or tightly regulated by the government? Would the meter reader then be considered a government employee? According to one court, "[M]ere employment by an arm of the government is not enough to make an actor a government agent for purposes of the Fourth Amendment. Rather, the nature of the actor's employment, his specific duties and authority to act for the State and the circumstances of the search are all taken into account in deciding whether a search was 'private' or governmental in nature" (*Commonwealth v. Cote*, 15 Mass. App. Ct. 229 [1983], p. 234).

3.3 The Scope of a Private Search   Yes. The police should have obtained a warrant in this instance because they subjected the dog biscuits to additional scrutiny (see *Walter v. United States*, 447 U.S. 649 [1980]). The biscuits were clearly handed over to the police by a private person, and assuming Olson's girlfriend acted without the knowledge or acquiescence of the police, the Fourth Amendment was not implicated. But when the law enforcement officers subsequently had the biscuits subjected to laboratory analysis, they significantly expanded the scope of the initial search. According to one court:

> No matter how egregious [the searcher's] actions may appear in a society whose fundamental values have historically included individual freedom and privacy, the exclusionary rule cannot be invoked by the defendant to bar the introduction of evidence that was procured by [persons] while acting as private citizens. . . . Similar principles do not, however, govern our review of the evidence-gathering techniques employed by the state. . . . [W]hen the governmental search significantly expands a prior private search . . . the independent governmental search is subject to the proscriptions of the Fourth Amendment. (*State v. Von Bulow*, 475 A.2d 995, 1012, R.I., *cert. denied*, 469 U.S. 875 [1984])

3.4 A "False Friend" Scenario   This is known in some circles as a "false-friend" scenario. Unfortunately for Quinn, his attorney will not succeed in having the statements suppressed. Quinn has no reasonable expectation of privacy in his jail cell conversations because when he conversed with the police officer, he assumed the risk that that individual would betray him. As the Supreme Court observed in *Hoffa v. United States* (385 U.S. 293 [1966]), the defendant "was not relying on the security of the hotel room; he was relying upon his misplaced confidence that [the labor union associate] would not reveal his wrongdoing" (p. 302). Later, in reaffirming the *Hoffa* decision, the Supreme Court stated that a person does not have "a justifiable and constitutionally protected expectation that a person with whom he is conversing will not then or later reveal the conversation to the police" (*United States v. White*, 401 U.S. 745 [1971]).

3.5 Is a Public Street an Open Field?   The answer is almost certainly no, for two reasons: First, the vantage point (the public sidewalk) is one from which the public has access. Second, the ladder cannot be considered an enhancement device. It should be underscored that even after seeing the marijuana plants, Officer Perez cannot then enter the backyard and seize the plants. According to the Supreme Court, "Incontrovertible testimony of the senses that an incriminating object is on the premises belonging to a criminal suspect may establish the fullest possible measure of probable cause. But even where the object is contraband, this Court has repeatedly stated and enforced the basic rule that the police may not enter and make a warrantless seizure" (*Coolidge v. New Hampshire*, 403 U.S. 443 [1971], p. 468). Instead, Officer Perez should use his firsthand observation of the marijuana plants as the basis to apply for a warrant.

3.6 Drug Dogs as Sensory Enhancement Devices   Drug dogs are controversial as so-called sensory enhancement devices. The courts have been particularly vocal, in fact, on when and where drug dogs can be used. Much to the woman traveler's chagrin, though, the court will uphold the narcotics officer's actions. The Supreme Court ruled in *United States v. Place* (462 U.S. 696 [1983]) that the presence of a drug dog at a public airport did not trigger the protections of the Fourth Amendment. What is important in this illustration is that the dog sniffed the woman's *luggage*, not the woman herself. Had the narcotics officer let the dog approach and sniff passengers as they moved throughout the terminal, the result would have probably been different. In *United States v. Beale* (736 F.2d 1289, 9th Cir., *cert. denied*, 469 U.S. 1072 [1984]), for example, it was ruled that when a dog sniffs a person instead of the person's luggage, the Fourth Amendment is implicated. Thus, law enforcement officers need justification in order to let drug dogs sniff people.

3.7 Informants and Probable Cause   This is a tough one. The answer could be yes or no, depending on the judge. Using the *Gates* test for totality of circumstances, the judge could conclude that even though the police officer's application for a warrant was deficient in explaining the details of the informant's past reliability, this weakness was compensated for by the informant's statements about how the gambling operation worked. Even so, the fact that the informant knew of an unlisted phone number, which was later corroborated by the police, does not necessarily suggest criminal activity was taking place. In fact, in the case on which this scenario is based, a U.S. district judge ruled that probable cause was lacking, even under the *Gates* standard set forth by the Supreme Court. In support of his position, the judge noted that the officer failed to establish the informant's past reliability, that the informant provided "fuzzy" details about the gambling operation, and that the unlisted phone number was not indicative of criminal activity (see *United States v. Turner*, 713 F. Supp. 714, D. Vt. [1989]).

3.8 Having Probable Cause to Arrest   Just because a person appears suspicious does not give rise to probable cause. A person who looks suspicious to one officer may look perfectly normal to another. Also, just because the person had a hand in his pocket and the clerk looked nervous when reaching into the register does not suggest that probable cause was in place. (Perhaps the suspect was reaching for his wallet and the clerk had poor social skills!) Probable cause must be based on more than a suspicion or hunch. According to Justice Warren's observation, the "demand for specificity in the information upon which police action is predicated is the central teaching of this Court's Fourth Amendment Jurisprudence" (*Terry v. Ohio*, 392 U.S. 1 [1968], p. 21, n. 18).

3.9 Is There Reasonable Suspicion?   The answer would seem to be an emphatic no, for these significant reasons: (1) A third party supplied the information; (2) the woman on the sidewalk did not describe how she knew that the driver would be in possession of a gun and narcotics; and (3) the officer's actions went beyond a stop-and-frisk (the intrusion that reasonable suspicion justifies) and, arguably, the officer engaged in a search when he reached into the driver's car for the gun. Despite these problems, which seem to suggest reasonable suspicion was never in place to begin with, the Supreme Court ruled in *Adams v. Williams* (407 U.S. 143 [1972]) that the officer's actions *were* lawful. The Court observed that the third-party information "carried enough indicia of reliability" (p. 148). Moreover, the Court said:

> [When] Williams [the man in the car] rolled down his window, rather than complying with the policeman's request to step out of the car so that his movements could more easily be seen, the revolver allegedly at Williams' waist became an even greater threat. Under these circumstances the policeman's action in reaching to the spot where the gun was thought to be hidden constituted a limited intrusion designed to insure his safety, and we conclude that it was reasonable. (p. 148)

3.10 Metal Detectors and Administrative Justification   By traditional Fourth Amendment standards, this search would almost certainly be judged unlawful. No justification was in place, and the search clearly intruded upon Marceau's person, an area in which the courts have consistently ruled that a person has an objectively reasonable expectation of privacy. However, traditional Fourth Amendment doctrine does not apply here because of administrative concerns. Since the primary purpose of metal detector searches at airports is to ensure public safety, not to target any particular person, the courts will uphold the search. What is shown in this instance is that the government's need to search (and, of course, the risk to public safety if people are allowed to board planes armed) outweighs the individual's right to be free from unreasonable searches and seizures. Thus, searches of this nature are permissible when "the privacy interests implicated by the search are minimal, and where an important governmental interest furthered by the intrusion would be placed in jeopardy by a requirement of individualized suspicion" (*Skinner v. Railway Labor Executives' Association*, 489 U.S. 602 [1989], p. 624).

■ CHAPTER 4 Searches and Arrests with Warrants

4.1 Who Was That Bald Man?   Absolutely. They can apply for a "John Doe" arrest warrant. Sufficient detail exists such that it is unlikely that the wrong person would be apprehended. Compare this fictitious case with the real-life case of *Commonwealth v. Crotty* (92 Mass. 403 [1865]). In that case:

Morris Crotty and others were indicted and convicted for a riot in resisting the arrest of Crotty upon a warrant commanding the arrest of "John Doe or Richard Roe, whose other or true name is to your complainant unknown." The conviction was set aside by the Supreme Judicial Court of Massachusetts, upon the grounds that the warrant was insufficient, illegal, and void, because it did not contain Crotty's name, nor any description or designation by which he could be known and identified as the person against whom it was issued, and was in effect a general warrant, upon which any other person might as well have been arrested, as being included in the description; and that "the warrant being defective and void on its face, the officer had no right to arrest the person on whom he attempted to serve it; he acted without warrant, and was a trespasser; the defendant whom he sought to arrest had a right to resist by force, using no more than was necessary to resist the unlawful acts of the officer; an officer who acts under a void precept, and a person doing the same act who is not an officer, stand on the same footing; and any third person may lawfully interfere to prevent an arrest under a void warrant, doing no more than is necessary for that purpose." (153 U.S. 78 [1894], p. 86)

4.2 The Fourth Amendment's Particularity Requirement This warrant almost certainly comports with the Fourth Amendment. Because the items in question are readily identifiable by trained law enforcement officers, the particularity requirement can be somewhat relaxed. However, if the warrant authorized the seizure of "stolen property," it would probably not be upheld on review. As one court observed, "[T]o describe in general items like guns and jewelry as 'stolen' adds nothing instructive to a description in a warrant" (*Commonwealth v. Rutkowski*, 406 Mass. 673 [1990], p. 676). In another case, a court held that a search warrant for the defendant's residence authorizing the seizure of stolen jewelry did not satisfy the Fourth Amendment's particularity requirement because it did not provide meaningful guidance to the officers conducted the search as to what items were to be seized (*Namen v. Alaska*, 665 F.2d 449 [8th Cir. 1985], p. 453).

4.3 What Type of Seizure? In *Hayes v. Florida* (470 U.S. 811 [1985]), the case on which this exercise is based, the Supreme Court held:

Where there was no probable cause to arrest petitioner, no consent to the journey to the police station, and no prior judicial authorization for detaining him, the investigative detention at the station for fingerprinting purposes violated petitioner's rights under the Fourth Amendment, as made applicable to the States by the Fourteenth; hence the fingerprints taken were the inadmissible fruits of an illegal detention. . . . When the police, without probable cause or a warrant, forcibly remove a person from his home and transport him to the station, where he is detained, although briefly, for investigative purposes, such a seizure, at least where not under judicial supervision, is sufficiently like an arrest to invoke the traditional rule that arrests may constitutionally be made only on probable cause. (p. 811)

However, the Court also noted, "We also do not abandon the suggestion in *Davis* and *Dunaway* that under circumscribed procedures, the Fourth Amendment might permit the judiciary to authorize the seizure of a person on less than probable cause and his removal to the police station for the purpose of fingerprinting. We do not, of course, have such a case before us" (p. 817). Thus, it would appear that certain investigative detentions based on less than probable cause are permissible.

4.4 Detention of a Third Party during an Arrest Unfortunately for the man, the courts will probably not grant his motion. This hypothetical case is similar to *Michigan v. Summers* (452 U.S. 692 [1981]), in which the Supreme Court upheld the detention of several individuals during the service of a search warrant, even though the police had no real justification to do so. The Court offered the following in support of its decision: "The detention of one of the residents while the premises were searched, although admittedly a significant restraint on his liberty, was surely less intrusive than the search itself. Indeed, we may safely assume that most citizens, unless they intend flight to avoid arrest, would elect to remain in order to observe the search of their possessions" (p. 701).

4.5 A Public or Private Arrest? The case in this exercise closely resembles the case of *United States v. Carrion* (809 F.2d 1120 [1987], a Fifth Circuit Court of Appeals decision. Interestingly, the court ruled that a warrant was not required. According to the court:

[W]hen agent Gee [one of the real agents] drew his weapon, aiming it at Solmor [the real suspect], and ordered him to raise his hands, Solmor must have understood that he was under arrest. . . . Thus, Solmor's arrest occurred as he stood in the doorway of his hotel room and was first confronted by agents Harrington and Gee, who were standing in the hallway. . . . Under this Court's decision in *United States v. Mason* (661 F.2d 45 [5th Cir. 1981]), Solmor had no protectible expectation of privacy at the open door to his hotel room. In *Mason*, a law enforcement agent had arrested the defendant Mason's common law wife or paramour Mitchell. "Accompanied by three colleagues, the agent then took Mitchell to the house where she and Mason were living. The agents had neither an arrest or search warrant. . . . Mason came to the front door as Mitchell and the agents approached the house." . . . The defendant Mason was arrested at the door. The *Mason* Court concluded that the defendant had been "permissibly arrested at the front door," noting that the "Supreme Court [had] found such a warrantless arrest consistent with the Fourth Amendment in *United States v. Santana* (427 U.S. 38 [1976]), 'because the defendant in *Santana* [had been] in a public place and had no protectible expectation of privacy.'" (p. 1120)

4.6 Serving a Search Warrant in a Third-Party Residence   As the Supreme Court ruled in *Steagald v. United States* (451 U.S. 204 [1981]), a separate search warrant is required in order to arrest a person in a third-party residence. However, in this scenario, there is additional information: Fred has resided with Sue for eight weeks, and he can enter the apartment at his leisure with the key given to him by Sue. Thus, the determinative question becomes, Whose residence is this? Even though Sue's name is on the lease, it is arguable that Fred is more than just a houseguest, given his long stay at her apartment. However, if Fred's stay is truly temporary, the courts will probably declare Fred's arrest unconstitutional. According to one court:

> We would impermissibly diminish the protection offered by *Steagald* were we told that, for purposes of the homeowner's Fourth Amendment rights, the dwelling is the 'home' of whoever happens to be staying there. . . . The Fourth Amendment right to be secure against warrantless searches within the home is too vital to justify entry without a search warrant to execute an arrest warrant upon a guest in the home. (*Perez v. Simmons*, 884 F.2d 1136 [9th Cir. 1988], pp. 1141–1142).

Assuming, then, that the prosecutor fails in her argument that Fred was a resident and not a guest, what other argument might she be able to make in support of the arrest?

4.7 A Properly Served Search Warrant?   At first glance, the answer would appear to be no. The agents and officers were technically not refused admittance. There was simply no answer. However, in *United States v. Kennedy* (32 F.3d 876 [4th Cir. 1994], the Fourth Circuit Court of Appeals declared that this action was appropriate, even though no clear exigencies existed. According to the court:

> It is true that the officers in this case broke into Kennedy's house immediately after knocking and yelling "Police," and failed to wait for an explicit refusal of admittance or the lapse of a significant amount of time before breaking into the premises. However, the officers' failure to wait for a response does not mandate a conclusion that the search was illegal. It is well-established that noncompliance with the knock and announce requirements may be excused where exigent circumstances render strict compliance imprudent. . . . Whether exigent circumstances existed at the time of the entry, and whether the degree of the exigency was sufficient to justify the extent of the noncompliance, is determined by an analysis of the facts of each case. . . . As a general matter, however, exigent circumstances have been found to exist where the officers at the *premises reasonably believed that waiting for a response before entering the premises would create an opportunity for the occupants to destroy relevant evidence or to prepare an attack against them.* (p. 882, emphasis added)

4.8 Deadly Force beyond Present Dangerousness   The Supreme Court has not confronted this question, and only one circuit court has come close to doing so. In *Wright v. Whiddon* (747 F.Supp. 694 [N.D. Ga. 1990]), Wright was being transported to court for a probation revocation hearing. The officer transporting Wright failed to secure him adequately, and as a result, Wright escaped and ran into the street. Officers gave chase. Wright was unarmed and made no threatening movements, but one of the officers fired a single shot, mortally wounding him. The court frowned on this action, noting that "previous attempts to apprehend Wright were successfully accomplished without the need to use force whatsoever." Had Wright been particularly violent in the past, however, deadly force may have been justified.

4.9   Defining *Daytime*   This exercise is based on Wyoming district court case *United States v. Porco* (842 F. Supp. 1393 [1994]). In it, the court noted that a Wyoming statute defines *daytime* as the hours between 6:00 a.m. and 10:00 p.m., so the defendants' argument was meritless. Indeed, the Wyoming statute's language is virtually identical to the federal provision embodied in Rule 41(c) of the *Federal Rules of Criminal Procedure*, which also defines the term *daytime* to mean the hours from 6:00 a.m. to 10:00 p.m. The court also cited *United States v. Keene* (915 F.2d 1164 [8th Cir. 1990]), in which the Eighth Circuit Court of Appeals held that a search that was conducted at 8:20 p.m. was a daytime search under Rule 41, even though the search occurred after sunset.

4.10   Where Can Police Reasonably Look?   Clearly, one could not reasonably look for a stolen circus elephant in a kitchen cupboard, but the koala question is different. Even so, it is unlikely that anyone would keep a koala (or any other animal, for that matter) in a cupboard. Some sort of enclosure would surely be desirable, but not one that denies the animal light and gives it little room for movement. On the other hand, though, someone unscrupulous enough to steal a rare koala may not really care. And what's more, since the warrant was being served at a taxidermist's house, the deputies may reasonably have expected that the poor animal was already dead and stuffed. The answer to this question, it seems, could go either way.

▪ CHAPTER 5 Searches and Arrests without Warrants

5.1   Timing of a Search Incident to Arrest   No, according to the Supreme Court in *United States v. Chadwick* (433 U.S. 1 [1977]). The facts of *Chadwick* were basically the same as those presented here, except the case dealt with federal agents searching a footlocker. In the Court's words:

> Here the search was conducted more than an hour after federal agents had gained exclusive control of the footlocker and long after respondents were securely in custody; the search therefore cannot be viewed as incidental to the arrest or as justified by any other exigency. Even though on this record the issuance of a warrant by a judicial officer was reasonably predictable, a line must be drawn. In our view, when no exigency is shown to support the need for an immediate search, the Warrant Clause places the line at the point where the property to be searched comes under the exclusive dominion of police authority. Respondents were therefore entitled to the protection of the Warrant Clause with the evaluation of a neutral magistrate, before their privacy interests in the contents of the footlocker were invaded. (pp. 15–16)

5.2   Proper Scope for a Search Incident to Arrest   The answer to the first question is a resounding yes. The court's decision in *Maryland v. Buie* (494 U.S. 325 [1990]) permits law enforcement officers to take two precautionary steps when making an arrest in a person's home: (1) to look in places immediately adjoining the place of arrest for persons that may inflict harm on them and (2) to conduct a protective sweep of the whole house if they have reasonable suspicion that other dangerous individuals are present. The sweep, however, is limited to a cursory search of the places in which such people may be found. In the exercise, the area upstairs was not adjoining the area in which Sheen was arrested. However, based on the information supplied by the neighbor, the officer who conducted the protective sweep of the house was more than justified in doing so. Also, because the drug paraphernalia was in plain view, the officer was justified in seizing it. Had the other two individuals not been accomplices (or had the officers not had reasonable suspicion to conduct a protective sweep), then their actions would not have been acceptable.

With regard to the second question, the officer's actions were not appropriate. The act of looking in a drawer goes beyond the definition of *cursory*. Obviously, a person could not hide in a drawer, so had the drug paraphernalia been seized from the drawer, it would not have been admissible in a criminal trial.

5.3   Exigent Circumstances and the Severity of the Offense   Perhaps a better question is whether burglary is a serious enough offense to justify an arrest based on exigent circumstances. According to an Illinois court, which decided the case on which this exercise is based, the answer to both questions is no. Citing a federal appellate opinion in *Dorman v. United States* (435 F.2d 385 [D.C. Cir. 1970]), the Illinois court observed:

> [T]he Fourth Amendment to our Federal Constitution requires scrutiny by a judicial officer before the police may enter a dwelling to effect an arrest unless exigent circumstances do not tolerate a delay and consequently a warrantless entry into a dwelling is justified. The case of *Dorman* set forth various factors to be considered in determining whether "exigent circumstances" are present. Included among those factors are the following: (1) whether a grave offense is involved, particularly one that is a crime of violence, (2) the suspect is reasonably believed to be armed, (3) there exists not merely the minimum of probable cause that is required when a warrant has been issued but beyond that a clear showing of probable cause including 'reasonably trustworthy information' to believe the suspect committed the crime involved; (4) strong reason exists to believe that the suspect is in the premises being entered; (5) there is likelihood the suspect will escape if not swiftly apprehended; (6) whether the entry is forceable or peaceful; and (7) the time of entry (day or night). . . . Applying the *Dorman* standards to the instant appeal we conclude that the circumstances did not justify a warrantless entry. The suspect Chambers was not involved in a grave offense of violence. There was no reason to believe that he was armed and it is difficult to conclude that he would have escaped during the delay occasioned by the procurement of a warrant. The record reflects that he had been in the same building as the victim of his burglary for a period of some three weeks after he committed the offense. The entry into the defendant's apartment was made during the night time. (pp. 9–10)

In short, not only was the underlying offense not serious enough, but there was no other evidence to suggest that exigent circumstances existed in this case.

5.4 Are Exigent Circumstances Present? Unfortunately for the robbery suspect, the arrest in the first scenario will be upheld. This is assuming, of course, that probable cause exists. As a general rule, the police may chase a suspect into a private place to effect an arrest that was initiated in a public place. As the Supreme Court noted in *United States v. Santana*, "[A] suspect may not defeat an arrest which was been set in motion in a public place, and is therefore proper under *Watson*, by the expedient escaping to a private place" (p. 43)

The second question can be answered, tentatively, with another question: Why did the police wait three hours? Arguably, hot pursuit was no longer an issue after three hours. And as the Supreme Court noted in *Minnesota v. Olson*, a warrantless entry in the absence of a hot pursuit, and given the minimal likelihood of the suspect escaping, is not valid.

The answer to the third question is a tough one. The Supreme Court has not confronted this issue head on, but one court has noted, as indicated earlier, that a hot pursuit, by itself, creates no necessity for abandoning the warrant requirement (*State v. Wren*). Thus, it would seem that a warrant is required before the police can lawfully act absent any exigent circumstances.

5.5 Immediacy and Evanescent Evidence In U.S. *v. Brock* (667 F.2d 1311 [9th Cir. 1982]), the case on which this exercise is based, the Ninth Circuit said yes:

> The issue is whether the search ought to have been deferred until after a warrant could have been obtained. Relying on [*United States v. Williams*, 630 F.2d 1322, 1327 (9th Cir. 1980)] the district court thought not. In *Williams* a finding of exigency to search a motor home five hours after the arrests was based on the need of agents to enter to check on the explosiveness of the chemicals. Here, the need to check was even more urgent. The agents knew that the parties in the motor home had been "cooking" chemicals and that Brock had rushed out of the motor home choking from the fumes. As the district court found, these facts, combined with the agents' knowledge of the explosiveness of the chemicals used in making methamphetamine, justified the agents' belief that the motor home had to be searched to avoid a possible explosion. Moreover, the agents were unaware exactly who was in the motor home and whether all occupants had exited. (p. 1318)

5.6 Police-Created Exigencies This exercise confronts the controversial issue of police-created exigencies. In *United States v. Munoz-Guerra* (788 F.2d 295 [5th Cir. 1986]), the case on which this exercise is based, the Fifth Circuit rejected the argument that officers acted properly because they feared the suspect may retrieve a gun from the other room:

> In *United States v. Thompson*, 700 F.2d 944, 950 (5th Cir. 1983), we held that the government could not justify a warrantless search on the basis of exigent circumstances of its own

making. . . . Agents Bryant and Keiffer [the real names of the officers] knew when they knocked on the patio door that, once having made their presence known to Munoz-Guerra [the real suspect] (and possibly to other occupants) it would be necessary to conduct a security search of the premises and to restrain the condominium's inhabitants. Warrantless entry was thus a foregone conclusion the instant the agents revealed themselves to Munoz-Guerra at the patio door. The question before this court, then, is whether exigent circumstances justified the agents' initial decision to approach the patio door. Our past opinions have consistently emphasized that without reason to believe that a criminal suspect was aware of police surveillance, the mere presence of firearms or destructible, incriminating evidence does not create exigent circumstances. *See, e.g., Thompson,* 700 F.2d at 948; *United States v. Webster,* 750 F.2d 307, 326 (5th Cir. 1984), *cert. denied,* 471 U.S. 1106, 105 S. Ct. 2340, 85 L. Ed. 2d 855 (1985); *United States v. Cravero,* 545 F.2d 406, 414–15 n.24 (5th Cir. 1976) (en banc), *cert. denied,* 430 U.S. 983, 97 S. Ct. 1679, 52 L. Ed. 2d 377 (1977). In the instant case, it was possible to secure the condominium covertly from the outside. There was no basis, on these facts, for believing that resort to a magistrate would have created risks of a greater magnitude than those which are present in any case where the police have probable cause but delay entry pending receipt of a warrant. . . . Had the police's necessary efforts to secure the premises been visible to the inhabitants or had there been reason to believe that someone within the condominium was in need of immediate succor, the government's position would have merit. The government's argument that swift and immediate action may have minimized risks to human life and physical evidence, however, misses the mark. Our Fourth Amendment jurisprudence contemplates that protection of individual rights of privacy will be achieved at some cost to society's interest in public safety; and, in the ordinary case the risk that a criminal suspect will become aware of covert surveillance is deemed insignificant in contrast to the more substantial benefits we all derive from the procedural safeguards of judicial process. (pp. 298–299)

5.7 A Twist on *Carroll* The original rationale for the automobile exception was the impracticality of obtaining a warrant. When cars are stopped on the open road, for instance, they can easily be driven off, so the Supreme Court said that search warrants were not necessary in such circumstances (*Chambers v. Maroney,* 399 U.S. 42 [1970]). It would seem, given the example, that the Court's original logic would not apply and that the search would be unlawful. This was the decision reached in the case on which this example is based. In *United States v. Williams* (827 F. Supp. 641 [D. Or. 1993]), the Court held that the car was considered immobile and that the automobile search exception did not apply: "A primary justification for the vehicle inspection, the inherent mobility of motor vehicles, is not present here. Without mobility or other exigent circumstances, the government may not invoke the vehicle exception to the warrant requirement" (p. 645). Contrast this decision with that in *United States v. Hatley* (999 F.2d 392 [9th Cir. 1993]), in which even though the defendant's car was inoperable in his driveway, the court held that it *appeared* to be mobile and that the search was valid.

5.8 Proper Scope for an Automobile Search This scenario mixes consent (discussed later) with the automobile exception to the Fourth Amendment's warrant requirement. On the one hand, it seems as though the highway patrol officer went a bit far during the course of this search. One has to ask, Did the officer exceed the scope of the consent given? This question will be reconsidered in the section on consent. However, even if the officer exceeded the scope of the consent given, he may still have been justified in cutting open the tire. As the Supreme Court noted in *Carroll v. United States,* the warrantless search of an automobile is permissible when (1) there is probable cause to believe the vehicle contains evidence of a crime and (2) securing a warrant is impractical. This includes any containers therein. Assuming the officer in this example had probable cause to search (i.e., given the unusual spare tire and the white powder), he was more than justified in doing so (see, e.g., *United States v. Strickland,* 902 F.2d 937 [11th Cir. 1990]).

5.9 Considering the "Immediately Apparent" Requirement for Plain View First, the initial seizure of the rifle would be unlawful because it was not immediately apparent to the officer that it was contraband. In other words, probable cause was not present to seize the rifle. *Probable cause* has been defined as "more than hunch, guesswork, and cop-on-the-beat intuition, but less than proof beyond a reasonable doubt or a near certainty that the seized item is incriminating. There must be enough facts for a reasonable person to believe that the items in plain view may be contraband or evidence of crime" (*United States v. Giannetta,* 909 F.2d 571 [1st Cir. 1990], p. 579). With regard to the second question, it does not matter that the rifle was not connected with the rape. If it was seized lawfully (i.e., if it was immediately apparent to the officer that the rifle was contraband), then the rifle could lawfully be introduced into evidence.

The answer to the third question hinges on the role of inadvertency. Until recently, inadvertency was a requirement for a lawful plain view seizure. However, as the Supreme Court decided in *Horton v. California* (496 U.S. 128 [1990]), inadvertency is no longer required. Thus, the fact that the officers knew of the rifle and did not obtain a warrant to seize it would not appear determinative. However, the *Horton* decision focused on inadvertency in the context of a search warrant, not an arrest warrant, as is the case here. The Supreme Court has not confronted this issue directly, and some states still require inadvertency under their own constitutions (e.g., *People v. Manganaro*, 561 N.Y.S.2d 379 [Sup. Ct. 1990]).

5.10 Plain Smell? The Supreme Court has not directly confronted the "plain smell" issue, which this example appears to resemble, but it has been willing to expand "plain view" to include other senses (such as feeling). As such, the seizure would probably be justified; the smell of marijuana is apparent to most laypersons, not just law enforcement officials. As one court prophetically observed:

> [B]ecause of their common doctrinal base, [the "plain view" and "plain feel" doctrines] will in all likelihood come to be seen, probably within a decade, as nothing more than instances or variations of an omnibus Plain Sense Doctrine or Plain Perception Doctrine, which will embrace plain view and plain feel and, by a logically compelling growth process, plain hearing, plain smell, and plain taste. (*State v. Jones*, 653 A.2d 1040 [Md. Ct. Spec. App. 1995], p. 1044).

CHAPTER 6 Actions Based on Reasonable Suspicion

6.1 Looking for Illegal Aliens This question was answered by the Supreme Court in *INS v. Delgado* (466 U.S. 210 [1984]). According to the Court:

> Interrogation relating to one's identity or a request for identification by the police does not, by itself, constitute a Fourth Amendment seizure. . . . Unless the circumstances of the encounter are so intimidating as to demonstrate that a reasonable person would have believed he was not free to leave if he had not responded, one cannot say that the questioning resulted in a detention under the Fourth Amendment. (p. 210)

Interestingly, in another factory seizure case, *Martinez v. Nygaard* (831 F.2d 822 [9th Cir. 1987]), the Ninth Circuit Court declared that worker was not seized, even when he was grabbed by the shoulder by an INS agent. The reason for the court's decision was that the agent was merely trying to get the worker's attention and thus released him immediately.

6.2 Creating a "Constitutionally Cognizable" Policy There is no easy answer to this question because the Supreme Court has stated that there are circumstances in which *any* detention implicates the Fourth Amendment and must be accompanied by the appropriate level of justification. For example, in *Brown v. Texas* (443 U.S. 47 [1979]), the Court ruled:

> In the absence of any basis for suspecting appellant of misconduct, the balance between the public interest and appellant's right to security and privacy tilts in favor of freedom from police interference. . . . [E]ven assuming that purpose is served to some degree by stopping and demanding identification from an individual without any specific basis for believing he is involved in criminal activity, the guarantees of the Fourth Amendment do not allow it. (p. 52)

This decision has been bolstered by the Court's decision in *Delaware v. Prouse* (440 U.S. 648 [1979]), in which it was held that even though spotchecks for drivers' licenses are minimally intrusive, they are nevertheless "constitutionally cognizable" and must be conducted in the presence of "articulable and reasonable suspicion" (p. 661).

6.3 Stretching the Time Limits of a Stop In the case on which this scenario is based (*United States v. Richards*, 500 F.2d 1025 [1974]), the Court of Appeals for the Ninth Circuit said, with regard to the officer's display of force:

We think the officers acted appropriately in accomplishing the stop. After approaching the aircraft, [the officer] displayed his badge and ordered appellant to shut down the plane's engines and disembark. This order was accompanied by no greater use of force than is involved in any request by a peace officer to stop and answer some questions. Agent Collins drew his gun and repeated the command only after appellant failed to comply with the first order. Otherwise, with nothing impeding the airplane, which was ready for take-off, the officers would have been powerless to prevent its flight. (p. 1028)

And with regard to the detention, the court declared:

The officers' inquiries of appellant . . . focused primarily on appellant's relationship to the aircraft. In light of the suspected use of the airplane and appellant's suspicious behavior, . . . these inquiries were within the scope of a routine on-the-scene police investigation. Appellant's implausible and evasive responses to these questions indicated that something was awry and created even more reason for the investigation being pursued further. (p. 1029)

Thus, a detention of more than one hour was permissible.

6.4   Was the Mobile Home Seized?   This situation blends the material from this chapter with the definition of a search/seizure posed in Chapter 3. Clearly, the deputies were government agents, but did their actions amount to a seizure? In the case on which this vignette is based, the court of appeals stated, "Because the officers had not entered Soldal's [the tenant's] house, rummaged through his possessions, or, in the Court of Appeals' view, interfered with his liberty in the course of the eviction, the Fourth Amendment offered no protection against the 'grave deprivation' of property that had occurred" (*Soldal v. Cook County*, 506 U.S. 56 [1992], p. 62). The Supreme Court disagreed, stating:

As a result of the state action in this case, the Soldals' domicile was not only seized, it literally was carried away, giving new meaning to the term "mobile home." We fail to see how being unceremoniously dispossessed of one's home in the manner alleged to have occurred here can be viewed as anything but a seizure invoking the protection of the Fourth Amendment. Whether the Amendment was in fact violated is, of course, a different question that requires determining if the seizure was reasonable. That inquiry entails the weighing of various factors and is not before us. (pp. 61–62)

6.5   What Constitutes a Proper Stop?   Officer Weber was certainly entitled to ask the driver some questions without any justification, but the encounter would need to remain voluntary. Arguably, the encounter in this scenario was not voluntary, as the driver was not free to leave because Weber had blocked the driveway with her cruiser. The question is, then, Did Weber have reasonable suspicion to stop the driver in the first place? That is, assuming that the encounter was a stop, thereby implicating the Fourth Amendment, was the officer justified in her actions? To answer this question requires looking at the specific facts known to Weber prior to the stop: (1) The car was in an area known for daytime burglaries, and (2) plastic trash bags of the type used in the burglaries were observed in the trunk. Weber *did not* know who lived at the residence, who the driver was, or even that the driver was nervous. This information was discovered *after* the stop. The facts that Weber possessed prior to the stop are therefore inadequate to support a showing of reasonable suspicion. For all Weber knew, the driver was leaving his house and taking some trash to the dump. Additionally, the after-the-fact knowledge Weber learned cannot be considered in determining the legality of the initial stop. Thus, the frisk was illegal because of the derivative evidence doctrine (discussed in Chapter 2).

6.6   The Permissible Scope of a Frisk   In evaluating the legality of a *Terry* stop such as this, the points to be considered are (1) whether there was reasonable suspicion and (2) whether the degree of intrusion was appropriate. Arguably, the officers had reasonable suspicion to stop Smith, but when they asked him to remove his shoes, they exceeded the permissible scope of a *Terry* stop. The Supreme Court has stated that "the least intrusive means reasonably available to verify or dispel the officer's suspicion in a short period of time" should be employed (*Florida v. Royer*, 460 U.S. 491 [1983], p. 500). In the case on which this scenario is based, *Commonwealth v. Borges* (395 Mass. 788 [1985]), the Massachusetts Supreme Judicial Court concluded that the stop effectively amounted to an arrest, requiring probable cause. The officers' conduct was not "reasonably related in scope to the circumstances which justified the interference in the first place" (*Terry v. Ohio*, 392 U.S. 1 [1968], p. 20).

6.7 A Vehicle Search   Unfortunately for the police officer, the evidence against the woman will almost certainly be excluded. The determinative factor in this scenario is that the search took place *before* the woman's arrest. Also, based on the information presented, the officer had no reason to fear for his safety. In the case on which this scenario is based, *Knowles v. Iowa* (525 U.S. 113 [1998]), the Supreme Court agreed, noting that "the threat to officer safety from issuing a traffic citation is a good deal less than in the case of a custodial arrest" (p. 113). The court also noted that a concern for officer safety during a routine traffic stop may justify the additional intrusion of ordering a driver and passengers out of the car and even conducting a search of the passenger compartment. However, these exceptions do not by themselves "justify the often considerably greater intrusion attending a full field-type search" (p. 113). Thus, the officer in this case was not justified in conducting a full-blown search.

6.8 The Bounds of a Proper Frisk   The evidence will almost certainly be suppressed because "[t]he search was not reasonably limited in scope to the accomplishment of the only goal which might conceivably have justified its inception—the protection of the officer by disarming a potentially dangerous man" (*Terry v. Ohio*, p. 65). In addition, the officer went beyond a lawful frisk by carefully feeling the lump in the gang member's pocket. Had the officer patted down the gang member without making the careful examination and immediately recognized that the package was crack, then she would have beeen justified by making the seizure. Doing so would be consistent with the Court's "plain feel" doctrine, established in *Minnesota v. Dickerson* (113 S.Ct. 2130 [1993]). As this scenario stands, though, the officer exceeded the bounds of a *Terry*-based frisk when she carefully examined the lump in the gang member's pocket.

6.9 Putting It All Together   It must be conceded that the act of pulling the truck over was a stop, requiring reasonable suspicion. Thus, the first question is, Did the officer have reasonable suspicion to stop the truck? The answer is almost certainly yes, despite the fact that the truck *did* have license plates, contrary to the report on the radio. It is reasonable to believe that the suspects could have put the license plates on the truck after the robbery so no one would be able to read the plates as they fled the scene of the crime. In a similar vein, the act of ordering the suspects out of the car was legal, even though one of the occupants was a woman. It is possible that witnesses mistook the woman for a man, and the fact that four people were in the truck supports the officer's actions of stopping the truck. Consider the Supreme Court's opinion in *United States v. Hensley* (469 U.S. 221 [1985]), in which it responded to arguments that the officer did not have enough information to conduct a lawful stop:

> In an era when criminal suspects are increasingly mobile and increasingly likely to flee across jurisdictional boundaries, [the information supplied to the officer over the radio] minimizes the volume of information concerning suspects that must be transmitted to other jurisdictions and enables police in one jurisdiction to act promptly in reliance on information from another jurisdiction. (p. 231)

Another significant factor in this scenario is that the information supplied to the officer came from other police officers (i.e., over the radio). Had the information been supplied by an anonymous informant, some additional information would probably have been needed for corroboration (see Chapter 3).

6.10 An Application of Drug Courier Profiling   There appears to be a great deal of suspicious conduct on the woman's part, but reasonable suspicion to stop someone must be established *prior* to the stop. That is, if there is reasonable suspicion to suspect the woman of criminal activity, it must be based on her conduct prior to the point that the agents approached her. She certainly matches some of the characteristics of the drug courier profile (e.g., traveling from a source city; appearing nervous), but many other travelers likely possess the same characteristics. However, if it is assumed that the woman was free to leave during the initial encounter and that the agents did not stop her, then their desire to further detain her may be justified. This is because of her failure to supply identification and the inconsistency between the information on her plane ticket and what she said regarding her travel plans. In fact, the Fifth Circuit Court of Appeals, in U.S. *v. Gonzales* (842 F.2d 748 [5th Cir. 1988]), a case with similar facts, found that the agents' suspicion was reasonable and that they were justified in detaining the suspect. In the court's words, "[L]aw enforcement officials are entitled to evaluate the specific and articulable facts known to them in light of their experience in narcotics enforcement, and we are inclined to give due credit to the experience and expertise of these officers" (p. 753).

▥ CHAPTER 7 Actions Based on
Administrative Justification and Consent

7.1 Inventoried and Inventoried Again   In *Florida v. Meyers* (466 U.S. 380 [1984]), the case on which this exercise is based, the Supreme Court upheld both searches:

> The District Court of Appeal either misunderstood or ignored our prior rulings with respect to the constitutionality of the warrantless search of an impounded automobile. In *Michigan v. Thomas*, 458 U.S. 259 (1982), we upheld a warrantless search of an automobile even though the automobile was in police custody and even though a prior inventory search had already been made. That ruling controls the disposition of this case. In *Thomas*, we expressly rejected the argument accepted by the District Court of Appeal in the present case, noting that the search upheld in *Chambers* was conducted "after [the automobile was] impounded and [was] in police custody" and emphasizing that "the justification to conduct such a warrantless search does not vanish once the car has been immobilized." 458 U.S., at 261. The District Court of Appeal's ruling that the subsequent search in this case was invalid because the car had been impounded is clearly inconsistent with *Thomas* and *Chambers*. (p. 382)

As to the second question, if only the second search was unconstitutional, something could be salvaged from this case: The first search could be upheld as a search incident to arrest, as discussed in Chapter 5.

7.2 Welfare-Related Home Inspections   In *Calabretta v. Floyd* (189 F.3d 808 [9th Cir. 1999]), the Ninth Circuit Court answered no:

> In our circuit, a reasonable official would have known that the law barred this entry. Any government official can be held to know that their office does not give them an unrestricted right to enter peoples' homes at will. We held in *White v. Pierce County*, . . . a child welfare investigation case, that "it was settled constitutional law that, absent exigent circumstances, police could not enter a dwelling without a warrant even under statutory authority where probable cause existed." . . . The principle that government officials cannot coerce entry into people's houses without a search warrant or applicability of an established exception to the requirement of a search warrant is so well established that any reasonable officer would know it. Under *White*, appellants' claim, that "a search warrant is not required for home investigatory visits by social workers," is simply not the law. (p. 813)

Furthermore, the court said:

> [I]n the case at bar, the report did not describe any evidence of physical abuse, and the social worker and police officer did not perceive any danger of injury to the children or loss of evidence if they secured a warrant. On her first visit four days after the call, ten days prior to her return with the police officer, the social worker wrote "Minors were easily seen and they did not appear to be abused/neglected." The only reason the social worker and police officer did not seek a search warrant was that their subjective opinion was that they did not need one. (p. 814)

7.3 Business Inspections   In *United States v. Argent Chem. Lab* (93 F.3d 572 [9th Cir. 1997]), the Ninth Circuit held that veterinary drug companies are closely regulated and thus subject to the so-called *Collonade-Biswell* exception to the Fourth Amendment's warrant requirement. In the court's words:

> Argent [the actual drug company] argues that, although the drugs were seized pursuant to a warrant issued in accordance with the Act, the seizure violated the Fourth Amendment's prohibition of unreasonable searches and seizures and its requirement that warrants issue upon probable cause. We conclude, however, that Argent's argument is defeated by the nature of its business and the regulation to which it is subject. (pp. 574–575)

7.4 Detecting Illegal Aliens   One of the main reasons for administrative searches is that they are aimed at protecting public safety, not at detecting evidence of a crime. Clearly, though, illegal aliens are evidence of a crime. Nevertheless, in *United States v. Martinez-Fuerte* (428 U.S. 543 [1976]), the Supreme Court upheld the legality of such checkpoints, even accompanied by brief questioning of the cars' occupants. The second question is a different story. While the purpose of such a checkpoint would appear to be the same (i.e., to detect illegal aliens), the tactics would be fundamentally different. Regardless of what such stops would do for traffic, searches of passenger compartments, trunks, and the like for the purpose of discovering illegal aliens are unconstitutional absent particularized suspicion. Searches of vehicles, which are far more serious intrusions than brief stops coupled with questioning, require probable cause (see, e.g., *United States v. Ortiz*, 422 U.S. 891 [1975]). The courts have also held that searches by roving patrols for the purpose of detecting illegal aliens must be predicated on, at the very least, reasonable suspicion (see *United States v. Brignoni-Ponce*, 422 U.S. 873 [1975]) and, most likely, probable cause (*Almeida-Sanchez v. United States*, 413 U.S. 266 [1973]).

7.5 A Constitutionally Valid Checkpoint? According to the Second Circuit Court of Appeals, the answer is yes. In the court's words:

> We conclude that, as planned, the Special Operation passed constitutional muster. First, the checkpoints in question served an important public concern in attempting to deter drive-by shootings that were, or were reasonably perceived to have been, connected with widespread drive-up drug purchases. Second, at the time of implementation, the checkpoints were reasonably viewed as an effective mechanism to deter criminal behavior in the barricaded area. . . . Third, the intended level of intrusion to motorists was minimal. No vehicle was to be stopped or its operation questioned unless entry into the cordoned-off area was desired. For those seeking entry, the stop was meant to be brief and was aimed solely at ascertaining the motorists' connection to the neighborhood. In *United States v. Martinez-Fuerte*, 428 U.S. 543, 49 L. Ed. 2d 1116, 96 S. Ct. 3074 (1976), the Supreme Court held that a checkpoint aimed at interdicting the flow of illegal aliens which involved "only a brief detention of travelers during which all that [was] required of the vehicle's occupants [was] a response to a brief question or two and possibly the production of a document evidencing a right to be in the United States" was not sufficiently intrusive so as to violate the Fourth Amendment. . . . Here, as in *Martinez-Fuerte*, the request for evidence of a legitimate reason to enter the barricaded area was not significantly intrusive. Moreover, because the plan here was to stop all motorists seeking entry, there was little concern that the stop would generate "fear and surprise." (p. 667)

Note that this checkpoint was upheld because the stops were not intended (not directly, anyway) to seek evidence of criminal activity.

7.6 Searches of Government Employees The answer is almost certainly no. In *United States v. Jones* (286 F.3d 1146 [2002]), the case on which this exercise is based, the Ninth Circuit held, in part, that "the search was not conducted by the [agency] in order to find a file or report necessary to carry out the agency's work. The search was carried out by federal agents to ensure that [agency] employees were not violating the subpoena and destroying potential evidence necessary in a criminal investigation" (p. 1150). Furthermore:

> The government's argument that retrieving official documents responsive to a subpoena is simply a "work-related" search is belied by the actions taken by the federal investigators. The immediate goal of the FBI was to secure documents relevant to a criminal investigation that could be admissible in subsequent criminal prosecutions. The federal investigators were involved at every step of the search. Federal investigators initiated the search of the [agency] offices. The agents directed the search and had [agency] employees point out offices and work areas relevant to the subpoena which they then proceeded to search. . . . Additionally, the FBI secured the building over the weekend and did not allow [agency] employees access to their offices. The extensive involvement of the federal agents did not make the search of Jones' office a routine file retrieval case under *O'Connor*. (pp. 1151–1152)

7.7 Drug Testing of Students According to the Seventh Circuit Court of Appeals, it does (*Todd v. Rush County Schools*, 133 F.3d 984 [7th Cir. 1998]). According to the court:

> [T]he difference between [*Vernonia* and other relevant precedent] and the present one is that here the testing is also required of those engaging in other extracurricular activities. However, we find that the reasoning compelling drug testing of athletes also applies to testing of students involved in extracurricular activities. Certainly successful extracurricular activities require healthy students. While the testing in the present case includes alcohol and nicotine, that is insufficient to condemn it because those substances may also affect students' mental and physical condition. (p. 986)

Furthermore, the court said,

> [T]he linchpin of this drug testing program is to protect the health of the students involved. As we have stated, "the plague of illicit drug use which currently threatens our nation's schools adds a major dimension to the difficulties the schools face in fulfilling their purpose—the education of our children. If the schools are to survive and prosper, school administrators must have reasonable means at their disposal to deter conduct which substantially disrupts the school environment." (p. 986)

7.8   What Constitutes Voluntary Consent?   According to the Supreme Court of Virginia, in *Lowe v. Commonwealth* (239 S.E.2d 112 [1977]), the answer is yes:

> The fact of custody alone is not enough in itself to demonstrate a coerced consent to search. . . . But the burden is on the Commonwealth to prove the voluntariness of any consent. . . . And whether the consent was actually freely given is a question of fact to be determined from "the totality of all the circumstances." *Schneckloth v. Bustamonte*, 412 U.S. 218, 227 (1973) . . . We think the evidence is sufficient in this case to support the trial court's ruling that the Commonwealth carried its required burden of proof. The testimony of the officers showed, and the defendant admitted during the suppression hearing, that the Consent to Search Form . . . was read to him; the officers stated that it was also explained to defendant. He was thus possessed of the knowledge that he had the right to withhold consent, yet the evidence is that defendant stated: "You go ahead and search. . . ." Moreover, there was positive testimony from the officers that their guns were not drawn at the time and that no threats or promises were made to defendant. As a matter of fact, when defendant learned before the consent that the officers suspected he was a drug user, defendant offered to obtain for the police his drug paraphernalia from the apartment bathroom. In sum, the record conclusively shows the Commonwealth met the test of voluntariness, approved in *Schneckloth*, 412 U.S. at 229, in that the consent was "the product of an essentially free and unconstrained choice by its maker" and that defendant's will had not "been overborne and his capacity for self-determination [had not been] critically impaired." (p. 678)

7.9   Scope of Consent   Based on the information provided, the answer to the first question is no. In *Florida v. Jimeno* (500 U.S. 248 [1991]), the Supreme Court noted:

> [T]he standard for measuring the scope of a suspect's consent under the Fourth Amendment is that of "objective" reasonableness—what would the typical reasonable person have understood by the exchange between the office and the suspect? The question before us, then, is whether it is reasonable for an officer to consider a suspect's general consent to a search of his car to include consent to examine a paper bag lying on the floor of the car. We think it is. (p. 251)

Since narcotics can be carried almost anywhere in a vehicle, the officers were justified in conducting an extensive search. In the second question, Lopez has not placed *direct* limits on the scope of the consent search but rather *indirect limits* on the scope of the search. It is doubtful that the officers could complete an exhaustive search inside five minutes, so it is likely that they wouldn't have the opportunity to search everywhere. Of course, as noted earlier, *theory* and *reality* often differ; the officers could potentially keep Lopez, regardless of his prior obligation. In addition, if probable cause to search develops anywhere along the way, then the scope of Lopez's consent will become largely irrelevant.

7.10   The Bounds of "Knock and Talk"   This is the worst form of "knock and talk." First, more than one officer has arrived at the scene, which could be construed as somewhat intimidating to the person at the door. Further, the officers lie to the person at the door by stating that they will obtain a warrant if he or she doesn't let them in. Finally, the person answering the door is visibly drunk and, quite possibly, not capable of giving valid consent. It is also possible that the person who answered the door does not even have the right to give consent. Based on this information, it is likely that any evidence turned up during the course of a search will be considered inadmissible under the totality of circumstances test that is required for determining whether consent is voluntary. At least one court has held, for example, that consent is not voluntary if police officers answering the question of whether a warrant will be obtained make no distinction between *seeking* a search warrant and *obtaining* one (see *United States v. Faruolo*, 506 F.2d 490 [2nd Cir. 1974]; *United States v. Boukater*, 409 F.2d 537 [5th Cir. 1969]).

■ CHAPTER 8 Interrogations and Confessions

8.1 Police Conduct and Voluntariness   Two questions need to be answered: (1) Did the police subject the suspect to coercive conduct? and (2) Did the coercive conduct result in the suspect making an involuntary statement? Only if both questions are answered yes will the confession be declared involuntary. Surprisingly, the Sixth Circuit Court of Appeals, in *McCall v. Dutton* (863 F.2d 454 [6th Cir. 1988]), the decision on which this example is based, stated that there was "no evidence that the officers used [their] weapons in any way to force a confession out of the petitioner" (p. 458). The court reasoned that the defendant offered a self-initiated confession and that the police conduct was "passive." This was a controversial decision, to say the least, and it does anything but clarify what constitutes coercive conduct. Had the officers resorted to threats or violence, the confession would have been involuntary (see *Bram v. United States*, 168 U.S. 532 [1897], pp. 542–543).

8.2 Suspect Characteristics and Voluntariness   As indicated in the text, rarely is mental condition enough for a confession to be declared involuntary. In the Supreme Court decision on which this example is based, *Colorado v. Connelly* (479 U.S. 157 [1986]), Justice Rehnquist argued that the confession was not a product of overreaching by the police. "Coercive police activity," the Court held, is a "necessary predicate to a finding that a confession is not 'voluntary' within the meaning of the Due Process Clause of the Fourteenth Amendment" (p. 166). Clearly, the confession obtained in the second scenario borders on involuntary. Yet even though the police arguably subjected Hornsby to coercive conduct, one must still ask the question as to whether the coercive conduct was enough to overcome Hornby's will.

8.3 Formal Criminal Proceedings   A key limitation associated with the Sixth Amendment right to counsel is that it exists only if formal adversarial proceedings have commenced. Eddie should have had counsel present for the questioning about the most recent burglary, but since he supplied no incriminating information about that crime, there was nothing to exclude from trial. Eddie could file a civil suit under Section 1983, however. As for the questioning about the earlier burglaries, Eddie enjoyed no Sixth Amendment protection because charges had not been filed. Of course, he could have enjoyed Fifth and/or Fourteenth Amendment protection. Indeed, *Miranda* most certainly applied.

8.4 The Nature of Custody   This example relates to the issues addressed in the discussion of government conduct in Chapter 3. However, the context here is that of *Miranda*, not the definition of a search. The specific question that needs to be posed, then, is, Does the law enforcement officers' reliance on an undercover agent to obtain a confession result in a custodial situation? On the one hand, this situation is clearly custodial; Reynolds is in a jail cell. On the other hand, she is not in the traditional *Miranda* environment. And according to the Supreme Court, this latter fact is determinative. In *Illinois v. Perkins* (496 U.S. 292), the Court relied on the original *Miranda* rationale to minimize the coercive aspects of police interrogation in a police-dominated environment. According to the Court, "*Miranda* was not meant to protect suspects from boasting about their criminal activities in front of persons whom they believe to be their cellmates. . . . Respondent viewed the cellmate-agent as an equal and showed no hint of being intimidate by the atmosphere of jail" (p. 298).

8.5 Can Reading *Miranda* Rights Create a Custodial Situation?   As a general rule, *Terry* stops (the case here) are treated as noncustodial for purposes of *Miranda* (*United States v. Galberth*, 846 F.2d 983 [5th Cir. 1988], p. 994). So, the question is, Does reading *Miranda* create a custodial situation? This is an important question because if, in fact, the confrontation is custodial and the suspect's waiver is not knowing, intelligent, and voluntary, then the confession (an important bit of evidence) will be excluded at trial. The Supreme Court has not addressed the question posed in this example, but at least one lower court has. That court held that the *Miranda* warning itself does not create custody (*United States v. Gordon*, 638 F.Supp. 1120 [W.D.La. 1986]). According to the court, "To suggest that the mere administration of the *Miranda* warnings converts a legally non-custodial situation into custody is to completely strip from *Miranda* its original intention which was to protect a citizen from the coercive effects of police custody" (p. 1133).

8.6 Incriminating Evidence and Interrogation   Clearly, Cheney was in custody when he was arrested. The pertinent question is, Did the officer's act of placing the marijuana plant in front of Cheney amount to interrogation, thus triggering *Miranda*? More specifically, did the police officer deliberately display the marijuana plant in an attempt to prompt a confession? Alternatively, should the officer have reasonably foreseen that a confession would result? On facts similar to those in the exercise, a Massachusetts court ruled that the display of incriminating evidence constituted interrogation (see *Commonwealth v. Rubio*, 540 N.E.2d 189 [Mass. App. 1989]). In another case, in which the police showed a suspect photographs of two suspected accomplices and told him "these two guys were arrested and you are going to be charged with robbery," his subsequent statement was excluded because the police activity in question amounted to interrogation (*State v. Ward*, 573 A.2d 505 [N.J. Super. A.D. 1990]).

8.7 Another Interrogation?   This example is identical to the case of *Arizona v. Mauro* (481 U.S. 520 [1987]). There, the Supreme Court held, "We doubt that a suspect, told by officers that his wife will be allowed to speak with him, would feel he was being coerced to incriminate himself in any way" (p. 528). Mauro, the defendant, was not subjected to coercive police action, psychological compulsion, or the like. Also determinative is the fact that the officer, though present, did not participate in the conversation. As such, Mauro's incriminating statement was considered admissible.

8.8 Were the *Miranda* Rights Read Properly?   According to the Supreme Court, *Miranda* requires that the suspect be warned "that he has the right to the presence of an attorney, *and that if he cannot afford an attorney one will be appointed for him* prior to any questioning if he so desires" (*Miranda v. Arizona*, 384 U.S. 436 [1966], p. 479; emphasis added). It would seem, based on a strict reading of *Miranda*, that Wentworth was not appropriately advised of his rights. At least one court has held, however, that omission of *Miranda*'s language concerning indigency does not require suppression of an incriminating statement (see *Chambers v. Lockhart*, 872 F.2d 274 [8th Cir.], *cert. denied*, 493 U.S. 938 [1989]). The Eighth Circuit did at least warn the police that *all* the *Miranda* warnings should be given and that they should not rely on their estimation of a suspect's financial status. Thus, in response to the second question, it should not matter, from a *Miranda* standpoint, whether a suspect appears to be rich or poor.

8.9 The Circumstances for a Voluntary Waiver   This example bears some resemblance to *Moran v. Burbine* (475 U.S. 412 [1986]), a case already discussed. The difference here, however, is that the police refused to let Nicholas meet with his attorney. In *Moran*, the Supreme Court noted that "events occurring outside of the presence of the suspect and entirely unknown to him surely can have no bearing on the capacity to comprehend and knowingly relinquish a constitutional right" (p. 421). Thus, it would seem that the attorney's attempts to contact his client were immaterial. Also, since Nicholas never *demanded* that his counsel be present, his waiver may be considered voluntary. Nevertheless, the police probably should have cut off questioning when Nicholas expressed his wish to have his counsel present, and at least one state court has decided similarly. In *State v. Reed* (627 A.2d 630 [N.J. 1993]), the court held that the suspect's knowledge that his counsel was attempting to contact him was essential to making a knowing and intelligent waiver. Further, when the police withhold such information, they violate the suspect's state constitutional rights (*People v. McCauley*, 645 N.E.2d 923 [Ill. 1994]).

8.10 Should the Exclusionary Rule Apply?   In *United States v. Cherry* (794 F.2d 201 [5th Cir. 1986], *cert. denied*, 479 U.S. 1082 [1987]), a statement obtained in violation of *Miranda* was excluded. However, the statement led the police to the murder weapon, and the court held that the murder weapon was admissible because it was nontestimonial. An important restriction on this and similar rulings, however, is that the statement must be obtained voluntarily. Clearly, in this exercise, the statement was not voluntary. The murder weapon would therefore not be considered admissible because it did not pass muster under the due process voluntariness test. Had the officer not played "Russian roulette" and had Richter's confession otherwise been voluntary, the murder weapon would have been admissible despite the clear-cut *Miranda* violation.

▓ CHAPTER 9 Identification Procedures and the Role of Witnesses

9.1 Counsel during a Lineup   No, counsel does not need to be present. The Sixth Amendment right to counsel is "offense specific." As the Supreme Court noted in *McNeil v. Wisconsin* (501 U.S. 171 [1991]), "The Sixth Amendment . . . is offense-specific. It cannot be invoked once for all future prosecutions, *for it does not attach until a prosecution is commenced, that is, at or after the initiation of adversary judicial proceedings—whether by way of formal charge, preliminary hearing, indictment, information, or arraignment*" (p. 175, emphasis added).

9.2 Altering the Suspect's Appearance   Requiring the suspect to alter his physical appearance appears incriminating, but the courts have ruled otherwise. Insofar as the Fifth Amendment's self-incrimination clause applies to testimonial, not physical, evidence, that provision is not violated. The Sixth Amendment does not apply, either, as no formal charges have been filed. A case in which the court upheld action similar to that described in the exercise was *United States v. Murray* (523 F.2d 489 [8th Cir. 1975]). It could be argued that the act of requiring the suspect to wear a wig "shocks the conscience," thereby violating the Fourteenth Amendment's due process clause (e.g., *Rochin v. California*, 342 U.S. 165 [1952]), but such claims rarely are successful. In *United States v. Brown* (920 F.2d 1212 [5th Cir. 1991]), for example, the Fifth Circuit Court of Appeals stated that requiring a suspect to dye his hair "reduce[d] the chance of misidentification" (p. 1215). Further, "the defendant has no right to disguise himself at the time of the crime, then refuse to do so again to confound identification" (p. 1215).

9.3 What Composes a Valid Showup?   Clearly, this police conduct seems questionable; at a minimum, this is a suggestive technique. Even so, the courts have not automatically rendered such identifications invalid. For example, in *Jackson v. United States* (412 F.2d 149 [D.C. Cir. 1969]), the court upheld a showup procedure in which the witness was brought to the suspect's hospital room for identification. The court frowned on this technique but stated that the witness's prior observations of the suspect minimized any suggestiveness in the hospital room:

> In other circumstances a remand might be required to determine how serious Jackson's [the defendant's] wounds were and whether a less suggestive confrontation could have been arranged within a few days. But the combination of several factors persuade the [c]ourt that the suggestive circumstances surrounding the confrontation were not so likely to lead to a misidentification as to require further proceedings. The victims of the robbery saw the suspect individually. They both testified that before the confrontation the police had told them neither that the suspect had been arrested near the Morgan Pharmacy, nor that almost $1,700, apparently the fruits of the crime, had been found on his person. Moreover, both victims had had an excellent opportunity to observe the robber under good lighting conditions, both during the crime and when he entered the store for the first time. Indeed, one employee had specifically remarked upon the robber's "weird" appearance after he had left the store for the first time and before the crime. Finally, both victims had given descriptions of the robber to the police immediately after the crime. In view of all these factors, we find no violation of due process confrontation arranged under the necessitous circumstances here. (p. 154)

Of course, this case does not address the specific details set forth in the exercise. A different decision might result in the workplace context, especially if the hospital identification was conducted because of the immobility of the suspect.

9.4 Making a Valid Identification   Although this scenario seems somewhat suggestive, several courts have upheld in-court identifications based on suggestive out-of-court chance encounters between a suspect and witness. For example, in *United States v. Pollack* (427 F.2d 1168 [1970]), a witness had been unable to identify the defendant in photographs presented to her but did recognize him in a courthouse encounter. Her subsequent in-court identification of the defendant was upheld. And in *United States v. Evans* (438 F.2d 162 [D.C. Cir. 1971]), the D.C. Circuit Court upheld the in-court identification of a defendant following an on-the-street encounter between him and the witness. Finally, in an earlier case, *United States v. Green* (436 F.2d 290 [1970]), the same court upheld a rape victim's in-court identification of the defendant based on a chance pretrial encounter:

> The victim observed her assailant closely and at length at the time of the crime, a fact which supports the conclusion that the in-court identification had an "independent source." . . . It

is true that a suggestive confrontation before trial may distort the recollection of a witness and impair the integrity of an in-court identification. That might be the case, for example, if the witness had had only a fleeting glimpse of the man she picked out on the street, and had felt the need to confirm her identification by a closer look. But in this case the victim took care to observe the suspect closely and verify her first impression before calling the police officers. Any distortion of her recollection must be attributed to the perfectly proper street identification, and not to the subsequent precinct confrontation. (pp. 292–293)

9.5 Creating a Valid Photographic Array   As for the first question, at least one court has upheld this type of photographic identification procedure. In *Chaney v. State* (267 So.2d 65 [Fla. 1972]), the Supreme Court of Florida permitted an identification of a rape suspect based on one photograph:

> It is true that a single photograph of Appellant was shown [to the victim] by the sheriff's deputy, because she told him Appellant had revealed to her he had been jailed for raping another girl. Pursuant to this revelation, it is logical that the police would show [the victim] a photograph of a suspect in another rape case who had been jailed as a lead in identifying and arresting the person suspected of committing the crime of rape. . . . Under these circumstances, it was not an abuse of due process rights to use the single photograph as a clue or lead in apprehending the rapist. . . . In fact, it would be unreasonable to preclude the use of such a photograph for this pre-arrest purpose. (p. 69)

With regard to the second question, this type of identification is, at the very least, less suggestive. Based on the *Chaney* court's decision, three photographs would seem more than appropriate. Nevertheless, the *Model Rules for Law Enforcement*[2] recommend that photographs of at least *seven* individuals of similar appearance be displayed to the witness in order to avoid suggestiveness.

The answer to the third question (and, indeed, the answers to the previous two) hinges on the totality of circumstances. In *Simmons v. United States* (390 U.S. 377 [1968]), the Supreme Court stated: "We hold that each case must be considered on its own facts, and that convictions based on eyewitness identification at trial following a pretrial identification by photograph will be set aside on that ground only if the photographic identification procedure was so impermissibly suggestive as to give rise to a very substantial likelihood of irreparable misidentification" (pp. 383–384). Not surprising, one court disapproved a photographic array in which the suspect's photograph was shown three times (*People v. Citrino*, 90 Cal. Rptr. 80 [1970]). In a similar vein, another court disapproved a photographic array in which the suspect's picture was altered to show a specific type of mustache (*State v. Alexander*, 503 P.2d 777 [1972]).

9.6 The Photo Array Revisited   If the police decide to tell each witness who the previous witness identified, this action will constitute suggestiveness of the first order and all but guarantee that any in-court identifications will be excluded. Compare the details of this exercise with those of the Supreme Court of Illinois's decision in *People v. Brown* (285 N.E.2d 1 [1972]). There, the police presented a witness with both a photographic array and a lineup. In neither situation was the witness directed to the suspect.

With regard to the second question, *King v. State* (306 A.2d 258 [1973]) is helpful in reaching a decision. Based on similar facts, the Court of Special Appeals for the state of Maryland stated:

> In our judgment, Mrs. Downey [the victim] was barraged with photographs of the appellant to the point of being brainwashed. After the three sets of photographs on December 16 in which the photograph of the appellant was the only one to recur, and in view of the repetitive exposure of Mrs. Downey to four separate photographs of the appellant on December 23 "to reassure her" that she would not "be sued for false arrest," we are not persuaded that the later lineup identification on January 5 and the later in-court identification were not the products of this repeated exposure. Looking at the totality of events between December 15 and December 23 as to photographic viewings, we are persuaded that the whole process, in the aggregate, was impermissibly suggestive. Evidence of it should have been excluded from the trial. (pp. 271–272)

[2]From Project on Law Enforcement Policy and Rulemaking, *Model Rules for Law Enforcement* series (Tempe, AZ: Arizona State University, 1974).

9.7 Identify the Leading Questions The first two questions are appropriate. The third question is not explicitly subjective, but it supplies enough detail that it almost suggests an answer. The fourth and fifth questions are classic examples of leading questions. The purpose of having the witness identify the defendant is just that: to have the witness make the identification, not the prosecutor. As such, steps should be taken to avoid leading the witness to identify any one individual. The same applies with pretrial identification procedures: Law enforcement officers should let witnesses make their own *independent* judgments.

9.8 Appropriate Questions on Direct Examination The first three questions are permissible, even though they appear leading. (Recall that leading questions are generally permissible only on cross-examination.) The purpose of these questions is to impeach the witness on the grounds that he or she could not have observed the events in question adequately. The fourth question, however, is irrelevant to the issue of identifying the robber, so it should not be asked.

9.9 When Is an In-Court Identification Tainted? On the one hand, the Supreme Court has stated that "the practice of showing suspects singly to persons for the purpose of identification, and not as a part of a lineup, has been widely condemned" (*Stovall v. Denno*, 388 U.S. 293 [1972], p. 302). On the other hand, in deciding the same case, the Supreme Court also stated that "a claimed violation of due process of law in the conduct of a confrontation depends on the totality of the circumstances surrounding it" (p. 302). Unfortunately, then, there is no easy answer to this question. In actuality, it depends on a great deal of information that is not included in the exercise. The appellate court that heard *Wright v. United States* (404 F.2d 1256 [D.C. Cir. 1968]), the case on which this exercise is based, stated:

> We are uninformed as to the characteristics which by Mrs. Vines' observation served to distinguish appellant from other persons. We know relatively little as to the similarities and the differences, respecting appellant and those in the room with him, in age, height, weight, dress and other physical features. We are not clear as to whether the contested identification was made before or after appellant was asked to stand. Nor can we tell whether, all circumstances considered, a lineup was feasible. These are but illustrative of relevant details we cannot fathom from what is before us. (pp. 1260–1261)

Only if such issues are thoroughly understood can a meaningful answer be reached.

9.10 When Is an In-Court Identification Valid? Usually, the courts are hesitant to exclude in-court witness identifications following illegal seizures of suspects. According to the Supreme Court in *United States v. Crews* (445 U.S. 463 [1980]), most witnesses are capable of giving testimony that is independent of any illegal search or seizure of the defendant. In *Crews*, the Court observed that "the robbery victim's presence in the courtroom at respondent's trial was surely not the product of any police misconduct. . . . She had notified the authorities immediately after the attack and had given them a full description of her assailant" (p. 471). Furthermore, according to the Court, "Nor did the illegal arrest infect the victim's ability to give accurate identification testimony. Based upon her observations at the time of the robbery, the victim constructed a mental image of her assailant" (p. 472) and simply recollected that image at trial. In this exercise, however, the events are somewhat different. Arguably, the witness is in the courtroom because of the illegal arrest. Further, it is likely that her testimony is not sufficiently independent of the unlawful arrest; it is based on a guess, not an accurate recollection of the defendant's identity. In sum, the witness in this exercise is a tainted witness.

■ CHAPTER 10 The Pretrial Process

10.1 The Probable Cause Hearing The *Gerstein* decision mentioned that the police can engage in certain "administrative steps" before bringing an arrestee before a magistrate to determine whether probable cause to arrest was in place. This example focuses on the meaning of the phrase *administrative steps*. In the case on which this example is based, *Sanders v. Houston* (543 F. Supp. 694 [1982]), a federal district court held that a delay of over 20 hours was acceptable:

> This Court concludes that "administrative steps" as used in Gerstein include more than transportation, booking, and filing charges. . . . The rights of a suspect are subject to limitations arising out of society's interest in police activity undertaken to aid in the identification of the

culprit and to obtain evidence which would aid in apprehending and convicting criminals. . . . Additionally, the procedures may provide significant proof of an exculpatory nature which would inure to the benefit of the arrestee. . . . Accordingly, it is the Court's determination that such activities—completing paperwork, searching the suspect, inventorying property, finger-printing, photographing, checking for prior record, laboratory testing, interrogating the sus-pect, verifying alibis, ascertaining similarities to other related crimes, and conducting line-ups—may be proper administrative steps incident to an arrest in a given case. (p. 700)

10.2 **Timing of the Probable Cause Hearing**   The facts in this exercise are virtually identical to those of a real-world case, *Kanekoa v. Honolulu* (879 F.2d 607 [9th Cir. 1989]). Here is the court's holding in that case:

> The length of appellants' detentions in this case was clearly unreasonable and violated their rights as a matter of law. All three men were detained for at least several hours after they could reasonably have been expected to be completely sober, and none of the three men was given a second intoxilyzer test. Melemai [one of the men] was detained for twenty hours. He was arrested at approximately 5:40 p.m. His blood alcohol level was found to be .14 per-cent when it was measured sometime between 6:15 p.m. and 8:00 p.m. An average man's blood alcohol level would drop from .14 percent to .05 percent, the level at which Honolulu Police Department regulations permit detainees to be interviewed [Red Brief at 16], within four hours, and would reach .00 percent in an additional three hours. . . . Therefore, Melemai was completely sober at the very latest by early morning, probably by 3:00 a.m. The defendants observe that no magistrates were available to conduct probable cause hearings between 6:00 p.m. and 8:00 a.m. Even if detainment until morning was justified by the unavailability of a magistrate, a question I do not address, Melemai's detention without a probable cause hearing until his release at 1:30 p.m. of the day following his arrest was unconstitutional. Melemai was delayed for approximately ten and one-half hours beyond the time he regained sobriety, and five and one-half hours beyond the time a magistrate was available. The police have failed to justify this delay by citing any "administrative step incident to arrest" that they needed to complete prior to presentment. Therefore, the judge's finding that Melemai's detention was reasonable was clearly erroneous. (p. 619)

10.3 **Amount of Bail**   As a general rule, equal protection is violated when bail is set beyond the ability of an indigent person to pay it. For this rule to apply, however, the indigent person must not be able to secure a bail bond. The Fifth Circuit's decision in *Pugh v. Rainwater* (557 F.2d 1189 [5th Cir. 1977]) is illustrative:

> We have been called upon to decide whether indigent pretrial detainees are deprived of Fourteenth Amendment equal protection of the law when they are imprisoned solely because they cannot afford money bail set under a system that does not require the judge first to con-sider less financially onerous conditions of release. In evaluating this problem, we have reached several conclusions: (1) When a judge sets money bail in Florida, he creates two *de facto* classes: non-indigents who presumptively can pay for their pretrial freedom and indigents who surely cannot; (2) This classification must be strictly scrutinized under the equal protec-tion clause because it discriminates against indigent criminal defendants and directly affects their fundamental right to be presumed innocent and to prepare an adequate defense; (3) Although Florida has a compelling interest in assuring a defendant's appearance at trial, (4) money bail is not necessary to promote that interest because the bail bondsman system eliminates the basic premise behind such bail; (5) Florida may promote its compelling interest through alternative forms of release that do not discriminate on the basis of wealth. These fac-tors lead inexorably to the conclusion that Florida's current bail system discriminates invidi-ously against indigents charged with crime. We hold that it violates the equal protection rights of such indigents. Our holding is not that money bail may never be imposed on an indigent defendant. The record before us does not justify our telling the State of Florida that in no case will money bail be necessary to assure a defendant's appearance. We hold only that equal pro-tection standards require a presumption against money bail and in favor of those forms of release which do not condition pretrial freedom on an ability to pay. (pp. 1201–1202)

10.4 **Preventive Detention**   This action was upheld in *United States v. Jessup* (757 F.2d 378 [1st Cir. 1985]), a decision handed down by the First Circuit Court of Appeals. The court held, among other things, that "the magistrate and district court have acted within their lawful authority in applying [Section 3142(e)], and related statutory provisions, to the . . . [defendant] Mark Jessup. We affirm the district court's decision to deny him bail and to hold him in custody pending his trial" (p. 379). The court upheld the trial judge's decision because he was unable to come up with a set of conditions that would guarantee Jessup's return. The judge's decision was also upheld because the offense Jessup was charged with was serious:

> [T]he offense was within Congress's definition of "dangerous federal offenses," the weight of the evidence against Jessup was strong (in particular, the evidence suggested to the magistrate that Jessup was a "trusted cohort" of his codefendant, who allegedly had been involved in cocaine dealing for some time) . . . Jessup had no relatives in Massachusetts, . . . Jessup had lived in Massachusetts for only two years, and . . . Jessup had been unemployed for six months before his arrest. (p. 388)

10.5 Financial Status and Bail Determination   Most bail decisions are pretrial in nature, but this example focuses on a bail decision *during* trial. The same issue arose during *Bitter v. United States* (389 U.S. 15 [1967]). There, the Supreme Court held that if bail is granted prior to trial, it can be revoked *during* trial "only when and to the extent justified by danger which the defendant's conduct presents or by danger of significant interference with the progress or order of the trial" (p. 16). By contrast, bail cannot be revoked for trivial infractions, such as failure to arrive at court on time. Indeed, a bail determination can also arise *after* trial, such as during the period between conviction and appeal. The Bail Reform Act of 1966 allowed for postconviction release if the convicted individual did not pose a danger to the community (18 U.S.C. Section 3148). However, under the Bail Reform Act of 1984, postconviction bail is not readily granted because judges must find by clear and convincing evidence that the convicted individual does *not* pose a threat to the community.

10.6 Treatment of Pretrial Detainees   In *Block v. Rutherford* (468 U.S. 576 [1984]), the Court upheld a detention facility's rule prohibiting contact visits, reasoning as follows:

> Here, the Central Jail's blanket prohibition on contact visits is an entirely reasonable, nonpunitive response to legitimate security concerns, consistent with the Fourteenth Amendment. Contact visits invite a host of security problems. They open a detention facility to the introduction of drugs, weapons, and other contraband. Moreover, to expose to others those detainees who, as is often the case, are awaiting trial for serious, violent offenses or have prior convictions carries with it the risks that the safety of innocent individuals will be jeopardized. Totally disallowing contact visits is not excessive in relation to the security and other interests at stake. There are many justifications for denying contact visits entirely, rather than attempting the difficult task of establishing a program of limited visits such as that imposed here. Nothing in the Constitution requires that detainees be allowed contact visits; responsible, experienced administrators have determined, in their sound discretion, that such visits will jeopardize the security of the facility and other persons. (pp. 585–589)

10.7 Preliminary Hearings   The Supreme Court has not answered this question, so for now, there are various rules and statutes both permitting and not permitting preliminary hearings for accused misdemeanants. Some states require preliminary hearings only for gross misdemeanors. Either way, case law is helpful. The Fifth Circuit stated, in *Pugh v. Rainwater* (483 F.2d 778), "No sufficient justification exists for disallowing preliminary hearings for misdemeanants [i.e., people charged with misdemeanors]. The plight of an accused misdemeanant incarcerated without a hearing is just as serious as that of an accused felon" (pp. 788–789). Further, "where misdemeanants are out on bond or are charged with violating ordinances carrying no possibility of pre-trial incarceration, they must be accorded preliminary hearings. In short, the offense charged is irrelevant to the man incarcerated prior to trial; he must, therefore, be afforded a preliminary hearing regardless of his status as an accused misdemeanant or an accused felon" (p. 789).

Postscript: Notice that *Pugh* was also cited in Decision-Making Exercise 10.3. The reason for this is that two issues were raised in that case: (1) denying bail for indigent defendants and, as here, (2) denying preliminary hearings for misdemeanants.

10.8 Prosecutorial Discovery   A question similar to this was addressed in *Fisher v. United States* (425 U.S. 391 [1976]). There, the Court held that the Fifth Amendment prohibits the prosecution from discovering potentially incriminating information that is (1) known *only* to the defense and (2) not going to be used as evidence at trial. Such information is protected by attorney/client privilege. By extension, this decision applies to lists of witnesses who will not testify—that is, potential witnesses that are known only to the defense. Importantly, if the prosecution learns of the identity of another individual (one who could, say, implicate the defendant in a criminal act) through another channel besides the defense (i.e., an independent source), then the Fifth Amendment will not be violated.

10.9 Defense Discovery The Jencks Act seems a little unfair to the defense because it places significant restrictions on discovery. And in the case on which this example is based, *United States v. Algie* (667 F.2d 569 [6th Cir. 1982]), the trial judge tried valiantly to force the prosecution to provide the requested information to the defense *prior* to the trial to assist in speeding things up and clearing the court's crowded docket. However, the Sixth Circuit Court of Appeals reversed the trial court judge's decision to require the prosecution to supply the government witness list and testimony prior to trial. In the court's words:

> Briefly put, the Judge's policy, as he outlines it, has been to order the United States Attorney to furnish statements taken by the government which would be covered by the Jencks Act five days in advance of trial, absent some specific reason to the contrary, and in any event, the night before the witness was to testify. Under this policy the District Judge cites statistics to indicate great progress in docket control and a substantial increase in numbers of pleas obviating any trial at all, and a substantial diminution in the length of trials which actually have occurred. . . . We emphasize that we heartily approve of the District Judge's objectives in seeking to bring about the disposition of his crowded docket, and applaud his efforts in this regard. We hope that will continue and that he will succeed in securing the maximum cooperation with his trial plans that it is possible to achieve from such voluntary cooperation as may be had from the United States Attorney. . . . It is, however, our manifest duty as we see it to say that the exigencies of court administration which the District Judge has cited do not authorize us to sanction any amendment of the mandatory language of the Jencks Act. (p. 571)

10.10 Disclosure of Exculpatory Evidence As noted in *Kyles v. Whitley* (514 U.S. 419 [1995]), the defendant is not required to show that the prosecution's remaining evidence would have been sufficient to prove guilt. Instead, the defense only needs to show that the exculpatory evidence would have raised a reasonable probability of a different outcome. This exercise is actually based on the *Kyles* decision. In that case, the Court stated:

> Because the net effect of the state-suppressed evidence favoring Kyles [the defendant] raises a reasonable probability that its disclosure would have produced a different result at trial, the conviction cannot stand, and Kyles is entitled to a new trial. . . . A review of the suppressed statements of eyewitnesses—whose testimony identifying Kyles as the killer was the essence of the State's case—reveals that their disclosure not only would have resulted in a markedly weaker case for the prosecution and a markedly stronger one for the defense, but also would have substantially reduced or destroyed the value of the State's two best witnesses. . . . Similarly, a recapitulation of the suppressed statements made to the police by Beanie [the informant]—who, by the State's own admission, was essential to its investigation and, indeed, "made the case" against Kyles—reveals that they were replete with significant inconsistencies and affirmatively self-incriminating assertions, that Beanie was anxious to see Kyles arrested for the murder, and that the police had a remarkably uncritical attitude toward Beanie. Disclosure would therefore have raised opportunities for the defense to attack the thoroughness and even the good faith of the investigation, and would also have allowed the defense to question the probative value of certain crucial physical evidence. . . . [Finally, w]hile the suppression of the prosecution's list of the cars at the crime scene after the murder does not rank with the failure to disclose the other evidence herein discussed, the list would have had some value as exculpation of Kyles, whose license plate was not included therein, and as impeachment of the prosecution's arguments to the jury that the killer left his car at the scene during the investigation and that a grainy photograph of the scene showed Kyles's car in the background. It would also have lent support to an argument that the police were irresponsible in relying on inconsistent statements made by Beanie. (p. 419)

■ CHAPTER 11 Prosecutors, Grand Juries, and Defense Attorneys

11.1 Reasons for Nonprosecution There are no Supreme Court cases prohibiting this type of decision, and there is nothing constitutionally wrong with the prosecutor relying on civil asset forfeiture in lieu of criminal prosecution. Typically, though, asset forfeiture is sought in conjunction with criminal prosecution or in cases in which there is not enough evidence for the prosecutor to mount an effective criminal case. Someone whose assets are targeted through forfeiture could argue that he or she was unfairly singled out (a topic that will be visited later in this book), but there appear to be no published court decisions addressing this possibility. By some estimates, there is no criminal prosecution in as many as 90 percent of all civil asset forfeiture actions.[3]

11.2 The Decision Not to Charge Actually, it is fairly difficult to answer this question without knowing the details of the investigation. In this case, the National Association for the Advancement of Colored People (NAACP) learned of the prosecutor's decision and actually sued (i.e., under several federal statutes), offering up several legal arguments, including that "the defendants acted in an arbitrary, capricious and discriminatory manner by failing to investigate the Russ shooting to determine if his constitutional rights and Federal statutes had been violated by Arkansas law enforcement authorities" (p. 1113). The decision reached by the court was that the defendants' motion to dismiss the cases should not be granted and, further, that the plaintiffs should have an opportunity to present their case in a civil trial. This is an important example of a court stepping in and providing a remedy for those who disagree with the nonprosecution of a certain individual or individuals.

11.3 Another Decision Not to Charge In *Town of Newton v. Rumery* (480 U.S. 386 [1987]), the Supreme Court upheld such an agreement but only because the defendant was not coerced into it. The Court held, in part:

> Although in some cases release-dismissal agreements may infringe on important interests of the criminal defendant and of society as a whole, the mere possibility of harm to such interests does not call for a *per se* rule invalidating all such agreements. The risk, publicity, and expense of a criminal trial may intimidate a defendant, even if he believes his defense is meritorious. But this possibility does not justify invalidating *all* release-dismissal agreements. In many cases a defendant's choice to enter into a release-dismissal agreement will reflect a highly rational judgment that the certain benefits of escaping criminal prosecution exceed the speculative benefits of prevailing in a civil action. Respondent's voluntary decision to enter into the agreement here exemplifies such a judgment. Respondent, a sophisticated businessman, was not in jail and was represented by an experienced criminal lawyer, who drafted the agreement. Respondent considered the agreement for three days before signing it. Because respondent voluntarily waived his right to sue under [Section] 1983, the public interest opposing involuntary waiver of constitutional rights is no reason to hold the agreement here invalid. (p. 386)

11.4 What Is Selective Treatment? Since traffic offenses of this nature are not criminal, Wise will not be able to allege unfair or selective prosecution per se. She could, however, probably present her claim in traffic court. And assuming she has the evidence to back up her contention, she would probably succeed. The Supreme Court has actually ruled on this matter but only in the criminal context. It has held that if a person is targeted for prosecution simply because of a controversial public statement he or she has made, then the First Amendment may be violated and charges may be considered inappropriate (e.g., *Federow v. United States*, 580 A.2d 600 [D.C.App. 1990]). Applying this decision, Wise may succeed in having the amount of her citation reduced. In short, the police and prosecutors alike cannot retaliate when people assert their First Amendment rights.

11.5 What Is Pretextual Prosecution? A somewhat related scenario came up in *United States v. Cammisano* (413 F.Supp. 886 [W.D.Mo. 1976]), in which a court concluded that selective prosecution *did* occur when a prosecutor charged an individual suspected of being involved in organized crime with a violation of the Federal Meat Inspection Act solely because there was not enough evidence to mount a more serious charge. However, the Ninth Circuit's decision in *United States v. Sacco* (428 F.2d 164 [9th Cir. 1970]) considered the practice of pursuing a lesser

[3]H. J. Hyde, *Forfeiting Our Property Rights,* (Washington, DC: Cato Institute, 1995).

charge perfectly acceptable. What makes this exercise different from *Sacco*, though, is that the crime Dwyer was charged with was *unrelated* to her alleged prostitution crimes. There do not appear to be any published decisions addressing facts quite like those presented in this exercise.

11.6 What Is Vindictive Prosecution? This exercise focuses on whether a prosecutor's threat to pursue more serious charges if a plea agreement is not accepted can be considered vindictive. Plea bargaining is considered further in Chapter 12, but for now, it is worth mentioning that if as part of a plea bargain, the defendant agrees to give up certain rights, he or she will not later succeed with a vindictive prosecution claim against the prosecutor for exercising those rights. To illustrate, in *Bordenkircher v. Hayes* (434 U.S. 357 [1978]), the prosecutor offered Hayes, the defendant, a 5-year term for a forged check charge. The prosecutor also threatened to prosecute Hayes as a habitual offender if he refused the agreement. Hayes refused the agreement and subsequently claimed vindictive prosecution. The Court held that due process is not violated when the "conduct engaged in by the prosecutor . . . no more than openly presented the defendant with the unpleasant alternatives of foregoing trial or facing charges on which he was plainly subject to prosecution" (p. 365). This is not to suggest, however, that prosecutors' plea-bargaining decisions are not restricted; again, those restrictions are considered in the following chapter.

11.7 Grand Jury Investigations Almost certainly not. The Supreme Court answered a question similar to this in *Hale v. Henkel* (201 U.S. 43 [1906]. There, it held, in part:

> Applying the test of reasonableness to the present case, we think the *subpoena duces tecum* is far too sweeping in its terms to be regarded as reasonable. It does not require the production of a single contract, or of contracts with a particular corporation, or a limited number of documents. . . . If the [subpoena] had required the production of all the books, papers and documents found in the office of the MacAndrews & Forbes Company, it would scarcely be more universal in its operation, or more completely put a stop to the business of that company. Indeed, it is difficult to say how its business could be carried on after it had been denuded of this mass of material, which is not shown to be necessary in the prosecution of this case, and is clearly in violation of the general principle of law with regard to the particularity required in the description of documents necessary to a search warrant or subpoena. Doubtless many, if not all, of these documents may ultimately be required, but some necessity should be shown, either from an examination of the witnesses orally, or from the known transactions of these companies with the other companies implicated, or some evidence of their materiality produced, to justify an order for the production of such a mass of papers. A general subpoena of this description is equally indefensible as a search warrant would be if couched in similar terms. (pp. 76–77)

11.8 Deciding on Variance The answer is almost certainly yes. Note first that the record of the grand jury proceeding can be shared with the two women because they will make "a showing that grounds may exist for a motion to dismiss the indictment because of matters occurring before the grand jury."[4] Indeed, even if they were denied access to the record of the grand jury proceeding, the indictments against them would point to the evidence on which the grand jury based its decision. Either way, according to the Supreme Court in *Russell v. United States* (369 U.S. 749 [1962]), if the defendant is "convicted on the basis of facts not found by, and perhaps not even presented to, the grand jury which indicted him," then the defendant is deprived "of a basic protection which the guaranty of the intervention of the grand jury was designed to secure" (p. 770). In other words, the women are all but guaranteed reversals of their convictions. Importantly, the prosecutor could not then go back to the grand jury with evidence that the women bought guns and seek a second indictment because of double jeopardy (see Chapter 14).

11.9 Right to Counsel in the Pretrial Phase The Supreme Court has answered this question no. As stated in *Gerstein v. Pugh* (420 U.S. 103 [1975]), a case discussed at some length in the previous chapter:

> Both the District Court and the Court of Appeals held that the determination of probable cause must be accompanied by the full panoply of adversary safeguards—counsel, confrontation, cross-examination, and compulsory process for witnesses. . . . These adversary

---

[4]*Federal Rules of Criminal Procedure,* Rule 6, issued by the 107th Congress, First Session, December 1, 2001. Available online: <www.house.gov/judiciary/crim2001.pdf>.

safeguards are not essential for the probable cause determination required by the Fourth Amendment. The sole issue is whether there is probable cause for detaining the arrested person pending further proceedings. This issue can be determined reliably without an adversary hearing. The standard is the same as that for arrest. That standard—probable cause to believe the suspect has committed a crime—traditionally has been decided by a magistrate in a nonadversary proceeding on hearsay and written testimony, and the Court has approved these informal modes of proof. (pp. 120–121)

11.10 Effective Assistance of Counsel   Probably not. The defendant should be able to point to specific errors, and neither of these alleged errors is specific enough. In *United States v. Cronic* (466 U.S. 648 [1984]), the case on which this exercise is based, the Supreme Court held that factors such as counsel's age and experience "may affect what a reasonably competent attorney could be expected to have done under the circumstances, but none identifies circumstances that in themselves make it unlikely that respondent received the effective assistance of counsel" (p. 666).

■ CHAPTER 12 Plea Bargaining and Guilty Pleas

12.1 What Constitutes Coercion?   As already noted in this text, psychological pressure can amount to coercion. Here, the question is, Did the prosecutor's offer *coerce* the defendant to plead guilty or *cause* him to choose between two alternatives? If the prosecutor's conduct amounts to coercion, then the defendant's subsequent conviction should be reversed. On the other hand, if the prosecutor simply informed the defendant of two choices and left it up to him to make the choice, the defendant's coercion argument will not succeed. The facts in this exercise point to coercion. Clearly, the prosecutor could have opted *not* to promise life in prison. Given that, it seems that the defendant was coerced into pleading guilty. As the Supreme Court suggested in *Brady v. United States* (397 U.S. 742 [1970]), the defendant could not rationally weigh the costs and benefits of going to trial versus pleading guilty. The defendant should therefore win his appeal.

12.2 Prosecutorial Deception   First and foremost, the defendant will only succeed with such an appeal if he knows and can prove that the prosecutor deceived him. If the prosecution permits discovery of the evidence in its possession, which it should (see Chapter 10), the defendant will probably have a solid case. Thus, it is quite likely that the defendant will succeed in having his conviction reversed. The prosecution cannot fabricate evidence or intentionally mislead the defendant into pleading guilty. As noted toward the end of this chapter, a valid guilty plea must be knowing, intelligent, and, perhaps most important, voluntary. The prosecutor will be hard pressed to show that the defendant pleaded guilty voluntarily.

12.3 An Inducement of Banishment   Banishment seems a little extreme but has been upheld in at least one court decision. In *Phillips v. State* (512 S.E.2d 32 [Ga. Ct. App. 1999], p. 33), a defendant filed a motion to strike various provisions of his plea agreement, including the banishment provision. The trial court denied the motion, and the appellate court affirmed. The latter court reached its decision despite the Georgia State Constitution's proscription against banishment. To support its decision, the court said that defendant effectively agreed to waive any right to challenge his agreement as a result of pleading guilty. In general, however, most states, the federal government, and some appellate court decisions have prohibited banishment as part of a plea agreement.

12.4 Judicial Inducements   A similar question was posed in *United States ex rel. Elksnis v. Gilligan* (256 F.Supp. 244 [S.D.N.Y. 1966]). There, a court held that a judge's explanation to the defendant that a more serious sentence would be imposed if he failed to plead guilty resulted in a coerced guilty plea. The court said:

> The unequal positions of the judge and the accused, one with the power to commit to prison and the other deeply concerned to avoid prison, at once raise a question of fundamental fairness. When a judge becomes a participant in plea bargaining he brings to bear the full force and majesty of his office. His awesome power to impose a substantially longer or even maximum sentence in excess of that proposed is present whether referred to or not. A defendant

needs no reminder that if he rejects the proposal, stands upon his right to trial and is convicted, he faces a significantly longer sentence. One facing a prison term, whether of longer or shorter duration, is easily influenced to accept what appears the more preferable choice. Intentionally or otherwise, and no matter how well motivated the judge may be, the accused is subjected to a subtle but powerful influence. A guilty plea predicated upon a judge's promise of a definite sentence by its very nature does not qualify as a free and voluntary act. The plea is so interlaced with the promise that the one cannot be separated from the other; remove the promise and the basis for the plea falls. (p. 254)

12.5 **Judicial Rejections** Yes, and several courts have held as such. For example, in *United States v. Crowell* (60 F.3d 199 [CA 5, 1996]), the court stated that "a district court's rejection of a plea agreement is reviewed only for abuse of discretion [and a] court may properly reject a plea agreement based on undue leniency" (pp. 205–206). Also, in *United States v. Brubaker* (663 F.2d. 764 [CA 7, 1981]), another court stated that the judge can reject a plea agreement when it restricts the court's sentencing discretion (p. 768). Clearly, the sentencing options for negligent manslaughter, as presented in this exercise, are less than for, say, first-degree murder.

12.6 **The Prosecutor's Duty to Fulfill the Bargain** No published decisions seem to address this issue directly; however, one case comes close. In *People v. Heiler* (79 Mich. App. 714 [1977]), a plea agreement was reached in which the defendant was to assist authorities in an investigation and in which the prosecutor later withdrew the plea. In that case, however, the defendant had taken no steps to assist in the investigation. (This aspect is different from the exercise, in which the defendant had proceeded to fulfill his end of the bargain.) In deciding *Heiler*, the court stated, "Absent any showing or allegation of prejudice to the defense resulting from the prosecutor's breach of faith, we decline to permit judicial intrusion upon the function of his office" (p. 722). To answer the question in this exercise, it must be decided whether what Leaves said in the investigation was prejudicial to his case. Assuming it was, then Leaves should be able to withdraw the plea.

12.7 **Two Prosecutors, One Bargain** The twist in this exercise is that a different prosecutor, Prosecutor 2, was present at the sentencing hearing—one who was less than enthusiastic about the terms of the agreement reached between the defendant and Prosecutor 1. However, in *United States v. Brown* (500 F.2d 375 [4th Cir. 1974]), the case on which this example is based, the court held that the prosecution failed to fulfill its end of the bargain and that the case should be remanded so a different judge could determine the appropriate sentence. In the court's words:

> [W]e believe that the government failed to keep its bargain. We have no occasion to consider the propriety of sentence, or recommendation as to sentence, as an element of a plea bargain, but it is manifest that the consideration which induced defendant's guilty plea was not simply the prospect of a formal recitation of a possible sentence, but rather the promise that an Assistant United States Attorney would make a *recommendation* on sentencing. This could reasonably be expected to be the sound advice, expressed with some degree of advocacy, of a government officer familiar both with the defendant and with his record and cognizant of his public duty as a prosecutor for the United States. (p. 377)

Further, the court stated, "[D]efendant does not seek to withdraw his guilty plea but only asks the lesser relief of 'specific performance' of the plea bargain. We thus have no need to consider a choice of remedies. In the light of defendant's position, we conclude that a remand for resentencing before a different district judge [is necessary]" (p. 378).

12.8 **Waiving Rights as a Consequence of Plea Bargaining** According to the Tenth Circuit Court of Appeals, which decided *United States v. Black*, it is perfectly acceptable for the defendant to give up his or her right to appeal. The court stated:

> Although the sentencing court may modify plea agreements in certain exceptional circumstances (for example, for reasons of public policy or in instances of fraud on the court, see, e.g., *United States v. Ready*, 82 F.3d 551 [2d Cir. 1996]), those circumstances are not present here. Accordingly, because the district court's remarks at sentencing could not have affected Mr. Black's decision to enter into the plea agreement and waive his right to appeal, and because the district court lacked the authority to modify the plea agreement in these circumstances, we conclude that the waiver-of-appeal provision should be enforced. (p. 1303)

12.9 A Valid Guilty Plea? This example is based on an actual case, *Hill v. Lockhart* (474 U.S. 52 [1985]), in which the Supreme Court held that the defendant need not be informed of his or her parole eligibility as part of the plea-bargaining process. Also, the Court stated that the petitioner failed to describe how defense counsel's flawed advise was prejudicial. The Court stated, in part:

> Petitioner did not allege in his habeas petition that, had counsel correctly informed him about his parole eligibility date, he would have pleaded not guilty and insisted on going to trial. He alleged no special circumstances that might support the conclusion that he placed particular emphasis on his parole eligibility in deciding whether or not to plead guilty. Indeed, petitioner's mistaken belief that he would become eligible for parole after serving one-third of his sentence would seem to have affected not only his calculation of the time he likely would serve if sentenced pursuant to the proposed plea agreement, but also his calculation of the time he likely would serve if he went to trial and were convicted. (p. 60)

12.10 Another Valid Guilty Plea? Similar facts were presented in *Peguero v. United States* (526 U.S. 23 [1999]). According to the Supreme Court:

> A district court's failure to advise a defendant of his right to appeal does not entitle him to habeas relief if he knew of his right and hence suffered no prejudice from the omission. Because Rule 32(a)(2) requires a district court to advise a defendant of any right to appeal his sentence, it is undisputed that the court's failure to give the required advice was an error in this case. However, as a general rule, a court's failure to give a defendant advice required by the Federal Rules is a sufficient basis for collateral relief only when the defendant is prejudiced by the error. . . . Because petitioner had full knowledge of his right to appeal, the fact that the court violated the Rule, standing alone, does not entitle him to collateral relief. The narrow holding in *Rodriquez v. United States*, 395 U.S. 327, 23 L. Ed. 2d 340, 89 S. Ct. 1715— that when counsel fails to file a requested appeal, a defendant is entitled to resentencing and an appeal without showing that his appeal would likely have merit—is not implicated here because the District Court found that petitioner did not request an appeal. (p. 23)

▨ CHAPTER 13 Rights at Trial

13.1 Putting Charges on Hold The question here is not whether O'Shea's right to a speedy trial was violated but whether the right applies. In light of the Supreme Court's decision in *United States v. Marion* (404 U.S. 307 [1971]), one must ask whether O'Shea was still accused once the *nolle prosequi* had been issued. According to the Supreme Court's decision in *Klopfer v. North Carolina* (386 U.S. 213 [1967]), the answer is yes. According to the Court:

> The petitioner is not relieved of the limitations placed upon his liberty by this prosecution merely because its suspension permits him to go "whithersoever he will." The pendency of the indictment may subject him to public scorn and deprive him of employment, and almost certainly will force curtailment of his speech, associations and participation in unpopular causes. (p. 213)

Further, as to defendant Klopfer's claim that his Sixth Amendment right was *violated*, the Court further stated:

> By indefinitely prolonging this oppression, as well as the "anxiety and concern accompanying public accusation," the criminal procedure condoned in this case by the Supreme Court of North Carolina clearly denies the petitioner the right to a speedy trial which we hold is guaranteed to him by the Sixth Amendment of the Constitution of the United States. (pp. 221–222)

13.2 When the Defendant Is Responsible for the Delay If the delay was caused by the defendant, a speedy trial claim will not likely succeed. If, as in this exercise, the defendant escapes from custody while awaiting trial, he will not succeed in claiming he was denied a speedy trial. Surprisingly, some defendants have tried! According to the Court in *United States v. Taylor* (487 U.S. 326 [1988]):

> Government was prepared to go to trial on the 69th day of the indictment-to-trial period, and it was respondent, not the prosecution, who prevented the trial from going forward in a timely fashion. Respondent argues that he has been charged separately and punished for his failure to appear for trial, that all the time he was at large has been excluded from the speedy trial calculation, and that the District Court therefore was correct in not considering his flight as a factor

in deciding whether to bar reprosecution. Respondent also observes that the Court of Appeals held, and the Government does not dispute here, that his failure to appear for a trial scheduled with only one day remaining in the indictment-to-trial period does not restart the full 70-day speedy trial clock. . . . That respondent's flight does not restart the clock, however, goes only to whether there has been a violation of the Act, and not to what the appropriate remedy should be. Respondent's culpable conduct and, in particular, his responsibility for the failure to meet the timely trial schedule in the first instance are certainly relevant as "circumstances of the case which led to the dismissal," . . . and weigh heavily in favor of permitting reprosecution. (pp. 339–340)

13.3 Court Backlog If the appellate court is reasonably attuned to Supreme Court precedent in this area, it will not agree with Bath's argument. First, she did not assert the right, which is one of the important criteria for judging a Sixth Amendment speedy trial claim (see *Barker v. Wingo*, 407 U.S. 514 [1972]). It is not clear whether the delay was prejudicial, but for the sake of this exercise, assume that it was not. Then, the length of the delay and the reasons for it must be considered. The length was not excessive based on past cases (e.g., *Loud Hawk*), and further, the reason for the delay—case backlog—seems legitimate enough. Unless Bath can find a better reason to appeal her conviction, she will likely remain in prison for some time.

13.4 Deceased Witnesses Bath's appeal is more likely to succeed this time, but the odds are still against her. While it may be true that the defense witness could have cast some doubt on Bath's involvement in the robbery, it is quite likely that bank security camera evidence, teller testimony, and perhaps customer testimony will be enough to convict her anyway. If no such evidence existed, then the delay *could* have been deemed prejudicial. Some court decisions have focused on witness memory loss as a result of delay (e.g., *Loud Hawk*), but none appear to have addressed facts similar to those presented here.

13.5 An Impartial Judge? Impartiality concerns have been raised in contempt hearings. Nothing prohibits judges from holding defendants, witnesses, counsel, and the like in contempt for any number of reasons. However, if a person insults the judge and the judge cannot make an objective decision on the contempt issue in light of this, the Supreme Court requires that the hearing be presided over by another judge (see, e.g., *Mayberry v. Pennsylvania*, 400 U.S. 455 [1971]; *Taylor v. Hayes*, 418 U.S. 488 [1974]). In *Mayberry v. Pennsylvania*, the Court vacated the contempt verdict, stating:

> Our conclusion is that by reason of the Due Process Clause of the Fourteenth Amendment a defendant in criminal contempt proceedings should be given a public trial before a judge other than the one reviled by the contemnor. . . . In the present case that requirement can be satisfied only if the judgment of contempt is vacated so that on remand another judge, not bearing the sting of these slanderous remarks and having the impersonal authority of the law, sits in judgment on the conduct of petitioner as shown by the record. (p. 466)

13.6 A Twist on the Six-Month Rule This exercise puts a twist on the *Lewis v. United States* (518 U.S. 322 [1996]) case cited in this subsection. It essentially asks, What if a defendant is charged with multiple counts of *contempt*, even though each count does not carry a penalty of more than six months in prison? This question was answered in *Codispoti v. Pennsylvania* (418 U.S. 506 [1974]). In that case, the defendants were each charged with several counts of contempt, none of which carried a penalty of more than six months in prison. The total sentence imposed, however, exceeded the six-month limit. In this situation, the Supreme Court held that the defendants were entitled to a jury trial. The Court permitted a jury trial in this context because it is usually not known in advance of a contempt hearing what the maximum penalty might be.

13.7 Small-Jury Voting Requirements Despite the majority views in *Johnson* and *Apodaca* that nonunanimous decisions are constitutional, the Court decided differently on the matter of six-member juries. In *Burch v. Louisiana* (441 U.S. 130 [1979]), the Court struck down a Louisiana statute that permitted nonunanimous decisions by six-member juries. In summary, the most divided verdict the Supreme Court will tolerate is 7 to 3. And if the jury size is less than 10, the Court would seem to favor unanimity. The Court stated, in part:

> The State seeks to justify its use of nonunanimous six-person juries on the basis of the "considerable time" savings that it claims results from trying cases in this manner. It asserts

that under its system, juror deliberation time is shortened and the number of hung juries is reduced. . . . Undoubtedly, the State has a substantial interest in reducing the time and expense associated with the administration of its system of criminal justice. But that interest cannot prevail here. First, on this record, any benefits that might accrue by allowing five members of a six-person jury to render a verdict, as compared with requiring unanimity of a six-member jury, are speculative, at best. More importantly, we think that when a State has reduced the size of its juries to the minimum number of jurors permitted by the Constitution, the additional authorization of nonunanimous verdicts by such juries sufficiently threatens the constitutional principles that led to the establishment of the size threshold that any countervailing interest of the State should yield. (pp. 138–139)

13.8 **What Composes a Distinctive Group?**   Treating groups besides women and minorities as distinctive could open a proverbial can of worms. To illustrate, in *Barber v. Ponte* (772 F.2d 982 [1st Cir. 1985]), the First Circuit pointed out potential problems with recognizing distinctive groups in different categories. In that case, the court was focusing on age as a criterion. It observed, "[I]f age classification is adopted, surely blue-collar workers, yuppies, Rotarians, Eagle Scouts, and an endless variety of other classifications will be entitled to similar treatment" (p. 999). However, the court also stated:

> That is not to say, however, that if a classification were *specifically* and *systematically excluded* from jury duty the same standard would be used as here, where defendant simply relies on a statistical disparity in the venires to challenge its constitutionality. If certain people are specifically and systematically excluded from jury duty, then the jury-administrating authority would have created its own group. Clearly, the state has no right to deliberately exclude specific classes or groups from juries without some very special reason. Thus, it may not *forbid* blue-collar workers, chess players, Masons, etc., from serving on juries. But if there are, as in the present case, mere statistical imbalances, unexplained, the problem is different. Statistical imbalances can be due to a host of factors—younger people may be away at school, serving in the armed forces, surfing in Hawaii, etc. Unless one is prepared to say that there is an affirmative constitutional duty to produce a true cross section on the venire for every imaginable group that exists in our complex society, something which no court has even come close to holding, we should avoid the overwhelming problems and sterile solutions that will result from attempting to subdivide a continuum of ages into "distinctive groups." (pp. 999–1000)

In short, Oki faces an uphill battle if her appeal is to succeed. In all likelihood, it will not.

13.9 **Strong Opinions on the Death Penalty**   As noted in *Witherspoon v. Illinois* (391 U.S. 510 [1968]), a statute providing for the exclusion of all potential jurors who express reservations concerning capital punishment was deemed unconstitutional. Here, however, there is someone who enthusiastically *supports* the death penalty. Further, the potential juror appears at least partly willing to set aside his or her personal convictions. As such, the resulting jury will probably conform to case law surrounding the Sixth Amendment's jury trial requirement. Indeed, as the Court argued in *Witherspoon,* "It is entirely possible . . . that even a juror who believes that capital punishment should never be inflicted and who is irrevocably committed to its abolition could nonetheless subordinate his personal views to what he perceived to be his duty to abide by his oath as a juror and to obey the law of the State" (p. 515, n. 7). The same could be expected to apply to someone who favors capital punishment.

13.10 **Appropriate Use of the Peremptory Challenge**   In *Purkett v. Elem* (514 U.S. 765 [1995]), the case on which this exercise is based, the Supreme Court sanctioned the prosecutor's use of peremptory challenges to exclude two black panel members. The prosecutor reasoned, in part, "I don't like the way they look, with the way the hair is cut on both of them. And the mustaches and beards look suspicious to me" (p. 771). The Court upheld the exclusions but only because the prosecutor seemed to be "genuine" in his argument. It stated:

> The prosecutor's proffered explanation in this case—that he struck juror number 22 because he had long, unkempt hair, a mustache, and a beard—is race neutral and satisfies the prosecution's step two burden of articulating a nondiscriminatory reason for the strike. "The wearing of beards is not a characteristic that is peculiar to any race." . . . And neither is the growing of long, unkempt hair. Thus, the inquiry properly proceeded to step three, where the state court found that the prosecutor was not motivated by discriminatory intent. (p. 769)

CHAPTER 14 More Rights at Trial

14.1   The Right to a Public Trial   In the case on which this exercise is based, *Press-Enterprise Co. v. Superior Court II* (478 U.S. 1 [1986]), the U.S. Supreme Court addressed whether the defendant's attempt to close a pretrial hearing and also whether the state supreme court's refusal to release the transcripts violated the First Amendment. There, the Court held:

> The qualified First Amendment right of access to criminal proceedings applies to preliminary hearings as conducted in California. First, there has been a tradition of public accessibility to preliminary hearings of the type conducted in California. As opposed to grand jury proceedings, preliminary hearings conducted before neutral and detached magistrates have been open to the public. Second, public access to such preliminary hearings is essential to the proper functioning of the criminal justice system. This proper functioning is not made any less essential by the fact that a preliminary hearing cannot result in a conviction and the adjudication is before a magistrate without a jury. The absence of a jury makes the importance of public access even more significant. (p. 1)

However, the Court also said:

> Since a qualified First Amendment right of access attaches to preliminary hearings as conducted in California, the proceedings cannot be closed unless specific, on the record findings are made demonstrating that "closure is essential to preserve higher values and is narrowly tailored to serve that interest" (*Press-Enterprise Co.* v. *Superior Court*, 464 U.S. 501, 510). If the interest asserted is the defendant's right to a fair trial, the preliminary hearing shall not be closed unless there is a "substantial probability" that that right will be prejudiced by publicity that closure would prevent and that reasonable alternatives to closure cannot adequately protect the right. (p. 501)

14.2   Gag Orders on the Media   This case, *Smith v. Daily Mail Publishing Co.* (443 U.S. 97 [1979]), went on to the Supreme Court, which struck down the statute that prohibited publishing the name of any youth charged as a juvenile offender without written order of the juvenile court. The Court stated:

> The magnitude of the State's interest in this statute is not sufficient to justify application of a criminal penalty to respondents. Moreover, the statute's approach does not satisfy constitutional requirements. The statute does not restrict the electronic media or any form of publication, except "newspapers," from printing the names of youths charged in a juvenile proceeding. In this very case, three radio stations announced the alleged assailant's name before the *Daily Mail* decided to publish it. Thus, even assuming the statute served a state interest of the highest order, it does not accomplish its stated purpose. (pp. 104–105)

14.3   Indigence and the Right to be Present   The Supreme Court granted *certiorari* (i.e., agreed to hear) in *Tacon v. Arizona* (410 U.S. 351 [1973]), the case on which this exercise is based, but it subsequently held that *certiorari* was "improvidently granted," meaning that the Court granted it mistakenly. Thus, the Arizona Supreme Court's decision in *State v. Tacon* (107 Ariz. 353 [1971]) must be examined. There, the court held:

> The defendant's [Tacon's] own testimony clearly shows he was aware that the trial was set for March 31st and that the trial would proceed without him if he failed to appear. The trial court was of the opinion that Tacon's absence was voluntary and there is substantial evidence in the record to support that opinion. Under these circumstances, we hold that Tacon's absence from his trial constituted a knowing and intelligent waiver of his right to be present at the trial and that the trial court, therefore, did not err in proceeding with the trial in his absence. (p. 357)

14.4   An Unavailable Witness   Surprisingly, in *Ohio v. Roberts* (448 U.S. 56 [1980]), the Court answered yes on similar facts. Part of the reason for this was that the witness's mother informed the prosecution that the witness was traveling. Even so, it is difficult to believe that the prosecution's decision to mail five subpoenas constituted a "diligent search." The dissent's argument was persuasive:

> In the present case, I am simply unable to conclude that the prosecution met its burden of establishing Anita Isaacs' [the witness's] unavailability. From all that appears in the record— and there has been no suggestion that the record is incomplete in this respect—the State's *total*

effort to secure Anita's attendance at respondent's trial consisted of the delivery of five subpoenas in her name to her parents' residence, and three of those were issued after the authorities had learned that she was no longer living there. At least four months before the trial began, the prosecution was aware that Anita had moved away; yet during that entire interval it did nothing whatsoever to try to make contact with her. It is difficult to believe that the State would have been so derelict in attempting to secure the witness's presence at trial had it not had her favorable preliminary hearing testimony upon which to rely in the event of her "unavailability." The perfunctory steps which the State took in this case can hardly qualify as a "good-faith effort." In point of fact, it was no effort at all. (pp. 79–80)

14.5 A Hearsay Exception? The Supreme Court affirmed, holding that the girl's statements did not contain particularized guarantees of trustworthiness. Specifically, the Court held:

> In admitting the evidence, the trial court identified only two factors—whether the child had a motive to make up her story and whether, given her age, the statements were of the type that one would expect a child to fabricate—relating to circumstances surrounding the making of the statements. The State Supreme Court properly focused on the presumptive unreliability of the out-of-court statements and on the suggestive manner in which the doctor conducted his interview. Viewing the totality of the circumstances, there is no special reason for supposing that the incriminating statements about the child's own abuse were particularly trustworthy. Her statement about her sister presents a closer question. Although its spontaneity and the change in her demeanor suggest that she may have been telling the truth, spontaneity may be an inaccurate indicator of trustworthiness where there has been prior interrogation, prompting, or manipulation by adults. Moreover, the statement was not made under circumstances of reliability comparable to those required, for example, for the admission of excited utterances or statements made for purposes of medical diagnosis or treatment. Because the State does not challenge the State Supreme Court's determination that the Confrontation Clause error was not harmless beyond a reasonable doubt, this Court will not revisit the issue. (pp. 825–827)

14.6 The Defendant's Right to Obtain Evidence In *Pennsylvania v. Ritchie* (480 U.S. 39 [1987]), the case on which this exercise is based, the Supreme Court agreed with the defendant but not completely. The Court affirmed, in part, and reversed, in part, the state supreme court's decision to grant the defendant's access to the records. The Court held:

> Criminal defendants have the right under the Compulsory Process Clause to the government's assistance in compelling the attendance of favorable witnesses at trial and the right to put before a jury evidence that might influence the determination of guilt. However, this Court has never held that the Clause guarantees the right to discover the *identity* of witnesses, or to require the government to produce exculpatory evidence. Instead, claims such as respondent's traditionally have been evaluated under the broader protections of the Due Process Clause of the Fourteenth Amendment. Compulsory process provides no greater protections in this area than those afforded by due process, and thus respondent's claims more properly are considered by reference to due process. (pp. 55–56)

The Court also held:

> Under due process principles, the government has the obligation to turn over evidence in its possession that is both favorable to the accused and material to guilt or punishment. Evidence is material only if there is a reasonable probability that, had the evidence been disclosed, the result of the proceeding would have been different. Although the public interest in protecting sensitive information such as that in CYS [the agency] records is strong, this interest does not necessarily prevent disclosure in all circumstances. Because the Pennsylvania Legislature contemplated *some* use of CYS records in judicial proceedings, there is no reason to believe that relevant information would not be disclosed when a court of competent jurisdiction determined that the information was "material" to the accused's defense. The Pennsylvania Supreme Court thus properly ordered a remand for further proceedings. Respondent is entitled to have the CYS file reviewed by the trial court to determine whether it contains information that probably would have changed the outcome of his trial. If it does, he must be given a new trial. If the CYS file contains no such information, or if the nondisclosure is harmless beyond a reasonable doubt, the trial court will be free to reinstate the prior conviction. (pp. 57–58)

14.7 Threatening a Witness   The Supreme Court answered yes and overturned the conviction. The Court said:

> The trial judge gratuitously singled out this one witness for a lengthy admonition on the dangers of perjury. But the judge did not stop at warning the witness of his right to refuse to testify and of the necessity to tell the truth. Instead, the judge implied that he expected Mills [the witness] to lie, and went on to assure him that if he lied, he would be prosecuted and probably convicted for perjury, that the sentence for that conviction would be added on to his present sentence, and that the result would be to impair his chances for parole. At least some of these threats may have been beyond the power of this judge to carry out. Yet, in light of the great disparity between the posture of the presiding judge and that of a witness in these circumstances, the unnecessarily strong terms used by the judge could well have exerted such duress on the witness' mind as to preclude him from making a free and voluntary choice whether or not to testify. (pp. 97–98)

Further, the Court said:

> [W]e conclude that the judge's threatening remarks, directed only at the single witness for the defense, effectively drove that witness off the stand, and thus deprived the petitioner of due process of law under the Fourteenth Amendment. The admonition by the Texas Court of Criminal Appeals might well have given the trial judge guidance for future cases, but it did not serve to repair the infringement of the petitioner's due process rights under the Fourteenth Amendment. (p. 98)

14.8 A Case of Double Jeopardy?   On one level, it would seem so; taking someone's property in addition to convicting him or her criminally seems like two punishments. However, the Supreme Court disagreed. It held in *Ursery*:

> The Double Jeopardy Clause provides: [N]or shall any person be subject for the same offense to be twice put in jeopardy of life or limb. . . . [I]n a long line of cases, this Court has considered the application of the Double Jeopardy Clause to civil forfeitures, consistently concluding that the Clause does not apply to such actions because they do not impose punishment. . . . It is the property which is proceeded against, and, by resort to legal fiction, held guilty and condemned as though it were conscious instead of inanimate and insentient. In a criminal prosecution it is the wrongdoer in person who is proceeded against, convicted, and punished. The forfeiture is no part of the punishment for the criminal offense. The provision of the Fifth Amendment to the Constitution in respect of double jeopardy does not apply. (p. 274)

14.9 Reprosecution after a Mistrial   The Court answered no. Namely:

> Where a defendant, by requesting a mistrial exercises his choice in favor of terminating the trial the Double Jeopardy Clause will not bar re-prosecution absent provocative or bad-faith conduct by the judge or prosecutor. *United States v. Dinitz*, 424 U.S. 600, 611. Here, as in *Dinitz*, the proceedings were terminated after jeopardy had attached at the defendant's request and with his consent, and there was no judicial or prosecutorial error that was intended to provoke the motion or that was otherwise motivated by bad faith. The prosecutor's failure properly to draft the information was at most negligent, and the District Court's failure to postpone the taking of evidence until it could fully consider petitioner's motion was entirely reasonable in light of the last-minute timing of the motion and defense counsel's failure to request a continuance or otherwise stress the importance to petitioner of not being placed in jeopardy on a defective charge. (pp. 33–34)

14.10 Outrageous Government Conduct   In this case, *United States v. Twigg* (588 F.2d 373 [3rd Cir. 1978]), the Court of Appeals for the Third Circuit decided that the government's conduct violated due process. The court concluded that the government's conduct reached a "demonstrable level of outrageousness." The court stated, in part:

> At the behest of the Drug Enforcement Agency, Kubica, a convicted felon striving to reduce the severity of his sentence, communicated with Neville and suggested the establishment of a speed laboratory. The Government gratuitously supplied about 20 percent of the glassware and the indispensable ingredient, phenyl-2-propanone. It is unclear whether the parties had the means or the money to obtain the chemical on their own. The DEA made arrangements with chemical supply houses to facilitate the purchase of the rest of the materials. Kubica,

operating under the business name "Chem Kleen" supplied by the DEA, actually purchased all of the supplies with the exception of a separatory funnel. . . . When problems were encountered in locating an adequate production site, the Government found the solution by providing an isolated farmhouse well-suited for the location of an illegally operated laboratory. Again, there was no cost to the defendants. At all times during the production process, Kubica was completely in charge and furnished all of the laboratory expertise. Neither defendant had the know-how with which to actually manufacture methamphetamine. The assistance they provided was minimal and then at the specific direction of Kubica. (pp. 280–281)

Again, the issue in this case was not entrapment but rather the government's outrageous conduct and violation of due process. The defendant's conviction was overturned by the court.

CHAPTER 15 Sentencing, Appeals, and *Habeas Corpus*

15.1 Death Penalty Sentencing   Not all states require that the jury decide if a death sentence is appropriate. As in this exercise, some states permit the jury to make a nonbinding recommendation to the trial judge, leaving it to the judge to decide whether a death sentence is in order. The Supreme Court has upheld state laws that give the final word to the judge. In *Harris v. Alabama* (513 U.S. 504 [1994]), the pertinent case, the Court held, in part:

> We have rejected the notion that "a specific method for balancing mitigating and aggravating factors in a capital sentencing proceeding is constitutionally required." . . . Equally settled is the corollary that the Constitution does not require a State to ascribe any specific weight to particular factors, either in aggravation or mitigation, to be considered by the sentencer. . . . To require that "great weight" be given to the jury recommendation here, one of the criteria to be considered by the sentencer, would offend these established principles and place within constitutional ambit micromanagement tasks that properly rest within the State's discretion to administer its criminal justice system. We therefore hold that the Eighth Amendment does not require the State to define the weight the sentencing judge must accord an advisory jury verdict. (p. 512)

Note again, however, that it is not appropriate for judges themselves to determine whether aggravating circumstances are present (see *Ring v. Arizona*, 122 S.Ct. 2428 [2002]).

15.2 Constitutional Rights during the Appeals Process   According to the Supreme Court's decision in *Griffin v. Illinois* (351 U.S. 12 [1956]), the answer is no. Further reaffirming this view, in *Draper v. Washington* (372 U.S. 487 [1963]), the case on which this exercise is based, the Supreme Court held that the judge's decision violated the equal protection clause of the Fourteenth Amendment: "By allowing the trial court to prevent petitioners from having stenographic support or its equivalent for presentation of each of their separate contentions to the appellate tribunal, the State of Washington has denied them the rights assured them by this Court's decisions in *Griffin*" (p. 497). Further, the Court stated, "In all cases the duty of the State is to provide the indigent as adequate and effective an appellate review as that given appellants with funds—the State must provide the indigent defendant with means of presenting his contentions to the appellate court which are as good as those available to a nonindigent defendant with similar contentions" (p. 496). Other cases affirming the decision in *Griffin* are *Entsminger v. Iowa* (386 U.S. 748 [1967]) and *Mayer v. Chicago* (404 U.S. 189 [1971]).

15.3 Effective Assistance of Counsel during the Appeals Process   In *Wainwright v. Torna* (455 U.S. 586 [1982]), the case on which this exercise is based, the Supreme Court decided against the petitioner. It held:

> In *Ross v. Moffitt*, 417 U.S. 600 (1974), this Court held that a criminal defendant does not have a constitutional right to counsel to pursue discretionary state appeals or applications for review in this Court. Respondent does not contest the finding of the District Court that he had no absolute right to appeal his convictions to the Florida Supreme Court. Since respondent had no constitutional right to counsel, he could not be deprived of the effective assistance of counsel by his retained counsel's failure to file the application timely. The District Court was correct in dismissing the petition. (pp. 587–588)

15.4 Retaliation for a Successful Appeal   According to the Supreme Court, the second prosecution was vindictive. The Court held:

> The prosecution of respondent for manslaughter, following his invocation of his statutory right to appeal his misdemeanor convictions, was unconstitutional as a violation of due process. . . . The fact that the proceedings before the Justice of the Peace were the county prosecutor's responsibility, whereas the felony indictment was obtained by the District Attorney, who was then involved in the manslaughter trial, may not make inappropriate the presumption of unconstitutional vindictiveness arising from obtaining that indictment. That presumption does not hinge on the continued involvement of a particular individual. In any event, here the county prosecutor was the State's sole representative at the arraignment on the felony indictment and, as required by statute, assisted at the manslaughter trial. (pp. 30–32)

15.5 An Appeal Prior to Adjudication   The Supreme Court has not decided on this issue, but at least one appellate court has. The Second Circuit actually dismissed the appeal, claiming as follows:

> We think the cases that have dismissed appeals by those under investigation, even in the absence of a pending criminal prosecution, have correctly applied the principles of *DiBella*. Where, as here, the party moving for return of seized property is the subject of a grand jury inquiry, allowance of an appeal from denial of the motion would interfere with the grand jury proceedings . . . and permit piecemeal appeals. . . . The term of the grand jury is limited. If its inquiry results in indictment, the lawfulness of the seizure will be fully considered upon a motion to suppress, and any ruling adverse to the defendant will be reviewable upon appeal from a final judgment; if the grand jury declines to indict the movant, or adjourns without indicting it, its property will most likely be returned, and if not, it can initiate an independent proceeding for its return. . . . Under *DiBella* a prompt appeal would be available after denial of a motion for return of property brought by a movant with no connection to either an actual or potential criminal case, a person not suspected of anything who happened to have on his premises property pertinent to an investigation or prosecution of someone else; a motion by one in that situation would be solely for the return of property. Because the appellant is not within that category, the denial of its motion is not a final order. (p. 156)

15.6 A Prosecution Appeal   According to the Supreme Court, the answer is yes. As decided in *United States v. Scott* (437 U.S. 82 [1978]), the case on which this exercise is based, the prosecution can appeal a judge's decision to dismiss the case against the defendant because a dismissal is not the same as an acquittal; thus, the double-jeopardy protection does not apply. In the Court's words:

> In a situation such as the instant one, where a defendant chooses to avoid conviction, not because of his assertion that the Government has failed to make out a case against him, but because of a legal claim that the Government's case against him must fail even though it might satisfy the trier of fact that he was guilty beyond a reasonable doubt, the defendant by deliberately choosing to seek termination of the trial suffers no injury cognizable under the Double Jeopardy Clause if the Government is permitted to appeal from such a trial-court ruling favoring the defendant. The Double Jeopardy Clause, which guards against Government oppression, does not relieve a defendant of the consequences of his voluntary choice. (p. 82)

15.7 A Harmless Error?   The only way to answer this question is to have a full understanding of what *other* evidence was used against the defendant. Only then, will it be possible to determine whether the error in question was harmful beyond a reasonable doubt. In *United States v. Hasting* (461 U.S. 499 [1983]), the case on which this exercise is based, the Supreme Court held that the error was harmless because the remaining evidence was sufficient for a conviction. The Court stated:

> *Chapman v. California*, 386 U.S. 18, held that a *Griffin* error is not *per se* error requiring automatic reversal and that a conviction should be affirmed if the reviewing court concludes that, on the whole record, the error was harmless beyond a reasonable doubt. It is the reviewing court's duty to consider the trial record as a whole and to ignore errors that are harmless, including most constitutional violations. Here, the Court of Appeals' analysis, in making passing reference to the harmless-error doctrine but not applying it, failed to strike the balance between disciplining the prosecutor on the one hand and the interest in the

prompt administration of justice and the victims' interests in not being subjected to the burdens of another trial on the other. (pp. 507–509)

Further, the Court said:

> On the whole record, the error identified by the Court of Appeals was harmless beyond a reasonable doubt. This Court has the authority to review records to evaluate a harmless-error claim, and the pertinent question here is whether, absent the prosecutor's allusion to the failure of the defense to proffer evidence to rebut the victims' testimony, it is clear beyond a reasonable doubt that the jury would have returned a guilty verdict. The victims' testimony negated any doubt as to identification, and neutral witnesses corroborated critical aspects of the victims' testimony, thus establishing a compelling case of guilt. On the other hand, the scanty evidence tendered by respondents relates to their claims of mistaken identity and consent. The patent inconsistency of these defense theories could hardly have escaped the jurors' attention. (pp. 510–512)

15.8 A Constitutional Question?

It depends. If Yu makes no constitutional claim, her petition will not be heard. According to the Supreme Court in *Townsend v. Sain* (372 U.S. 293 [1963]), "[T]he existence merely of newly discovered evidence relevant to the guilt of a state prisoner is not a ground for relief on federal *habeas corpus*" (p. 317). However, if Yu crafts her petition in constitutional terms, a hearing could be granted to determine the constitutionality of her confinement. It is, therefore, important that a *habeas corpus* petition raises constitutional questions. Citing *Price v. Johnson* (334 U.S. 266 [1948]), the Court further stated, "The primary purpose of a *habeas corpus* proceeding is to make certain that a man is not unjustly imprisoned. And if for some justifiable reason he was previously unable to assert his rights or was unaware of the significance of relevant facts, it is neither necessary nor reasonable to deny him all opportunity of obtaining judicial relief" (p. 291).

15.9 Timing of a Habeas Corpus Petition

No. The Supreme Court held in *Schulp v. Delo* (513 U.S. 298 [1995]), the case on which this exercise is based:

> The standard of *Murray v. Carrier* . . . —which requires a habeas petitioner to show that "a constitutional violation has probably resulted in the conviction of one who is actually innocent" . . . —rather than the more stringent *Sawyer* standard, governs the miscarriage of justice inquiry when a petitioner who has been sentenced to death raises a claim of actual innocence to avoid a procedural bar to the consideration of the merits of his constitutional claims. (p 298)

The Court also stated:

> *Carrier*, rather than *Sawyer*, properly strikes the balance between the societal interests and the individual interest in justice, when the claimed injustice is that constitutional error has resulted in the conviction of one who is actually innocent. Though challenges to the propriety of imposing a death sentence are routinely asserted in capital cases, a substantial claim that constitutional error has caused the conviction of an innocent person is extremely rare and must be supported by new reliable evidence that was not presented at trial, evidence obviously unavailable in the vast majority of cases. Thus, the threat to judicial resources, finality, and comity posed by actual innocence claims is significantly less than that posed by sentencing claims. More importantly, the individual interest in avoiding injustice is most compelling in the context of actual innocence, since the quintessential miscarriage of justice is the execution of an innocent person. The less exacting *Carrier* standard of proof reflects the relative importance attached to the ultimate decision. Application of the stricter *Sawyer* standard would give insufficient weight to the correspondingly greater injustice that is implicated by an actual innocence claim. (pp. 323–327).

15.10 Were All State Remedies Exhausted?

No. In *Anderson v. Harless* (459 U.S. 4 [1982]), the case on which this exercise is based, the Supreme Court held, "The requirement . . . that the state courts must have been provided a 'fair opportunity' to apply controlling legal principles to the facts bearing upon the federal habeas petitioner's constitutional claim was not met here. The 'substance' of respondent's federal *habeas corpus* claim was not fairly presented to the state courts so as to meet [the] exhaustion requirement" (p. 4). In other words, because the petitioner failed to present the due process claim to the state-level appellate courts, he failed to meet the exhaustion requirement, as initially set forth in *Ex parte Hawk* (321 U.S. 114 [1944]).

CASE INDEX

Note: **Bold** entries indicate Key Cases.

A

Abney v. United States, 431 U.S. 651 (1977), 449

Ackies v. Purdy, 322 F. Supp. 38(S.D. Fla. 1970), 290

Adams v. Williams, 407 U.S. 143 (1972), 90, 154, 170, 175

Adamson v. California, 322 U.S. 46 (1947), 6

Adarand Construction, Inc. v. Pena, 515 U.S. 200 (1995), 157–158

Agnello v. United States, 269 U.S. 20 (1925), 55

***Aguilar v. Texas,* 378 U.S. 108 (1964), 84, 85**

Air Pollution Variance Bd. v. Western Alfalfa Corp., 416 U.S. 861 (1974), 78

Ake v. Oklahoma, 470 U.S. 68 (1985), 335

Alabama v, Shelton, 535 U.S. 654 (2002), 332

***Alabama v. White,* 496 U.S. 325 (1990), 90**

Albernaz v. United States, 450 U.S. 333 (1981), 429

Albertson v. Subversive Activities Control Board, 382 U.S. 70 (1965), 230

Albright v. Oliver, 510 U.S. 266 (1994), 87

Alcorta v. Texas, 355 U.S. 28 (1957), 301

Alderman v. United States, 394 U.S. 165 (1969), 128

Allen v. Illinois, 478 U.S. 364 (1986), 232

Almeida-Sanchez v. United States, 413 U.S. 266 (1973), 207

Anaya v. Hansen, 781 F.2d 1 (1st Cir. 1986), 393

***Andersen v. Maryland,* 427 U.S. 463 (1976), 101**

Anderson v. Creighton, 483 U.S. 635 (1987), 45

Apodaca v. Oregon, 406 U.S. 404 (1972), 387

Argersinger v. Hamlin, 407 U.S. 25 (1972), 332

Arizona v. Evans, 514 U.S. 1 (1995), 61

***Arizona v. Hicks,* 480 U.S. 321 (1987), 163**

Arizona v. Youngblood, 488 U.S. 51 (1988), 304

Arkanwas v. Sanders, 442 U.S. 753 (1979), 153

Ashcraft v. Tennessee, 322 U.S. 143 (1944), 235, 236

Atkins v. Virginia, 122 S.Ct. 2242 (2002), 441

***Atwater v. City of Lago Vista,* 532 U.S. 318 (2001), 110–111**

Atwater v. City of Lago Vista, 533 U.S. 924 (2001), 9

Austin v. United States, 509 U.S. 602 (1993), 133

B

Baker v. Putnal, 75 F.3d 190 (5th Cir. 1996), 45

***Baldwin v. New York,* 399 U.S. 66 (1970), 381**

Ballew v. Georgia, 435 U.S. 223 (1978), 387

Barber v. Page, 390 U.S. 719 (1968), 413

***Barker v. Wingo,* 407 U.S. 514 (1972), 371, 374–375, 376**

***Batson v. Kentucky,* 476 U.S. 79 (1986), 398–399**

Baxstrom v. Herold, 383 U.S. 107, 15L.E.2d 620, 86 S.Ct.760 (1966), 425

Beard v. Banks, 542 U.S. 406 (2004), 465

***Beck v. Ohio,* 379 U.S. 89 (1964), 81**

Beckwith v. United States, 425 U.S. 341 (1976), 107, 240

Beecher v. Alabama, 408 U.S. 234 (1972), 236

Bell v. Cone, 535 U.S. 685 (2002), 339

***Bell v. Wolfish,* 441 U.S. 529 (1979), 284, 291**

***Benton v. Maryland,* 395 U.S. 784 (1969), 7, 424**

Berger v. New York, 388 U.S. 41 (1967), 126

***Berkemer v. McCarty,* 468 U.S. 420 (1984), 240**

Berry v. Cincinnati, 414 U.S. 29 (1973), 454

Betts v. Brady, 316 U.S. 455 (1942), 331

***Bivens v. Six Unknown Named Agents,* 403 U.S. 388 (1971), 44**

Blackledge v. Allison, 431 U.S. 63 (1977), 347

Blackledge v. Perry, 417 U.S. 21 (1974), 318, 448

Blake v. Cich, 79 F.R.D. 398 (D. Minn. 1978), 273

Blakely v. Washington, 542 U.S. 296 (2004), 400

Blanton v. City of North Las Vegas, 489 U.S. 538 (1989), 386

Blockburger v. United States, 284 U.S. 299 (1932), 426

Blum v. Yaretsky, 457 U.S. 991 (1982), 38

Board of Commissioners of Bryan County v. Brown, 520 U.S. 397 (1997), 41

***Board of Education v. Earls,* 536 U.S. 822 (2002), 215**

***Bordenkircher v. Hayes,* 434 U.S. 357 (1978), 310, 353, 354**

Bounds v. Smith, 430 U.S. 817 (1977), 464

Bousley v. United States, 523 U.S. 614 (1998), 465

Boyd v. United States, 116 U.S. 616 (1886), 54

***Boykin v. Alabama,* 395 U.S. 238 (1969), 362, 364**

Bradley v. Fisher, 80 U.S. 335 (1871), 44

***Brady v. Maryland,* 373 U.S. 83 (1963), 302**

***Brady v. United States,* 397 U.S. 742 (1970), 351, 352**

Brecht v. Abrahamson, 507 U.S. 619 (1993), 461

***Breithaupt v. Abram,* 352 U.S. 432 (1957), 144–145**

***Brewer v. Williams,* 430 U.S. 387 (1977), 237**

***Brinegar v. United States,* 338 U.S. 160 (1949), 81**

Brogan v. United States, 522 U.S. 398 (1998), 229

Brooks v. Tennessee, 406 U.S. 605 (1972), 298

Brown v. City of Oneonta, 195 F.3 111 (2nd Cir. 1999), 159

Brown v. Illinois, 422 U.S. 590 (1975), 63

Brown v. Louisiana, 447 U.S. 323 (1980), 454

***Brown v. Mississippi,* 297 U.S. 278 (1936), 234**

Brown v. Ohio, 432 U.S. 161 (1977), 427

Brown v. Texas, 443 U.S. 47 (1979), 90–91, 192

Brown v. United States, 356 U.S. 148 (1958), 228

Bumper v. North Carolina, 391 U.S. 543 (1968), 220

***Burdeau v. McDowell,* 256 U.S. 465 (1921), 70**

***Butterworth v. Smith,* 494 U.S. 624 (1990), 326**

Butz v. Economou, 438 U.S. 478 (1978), 44

527

Evitts v. Lucey, 469 U.S. 387 (1985), 447
Ex parte Hawk, 321 U.S. 114 (1944), 462
Ex parte Young, 209 U.S. 123 (1908), 45

F

Fare v. Michael C., 442 U.S. 707 (1979), 236n, 246, 248
Faretta v. California, 422 U.S. 806 (1975), 334
***Fay v. Noia,* 372 U.S. 391 (1963), 461, 463**
FDIC v. Meyer, 510 U.S. 471 (1994), 44
Felker v. Turpin, 518 U.S. 651 (1996), 467
***Ferguson v. Charleston,* 532 U.S. 67 (2001), 214**
Fikes v. Alabama, 352 U.S. 191 (1957), 234, 235
Fisher v. United States, 425 U.S. 391 (1976), 233
Fiske v. Kansas, 274 U.S. 380 (1927), 7
Flanagan v. State, 586 So.2d 1085 (Fla. Dist. Ct. App. 1991), 188
Flores v. Superior Court, 17 Cal.App.3d 219 (1971), 82
***Florida v. Bostick,* 501 U.S. 429 (1991), 80, 173, 188**
***Florida v. Jimeno,* 500 U.S. 248 (1991), 221**
Florida v. Nixon, 543 U.S. 175 (2004), 339
Florida v. Riley, 488 U.S. 445 (1989), 77
Florida v. RodriguezI, 469 U.S. 1 (1984), 172
***Florida v. Royer,* 460 U.S. 491 (1983), 105–106, 173, 174, 189, 192–193**
Ford v. Seabold, 841 F.2d 677 (6th Cir. 1988), 393
Ford v. Wainwright, 477 U.S. 399 (1986), 441
Frank v. Maryland, 359 U.S. 360 (1959), 203
Franks v. Delaware, 438 U.S. 154 (1978), 87–88
Frazier v. Cupp, 394 U.S. 731 (1969), 235
Fugate v. New Mexico, 471 U.S. 1112 (1985), 427
***Furman V. Georgia,* 408 U.S. 238 (1972), 440**

G

Gagnon v. Scarpelli, 422 U.S. 778 (1973), 333
Gannett Co., Inc. v. DePasquale, 443 U.S. 368 (1979), 405
***Garner v. United States,* 424 U.S. 648 (1976), 228, 229**
***Garrity v. New Jersey,* 385 U.S. 493 (1967), 230–231**
***Geddes v. Northwest Missouri State College,* 49F.3d 426, 8th Cir. (1995), 5, 44**
Gentile v. Nevada State Bar, 501 U.S. 1030 (1991), 407
Georgia v. McCollum, 502 U.S. 1056 (1992), 399
***Gerstein v. Pugh,* 420 U.S. 103 (1975), 108, 282, 292, 332**
***Gideon v. Wainwright,* 372 U.S. 335 (1963), 7, 331, 332, 442, 453**
Giglio v. United States, 405 U.S. 150 (1972), 302
Gilbert v. Mara, 410 U.S. 19 (1973), 233
Gillett v. State, 588 S.W.2d 361, (Tex.Crim.App. 1979), 71
Glasser v. United States, 315 U.S. 60 (1942), 392
Globe Newspaper Co. v. Superior Court, 457 U.S. 596 (1982), 405
G.M. Leasing Corp. v. United States, 429 U.S. 338 (1977), 206
Godinez v. Moran, 509 U.S. 389 (1993), 334–335
Goldman v. United States, 316 U.S. 129 (1942), 126
Goldsby v. United States, 160 U.S. 70 (1895), 293
Gollaher v. United States, 419 F.2d 520 (9th Cir. 1969), 328
Gonzalez v. Crosby, 125 S.Ct. 2641 (2005), 467
***Gooding v. United States,* 416 U.S. 430 (1974), 120**
Government of Virgin Islands v. Grant, 938 F.2d 401 (1985), 273
***Graham v. Connor,* 490 U.S. 386 (1989), 24, 43, 50, 115**
Granberry v. Greer, 481 U.S. 129 (1987), 462
***Gray v. Mississippi,* 481 U.S. 648 (1987), 400**
Green v. United States, 355 U.S. 184, 187-188 (1957), 424
***Gregg v. Georgia,* 428 U.S. 153 (1976), 440**
Griffin v. California, 380 U.S. 609 (1965), 411
***Griffin v. Illinois,* 351 U.S. 12 (1956), 444, 464**

***Griffin v. Wisconsin,* 483 U.S. 868 (1987), 93, 215, 216**
Griffith v. Kentucky, 479 U.S. 314 (1987), 454–455
Groh v. Ramirez, 540 U.S. 551 (2004), 101
Grosso v. United States, 390 U.S. 62 (1968), 230

H

***Hale v. Henkel,* 201 U.S. 43 (1906), 328–329**
Haley v. Ohio, 332 U.S. 596 (1948), 235–236
Ham v. South Carolina, 409 U.S. 524 (1973), 396
Hamling v. United States, 418 U.S. 87 (1974), 394
***Hampton v. United States,* 425 U.S. 484 (1976), 430, 431**
Harlow v. Fitzgerald, 457 U.S. 800 (1982), 24, 44, 45
Harmelin v. Michigan, 501 U.S. 957 (1991), 441
***Harris v. New York,* 401 U.S. 222 (1971), 252**
***Harris v. United States,* 331 U.S. 145 (1947), 122**
Hayden v. County of Nassau, 180 F.3d 42 (2nd Cir. 1999), 157
***Hayes v. Florida,* 470 U.S. 811 (1985), 195, 260, 262**
Haynes v. United States, 390 U.S. 85 (1968), 230
Heller v. Doe, 509 U.S. 312 (1993), 157
Helvering v. Mitchell, 303 U.S. 391 (1938), 425
***Henderson v. Morgan,* 426 U.S. 637 (1976), 363**
Henry v. United States, 361 U.S. 98 (1959), 87, 104
Hernandez v. New York, 500 U.S. 352 (1991), 399
***Herrera v. Collins,* 506 U.S. 390 (1993), 460**
Hilbel v. Sixth Judicial District of Nevada, 5YZ U.S. 177 (2004), 173
Hill v. California, 401 U.S. 797 (1971), 116–117
Hill v. Lockhart, 474 U.S. 52 (1985), 352
***Hill v. United States,* 368 U.S. 424 (1962), 461**
***Hoffa v. United States,* 385 U.S. 293 (1966), 74**
Holland v. Illinois, 493 U.S. 474 (1990), 399
Holt v. United States, 218 U.S. 245 (1910), 233
***Horton v. California,* 496 U.S. 128 (1990), 155, 164**
Horton v. Goose Creek Independent School District, 690 F.3d 470 (5th Cir. 1982), 212
Howard v. Grinage, 82 F.3d 1343 (6th Cir. 1996), 44
***Hudson v. McMillian,* 503 U.S. 1(1992), 43**
Hudson v. Palmer, 468 U.S. 517 (1984), 291
Hunter v. Underwood, 471 U.S. 222 (1985), 157
***Hurtado v. California,* 110 U.S. 516 (1884), 6, 321**
Husty v. United States, 282 U.S. 694 (1931), 152–153

I

Idaho v. Wright, 497 U.S. 805 (1990), 414
***Illinois v. Allen,* 397 U.S. 337 (1970), 407, 410**
Illinois v. Andreas, 463 U.S. 765 (1983), 207
Illinois v. Caballes, 543 U.S. 405 (2005), 154
***Illinois v. Gates,* 462 U.S. 213 (1983), 85**
***Illinois v. Lafayette,* 462 U.S. 640 (1983), 92, 201**
***Illinois v. Lidster,* 540 U.S. 419 (2004), 209**
***Illinois v. Rodriguez,* 497 U.S. 177 (1990), 222**
Illinois v. Somerville, 420 U.S. 458 (1973), 428
Illinois v. Wardlow, 528 U.S. 119 (2000), 91
In re Bradley, 318 U.S. 50 (1943), 429
In re Brian A., 173 Cal.App.3d 1168 (1985), 83
In re Frank V., 233 Cal.App.3d 1232 (1991), 83
***In re Gault,* 387 U.S. 1 (1967), 232**
In re Groban's Petition, 352 U.S. 330 (1957), 328
In re Johnathan, M., 117 Cal.App.3d 530 (1981), 83
In re Marcellus L., 279 Cal. Rptr. 901 (Ct. Spp. 1991), 218
***In re Oliver,* 333 U.S. 257 (1948), 7, 404**
In re Trinidad V., 212 Cal.App.3d 1077 (1989), 82
INS v. Lopez-Mendoza, 468 U.S. 1032 (1984), 60

*Note: **Bold** page numbers indicate citations of key terms.*

protective sweeps of, 183–184
third-party, arrests in, 109–110
hospital patients, drug and alcohol testing
of, 214
hostile witness, 260
hot pursuit, searches and, 143–144
house. *See also* homes
definition of, **69**

I

identification procedures, 256–279
constitutional restrictions on, 258–260
exclusionary rule and, 275, 277–278
illegal searches and seizures and,
277–278
pretrial, 261–266
tainted, **276,** 278
during trial, 266, 268–275
illegal immigrant checkpoints, 207–208
"immediately apparent" requirement, of
"plain view" doctrine, 163–164
Immigration and Naturalization
Service, deportation hearings of,
exclusionary rule and, 60
immunity
grants of, 231, 329
qualified, **45**–46
sovereign, **44**–45
impact, disparate, **158**
impartial judge, **379**
right to, 379–381
impeachment cases, confessions and exclusionary rule and, 251–252
impeachment exception to
exclusionary rule, **61**–62
impeachment of witness, **274**
in-court showup, **263**–264
inadvertency
Eighth Amendment and, 43
in "plain view" doctrine, 164
incapacitation, as goal of sentencing, **436**–437
incorporation, of federal laws to states
constitutional provision for, 4
controversy over, 5–6
definition of, **5**
fundamental rights perspective on, 6–7
selective, 6
total, 6
views on, 6
incriminating evidence, interrogation and,
242
independent source exception to "fruit of
the poisonous tree" doctrine, **64**
indeterminate sentencing, **437**
indictment
by grand jury, 31
plea bargaining and, 363
speedy trial and, 373
indifference, deliberate, 43
indigent defendant, right to counsel of, 335
individual liability, **42**–44

inevitable discovery exception to "fruit of
the poisonous tree" doctrine, 64
informants
probable cause and, 84–86
searches and, 74–75
information
communicative, 232–233
mistaken, reasonable reliance on, 87
prosecution by, 31
injunctive relief, **36**
inspections, **202**–207
business, 204–206
fire, 206
home, 203–204
international mail, 206–207
welfare, 204
institutional agents, searches and, 74–75
intent, Eighth Amendment and, 43
intentional tort, **46**
interlocutory appeal, **449**
Internal Revenue Service actions,
exclusionary rule and, 59–60
internal review of law enforcement, **51**–52
international mail inspections, 206–207
interrogations, 234–252. *See also* confession(s)
definition of, **242**
general questioning distinguished from,
243
incriminating evidence and, 242
Miranda approach to, 242–243. *See also*
Miranda warnings/rights
Sixth Amendment approach to, 237–239
inventory searches, **200**–202
person, **201**–202
vehicle, 200–201, 202–203
investigative detentions, 195
definition of, **195**
in drug courier profiling, 188–189
investigative powers, of grand jury, 328–329

J

joinder, 309, **319**–321
judge(s)
code of conduct for, 382–385
impartial, right to, 379–381
not impartial, methods
of removing, 380–381
questioning by, in jury selection, 394, 396
judgment
collecting, in civil lawsuit, 39
summary, in civil lawsuit, 39
judicial activism, **25**
judicial inducements, for plea bargaining,
356–357
judicial restraint, **25**–26
juror selection, 391–400
equal protection challenges to, 392–394
fair cross-section challenges to, 392–394
voir dire process in, 394–400. *See also voir
dire* process
jury duty, 391

jury list, **391**
jury panel, **391**
jury pool, 391
jury sequestration, media and, **406**
jury trial(s)
impartial nature of, right to, 381, 384–400
right to, waiving, 390–391
right to impartial judge in, 379
selection of jurors for, 391–400. *See also*
juror selection
size of juries for, 387, 388
voting requirements for, 387, 389–390
jury waiver, plea bargaining and, 350
justification, administrative, 198–225. *See
also* administrative searches
justification doctrine, 81–93
administrative justification and, 91–93
definition of, **81**
probable cause and, 81–88. *See also* probable cause
reasonable suspicion and, 88–91

K

"knock and announce" requirement
for arrest warrant, **112**–113
for search warrant, 119
"knock and talk" consent searches, **222**–223
knowledge, firsthand, probable cause and,
86–87

L

law, color of, **37**–38
law enforcement
civilian review of, **52**
conduct of, voluntariness and, 235
faith in, 24–25
force used by, 50
internal review of, **51**–52
mediation and, **53**
in pretrial process, 30
reasonable suspicion and, 88–89
lawful access requirement, of "plain view"
doctrine, 162–163
lawyer's letter, in civil lawsuit, 38
leading question, **268**–270
legal cases
finding, 17–18
parties of, 19
publications containing, 18
route of, to Supreme Court, 20–22
tracing progress of, 18–20
legal citations, 17
legal remedies, **35**. *See also* remedies for constitutional violations
legal research, 14, 17–22
liability
civil, Section 1983, defenses to, 44–46
county, **40**–42
individual, **42**–44
municipal, **40**–42
supervisory, **40,** 41
theories of, **39**–44

physical characteristics and, 75–76
   reasonable expectation of, **69**, 73–79
   right to, **27**
privacy doctrine, 26
pro se defense, **334**
probable cause, 81–88
   arrest warrants and, 99
   arrests and, 84
   definition of, **81**
   determination of, 31, 87–88
   firsthand knowledge and, 86–87
   home inspections and, 203
   "immediately apparent" and, 163
   informants and, 84–86
   justification doctrine and, 81–88
   preliminary hearing and, 292–294
   prudent man concept and, 82–83
   reasonable reliance on mistaken
      information and, 87
   reasonable suspicion vs., 88–89
   search warrants and, 99
   searches and, 81–84
   third parties and, 84–86
probable cause hearing, **282–284**
probation supervision searches, 215–219
procedural due process, **5, 44**
profiling
   drug courier, 188–195. *See also* drug
      courier profiling
   racial, **155**–160. *See also* racial profiling
property
   damage to, during execution of
      arrest warrant, 114
   seizures of, **80**
prosecutorial discretion, **310**
prosecutorial inducements, **352**–354.
      See also plea bargaining
prosecutors/prosecution, 310–321
   appeals by, 451
   charging decision by, 310
   decision not to prosecute by, 310–315
   definition of, **19, 310**
   discovery by, 295–299
   in disregard of legislative intent, 319
   duty of
      to disclose exculpatory evidence,
         301–303
      to preserve evidence, 303–304
   effects of plea bargaining on, 359–361
   filing methods on, 31
   joinder and, 309, **319**–321
   peremptory challenges by, 398–399
   pretextual, **317**–318
   restrictions on bringing charges and,
      316–319
   standards of conduct for, 313
   unfair and selective, 316–318
   vindictive, **318**–319
protective sweeps
   definition of, **183**–184

of residences, 183–184
   during searches, **140**
public defenders, code of conduct for,
      336–337
public duty defense, **49**
public duty doctrine, **46**
public safety exception, to *Miranda* rights,
      249–250
public trial, right to, **404**–407
   First Amendment and, 405–407
   inapplicability of, 404–405
punishment, capital, 441
"purged taint" exception to "fruit of the
      poisonous tree" doctrine, **63**
pursuit, seizure by, 80–81

Q

qualified immunity, **45**–46
questions/questioning. *See also*
      interrogations
   after asserting right to remain silent,
      248–249
   compulsion during, 228–229
   functional equivalent of, **242–243**
   general, interrogations distinguished
      from, 243
   leading, **268**–270
   specific, **268**
   of witnesses, forms of, 268–272

R

race
   as criterion for conducting stop, guide-
      lines for, 156
   drug courier profiling and, 194–195
racial profiling, **155**–160
   case law on, recent developments in,
      159–160
   Fourteenth Amendment equal
      protection claims and, 157–158
   Title VII of Civil Rights Act of 1964 and,
      158–159
real property, forfeiture of, 133
real world, of criminal procedure, **9**–10
reasonable expectation of privacy, **69**
   infringement of, search as, 73–79
reasonable suspicion
   actions based on, 169–197
   definition of, **89, 169**
   Fourth Amendment and, 88–91
   investigative detentions and, 195
   "knock and announce"
      requirement and, 113
   stop-and-frisk and, 170
   stop based on, 170–178. *See also* stop(s)
reasonableness
   objective. *See also* objective reasonableness
   of search or seizure, **69**–70
   subjective, **23**–24
reasonableness clause of Fourth
      Amendment, **67**
recross-examination of witnesses, **416**–417

redirect examination of witnesses, **416**
rehabilitation
   as goal of sentencing, **436**
   of witness, **274**–275
Rehnquist, William H., 25
release
   on own recognizance (ROR), **288**
   pretrial, 284–292. *See also* pretrial release
remands, of case back to lower court, **19**
remedies for constitutional violations,
      34–36. *See also* civil remedies for
      constitutional rights violations
   civil, 37–48
   criminal, 48–50
   definition of, **35**
   exclusionary rule and, 54–64.
      See also exclusionary rule
   extralegal, **35**
   legal, **35**
   nonjudicial, 51–54
reprosecution, after mistrial, 428
research, legal, 14, 17–22
residences. *See* homes
respondent, definition of, **19**
restraint, judicial, **25**–26
retribution, as goal of sentencing, **436**
reversals, of lower court decision, **19**
rights, constitutional, violations of, reme-
      dies for, 34–65. *See also* remedies for
      constitutional violations
risk, assumption of, 48
ROR (release on one's own
      recognizance), 288
rule of four, **21**

S

safety checkpoints, 209
same offense, definition of, **426**
sanctions, noncriminal, threats of, 230–231
school disciplinary searches, **211**–212
school students, drug and alcohol testing of,
      214–215
search(es)
   administrative, 92–93, 198–219. *See also*
      administrative searches
   consent, **220**–223
   consent for, drug courier profiling and, 188
   definition of, **69**, 94
   enhancement devices in, 78–79
   exigent circumstances and, 142–148.
      See also exigent circumstances
   as government action, 70–73
   illegal, identifications resulting from,
      277–278
   incident to arrests, **138**–142
   inventory, **200**–202
   locker, 212
   manner of, 122
   pat-down, 182. *See also* frisk(s)
   privacy and, 73–79
   private, acts authorized by, 72–73

542   *Subject Index*